PIONEERS OF LAW AND ECONOMICS

Pioneers of Law and Economics

Edited by

Lloyd R. Cohen and Joshua D. Wright

George Mason University, USA

Edward Elgar

Cheltenham, UK • Northampton, MA, USA

Published by
Edward Elgar Publishing Limited
The Lypiatts
15 Lansdown Road
Cheltenham
Glos GL50 2JA
UK

Edward Elgar Publishing, Inc.
William Pratt House
9 Dewey Court
Northampton
Massachusetts 01060
USA

Paperback edition 2011

A catalogue record for this book is available
from the British Library

Library of Congress Control Number: 2009930865

MIX
Paper from
responsible sources
FSC
www.fsc.org   FSC® C018575

ISBN 978 1 84720 479 0 (cased)
ISBN 978 0 85793 544 1 (paperback)

Typeset by Cambrian Typesetters, Camberley, Surrey
Printed and bound by MPG Books Group, UK

Contents

Contributors

Harold Demsetz UCLA
Nuno Garoupa University of Illinois College of Law and University of Manchester
    School of Law
Fernando Gómez-Pomar Pompeu Fabra University School of Law
Mark F. Grady UCLA School of Law
Thomas W. Hazlett George Mason University
Keith N. Hylton Boston University School of Law
Katherine V. Litvak University of Texas School of Law
Andrew P. Morriss University of Illinois College of Law
Sam Peltzman University of Chicago
John F. Pfaff Fordham University School of Law
Larry E. Ribstein University of Illinois College of Law
Stephen M. Stigler University of Chicago
Robert D. Tollison Clemson University
Thomas S. Ulen University of Illinois College of Law
Susan Woodward Sandhill Econometrics
Joshua D. Wright George Mason University School of Law

Introduction

Lloyd R. Cohen[1] *and Joshua D. Wright*[2]

Some time back, while a candidate for a position as a professor of law and economics, one of us was challenged by an interviewer who opined that the great recent success and influence of law and economics could be likened to a Kuhnian revolution.[3] We were taken aback at the time. Now fifteen years later we have occasion to offer a response.

No it isn't. In a very fundamental sense law and economics is nothing new – and that is what explains its great success. Scholars of the law – certainly in the English tradition – have always been concerned with three questions seen as central to the law and economics enterprise. First, what is the effect of a given law? How will people behave in response to it? Second, what should the law be? By some metric of the good, the just, and the salutary, what law will maximize the maximand? Third, given the institutions of law-making, what can we expect the law to be? What explains both the broad structure and the subtle texture of the law we observe? These questions are the core subjects of law and economics: positive law and economics; normative law and economics; and public choice.

So, then, what is new and pathbreaking in law and economics? The story is told of the late great price theorist Charles Ferguson who wrote one of the first standard textbooks in microeconomics that his wife, having perused the manuscript, offered the view that it amounted to nothing more than common sense, to which Professor Ferguson – his nose slightly out of joint – responded '*refined* common sense!' And so it is. While the questions addressed by law and economics may not be especially new, the rigor and care with which they are analyzed by economists we think sufficiently distinguishable from what came before to properly be viewed as pathbreaking.

But that said, the economic analysis of the law did not simply appear out of the blue in the second half of the 20th century. Nor can the origin of law and economics be traced to some unique moment in history, such as Holmes's observation that 'the man of the future is the man of statistics and the master of economics'.[4] Rather, it was an organic outgrowth of the intellectual development of its two constituent disciplines. This renders it a difficult, if not impossible, task to identify a finite set of 'Pioneers of Law and Economics' without excluding some extremely influential 'economists' in the broadest sense of that term.

With much justice one could trace this hybrid back to the pioneering scholarship of Adam Smith, Jeremy Bentham or even Niccolo Machiavelli. And, were there no constraints and no

---

[1]   Ph.D. J.D., Professor of Law, George Mason University School of Law, LCohen2@GMU.EDU.

[2]   Ph.D. J.D., Assistant Professor of Law, George Mason University School of Law, JWrightg@GMU.EDU.

[3]   Thomas S. Kuhn, *The Structure of Scientific Revolutions* (1962).

[4]   Oliver Wendell Holmes, 'The Path of the Law', 10 *Harvard Law Review* 457, 469 (1897).

opportunity costs, we would have relished including them. But constraints and opportunity costs are the nature of the world and the subject of our discipline, so we have limited the era of the subjects of the principal essays to the era generally viewed as the period of the flowering of the movement, the second half of the 20th century. Even with this restriction, the scope of modern law and economics is quite broad, continuously expanding and without sharply marked borders. The expansion is likely attributable to the power of economic tools, and more importantly the generality of its principles. These twin characteristics have allowed for its successful invasion of intellectual territory once thought outside the realm of the discipline. No longer is law and economics limited to areas considered to involve commercial activity, such as antitrust, securities regulation and commercial law. Recent times have seen the expansion of economic analysis into areas such as family law, constitutional law, and discrimination.

As editors we are economists, and as such our primary challenge has been to economize: on space, on talented authors, and on honors to be bestowed. Perhaps out of an excess of economy we have neglected to include a number of talented imaginative contributors. In addition, in the case of several essays, we have asked the author to write on the contributions of two personalities. Such a grouping would be not merely odd, but incomprehensible, were these essentially biographical essays. But they are not. They are meant to capture and honor pathbreaking work by leading contributors to the field. While each of the subjects has written a great deal of individually authored work, or work co-authored with others, where their principal contributions to law and economics were co-authored with another towering figure in the field, we thought it informative, efficient and just to combine them into a single chapter (albeit one that might be of greater length). We trust that our intelligent readers will not draw the incorrect inference that this implies any denigration of the contributions of the individual subjects. No slight was intended. Our motives were pure. Where a large body of work was produced by two distinguished contributors, it seemed economical in space, and more importantly, in authorial talent, to have one author write on both subjects in a single essay. If we were mistaken in this, for this and all our other sins of omission and commission we humbly apologize.

Consistent with this era of economic imperialism, we've adopted an approach to this volume which embraces a view of law and economics that is inclusive of not only a broad scope of issues, but also economic methods. Some of the pioneers featured in this volume might be counted as economic theorists, others public choice scholars, and still others lawyers and judges applying economic insights to the law and legal institutions. Likewise, the contributors to the volume include other pioneers, former students and clerks, colleagues, and influential scholars in the field of law and economics. It is now time to let the chapters and their subjects speak for themselves. Beyond ordering them more or less chronologically, our job is done.

Lloyd R. Cohen
Joshua D. Wright

1 Ronald H. Coase

Thomas W. Hazlett[1]

Professor Coase possesses an unusual mind. In addressing some of the most basic issues of the day, he manages to transform the dialogue permanently. He has done this not once but repeatedly. The formula evidently entails first thinking the unthinkable, then penetrating and examining its essence, and finally explicating the issues in a more fundamental way than was hitherto possible.

　　To be sure, this can be embarrassing to others. What is one to do with a 'gift' that is patently right, eludes analysis, and upsets foundations?[2]

Paradox swirls about the scholarly contributions of Ronald H. Coase.

A stunningly original thinker whose work changed the course of economic analysis, he spent most of his academic life in a law school.[3] His influence among scholars is vast, with his curriculum vitae featuring two of the ten most-cited articles of all time – including the top entry.[4] But that article would never have been written if the editors at the *Journal of Law & Economics* did not think his previous contribution contained a fatal error.[5]

Coase is commonly credited as being instrumental in the creation of 'law and economics'[6] and then the New Institutional Economics,[7] yet he has roundly dismissed the application of microeconomic analysis, and the rationality assumption on which it rests, to worlds beyond traditional economic markets.[8] There is no one who has done more to bring attention to the issue of transaction costs, yet his most compelling and well-read work is best

---

[1]　The author wishes to thank Arthur Havenner, Vernon L. Smith and Dennis Weisman for insights on the subject of this chapter. The usual disclaimer applies, although the author wishes it did not.

[2]　Oliver E. Williamson, 'Preface', in O. E. Williamson and S. G. Winter, eds, *The Nature of the Firm: Origins, Evolutions, and Development* (New York: Oxford University Press, 1993), p. v.

[3]　Coase became a faculty member at the University of Chicago Law School in 1964. While he retired in 1982, he continues to hold the title of Clifton R. Musser Professor of Economics Emeritus, giving him over four decades as a law school professor.

[4]　A survey of the most influential economic studies, as judged by number of citations in the calendar year 1987, found that Coase had two articles in the top 10, calling him 'The citation superstar of the list'. His 1960 article, 'The Problem of Social Cost', was cited 1,005 times, far ahead of the second most-cited paper – Pratt's 1965 article on risk aversion in *Econometrica* – which garnered 671 citations. Arthur M. Diamond, Jr, 'Most-Cited Economics Papers and Current Research Fronts', *Current Comments* (January 9, 1989).

[5]　R.H. Coase, 'Law and Economics at Chicago', 36 *Journal of Law & Economics* 239 (April 1993), p. 250.

[6]　Richard Posner credits the birth of the sub-discipline 'law and economics' to the publication of key papers by Ronald Coase and Guido Calabresi. Richard A. Posner, *The Economics of Justice* (Cambridge: Harvard University Press, 1983).

[7]　Coase served as the first president (1996–97) of the International Society for New Institutional Economics; http://www.isnie.org/about-html.

[8]　Coase 'will have no truck with applying economics outside its conventional domain of explicit markets'. Posner (1993), p. 200.

known for a theorem that employed an assumption that transaction costs are zero. And while few have contributed more to economic theory, Coase has always thought of himself as an empiricist,[9] a scholar who merely set out to investigate the actual way markets operated, an analyst 'looking for results'.[10]

Still, Professor Coase's most serious empirical investigation was undertaken as a 20-year-old undergraduate conducting interviews with business executives. 'Coase's work is unusual because it contains almost no mathematics or sophisticated statistical analysis.'[11] Coase himself bemoaned, in 1988, that, 'My point of view has not in general commanded assent, nor has my argument, for the most part, been understood'.[12] The following year, law and economics scholar Stewart Schwab flatly predicted: 'Coase will never win the Nobel Prize for Economics'. Coase was, in fact, awarded the Nobel Prize in Economics in 1991.

The irony of which makes for a fascinating story of thought, discovery, and intellectual intrigue.

1   A young socialist discovers the capitalist firm

Ronald Harry Coase was born in England on December 19, 1910, and soon assigned to a school for 'physical defectives' due to his use of leg braces. This, as per the policy of the day, placed the youngster in class with 'mental defectives'.[13] Finally, at age 12, the system admitted him to the main educational track, and the precocious pupil achieved sufficient catch-up to enroll at the London School of Economics. There, while thinking himself a socialist, he landed in the class of Professor Arnold Plant, a noted classical economist just arrived from the University of Cape Town. Coase was struck by Plant's description of spontaneous order, what Coase would later call 'the price system'. This triggered a host of questions in the student, whose University of London grant funded a tour of American businesses in 1931–32 to answer them.[14] Specifically, how did firms, or the business executives who ran them, understand when to produce items themselves, and when to buy them from others?

That investigation, eventually published in 1937 as 'The Nature of the Firm',[15] triggered a fresh view of enterprise and the organization of markets. It brought into focus the centrality of transactions and teamwork. When teams afforded advantages, transactions would be structured so as to tie inputs together in packages, giving scope to firms. When such relations were less helpful, inputs could be efficiently assembled using 'the price system'.

This interface between the firm and the market, happened upon in a quest to understand the contours of either, constituted a major advance. Economists had been little concerned

---

[9]   Albeit an empiricist who dismissed econometrics as a demonstration that 'if you torture the data enough nature will always confess'. Richard A. Posner, 'Ronald Coase and Methodology' 7 *Journal of Economic Perspectives* 195 (Autumn 1993), p. 199.

[10]   Thomas W. Hazlett, 'Looking for Results: Nobel Laureate Ronald Coase on Rights, Resources and Regulation', *Reason* (January 1997); http://www-reason.com/news/show/30115.html.

[11]   Posner (1993), p. 199.

[12]   R.H. Coase, *The Firm, the Market, and the Law* 1 (1988), Chicago: University of Chicago Press.

[13]   Hazlett (1997).

[14]   Steven N.S. Cheung, 'The Contractual Nature of the Firm', 26 *Journal of Law & Economics* 1 (April 1983).

[15]   R.H. Coase, 'The Nature of the Firm', 4 *Economica* 386 (1937).

with the creation or internal functioning of firms, picking up their stories of market structure once firms were already in place. Firms were units of production, 'black boxes' set to the side, while economics[16] – 'the science of choice'[17] – turned its attention to trades between firms and their customers. What effort had been made to peer into the firm had been strangely non-economic, as in the categorical assertion by Adolph Berle and Gardiner Means (1932)[18] that corporate managers would systematically appropriate shareholders, leaving unexplained why equity owners would so willingly finance this arrangement.[19]

Coase, perhaps naively and without the intellectual baggage of his elders, ventured forth with the basic tools of price theory. Alternatively, the fresh look at firms was driven by an ideology of its own: 'Perhaps because of Coase's socialism, *The Nature of the Firm* emphasized the costs of markets'.[20] Whatever the source of his inspiration, it flashed the trademark of important economic discoveries: radically controversial as an initial proposition, but utterly unobjectionable once understood. 'My contribution to economics', notes Coase, 'has been to urge the inclusion in our analysis of features of the economic system so obvious that, like the postman in G.K. Chesterton's Father Brown tale, "The Invisible Man," they have tended to be overlooked'.[21]

In the mind of its author, the mission was always simple: 'Our task is to attempt to discover why a firm emerges at all in a specialized exchange economy'.[22] The analytical entrée was equally straightforward. The tasks performed by firms, production and exchange, can also be performed by individuals transacting in the market. Why do companies organize to produce what could be produced without such formal relations? 'Outside the firm, price movements direct production . . . Within a firm, these market transactions are eliminated and in place of the complicated market structure with exchange transactions is substituted the entrepreneur-co-ordinator, who directs production.'[23] This investigation would, Coase hoped, reveal the boundaries of the firm and its determinants.

The high-level answer was virtually tautological: firms expand internally when it is more efficient than using the market.[24] The logic nonetheless generated remarkable influence and, after a long lag, academic productivity. Specifically, it steered economists

---

[16]   'It is a mistake to confuse the firm of economic theory with its real-world namesake. The chief mission of neoclassical economics is to understand how the price system coordinates the use of resources, not the inner workings of real firms.' Harold Demsetz, 'The Structure of Ownership and the Theory of the Firm', 26 *Journal of Law & Economics* 375 (June 1983), p. 377.

[17]   Oliver E. Williamson, 'The Theory of the Firm as Governance Structure: From Choice to Contract', 16 *Journal of Economic Perspectives* 171 (Summer 2002).

[18]   Adolph A. Berle and Gardiner C. Means, *The Modern Corporation and Private Property* (revised edition, 1991): Edison, NJ: Transaction Publishers.

[19]   Harold Demsetz, 'The Structure of Ownership and the Theory of the Firm', 26 *Journal of Law & Economics 375* (1983).

[20]   Guido Calabresi, 'The Pointlessness of Pareto: Carrying Coase Further', 100 *Yale Law Journal* 1211 (1991), p. 1212.

[21]   Ronald. H. Coase, 'The Institutional Structure of Production', 82 *The American Economic Review* 713 (Sept. 1992), p. 713. This article was Coase's Nobel Lecture.

[22]   Coase, 'The Nature of the Firm', p. [74].

[23]   Ibid., p. [73].

[24]   But not quite tautological, argues Steven Cheung (1983), p. 4. Oliver Williamson takes the other side: 'The transaction cost logic of economic organization had its origins in a tautology which Ronald Coase wryly defines as "a proposition that is clearly right"'. Williamson (1993), p. 90.

towards the examination of trade-offs faced by firms. The black box was pierced; the choice margins to be studied then multiplied. Comparative economic strategies and conditions were revealed in intra-firm and inter-firm differences. The distribution of organizational modes across ownership structures – proprietary firms, partnerships, co-ops, public corporations, and non-profit enterprises – offered rich sources of additional data. The notion that the firm was itself a market institution, organically born and persistently adjusting to changing competitive constraints, brought the subject matter squarely within the microeconomic analysis. As Harold Demsetz would write, the firm is 'an endogenous outcome of a maximizing process'.[25]

Coase found that the complexity of organizations was associated with the pursuit of efficiencies. That decentralized firms would understand the relevant costs and benefits embedded in 'make or buy' decisions illuminated new terrain for market forces. The 'invisible hand' applied not just to inter-firm or firm-to-consumer market transactions, but to the internal organization of business enterprises (or public bureaucracies) themselves. This perspective was not immediately heralded: 'the state of transaction cost economics in 1972 was approximately where Coase had left it in 1937'.[26] But interest was about to skyrocket.[27] The 'theory of the firm' led to valuable discoveries and productive new research programs concerning governance structures, contracts, and property rights.[28] When explaining 'the firm in economic theory', households came to be included as objects of study, contrasting with the pre-Coasean tradition of treating them as holistic decision-making units that 'distorts some characteristics of real families and real firms'.[29] The growing use of price theory to explain social behavior beyond the narrowly economic was a logical extension. On the 50th anniversary of its publication, 'The Nature of the Firm' was widely cited in papers dealing with diverse questions of social organization, was the topic of special issues in prestigious journals,[30] and was soon to spur the creation of the Society for New Institutional Economics, which Coase served as Founding President (1996–97).

The 'Nature of the Firm' helped demolish analytical walls by revealing the generality of the constraints on decision-makers across institutions. As Guido Calabresi explains,

> A full understanding of the *costs* and *possible benefits* of markets requires us to accept something which runs against some of our most basic presuppositions. It requires us to realize that neither market nor nonmarket forms of organization are primary; rather, they are two approaches which interrelate in oddly symmetrical ways as (a) people seek to find the most efficient (least costly) way of structuring their relationships, and, given that both approaches exist, (b) people try to use the power (wealth or authority) which each approach gives them to accrue maximum benefits to themselves.[31]

---

25   Harold Demsetz (1983), p. 377.
26   Oliver E. Williamson, 'The Logic of Economic Organization', in Williamson and Winter (1993), p. 90.
27   Citations tracked by the Social Science Citation Index to 'The Nature of the Firm' had the following pattern: '1966–70, 17 citations; 1971–75, 47 citations; and 1976–80, 105 citations'. Cheung (1983), p. 1.
28   For an overview of this evolution, see Williamson (2002).
29   Demsetz (1983), p. 378.
30   See, e.g., 4 *Journal of Law, Economics, and Organization* 1 (Spring 1988).
31   Guido Calabresi, 'The Pointlessness of Pareto: Carrying Coase Further', 100 *Yale Law Journal* 1211 (1991), p. 1214 (emphasis in original).

This protean insight would later undermine Coase's own preference that microeconomic analysis be confined within the standard domain of economic markets.[32] But even more ironic is the fact that Coase's own perspective on firms was at odds with the methodology he devised. Where Coase launched his investigation of firms by asking about how transactions within firms differ from market transactions outside of them, the bright lines he imagined do not exist. Coase's paper, so fundamental in showing others how the general cost-benefit framework applied elsewhere would yield fruit in explaining the coordination process within firms, was based on a sharply asymmetric view of the price system.

Once it is seen that the decisions made by firm managers conform to the laws of economic analysis, it is then seen that all choices – transactions within firms as well as those bridging them – are subject to the constraints of the price system. The apparent difference is of form rather than substance. Coase, however, posited a highly artificial world in which the delineations of the firm were bright; activities inside those boundaries were planned, while those outside were spontaneous. Steven Cheung identifies 'Coase's "firm" ' as an unrealistic construct. 'Coase's central thesis is that differences in the costs of operating institutions (transaction costs) lead to the emergence of a firm to supersede a market.'[33] But the firm's choices are constrained by conditions of supply and demand. To view the manager as coordinating production by 'ordering' workers to perform certain tasks is to mistake the location of choice with the nature of choices. Alchian and Demsetz (1972) noted that this approach failed to incorporate the ubiquitous influence of market forces.[34]

No matter. Other economists saw the 'Coasean' implications that Coase did not; the 'Theory of the Firm' motivated research into the contractual nature of economic relations. What set this research in motion, and indeed turned Coase to productive new inquiries, was the prominence that 'The Nature of the Firm' gave to transaction costs. The ability to find, negotiate, and consummate contracts was seen as being of central importance in the pursuit of efficiency. This new perspective pointed the way to even larger breakthroughs in economic theory.

2   The dynamic role of prices

Long before 'The Nature of the Firm' gained academic currency, Coase dove into an interesting theoretical debate. In 'The Marginal Cost Controversy',[35] he disputed the policy proposed for high fixed-cost industries put forth by Harold Hotelling.[36] This analysis had garnered widespread support, and was referenced by Coase as the Hotelling-Lerner thesis.[37] This paradigm proposed that the efficient manner of dealing with firms where marginal cost generally falls below average cost, due to the presence of substantial fixed costs, is via a combination of price controls and subsidies. The price control was necessary to constrain prices to the level of marginal cost. Firms would not price at marginal cost

---

[32]   Posner (1993), p. 207.
[33]   Cheung (1983), p. 3.
[34]   Armen A. Alchian and Harold Demsetz, 'Production, Information Costs, and Economic Organization', 62 *American Economic Review* 777 (1972), p. 783.
[35]   R.H. Coase, 'The Marginal Cost Controversy', 13 *Economica* 169 (August 1946).
[36]   Harold Hotelling, 'Stability in Competition', 39 *Economic Journal* 41 (1929).
[37]   The Lerner embrace is given in Abba P. Lerner, *The Economics of Control: Principles of Welfare* (1944), New York: Macmillan.

voluntarily, both due to the market power created by increasing returns and by virtue of the fact that companies could not profitably sustain themselves by pricing below their average cost. The Hotelling solution was to nonetheless force suppliers to price at marginal cost, and to then compensate losses through state subsidies sufficient to achieve break-even profits for the firm.

Coase objected. Hotelling's model was logically inconsistent, seeing prices as yielding essential information about costs and values in the one setting but then unnecessary in directing the creation of economic structures in another. The result was that the postulated maximization problem artificially excluded vital considerations. 'Any actual economic situation is complex and a single economic problem does not exist in isolation'.[38] Price controls and subsidies, designed to achieve the benefits of output expansion, also carried costs – yet only the benefits formally entered the Hotelling-Lerner analysis. Specifically, costs would be borne when firms' profit-pursuing discoveries were supplanted by administered prices. Lacking market-generated information, how would the state know where to set prices, which firms to fund, and how much to pay? Coase, then teaching at the London School of Economics, was clearly influenced by F.A. Hayek and the informational challenges he stressed.[39] It led Coase to realize that the Hotelling-Lerner solution contradicted itself, arguing for the superior efficiency of price signals in one context but then inexplicably discarding them – without cost – in another:

> If it were possible to make such estimates, at low cost and with considerable accuracy . . . this would be likely to lead, in my opinion, not to a modification of the pricing system but rather to its abolition. . . . Indeed, Professor Lerner in an earlier section of his book argues for a pricing system on precisely the grounds that it is impossible for a Government to make such estimates.[40]

The important enterprise that Coase again pursued was generalization, bringing new institutions within the purview of economic analysis. Government was not something separate and apart from the marketplace, stocked with data unknown to others and operated by selfless calculators immune to error. Coase's later hostility to public choice and its use of the rationality assumption in modeling political behavior is remarkable given the service he rendered in its development.

Perhaps Coase was thinking about the policy more carefully than the politics. By the 1940s, it is clear from his writings that the socialist leanings of his youth were fading, perhaps a contrarian response to the opposite drift of his academic colleagues. Of course, the Great Depression had had a profound impact on the policy debate. The 1934 tract written by Henry Simons, *A Positive Program for Laissez Faire: Some Proposals for a Liberal Economic Policy*, was considered the pro-market position – and advocated nationalization of railways, utilities, and other industries, while granting vast new powers to the Federal Trade Commission to deconcentrate private industry:

38   'Marginal Cost Controversy', op cit., p. 170.
39   F.A. Hayek, 'The Use of Knowledge in Society', 35 *American Economic Review* 519 (Sept. 1945).
40   'Marginal Cost Controversy', op cit., p. 175.

There must be an outright dismantling of our gigantic corporations. . . . their existence is to be explained in terms of opportunities for promoter profits, personal ambitions of industrial and financial 'Napoleons', and advantages of monopoly power.[41]

Simons was a well-known member of the 'Chicago School', but Coase – long an admirer of Chicago's Frank Knight – was unimpressed. When Simons expressed hostility to private enterprise on the grounds that 'most of our resources are utilized in persuading people to buy one thing rather than another, and only a minor fraction actually employed in creating things to be bought',[42] Coase found the methods – not to mention the policies – wanting. As he later wrote:

[I]n dealing with industrial organization, Simons provides no empirical backing for his contentions, makes no serious investigation of what the effects of his proposals would be in the efficiency with which the economic system would operate, nor does he consider whether the Federal Trade Commission would be likely to do what he wanted or whether, even if it wanted to do so, it would be possible for it to acquire the information necessary to implement his proposals. Simons's approach is the very antithesis of that which was to become dominant as a result of the emergence of that new subject, law and economics. Stigler's description of Simons is eminently just: Simons was a utopian.[43]

Assigned with teaching public utility pricing at the LSE, Coase had years to contemplate how regulators carried out their duties, how firms responded, and how consumer welfare was impacted. Government subsidies could be provided to an infinite number of public utilities; sorting through to implement just the productive funding options was a job for competitive markets just as prices revealed relative values. This insight led Coase to see the trade-offs attendant upon the proposed public financing scheme, presaging the Coase Theorem years later.

In particular, Coase argued that, while private (unsubsidized) solutions might be statically inefficient, there was no free lunch: government subsidy had efficiency costs of its own. First among these was the information lost when the feedback loop of profit was jettisoned in favor of public sector selection. Further, Coase sought to infer how private firms did, in fact, deal with static inefficiencies. He observed that customers often paid prices approximating marginal cost for marginal units under multi-part tariffs that allowed suppliers to recoup fixed costs via fixed periodic (say, monthly subscriber) charges.[44] Not only did Coase grasp such pricing schemes as a way to improve on textbook inefficiency, he recognized the underlying forces at work. Facing unexploited gains from trade, market actors created innovative solutions unanticipated by economists. The centrality of Adam Smith's 'invisible hand' in Coase's economics was evident.[45]

---

[41]   Henry Simons (1934), pp. 19–21; quoted in Coase (1993), p. 241.
[42]   Simons (1934), pp. 31–2; quoted in Coase (1993), p. 241.
[43]   Coase (1993), p. 242.
[44]   The modern cellular telephone network displays the multi-part price schedule in simple terms. Monthly subscribers pay a fixed fee in exchange for 'buckets' of minutes wherein the marginal cost of a minute is zero. Moreover, such subscribers are offered 'free minutes' during off-peak times, thus raising demand for subscriptions.
[45]   Coase notes, in his Nobel Lecture, that Professor Arnold Plant introduced him to Adam Smith in 1931, and that he was instantly impressed by the concept of the 'invisible hand'. Richard Posner

3   Property rights and radio spectrum

If Adam Smith provided the impetus for Coase to rethink the utility pricing paradigm, he would also prove essential in helping Coase understand how radio waves were regulated. Undertaking a decade-long investigation of the matter, Coase began with an inquiry into the British Broadcasting Corporation, holding a then-monopoly over radio and television broadcasting in the United Kingdom. His book, *British Broadcasting: A Study in Monopoly*, was published in 1950. Then Coase, migrating to the University of Buffalo in 1951, shifted his attention to US institutions.

His thinking took a sharp turn at about this time with the provocative analysis offered by Leo Herzel, a law student writing in the *University of Chicago Law Review*.[46] Herzel argued that radio waves should be allocated not by regulators at the Federal Communications Commission (FCC), but by sale to the highest bidder. This departure from orthodoxy elicited a wild attack by Dallas Smythe, a former FCC Chief Economist.[47] Smythe belittled Herzel's expertise, asserting that the technical properties of radio spectrum did not admit to private ownership or, therefore, market allocation. Smythe then taunted the law student: 'Surely it is not seriously intended that noncommercial radio users (like police) . . . should compete with dollar bids against the broadcaster users for channel allocations'.[48] To which Herzel, in his Rejoinder, offered: 'It certainly is seriously suggested. Such users compete for all other kinds of equipment or else they don't get it. I should think the more interesting question is, Why is it seriously suggested that they shouldn't compete for radio frequencies? . . . The result would be that government would be saved from the self-knowledge of what such services cost and, unlike other consumers, would not have to decide whether they were really worth it in comparison with available substitutes.'[49]

The Herzel-Smythe exchange was enlightening for Coase, who was treated to an extremely weak argument for government regulation of externalities. The traditional view supported central planning in airwaves as the only reasonable way to deal with endemic spillovers. These third-party effects were allegedly due to the nature of wireless, a technological reality beyond the reach of economics. But the argument was obviously confused. Even a young law student understood that arguing for non-market allocations on distributional grounds constituted a *non sequitur* in a debate over efficiency. Something was amiss, and Coase pondered it.

He did not instantly discover the full scope of the error. While intrigued by Herzel's argument for market allocation,[50] Coase was uncertain as to its correctness. 'It was neces-

---

writes that Coase, much later in his career, was of the opinion that virtually everything interesting in economics had been included in *The Wealth of Nations*. Posner (1993), p. 203.

46   Leo Herzel, ' "Public Interest" and the Market in Color Television', 18 *University of Chicago Law Review* 802 (Summer 1951).

47   Dallas W. Smythe, 'Facing Facts about the Broadcast Business', 20 *University of Chicago Law Review* 96 (Autumn 1952).

48   Ibid., p. 100.

49   Leo Herzel, 'Rejoinder', 20 *University of Chicago Law Review* 106 (1952), p. 106.

50   While Coase initially assumed that the argument had been gleaned from Milton Friedman or Aaron Director at the University of Chicago Law School, where Herzel was a student, he was wrong. Herzel's thinking was motivated by his undergraduate reading of Lerner (1944), 1. See Leo Herzel, 'My 1951 Color Television Article', 41 *Journal of Law & Economics* 523 (Oct. 1998). See also Coase (1993).

sary to take into account the existence of transaction costs.'[51] What ultimately won the day were 'the incredibly feeble arguments' put forth by Professor Smythe, an acknowledged broadcast policy expert and Professor of Economics at the University of Illinois. In his exuberance to trounce the law student, the infirmities of his position were revealed: Smythe failed to grasp the generality of the economic problem. Coordinating use of radio spectrum, a medium where rival users have the potential to conflict with one another, required judgments as to relative values. Was the performance of a radio station in Cincinnati, aided by higher power, worth the degradation of signals for listeners in Frankfurt, Kentucky?

The government could decide the question by fiat, as the Federal Communications Commission did. Given the subject matter, which has a technical component, and the seemingly ubiquitous nature of the spillover problem attendant to 'interference' between radio users, that approach looks reasonable, even essential. So wrote Justice Felix Frankfurter in the 1943 Supreme Court case establishing the legality of government spectrum allocation under the 1927 Radio Act:

> The plight into which radio fell prior to 1927 was attributable to certain basic facts about radio as a means of communication – its facilities are limited; they are not available to all who may wish to use them; the radio spectrum is simply not large enough to accommodate everybody. There is a fixed natural limitation upon the number of stations that can operate without interfering with one another. Regulation of radio was therefore as vital to its development as traffic control was to the development of the automobile. In enacting the Radio Act of 1927, the first comprehensive scheme of control over radio communication, Congress acted upon the knowledge that, if the potentialities of radio were not to be wasted, regulation was essential.[52]

This rendition of the commons problem[53] spurred Coase to fundamentally rethink the basic economic problem: how society rations access to scarce resources. The result was a fresh look that would soon force microeconomic textbooks to be rewritten.

Coase reasoned that while administrative controls could mitigate conflicts between airwave users, government could not eliminate the trade-offs faced. To limit one set of airwave uses could protect the value of others, but the restrictions themselves imposed costs. There is no such thing as a free interference constraint. Moreover, the costs of coordinating activities were not qualitatively altered when the state assumed spectrum management duties. Government regulators were forced to choose between competing alternatives. But there were other rationing devices.

Coase recognized the airwave allocation problem as generic and, therefore, the administrative allocation scheme as peculiar. Economies routinely employed the price system to make the choices that the Federal Communications Commission was imposing. The argument made for this system boiled down to the view that markets could not work because

---

[51] Coase (1993), p. 249.

[52] *National Broadcasting Co. v. United States*, 319 US 190, 213, 215–17 (1943).

[53] Not only was the theory wrong, as Coase would show, but the description of the US radio market prior to the 1927 Radio Act was factually inaccurate. The initial regime policing wireless used common law rules of first appropriation, with enforcement by the US Department of Commerce. Coase structured his analysis, and ultimately his published argument, based on this flawed history. See Thomas W. Hazlett, 'The Rationality of U.S. Regulaion of the Broadcast Spectrum', 33 *Journal of Law & Economics* 133 (April 1990). See, also, Clarence C. Dill, *Radio Law* (Washington, D.C.: National Law Book Co., 1938).

markets required owners, and 'private property rights in the electromagnetic spectrum are too difficult to define and enforce, given the invisible nature of the resource and our limited understanding of the circumstances in which one type of broadcast activity will interfere with another'.[54] These spillovers would result in 'chaos', as was assertedly the case previous to the 'public interest' licensing scheme instituted in the 1927 Radio Act.

Coase saw this argument, resting on the technical attributes of spectrum – 'certain basic facts about radio' – as logically flawed. Wireless emission rights needed to be delimited in law. Such rights could be assigned to private parties or, alternatively, to government agencies. In the former, the price system could operate, with spectrum utilized according to the highest bids. In the latter instance, government agencies would exercise their judgment as to the 'public interest'. These formed the relevant choices.

Chaos would occur wherever scarcity obtained and constraints on resource appropriation were lacking. This crucial fact had been overlooked in economics; the model of perfect competition, assuming perfect information, skipped right past the institutional details of how trades were consummated. Here Coase was forced to confront it directly. The result was a seminal article that today places the 'broadcast spectrum in a high, almost holy place, in the economic analysis of law and the economics of property rights'.[55] The gist of the argument is captured in a rejection of radio waves as a special case:

> [I]f no property rights were created in land, so that everyone could use a tract of land, it is clear that there would be considerable confusion and that the price mechanism would not work because there would not be any property that could be acquired . . . But it would be wrong to blame this on private enterprise and the competitive system. A private enterprise system cannot function unless property rights are created in resources, and, when this is done, someone wishing to use a resource has to pay the owner to obtain it. Chaos disappears; and so does the government, except that a legal system to define property rights and to arbitrate disputes is, of course, necessary.[56]

Coase proposed that a system of property rights in radio spectrum replace administrative allocation. The recommendation was hugely controversial. Asked to present his ideas to the Federal Communications Commission at a 1959 hearing, Commissioner Philip S. Cross began the questioning with, 'Are you spoofing us? Is this all a big joke?'[57] Shortly thereafter, Coase and two co-authors were commissioned to write a study of private property rights in spectrum by the Rand Corporation. The project was funded and the paper written, but then abruptly abandoned. The think tank refused to publish their own research when a reviewer stressed Rand's own 'vulnerability. . . . to the fire and counterfire from

---

54   Thomas W. Merrill and Henry E. Smith, 'What Happened to Property in Law and Economics?' 111 *Yale Law Journal* 357 (2001).

55   Dean Lueck, 'The Rule of First Appropriation and the Design of the Law', 38 *Journal of Law & Economics* 393 (April 1995), p. 419.

56   R.H. Coase, 'The Federal Communications Commission', 2 *Journal of Law & Economics* 1 (1959).

57   'I was completely taken aback but I managed to reply: "Is it a joke to believe in the American economic system?" Later Commissioner Cross said that mine was "the most unique program yet presented." ' R.H. Coase, 'Comment on Thomas W. Hazlett: Assigning Rights to Radio Spectrum Users: Why Did FCC License Auctions Take 67 Years?' 41 *Journal of Law & Economics* 577 (1998), p. 579.

CBS, FCC, Justice, and most of all – Congress'. Releasing the study would simply be 'asking for trouble in the Washington-Big Business maelstrom . . .'.[58]

Coase had spent years studying radio spectrum and its regulation, and was deeply into the topic when, having by then left Buffalo for the University of Virginia, he spent 1958 at Stanford University's Center for Advanced Study in the Behavioral Sciences to focus on the question. The investment paid dividends.[59] In fashioning a policy position on frequency allocation, he pioneered a new path in economics.

First, he had seen that the government's resource allocations faced the same trade-offs as those made in the private sector. Either approach had to choose between valuable, mutually exclusive options. Second, 'spillovers' were not one-way, but reciprocal conflicts. When Station A's broadcasts diminish the listening experience of Station B's audience, it is said that A interferes with B. But it is equally true that when a rule (or contract) then limits or silences Station A to protect B's listeners, B interferes with A. Third, spillovers were not economically exogenous properties associated with particular products or services, but core resource choices. The use of economic resources to pursue one set of goals limits their use for others. Nothing technical. Just economics.

These insights revealed that the task at hand was not to eliminate spillovers but to help economic agents markets discover the optimal level. This was Coase's *Eureka!* moment:

> It is sometimes implied that the aim of regulation in the radio industry should be to minimize interference. But this would be wrong. The aim should be to maximize output. All property rights interfere with the ability of people to use resources. What has to be insured is that the gain from interference more than offsets the harm it produces.[60]

In hindsight, this is utterly obvious. It was anything but obvious at the time. Indeed, the editors of the *Journal of Law & Economics* thought the argument was in error, violating the Pigouvian principle that externalities could not be accounted for by private exchange. Coase persuaded the editors to publish his FCC paper, and 'its attack on A.C. Pigou', on the grounds that 'even if my argument was an error, it was a very interesting error'. Hence, Coase was invited to explain his position more thoroughly. He then composed what was to become the most cited scholarly paper in economics, which was published by the *JLE* in 1960. 'Had it not been that these Chicago economists thought that I had made a mistake in the article on "The Federal Communications Commission" ', claims Coase, 'it is probable that "The Problem of Social Cost" would never have been written'.[61]

---

58   In Coase (1998), p. 580, quoting a referee's report submitted to Rand. The Rand paper written by Coase, William Meckling, and Jora Minasian, was finally released in 1995 – the year after FCC license auctions were instituted.

59   'An economist who, by his efforts, is able to postpone by a week a government program which wastes $100 million a year (what I consider a modest success) has, by his action, earned his salary for the whole of his life.' Ronald H. Coase, 'Economists and Public Policy', in J. Fred Weston, ed., *Large Corporations in a Changing Society* (New York: NYU Press, 1975); reprinted in Daniel B. Klein, *What Do Economists Contribute?* 30 (New York: NYU Press, 1999), p. 44.

60   Coase (1959), p. 28.

61   Coase (1993), p. 250.

Before discussing that famous paper, a brief assessment of Coase's contribution to spectrum policy is warranted. His 1959 analysis[62] suggested a research agenda for communications scholars that continues to bear fruit. Spectrum liberalization has occurred in the intervening decades, with private property institutions widely introduced in wireless markets. This trend is likely not due to Coasean intellectual trends alone, but also to the advent of more sophisticated wireless technologies which have made the high costs of administrative allocation more socially expensive, coupled with the fading political significance of traditional (radio and television) broadcasting.[63] Whatever the policy dynamics, Coase's conjecture regarding market allocation of radio spectrum has proven correct. Not only have auctions successfully been used in at least 30 countries to assign wireless licenses, the licenses issued grant broader, more flexible use rights. These delegate wide discretion to licensees, tantamount to granting (for the frequency spaces allotted to the license) private property rights in spectrum.[64] This is not to say that most nations have adopted the private property rights model generally, although a few have attempted to do something close to this.[65] Rather, the model is employed on a case-by-case basis for the most valuable wireless services, those providing mobile voice and data.

Coase argued for application of this model on theoretical grounds. What evidence Coase could have reviewed – the use of common law property rights to allocate airwaves prior to the 1927 Radio Act – he largely overlooked and then misunderstood.[66] He took no account of it in advocating that policy makers define property rights in spectrum and then let band owners bargain to determine the most productive applications from there. It was an extremely leveraged position, particularly considering its denunciation by experts in the field. But Coase's normative argument, rooted in Adam Smith, triumphed in the decades to follow. What Coase supposed about the superior efficiency of market allocation of radio spectrum has been proven correct. The productivity of advanced wireless networks, to take one important and obvious example (serving an astounding four

---

62   In 1965 Coase commented more directly on the operational elements of the 'public interest' licensing system. R.H. Coase, 'Evaluation of Public Policy Relating to Radio and Television Broadcasting: Social and Economic Issues', 41 *Land Economics* 161 (May 1965).

63   Thomas W. Hazlett, 'Assigning Property Rights to Radio Spectrum Users: Why Did FCC License Auctions Take 67 Years?' 41 *Journal of Law & Economics* (October 1998); Hazlett, *The Wireless Craze . . .* 14 *Harvard Journal of Law & Technology* (Spring 2001).

64   Hazlett (2001); Thomas W. Hazlett, 'Optimal Abolition of FCC Spectrum Allocation', 22 *Journal of Economic Perspectives* 103 (Winter 2008a).

65   See Thomas W. Hazlett, 'Property Rights and Wireless License Values', 51 *Journal of Law & Economics* 573 (August 2008b).

66   Hazlett (1990). See, also, Coase (1998). Here Coase responds to the argument that property rights in spectrum were well understood (and in use) in the run-up to the 1927 Radio Act, but rejected due to the success of a distributional coalition – combining the interests of incumbent radio broadcasters and policy makers – that wanted to create and then share rents. He clings to an 'error theory' explanation, that 'public interest' licensing was mistakenly instituted because the property rights alternative was not grasped. Yet Coase then presents compelling information showing how his 1962 Rand Corporation property rights study was suppressed due to strategic opposition by broadcasters, regulators, and Congress. In this, Coase demonstrates the paradox that, while his work did so much to extend economic analysis to 'non-market' institutions, his own perspective remained unrepentantly hostile to such analysis (including public choice).

billion subscribers globally[67]), rests on the spectrum property rights granted to mobile carriers.

Coase's normative prescriptions also hold up against a more recent assault. The 'spectrum commons' argument asserted by various law professors holds that the advent of 'smart radios' that adroitly dodge rival airwave traffic make 'open access' spectrum regimes the newly efficient default solution.[68] Spectrum sharing has surpassed spectrum partitioning, reducing the value of exclusive spectrum rights or making them altogether obsolete. 'The property approach made sense in 1960, but is now questionable.'[69]

In fact, the critique flounders. Owners of exclusive spectrum rights deploy precisely the advanced technologies cited as game-changing. The most intensely shared bands are those where de facto ownership rights are granted. Exclusive control over spectrum enables coordination between investors, technology suppliers, application venders, and customers. The expensive, complex networks developed there are unseen either in traditionally licensed bands such as broadcasting, or in unlicensed bands (analogized to 'spectrum commons') which rely on government standards and power limits ('governance' in Henry Smith's apt taxonomy[70]) to mitigate conflicts.[71] Overall, the social value of exclusive frequency rights far surpasses what is generated by rival regimes.[72]

Three aspects of the debate are of note. First, 'Digital Coase' survives intact, despite the fact that Coase staked out policy positions that were necessarily naïve with respect to modern technology.[73] That implies a powerful theoretical construct. Another irony strikes. Coase's methodological claim is that facts and institutions should rule economic analysis. But here Coase's normative model is revealed to be sound precisely because it rested on solid theory. Moreover, despite Coase's ostensible emphasis on marketplace data, his FCC article contained virtually no specific, technical information about government or market institutions or the choices they faced.[74] Instead, his analysis presented a logical critique of

---

[67] International Telecommunications Union, World Telecommunication/ICT Indicators (WTI) database (2008).

[68] Yochai Benkler, 'Overcoming Agoraphobia: Building the Commons of the Digitally Networked Environment', 11 *Harvard Journal of Law & Technology* 287 (Fall 1998); Lawrence Lessig, *The Future of Ideas* (New York: Random House; 2001); Kevin Werbach, 'Supercommons: Toward a Unified Theory of Wireless Communication', 82 *Texas Law Review* 863 (March 2004). For a good summary of these arguments, see Stuart Benjamin, 'Spectrum Abundance and the Choice between Private and Public Control', 78 *New York University Law Review* 2007 (December 2003), pp. 2014–16.

[69] Werbach (2004), p. 867.

[70] Henry E. Smith, 'Exclusion Versus Governance: Two Strategies for Delineating Property Rights', 31 *Journal of Legal Studies* S453 (June 2002).

[71] Thomas W. Hazlett, 'The Spectrum-Allocation Debate: An Analysis', 10 IEEE *Internet Computing* 68 (September/October 2006).

[72] Thomas W. Hazlett and Matthew L. Spitzer, 'Advanced Wireless Technologies and Public Policy', 78 *Southern California Law Review 595* (March 2006).

[73] Thomas W. Hazlett, 'Ronald Coase and the Spectrum Question', Beesley Lecture, London Business School, published in Colin Robinson, ed., *Utility Regulation in Competitive Markets* (Edward Elgar, Cheltenham, UK and Northampton, MA, USA: 2007).

[74] Coase (1959) is cited by contemporary spectrum policy experts as 'a scathing critique of spectrum regulation'. Phil Weiser and Dale Hatfield, 'Property Rights in Spectrum: Taking the Next Step', *IEEE Xplore* 43 (2005), p. 44. In fact, Coase presented 'a scathing critique' of the arguments justifying the imposition of administrative allocation, but offered little if any evidence that the system in place had inefficiently allocated radio spectrum.

the arguments put forward to defend administrative allocation of airwaves, buttressed by analogies from how the price system works to make efficient resource choices elsewhere. This proved sufficient to craft an argument that would stand up to mesh networks, array antennae, and ultra-wideband radios two generations later.

Second, the 'commons' attack on Coase is of a piece with a general line of thought in the 'evolution of property rights' literature.[75] While Coase did not himself overturn the transaction cost rock, he suggested that it would be interesting to look there. Harold Demsetz took him up on this in a seminal 1967 paper.[76] He posited that property rights were created when the benefits they delivered, improving social coordination and boosting productivity, justified the costs of defining and enforcing such rights. Terry Anderson and P.J. Hill then supplied an iconic example of technology shifting such an equilibrium, arguing that the introduction of barbed wire in the 1880s made land rights cheaper to delineate in the American West, thus prompting a widespread shift from open pastures to private farms.[77]

This places the current spectrum property rights debate – a 'barbed wireless' controversy – within a burgeoning literature that attempts to understand how rights regimes shift in response to economic, technological, or other social factors.[78] Gary Libecap,[79] Carol Rose,[80] and Elinor Ostrom,[81] among others, notably contribute to this inquiry. There is consensus on just where this inquiry began: 'The economics of property law begins with Coase (1960)'.[82] That Coase's story about spectrum property rights can today be fruitfully evaluated within a framework that defines the institutional elements separating open access, state property, common property, and private property regimes underscores the impressive intellectual progress triggered by his work.

4   The Coase Theorem: 'a very interesting error'

Economists, led by A.C. Pigou,[83] traditionally saw the interference problems such as occurred with radio frequencies as 'externalities'.[84] Economic choices were made without regard to the interests of third parties when uncompensated costs or benefits resulted. The

---

[75]   Not that the 'commons' argument is explicitly put forward in this manner.

[76]   Harold Demsetz, 'Toward a Theory of Property Rights', 57 *American Economic Review: Papers and Proceedings* 347 (May 1967).

[77]   Terry L. Anderson and Peter J. Hill, 'The Evolution of Property Rights: A Study of the American West', 18 *Journal of Law & Economics* 163 (April 1975).

[78]   For an excellent overview, see Dean Lueck and Thomas J. Miceli, 'Property Law', in A.M. Polinsky and S. Shavell, eds., *The Handbook of Law and Economics Volume 1* 183 (Amsterdam: North Holland, 2007).

[79]   See, for example, Gary Libecap, *Contracting for Property Rights* (New York: Cambridge University Press, 1989).

[80]   See, for example, Carol M. Rose, 'Evolution of Property Rights', in P. Newman, ed., 2 *The New Palgrave Dictionary of Law and Economics* 93 (New York: Stockton Press, 1998).

[81]   Elinor Ostrom, *Governing the Commons: The Evolution of Institutions for Collective Action* (New York: Cambridge University Press, 1990).

[82]   Lueck and Miceli (2007).

[83]   A.C. Pigou, *The Economics of Welfare* (1920), London: Macmillan and Co.

[84]   The term was coined by Paul Samuelson in the 1950s. R.H. Coase, 'The Firm, The Market, and the Law', Ch. 1 in R.H. Coase, *The Firm, the Market, and the Law* 1 (Chicago: University of Chicago Press, 1988), p. 23.

problem derived from resources prone to endemic spillovers. Pigou proposed a system of government taxes and subsidies to force decision-makers to take such effects into account, steering the economy back to efficiency.

Coase's look at the FCC gave him a radically different vantage point. Rather than policies to reduce or eliminate spillovers, the economic objective was to discover the right mix of mutually exclusive activities. Normally such balancing is achieved via trading, such that the most valuable deployments are discovered by the high bids they attract. The simplest way to show this was to take Pigou's tax solution, which assumed zero transaction costs (including those required for the government to define and impose efficiency-creating taxes), and to note that private, unregulated markets would likewise optimize resource use. Rights to pollute, for instance, would be sold to those willing to pay the most. Abstracting from wealth effects (that is, a change in demand or supply when the distribution of wealth is altered), it made no difference who was initially awarded such rights. Efficient, wealth-maximizing outcomes would obtain by virtue of a frictionless auction.

This was considered an error by George Stigler and Milton Friedman, as well as their colleagues: 'Chicago economists could not understand how so fine an economist as Coase could make so obvious a mistake'.[85] To answer their objections, Coase wrote a new paper that he was invited to present at the home of University of Chicago Law School Professor Aaron Director. What there transpired was momentous, as colorfully described by Stigler:

> Ronald asked us to believe . . . [in] this world without transaction costs: Whatever the assignment of legal liability for damages, or whatever the assignment of legal rights for ownership, the assignments would have no effect upon the way the economic resources would be used! We strongly objected to this heresy. Milton Friedman did most of the talking, as usual. He also did much of the thinking, as usual. In the course of two hours of argument the vote went from twenty against and one for Coase to twenty-one for Coase. What an exhilarating event! I lamented afterward that we had not the clairvoyance to tape it.[86]

Stigler went on to dub the proposition 'the Coase Theorem'.[87] This awarded Coase a valuable property right, as the Theorem became one of the most widely known paradigms in the social sciences. But it does a great disservice to the pathbreaking significance of Coase's 1960 article on which it is based.[88] Coase did not mean to put his readers in the 'zero transaction world' and leave them there. Instead, he used the hypothetical model to answer Pigou's *deus ex machina*: an exogenous government agency cleanly dropped into the marketplace to set prices so as to equate social cost with private cost. If that solution is free, reasoned Coase, it would be unnecessary. Markets, under the same analytical construction, would optimize on their own.

The point was not that real-world markets *would* get there, and Coase made no such claim. Rather, he fashioned an apples-to-apples comparison of institutional responses, revealing something much deeper: taxes and subsidies were not the sole solution, nor were

---

85   George J. Stigler, *Memoirs of an Unregulated Economist* (New York: Basic Books, 1988).
86   Stigler (1988), p. 76.
87   'This proposition, that when there are no transaction costs the assignments of legal rights have no effect on the allocation of resources among economic enterprises, . . . I christened . . . the Coase Theorem.' Ibid., p. 77.
88   R.H. Coase, 'The Problem of Social Cost', 3 *Journal of Law & Economics* 1 (1960).

they costless. Echoing his 'Marginal Cost Controversy' paper, Coase saw that the economic analysis properly focuses, first, on the ability of decentralized agents to deal, and then, second, inquires as to how the environment for bargaining might be improved. Policies to be considered include, but are not limited to, Pigouvian taxes. Efficiency is then assessed with respect to the costs and benefits of alternatives, apples to apples. Carl Dahlman explained the Coase contribution this way:

> The difference between private and social cost is simply postulated . . . If the government, or some other nonmarket force, cannot do it at cheaper cost than the market, then there is no difference at all between private and social cost. From Pigou's assertion that there is such a difference we must infer that he believes that the government can take the social cost into account better than the market can. But, in the absence of an analytical proof, it remains an assertion, to be taken on faith.[89]

Unraveling the positive from the normative, Coase performed radical surgery on micro-economic theory. *Spillovers* had been cast as one-way effects, technical problems affecting certain types of products or processes. The divergence between private and social cost obtained whenever a person not participating in a transaction was nonetheless impacted. Coase saw that view as highly misleading. Such third-party effects, ubiquitous in the economic system, do not imply systemic failure. Indeed, it would be inefficient to eliminate such effects – as when FCC regulators represented their task as protecting against 'harmful interference' to radio or TV stations. Coase saw the error: such effects were inputs to be optimally deployed, not spillovers to be categorically reduced.

The use of any scarce resource impacts third parties. Harry eats the cheeseburger; the burger joint gains from the sale of the burger; but hungry third-party Sally goes without. This constitutes a 'spillover' just as do the sparks a train spews onto crops grown adjacent to the rail line. In either instance scarce resources are consumed by one activity instead of another. Sally can potentially outbid Harry for the cheeseburger. The farmer may pay the train to keep its sparks from flying onto its crops.

Coase avoided the term 'externality' in his 1960 paper, focusing instead on 'harmful effects' and 'whether decisionmakers took them into account or not'.[90] That is because one of his 'main aims' in the paper 'was to show that such "harmful effects" could be treated like any other factor of production . . .'.[91] Such inputs would generally be used when their employment led to the creation of benefits exceeding their cost.

This shifted attention to the reasons that potentially positive-sum transactions might not be made. By labeling certain effects as 'externalities', economists leapt past this, attributing spillovers to the nature of particular activities and then embracing non-market remedies. Coase sharpened and yet generalized the analysis, zeroing in on the economic actors, including regulators. He saw how market trades could mitigate 'harmful effects'. He saw how regulatory choices might fail. The difference between Sally's bidding opportunity and that of the farmer's was not the unique presence of a 'harmful effect' from the railroad but found in the nature of the respective property rights. With the rights to the resource firmly

---

[89]   Carl Dahlman, 'The Problem of Externality', 23 *Journal of Law & Economics* 141 (April 1979), p. 155.

[90]   Coase (1988), p. 26.

[91]   Ibid.

established, Sally's bid was easily registered. Her failure to oputbid Harry posed no inefficiency. The 'externality' did not constitute a market failure.

Were the 'sparks' also for sale, the farmer and the railroad could transact similarly.
Perhaps, however, such rights were prohibitively costly to package and trade. Then the
auction mechanism breaks down. But, the verdict of inefficiency is premature. Only if
some alternative mechanism – say, Pigouvian taxes – is able to produce outcomes at a cost
lower than their benefit can efficiency be improved. 'The essence of Coase's insight is that
transaction costs are no different from any other costs.'[92] This break-through was motivated by his strong reaction to the costless and omniscient regulator relied on by economic
theory.

With the costs of using rival institutions front and center, Coase's 'Eureka!' flashed.
'Coase, in his great articles, focused on the symmetry between command and market
systems where the object was the establishment of efficient ways of achieving mutually
desired ends.'[93] This is what the 'Coase Theorem' should describe: the centrality of transaction costs in determining economic efficiency, and the ubiquity of such costs. Rather than
postulate a logical result in a frictionless world, Coase sought to push economic analysis
into actual markets. By evaluating the effectiveness of various legal regimes in enabling
decision-makers to bargain, economists could help formulate policies to maximize wealth.

As with Hotelling's plea to enforce marginal cost pricing, Coase had been inspired by
the asymmetry of Pigou's theory. With perfect information, policy interventions solve
'market failures' by assumption. Yet such failures would themselves be absent were market
actors encased in the same theoretical cocoon as occupied by state price setters. This was
poor theory. Responding to it, Coase aimed to generalize the analytical problem.

He has not fully succeeded. Some years after 'The Problem of Social Cost' was
published, Harold Demsetz observed generous use of what he labeled the 'Nirvana Fallacy'
in the policy pronouncements of such a sophisticated theorist as Kenneth Arrow.[94] Coase
personally laments his lack of influence.[95]

5   The study of property rights

5.1   *Exogenous rights creation*

Ronald Coase's modesty is disputed by the heavy volume of productive scholarship found
in his wake. The stream is particularly thick in the study of property rights. The 'Social
Cost' paper revealed the importance of transaction costs, and how differently defined property rights will alter them. It also, via the Coase Theorem's invariance result (with zero
transaction costs or wealth effects, it makes no difference in the final allocation of
resources which party is awarded the rights), encouraged scholars to examine how rights or
liabilities be assigned so as to minimize transaction costs.

Ronald Coase did not get very far on these questions. The FCC and 'Social Cost' papers
both rely on the creation and assignment of private ownership in resources, but assign that

---

92   Calabresi (1991), p. 1218.
93   Calabresi (1991), p. 1214.
94   Harold Demsetz, 'Information and Efficiency: Another Viewpoint', 12 *Journal of Law &
Economics* 1 (April 1969).
95   Coase (1988).

function to courts or legislators without formally investigating the manner in which such assignments occur. This left a sizeable gap.

It is being filled by two branches of the law and economics literature.[96] The first seeks to track how property regimes evolve over time. It symmetrically applies a cost-benefit framework to compare alternative rules.[97] The second focuses on how to award property rights – or assess liability – when courts hear tort or nuisance cases. Two important 1972 papers – Demsetz's 'When Does the Rule of Liability Matter?'[98] and Calabresi's and Melamed's 'One View of the Cathedral',[99] pick up where 'Social Cost' leaves off. In a positive transaction costs environment, the efficient rule is to assign property rights, all else equal, to the party that would end up with them were transactions costs low. (This is equivalent to assessing accident liability to the 'least cost avoider'.) This economizes on the resources used to create the optimal deployments, reducing transactions and, in fact, salvaging efficient outcomes when transactions costs might prevent them altogether. David Friedman sums up the simple logic about rights creation when discussing the fragmentation issue:

> When constructing bundles of rights the first question becomes 'Which rights belong together?' If I own the right to farm the land, the right to walk on the land is worth more to me than to anyone else, so the two belong in the same bundle. Since it is hard to grow crops if other people are free to tramp through your fields, the right to exclude trespassers probably belongs in the bundle as well. But that depends in part on how the land is going to be used. If it is timber instead of corn, the argument is not so clear. In some legal systems ownership of land implies only a very limited right to exclude trespassers.[100]

A similar logic applies to the use of liability rules in place of property ownership when transactions are relatively costly. This can occur due to the presence of free riders or large-number coordination problems. Legal scholarship has grasped the importance of the framework for deciding a wide range of cases, and the flurry of intellectual activity there likely dominates whatever influence Coase may lay claim to among his fellow economists.[101]

Three developments merit attention here. First is the problem buried in the 'Social Cost' paper regarding Coase's treatment of the creation of property rights. Because he found it heuristically convenient to separate this operational question from the theoretical discussion he was engaged in, he relegated transactions cost to exogeneity. When the costs of using the market were relatively high, then the relative benefits associated with regulation or other policies to augment or substitute for standard trading mechanisms tended to

---

96   I have heard Harold, on more than one occasion, joke that he should have won Coase's Nobel Prize on the grounds that he has published the Coase Theorem paper so many more times than has Ronald.

97   See discussion, *infra* at notes 75–81.

98   Harold Demsetz, 'When Does the Rule of Liability Matter?' 1 *Journal of Legal Studies* 13 (January 1972).

99   Guido Calabresi and Douglas Melamed, *Property Rules,* 'Liability Rules, and Inalienability: One View of the Cathedral', 85 *Harvard Law Review* 1089 (April 1972).

100   David D. Friedman, *Law's Order* (Princeton: Princeton University Press; 2000), p. 113.

101   In his 1991 Nobel Lecture, Coase exhibited just this view. Referencing his 'Social Cost' paper, he noted that, 'its influence on legal scholarship . . . has been immense . . . [while] its influence on economics . . . has not been immense'.

become more desirable. But this left the impression that the costs of using the market to organize economic activity were unrelated to the manner in which the property rules were crafted.

Harold Demsetz has recently returned to the issue and found Coase's approach a source of some mischief.[102] Scholars have taken the presence of positive transaction costs as sufficient justification for abandoning property rules in favor of liability rules, regulation, or Pigouvian taxes. Indeed, Coase himself has been quick to suggest that regulation may be the preferred alternative when large numbers of agents need to transact. Demsetz notes this default position for dealing with high transaction costs omits a crucial analysis: how the creation of property rights can raise or reduce transaction costs. For instance, to eliminate the demand for transactions, policy makers can assign potentially conflicting property rights to one rather than multiple parties. This allows a single enterprise to optimize with respect to 'harmful effects.' So, for instance, instead of issuing 10 licenses allocated to 10 adjacent 1 MHz bands, inviting costly delineation of rights contours and potentially producing tragedy of the commons, resources can be economized by allocating one license with the right to control the entire 10 MHz band.[103]

Yet, suppose rights are allocated to 10 different enterprises, and that prohibitively costly transactions then prevent efficient social coordination. Rather than identifying this as an 'externality' problem, Demsetz first inquires as to why the parties do not merge: '[T]here is no externality if ownership is unified.'[104] The answer must focus on the costs of bringing complementary rights into a single enterprise. That involves the loss of specialization gains, potentially increasing 'management costs'. Market transactions, including mergers, reflect a balancing test: the existence of spillovers implies that the costs of remedying such 'inefficiencies' exceed the benefits generated by ameliorating them. Given the distribution of property rights, this outcome is optimal. What remains to be fixed is not 'market failure', but the path taken by legal institutions assigning rights. Coase's *Social Cost* paper, treating this process as exogenous, fails to bring these economic considerations into the analysis. That, in turn, unleashes a premature embrace of alternative methods for dealing with externalities, despite the fact that wealth-maximizing solutions may be achieved with a more productive delineation of initial rights.

A related issue is Coase's focus on the importance of well-defined property rights for market transactions. Policy makers cite Coase for the proposition that, where property rights have not been well-defined, market transactions will fail. The implication is thus gleaned that property rights should not be awarded until legal authorities can meticulously

---

[102]   Harold Demsetz, 'Ownership and the Externality Problem', in Fred McChesney and Terry Anderson, *Property Rights: Cooperation, Conflict, and Law* (Princeton: Princeton University Press, 2003); Demsetz, 'Ownership and Exchange', Ch. 6, and 'Reinterpreting the Externality Problem', Ch. 7, in Harold Demsetz, *From Economic Man to Economic System* 90 (Cambridge: Cambridge University Press, 2008). See also, Fred McChesney, 'What I'd Say? Coase, Demsetz and the Unending Externality Debate', 26 *Cato Journal* 179 (Winter 2006).

[103]   Of course, the distribution of equity shares can substitute for the distribution of multiple property right. So, ownership of the 10 MHz license might be awarded to 10 different parties. The result is that the partitioning of equity ownership substitutes for the partitioning of resource ownership. Where the costs of adjudicating spillovers ('interference') are high relative to the costs of equity ownership deconcentration, the approach can produce efficiencies.

[104]   Demsetz (2003), p. 287.

refine them. As the Federal Communications Commission, now embracing Coase, wrote in 2002: for markets to work the government must '[c]learly and exhaustively define spectrum users rights and responsibilities'.[105] Phil Weiser and Dale Hatfield expand on this theme.[106]

This categorical position violates the analytical symmetry that the FCC and 'Social Cost' papers (and 'The Nature of the Firm' and 'The Marginal Cost Controversy', for that matter) did so much to establish. The costs of delineating clearer, more detailed rights are positive; investing those costs must deliver benefits of larger magnitude or the effort is a net social loss. Wireless markets, depending on inputs allotted by regulators, have historically been plagued by artificial spectrum scarcity.[107] Frequency rights have often been defined such that common interest tragedies obtain.[108] Alternatively, when broad but incomplete spectrum ownership rights packages have been issued, private licensees have frequently produced the necessary transactions to achieve substantial gains from trade.

An illustration is offered by a mobile television service created by Qualcomm, which in 2003 purchased rights to the frequencies allotted to TV Channel 55. The rights conveyed broad, exclusive control of the 6 MHz band to the licensee, but did not specify frequency contours. Interference with TV viewers of stations using the same or adjacent airwaves, particularly Channels 54, 55 and 56, was possible. Qualcomm and the TV Stations, with incentives to internalize gains, however, negotiated; Qualcomm paid scores of TV licensees to accept interference. Qualcomm's new service, MediaFLO, began nationwide service in 2007.[109] The importance of equipping market actors with rudimentary property rights so as to enable the negotiations that will create efficient spectrum sharing rules has long been known to economists. They have promoted the use of 'overlay rights' – where existing radio users are grandfathered but new rights to surrounding frequency space are assigned to licensees with broad, imperfectly defined spectrum rights – to move spectrum

---

[105]   Federal Communications Commission, *Spectrum Policy Task Force Report* (November 15, 2002).

[106]   Philip J. Weiser and Dale Hatfield, 'Spectrum Policy Reform and the Next Frontier of Property Rights', 15 *George Mason University Law Review* 549 (Spring 2008), pp. 591, 608. See also, Thomas W. Hazlett, 'A Law & Economics Approach to Spectrum Property Rights: A Response to Professors Weiser and Hatfield', 15 *George Mason University Law Review* 975 (Summer 2008).

[107]   See, for example, Bruce M. Owen and Gregor L. Rosston, 'Spectrum Allocation and the Internet', in W. Lehr and L. Pupillo, eds, *Cyber Policy and Economics in an Internet Age* (Springer, 2002, p. 197); Hazlett (2008a). This performance verdict strongly supports Coase (1959).

[108]   Thomas W. Hazlett, 'Spectrum Tragedies', 22 *Yale Journal of Regulation* 242 (Spring 2005). See also, Michael Heller, *The Gridlock Economy* (New York: Basic Books, 2008).

[109]   It should be noted that TV licenses are issued across 210 local markets in the US. Stations generally have different owners, making negotiations costly. The TV stations involved included many on Channel 55 itself; all stations on Channels 51–69 were analog broadcasters due to go dark in 2009. Hence, Qualcomm paid not only adjacent stations to accept interference, it also paid a number of Channel 55 broadcasters to terminate their analog signals prior to the mandated 'digital switchover'. Through this, the FCC maintained the procedural fiction that it was administratively designing the interference parameters adopted. In fact, the FCC did conduct a rulemaking, begun in January 2005 and concluded in October 2006, which set forth frequency border conditions. The rules were selected from the proposal put forward by Qualcomm, however, which was forced by law to submit the agreements struck with TV stations for regulatory approval. Agreements were negotiated prior to the FCC rules, and then formed the basis for the rules that the FCC adopted. Thomas W. Hazlett, 'A Law & Economics Approach to Spectrum Property Rights: A Response to Professors Weiser and Hatfield' 15 *Geo Mason U.L.R.* 975 (Summer 2008), pp. 999–1004.

into more valuable deployments. The proposal had great success in the Personal Communications Services (PCS) band, where licenses were first auctioned in 1995, is currently being used in the Advanced Wireless (AWS) band, where licenses were auctioned in 2006, and is proposed for use in reallocating the digital TV band.[110]

Demsetz's critique contrasts the endogeneity of transaction costs with Coase's assumption that well-defined property rights are necessary for market transactions. When market failure is said to exist in the presence of high transaction costs, it obscures the fact that high transaction costs may reflect inefficient rights definitions. The analysis of the rival institutional options suffers. Indeed, when Coase's initial property rights discovery was made in radio spectrum, it was to observe that tragedy of the commons – 'chaos' – was a product of there being 'no property rights'.[111] What he failed to incorporate was that private property rights in spectrum, under priority-in-use rules from common law, had successfully coordinated the 1920s radio market, but were abandoned by policy makers in favor of administrative allocations for political (distributive) reasons.[112] The 'period of the breakdown of the law', which obtained from July 1926 when the U.S. Commerce Department refused to enforce the established property regime, constituted non-market failure.[113] To assert, as did Coase, that the regime switch to central allocation following the 'breakdown' was the result of analytical error was not empirically established or even investigated. Coase abstracted from the process of rights creation, and hence overlooked key elements of the institutional options available.

Fred McChesney charts the Demsetz critique, giving it its due, but concluding that the answers are themselves found in Coase's work. This is a correct, if once again ironic, assessment.[114] Coase has often refused to follow his own star, innovatively extending marginal analysis to the internal organization of firms, but then bringing his project to a halt at other arbitrary boundaries. In general, he has declined to model the behavior of judges, legislatures, or other government decision-makers as rationally self-interested. But by Coase's own lights, there is no such thing as a free property right. To view ownership rules as exogenously determined by actors operating without regard to self-interest is to resurrect the analytical asymmetries of Harold Hotelling or A.C. Pigou.

5.2   Bundle of sticks[115]

One of the most influential intellectual currents in the work of Ronald Coase is reliance on a 'bundle of sticks' approach to property rights. This is associated with the legal concept of *in personam*, where ownership inheres not in 'things' or 'property' but in particular activities. The bundle of sticks refers to the set of actions the owner may engage in. This contrasts with *in rem* rights, which start from the polar position that the owner possesses

---

110   Thomas W. Hazlett and Vernon L. Smith, 'Don't Let Google Freeze the Airwaves', *Wall Street Journal* (October 3, 2008).

111   'Professor Siepmann seems to ascribe the confusion which existed before government regulation to a failure of private enterprise and the competitive system. But the real cause of the trouble was that no property rights were created in these scarce frequencies'. Coase (1959), p. 14.

112   Hazlett (1990).

113   Ibid.

114   McChesney (2006).

115   This subsection is based on the excellent treatment in Thomas Merrill and Henry Smith (2001).

the thing itself and all uses associated with it. This does not preclude the partitioning of some use rights to others. Land rights are generally considered *in rem,* but reflect the existence of easements or liabilities that encroach.

The important difference between the approaches is that they feature distinct default points in defining rights. With *in personam,* a bundle is built up with the addition of articulated rights. With *in rem,* ownership begins broad and wide, and then is whittled down. For heuristic reasons, Coase adopted – at most points – the *in personam* approach. This was convenient in that the informational requirements, in an academic treatment, were less. There was no reason to explain the scope of property rights, only to consider the trading of specific use rights and to treat packages of rights as 'ownership'.

Yet, when constructing property rights via legal institutions, *in rem* informational requirements can be substantially lower. Again, the fortuitous example is found in radio spectrum. Coase's 1959 paper was motivated by his response to the claim that airwave chaos was a product of private enterprise, and required central planning of wireless activities for efficient operation. Taking the traditional history as given, Coase presented the standard market solution to frequency rights as *in rem,* via a land ownership analogy[116]:

> We know from our ordinary experience that land can be allocated to land users without the need for government regulation by using the price mechanism. But if no property rights were created in land, so that everyone could use a tract of land, it is clear that there would be considerable confusion and that the price mechanism could not work . . . But it would be wrong to blame this on private enterprise and the competitive system. A private-enterprise system cannot function properly unless property rights are created in resources, and, when this is done, someone wishing to use a resource has to pay the owner to obtain it. Chaos disappears; and so does the government except that a legal system to define property rights and to arbitrate disputes is, of course, necessary.

The utility of this approach, in theory and in practice, is that it vests spectrum owners with broad rights, enabling rival users to execute trades that establish optimal 'interference' levels. The reason *in rem* rights are key is that the trades will necessarily deal with a host of dynamically changing uses unknown ex ante. Legal authorities can delegate broad rights to owners via *in rem,* allowing imperfect but relatively simple property lines to set a basis for negotiation. This approach encourages wealth-creating resource sharing, à la Coasean bargains. It also provides incentives for innovation, as residual claimants – those with *in rem* ownership – internalize gains from discovering productive new wireless applications. The residual claimant holding yet undiscovered *in personam* rights, however, is the regulatory authority. Because agency decision-makers do not internalize costs or benefits of innovation, the property rights structure imposes net social costs as an alternative to the *in rem* regime.

In radio spectrum, those costs have proven onerous. Plagued by high informational requirements and constrained by the rent-seeking behavior of interests resisting rent-dissipating competition, the well-established equilibrium in FCC spectrum regulation constitutes an extremely expensive way to coordinate resource use. Coase implicitly made this point, not on empirical grounds, but on the theory that an 'invisible hand' could more efficiently allocate spectrum between competing alternatives than could a central planner.

---

116   Coase (1959), p. 15.

Hence, Coase's normative policy recommendation required *in rem* rights. That is why, years after the FCC paper, Coase reverted to an *in rem* regime in suggesting the sale of 'radio frequencies' when outlining the efficient public policy:

> I have proposed that radio frequencies should be disposed of to the highest bidder because it would avoid the costs of the present procedure, would tend to allocate these frequencies to those who could use them most efficiently, would prevent the unjustifiable enrichment of those (commonly wealthy) private individuals who obtain these grants from the FCC, and would facilitate changes in the use of radio frequencies when this seemed to be called for.[117]

Given this, Coase's 'bundle of sticks' approach appears puzzling. The confusion appeared in this passage:

> If one person could use a piece of land for growing a crop, and then another person could come along and build a house on the land used for the crop, and then another could come along, tear down the house, and use the space as a parking lot, it would no doubt be accurate to describe the resulting situation as chaos.[118]

Actually, no. Were such rights exclusively issued, the owners would negotiate to arrange for the highest valued employment(s). What is the potential failure? It arises in one of two situations.[119] First, where the property rights are non-exclusive, the standard tragedy of the commons ensues. Second, where the most valuable rights are not issued to private parties, they cannot be employed. This is the situation when new resource uses dynamically emerge but cannot be legally defined and distributed to owners at low costs (or costs low enough to beat the *in rem* alternative). This too constitutes a tragedy of the commons, albeit one unfamiliar to those looking for over-grazing.[120]

Private markets cannot bid resources into their highest valued employments when the relevant rights are held (or withheld) by regulators. Coase's FCC article, while explicitly motivated by the *in rem* concept of land ownership and relying upon the distribution of *in rem* rights to private parties, abandons the regime. Late in the analysis, it rejects the view that radio spectrum constitutes a resource to be owned, arguing for a system of specifically defined use rights:

> What does not seem to have been understood is that what is being allocated by the Federal Communications Commission, or, if there were a market, what would be sold, is the right to use a piece of equipment to transmit signals in a particular way. Once the question is looked at in this way, it is unnecessary to think in terms of ownership of frequencies or the ether.[121]

---

117   R.H. Coase, 'The Economics of Broadcasting and Government Policy', 54 *American Economic Review* 440 (March 1966), p. 445.

118   Coase (1959), p. 15.

119   This tragedy directly reflects the insight of Coase (1960) that the cost of restricting economic activity to avoid a harmful effect is the mirror image of costs imposed by productive activity that impose, as a byproduct, a harmful effect.

120   Note that the example, which features just three individuals with overlapping rights to the same resource, implies that negotiations would not be prohibitively expensive.

121   Coase (1959), p. 33.

Coase claimed that thinking of spectrum ownership 'tends to obscure the question that is being decided'. He illustrated this by writing that, 'whether we have the right to shoot over another man's land has been thought of as depending on who owns the airspace over the land. It would be simpler to discuss what we should be allowed to do with a gun.'[122] But the analogy is dubious. The use of a gun often involves sporadic, spontaneous use of airspace, and transactions between gun users and property owners are relatively expensive. The passer-by pulling out a gun to defend himself is not in a position to bargain. Behavioral rules on gun use generally appear appropriate. But not always. Where a landowner seeks to supply fee hunting or a shooting range, the rights to determine what bullets go through 'her' airspace are tied to the land, and efficiently so. The land uses and the adjacent airwave uses are highly complementary, and would likely be held by a single enterprise in a low transactions cost environment.

Limiting wireless applications to those enabled by 'the right to use a piece of equipment to transmit signals in a particular way' appropriates just the choices that the Coase Theorem requires markets to trade. Coase's logic in arguing for market allocation to replace administrative allocation of spectrum, in fact, has been strongly supported by scholarship revealing how FCC rules stymie competition, innovation, and productivity.[123] The reason for this is that the issuance of narrow use rights or 'operating permits', as distinct from 'spectrum licenses' or frequency ownership, does not allow private parties scope for innovation either in the introduction of new technologies, services and business models, or in the allocation of spectrum. Indeed, when rent-seeking dynamics are included in the analysis, licensing restrictions closely resemble cartel enforcement devices, limiting competitive rivalry via rules promoted by industry incumbents.[124]

Imagine that Band A's owner asks adjacent Band B's owner to deploy a new radio system, which A will pay for, allowing B's customers to remain unaffected while A's wireless network upgrades to a new architecture, doubling the value of the service to A's customers. The transaction is prohibited under *in personam* rights – which constitute the traditional regulatory regime that Coase critiqued. This regulatory structure is called 'command and control' by the agency itself.[125]

FCC economists arguing for market allocation of radio spectrum rightly emphasize the key reform: liberalizing licenses to convey 'flexible use' rather than specific use rights.[126] Such reforms have been undertaken, implicitly in the US,[127] explicitly in countries such as Australia and Guatemala. Neither the informational requirements nor administrative costs have proven onerous.[128]

---

[122]   Coase (1959), p. 34.

[123]   Thomas W. Hazlett, 'The Wireless Craze, the Spectrum Auctions Faux Pas, the Unlimited Bandwidth Myth, and the Punchline to Ronald Coase's "Big Joke": An Essay on Airwave Allocation Policy', 14 *Harvard Journal of Law & Technology* 335 (Spring 2001).

[124]   Hazlett (1990). Of course, the classic description of regulatory capture is found in George J. Stigler, 'The Economic Theory of Regulation', 2 *Bell Journal of Economics & Management Science 3* (Spring 1971).

[125]   FCC SPTFR (2002).

[126]   Evan Kwerel and John Williams, 'A Proposal for a Rapid Transition to Market Allocation of Spectrum', FCC Office of Plans & Policies, Working Paper No. 38 (November 2002).

[127]   Hazlett and Spitzer (2006).

[128]   Hazlett (2008b); Thomas W. Hazlett, Giancarlo Ibarguen and Wayne Leighton, 'Property

Arguing for *in personam* rights, Coase advanced a policy prone to common interest tragedies,[129] sabotaging his normative argument. It is notable that Coase limited his discussion of negotiated solutions, both in the FCC paper and in 'Social Cost' paper, to two-person bargaining situations, while suggesting that multi-party conflicts would tend to be resolved by regulation. 'When large numbers of people are involved, the argument for the institution of property is weakened and that for general regulations becomes stronger . . .'.[130] The Demsetzian critique cuts here. Defining property via *in rem* rights is a standard way to mitigate large numbers bargaining costs; Coase, in abstracting from the relationship between rights construction and transaction costs, nonetheless falls prey to their connection. Reality forced him back to the broader view of property. In his (suppressed) 1962 Rand study, as in his 1966 AER paper, he reverted to an *in rem* formulation of spectrum rights.[131]

But the damage was done. The law and economics literature followed Coase's *in personam* preference as the default rights construction path. It is commonly assumed that property rights are best characterized as 'bundles of sticks'. Thomas Merrill and Henry Smith express concern with the implications.[132] Important trade-offs embedded in the choice of property model go unexamined. Coase, the pre-eminent expositor of the property rights solution to tragedy of the commons, plays a key role in its re-emergence.

5.3   Looking under the light(house)

The standard-issue professional joke is that economists look to find the coin they're missing not where they remember dropping it but in the area illuminated by the street lamp – 'the light's better there'. Coase might supply a different punchline: leading economists would not have bothered looking for the lost coin – it's location was simply an empirical issue.

Instead, they would craft a theory. Coase was animated by such theories; he thrilled at the challenge of roping them, and then dragging them back to the marketplace. That is where he checked out their examples. He was inevitably surprised and delighted by what he found.

In many respects, this was his motivation for accepting the offer to serve as editor of the *Journal of Law & Economics* (*JLE*) in 1964.[133] What was needed was a forum for high-quality fact-checking. Coase summarized his *modus operandi* as 'looking for results'.[134]

Rights to Radio Spectrum in Guatemala and El Salvador: An Experiment in Liberalization', 3 *Review of Law & Economics* 2 (2007).

[129]   See Heller (2008), Ch. 4.

[130]   Coase (1959), p. 29.

[131]   In formulating property rights to replace administrative allocations, Coase and his Rand colleagues attempted to define spectrum boundary conditions inside of which '[t]he right holder shall have the right to refuse others permission to radiate energy . . .' and wherein '[t]he uses to which a right holder puts his property shall be determined by him . . .' Ronald Coase, William H. Meckling and Jora Minasian, *Problems of Radio Frequency* (Santa Monica: Rand Corporation, Sept. 1995), p. 101.

[132]   They cite prominent work in which the bundle of sticks approach to property rights is prominent, including Robert Cooter, 'Unity in Tort, Contract, and Property: The Model of Precaution', 73 *Cal. L. R.* 1 (1985); Calabresi and Melamed (1972); and Yoram Barzel, *Economic Analysis of Property Rights, Second Edition* (Cambridge: Cambridge University Press, 1997).

[133]   Hazlett (1997).

[134]   Ibid.

One result that he found interesting was that economic theorists from John Stuart Mill to Paul Samuelson had employed the lighthouse as a paradigmatic public good impossible to privately finance and supply. The navigational beam offered to sailors being a non-excludable, poorly targeted utility, its productive contribution to shipping would go predictably uncompensated due to endemic free riding.

Game on. Coase, investigating the matter, emerged triumphant.[135] The fact was that lighthouses in England had, for large stretches of history, been constructed by private investors and were operated by for-profit companies. Excludability had been created through legal institutions, entitling lighthouses the right to collect fees. The light beam supplier was then able to obtain recompense.

> The early history shows that . . . a lighthouse service can be provided by private enterprise. In those days, shipowners and shippers could petition the Crown to allow a private individual to construct a lighthouse and to levy a (specified) toll on ships benefiting from it. The lighthouses were built, operated, financed, and owned by private individuals . . . The role of the government was limited to the establishment and enforcement of property rights in the lighthouse.[136]

After the 1830s, rules changed, yet certain fundamental institutional aspects remained the same. The British government mandated that British ships pay duties. Fees, set to cover costs, were then distributed to lighthouses. The pricing schedules were not linear, but multi-part; most shipowners maxed out and then paid nothing for the marginal ship. This was efficient, overcoming the output restriction that Samuelson had advanced as the rationale for state-owned enterprise. Coase noted that shippers setting tariffs and then paying them were far more likely to efficiently police suppliers than government administrators lacking financial interest in the matter.

Some have criticized Coase's analysis as overplaying the role of the market and under-playing the role of the state.[137] The rejoinder is weak. Coase's analysis underscored the role of legally created and enforced property rights. Moreover, it stressed that the existence of a possible private solution did not decide the matter; further empirical evidence would be helpful there, too. But the finding that the historical market organization was not based on public financing via taxpayer subsidies – the enterprise advocated by Samuelson – showed that the structural efficiency case had not met its burden. There was scope for private finance and supply, and more information was necessary to compare that policy solution with the performance of alternatives.

Coase thought the finding important for economic theory and public policy:

> How is it that these great men have . . . been led to make statements about lighthouses which are misleading as to the facts, whose meaning, if thought about in a concrete fashion, is unclear, and which, to the extent that they imply a policy conclusion, are very likely wrong? . . . Despite the

---

[135]   Ronald H. Coase, 'The Lighthouse in Economics', 17 *Journal of Law & Economics* 357 (October 1974).

[136]   Coase (1974), p. 375.

[137]   Andrew Odlyzko, *Pricing and Architecture of the Internet: Historical Perspectives from Telecommunications and Transportation* (August 29, 2004), http://www.dtc.umn.edu/~odlyzho/doc/pricing.architecture.pdf.

extensive use of the lighthouse example in the literature, no economist, to my knowledge, has ever made a comprehensive study of lighthouse finance and administrations. The lighthouse is simply plucked out of the air to serve as an example.[138]

Coase's empiricism was informal. But it fleshed out an important example, presenting a compelling historical narrative, and challenged economic theory.[139]

Such work opened the door for much more 'fact-checking' research – much of it published in the *JLE*. Two such studies merit mention.

Steven Cheung's 1973 essay, 'The Fable of the Bees',[140] deconstructed another iconic example in economic theory, the 'ownership externality' associated with 'apples and bees'. Due to the complementary nature of honey and apple production, combined with the implicit assumption that the positive contribution to honey output made by apple producers, and vice versa, will thereby be uncompensated in the market,[141] economists widely referenced the example as an illustration of market inefficiency. Cheung took a look at actual markets and found something quite different. Contracts between farmers and beekeepers were widely offered and executed, optimizing the use of productive inputs across firms.[142]

In 1990, Stanley Liebowitz and Stephen Margolis published another *JLE* article in this genre. 'The Fable of the Keys'[143] quickly became a classic. It responded to the well-known story about the development of the QWERTY typewriter keyboard. As relayed by Paul David in 1985,[144] the QWERTY layout was highly inefficient for modern typewriting machines, but had been adopted in the 19th century as a method for slowing down typists in order to reduce jamming. While better technologies made the jamming concern obsolete, the fact that millions of people had learned the QWERTY system kept superior keyboards (enabling faster typing) off the market.

---

[138] Coase (1974), pp. 374–5.
[139] Today that non-technical contribution can scarcely be made in the *JLE*, let alone another highly regarded economics journal, but is the domain of the law review. It is appropriate to note, however, that the American Economics Association has published the *Journal of Economic Perspectives* since 1987, presumably designed to fill just such a gap (or some small part of it) in satisfying the demand for economics articles devoid of technical analysis or specialized jargon. Other AEA journals have more recently emerged with seemingly similar missions, including the policy-oriented *Economists' Voice*.
[140] Steven N.S. Cheung, 'The Fable of the Bees: An Economic Investigation', 16 *Journal of Law & Economics* 11 (April 1973).
[141] Francis M. Bator, 'The Anatomy of Market Failure', 72 *Quarterly Journal of Economics* 351 (1958).
[142] Many studies of these interesting contractual arrangements have added greater detail to the economic forces at work. See Alan L. Olmstead and Donald B. Wooten, 'Bee Pollination and Productivity Growth: The Case of Alfalfa', 69 *American Journal of Agricultural Economics* 56 (February 1987); Mary K. Muth, Randall R. Rucker, Walter N. Thurman and Ching-Ta Chuang, 'The Fable of the Bees Revisited: Causes and Consequences of the U.S. Honey Program', 46 *Journal of Law & Economics* 479 (October 2003).
[143] S.J. Liebowitz and Stephen Margolis, 'The Fable of the Keys', 33 *Journal of Law & Economics* (April 1990).
[144] Paul David, 'Clio and the Economics of QWERTY', 75 *American Economic Review* 332 (May 1985).

The example formed the factual crux of a broad argument for market failure. Path dependency put unregulated economic markets in a rut. Citing a collective action problem in efficiently shifting systems, David called on more liberal use of government regulation to set standards. Paul Krugman's 1994 *Peddling Prosperity*,[145] in a chapter entitled, 'The Economics of QWERTY', boldly upped the ante. Extrapolating the path dependence problem, Krugman argued that, while the city of Cleveland may have been optimally located when founded, it could well be located in an unproductive spot now. But inertia doomed any relocation project. He generalized: this was an example of endemic market failure.

Liebowitz and Margolis persuasively demolished QWERTY path dependence. The typing standard did not block progress; the historical record showed that no alternative would have been more efficient. Moreover, it launched a compelling analysis of the costs and benefits of standards. Economists were forced to reconsider their policy pronouncements, and to recognize that the options taken – sacrificing better visibility as to changing conditions in the future – were themselves valuable. In 1998, Krugman reversed course, conceding that were substantial efficiency gains available, the investment in switching costs would likely have been made by private parties.[146]

6   Conclusion

'Creativity often, and perhaps usually, consists of looking at familiar things or ideas in a new way.'[147]

A.C. Pigou reasoned that, 'in some occupations, a part of the product of a unit of resources consists of something, which, instead of coming in the first instance to the person who invests the unit, comes instead . . . as a positive or negative item, to other people'.[148] He thus saw the externality as a condition affecting a certain class of industry or behavior. This dysfunction was the product of standard, off-the-shelf economic theory. Routinely, potential gains escaped the system, were scattered and were lost.

But where did they go? Coase was never possessed by the formalities of the micro-maximization problem. He was, in Karl Brunner's warm words, 'an old-fashioned economist'.[149] He reveled in the prose of Adam Smith, and was motivated by the idea of gains from trade. This perspective opened vistas. Coase took in more; he more easily grasped essentials; he then displayed a facility for lucidly explaining them.

All economic choices incur costs in order to create benefits. These effects are prompted by decision-makers, but extend beyond the party 'who invests the unit'. The social efficiency question concerns what mechanisms are in place to link those affected, such that net gains are reliably positive. Coase recognized the fundamental role of property rights in

---

[145]   Paul Krugman, *Peddling Prosperity* (New York and London: W.W. Norton, 1994).

[146]   Lee Gomes, 'Economists Decide to Challenge Facts of the QWERTY Story', *Wall Street Journal* (February 25, 1998).

[147]   George Stigler, discussing the Coase Theorem; Stigler (1988), p. 79.

[148]   A.C. Pigou, *The Economics of Welfare* (London: Macmillan & Co., 1924), p. 174.

[149]   Karl Brunner, 'Ronald Coase: Old-Fashioned Scholar', 94 *Scandinavian Journal of Economics* 7 (March 1992).

supplying such a communications grid. This led him to contrast regimes where market coordination produces efficient exchanges with those that fail to do so. Coase followed the spillovers to see where they came from and where they went.

Pigou focused on a narrow maximization problem. While analytically sophisticated, it proved operationally simplistic. Once certain arguments were found to be missing from the relevant optimization problem, the logic of market failure was inescapable. The existence of externalities was a generic system defect. From the confines of a model which excluded the details of institutions, the error was compounded by importing a *deus ex machina* solution. That the very same incentive or informational infirmities that had caused the identified market failure might apply to the proffered non-market solution was not evident. Until Coase.

The opportunity he found was productively exploited. By simply taking the path less traveled, inquiring as to how transactions did – or could – resolve resource misallocation, he was able to write the same seminal paper on repeated occasions. As he has himself noted, 'The Nature of the Firm', 'The Marginal Cost Controversy', and 'The Problem of Social Cost' 'all embody essentially the same point of view'.[150] These contributions, separately and together, properly focused attention on the fundamental importance of the property rights regime in efficiency-enabling transactions. Notwithstanding the zero-cost tautology that Stigler has dubbed the Coase Theorem, the work proved 'a stepping stone on the way to an analysis of an economy with positive transaction costs'.[151]

The dean of modern law and economics scholars, judge Richard J. Posner, calls Ronald Coase 'the George Orwell of modern economics'.[152] This Orwell has extended one of the simplest maxims in the science, what Guido Calabresi labels 'Coase's insight – there is no free lunch'. His work reminded those recommending this or that policy that 'Everything has costs: There is a cost to liability ways of shifting entitlements, and there is also a cost to any other way of doing it'.[153]

This symmetry takes economics from categorical to incremental choices, illuminating actual trade-offs. Policy decisions necessitate the comparison of institutional options, fully assessing alternative pathways. This contribution, wide and deep, has been touched by paradox at virtually every turn. And there is one more to mention. In Coase's Nobel Lecture and in other writings, he bemoans his lack of influence. 'My point of view has not in general commanded assent, nor has my argument, for the most part, been understood.'[154]

It is easy to mock the assertion, as Robert Ellickson does.[155] But there is also a ring of truth to the statement, as Ellickson also elucidates. 'Coase's name is consistently attached

---

[150]   Coase (1988), p. 1.

[151]   Nobel lecture, p. 9.

[152]   Posner (1993), p. 205.

[153]   Guido Calabresi, 'Remarks: The Simple Virtues of the Cathedral', 106 *Yale Law Journal* 2201 (May 1997), p. 2206.

[154]   Coase (1988), p. 1.

[155]   'One can imagine the muttering that Coase's plaint will provoke in the university towns across America. "Wait a minute, buster," will grouse the professors. "It must be tough when you've merely written the most cited article in the legal literature".' Robert C. Ellickson, 'The Case for Coase and Against "Coaseanism",' 99 *Yale Law Journal* 611 (December 1989), p. 611 (footnote omitted).

to propositions that he has explicitly repudiated.'[156] This surely frustrates Coase. But it goes with the turf. When one offers such broad insights that touch so many corners of the enterprise, the period for integrating such perceptiveness is long. Forgive those who advance 'propositions that he has explicitly repudiated'. Even, on occasion, Coase himself.

---

[156]   Ibid.

2 Aaron Director remembered*

Stephen M. Stigler

The faculty of the University of Chicago Law School is, and has been for some time, an extraordinary group. Aaron Director was unusual even within this group. In a group where the average annual number of publications per single faculty member exceeds that of the whole of many law schools, Aaron published next to nothing – a coauthored book and a pamphlet on unemployment in 1932 before he hit his stride and little more than a few book reviews after that. In a group decorated by all manner of academic honors (even a Nobel Prize), Aaron did not even have a Ph.D. In a group of forceful and dynamic intellects, Aaron never raised his voice, and casual observers might well have overlooked him, unless they noticed his colleagues lowering their own voices to hear what Aaron had to say.

And of course he was remarkable, or we would not be recalling him 40 years after he retired and moved to California, where he lived until his death in September 2004. A reader would be entitled to ask, what can I, a statistician who came to Chicago 14 years after Aaron left for California, what can I usefully add to a discussion of this remarkable man? I could tell you that I am writing because in the early 1930s Aaron taught statistics at this university. He did do that, but that is not the real reason, which derives from the fact that my father, George Stigler, was, from the late 1950s until he died in 1991, Aaron's best friend.

My father and Aaron first became closely acquainted in 1947 when they were invited (with Milton Friedman, already by then Aaron's brother-in-law) to the first meeting in Switzerland of the Mont Pelerin Society. In pictures from that time they look like three mischievous East German spies. That society was formed by Friedrich Hayek to celebrate classical liberalism, and Aaron had met Hayek in 1937 during a year-long stay at the London School of Economics. Aaron played a pivotal role in getting the University of Chicago Press to publish Hayek's influential 1944 attack on government intervention in economic affairs, a book called *The Road to Serfdom*.

When my father returned to the University of Chicago in 1958, he and Aaron and Milton were reunited on one campus, and they shared an extraordinary level of discourse, and lighter moments as well. When Milton visited the U.S.S.R., he sent my father a postcard with a picture of Karl Marx. My father was chagrined that he had no comparable postcard of Adam Smith to respond with. He and Aaron went to remedy this and learned something about practical price theory in the process. First, postcards were printed in sets of five, so they had to identify four more worthy subjects to go with Adam Smith. And second, while it cost $100 to produce 100 sets of postcards, it cost only $101 to produce several thousand sets. I still have a cabinet full of the results of this lesson. They had other adventures in practical

* Based on a talk given on February 2, 2005, at the University of Chicago Law School. Reprinted with permission from the *Journal of Law and Economics*, 48 (October 2005, 307). © 2005 by The University of Chicago. All rights reserved. 0022-2186/2005/4802-0013$01.50.id.

economics, including an ill-timed entry into the silver futures market, which was even less profitable than the postcard venture.

After Aaron retired from the University of Chicago in 1965, my father began a long series of academic visits to Stanford University's Hoover Institution, where the chance to visit with Aaron was a distinct highlight. It was only in the early 1980s that I got to know Aaron more than casually.

Despite a 40-year difference in our ages, I was attracted by the same qualities my father saw in Aaron: his curiosity, his interest, his understanding, his humor, all this together with an intellect of the highest quality and no pretense. My father once likened him to Socrates, but if that conjures up an image of the much-feared Socratic method, it misses the point. Not that his comments couldn't be disquieting. I recall once complaining to him about how much I was spending on income taxes. He was comforting: 'Yes, too bad about all that pesky income.' Aaron had a keen eye for superficial analysis.

My frequent visits with Aaron dated from the mid-1980s, when I first joined the board of the Center for Advanced Study in the Behavioral Sciences at Stanford. Aaron and I had wide-ranging discussions on many subjects, and it appeared to me that there was no limit to his intellectual resources. I became more curious about his background, and in the early 1990s I began to quiz him on his life and kept notes as best I could on what I learned. I shared a version of these notes with Ronald Coase, and he was able to use and build on them in his fine biographical article about Aaron for the *New Palgrave Dictionary of Economics and the Law*, which was published in 1998.

Aaron was born in a small town in what is now Ukraine, about 40 miles south of Pinsk, on an uncertain date in 1901. When Aaron emigrated to the United States in 1914 with his mother and siblings, to settle in Portland, Oregon, where his father had set up a precarious existence, he was required to choose birthdates for himself and his siblings; he chose the fall equinox for himself and Christmas Day for his baby sister Rose. It was in Portland as a teenager that he first encountered the English language, and it is a tribute to his remarkable intelligence that within 6 years, English was his specialty and he was made the editor of the Lincoln High School yearbook.

That yearbook contains what may be Aaron's first publication in law and economics, written at the tender age of 20. It bears the hallmark of Aaron's keenly analytical mind and is entitled 'Blue Sunday Madness'. At that time, a 'Blue Sunday' law was being considered in Portland, one that would ban work on Sunday and, among other things, halt all trains on Sundays. Rather than attack the proposed law, Aaron examined its consequences. He began by imagining a train approaching Portland on a Sunday and stopping 7 miles out of town, where the conductor informed the passengers they would remain there until Monday. Aaron granted that in olden days the law would work no hardship – 'The nomads of old,' he wrote, 'marching through the wilderness, might without any disadvantages stop marching on Sunday. They might also feed their cattle on Saturday and tell them they must go hungry on Sunday. They could also feed themselves and diplomatically inform their stomachs that eating on Sunday was work and therefore forbidden'. Aaron allowed that similar accommodations were feasible in the modern age and that some relief was available by the planned exemption of automobiles from the law. 'You may ask,' he wrote, 'why Fords are allowed to be used on Sunday while trains are not. Every Ford owner will inform you that Fords carry special privileges, as it takes no work to drive one.' But in industry and shipping and communications, he noted that more serious economic consequences would be encountered, such as shutdown costs in heavy industry, boats forced to stop on Sunday regardless of the wind, and the need to recall wireless transmissions that would otherwise arrive on Sunday. Still, he ended on an optimistic note: if the law were approved it would still be possible, he said, to 'live – if not happily at least live ever afterward'.

Aaron graduated from Lincoln High in January 1921, and about that time the Yale University dean of admissions visited the school, with the result that Aaron and a slightly younger friend enrolled in Yale in the fall of 1921 as scholarship students. The younger friend was Mark Rothkowitz, later famous as an abstract painter under the name Mark Rothko. While at Yale, Aaron and Mark Rothko published an underground newspaper called the *Saturday Evening Pest* from February to May 1923. Its motto was, 'The beginning of doubt is the beginning of wisdom', and the first issue announced this credo:

> We believe
>   That in this age of smugness and self-satisfaction, destructive criticism is at least as useful, if not more so, than constructive criticism.
>   That Yale is preparing men, not to live, but to make a living.
>   That the life of the average undergraduate is stupid, empty, and meaningless.
>   That the literature of the undergraduate consists chiefly of our contemporary, *The Saturday Evening Post*.
>   That athletics hold a more prominent place at Yale than education, which is endured as a necessary evil.

They evidently came under fire from the administration; their last issue contains a supporting letter solicited from Sinclair Lewis, a distinguished alumnus of Yale. Rothko did not return the next fall, and Aaron graduated in 1924 after only 3 years, probably to the relief of the Yale administration.

Aaron was a bit of a radical at Yale, and for the next year and a half he traveled, working as a migrant laborer in Midwestern wheat fields and New Jersey textile mills, even in a Pennsylvania coal mine, as he crossed the country studying American labor from the inside. He taught at a labor college in New Jersey, and he traveled to Europe, to England, and as far to the east as Czechoslovakia, before returning to Portland as an educational director at the Portland Labor College. In 1927 he decided to come to Chicago for graduate study in labor economics with Paul Douglas, then a member of our economics department and later a U.S. senator from Illinois. After 3 years as a student, Aaron joined the staff in 1930, teaching and assisting Douglas on a book on unemployment. Aaron was evidently a very effective teacher – the Nobel economist Paul Samuelson recalls that it was a course of Aaron's that introduced him to economics when he was a college student here and that course first excited his interest in the subject.

The next few years after 1934 Aaron was a migrant worker of a different sort: 2 years in Washington at the U.S. Treasury Department, then back to Chicago to work with Jacob Viner, then in 1937 a year at the London School of Economics researching for a dissertation that was planned to be on the Bank of England but never finished, then back to Chicago, then off to Washington, this time to work successively in the War Department, the Alien Properties Bureau, and the Commerce Department on International Trade. And then in 1946, he was back to Chicago, to teach in the law school, an appointment he owed to the high opinions of him held by Henry Simons and Friedrich Hayek.

Over this period, Aaron maintained his silence in publication, at least under his own name.

But he told me a story about how he had once written a syndicated column for Scripps-Howard that appeared in such papers as the *New York World Telegram* in the early 1940s. It was published on the opinion page, immediately beneath the column of Westbrook Pegler and just above Eleanor Roosevelt's daily diary, a column she called 'My Day'. You would not discover this from reading the newspaper since Aaron's name did not appear; the columns were attributed to General Hugh S. Johnson ('Old Ironpants'), the man who had run Roosevelt's National Recovery Administration until it was canceled by the Supreme Court in 1935 as unconstitutional. The story Aaron told me was that in 1942 he had become friends with Johnson's son Kilbourne while working in Washington. In March and April, Hugh Johnson was taken by a serious bout of pneumonia and had trouble keeping up with his daily column, and the son asked Aaron to ghostwrite a few columns, and he did. Hugh Johnson died of the pneumonia in the early morning of April 15, and the next issue of *Time* magazine carried a long obituary. In the course of the obituary the writer remarked that there was no sense of imminence in Johnson's last column, a column on taxes and prices that appeared the day of his death. And the writer quoted the opening sentence of the column. Yes, the column was one that Aaron had written; the opening sentence was pure Aaron: 'There appears to be no end to the lack of frankness and coordination among high government officials'.

My father wrote several times of his great admiration and warm affection for Aaron, describing him as 'a paragon of all collegial virtues', and described his mind as a 'probing intelligence that thinks its way to the bottom – or at least to an unfamiliar depth – of many questions'. Aaron always protested at statements that exceeded logical limits or available evidence, and in this last sentence I can see my father pausing after 'thinks its way to the bottom' and, realizing that Aaron would not approve, adding 'or at least to an unfamiliar depth'. Aaron was an extraordinary man, and we should be proud of his influential association with the University of Chicago.

3 Aaron Director's influence on antitrust policy*

Sam Peltzman

Aaron Director was born in Charterisk, which is now in Ukraine, in 1901. He died in Los Altos Hills, California, on September 11, 2004. His life was long, his vita was short, and his influence on US antitrust policy was profound. He was the intellectual progenitor of what is sometimes called the 'Chicago School' of antitrust policy. Some of the seminal contributions of this school appeared in the *Journal of Law and Economics,* of which Director was the founding editor. In this memorial essay I will review his life briefly, but I will focus mainly on his contribution to the economic and legal analysis of antitrust issues.

Aaron Director came to the United States in 1913 with his family. He spent his formative years in Portland, Oregon, where the family ran a furniture store. In 1921 he was awarded a scholarship to attend Yale University, from which he graduated in 1924. At this time of his life, Director fancied himself a socialist and conducted himself accordingly, dabbling at various blue-collar jobs and teaching at a school affiliated with the Oregon Labor Party. These radical beliefs were eventually to be altered radically. This pattern of early infatuation with socialism and its subsequent rejection was later to be mirrored in several of his influential students.

Director first arrived at the University of Chicago in 1927 with a fellowship to study labor economics under Paul Douglas (co-parent of the Cobb-Douglas production function and later US senator from Illinois). However, the greater intellectual influence on his life would come from Frank Knight and Jacob Viner. Director was a graduate student and part-time instructor at Chicago until 1934, but he never completed a doctoral dissertation. It was during this period that he persuaded his sister, Rose, to join him as a graduate student, where she met her future husband, Milton Friedman. This was also the time when Milton Friedman, Aaron Director, and fellow student George Stigler formed a powerful tripartite intellectual relationship that was to endure for the entirety of their careers.

Director was in some ways the odd member of this triad. Friedman and Stigler tended to dominate any room they entered; Director was relentlessly uncharismatic. His two friends were masters of the quick repartee; Director was, at least in my memory, slow and thoughtful.[1] Friedman and Stigler tended toward impatience and a desire to move on. By contrast, a conversation with Director could be punctuated by long silences that often began with one question and ended in another.

---

* I am indebted to Dennis Carlton and Douglas Lichtman for their comments on an earlier version and to Sharon Jennings for bibliographic assistance. Reprinted with permission from the *Journal of Law and Economics,* 48 (October 2005, 313). © 2005 by The University of Chicago. All rights reserved. 0022-2186/2005/4802-0013$01.50.

[1] So much so that the actual publication dates of the early volumes of the *Journal of Law and Economics* lagged well behind the dates on the cover.

The period of Director's great influence on economics and law began in 1947 with his appointment to the faculty of the University of Chicago Law School. He was the successor to Henry Simons, who served only briefly as the first economist on a major law school faculty before his untimely death. Director retired from the university in 1966 and spent the rest of his life in the Bay Area of California, where he was affiliated with the Hoover Institution.

None of Director's innovations appear under his own name. They were transmitted in two ways – in the classroom where he co-taught the law school's antitrust course and from collegial interaction. Director's conversations with colleagues sometimes resulted in seminal articles. But other of his ideas were broadcast less formally, often by Friedman or Stigler or, later, by Ronald Coase.[2] His influence on the law students was more direct, since some were destined to become influential judges or legal scholars or both. This history raises obvious problems of attribution. When I subsequently link an idea to Director, I will be conveying my sense of the 'oral tradition' that produced the idea.

Director's most important influence on antitrust policy occurred in three areas: predatory pricing, vertical restraints in distribution, and tied or bundled sales of multiple products. These contributions arose out of his broader interest in what is sometimes called 'business practices'. These are the myriad ways in which real-world businesses behave differently from the caricature found in textbooks. Those differences sometimes arouse a suspicious response from economists. Visions of 'market power' and 'deadweight loss' triangles dance in their heads, and some of the suspect practices have been constrained by antitrust policy. Director rejected this kind of intellectual laziness, and he sought, sometimes successfully, to inoculate those around him against it.[3]

Director approached all business practices with a methodology that entailed asking very basic questions and answering them with a rigorous logic that appealed ultimately to facts. The style was verbal – some combination of Socratic dialogue and Adam Smith. This style had the disadvantage of producing few closed-form solutions. But it had the advantage of permitting analysis of the kind of problems that elude simple solutions. Indeed, I believe that one reason for Director's lasting influence is that he was able to show that simple judgments about business practices often cannot withstand rigorous scrutiny.

I have already alluded to one such judgment – that the default answer to why a hard-to-understand business practice exists is 'monopoly' and that the default policy response is 'call the cops'. Director's academic career coincided with the highwater mark of the influence of that kind of analysis on antitrust policy. Most of the change – in both the way economists analyzed business practices and antitrust policy – would come after his retirement in 1966.

In the remainder of this essay, I will focus on the practices in which Director's influence on either economic analysis or policy was most significant. I will try to summarize his analysis in the context of my lay understanding of the prevailing antitrust policy. Later, I will

---

2   For example, I first encountered Director's now-conventional analysis of tie-in selling as a homework problem in Milton Friedman's price theory class. We were, one by one, called into Friedman's office to be duly impressed by the deficiencies of our own answers and by the elegance of Director's answer.

3   Interestingly, an excellent example of the kind of analysis Director was reacting against was the work of his immediate predecessor, Henry Simons (1934), who proposed remedies for perceived deficiencies in competition such as taxes on advertising (because it distorted preferences) and administrative limits on firm size (to preserve the textbook Garden of Eden populated by atomistic price-taking firms).

discuss how, if at all, the analysis might have contributed to changing the policy, and I will explore the issue of why this influence on policy was greater in some areas than others. My goal is not to give a comprehensive treatment of either the theory or its connection to policy. Nor will I discuss much of the post-Director development of the theory. Rather, I want to provide enough summary to place Director's contribution in a historical context.

1 Three main contributions to economic analysis

Predatory pricing
The large firm that crushes small rivals with ruinous bouts of below-cost prices is a durable part of the folklore of American capitalism. The story evokes images of late nineteenth-century robber barons swashbuckling their way to monopolies; the specific example of John D. Rockefeller and the Standard Oil Trust probably comes most readily to mind. That example is also important because the practice is illegal and played a role in the antitrust case that broke up Standard Oil. The idea that predatory practices of one sort or another are an important source of monopoly continues to exert a powerful hold both inside and outside the economics profession.

The locus classicus of historical revisionism in these matters is John McGee's article on the *Standard Oil* case in the first volume of the *Journal*.[4] In this case, we have the author's summary of Director's influence on the article:[5]

> I am profoundly indebted to Aaron Director, of the University of Chicago Law School, who in 1953 suggested that this study be undertaken. Professor Director, without investigating the facts, developed a logical framework by which he predicted that Standard Oil had not gotten or maintained its monopoly position using predatory price cutting. In truth, he predicted, on purely logical grounds, that they never systematically used the technique at all. I was astounded by these hypotheses, and doubtful of their validity, but was also impressed by the logic that produced them. As a consequence, I resolved to investigate the matter, admittedly against my better judgment; for, like everyone else, I knew full well what Standard had really done.

The logic that astounded McGee could have come from a dialogue something like this (except that Director rather than McGee would be asking most of the questions):

McGee (JM): Do you mean to deny that a dominant firm would rather have fewer rivals than more?
Director (AD): No.
JM: Do you mean to deny that the dominant firm will be generating more monopoly rents than any small rival?
AD: Let us assume that is the case.
JM: Fine. Cannot the dominant firm use part of its rents to endure a bout of localized below-cost pricing that drives its rival from the market?
AD: Sometimes.

---

[4] McGee (1958).
[5] *Id.* at 138.

JM: Only sometimes? Then you think there are conditions where predatory price cutting cannot work at all?

AD: Correct. Think of the simplest case: the predator has no cost or demand advantage of any kind over the prey (otherwise it could achieve monopoly without predation). Importantly, it has no cost advantage in accessing capital. In this case, predation cannot succeed.

JM: Why not?

AD: Successful predation means that the predator will be able to recoup short-run losses by generating more monopoly rents than otherwise in the future, enough more to pay, in present values, for the short-run losses. If the predator could succeed in this sense, so too could the prey in this simple case.

JM: How so?

AD: By following a matching strategy. Match the predator's price. Borrow (at the same marginal borrowing/lending rate as the predator) to finance short-term losses. Wait for the predator to raise price and match that. If the present value of the predator's cash flows is positive, so too will be that of the intended prey. Indeed, the prey can do even better: the prey can avoid the short-run losses by shutting down and letting the predator enforce the below-cost price. Thus, the simple case involves a logical contradiction – a price path that is at once profitable for the predator and not profitable for the prey.

JM: So predation can succeed only if the predator has some kind of cost advantage.

AD: Correct. But pause to note that if the predator has a cost advantage, then we are back in the case where the predator can achieve monopoly without predation. This should illustrate for you the logical swamp into which predation arguments lead: predation is impossible without a cost advantage and unnecessary with one.

JM: Noted. But let us go on. What kind of cost advantage do you have in mind?

AD: The prey has to face higher marginal borrowing costs than the predator. I could take you further into the logical swamp by asking why the predator has such an advantage. But let's just assume it's there and move on.[6]

JM: OK. Why does the success of predation depend on this capital cost difference?

AD: Because the matching strategy will no longer necessarily preclude successful predation. For example, suppose the predator can borrow at (or sacrifice a return of) 10 percent per year to finance a price war while the prey would have to pay 15 percent. Suppose further that eliminating the prey allows a price increase that generates a gross return of 14.99 percent per year on the funds invested in a price war and that the 4.99 percent margin over the cost of capital is sufficient to make predation more profitable than the status quo. Then predation could succeed, because a 14.99 percent return on 15 percent money cannot be profitable for the prey.

JM: You said 'could succeed.' Why not *would* succeed?

AD: Because the requirements for success are more stringent than I have let on. For example, it has to be the case that all other potential players, including firms in other industries, face 15 percent marginal borrowing costs. If any outsider faces 10 percent, like the predator, the matching strategy rears its ugly head: the outsider will buy the assets, reenter this industry, and match the 14.99 percent price.

---

6   Director liked to talk about 'price discrimination' in the credit market in this context. This vagueness may have been deliberate. If the cost difference reflected risk or information cost differences, then we are perilously close to an ordinary competitive process in which a lowcost rival supplants a higher-cost rival.

JM: But since you do admit that predation might succeed, isn't it plausible that Standard Oil (and other large firms with lower borrowing costs than rivals or new entrants) fit the requirements for success?

AD: Let us assume so. The case is still not closed.

JM: Why not?

AD: If Standard could win a price war, both it and the intended prey can do better by merging before the war takes place. After all, the main gain from the war goes to consumers who pay bargain prices. By merging, Standard and its intended victim can avoid transferring wealth to consumers and share it for themselves. If you will go back to the record of the case, you should find that merger was a more important source of Standard's growing market share than predation, and you will find that the prices paid for rivals were hardly stingy.

Apparently McGee took the advice and verified Director's prediction. Virtually all subsequent discussion of predation must somehow come to grips with the logic summarized above.

That logic is sometimes interpreted as an impossibility theorem. That interpretation is wrong, as Director was always careful to point out. For example, I can recall the day he led his class in a discussion of a case in which the defendant was charged with predation.[7] He sat serenely puffing on his pipe (quite permissible in that era) as he walked us through the damning facts one by one and asked us to interpret each of them. The students, intoxicated by the then-novel McGee article, would try mightily to fit each fact into a nonpredation model. But in the end Director brought us to see that the defendant most likely was guilty as charged. And he resisted our desire to inquire further as to why the defendant might have followed a predatory strategy.

The point of that exercise was, I think, to put the theory into perspective. The theory was a guide to the facts, not a substitute for them. The theory did not rule out predation on logical grounds. It did say that the practice would probably not be the typical mode of interaction between firms, just as wars would not be the common outcome of international negotiations nor strikes the usual outcome of labor bargaining. But we needed to be reminded that wars, strikes, and predation did occasionally occur.

Vertical restrictions in distribution

Attempts by manufacturers to attenuate competition among their distributors remain under a legal cloud. Perhaps the most durable example of this legal hostility is the prohibition on resale price maintenance (RPM), the contractual restriction on the right of a retailer to charge less than a specified price for the manufacturer's product. The common sense of the legal hostility to the practice is easy enough to apprehend: RPM is price fixing, and isn't price fixing bad for consumers? The surprisingly qualified answer that emerged from Chicago was Lester Telser's classic article in the *Journal of Law and Economics*.[8] The article's title rephrases the question as 'Why Should Manufacturers Want Fair Trade?' ('fair trade' was a contemporary euphemism for RPM).

According to Telser,[9] this refocus of the question was Director's main influence on the

---

7   Regrettably, I cannot recall any of the facts of the case, except that it occurred early in the twentieth century and the defendant was Corn Products Refining.

8   Telser (1960).

9   Lester G. Telser, personal communication, May 16, 2005.

article. As with the analysis of predation, Director felt that the analysis had to begin with a clear specification of how the suspect behavior could be consistent with profit maximization. In this case, Director impressed on his students and colleagues the need to distinguish ordinary price fixing by retail cartels from RPM, which was a contractual restriction desired and often enforced by manufacturers on retailers. The former was adequately handled by the conventional wisdom about price fixing, but RPM could not be so easily reconciled with profit maximization.

Specifically, the practice did not generally seem in the best interest of manufacturers. A non-price-taking manufacturer's first-order interest could be attained by setting a profit-maximizing wholesale price (W^*). Conceptually, W^* could be derived from the monopoly retail price (P^*) as $W^* = P^* - m$, where m is the marginal cost of providing retail services. That is, the manufacturer's first-order interest was to maximize the monopoly rent extracted from consumers and then cede just enough to retailers to cover their cost of delivering the monopoly output to consumers. That interest seemed adequately served by retail competition. Presumably, free entry and competition would drive retail margins to marginal cost and thereby permit the manufacturer to charge W^*.

Resale price maintenance seemed contrary to this first-order interest of the manufacturer. If competition would yield retail margins of m, and thus P^* given W^*, then an effective RPM contract would yield a retail margin greater than m – that is, the contract would constrain some retailer from reducing its margin by offering a lower price. Logically, that inflated retail margin would have to come out of potential manufacturer profits. For example, if the actual margin was constrained to exceed m, then the actual W would have to be below W^* if the contract specified P^*. Hence the question that is the title of Telser's article.

The answer, according to the preceding logic, had to focus on special circumstances in which the practice could provide particular benefits that overcame the first-order loss to the manufacturer from suppressing retail competition. According to Telser,[10] Director's first instinct in this matter was to look for an anticompetitive rationale. So he asked Telser to read the record of an antitrust case against General Electric and other light bulb manufacturers in which the manufacturers agreed to impose RPM on retailers and also agreed to divide retail outlets among themselves. This ultimately led to a rationale for the twin practices of RPM and exclusive dealing in terms of cartel enforcement costs: the cartel is primarily interested in the right wholesale price, but suppose it cannot easily enforce this price directly because of the ease of concealing transaction prices at the wholesale level. By contrast, RPM is enforceable because the nature of retail markets (many casual customers paying a price that is prominently displayed) renders deviations from RPM (and exclusive-dealing arrangements) easily detectable. That ease of detection means that RPM cum exclusive dealing is less likely to be violated than an upstream price agreement. If the downstream agreements are not violated, then upstream price cutting is also deterred. The reason is that upstream price cutting will not lead to higher retail sales, which require lower retail prices for a brand or more retailers stocking it or both.

The enduring effect of Telser's article, however, rests on another rationale for RPM, which has a much different domain of application and much different welfare implications than the cartel story. This is the 'service argument', which focuses on the provision of point-of-

---

[10]   *Id.*

purchase information services that enhance the value of a good by more than the costs of producing the information. Telser had in mind complicated durable search goods such as consumer electronics, appliances, cameras, and the like, where the buyer relies on retailers to learn about the relevant features, make brand and model comparisons, and so on. Telser's key insight was that the retailer that provides such services obtains compensation for them only if the consumer buys the product at that location.

Here there is a potential public-good problem. Retailers who do not incur the costs of providing the information can reap some of the benefits. They can discount the price at full-service retailers and thereby win the business of customers who have availed themselves of the services of full-line retailers. Such competition from 'free riders' will lead to the usual result of an undersupply of the point-of-purchase services in equilibrium. Resale price maintenance potentially overcomes the free-rider problem by fixing a retail margin sufficiently high to pay for the full-line retail services and diverting retail competition from price to nonprice attributes, including importantly the quality of the point-of-purchase services provided by retailers.

Subsequent development of Telser's service argument showed how other vertical restrictions on retailers could either complement or substitute for RPM. For example, numerical restrictions on retailers (authorized dealers, territorial franchises, and the like) could reduce free riding by reducing the number of potential free riders and thereby better align the interests of retailers and manufacturers – and consumers. This line of analysis had of course quite different welfare implications than simple restraints on retail competition. Without the vertical restrictions, consumers would be worse off owing to the resulting underprovision of point-of-purchase information. At the same time, as Telser's cartel explanation of RPM had already hinted, most retail numerical restrictions could also complement cartel enforcement by attenuating the ability of rivals to shift customers from one to another.

Tie-in selling

The sale of one product (X) conditional on the purchase of another (Y) comes in several varieties. For example, X might be a machine that uses various amounts of Y in a production process. In a 'requirements' tie-in, the purchaser or lessor of an X must use only that seller's brand of Y in the machine. Or X and Y could be two different machines that are both useful to a group of buyers. Bundling or full-line forcing occurs when a producer of X requires customers to buy a package of X and Y at a bundled price.

Tie-ins have been legally problematic when the seller of X (or Y) is a monopoly, for example, when X is protected by a patent or copyright. In such cases, the courts have sought to prevent monopolistic leverage – the use of the X monopoly to secure another monopoly in Y. If one monopoly is good for the monopolist and bad for the consumer, two monopolies must be better for the monopolist and worse for the consumer. Aaron Director rejected this commonsense reasoning, just as he had rejected the easy logic of widespread predation and the reflexive condemnation of resale price maintenance. He did this by paying attention to some important facts about the way tie-ins worked in practice, facts that were not adequately captured by received theory.

The general idea that a monopolist might prefer to set two prices rather than only one was not novel to economists of Director's era. Specifically, it was understood that a monopolist of X (say, coffee) would also like to have a monopoly of related goods – substitutes (tea) or complements (sugar). If Y was a substitute like tea, consumers would tend to be worse off with an X-Y monopoly than with an X-only monopoly, because the former would set a higher monopoly price of X than the latter and would extract monopoly rents from consumers of Y as well. If Y was a complement like sugar, the welfare effects were murkier. If the complementarity is strong enough, then both prices could be lower under dual monopoly than under separate monopoly. Indeed, the possibility that an X-Y monopolist would sell, say, coffee below cost to promote sales of monopoly-priced sugar could not be ruled out. For drinkers of black coffee, such a state of affairs would be preferable even to a competitive coffee market.

Director had no quarrel with the logic underlying such theoretical propositions, nor did he reject as a broadly valid generality that, with exceptions such as the case of complements just discussed, two monopolies were worse for consumers than one. The problem with both the theory and the courts' fear of monopolistic leverage was their excessive scope in light of facts about the markets in which tying is found.

There is, unfortunately, nothing comparable to McGee or Telser that writes down and elucidates Director's ideas on tying.[11] Accordingly, I will try to summarize the relevant oral tradition as I remember it.[12]

For the sake of brevity, I will focus on requirements tie-ins here. Here one factual problem concerned the plausibility of the notion that the X monopoly could actually secure the Y monopoly by imposing the tie-in. Sometimes this was plausible, particularly if one took a sufficiently narrow view of the market for Y. Thus, when IBM patented a punch-card processing machine and tied the sale of cards to leases on the machine, all significant competition in the cards that these machines processed was precluded. But what are we to make of International Salt, which patented a salt-dispensing machine used by food processors and tied the sale of salt to dispensingmachine leases? Or what of United Shoe Machinery, which tied sale of thread to the lease of a patented sewing machine? In both cases, the tied sales (of salt and thread) were a small fraction of total consumption of these items. The notion that International or United could leverage their patents into monopolies of salt or thread was fanciful.

Another problem, this time emanating from the theory, was the overwhelming prevalence of complementarity between the tying good (X) and the tied good (Y). The theory suggests that the tied good could as easily be a substitute for X, but IBM apparently never contemplated tying accounting ledgers, nor did International Salt tie the sale of other spices. Indeed, by 1960 the theory had been broadened to include utterly unrelated goods as candidates for Y. Thus, M. Burstein wondered why IBM did not tie the sale of salt to its machine leases.[13] Director may have wondered about such matters too, but he knew that, while we awaited resolution of Burstein's conundrum, a good theory had to recognize the fact that Y almost always was a complement to X.

---

[11]   McGee, *supra* note 4; Telser, *supra* note 8. Perhaps Bowman (1957), comes closest, but it focuses more on the law than on systematizing the economic analysis. Also Director set out the basic idea that I summarize here in Director and Levi (1956).

[12]   Here the memory of Friedman's unsparing criticism of my answer to his homework problem proves useful. As he went over my answer, it became clear that I had managed on my own to reproduce the conventional theory of complements and substitutes that is summarized above. This feat did not impress Friedman, because, as he stated unhesitatingly, that theory was completely wrong. Much of what follows was in Friedman's subsequent elaboration of the correct theory that he had gleaned from his conversations with Director.

[13]   Burstein (1960).

Indeed, Y was most often not just any complement, such as sugar for coffee. It was most often part of a joint-service arrangement in which either X or Y or both were valueless without the other. The lessees of IBM machines wanted to process cards. The machines without cards or the cards without a machine were valueless. Salt may be valuable without a patented salt dispenser, but the latter is worthless without the former. Any good theory of tie-ins had to come to grips with the prevalence of joint-service arrangements among actual requirements tie-ins, even if it could not tell us why weaker complements like coffee and sugar are not tied.

Director then uncovered a major obstacle to developing such a theory, which I will illustrate with the canonical IBM example. We can express a user's demand for that joint service in terms of the processing of cards per machine per unit time. That demand is satisfied by machines and cards, which can be supplied separately or via a tie-in. Assume that a potential customer has a demand for processing given by $q = 1 - p$, where q is the number of cards processed per machine hour and p is either the price per card processed or the marginal value of processing. For simplicity, assume that both cards and machine are costless and that any customer will use one machine to process cards. The purpose of setting the problem up this way is to focus attention on the question: how should IBM optimally exploit the processing demand if it has a monopoly on the machine?

The answer here is to rent the machine for $0.50 per hour and give the cards away – or, more simply, allow them to be supplied by a competitive card industry at a value of p equal to marginal cost, which equals zero. Here an effective tie-in, which set a positive price on cards and precluded competitive purchases, would actually be counterproductive, because the sum of IBM's card sales and machine rental income would be less than $0.50 per hour.[14] This answer, of course, turns a monopoly pricing problem into a paradox. The real IBM did enforce a tie-in. More broadly, the common pattern in joint-service arrangements is not to collect all monopoly profit in the charge for the fixed component (the machine). Rather, it is to underprice the fixed component – in the extreme, give it away – and thereby leave surplus to be extracted in sales of the variable component (the cards) at supramarginal cost prices. This is what International did with its salt and United with its thread. This is what another canonical example, Gillette, did with its razors and patented blades, not by contract but by the design and pricing of the components.

Director resolved the paradox by considering the effect of differences among customers in their demand for the joint service. So, suppose only half the consumers had the demand in the previous example, $q = 1 - p$, while the remaining half had the demand, $q = 2(1 - p)$. Think of this second group as high-intensity users (H), who would process twice as many cards per hour at any price per processed card as the low-intensity users (L). This complexity does not by itself change the essential nature of the first-best solution to IBM's pricing problem. It is still profit maximizing to extract all profits in machine rentals and none from card tie-ins. The only wrinkle here is that the machine rentals have to discriminate between the L, who

---

[14]   Director himself used inelastic demand to illustrate the paradox emerging from the example. So, suppose the customer valued the joint service at $0.50 per card processed, up to one card per hour, and zero for each additional card. In this case, IBM can also obtain $0.50 per hour from untied machine rentals. He then pointed out that IBM would be indifferent between any combination of machine rental and card prices that summed to $0.50 per hour. For example, if IBM enforced a tie-in at a price of $0.10 per IBM-supplied card, then the surplus leftover for exploitation by a machine rental would be only $0.40.

continue to be charged $0.50 per hour, and the H, who are charged $1.00 per hour. Director then focused on the second-best problem: suppose explicit price discrimination is infeasible. Maybe IBM is unable to overcome the usual arbitrage problem whereby the H would try to sublease from the L or masquerade as L. More important, perhaps IBM may not know which customers are H and which L in advance of contracting with them.

Accordingly, Director reformulated IBM's problem as a second-best choice between two nondiscriminatory arrangements. Suppose IBM had to choose between just setting a nondiscriminatory machine rental or offering a nondiscriminatory tie-in arrangement. Between these two, the tie-in wins out. Specifically, the profit-maximizing tie-in would have IBM rent machines to all for $0.28125 per hour provided the renter agreed to buy all cards the machine would process from IBM at $0.25 per unit. This arrangement would produce total revenues of $1.125 per pair of H and L customers. This is less than the $1.50 under first-best discrimination, but it beats the $1.00 maximum from nondiscriminatory machine rental without a tie-in.[15] The tie-in works here because it mimics the pattern that underlies the superiority of first-best discrimination: an H pays more monopoly rent ($0.65625 per hour) than an L ($0.46875). But the tie-in avoids all of the problems specific to the firstbest solution – the need to distinguish customers and to prevent arbitrage. (Of course, the tie-in entails enforcement problems of its own, because any customer would prefer to evade the tie-in restriction.)

More generally, the tie-in is acting as an implicit metering device. It is measuring the intensity with which the customer is employing the machine in circumstances in which the more intensive user (H) also places the highest valuation on the joint service. It is this positive correlation between intensity of use and valuation that drives the superiority of tie-ins to untied rentals. Director then went on to develop a complementary rationale for the other major form of tying – full-line forcing or bundling. Again, he rejected the simple leverage argument in favor of an analysis in which bundling is a second-best arrangement that exploits valuation differences when explicit discrimination is infeasible. Specifically, he showed how bundling tended to better exploit negative correlations across customers in their valuation of components (those with high valuations of one component had low valuations of the other, and vice versa) than nondiscriminatory pricing of the separate components.

A common Socratic thread runs through the three analyses I have sketched. All begin with a seemingly innocuous question: would a deep-pocketed dominant firm wish to set predatory prices? Would manufacturers want resale price maintenance? Are two monopolies better than one? The questions seem almost rhetorical, but they are not. Rather, they are meant to bring into focus the need to examine carefully the implications of profit maximization for the business practice under study. By contrast, the then-prevailing commonsense approach to these practices tended to jump to the rhetorical answer: we 'knew full well what Standard had done'. In all three cases, careful analysis shows that such obvious answers are wrong, because they are not generally consistent with the interest of the perpetrator. Proper resolution of the apparent paradox then requires further analysis that appropriately restricts the domain of the practice (to a subset that excludes mergers and similarly situated prey in the case of predatory pricing, to complex search goods in Telser's special-services rationale for RPM, and to joint-

---

[15]   This could be achieved by renting machines at $0.50 per hour, in which case both H and L rent, or by charging $1.00 per hour, which induces the L to exit the market.

service arrangements in which value and use intensity are directly related for requirements tie-ins). I argue later that this method of analyzing policy-relevant issues proved influential even when the resulting paradox was not resolved by Director or his colleagues and students.

2 The effect of the analysis on antitrust policy

Antitrust policy changed after Director left active scholarship. Director's work contributed to the intellectual climate within which that change occurred. This is not the place to weigh the many factors contributing to the change in policy. Rather, I address an easier question: how far did antitrust policy change in the direction suggested by Director's analysis? The answer is mixed.

The largest change has occurred in predatory-pricing cases. The law here has not changed: predatory pricing remains illegal. But the skepticism of the courts and the reluctance of the antitrust agencies to bring such cases have increased considerably. Most such cases are now initiated by the defendant's competitors, and these have a tougher gauntlet to run than in the past. The gauntlet will today often include, however implicitly, the need to overcome the arguments in McGee:[16] is predatory pricing a positive net present value strategy for the predator? What about the (re)entry problem? And so forth. For example, the Supreme Court used the present value test in the 1986 *Matsushita v. Zenith* case to support its rejection of a predation charge against Japanese television manufacturers.[17] It made the test a central feature in another landmark case that rejected a charge of predation in the cigarette industry.[18] Cases like these have greatly lengthened the odds against success for plaintiffs in predation cases.

Vertical restrictions on distribution represent a partial victory for the analysis inspired by Director. Resale price maintenance remains a per se violation. Indeed, even informal pressure from manufacturers against retailers' price reductions can be problematic, as in the recent *Nine West* case.[19] The courts have persisted in lumping RPM with horizontal price fixing and have not made a distinction between the beneficial and harmful varieties of RPM. However, policy on vertical restrictions that are substitutes for RPM has become substantially more permissive. Cases such as *GTE-Sylvania*[20] and *White Motor*[21] made clear that manufacturers could restrict the number and territorial boundaries of their distributors. These rulings recognized both the importance of interbrand competition for consumers and the role of vertical restrictions in fostering such competition.[22] In a recent twist, the Supreme Court reversed (in *State Oil v. Khan*)[23] a long-standing policy against maximum-price restrictions by manufacturers on their numerically restricted retail networks. The occasional need for this form of price fixing in such cases is implied by the line of theory begun by Telser.[24] So, from the

---

16   McGee, *supra* note 4.
17   *Matsushita v. Zenith*, 475 US 574 (1986).
18   *Brooke Group v. Brown & Williamson Tobacco*, 113 S. Ct. 2578 (1993).
19   In re *Nine West Shoes Antitrust Litig.*, 80 F.2d. Supp. 181 (2002) (in which a shoe manufacturer threatened to reduce supplies of its brand to the errant retailers).
20   *Continental T.V. v. GTE Sylvania*, 433 US 36 (1977).
21   *White Motor v. United States*, 372 US 253 (1963).
22   The emphasis on interbrand competition in these cases may be too restrictive. A monopoly manufacturer may also face downstream free-rider problems that can be alleviated by vertical restrictions, and these can provide net benefits to the monopolist's consumers.
23   118 S. Ct. 275 (1997).
24   Telser, *supra* note 8. Briefly, the manufacturer (and consumer) is happy that the vertical restriction reduces free riding but is unhappy if the resulting downstream market power is utilized fully.

standpoint of that theory, the policy response seems a crazy quilt: one solution to the free-rider problem (RPM) remains illegal to this day. Another (numerical restrictions) became legal shortly after, but a complementary policy (price maxima) remained illegal for another 30 years or so.[25] The theory would have suggested permissiveness about price maxima[26] and a rule-of-reason approach to both RPM and numerical restrictions.[27]

The court treatment of tying cases bears the least imprint of Director's analysis. The leverage doctrine has not been seriously modified or embellished. So defense of the practice remains, as it was before, an exercise in defusing leverage arguments. For example, in the recent *Microsoft* case,[28] the bundling of an internet browser with other software was defended on grounds of consumer convenience, ease of replacement with competitive browsers, and so forth. There was no serious discussion of the role of differences in demand across customers, which is the central feature of Director's analysis. This focus on leverage also creates apparent oddities. For example, it is perfectly legal for a machine monopolist to meter the use of the machine and levy a two-part price that increases with machine usage. However, the analytically equivalent (according to Director's theory) tied sale of a complement in a joint-service arrangement would be illegal. It is also usually legal to design the fixed component of a joint service to accomplish the same goals as an illegal tie-in contract. Thus, for example, Hewlett-Packard's strategy of designing printers that can function only with Hewlett-Packard ink cartridges does not attract antitrust scrutiny.[29] In such joint-service arrangements, Director's theory suggests that neither the tie-in nor the metering nor the product design can reduce competition by itself,[30] so the theory would seem to imply symmetric legal treatment of the three.

I can only venture a tentative rationale for this mixed pattern in the influence of Director's idea on antitrust. It is related to the deleterious effects on competition of enforcing an erroneous theory. Briefly, the worse the potential effects on competition from continued enforcement of the erroneous theory are, the more willing the courts seem to overturn the theory. These deleterious effects seem clearest in the case of predatory practices. Vigorous enforcement of restrictions on price cutting can stifle competition by protecting high-cost competitors and making large firms hesitant about pressing competitive advantages. A court seeking to uphold the larger intent of the antitrust laws will have to weigh this possible anticompetitive effect of punishing low prices seriously. The court's trepidation here will be reinforced by the fact that the typical complainant these days is a competitor rather than a consumer.

---

[25]   Until an intellectual descendant of Director, Judge Richard Posner, in upholding the precedent on this matter, explained to the Supreme Court why his doing so made no sense, and the Court obliged by overruling him.

[26]   They reduce consumer prices and increase output.

[27]   Both RPM and numerical restrictions can be used to reduce competition in roughly similar circumstances (when enforcing an upstream cartel agreement is more costly than enforcing the downstream agreement and where the provision of downstream point-of-purchase services is unimportant). Both of them can also increase competition or output in roughly similar circumstances (where free riding can result in suboptimal provision of retail services).

[28]   *United States v. Microsoft*, 346 US App. D.C. 330 (2001).

[29]   But Microsoft's integration of the browser with other software did attract such scrutiny.

[30]   Indeed, all three arrangements provide increased incentives for entry into the high-value, high-use segment of the market.

There is also a potential adverse effect on competition from outlawing RPM. This comes from eliminating a mechanism that enhances interbrand competition. However, this adverse effect has been mitigated by the loosened legal restrictions on good substitutes for RPM and by the continued lack of significant antitrust constraints on other substitutes, such as advertising. Accordingly, the net effect on competition of maintaining the RPM restriction may be minor even if it is negative.

Director's analysis of tying presupposes monopoly, often by patent or copyright. Accordingly, there is no direct effect on competition of restricting tie-ins. The main effect of the restriction, according to the theory, is on the ability of the monopolist to extract rent from consumers, and the implications of this for output or overall consumer welfare are ambiguous. There may also be indirect effects on competition from restricting tie-ins, such as a reduced incentive for invention. But courts are generally reluctant to consider such secondary effects.[31] Accordingly, the courts can persist in enforcing an erroneous theory in this case without thereby systematically harming competition.

3 Summary and conclusion

Aaron Director made important contributions to the analysis of business practices. None was ever published under his name. Accordingly, economists today often do not know how much their discussion of these practices has been influenced by Director. I hope that ignorance has been partly redressed by this essay, at least in the areas of predatory pricing, vertical restraints on distribution, and tie-in sales on which I have focused. I have also tried to show how some of the changed antitrust policy in these matters finds roots in Director's analysis. However, I think that Director's influence on economic and legal analysis goes beyond the specific business practices where he had his greatest success.

That broader influence is rooted in his rigorous approach to business practices and related antitrust issues. On the whole, I believe that approach contributed to an increased skepticism among economists and policy makers about 'activist' antitrust policy more generally. A full discussion of this shift is beyond the scope of this essay, and Director's contribution to much of it has to be indirect. For example, horizontal merger policy became less mechanical and less restrictive, but as far as I know Director had little to say about this area of policy.[32] Director's contribution to the broader shift in the intellectual climate was more one of analytical style than anything else.

Looking back now, it is hard to imagine how little rigor underlay the analysis of antitrust issues in Director's day. I have already alluded to how commonsense aversions to price fixing continue to inform restrictions on RPM, how similarly intuitive distaste for so-called cutthroat competition was given great weight, and so forth. That style was pervasive. For example, restrictive merger policy was mainly supported by a simple view that more competitors

---

[31] For example, the same Schumpeterian argument could justify permitting price-fixing agreements.

[32] Informally he always seemed more skeptical than his colleagues about merger restrictions. But any such skepticism was hardly infectious. As late as 1969, the president's Neal Commission, chaired by the law school colleague with whom he co-taught the antitrust course and including among its members his close friend George Stigler, recommended special legislation to generally limit the four-firm concentration ratio to 70 percent. See White House Task Force on Antitrust Policy, CCH Trade Reg. Rep. No. 415 (Supp. May 26, 1969).

meant more competition.[33] Director's students and colleagues learned to be dissatisfied with this insubstantial mode of analysis. They would be trained to ask many tough questions, and even if they could not answer them, they would be skeptical about the easy answers.

One example of this that I can recall is vertical integration policy. The specific issue was the acquisition by an upstream firm of downstream distributors.[34] At the time, this was viewed with alarm as a possibly predatory practice: surely the acquirer would deny the distribution outlets to upstream competitors and thereby hobble or destroy them. Director never had a good general story about such mergers, but then no other economist has one either. However, he forced you to ask enough questions to see that the predatory story was nonsense: does that story not presuppose that the distributor has market power? If handling the upstream competitor's product maximizes the distributor's monopoly or monopsony rent, then would not a merger for the sake of vertical foreclosure sacrifice some monopoly rent? If so, would not a better use of the distributor's market power be to (continue to) charge the upstream competitor a premium price for access that reflects the superior value of the competitor's product? If that does not happen and you see what looks like foreclosure, should you not expect that this is value and/or rent maximizing? Or should we assume that the upstream firm also has market power? Then the vertical merger may indeed discomfort upstream rivals, but retail prices would be reduced.[35] Should antitrust policy then block a merger that lowers price and raises output?

This hardly hypothetical interchange illustrates some broad features of Director's influence on those around him. You needed to start with the most basic question: how can a particular business practice maximize the value of the practitioner? You then needed to explore rigorously all the implications of the answer to that question. Even if you could not figure out all the implications or answer all the questions, you probably would have eliminated the monopoly answer or relegated it to a special case. The residual ignorance would then lead you to a greater weight on an efficiency rationale even if you could not articulate one explicitly. At the end of the day, Director had a simple test that could (at least in principle) distinguish among efficiency and monopoly stories: does the practice lead to higher or lower output? This test was perhaps simple and incomplete, but it is far more coherent than what went before.

This shifting of weight from monopoly to efficiency explanations as the primary motive for a business practice has, I think, been permanent among economists and policy makers. This broader change in the framework of our analysis owes much to Aaron Director. It may be his most important intellectual legacy.

Bibliography
Bowman, Ward S., Jr. 'Tying Arrangements and the Leverage Problem'. *Yale Law Journal* 67 (1957): 19–36.
Burstein, M. L. 'The Economics of Tie-in Sales'. *Review of Economics and Statistics* 42 (1960): 68–73.
Director, Aaron, and Levi, Edward. 'Law and the Future: Trade Regulation'. *Northwestern University Law Review* 51 (1956): 281–96.

---

[33]   There was, of course, some nuance: firms had to be bigger than minimum-efficient scale. And there was a growing, ultimately controversial, empirical literature showing higher profits in more concentrated industries that provided something of a rationale for restrictive policy on mergers.

[34]   It could as easily have been the downstream firm acquiring the upstream firm.

[35]   By eliminating double markups in independent wholesale and retail transactions.

McGee, John S. 'Predatory Price Cutting: The Standard Oil (N.J.) Case'. *Journal of Law and Economics* 1 (1958): 137–69.
Simons, Henry C. *Positive Program for Laissez Faire: Some Proposals for a Liberal Economic Policy*. Public Policy Pamphlet No. 15. Chicago: University of Chicago, 1934.
Telser, Lester G. 'Why Should Manufacturers Want Fair Trade?' *Journal of Law and Economics* 3 (1960): 86–105.

4 George J. Stigler and his contributions to law and economics

Harold Demsetz

George J. Stigler, outstanding economist and essayist, should be easy to write about. He is not. So much already has been written about him by others, by me, and even by him in his autobiography, that it is difficult to give the reader something not already known or easily found. And, indeed, this essay begins with summary biographical facts about Stigler that will be familiar to several readers. However, Stigler's role as a pioneer in law and economics has not yet received the attention it deserves. I remedy the oversight here.

Stigler was born in 1911 in Renton, Washington, near Seattle, to parents who had recently emigrated from Europe. He remained in the northwest until he completed undergraduate work at the University of Washington. Business administration and political science were his major interests. His plan upon graduation was to enter the world of business but the depression-caused lack of opportunities led him to continue his education instead. He sought, and received in 1933, an MBA degree from Northwestern University. During his time at Northwestern he developed a deepening interest in economics. He pursued this by entering the University of Chicago's graduate program in economics, from which he received a doctorate in 1936. While at Chicago he became close friends with fellow students Milton Friedman and W. Allen Wallis; he also met Margaret Louise Mack, who would later accept Stigler's proposal of marriage.

Three members of Chicago's economics faculty were important to Stigler and his friends: Frank Knight, Jacob Viner, and Henry Simons. Knight, philosophically and conceptually inclined, Viner, a theorist with empirical leanings, and Simons, who dealt in matters of policy, gave these young men high quality exposure to the world of economics. Stigler chose to write his dissertation under the direction of Knight. Knight's reputation for toughness and high standards discouraged most students from choosing him as thesis director. However, of the three mentors, Knight offered the greatest depth of thought about the history of economic thought, and this had become one of Stigler's leading interests. Stigler's dissertation, titled 'Production and Distribution Theories: 1870–1895', reveals this, as does his first published article, 'The Economics of Carl Menger' (1937).[1] History of thought remained an interest throughout his career. It reveals itself not only in papers written for those specialized in this topic but also in quotations from the masters that appear in his essays and his articles in industrial organization. This work, however, is not where his contributions to law and economics are found. Accordingly, I do not consider it beyond this point.

Doctorate in hand, Stigler joined the faculty of the Iowa State College and then, in fairly quick succession, he moved to the University of Minnesota, Brown University, and Columbia University. He took leave from the University of Minnesota during World War II to be at the

---

[1]   The dissertation was published as a book by Macmillan in 1946.

National Bureau of Economic Research (NBER) and to work in the Office of Price Administration. He then became a member of Columbia University's Statistical Research Group, led by Allen Wallis and including Friedman. The group dealt with war-associated problems such as that of determining the correct firing distance to be used by a fighter pilot when attacking an enemy bomber. In 1945, at the end of the war, Friedman returned with Stigler to Minnesota. A year later, they both moved on, Stigler to Brown University and Friedman to Chicago. Stigler then joined the faculty at Columbia University and remained for eleven years before accepting appointment, in 1958, to the University of Chicago where he became the first Charles Walgreen Distinguished Service Professor. He remained active at Chicago until his death in 1991 at age 80.

Stigler found Friedman and Wallis already entrenched at Chicago when he arrived, Friedman in the Economics Department and Wallis, as Dean, in the Graduate School of Business. Chicago had considered hiring Stigler earlier, in 1946, but the President of the University, after interviewing him, thought he was too empirical for Chicago and decided to veto the offer his Economics Department sought to make. This was a mistaken view of Stigler's work and a mistaken view of Chicago's needs. Although Stigler's work did reflect his commitment to measurement and evidence gathering, he always linked this commitment to theory. After Chicago decided against hiring Stigler, it extended an offer to Friedman; hence, Friedman's presence at Chicago when Stigler arrived in 1958. During their time at Chicago, Friedman and Stigler became Presidents of the American Economics Association, Nobel Laureates, and two of the highest ranking American economists.

Stigler, I think, never contemplated leaving the University of Chicago. If a university and its traditions can become objects of affection, I would say Stigler dearly loved Chicago. It seemed to come closest to meeting his notion of what a great university should be, an institution concerned with the discovery and improvement of knowledge and not with much else. He thought, for example, that active pursuit of political objectives and of various other 'causes' only diverts a university from this mission.

He held appointments in both the Economics Department and the Graduate School of Business. He effectively served each institution. His broad influence at home and abroad surely derived from his writings, but, especially at home, not only from these. Within the smaller sphere of the University, his influence also came from the services he rendered Chicago. These included the long period he served as editor of the *Journal of Political Economy*, the creation and direction of the Center for the Study of Economy and State (which now bears his name), and the industrial organization workshop he founded and led for many years. His persuasive personality, keen humor – occasionally a bit sharp – and his skills as debater and writer were of great help to him also. His humor is evident in his professional articles, essays, and correspondence. Allen Wallis (1993) illustrates Stigler's humor with a note he received from Stigler when attempting to bring him to Chicago from Columbia:

> Dear Allen:
>   It is always hard for me to begin a letter which conveys bad news to a friend. I know that it is preferable to be explicit and direct, 'to get it over with,' as the popular expression has it, but it is easier to give such uncongenial advice than to follow it. Especially is the task more difficult when the bad news is of the writer's own making, as to a large degree, but not exclusively, it is in the present case. In short, I shall be happy to accept the professorship at Chicago.
>   Cordially,
>   George Stigler

At times, as noted, Stigler's humor had a sharpness to it. This sometimes offended, but the humor was good enough to be worth its sting, especially if you were just a bystander. He once offered to his audience a proposition that he had gleaned from his study of the history of thought: All good economists are tall. To this, he added, he knew of only two exceptions, Milton Friedman and John K. Galbraith. One day, while I was chatting with him in his office, a student requested an audience. He entered and quickly claimed that Stigler had graded him unfairly. Stigler agreed and apologized, and then claimed the university simply did not allow the lower grade that was deserved.

Despite this sharpness, Stigler truly was thoughtful of and generous to others. He used inordinate amounts of his valuable time to give manuscripts of colleagues a careful reading. He did not indulge his humor if the behavior and utterances of others did not make them fair game. I do not remember him aiming his barbs at colleagues like R.H. Coase, Aaron Director, and Friedman. He made sure, through cajoling and transporting, that his now old and retired teacher Frank Knight came to lunch at the Quadrangle Club every now and then, where they joined others who were still active. Stigler might have fun with the young economists present at such lunches, but he always treated his teacher with great respect. Knight, though then in his eighties and in the last decade of his life, retained his alertness and feistiness. Occasionally, he would lift an eye brow and grump 'Humph!' when others made statements he thought foolish. Stigler's generosity and sympathetic feeling toward those experiencing real difficulties surfaced time and again.

But, so did his toughness. This was at its most obvious to me at faculty meetings that dealt with appointments and promotions in the Graduate School of Business. At these meetings, Stigler would stand his ground with skill and wit, and he did so even though good friends and quality colleagues championed opposing positions. He persisted in the effort to maintain faculty of the high quality that he thought Chicago merited, even though, by my memory count, he lost more battles than he won. I have been asked several times what it takes to make a great university. Money helps, and Rockefeller provided this to Chicago. Leadership helps, and Chicago's first president, Rainey Harper, provided this, first by being willing to use Rockefeller's money to make good appointments and second by convincing Rockefeller to leave the running of the University to Harper. These give a university a good start, but just as important, perhaps even more important, a university seeking to maintain greatness needs at least a small group of distinguished scholars who are willing to go out of their way to preserve and improve faculty quality. Chicago had more than the usual share of such people through a long stretch of time. They included Knight, Viner, Wallis, Friedman, Stigler, Coase, Gary Becker and others. A university, with its tenure entitlement, is an institution riddled with free rider problems that encourage people to sit back and to let others do the difficult work. A university retains greatness only if has these 'others' who are willing to bear personal costs to pass a better university on to future generations. Poor appointments and undeserved promotions get locked in by tenure, whereas an occasional failure to secure someone who turns out to be very good can be rectified (as Chicago did by going after Stigler after first rejecting him). No one, during my tenure at Chicago, was more willing than was Stigler to stand against those who, through concern for present comforts with others, undermine the future by being too willing to go along with this and that exception.

It was in 1963, while a member of the UCLA faculty, that I first met Stigler. I had received an invitation to present a workshop paper at Chicago. The invitation came from Reuben Kessel who had heard my UCLA colleague Armen Alchian mention me as a promising young economist (I was then 33). Chicago had a double allure for me, first because of the university's quality, although, at the time, I had no deep knowledge about this, and second because the city was home for my wife and me. Sitting at the back of the seminar room in which I presented my paper was a tall man who, once I began to speak (no doubt a serious mistake), began to launch a series of questions that dealt with issues I had not contemplated when I wrote this paper but which, nevertheless, were germane to it. The questioner, of course, was Stigler, whom I would meet at a dinner hosted by Merton Miller at his home on the evening of the workshop. Stigler came a bit late, but he quickly took center stage and proceeded to dominate the evening's conversation. The dinner guests, mostly faculty, neither shy nor backward, seemed quite willing to sit back and enjoy the entertainment along with the food. Miller could have collected a cover charge at the door. Perhaps he did. This social showmanship role, I came to think, became a burden to Stigler later in life, one borne because others expected it of him and not because, as in earlier times, he enjoyed performing.[2]

Regular attendees at the industrial organization workshop throughout the time of my years at Chicago constituted a formidable group. Usually present, in addition to Stigler, were R.H. Coase, Aaron Director, Reuben Kessel, Lester Telser, Peter Pashigian, Richard Posner, and, toward the end of my stay at Chicago, Gary Becker. Other Chicago faculty came to the workshop when the speaker or the subject interested them. Unlike workshop participants at most places, many if not all regular attendees would have read the paper thoroughly before the speaker actually gave it. This made them less willing to sit still for a presentation that very probably would only repeat what they already knew. Anxious to get to what they perceived to be the central issues raised in the paper, they would begin asking questions soon after the speaker gave his opening remarks. Speakers often thought they were not given the time needed to explain their paper properly, but since the paper already had been thoroughly read, they had been given a full reading if not a full listening. Stigler often asked the first question and, for a time, but not a long time, this set the tone of discussion. Others would soon join in, sometimes disagreeing with Stigler, but more often raising points different from those made by him. Not everyone shared in this style. Coase and Director would usually sit back and listen quietly to the speaker and the questioners, but then, toward the end of the workshop, after listening to everyone else, they often quietly made the most penetrating observations of the seminar.

I describe the workshop to illustrate the atmosphere at Chicago and to highlight the central role played by Stigler who often, just prior to the workshop, entertained the speaker and some workshop regulars at lunch. But mainly, I want the reader to notice the cast of characters. Among them are those few who were to play lead roles in what was to become the new discipline of law and economics: fertile soil in which to plant and nurture a new field.

If one were to choose the person whose work has been most central to the development of law and economics, the choice most surely would be R.H. Coase, a choice reinforced in Stigler's article 'Law or Economics?' (1992). He notes in this article how little interaction there was between law and economics prior to Coase's work on social cost, and how much more interaction there was after Coase wrote his famous 'The Problem of Social Cost'

---

[2]   As it turned out, I did get the offer from Chicago and remained there, learning, for about eight years. During my stay, on some occasion I cannot remember, but perhaps at dinner over some wine, George (if I may) told me he supported making an offer to me because he liked the way I handled myself at the workshop and not because he liked my paper. Well, one out of two with George isn't so bad.

(*Journal of Law and Economics*, 1960). Stigler thought of law and economics in his article as the application of economics to the analysis of contract, property, externalities, and torts. However, the field properly includes antitrust, regulation, the law-making process, and law enforcement. In this sense of law and economics, Stigler's work also plays a large role, not only in influencing economists, but also in influencing political and legal scholars. Some of the work that had this impact pre-dated, and some post-dated, the formal emergence of the new field. In this more complete arena, Stigler as a pioneer of law and economics merits a rank only a notch below Coase's.

The importance of Coase and Stigler to law and economics comes mainly, but not exclusively, from published writings. Aaron Director, on the other hand, did not publish much, although law school students learned much from him and did produce a sizeable quantity of good work. Director contributed to the emerging field by creating and editing the *Journal of Law and Economics*. Stigler had met Director long before the two became colleagues at Chicago when, shortly after World War II, both attended the first meeting of the then newly forming Mont Pelerin Society. The two became close friends after Stigler joined Chicago's faculty. I strongly suspect, on the basis of comments and conversation but not hard facts, that Stigler was of great help to Director in establishing the new journal, supporting him morally, institutionally, easing his way to funds, and in yet another important way: he willingly 'underplaced' manuscripts by putting them into this new and untried journal when they easily could have found their way into established, large circulation journals. In doing this, I do not think Stigler thought he was helping to create a new field of inquiry. He simply sought to help a close friend. Nonetheless, his name in this journal got it off to an exceptionally good start. He did this several times during the history of the journal, helping the journal to continue its progress when Coase became its second editor. The explicit roles played by Director and Coase as editors are widely known, but the support Stigler gave them has gone largely unrecognized.[3]

Stigler's professional output at the beginning of his career (from 1937 to 1942) dealt mainly with history of thought, labor supply and employment, and price theory; he published a textbook in 1942, *The Theory of Competitive Price*, that would come to dominate the teaching of price theory to students for many years. High quality work, no doubt. Great competence in price theory can be seen in it. So can an interest in empirical studies. However, none of it constitutes a solid basis for anticipating future contributions to law and economics.

A hint of future concerns with the interaction between economy and state is offered in 1946, when Stigler published 'The Economics of Minimum Wage Legislation'. Here, Stigler brings price theory to the task of demonstrating the consequences of legislated non-market-clearing prices. The hint is reinforced more strongly in 1949, when he published 'A Theory of Delivered Price Systems', an article written in the context of the ongoing antitrust debate about pricing practises, used in the sale of steel, cement, and bituminous coal, that resulted in identical prices in a given location for a given commodity produced by different sellers whose

---

[3]   There is also the task of disseminating the thoughts and findings of the new discipline. Journal articles sufficed for those who already were keyed into what was happening at Chicago. Those still on the outside needed other sources. One major source was the first text in law and economics, written by Posner. A second source had no connection to this workshop but did have a connection to Chicago's Law School. Henry Manne, who had been a student of Director, created and directed a law and economics center at the University of Rochester through which hundreds of law professors and Federal judges would ultimately learn about law and economics.

production locations were not the same distance from the buyer's location. Theoretical pronouncements populated this debate without introducing, let alone testing, a coherent theory for this pricing practice. Stigler sets forth an innovative theoretical explanation of the practise that makes it a preferred method of setting price in situations in which production is subject to considerable scale economies and in which the demand for the good is subject to fluctuations across geographical locations that are not highly correlated. He sees the delivered price system as a way of shifting production to least-cost producers when demands rise in one region relative to another. A region in which demand is low will have unutilized excess capacity (subject to scale economies), while a region in which demand is high will be straining its productive capacity. A delivered price system will shift production from the second region to the first.[4] He uses data to see if empirical implications of this theory are supported. He finds moderate support for his theory. Empirical support, however, is not as important as is his demonstration of the advantages of formulating a testable theory and then actually testing it. The usefulness of this paper to law and economics will be apparent to those who have read antitrust cases in which delivered price systems were relevant. In 'Monopoly and Oligopoly by Merger', Stigler (1950) adopts the same technique to explain the conditions under which merger is the privately preferred way to acquire pricing power. These two papers mark a shift in Stigler's interest toward problems that then would have been classified as in industrial organization but, because they began to bring economics to bear on legal issues, they also mark the beginning of Stigler's contributions to law and economics.

In the well-known published collection of his writings in industrial organization, Stigler (1968) introduces the volume with the following statement: 'Let us start this volume on a higher plane of candor than it will always maintain: there is no such subject as industrial organization'. He then describes the field's interests as largely the same as that of price or resource allocation theory. I note the wisdom Stigler exhibited in denying the existence of a field that he had been busy creating. He then goes on to justify a distinction between what is called industrial organization and price theory, arguing that the formal generality of price theory makes it difficult for price theorists to deal with specific cases of business organization and with public policies that affect this organization. This second justification, and the contents of his collection, indicate Stigler's newly acquired interest in bringing economics to bear on policy and, therefore, on law. Among his papers, in addition to those already cited, those that bear on antitrust are:

- 'A Note on Block Booking' (1963), in which Stigler wrestles (unsuccessfully in my judgment) with the practice used by the movie industry that required distributors of film to purchase a bundle of movies.
- 'A Theory of Oligopoly' (1964), an innovative theory (tested with data) that asks how the number and permanence of buyers of a product affect the probability that sellers will cheat on a collusive agreement they have made.
- 'The Dominant Firm and the Inverted Umbrella' (1965), a paper that relates to the profitability of a market strategy supposedly used by the US Steel Corporation, a strategy discussed in the context of antitrust attacks on the Corporation.

---

4   I note that this 'shifting' property is not sufficient to establish collusion. It would occur even if prices are set competitively. The test for collusion is whether price on average exceeds production cost.

- 'The Economic Effects of the Antitrust Laws' (1966). In this important article, Stigler looks abroad, to England, for a control by which to judge the efficacy of American antitrust policy. At the time Stigler wrote, England had no antitrust law.

The last listed article merits further description because of the way it fits into the pattern of interpretation Stigler began to apply to economic regulation. He gathered data on comparable industries, one set of which are based in England and the other set in the USA, and then proceeded to examine the market structure of these industries, assuming here that the goal of antitrust is competition and that competition inversely relates to market concentration. Although some industries in England exhibit different degrees of market concentration from those exhibited by their counterparts in the USA, market concentration is not systematically greater in England. Hence, Stigler concludes that America's antitrust policy does not accomplish its avowed objective of increasing the intensity of competition.[5]

What accounts for Stigler's enthusiasm for topics germane to antitrust? Well, it is an area in which data are available or can be mustered. It therefore caters to Stigler's desire to bring data to bear on a problem. It is application of price theory, in which Stigler already had proved to be a master. It is an area that, before Stigler, was laden with unscientific discussions and therefore ready for a strong dose of scientific method. All in all, it was an area of economics waiting for someone like Stigler, and there was no one more like Stigler than was Stigler. But I think there is another reason for his involvement. Antitrust was the area in which Aaron Director worked most in the Law School. He already was complaining to Law School students about the nonsense being peddled in antitrust cases and about how a person could make sense of some marketing and pricing practices by applying price theory. Although he was not a writer of articles, he was finely tuned to questions that needed answers. These he readily discussed with the man who, after his arrival in 1958, became his close friend and colleague. I am sure that their discussions led Stigler into this particular area of application of economic and statistical methods. Four of the six articles mentioned in preceding parts of this essay as relevant to antitrust appeared after Stigler returned to Chicago. If there be life after death, Stigler and Director are together again, Stigler speaking without hesitation and Director quietly puffing his pipe and occasionally interrupting with a question or observation. No doubt, they are striving to make sense of their new surroundings.

On arriving at Chicago, Stigler began to execute a research program that he implicitly revealed to fellow economists in 1964 when he issued a clarion call to them in the presidential address delivered at American Economic Association annual meeting (and published in 1965 under the title 'The Economist and the State'). He urged economists to become more scientific. To do this, he said, they would need to bring data to bear on theories that are modeled in ways that made them testable. Theory alone, he observed, generates no great confidence if it has not undergone testing, and it smacks of ambiguity if its variables and coefficients have not been defined well enough to be measured. He emphasized in this address the need for a scientific approach to the task of giving political advice, and he even used the writings of our hero Adam Smith to illustrate just how unconvincing is advice-giving unsupported

---

5   It is plausible that a goal of antitrust is keeping markets from becoming highly concentrated, and in this sense Stigler's conclusion that antitrust has not been effective is well taken. However, as I have argued elsewhere, and as Stigler would later come to believe, the connection between market structure and market competitiveness is not reliable.

by evidence. He noted that Democrats and Republicans alike will find measures of elasticity of demand useful. One may forgive Stigler the overly optimistic view he presented about the power of statistical evidence, claiming that the influence of economists on policy would be greatly enhanced if only they would bring sound theory backed by hard statistical evidence to the discussion. On this occasion, after all, he was a missionary. Nonetheless, such over-optimism aside, the work he did in the context of demonstrating to others the proper approach to take to a problem often was of 'breakthrough' quality, and it did alter the way economists, legal scholars and political scientists approach topics in law and policy.

By the time he delivered this address, he had already broken free from the antitrust 'box' that contained much of this applied work. Especially important was the article he co-authored with Claire Friedland, 'What Can Regulators Regulate? The Case of Electricity'. This examined price regulation, which is quite different from antitrust. He also published, as sole author, a paper on the 'Pubic Regulation of the Securities Markets' (1964).

'What Can Regulators Regulate?' measured the consequences of the public regulation of electricity prices. This brought a fresh view to the prevailing belief that regulation, although it might well be poorly executed, would at least succeed partly in achieving its objective, which was to hold electricity prices closer to the cost of producing electricity than they might be otherwise. Stigler and Friedland challenged this complacent view by showing that electricity prices, properly adjusted for input prices and for variations across the state in per capita income, are not systematically higher in states that did not regulate than in states that did. The implication was that regulators are powerless to achieve their objectives even partly. Economists and regulators were stunned by the evidence.[6] Stigler repeated a test of the potency of regulation in 'Public Regulation of the Securities Markets' and found, once again, that regulators, here the Securities and Exchange Commission (SEC), failed to achieve their ostensible goal of making better investors of the general public. He reached this conclusion by comparing the variance in stock prices before and after the SEC came into existence. He found no systematic difference. He repeated the test once again in 1966, in 'The Economic Effects of the Antitrust Laws', and again found no regulatory effect.

Stigler by this time had produced a series of articles demonstrating the impotence of economic regulation, whether this involved antitrust, price setting, or security information provision. He began to puzzle about this lack of potency, and, now, so did others. The specific results produced might need adjusting, or even rejecting, but the work succeeded in ending a long period during which economists and political scientists took the efficacy of regulation for granted. He had succeeded in transforming a habit of thinking about regulation on the basis of a myth to one of scientific investigation, surely a major contribution to law and economics.

The energies of other economists now went into the examination of regulation and into the re-examination of the work done by Stigler and Friedland. Data errors were found. The correction of these led to a revision of the conclusions they had reached about the regulation of electricity prices. Regulation, it seems, did reduce electricity prices somewhat, but not by an amount that was statistically very significant. More important than this revision was the work being done by others that began to show a systematic effect on prices of a variety of

---

6   See Peltzman (1993) for a good discussion of the importance of 'What Can Regulators Regulate?'

types of regulation, but surprisingly, an effect that was the opposite of that intended. Regulation generally made prices higher, not lower. Before these studies had been undertaken, Stigler puzzled about how to explain the impotency of regulation. After these studies, his puzzle became how to explain the perverse consequences of regulation. This led Stigler to write a second breakthrough article, 'The Theory of Economic Regulation' (1971). He proposed a capture theory of regulation, in which regulated industries capture the policies of regulators by standing ready to give or not to give financial aid to regulators who are elected to their posts; by offering employment to regulators who retire; and by supplying argument, facts, and studies to regulators that bolster positions sought by the regulated. Again, his work prompted the work of others, some of whom were close colleagues of Stigler. While not denying the regulated an influence over the regulators, this work offered theory and some evidence that voters in a democracy and customers in a market do have some influence over the behavior of regulators. No matter, regulation now remains fit for study and fit for skepticism.

'The Theory of Economic Regulation' was preceded by two articles that are relevant to Stigler's role in law and economics, 'The Optimum Enforcement of Laws' (1970) and 'Director's Law of Public Income Redistribution' (1970). The first makes readers cognizant of the important role played by enforcement cost in a meaningful theory of law enforcement and discusses novel ways of reducing this cost; it was followed later by 'Law Enforcement, Malfeasance, and Compensation of Enforcers', co-authored with Gary Becker (1974), in which, among other things, the authors propose letting anyone, not just officers of the law, enforce the law. The second 1970 article presaged 'A Theory of Regulation'. It pursued and modestly tested Director's idea that income distribution would favor the income category that offers politicians the most voters. In general, this would be the middle class; tax law, Stigler demonstrated, did indeed favor the middle class if one notes who benefits from tax expenditures as well as who pays taxes. Here we see who possibly influenced Stigler when he thought about the regulated controlling the regulators in his 'The Theory of Economic Regulation'.

Stigler's work may be distinguished from the earlier contribution to political economy made by Buchanan and Tullock in their important book *The Calculus of Consent* (1962). The subtitle of this book, 'Logical Foundations of Constitutional Democracy', indicates the difference. Buchanan's and Tullock's work is a logical and insightful rationalization of democratic political governance and also a brilliant inquiry, based on the individualistic postulate of (political) behavior, into the inner workings of political institutions. Their work created the new field of public choice, but, as the book claims, it is a treatise based in logic and economic theory; it is not the equivalent of the type of the scientific work done by Stigler, although it set in place the logic on which such work could be based. Stigler first examined the consequences of regulation through the lens of theory-guided statistical work. His first findings were partly undermined by those of others. He accepted their critiques and findings and began to think about how to revise theory to accord with these. He came up with his captive theory of regulation. This led to more critiques and to modifications made by others, among them close colleagues, that produced a more general and testable model of political behavior. This, too, has been and is being subjected to empirical testing. His work and his reactions to the works of others brought scientific (positive) economics to law, regulation and politics. His greatest success is that his call for scientific work, issued in his 1964 Presidential Address, has been answered, and not just in the field of law and economics.

References

Stigler, G.J. (1937), 'The Economics of Carl Menger', *Journal of Political Economy*, April.
Stigler, G.J. (1946), 'The Economics of Minimum Wage Legislation', *American Economic Review*, June.
Stigler, G.J. (1949), 'A Theory of Delivered Price Systems', *American Economic Review*, December.
Stigler, G.J. (1950), 'Monopoly and Oligopoly by Merger', *Papers and Proceedings, American Economic Review*, May.
Stigler, G.J. (1963), 'United States v. Loew's Inc.: A Note on Block Booking', *The Supreme Court Review*.
Stigler, G.J. (1964), 'Public Regulation of the Securities Markets', *Journal of Business*, April.
Stigler, G.J. (1964), 'A Theory of Oligopoly', *Journal of Political Economy*, February.
Stigler, G.J. (1965), 'The Economist and The State', *American Economic Review*, March.
Stigler, G.J. (1965), 'The Dominant Firm and the Inverted Umbrella', *Journal of Law and Economics*, October.
Stigler, G.J. (1966), 'The Economic Effects of the Antitrust Laws', *Journal of Law and Economics*, October.
Stigler, G.J. (1968), *The Organization of Industry* (Homewood, Ill.: Richard D. Irwin).
Stigler, G.J. (1970), 'Director's Law of Public Income Redistribution', *Journal of Law and Economics*, April.
Stigler, G.J. (1970), 'The Optimum Enforcement of Laws', *Journal of Political Economics*, May/June.
Stigler, G.J. (1971), 'The Theory of Economic Regulation', *Bell Journal of Economics and Management Science*, Spring.
Stigler, G.J. (1992), 'Law or Economics', *Journal of Law and Economics*, October.
Stigler, G.J. and Becker, G. (1974), 'Law Enforcement, Malfeasance, and Compensation of Enforcers', *Journal of Legal Studies*, January.
Stigler, G.J. and Friedland, C. (1962), 'What Can Regulators Regulate? The Case of Electricity', *Journal of Law and Economics*, October.
Peltzman, S. (1993), 'George Stigler's Contribution to the Economics of Regulation', *Journal of Political Economy*, October.
Wallis, W.A. (1993), 'In Memoriam', *Journal of Political Economy*, October.

5 The enduring contributions of Armen Alchian

Susan Woodward

Armen Alchian's work of lasting influence in law and economics falls into three areas. First (in time) is his evolutionary explanation as to why rationality is a reasonable hypothesis from which to begin economic reasoning. Second is his work on property rights, which explores how assignments of property rights and decision rights influence how resources are used, with the central theme that incentives matter. Third is his work on why particular combinations of assignments of property and decision rights are so often seen, in particular how these are shaped by the potential for opportunistic behavior.

For law and economics, the third area is the most important. Here Alchian explored why some people give directions while others take them, why certain groups of assets are jointly owned, why we see long-term contracts, vertical integration, first refusal rights, posted prices, credible threats, hostages to exchange, and more. Each of these different aspects of firm organization involves either contractual or organizational restraints on behavior. Many of these restraints, including vertical integration, exclusive contracts, long-term contracts, posted prices, and first refusal rights had previously been seen as monopolistic, inhibiting the operation of free markets. Alchian helped us understand how contractual restraints could promote competition and efficiency, indeed in some settings were essential to commerce in the sense that without the restraints, investment might not occur. This third area identifies two different kinds of transactional frictions – often called vulnerability to opportunism – that shape contracts among and organization within firms: (1) moral hazard, and (2) hold-up. Alchian's contributions to these two discussions came separately, six years apart, and were united, providing further insights, a few years later.

In the background of all three themes in Alchian's work is a theory of ownership, that is, a theory of who ends up owning (and directing) what resources. A theory of ownership was never the goal of this work. Instead the goal was to better understand how we get from a set of property and rights assignments to an economic outcome. The pattern of ownership is a feature of the outcome.

Alchian's work provides answers to this seemingly unrelated set of questions:

(1) In small businesses, the person who owns the company also directs the efforts of employees, but in large companies, shareholders hire a manager. Why this difference?

(2) Why would a company like McDonald's, which has access to capital via the stock market, franchise its restaurants, asking the franchise owners, whose access to capital is surely not as good as McDonald's, to fund the operation of the local restaurant?

(3) Why do newspapers always own their printing presses, while book publishers almost never do?

(4) Why (prior to cell phones) did fish canneries post prices for fishermen bringing their catches?

(5)   Why are steel manufacturers diffusely held and funded with substantial debt while pharmaceutical companies are relatively closely held and have virtually no debt?

(6)   Why is free contracting, not necessarily free markets, the key to efficiency?

(7)   Why do doctors want much longer-term leases on their office space than dress shops do?

(8)   Why are country clubs owned by their members instead of outside investors?

(9)   Why do people buy insurance for small risks like auto towing?

In his evolution paper[1] ('Uncertainty, Evolution, and Economic Theory', 1950), Alchian discusses how the dominant features of all organizations that allocate resources – who decides, who performs, and who collects the residual value – are at all times under pressure from competition. The pressure comes from customers of the products produced and also from those who seek the rights to decide, perform, and collect the residual value from production. Organizations that do not get these features right do not survive. It does not matter whether their allocative decisions were made randomly or via a system of conscious, focused profit maximization, or something in between. However the decisions are made, the more profitable – the more fit – prevail, and the less fit are weeded out by market forces. And of course, those not weeded out will end up owning more resources. Market forces push firms in directions consistent with profit maximization by awarding more resources to those successful in making profits and by bidding away or dissipating resources from those who do not.

The second set of ideas concerns how incentives matter, or more formally, how assignments of property rights and decision rights influence how resources are used. These themes do not concern the 'optimal' set of property rights ('optimal' is a word Alchian uses sparingly), or set out to defend private property, but are analyses of how decisions actually made will depend on the costs and benefits to those who are assigned the decision rights and residual claims. Substantial attention to property rights and decision rights makes for much of the originality and power in university economics (the title of my own first textbook in economics in 1967).

The third area of influence concerns economic institutions both private and public, of contract and law, and focuses on how the organization of activity within a firm and between firms supports commerce which requires investments that are vulnerable to opportunism ('Production, Information Costs, and Economic Organization', 1972[2], 'Vertical Integration, Appropriable Rents, and the Competitive Contracting Process', 1978[3], and 'Long Live the Firm', 1988[4]). This thinking developed in three waves. The first (1972), with Demsetz, was about the form of opportunism we call moral hazard or shirking. Morally hazardous opportunism occurs when it is costly for a principal (for example, owner and manager) to observe

---

[1]   Alchian, A.A., 1950, 'Uncertainty, Evolution, and Economic Theory', *Journal of Political Economy*.

[2]   Alchian, A.A. and Demsetz, H., 1972, 'Production, Information Costs, and Economic Organization', *American Economic Review*.

[3]   Klein, Benjamin, Robert G. Crawford and Armen A. Alchian, 1978, 'Vertical Integration, Appropriable Rents, and the Competitive Contracting Process', *Journal of Law & Economics*, 21(2), 297–326.

[4]   Alchian, A.A. and Woodward, S.E., 1988, 'The Firm is Dead: Long Live the Firm: A Review of Oliver Williamson's *The Economic Institutions of Capitalism*', *Journal of Economic Literature*, March.

or measure the performance of an agent (employee). The presence of moral hazard and shirking helps us understand why production is organized as it is, with various combinations of separated or combined ownership and management, and with managers and workers.

The second wave (1978) examines the potential for hold-up. Hold-up occurs when at least one party makes an irreversible long-term investment whose value depends on someone else's performance. When an investment that creates joint value is made, and the resources contributed are possessed[5] by at least two different parties, one party can threaten the other with departure unless it receives a larger share of the joint value. Which party has the stronger position to threaten hold-up and extract a higher share depends on the alternatives available to each. Both moral hazard and hold-up can inhibit commerce, but markets seek to prevent them from doing so in very different ways. Preventing moral hazard from destroying joint value requires monitoring (collection of costly information). Hold-up does not so much destroy joint value as discourage its creation when the potential for hold-up is anticipated. The threat of hold-up can be dulled with long-term contracts, joint ownership of assets, posted prices, first refusal rights, and more. Along with this comes the idea that it is in free *contracting*, not necessarily free *markets*, where efficiency lies.

Without irreversible investments there can be no hold-up. Without assets whose creation cannot be undone, the potential for disputes to arise over division of the rents is nil. Alchian emphasizes how long-term contracts and other mutual, voluntary obligations among transactors inhibit behavior that otherwise threatens to preclude the creation of joint value, and promotes behavior that builds it.

The third wave of thinking brought the discussion of these two kinds of opportunism together for a more comprehensive view of the firm, combining both the organization as well as the financing of production, in 'Long Live the Firm'. Alchian and Woodward (1988) extend and clarify Williamson, distinguishing between the two kinds of opportunism – moral hazard and hold-up – and how firms address these two forms of opportunism in different ways.

All three lines of thought – evolution towards efficient assignments of property and decision rights, how incentives depend on rights, and how markets cope with opportunism (shirking and reneging) – lead to a theory of ownership. The ownership of assets and decision rights is not random or merely historical, but tends to move, gravitate, or evolve in the direction most effective at organizing, directing, and encouraging the creation of value and restraining opportunistic behavior that threatens joint value. The technology of contracts and rights assignments are at least as important as production technologies in shaping economic activity. Technologies are known or knowable worldwide, but we observe vast variation in income across countries. The variation in income across countries cannot be explained by variation in access to technical knowledge. The best evidence suggests that the differences in economic institutions, especially the protection of property rights, including the absence of corruption in government, are the source of the variation.[6]

---

[5]   I use 'possess' rather than 'own' because most forms of human capital are inalienable (cannot be transferred, surrendered, or sold), a quality not suggested by 'own'.

[6]   Hall, Robert E., and Charles E. Jones, 1999, 'Why Do Some Countries Produce So Much More Output than Others?' *Quarterly Journal of Economics*.

Evolution

Kenneth Arrow claims,[7] and Earl Thompson agrees, that Alchian's 1950 evolution paper was the source of Alchian's original fame. The proposition is that evolutionary forces, in the form of 'adaptive, imitative, trial-and-error' behavior, will eventually lead to outcomes that appear to be the result of rational, maximizing behavior. The notion that evolutionary forces would push firms in the direction of what look to be rational decisions brought around many who were repelled from economic reasoning by the bumptious assumption of rational optimization. The evolutionary view allowed for incomplete knowledge, mistakes, short-sightedness, experiments, and even stupidity, all of which seem to be abundant to most normal observers of life, but still arrived at a result consistent with rationality.

The innovations firms make are mainly not random, but conscious and forward-looking. If decisions were chosen at random, surely more would fail than we see fail, as the great proportion of random mutations in nature fail. Evolution happens faster if the mutations are chosen with some foresight. But, as Alchian emphasizes, even when choices are imitative and forward-looking, they still have a random element arising from mistakes and surprises.

Alchian's point, however, was that even if the decisions were random, what will give order to the outcomes is the constraints – the scarcity – under which they operate. Out of potentially chaotic choice will emerge the order of successful choices, those with cost no higher than price. The test of the merit of the theory should not lie in an examination of the rationality of the choices, but whether the *outcomes* fit the theory. Behind Alchian's thinking is a clear philosophy of science.

Discussions combining the words evolution and economics were not new in 1950. Even before 1910 we see pieces such as 'American Shoemakers, 1648–1895: A Sketch of Industrial Evolution',[8] *Evolution of Credit and Banks in France*.[9] These and similar works were mainly about how industries and production processes changed over time, incrementally, and for the better, but none made the connection between evolution in economic institutions and the reasonableness of rationality. That connection was Alchian's contribution.

Alchian's thinking on evolution was to some merely a comfort, but to others, a salvation of economics. In the economics literature there was much discussion of irrational economic behavior, not entirely unrelated to what we read in behavioral economics today. The main difference is that today's behavioral economics is more disciplined, with organizing themes of different forms of irrationality (framing, impatience, an assortment of cognitive biases), while the older version was more just a list of decision failures. And I believe that as the economics of 'behavioral behavior' develops, it will be revealed as yet another aspect of optimization – doing the best we can with our scarce resources, where attention, processing time, focus, and willpower are counted among the scarce resources. Psychologists have now demonstrated experimentally that 'willpower' is a scarce resource, the depletion of which is costly. The cognitive processes of people who have exerted more self-control are less accurate than those who have exerted less. Subjects put in a position to resist temptation (to not eat freshly baked chocolate chip cookies sitting in front of them), to inhibit expressions of

---

7   See the Fall 2001 Newsletter of the ISNIE at www.isnie.org for this discussion.
8   Commons, J.R., 1909, *Quarterly Journal of Economics*.
9   Liesse, Andre, 1909, *Evolution of Credit and Banks in France*, Washington DC: Government Printing Office. http://socserv2.McMaster.ca/mecon/ugcm/3113/liesse/EvolutionCreditBanksFrance.pdf.

emotion during a gory movie, even to merely direct attention in some way, do unambiguously worse on cognitive tests immediately after these efforts than controls not similarly burdened. Moreover, the 'power' in willpower is not just a metaphor, but a physical expenditure of fuel (glucose) that powers the brain.[10] From here it cannot be far to a measurement of the cost of attention and self-control. Attention is a scarce resource.

In 1950 when Alchian's evolution paper was published, critics of economics would look to this irrationality literature to discredit economics generally or to undermine the legitimacy of capitalist institutions. Alchian's point was that the decisions of those who directed resources did not have to be perfect or optimal, but only had to move things towards efficiency. This interpretation of rationality made economics more acceptable as a discourse.

A considerable literature has grown up around evolution and economics devoted to evolutionary game theory. Much of this literature attempts to show the conditions necessary for an efficient equilibrium in social institutions. Alchian was never so ambitious. He never claimed optimality or efficiency for any set of forces for allocating resources, either in the form of firms or larger social institutions such as government. His logic was about the *direction*, not the destination or the speed. More efficient institutions would survive, the less efficient would not. He had little patience for the precise assumptions necessary to get from improvements to perfection.

It is not clear that Alchian would have any interest in claiming this game theory literature as his progeny, because of its focus on optimality. But those who work in the area these days have mainly forgotten Alchian. Despite Ken Arrow's protestations in earlier Alchian appreciations, there are few references to Alchian's 1950 evolution paper now.

Property rights
Alchian's work on property rights and decision rights is the foundation of his most important contributions to economic thinking, especially the theory of the firm. This work also made him popular with conservative organizations such as the Liberty Fund, the Olin Foundation, and the Lilly Foundation. Olin and Lilly gave money to various kitties the Economics Department had for subsidizing students and young professors, some even not-so-young professors, and the Liberty Fund organized many conferences and published Alchian's collected works in two handy volumes, bless them. Little did they realize what a subversive he was! If they had read his stuff more carefully, and realized that he viewed private property as simply one of many alternative forms of coercion (and there is no coercion-free social life), they might have been alarmed.

It is not difficult to see what appealed to them: Alchian compared the incentives in privately owned firms, jointly owned firms, non-profit organizations, publicly regulated firms, socialist firms, cost-plus compensation arrangements, and different legal rules for addressing externalities. He drew the different outcomes that could be expected given the incentives of each organizational form. He did not argue from oughts and shoulds, but simply from what was valued by those making decisions (what were their utility functions – a topic

---

10   Gailliot, M.T., and Baumeister, R.F., DeWall, C.N., Maner, J.K., Plant, A.E., Tice, D.M., Brewer and L.E., Schmeichel, B.J., 2007, 'Self-Control Relies on Glucose as a Limited Energy Source: Willpower is More than a Metaphor', *Journal of Personality and Social Psychology*, 92, 325–36. See also Baumeister, R.F., Bratslavsky, E., Muraven, M. and Tice, D.M., 1998, 'Ego Depletion: Is the Active Self a Limited Resource?' *Journal of Personality and Social Psychology*, 74, 1252–65.

whose meaning he explored at some length) and how the organizational forms would determine the set of decisions available. Alchian leads his readers from decision rights to how decision-makers deploy resources to obtain what *they* value (what is in their personal utility functions), and how this determines what is produced and whether there is any residual value, and if so, who receives it. At this time the battle between capitalism and socialism (or communism) for hearts and minds was still raging (as opposed to its now mainly settled character since the collapse of the Soviet Union), so a clear voice in favor of the outcomes of capitalism was welcome. This work had grown out of his work at the Rand Corporation, where he pondered topics such the design of military procurement contracts.

Ironically, Alchian did little to defend capitalist institutions directly, although many things he has written suggest he believes they are better than others. Indeed, he pointed out that a system of private property was not less coercive than other systems, it was simply a *different form* of coercion. But he does believe that a given a choice, considering various systems, most people, especially smaller, weaker people – like women – would choose to live with the coercion of private property, in which the state helps us defend our property (by coercing others on our behalf) and restrains (coerces) us from taking the property of others. In such a system, being big and strong is less of an advantage than it would be in many other systems we might imagine.

Is the alignment of incentives with profits all good? Well, no. Why not? Because incentives matter, and incentives aligned with current profits or the current stock price can produce behavior inconsistent with greater profits in the long run. Aligning incentives perfectly is difficult.

The organization of mortgage loan origination is illustrative. Before 1990, nearly all mortgage loans were originated in a lender's office by employees of the lender known as loan officers. Loan officers are generally paid a salary, possibly plus a bonus for a higher volume of loans made. By the mid-1990s, mortgage brokers had become an important part of mortgage lending. Mortgage brokers are independent agents who are true middlemen. Compensation for mortgage brokers is the simple difference between retail (what the broker can negotiate from a borrower) and wholesale terms (which look like posted prices, generally not seen by borrowers). The outcomes of loans written by loan officers who are employees of the lender are different in predictable ways from those originated by mortgage brokers. Brokered loans prepay faster (to the disadvantage of the wholesale lender) and default with higher frequencies than do mortgages originated by loan officers.[11] Brokered loans are more expensive for borrowers on average than loans written by loan officers.[12] Mortgage brokers' incentives are simply more focused on pure profitability, sort of an 'eat what you kill' model of compensation, than are those of loan officers. In the secondary market for mortgages, the average differences (in prepayments and defaults) between lender-originated loans and broker-originated loans are priced, and less is paid for brokered loans than those originated in lenders' offices. Should we, having read Alchian, be surprised that mortgage brokers manage to extract a bit more from both lender and borrower than do

---

[11]   Alexander, W.P., Grimshaw, S.D., McQueen, G.R., and Slade, B.A., 2002, 'Some Loans are more Equal than Others: Third-Party Originations and Defaults in the Subprime Mortgage Industry', *Real Estate Economics*, Winter.
[12]   Woodward, S.E., 2008, 'A Study of Closing Costs for FHA Mortgages', US Department of Housing and Urban Development. http://www.huduser.org/ Publications/pdf/FHA_closing_cost.pdf.

loan officers? No. However, wholesale lenders, who are attentive repeat dealers, know what differences to expect on brokered loans, and price accordingly. It is not so clear that borrowers are similarly well-informed.

Another illustration lies in the empirical research on accounting fraud. Many financial economists promoted options on company stock as a beneficial form of compensation to high-level executives in order to align their incentives with value creation. It does align incentives, but sometimes perversely. When executives receive more compensation in the form of options on the value of their firm, the incidence of overstated earnings (later restated lower), is higher.[13] The incidence of back-dated options (a specific form of under-reported costs) is also higher. Incentives matter. Executives with more options not only have more incentive to make their firms profitable but also more incentive to overstate those profits.

Pure (100 per cent) long-term ownership on the part of managers should get the incentives for true profits right. This comes at the cost to owners of having too many eggs in one basket, an under-diversified portfolio. But this idea skips ahead to the later Alchian work.

Alchian's work on property and decision rights began to give microeconomics insight into the organization of production, not just the technology. In the technological treatment, 'the firm' was simply a production function with incentives unquestioned. Intermediate price theory textbooks maximized utility given prices, and maximized profits subject to prices and production technology, explored economies of scale and scope, and discussed potential for monopoly when scale economies were present. I have in mind especially the more mathematical treatments, textbooks such as Henderson and Quandt (1958),[14] which dazzled the student with the elegance of mathematical descriptions of total, average, and marginal cost and output, economies of scale and scope, and substitutability of inputs. The merit of the mathematical treatment is that a student cannot leave them without becoming very clear on average versus marginal, and short-run versus long run.

A deep understanding of the production function is important, but it offers little to explain organizations and hierarchies, and the presence of a residual claimant, all presumed that if the objective function writ down was profit maximization, profits would be maximized. A student could come away with the impression that production could be directed by someone who knew a lot of calculus and could figure out what inputs to buy, hand out sheets with instructions, and be done. What Alchian suggested (for example) was that we cannot expect the same outcomes from a firm that is operated as a non-profit cooperative from one with owners who are residual claimants, even if the production processes (production functions) are identical. A student could have been left believing that a socialist firm instructed to maximize profits would make the same decisions as a privately owned capitalist firm.

Alchian's discussions of the incentives created by property and decision rights led naturally and directly to his insights on the organization of firms. Though the word 'shirk' does not appear in Alchian's early papers on property and decision rights, the idea (notion? concept?) of shirking is clearly present in Alchian's discussion of for-profit versus non-profit

---

13   Johnson, S.A., Ryan, H.E. and Tian, Y.S., 2005, 'Executive Compensation and Corporate Fraud', working paper, Texas A&M U., and Gao, P., and Shrieves, R., 2002, 'Earnings Management and Executive Compensation: A Case of Overdose of Option and Underdose of Salary?' SSRN working paper, July.
14   Henderson, James, and Quandt, Richard, 1958, *Microeconomic Theory: A Mathematical Approach*, New York: McGraw-Hill.

firms. Alchian predicts that managers who are owners will allocate resources differently from managers who are not owners because all value leisure, but owners benefit from giving up leisure more than non-owners do. This discussion shows a clear focus on the conflict of interest between between owners and managers, and the possibility of shirking on the part of non-owner managers.

Property rights, incentives, opportunism, and the firm: moral hazard and information costs

The big new idea in 'Production, Information Costs, and Economic Organization' (1972), is to make the management of opportunism in the form of moral hazard the central force in the organization of economic activity. The lower effort of the non-owner manager, discussed in the property and decision rights papers, is called shirking. It is a clear next step to discuss how the cost of monitoring (information costs) in different kinds of production processes will result in different organizations of productive activity in order to inhibit shirking.

Coase had provided key insights into the firm by showing the importance of joint ownership of assets for efficient control of externalities. When externalities are present in the production of inputs common to an end product, we need either a contract (likely long term) or joint ownership to efficiently control the externalities. Whether a contract or joint ownership was better depended on the transaction costs of each. Coase acknowledged transaction costs within firms, but did not focus on the control of shirking as a central role for the firm or a cost of doing business, nor on the potential for hold-up among mutually dependent resources. One example Coase discusses in his theory of the firm concerns the buying of theft insurance on a building and how it changes incentives. Incentive issues are everywhere. If a firm orders a fence rather than buying insurance, should it use a fixed-price contract or pay by the hour to build the fence? The choice will change incentives. Coase saw shirking as one among many costs and did not give it first priority as a source of explanation. Alchian, Williamson, and others saw it as a primary force.

The idea of moral hazard was not new; it was already well understood in the context of insurance. That the post-insurance probability of loss was higher than the pre-insurance probability of loss was acknowledged, as were its efficiency properties. Without insurance, the insured's only opportunity for reducing risk is to take care. By insuring a loss, the insured not only lays off risk but also is relieved of an inefficiently high level of care-taking. If insureds are risk-averse, they may spend more resources on care-taking than the expected value of the loss. Insurance clearly makes them better off. Some reduction in care-taking behavior is efficient. The trouble comes when insureds reduce care-taking beyond the point where their own marginal contribution to losses in the risk pool is greater than the marginal amount they pay into the risk pool. Ideally, that is if information costs were zero, marginal risk and marginal contribution would be equated. An insurer who could costlessly monitor the activity of insureds and adjust insurance premiums accordingly could achieve such an equality, efficiently reducing the insured's level of care-taking. But monitoring is costly, so there is some 'inefficiency' in insurance compared to a free-information, or zero-monitoring cost, ideal. Acknowledging the cost of monitoring, we still have an efficient insurance equilibrium, despite some 'moral hazard loss'. In principle, such a loss is 'merely' a transaction cost.

This analysis of costly monitoring and moral hazard as transaction costs in insurance carries over directly to the firm. 'Management' will give directions to and monitor 'labor'. Owners will monitor managers. If the success of management can be cheaply monitored (observed), then ownership and management can be separated with little loss. From an owner's point of view, both labor and management are 'labor', but have different skills, and owners provide the capital and make the decisions regarding whom to hire and keep as management. If monitoring management is too costly, then ownership and management cannot be separated, and owners must *be* managers – as in the case of venture capital start-ups.[15] Even this – the importance of owners having a day-to-day role in operations – is a matter of degree. The importance of owners, of course, is that they are residual claimants, and thus own whatever is left over after the product has been sold and other contributors have been paid.

Some fans of 'Production, Information Costs, and Economic Organization' (1972) have even suggested this paper introduced the term 'residual claimant'.[16] It is not so. The earliest cite I can find (without trying awfully hard – search via Google Scholar) is in the work of F.A. Walker,[17] *Land and its Rent* (1883), nearly a hundred years prior. The annual level of cites was rising over time, but it exploded after 1972.

Thus, the concept of moral hazard was already understood in a sophisticated way. The notion of a residual claimant had been around since at least 1883. Alchian had already written about how property and decision rights assignments influenced economic outcomes. By making opportunism and monitoring central, Alchian shows us that ownership is not simply the haves giving orders to the have-nots, but economic forces pushing ownership in a direction such that those who are more talented at directing resources end up owning more of them. What had not happened prior to the 1972 paper was to combine uncertainty, moral hazard, and monitoring in an analysis of relations among owners, employers, and employees (and all other claimants on a given economic activity), and thus to draw out the implications of monitoring costs in production, and the forms taken by various economic organizations depending on the shape and size of monitoring costs. Because Alchian had already devoted considerable thought to how incentives shape outcomes, beginning with his thinking on how to structure military procurement contracts, it was natural that such thinking would lead him to the ideas that came to him.

The presence of moral hazard helps us understand why the rights to direct resources are often accompanied by ownership of the resources themselves. Two forces operate towards the use of non-owner managers. One is the measurability of output (information costs) and another is economies of scale. When an enterprise is not efficient except on a large scale, and requires the resources of many individuals for its undertaking, it becomes less feasible for a single person or family to amass the necessary resources.

Alchian is a thinker who is both open-minded and truth-seeking. In a later paper on moral hazard, 'Specificity, Specialization and Coalitions' (1984),[18] Alchian acknowledged that Williamson (1975)[19] was right and Alchian and Demsetz (1972)[20] were wrong about the

---

15   Hall, Robert E., and Woodward, Susan E., 2008, 'The Burden of the Nondiversifiable Risk of Entrepreneurship', July, NBER Working Paper 14329.

16   Thomas Merrill, 2007, 'Establishing Ownership: First Possession and Accession', Law and Economics Workshop, UC Berkeley, February, 2007, footnote 41.

17   Published by Little, Brown, and Company, Boston.

18   Alchian, Armen, 1984, 'Specificity, Specialization and Coalitions', *Journal of Institutional and Theoretical Economics*, no. 140, pp. 34–49.

19   Oliver Williamson, 1975, *Markets and Hierarchies, Analysis and Antitrust Implications, a Study in the Economics of Internal Organization*, New York: Free Press.

20   Alchian and Demsetz, 1972, 'Production, Information Costs, and Economic Organization', *American Economic Review*.

importance of long-term contracts between workers and owners. Alchian and Demsetz dismiss the importance of a long-term relationship: 'neither employee nor employer is bound by any contractual obligation to continue their relationship'. In 'Specificity' (1984), Alchian acknowledges that there is a strong expectation by both employer and employee of a long-term relation, and that this expectation influences the behavior of both. Employers treat employees better and employees are more loyal because both value their mutual relationship and want it to continue. As Alchian said, 'It might make Harold mad, but it is true'.

Property rights, incentives, opportunism, and the firm: hold-up
'Production, Information Costs, and Economic Organization' (1972) was a big step forward from the firm as merely a production function, but another big piece was to be added by introducing another form of opportunism: hold-up. Costly information and the necessity of monitoring to restrain moral hazard could not explain many features of firms. For example: why do newspapers always own their own printing presses, but book publishers almost never do?

The epiphany to explain this and similar phenomena came in 1978, in 'Vertical Integration, Appropriable Rents, and the Competitive Contracting Process', with Robert Crawford and Benjamin Klein (*Journal of Law and Economics*). 'Production, Information Costs . . .' contains no hint of the possibility of opportunistic attempts to seize the joint value (hold-up) created by an investment as a force in shaping the firm. Combining hold-up and moral hazard, two quite different forms of opportunism, gave us an even richer theory of the firm.

In particular, for the question of press ownership: if the presses of newspapers were owned separately from the provider of content, the printing press would have the opportunity to extract rent from the content provider. 'Pay us more now or we don't print tomorrow's paper' is a threat for more compensation in the same way as labor, which cannot be owned by a firm, threatens firms such as airlines and trash collection, for more compensation. A book publisher is not similarly vulnerable. It can negotiate a deal for printing well in advance of its printing needs, and does not need the continuous services of a press. And if the press attempts to hold up a publisher at the last minute, the loss to the publisher of simply turning to another printer is not so great as the loss for a newspaper, because the news is more perishable than a book. The newspaper could have a long-term contract with a printer also, but it would be subject to repeated renewal and possibly renegotiation. If the costs of renegotiating are non-trivial, combining ownership of content and press dominates for the newspaper, but does not for the book publisher.

The other example of hold-up-driven asset holdings discussed at length in 'Vertical Integration' is the acquisition of Fisher Body by General Motors.[21] General Motors was not unhappy with the quality of products it was getting from Fisher. Information costs of assuring quality were not the issue. Instead, the issue was that when Fisher designed an especially appealing body, it attempted to raise the price to GM more for the updated models. In other words, when Fisher created a body with unusually high rents, Fisher would attempt to extract

---

[21] These facts may be more stylish than factual. Coase and Klein have disputed whether there was actual hold-up by Fisher. Klein maintains that there was. The interested reader should review both Coase and Klein. See Klein, Benjamin, 2007, 'The Economic Lessons of Fisher Body–General Motors', *International Journal of the Economics of Business*, February.

the rent from GM by charging higher prices for updates, producing a costly negotiation with GM over price. Like gathering information, negotiating can be costly. The costly negotiation could be eliminated by having body production and the rest of auto production jointly owned. This potential for hold-up, and the attendant costs of negotiating a new price, was the force that impelled GM to buy Fisher.

Hold-up potential is key to understanding the joint ownership of certain assets and the use of vertical restraints of trade. The contribution to antitrust analysis is especially great, because many instances of vertical integration and vertical restraints had been interpreted as monopolistic and nothing more. With the understanding of the creation of joint value and future disputes over its division, we now see that such restraints are not monopolistic, but essential for effective competition, even for the existence of some kinds of investments.

As moral hazard was previously understood in the context of insurance (but not as a force shaping firms) the potential for hold-up was also known prior to the publication of 'Vertical Integration'. It had been discussed by Alfred Marshall, in some detail, and I remember Alchian recounting Marshall's story many times. Marshall imagined a manufacturing plant locating near a public utility in order to be able to obtain power cheaply. Once the manufacturing plant's investment was made, the utility could raise the price of power to the plant and extract the quasi-rents of the sunk costs. Marshall saw the resolution in 'bargaining' (not further specified) and 'doing the right thing' (whatever that is). Alchian, Crawford and Klein saw that this hold-up potential was not an isolated situation, but a set of conditions common to many kinds of economic activity, and an important force determining the size and shape of firms.

There are many additional compelling examples of hold-up to demonstrate its force in shaping transactions. One is towing insurance. How many people really spend enough on towing to make it worth insuring? Surely it is a tiny fraction of nearly everyone's permanent income. Risk-aversion to a large potential loss is not the issue. The AAA (American Automobile Association) has long-term contracts with both auto owners (for towing insurance) and auto-towing establishments. It negotiates a price for towing with towers, and relieves auto owners/users from potential hold-up when they have a breakdown. Towing insurance exists to provide a negotiated price ahead of your need for service to preclude hold-up when you are in need. Long-term contracts between studios and performers prevent a star from holding up a studio for a show's rents, when it is the studio's investment that made the star a star. An investor who builds a building on rented land (not an uncommon situation, perhaps due to taxes on capital gains) needs a very long-term contract to protect the investment, which is mainly a sunk cost, from the hold-up of land rent increases that could extract the value of the investment.

Combining moral hazard and hold-up
Bringing together moral hazard (or shirking) and hold-up, the two forms of opportunism, came when Alchian was invited to review Williamson's *The Economic Institutions of Capitalism*.[22] This assignment, and my enlistment, provoked both of us to read *Institutions* carefully and find that while both forms of opportunism were present in Williamson's think-

---

[22]   Williamson, Oliver, 1985, *The Economic Institutions of Capitalism: Firms, Markets, and Relational Contracting*, New York: Free Press.

ing, they were not crisply distinguished, and that while they were crisply distinguished in Alchian's two papers, they were not integrated and discussed together as they were in Williamson. Indeed, the literatures on moral hazard and hold-up were almost entirely disjoint. The goal of the book review, 'Long Live the Firm' (1987), was to pull the ideas all together. 'Long Live' introduces the concept of asset plasticity. Assets are plastic when they can be used in many different ways (having different costs and different risk profiles). Assets are implastic when they are good for only a few things and not much subject to alteration. Plasticity ties into both moral hazard and hold-up potential.

For example, the assets of a steel-manufacturing firm are highly implastic and firm-specific. There is not much that can be done with them but produce steel, and they offer few options, and little discretion, in how this is done. Steel plants are among the most fixed of fixed assets. The riskiness of the outcomes will be mainly driven by fluctuations in demand for the product, not by manager's decisions about how the assets are used. This influences the firm's organizational and financial features. Thus, separating management from owner-ship is feasible because monitoring costs of managers by owners are low. In addition, since output is very measurable, monitoring of employees by managers is also relatively inexpensive.

The manufacturing assets of the steel mill are implastic, and the cost of their creation is a sunk cost. Sunk costs create vulnerability to hold-up. The manufacturing plant will likely be owned by the same party that operates the plant, otherwise the operators would be subject to hold-up by the owners of the plant and vice versa. The scale economies of such manufacturing processes are often substantial. The scale economies call for aggregating the resources of many investors to agglomerate the required capital and to diversify risk. The firm can be funded by both equity (the residual claimant) and debt. The debt-holders need not fear that the equity-holders will exploit them by increasing the risk of the underlying assets because the physical nature of the assets inhibits this.

The firm will be organized with limited liability to accommodate transferable shares. Without limited liability, the debt-holders would have an interest in the identity and wealth of individual equity-holders, and also an interest in inhibiting the sale of equity from a wealthier to a less-wealthy shareholder. Limiting liability eliminates the wealth of individual shareholders as an issue in the dealings between debt-holders and the firm. Yes, there are fewer resources to repay debt-holders, and so debt-holders require a larger premium for risk as a result. The equity-holders, not the debt-holders, bear the cost. Limited liability thus accommodates both risk-sharing and spontaneous consumption (buying and selling shares) decisions by shareholders. It is transaction costs, not risk-avoidance, that give rise to limited liability. Debt-holders are not exploited by limited liability, but are eyes-wide-open, strategic, price-influencing parties to a transaction that limits liability and improves joint welfare.

Establishing a policy of paying dividends to equity-holders can have two benefits. First, it constrains management from using cash in other ways, tying the hands of management. Second, it provides a means of not accumulating cash which might give bond-holders less exposure to risk than they are being paid to accept.

We are not done yet! Another set of claimants can potentially hold up the firm: labor. The firm can create a defined-benefit pension plan so that not just current wages, but the long-term income of employees depends on their continued association with the firm, essentially delaying some compensation so that employees stay around to collect it. Moreover, the firm might under-fund the pension plan, essentially making the pension plan a subordinated debt-holder, to inhibit a labor union from raising wages and threatening the quasi-rents of the enterprise.[23]

In contrast, the large pharmaceutical manufacturers are mainly organized with a strong involvement of owners in management (even to the degree of being controlled by involved families); they are closely held compared to most public firms, they have little by way of debt financing, and they pay low, if any, dividends. We suggested this results because their assets (laboratories and intellectual property) are more difficult to describe, and useful for a wide assortment of different activities (they are plastic, and can be used for more risky and less risky endeavors). In particular it is difficult to be precise about what bond-holders own if the firm defaults. (Williamson would call this a case of impacted information.) Thus, the moral hazard cost of debt is so high that it precludes the existence of much debt.

Contrast both with restaurants. Restaurants have some fixed costs, but the fixed assets (stoves, refrigerators, etc.) are not unique (not firm-specific) and are easily saleable. Restaurants are nearly always run by owners, even when they are franchised operations with national brand names, suggesting that the continuing presence of a residual claimant is essential for productive outcomes. Potential problems include monitoring the quality of the food produced, assuring that dinner plates are heated and salad plates are chilled, creating a convivial, welcoming atmosphere for customers, assuring that inputs (steaks, shrimp, bottles of olive oil) are not carried away by employees, and surely more.

This work goes on to extend these ideas to other social institutions (country clubs, social ostracism, moralistic aggression, the raising of children). The curious reader can retrieve the 1987 *Journal of Economic Literature*.

One more topic: Alchian also touched on one more law and economics topic, price discrimination, in an analysis of trading stamps (with Benjamin Klein). This was at a time when economists were enchanted with every new instance of price discrimination identified. Alchian and Klein[24] suggested that those assigning a lower value to their time would collect and redeem the stamps, while others would not, resulting in people with low time value paying a lower price than those with high time value. They missed the single most important aspect of trading stamps, which can be learned from studying the items available in redemption catalogs: they were mainly for the home – things women wanted. Even the items that men might want were those that women approved of men having (barbeques, power tools). Yes, the price discrimination was in favor of those with lower-valued time, but trading stamps also gave women a tool to re-allocate family income to themselves. Trading stamps enabled opportunism in the home. As women went to work, trading stamps died. There was still plenty of variance in the distribution of time value, but women now had their own paychecks. Coupons were as good as trading stamps for exploiting the differences in time value and did not have to be stuck into books.

---

[23]   This idea was contributed by Richard Ippolito, who was the first to realize that the reason all of the long-term systematic under-funding of pension plans was associated with heavy (large sunk cost) manufacturing was to inhibit the unions from appropriating a large fraction of the quasi-rents present when fixed costs are large. See Ippolito, Richard, 1985, *Pensions, Economics, and Public Policy*, Pension Research Council Publications, Philadelphia: University of Pennsylvania Press.

[24]   'Vertical Integration, Appropriable Rents, and the Competitive Contracting Process', Klein, Benjamin, Robert G. Crawford and Armen A. Alchian, 1978, *Journal of Law and Economics*.

Reflections

Alchian's work influencing law and economics is extraordinary in its thematic consistency. The papers together present a coherent, unfolding, and ever richer view of the firm and other social institutions. Each set builds on what came before. Though all the writings have something to teach, the later ones are more mature, showing more respect for notions such as 'fairness', 'doing the right thing' (often dismissed earlier by economists), and reciprocal social altruism (sounds much better than merely doing the right thing). Instead of criticizing practices such as not paying college athletes their marginal product, Alchian seeks to understand why this is not done.

Yet, frustrations abound in trying to chronicle Alchian's contributions. They arise from his style. He had little patience or respect for provenance. He cared about what was already understood, and was eager to give credit to those who contributed, but cared little for the various ways in which misunderstanding prevailed or who misunderstood in what ways. He discussed only the most important misunderstanders. He cared about understanding the world better. Some believe he was lazy (he *did* play a lot of golf), but when he was not playing golf, he was always thinking about the world and why it worked the way it did. Actually, even when he was playing golf, he was often thinking, and talking, about how things worked. Alchian often played golf with Bill Meckling, of Jensen and Meckling,[25] whose seminal work on the theory of the firm appeared in 1976, just after Alchian's 1972 paper with Demsetz.

Despite property rights being his favorite topic and that on which he contributed the most, he put little effort into establishing his property rights over ideas. He was not at all an operator. He had no interest in running things, escaped being editor of a journal, was eager to relinquish the responsibility for choosing faculty when he formally retired, paid little attention to who cited him, did not even care much about the prestige of the places where his work was published. He pulled accepted papers from prestigious journals (the *American Economic Review*) to contribute them instead to volumes in honor of friends. As a result, though he is much loved by those whom he taught, organized appreciations are limited. His attitude was that there were better ways to spend time than to lobby. Lobby for ideas, yes; but lobby for his stamp on them, not worth the time. Thus, this contribution is mainly about what was new in Alchian's work, not about the record of who learned what from him when, or who owes him. To Alchian, ideas are much more important than being important. His contribution is the greater for it.

---

25   Meckling, William H. and Michael C. Jensen, 1976, 'Theory of the Firm: Managerial Behaviour, Agency Costs and Ownership Structure', *Journal of Financial Economics*, Vol 3, no. 4.

6   Harold Demsetz
*Mark F. Grady**

1   How I met Harold Demsetz

I first met Harold Demsetz when I enrolled in his law and economics course at the UCLA law school. The year before he had returned to UCLA from the University of Chicago and was for the second time a member of the UCLA economics faculty. To my knowledge, he has been the only member of the department of economics ever to teach a class at the law school. There were about 40 students in the class, and the readings were from the early law-and-economics literature, mainly articles from the *Journal of Law and Economics*. We started with Ronald Coase's 'Theory of Social Cost'[1] and soon moved from there to various contributions by the other pioneers of law and economics.

The class was being offered during the last years of the Vietnam War and because of that war, and its demonstrations, our sessions divided themselves into two parts. In the first part, Demsetz taught us how to understand law and economics ideas and how to critique them, which, it soon was apparent, he thought were the same. He would explain his premises and then proceed formally, step-by-declared-step, to his conclusion. Some of his conclusions – those of the early law-and-economics literature – were revolutionary. For instance, the Coase Theorem, on which we spent a few class sessions, famously provides that the liability rule makes no allocative difference when transaction costs are low. To Demsetz this 'theorem' was exactly what its name suggested: a formal statement that could be derived by using the rules and axioms of a deductive system, namely, economics. It could also be defended in the same way, as he demonstrated to us when we would challenge his conclusions, challenges that he invited.[2]

Chicagoans – and not only University of Chicagoans – have the reputation of being plain-spoken people with practical concerns. Demsetz is of course a native-born Chicagoan and speaks with a Chicago accent, though now somewhat attenuated. However familiar they may be with the Windy City and its denizens, most people would probably not expect to meet a Chicagoan who, though retaining his characteristic speech and outlook, nevertheless lectured and argued in the way one would expect from a Cambridge professor of logic. As a young Californian with little outside experience, I had no premonition that such a combination was possible. Demsetz, though not an historian of economic thought, explained to us pretty clearly that Adam Smith's philosophy had become highly developed through the contributions of many great minds. More through his dedication and intensity than anything else, Demsetz told his students that our law and economics course was addressed to the leading issues in that evolved system of knowledge. Amazingly, this claim turned out to be true.

---

*   Professor of Law and Director, Center for Law and Economics, UCLA School of Law.

[1]   3 *Journal of Law and Economics* 1 (1960).

[2]   Demsetz was an early expositor and developer of the Coase Theorem. See Harold Demsetz, 'When Does the Rule of Liability Matter?', 1 *Journal of Legal Studies* 13 (1972); Harold Demsetz, 'Wealth Distribution and the Ownership of Rights', 1 *Journal of Legal Studies* 223 (1972).

The second part of Demsetz's law and economics course occurred that year without his planning for it. In the middle of that spring quarter (May of 1972), the Vietnam War ground toward its conclusion with the Nixon Administration's adoption of a hard line in which the US government suspended the Paris peace talks and mined Haiphong harbor in order to seek more concessions at the bargaining table. The ensuing protests, led by the Students for a Democratic Society, changed our once tranquil campus into a combat zone with daily clashes between the protesters and the LAPD SWAT troops. Soon, new students appeared in our classroom.

Up to that point, as I've said, Demsetz had been speaking with us – really arguing with us – about the Coase Theorem, the theory of property rights, and related matters. Now, at the beginning of each session, the new students would shout questions at him before he could introduce his own subjects. Perhaps they expected that a professor of 'law and economics' wouldn't have considered issues of the same rank that Karl Marx and other socialist economists had written about. In any event, the new students began to ask really basic questions, such as 'What is the purpose of the economy?' and 'How does the system of private property support capitalism?' Demsetz gave the new students – and the rest of us – an amusing surprise. No matter what the tone of the speaker, Demsetz always took their queries to be academic, and he answered each one as if it were an interesting point raised in seminar. More than that, he treated the protesters as if they were prize students, with the daring and wit to ask really important questions.

As I've already suggested, Demsetz was – and still remains – a master of rhetorical technique, presumably having sharpened his skills at University of Chicago workshops. In those classes, however, his most basic weapons were his civility, his close logic, and his careful attention to the details of economic arguments – both his own arguments and those of the protesting students. Many of his responses to the questions examined the question's implicit premises or the questioner's logic in following premises to a conclusion. We learned more than we had bargained for, and that second part of the course left us little doubt that the truly big economic questions were exactly those that Demsetz most enjoyed debating. I think we were all gratified that he thought so much of us that he had invited us into the game and taught us how it was really played.

2   An overview of Demsetz's scholarly work

To my knowledge, Demsetz has never explained exactly what scientific concept has animated his work, but that concept becomes clear from reading even a few of his important contributions. He has consistently sought to uncover the simplest economic ideas that have the greatest explanatory power. Here is a sample: private property arises when externalities become costly; monopoly power depends more on transaction costs than on industry structure; the business firm is concerned with team production and is beset by agent shirking.[3] All of these important economic ideas have spawned huge literatures that have explored and extended them. Moreover, even though Demsetz published some of these ideas over 40 years ago, they all continue to guide vast research agendas by hundreds of scholars. Citations to Demsetz's original descriptions of these ideas still generally increase from year to year. For instance, in

---

[3]   This last idea resulted from a collaboration between Demsetz and his friend and colleague Armen Alchian. Although Demsetz's ideas are indeed simple, he has always carefully explained them as well as their important implications.

the WESTLAW journals database, Demsetz's 'Toward a Theory of Property Rights'[4] was cited 22 times in 1997 and 42 times in 2007.[5] The article was published in 1967 and has approximately 530 citations total. If we do the math, approximately 8 per cent of the total citations to this article occurred in the last of the 40 years in which a citation was possible. In our current era, Demsetz's ideas remain growing ideas, even his relatively old ideas.

It is impossible here to survey all of Harold Demsetz's work, so I will confine myself to his most important contributions to the law and economics literature. These scholarly works fall into four areas: the theory of property; industrial organization; the theory of the firm; and financial economics.

3 Demsetz's theory of property

From a purely law and economics perspective, Demsetz's most important contribution to economics has almost certainly been his theory of property.[6] Besides having been cited many times, the piece was the subject of a 2002 symposium published in the *Journal of Legal Studies*.[7] Even since that relatively recent gathering, the piece continues to organize modern legal scholarship in the area of property and especially on the question of the evolution of property rights.[8]

The chief importance of the article lies in a realm that few have stressed, not even Demsetz himself. It was the first positive economic theory of law. The prior law and economics literature had been exclusively normative. Aaron Director's work – both his own published work and that which he inspired others to undertake – seems to have been economic critiques of laws and legal doctrines.[9] Demsetz's great friend, George Stigler, captured the normative perspective of the early Chicagoans with his amusing story that Aaron Director, the founding editor of the *Journal of Law and Economics*, originally wanted to call it the *Journal of Law*

---

    4   57 *American Economic Review Papers and Proceedings* 347 (1967).
    5   Search conducted on January 28, 2008. Here are the citation numbers of this article for other years, all in the WESTLAW journals database, which makes it easy to collect these yearly numbers:

        2007:   42;
        2006:   34;
        2005:   47;
        2004:   46;
        2003:   31;
        2002:   30;
        2001:   28;
        2000:   30;
        1999:   29;
        1998:   21;
        1997:   22.

    6   Harold Demsetz, 'Toward a Theory of Property Rights', 57 *American Economic Review Papers and Proceedings* 347 (1967). The mature analysis contained in this article was prefigured by an even earlier piece. See Harold Demsetz, 'The Exchange and Enforcement of Property Rights', 7 *Journal of Law and Economics* 11 (1964).
    7   Symposium, 'The Evolution of Property Rights', 31 *Journal of Legal Studies* S331 et seq. (2002).
    8   See, for example, Katrina Miriam Wyman, 'From Fur to Fish: Reconsidering the Evolution of Private Property', 80 *New York University Law Review* 117 (2005).
    9   Aaron Director and Edward H. Levi, 'Law and the Future: Trade Regulation', 51 *Northwestern University Law Review* 281 (1956).

or Economics.[10] Director's successor, Ronald Coase, had a similarly normative bent. In his 'Problem of Social Cost',[11] Coase's lengthy analysis of legal doctrines, ranging from the law of nuisance[12] to the law of coneys,[13] claimed that courts' painstaking decisions amounted to economic nullities and that their evolved legal rules contained nonsensical and even humorous distinctions.[14] The revolutionary contributions of these early law and economics scholars came from their normative perspectives on the courts and on the law.

When Demsetz began work on his theory, property was already a central concern among socialist philosophers and economists, another point that Demsetz himself has never stressed. Proudhon had famously equated private property with theft,[15] and Marx had seen it as the antithesis between labor and capital,[16] whatever that may mean. Although Locke had provided a liberal theory of property,[17] before Demsetz wrote, neoclassical economists lacked any theory of their own.

---

[10]   George J. Stigler, 'Law or Economics', 35 *Journal of Law and Economics* 455 (1992).

[11]   3 *Journal of Law and Economics* 1 (1960).

[12]   Id. at pp. 8–35.

[13]   Coase's review of the legal rules governing invading rabbits was motivated, as he said, by A.C. Pigou's choice of this example as an 'uncharged disservice' – what we would now call a negative externality. See Coase, 'Problem of Social Cost', at pp. 35–9.

[14]   Coase concluded one such analytical passage as follows:

The reasoning employed by the courts in determining legal rights will often seem strange to an economist because many of the factors on which the decision turns are, to an economist, irrelevant. Because of this, situations which are, from an economic point of view, identical will be treated quite differently by the courts.

Id. at p. 15.

[15]   Here is a memorable passage:

Reader, have you ever been present at the examination of a criminal? Have you watched his tricks, his turns, his evasions, his quibblings, his equivocations? Beaten, confounded in all his assertions, pursued like a wild animal by the inexorable judge, tracked from hypothesis to hypothesis, he makes his statement, then corrects it, retracts it, contradicts it; he exhausts all the tricks of dialectics, more subtle, a thousand times more ingenious than the one who invented the seventy-two forms of the syllogism. So the proprietor does when called upon to defend his right: first he refuses to reply, he exclaims, he threatens, he defies; then, forced to accept the discussion, he arms himself with chicanery, he surrounds himself with formidable artillery, crossing his fire, opposing one by one and all together occupation, possession, prescription, contracts, immemorial custom, and universal consent. Conquered on this ground, the proprietor, like a wounded boar, turns on his pursuers . . . .

Pierre-Joseph Proudhon, 'What Is Property?' at p. 68 (1840) (*Cambridge Texts in Political Thought*, D.R. Kelley and B.G. Smith, eds and trans, 1994).

[16]   This simple statement is perhaps a misinterpretation of Marx's actual view on this point, which he expressed as follows:

The antithesis of *propertylessness* and *property* so long as it is not comprehended as the antithesis of *labour* and *capital*, still remains an antithesis of indifference, not grasped in its *active connection*, its *internal* relation – an antithesis not yet grasped as a *contradiction*. (emphasis in original)

Karl Marx, 'Private Property and Communism', Economic and Philosophic Manuscripts of 1844, reprinted in Robert C. Tucker, *The Marx-Engels Reader* (New York: W.W. Norton & Co., 2d ed., 1978), at p. 81.

[17]   John Locke, 'Second Treatise of Government' (1698), reprinted in John Locke, 'Two Treatises of Government', at pp. 285–302 Cambridge [England]; New York: Cambridge University Press. (*Cambridge Texts in the History of Political Thought*, P. Laslett, ed., 1988).

Coase's 'Problem of Social Cost', published in 1960, made externalities central to that decade's law and economics scholarship. Coase had famously demonstrated that A.C. Pigou's analysis[18] of the problem of the sparking locomotive was incomplete or worse, that causation was reciprocal, and that in the low-transaction-cost case it didn't even matter whether the railroad was liable or the farmer. The dominant theme of Coase's work was that it would be far easier for the courts and regulators to worsen the situation than to improve it.

Against this backdrop, Demsetz provided his own revolutionary theory that property was the means by which externality problems were typically solved in the real world. Without property, there could be no contract. Both were correlative parts of private solutions to an enormous range of problems – problems that Pigou and the prior generation of welfare economists saw as inevitably demanding active regulation, such as a government-calculated tax on each train that left the station. Demsetz was also the first to see that society modulated the concept of property – made it more or less private – depending on the value of the underlying scarcities and the administrative costs that would need to be incurred in order to enforce property rights of different degrees.

If we read Coase in retrospect, some idea of property must have been implicit in his analysis although it was nowhere declared or analyzed. It seems impossible, however, that Coase could have had in mind anything similar to Demsetz's theory of property because Coase's theory of legal institutions was relentlessly normative – a description of judicial errors made and false pretensions assumed.

In addition, because Demsetz saw his own theory as potentially falsifiable, the way all good positive theories are, Demsetz actually provided evidence in support of it. Coase had never thought that his theory needed any support beyond the formidable logic that he deployed to explain and defend it. Because Coase's theory lived entirely in the realm of logic, it was not falsifiable in the positive sense; at its inception, it was either true or false depending on the soundness of its own internal logic. That is why George Stigler quite properly called it a 'theorem'. Demsetz's own empirical evidence is now so well known it hardly bears repeating. It bears some stress, however, that this was the first empirical evidence ever marshaled in support of a positive economic theory of law. Before the fur trade opened, Canadian aboriginal hunters possessed no property over hunting grounds. After the French developed this trade, the fur-bearing animals became increasingly scarce, and property institutions emerged to manage the scarcity.

Demsetz's theory possesses enormous scope and power. For instance, in the eastern United States, water tends to be abundant and the property right system tends to be communal. In the southwestern United States, water is much scarcer, and, just as the theory predicts, property over it tends to be more private even as the administrative costs of this more privatized system tend to be much greater, which was a point Demsetz also stressed.[19] Consider an apparently different problem but actually the same problem in a different guise. When practically no one wants to put your image on a tee-shirt, you have few property rights to stop

---

18   A.C. Pigou, *The Economics of Welfare* (4th ed., 1932), London: Macmillan and Co.

19   See generally Jedidiah Brewer, Robert Glennon, Alan Ker and Gary Libecap, 'Transferring Water in the American West: 1987–2005', 40 *University of Michigan Journal of Law Reform* 1021 (2007); Nicole L. Johnson, 'Property Without Possession', 24 *Yale Journal of Regulation* 205 (2007) and sources cited therein.

them from doing so.[20] When just about everyone wants to put your face on a tee-shirt – and thereby use up your publicity asset much too quickly and inappropriately – you have comprehensive property rights to stop them.[21] The idea that economic ideas could be used to explain law was at the time Demsetz wrote totally novel.

Like all great positive theories, Demsetz's theory is at the same time general and parsimonious, the hallmark of all of his work, whether positive or normative. His theory of property is in fact so simple that it verges on tautology, yet stops short of that and becomes a powerful and falsifiable explainer of a vast range of human institutions. Some have sought to make his theory more complicated,[22] but complication has never been Demsetz's scholarly ambition.

---

20   See Mark F. Grady, 'A Positive Economic Theory of the Right of Publicity', 1 *UCLA Entertainment Law Review* 97 (1994). The example of tee-shirts comes readily to mind because this past academic year Demsetz received a request from a large class of first-year property law students to use his own image on a tee-shirt. They explained that their professor parried all of their questions with the retort, 'What would Demsetz say?' With Demsetz's permission they made a tee-shirt with his picture on it and their professor's constant question as the legend.

21   Id.

22   See William H. Riker and Itai Sened, 'A Political Theory of the Origin of Property Rights: Airport Slots', 35 *American Journal of Political Science* 951 (1991). Here is their theory, which they base on Demsetz's work, explaining when airport land rights become private:

> [W]hat are the necessary conditions for the emergence of a right? We have already inferred one condition.
> **Condition 1:** Scarcity. The content of the right is scarce, driving its value above enforcement costs. Without such value, control is pointless.
> Further necessary conditions are that private property is to actors' advantage.
> **Condition 2:** Right-holders [for example, airlines in the case of takeoff and landing slots] desire the right. If this condition is not satisfied, holders do not seek the right; hence, it does not emerge.
> **Condition 3:** Rule makers [for example, the FAA and DOT] desire to recognize the right. This condition is necessary because a right unproclaimed by enforcers is not ultimately enforceable.
> Since rule makers are [. . .] the enforcers, they must wish to establish and maintain the right to obtain their net benefits of enforcement (i.e., tax income and the gratitude of right-holders and others who consciously gain from efficiency, less the cost of enforcement). Condition 3 is crucial to differentiate our theory from a strictly economic one like Demsetz's, in which scarcity is sufficient. According to our theory, even with scarcity, rights do not emerge unless officials are advantaged by them.
> **Condition 4:** Duty-bearers [for example, pilots who do not have landing rights] respect the right. This is a necessary, but often unnoticed, condition.
> [. . .]
> We summarize our model by stating explicitly our theory of the emergence of rights: rights originate in a historical event. As such there are identifiable actors with identifiable motives, who create rights. Rule makers grant a right to grantees, the Hohfeldian right-holders. By so doing they guarantee the right-holders a permanent claim over the content of the right, and they impose on the duty-bearers the duty to respect the holders' claim. Since the grantor thereby commits itself to police continually, it undertakes this obligation only if the gain from tax income and gratitude exceeds the cost of enforcement. Similarly, right-holders value the right only if the benefit from the enforced right exceeds the cost in taxes and gratitude. And duty-bearers respect the right only if enforcement eliminates the marginal benefits of not respecting it.

Id. at 955–6.

Their theory is (intentionally) much less parsimonious than Demsetz's theory and for that reason less falsifiable. For instance, if private property does not emerge even after externalities become costly and when enforcement of a private right has become economic, it could be because 'rule makers' do not 'desire to recognize the right'. This complication of the theory gives the theorist too many ways of wiggling out of a defective theory.

Some law and economics scholars have given Demsetz credit for providing the first positive economic theory of law,[23] but maybe not as much as he deserves. Two developments may have hindered his recognition as the founder of an important branch of economics. First, we live in a normative legal world. Since the 1920s, the conventional and still dominant patterns of legal scholarship see law criticism and law reform as pre-eminent.[24] Any attempt to account in general theoretical terms for how law actually solves social and economic problems is often seen as conservative or even retrograde.[25] Second, most of the positive theories of law following Demsetz have used a game-theoretic approach. However great its virtues in other areas, game theory has usually not produced the same fresh insight one gets from Demsetz's ideas.

4   Industrial organization

Demsetz has made a number of striking contributions to the theory of industrial organization. His two most important ideas, when viewed in retrospect, are that markets can be fully competitive even when industry structure is highly concentrated and that high concentration can be a sign that leading firms have been highly efficient.

In his leading article 'Why Regulate Utilities?',[26] Demsetz fundamentally revised the prior conception of monopoly. At the time he wrote, the orthodox view was that monopoly must occur in an industry characterized by continuously declining average costs. Reasoning from basic economic principles, he was able to demonstrate that no necessary connection existed between economies of scale and monopoly pricing. Demsetz gave the example of license plate manufacture as the type of industry that might hypothetically exhibit declining costs. Still, if buyers are able to solve a transaction-cost problem and call for bids from potentially competing manufacturers, there is no necessity for them to pay a monopoly price. Their ability to organize a collective bid would create – to use the modern term – a fully contestable market[27] in which the price actually charged could easily be a competitive price. Under the

---

[23]   See, for example, William M. Landes and Richard A. Posner, 'The Positive Economic Theory of Tort Law', 15 *Georgia Law Review* 851, 855, n. 14 (1981) (citing to a lesser known work by Demsetz but still characterizing it as an early positive economic theory).

[24]   See generally Karl N. Llewellyn, 'Some Realism about Realism', 44 *Harvard Law Review* 1222 (1931); Felix S. Cohen, 'Transcendental Nonsense and the Functional Approach', 35 *Columbia Law Review* 809 (1935).

[25]   See, for example, J.M. Balkin, 'Too Good to Be True: The Positive Economic Theory of Law', 87 *Columbia Law Review* 1447 (1987) (review of *The Economic Structure of Tort Law* by William M. Landes and Richard A. Posner. Cambridge, Mass.: Harvard University Press, 1987).

[26]   Harold Demsetz, 'Why Regulate Utilities?', 11 *Journal of Law and Economics* 55 (1968).

[27]   Although the article that coined this term did not cite to Demsetz (see William J. Baumol, Elizabeth Bailey and Robert D. Willig, 'Weak Invisible Hand Theorems on the Sustainability of Multiproduct Natural Monopoly', 67 *American Economic Review* 350 (1977)), subsequent articles have done so. See William J. Baumol, 'Contestable Markets: An Uprising in the Theory of Industry Structure', 72 *American Economic Review* 1 (1982) (AEA presidential address). Elizabeth Bailey has written: '[T]he theory of contestable markets builds on the tradition of Harold Demsetz, who first pointed out that it is sunk costs not economies of scale which constitute the barrier to entry that confers monopoly power'. Elizabeth E. Bailey, 'Contestability and the Design of Regulatory and Antitrust Policy', 71 *American Economic Review Papers and Proceedings* 178, 178 (1981).

Demsetz did not say, however, that contestable markets depend on the absence of sunk costs. Instead, he argued that durable capital goods created an obstacle to long-term contracts – a formulation that remains more accurate and more general. See Demsetz, 'Why Regulate Utilities?', 11 *Journal of Law*

old conception, monopoly depended on industry structure, which in turn dictated conduct and performance. Under Demsetz's totally novel view, monopoly depends on transaction costs.[28] That this idea was indeed a radical reconstruction of economic thought is shown by the fact that it took approximately ten years for even the leading economists of that era to understand this deceptively simple point and to begin to extend it. Now, as compared to then, transaction-cost economics is a major part of industrial organization theory.

Although Demsetz's article led to a basic revision of the problem of monopoly, it also had another impact, which seems modest only in comparison. The article led to an equally new conception of economic regulation and of the possibilities for regulatory reform. Building on Demsetz's idea of how the market for license plates could be made contestable, others have formulated actual regulatory reform proposals and programs based on the idea of the 'Demsetz auction', as it is now known.[29]

Demsetz's second major contribution to the industrial organization literature has been only slightly less important than his first. As already mentioned, before Demsetz's reconceptualization of monopoly as a problem of transaction costs, practically all economists had seen it as a matter of industrial structure. When industries were concentrated – so the theory ran – firms would engage in monopolistic conduct and market performance would be poor. The theory led to a number of government antitrust cases that sought to 'deconcentrate' concentrated industries largely because they were concentrated.[30]

This so-called 'market concentration doctrine', or the 'structure-conduct-performance' view of antitrust policy, was based on both theoretical contributions to economics[31] and empirical studies.[32] Some empirical studies did indeed show a modest correlation between higher concentration levels and industry profitability, and supporters of the theory based their deconcentration proposals on these studies. Many of them believed that the reported correlations were modest only because the data were confounded by multiple lines of business. For

---

and Economics at p. 64. Demsetz's insights on the importance of durability to the problem of monopoly were subsequently extended by Ronald Coase. See R.H. Coase, 'Durability and Monopoly', 15 *Journal of Law and Economics* 143 (1972).

[28]   See, for example, Oliver J. Williamson, 'The Vertical Integration of Production: Market Failure Considerations', 61 *American Economic Review Papers and Proceedings* 112, 114–15 (1971) (discussing Demsetz's transaction-cost theory of monopoly).

[29]   See, for example, Daniel G. Swanson and William J. Baumol, 'Reasonable and Nondiscriminatory (Rand) Royalties, Standards Selection, and Control of Market Power', 73 *Antitrust Law Journal* 1, 15 (2005).

[30]   See, for example, Exxon Corp., 98 FTC 453, 456–59 (1981) (complaint alleging agreement to monopolize and maintenance of a noncompetitive market structure); *United States v. IBM Corp.*, [1961–1970 Transfer Binder] Trade Reg. Rep. (CCH) ¶ 45,069 (SDNY filed January 17, 1969) (complaint alleging monopolization and attempted monopolization); *Xerox Corp.*, 86 FTC 364, 367–8 (1975) (complaint alleging monopolization, attempted monopolization, and the maintenance of a highly concentrated market structure); *Kellogg Co.*, 99 FTC 8, 11–16 (1982) (complaint alleging maintenance of a highly concentrated, noncompetitive market structure, and shared monopolization). These government 'deconcentration' complaints were filed in the 1960s and 1970s and were dismissed after Demsetz's work became understood.

[31]   See generally Joe S. Bain, *Barriers to New Competition* (1956), Cambridge: Harvard University Press; Richard Caves, *American Industry: Structure, Conduct, Performance* (1967), Englewood Cliffs, N.J.: Prentice-Hall..

[32]   See generally *Industrial Concentration: The New Learning* (H. Goldschmid, H. Mann and J. Weston, eds., 1974), Boston: Little Brown.

instance, concentration in the transparent tape industry could be very high, but 3M operates not just in this industry but also in many others. The persistent economic argument was that if various lines of business could be statistically separated – if transparent tape could be separated from duct tape – then we could clearly see both the high concentration in the transparent tape industry and that profitability was strongly correlated with it. To that end, the Federal Trade Commission launched a large and expensive program asking companies to report their sales and profits by 'line of business'.[33]

Just at this point, Demsetz published his paper 'Industry Structure, Market Rivalry, and Public Policy'.[34] The then-orthodox 'structure-conduct-performance' view of antitrust posited that higher concentration in an industry led to higher profits because, with fewer actors, collusion, or 'oligopolistic pricing', would become more possible. That is why, these economists argued, a positive correlation existed between industry concentration and industry profitability – and they also believed that when the FTC finished its line-of-business statistical project, the correlation would appear stronger still. Against this dominant view, Demsetz proposed that causation actually ran in the opposite direction. Firms were not more profitable because they lived in concentrated industries; instead, industries became concentrated because some firms had achieved exceptional profitability.

In a theoretical statement that anticipated his later work on the theory of the firm, Demsetz reasoned that some firms would occasionally develop techniques that would reduce costs, improve products, or both at the same time. Moreover, these efficiencies might not swiftly erode because they could depend on what we would now call firm-specific assets – perhaps an exceptionally able management team that one firm had assembled and which its rivals could not easily copy. Such a superior firm would then expand at the expense of its rivals, and its profitability might well remain high even as its market share increased. In the usual case, the firm's industry would then become more concentrated, and the industry itself would simultaneously become more profitable. Average industry profitability in this newly concentrated market would rise not because of greater opportunities for 'oligopoly' but because the industry's total profits would now include the supranormal returns of the expanded superior firm.

If Demsetz's hypothesis were true, then a deconcentration policy would set its sword against efficiency instead of monopoly. He proposed a simple empirical test. If the 'structure-conduct-performance' economists were right, then the *small* firms in concentrated industries should fare better than the small firms in unconcentrated industries because all firms, large and small, benefit from a monopoly – or 'oligopoly' – price. On the other hand, if the 'superior ability' hypothesis was right, smaller firms should fare worse in concentrated industries than in unconcentrated industries because in the usual case these smaller firms would be especially afflicted by the firm-specific efficiencies of their already expanded rivals.

Demsetz's empirical results, published in the same paper, supported his own theory better than the orthodox theory of market concentration. He found that the largest firms in various industries were generally more profitable the higher the rate of concentration. Nevertheless, when market concentration increased, smaller firms failed to gain the benefit predicted for

---

[33]   See G.J. Benston, 'The Validity of Profits-Structure Studies with Particular Reference to the FTC's Line of Business Data', 75 *American Economic Review* 37 (1985) and sources cited therein.
[34]   16 *Journal of Law and Economics* 1 (1973).

them by the orthodox theory. The profitability of the smaller firms was either the same or slightly lower in more concentrated as compared to less concentrated industries.[35]

Demsetz acknowledged that it was difficult to understand the nature of the equilibrium in industries populated by firms of differing abilities, but that complication did not detract from the larger contribution his study made. It was a significant blow to the structure-conduct-performance view of antitrust policy, which has been on the wane ever since. The study moreover refined Demsetz's idea that monopoly was more about transaction costs than industry structure and also demonstrated that if antitrust enforcers were to focus in any single-minded way upon market concentration they could easily do more harm than good.

5   The theory of the firm

In 'Production, Information Costs, and Economic Organization',[36] Demsetz, collaborating with his colleague and friend Armen Alchian, created the modern theory of the firm. The ideas are again startlingly simple. Firms arise because of 'team production', which occurs when two people join together to produce an output and when it is difficult to define or determine each individual's contribution.[37] The authors give the now celebrated example of two men who jointly lift heavy cargo into trucks. Solely by observing the total weight loaded per day, it would be impossible to determine each worker's marginal productivity. This common situation creates the inducement to firm organization because someone has to assess and monitor the contributions of each worker in order properly to reward each one. Theoretically the workers could hire a monitor themselves and agree to abide by the monitor's assessments, but then the monitor might have an incentive to shirk or to collude with a shirking worker. The common solution is to make the monitor the residual claimant of the surplus value of the team's output, which firm organization routinely accomplishes. Indeed, viewed through the lens of this theory, it is easy to see people creating them with this particular purpose in mind. In fact, now that we have the Alchian-Demsetz theory, the largest problem is to remember that economists previously possessed other ideas about why firms existed.

This article has been enormously influential by any standard. For instance, the JSTOR scholarly database includes 629 articles that include the words 'team production' and 'Demsetz'.[38] The same search of the WESTLAW journals database, which contains law and law-related journals, yielded 175 articles,[39] including a highly influential article by law professors Margaret Blair and Lynn Stout that develops a theory of corporate law around Alchian and Demsetz's team production idea.[40]

---

[35]   Id. at 5–7.

[36]   62 *American Economic Review* 777 (1972).

[37]   As Alchian and Demsetz stress, team production may encompass not only human inputs but also other types. They write:

> Team production [. . .] is production in which 1) several types of resources are used and 2) the product is not a sum of separable outputs of each cooperating resource. An additional factor creates a team organization problem – 3) not all resources used in team production belong to one person.

Id. at 779.

[38]   Search conducted January 28, 2008.

[39]   Search conducted January 28, 2008.

[40]   See Margaret Blair and Lynn Stout, 'A Team Production Theory of Corporate Law', 85 *Virginia Law Review* 247 (2001).

Besides seeing team production as the basic motive of the firm, Alchian and Demsetz also described the firm's essential problem, namely, to monitor shirking on the part of its agents, which seems to have been a totally novel idea in 1972. This 'principal-agent' problem – as it is now called – has been, if anything, more influential than their correlative idea of team production. Jensen and Meckling are widely credited for their pathbreaking exploration of how agency costs influence all aspects of the firm behavior and organization, and they explicitly founded their analysis on Alchian and Demsetz's economic theory.[41]

6 Financial economics

Demsetz's earliest published work was empirical,[42] and his article on 'The Cost of Transacting'[43] is another important example. Much of Coase's reasoning, both in his theory of the firm and in his theory of social cost, revolved around impediments to the use of the price system, that is, around the cost of transacting. Coase, however, provided little guidance as to what affected this cost.

In the 'Cost of Transacting', Demsetz provided the earliest careful examination of transaction costs and their behavior. The study design was typically ingenious. Demsetz reasoned that in stock transactions on the New York Stock Exchange, the principal parts of the transaction cost would be the bid-ask spread and the brokers' commissions. The bid-ask spread was in effect the price that the buyer paid for immediacy. For instance, if he had just purchased stock and wanted to sell immediately, he would lose the bid-ask spread. Thus, under Demsetz's simple reasoning, the determinants of these bid-ask spreads represented the determinants of transaction cost in at least one important setting. Demsetz found that in this market at least, transaction costs were subject to economies of scale. The more shares outstanding and the more transactions, the lower the bid-ask spread. This seminal article, as it has been called, has been cited by literally hundreds of other articles, mostly in the area of financial economics.[44]

---

[41]   In their pioneering article, Jensen and Meckling wrote:

[I]t is clear that our definition of agency costs and their importance to the theory of the firm bears a close relationship to the problem of shirking and monitoring of team production which Alchian and Demsetz (1972) raise in their paper on the theory of the firm.

M.C. Jensen and W.H. Meckling, 'Agency Costs and the Theory of the Firm', 3 *Journal of Financial Economics* 305, 309 (1976).

[42]   Harold Demsetz, 'The Effect of Consumer Experience on Brand Loyalty and the Structure of Market Demand', 30 *Econometrica* 22 (1962).

[43]   Harold Demsetz, 'The Cost of Transacting, 82 *Quarterly Journal of Economics* 33 (1968).

[44]   On December 20, 2007, JSTOR reported 119 cites to this article. Most have extended its ideas. An example is Allen B. Atkins and Edward A. Dyl, 'Transactions Costs and Holding Periods for Common Stocks', 52 *Journal of Finance* 309 (1997). The first sentence of this article reads:

Early articles by Harold Demsetz (1968) and Jack Treynor, writing under the pseudonym Walter Bagehot (1971) examine the importance of transactions costs and, in particular, the bid-ask spread, for investment decisions. These seminal papers gave rise to much research regarding the determinants of the bid-ask spread, the size of bid-ask spreads in various markets, the role of bid-ask spreads in explaining so-called stock market anomalies, and the effect of bid-ask spreads on returns from common stock. (footnotes omitted)

Id. at 309.

In 'The Structure of Corporate Ownership: Causes and Consequences',[45] Demsetz and a co-author, Kenneth Lehn, built on Alchian and Demsetz's earlier theory of the firm and examined whether the costs and benefits of agent monitoring affected the firm's financial structure. Demsetz and Lehn reasoned that the less stable the environment in which a firm operated, the more costly it would be for a firm's owners to monitor management and other firm agents. Nevertheless, the owners would also be subject to shirking on this monitoring task to the extent that they shared ownership with each other. With divided ownership, each owner would capture only a portion of the benefit from the owner's own increased monitoring of agents, and the rest would be captured by other owners. They reasoned that a solution to this free-rider problem would be for owners to increase their stakes. Thus, Demsetz and Lehn predicted that firms operating in unstable or 'noisy' environments should be owned by fewer individuals, which would increase the return to monitoring for each owner. Their empirical results supported this prediction, and as a result recast economists' understanding of the firm and how firms actually solve the agency problems that beset them. In the process, the article cast doubt on the earlier theory of corporate ownership, developed by Berle and Means,[46] which asserted that lower ownership concentration should be associated with lower profitability. Demsetz and Lehn reasoned that no necessary relationship existed between the two because investors would not willingly sacrifice rates of return in order to acquire a more diffuse share. In equilibrium, if more diffuse ownership is associated with poorer management performance, owners would need to be compensated for these lost returns.

In a closely related piece published the following year, Demsetz theorized that insider trading could be a way of rewarding owners who take large stakes in firms so as to be able to monitor their managers and other agents more economically.[47] One collateral cost of taking a large ownership stake, Demsetz theorized, was 'firm-specific' risk. Nevertheless, if these same investors could also trade on firm-specific information, it might compensate them for the firm-specific risk that they must bear (and that minority shareholders do not bear). In the paper Demsetz provided some empirical support for his claim and invited others to investigate the question more intensively.

A full investigation has yet to occur. For instance, Banerjee and Eckard[48] have found that insider trading did not produce too many losses to outsiders even before it was regulated. They cite to Demsetz's paper for the proposition that 'insider gains, as implicit compensation, also enhance efficiency by reducing agency costs and promoting value-maximizing behavior by managers', but then say that their own study sheds little light on this hypothesis because in the study period (1897–1903) 'substantially greater ownership points to lower agency costs and a correspondingly less important role for insider trading'.[49] Demsetz's theory was, however, different from their characterization of it. He did not say that insider trading was an

---

[45] Harold Demsetz and Kenneth Lehn, 'The Structure of Corporate Ownership: Causes and Consequences', 93 *Journal of Political Economics* 1155 (1985).
[46] Adolf A. Berle and Gardiner C. Means, *The Modern Corporation and Private Property* (New York: Macmillan, 1933).
[47] Harold Demsetz, 'Corporate Control, Insider Trading, and Rates of Return', 76 *American Economic Review of Papers and Proceedings* 313 (1986).
[48] Ajeyo Banerjee and E. Woodrow Eckard, 'Why Regulate Insider Trading? Evidence from the First Great Merger Wave (1897–1903)', 91 *American Economic Review* 1329 (2001).
[49] Id. at 1334, n. 18.

antidote for positive agency costs. He theorized instead that insider trading could compensate large-block owners who want to manage the company themselves or invest in it for other reasons. Although Bill Gates may or may not face large agency costs in connection with his ownership of Microsoft stock, he surely bears a large firm-specific risk. To the extent that large-block ownership is useful, as by substituting for greater monitoring efforts, the firm-specific risk must be compensated or else this potentially valuable ownership structure will be underproduced.

7   Conclusion

I hope that this review of Harold Demsetz's work demonstrates that he has been one of the most productive pioneers of law and economics. He originated the positive economic approach to law and has contributed strikingly novel ideas in a number of areas, ideas that continue to frame the entire field.

7 Benjamin Klein's contributions to law and economics
*Joshua D. Wright**

1 Introduction

Benjamin Klein's influential contributions to industrial organization, the theory of the firm, and the economics of contracts are widely recognized by economists. A recent analysis of articles published in peer-reviewed economics journals since 1970 reveals two of Klein's publications among the top 60 cited. Klein, along with Oliver Williamson, is also credited with explaining the economic relationship between asset specificity and vertical integration that has been described as 'one of the great success stories in industrial organization over the last 25 years'.

While Klein's contributions to the economics of contracts and to the theory of the firm are widely recognized in the economics literature, Klein's work has also been highly influential in the economic analysis of the law. This essay explores the intellectual foundations of these contributions, their impact on law and economics, and considers some potential applications of Klein's insights to contract interpretation.

It is customary in essays of this genre to define the scope of the project and issue some disclaimers about obvious omissions. The primary purpose of this essay is to identify and explore the intellectual foundations and themes in Klein's pioneering work in law and economics. In order to economize on page constraints, I will focus almost exclusively on Klein's contributions to the law and economics of contracts. 'Contracts' is defined broadly in this setting to include implicit and self-enforced agreements, specific contract terms, and particular contractual arrangements such as franchising and vertical integration.

This organizational framework omits some important work that would obviously merit inclusion in an essay cataloging Klein's contributions to law and economics. If the weight of an intellectual contribution was properly weighted by citation or some other metric of scholarly impact, one might reasonably start a chapter such as this with Klein's seminal analysis of litigation and settlement with George Priest, *The Selection of Disputes for Litigation*. Priest and Klein (1984) has proven to be one of the most influential articles in legal scholarship, and is certainly part of the law and economics canon.[1] The Priest-Klein litigation model explored the systematic differences between litigated and settled cases and generated, amongst other insights, the well-known and much tested prediction that plaintiffs will prevail at trial 50 percent of the time under certain conditions, regardless of the likelihood with which they would have won the underlying cases they settled. Subsequent researchers have built upon,

* Visiting Professor, University of Texas School of Law; Assistant Professor, George Mason University School of Law (on leave). I thank Benjamin Klein and Scott Masten for valuable comments and suggestions. Brandy Wagstaff provided excellent research assistance.

[1] See, for example, Shapiro (1996) (ranked 99th out of all law articles); Krier and Schwab (1997) (ranked 81st of all law articles); Landes andd Posner (1996) (ranked 28th of all law articles).

modified, extended, and tested the Priest-Klein model in various ways.[2] Despite the Priest-Klein model's obvious importance in the development of an economic analysis of settlement and litigation, it will not be covered in detail in this essay.

A second important omission of a pathbreaking analysis is Granitz and Klein's (1996) account of the famous Standard Oil monopoly. Contrary to the conventional wisdom in McGee's (1958) classic article that Standard Oil owed its success to serial mergers and acquisitions executed at or above market prices, Granitz and Klein convincingly document that Standard Oil's monopolization strategy involved Rockefeller's cartelization of the railroad industry by serving as the 'cartel ringmaster'. In other words, Standard Oil used its dominance in refining to effectively police the railroads in order to stabilize the petroleum cartel. Granitz and Klein's analysis of Standard Oil continues to be one of the only convincing empirical examples in the literature of the well-known 'Raising Rivals' Costs' phenomenon. As Klein (2003) points out in relationship to theories of exclusion, the relative absence of empirical proof combined with the fact that the Standard Oil example involved a *horizontal* conspiracy suggests that antitrust policy that expends significant resources attempting to identify potentially anticompetitive vertical agreements is not yet empirically justified. As with Priest and Klein (1984), and with apologies to the interested reader, a more detailed discussion is omitted.

One additional task remains before we turn to Klein's scholarly contributions to the law and economics of contracts. Contributions to law and economics can come in many forms other than scholarship. I mention some of Klein's important contributions of this variety before moving on to the heart of the essay. Klein currently serves on the board of editors of several academic publications focusing on economic analysis of law, including *Supreme Court Economic Review*, *Antitrust Law Journal*, and the *Journal of Law, Economics and Organization*. Klein is also on the Advisory Board of the *New Palgrave Dictionary of Economics and Law*. Klein has also served as a consultant to the Federal Trade Commission (FTC) and the Department of Justice Antitrust Division and taught at the Economics Institute for Federal Judges. Klein also served as the Economics Director for the once active Joint Degree Program in Law and Economics at UCLA. Klein has also had considerable influence over subsequent generations of law and economics scholars who were former students at UCLA, including the author. Timothy Muris (2003), a former student and the former Chairman of the FTC, singles out Klein's contributions to law and economics as having substantial influence on the development of modern competition policy.

I would also be remiss if I did not take this opportunity to acknowledge and express gratitude for Klein's contribution to my own academic career as an economics graduate student at UCLA, a research assistant, and later as a co-author and mentor. Perhaps the most important lesson I learned was that economics was not about theoretical blackboard exercises, mathematical models, or regressions, but using all of the available tools to explain real world phenomena. Economics is at its best when it is used to shed light on and increase our understanding of actions, relationships, and institutions that are not well understood. There is an especially significant cost to theoretical abstraction in the world of law and economics

---

[2]   Empirical work includes Priest (1987); Eisenberg (1990); Waldfogel (1995); Kessler, Meites, and Miller (1996); Siegelman and Donohue (1995); and Froeb (1993). Theoretical contributions include Grossman and Katz (1983); Hylton (1993); Shavell (1995); Spier (1992); and Nalebuff (1987).

because institutions, the content of the law, and how courts enforce the law affect the incentives of the firms and individuals and economic agents being studied. I was taught that economic analysis is a process that requires 'getting one's hands dirty' with the facts and viewing and interpreting those facts through the lens of economic theory. While I consider myself fortunate to have received these lessons in the classroom, they are evident in Klein's approach to economics, and, as we shall see, apparent in his body of work.

Klein's approach to economics, in turn, no doubt began with his economics training at the University of Chicago, under the tutelage of two of the primary intellectual influences in his career: Milton Friedman, his dissertation advisor, and George Stigler. As one might predict from a student of Friedman and Stigler, Klein's two primary fields were monetary theory and industrial organization. Klein's dissertation, 'The Payment of Interest in Commercial Bank Deposits and the Price of Money: A Study of Demand for Money', reflected Klein's interest in each of these fields and would later be published in the *American Economic Review* as 'Competitive Interest Payments on Bank Deposits and the Long-Run Demand for Money'. Klein's analysis corrected previous attempts to estimate the demand for money by estimating and allowing for perfectly competitive interest payments on commercial bank deposits, allowing own price and a cross price to have separate influences, and assuming that the prohibition of interest payments is totally ineffective.

Little in the topic of that particular publication would allow the casual observer to confidently predict Klein's subsequent contributions to industrial organization, contracts, antitrust, or law and economics. Nonetheless, the dissertation is notable for two reasons. First, it identifies Friedman and Stigler as two significant intellectual influences in Klein's work. Second, Klein's work in monetary theory is relevant to this essay because it provides the seeds for what would ultimately produce his major contributions to law and economics. Specifically, the origins of Klein's framework for analyzing contractual relationships can be found in the dissertation's second chapter, later published in the *Journal of Money, Credit, and Banking* as 'The Competitive Supply of Money'.

In that paper, Klein explored the widely accepted notion that government intervention in the money industry was justified. What were the money industry's unique characteristics that required the monopolistic supply of currency? Klein argued that a system of competing money suppliers would not necessarily generate a hyper-inflation and an infinitely high level of money prices so long as the firms were able to prevent counterfeiting. Where the private supply of money raises the opportunity for the firms to 'deceive' customers by supplying more money than anticipated ex ante, firms can rely on their brand name as a capital asset that facilitates performance. Klein's work over the next several years would be largely devoted to building upon that framework, which would be incomplete without the combination of two fundamental economic insights involving the role of contract terms in facilitating contractual performance.

The first key insight comes from Klein's work with Armen Alchian and Robert Crawford ('KCA') on asset specificity and the economic forces creating the well-known 'hold-up' problem. While often described as an analysis of the existence of or conditions that give rise to the hold-up problem, a more precise description is that it was an attempt to provide a framework for understanding the contractual responses of transactors anticipating potential hold-up problems. KCA explain the use of vertical integration as an efficient contractual response to potential hold-up problems associated with asset-specific investments. While this analysis is properly viewed as a seminal contribution to the theory of the firm, it is important to also recognize it as the first step in the development of a broader analytical framework for understanding the role of contract terms in facilitating contractual performance.

Klein and Leffler (1981) extend this framework by analyzing private contract enforcement mechanisms. Because private enforcement capital is limited, and written contracts are necessarily imperfect and incomplete, transactors must combine both court-enforced written terms with self-enforced unwritten terms to define what Klein calls the contractual relationship's 'self-enforcing range'. Written contract terms commit the parties with respect to certain actions that might effectuate a hold-up at the cost of creating contractual rigidity. In many cases, transactors may elect to avoid the costs associated with court enforcement of written contract terms by intentionally leaving elements of performance unspecified and enforced through private enforcement mechanisms.

Together, these two economic insights would be used to analyze the role of contract terms in facilitating self-enforcement and become a fertile basis for increasing our knowledge about contracts and the contracting process when applied to specific settings. For example, the self-enforcement framework would provide the basis for contributions to the theory of the firm, the economics of vertical restraints, franchises, block booking, exclusive dealing, slotting contracts, and various 'non-standard' contract terms in facilitating contractual performance.

Section 2 traces the intellectual history of the self-enforcement framework, emphasizing the role of brand names in facilitating contractual performance and contrasting the role of contract terms in the self-enforcement framework with the standard economic view. Section 3 examines Klein's contributions to the theory of the firm and vertical integration as a response to the hold-up problem. Section 4 considers applications of these insights to specific contractual arrangements, including: franchising, block booking, vertical restraints, exclusive dealing, and slotting contracts. Section 5 examines some virtues of the self-enforcement framework as a framework for understanding and analyzing contract law and contract interpretation. Section 6 offers some concluding remarks and observations.

2 Brand names, incomplete contracts, and private enforcement

The starting point for modern economic analysis of contracts is recognition that the costs associated with contractual specification result in incomplete contracts. The standard economic framework envisioned contracts as written documents that fully defined future performance. To the contrary, most real world contracts are designed with the intent to leave many elements of anticipated performance unspecified but understood.

As is now well recognized in the law and economics literature, contractual incompleteness does not merely result from the ink costs of writing down additional terms. Complete contractual specification is prohibitively costly for several reasons unrelated to the costs associated with drafting additional terms. First, complete contractual specification involves wasteful search and negotiation costs associated with identifying and negotiating contract terms for all potential contingencies. While discovering and negotiating specific responses to unlikely contingencies are likely to have substantial redistributive consequences, and thereby give parties an incentive to expend resources in an attempt to gain advantages over their trading partners during the contract negotiation process, resources devoted to this purely redistributive effort result in a wasteful dissipation of rents. Second, even if the transacting parties were determined to write a fully contingent contract in which a pre-specified response was drafted for each possible future state, the written agreement would still be incomplete because of measurement costs associated with specifying certain elements of performance (for example, the taste of a hamburger) in a legally enforceable manner. Finally, using written terms also imposes the additional cost of rigidity. In other words, because contract terms are necessarily imperfect, transactors can engage in hold-up by rigidly enforcing terms that may be contrary to the parties' intent. This type of hold-up is what occurred in the much discussed Fisher Body-General Motors case discussed in Section 3.

The world of incomplete contracts is also the starting point for Klein's analysis of the role of brand names and contract terms in facilitating contractual performance. The fact that many unspecified but understood elements of contractual performance exist, begs the question as to how these elements are enforced. Macaulay (1963) and others had demonstrated that reliance on court enforcement of contract terms was rare. A key analytical feature of Klein's theory of contractual performance was that it reconciled both real world phenomena: the prevalence of intentionally incomplete contracts and self-enforcement.

Klein's answer to the question of how these unspecified elements of performance could be enforced was the brand name enforcement mechanism. Klein and Leffler (1981) derive, and Klein and Murphy (1988) extend, the analysis of the use of privately imposed brand name sanctions to impose a capital loss for the party violating the contractual understanding.[3] The capital loss is created by the future losses associated with the termination of the relationship in the form of the quasi-rents on the non-salvageable relationship-specific investments that are lost upon termination (the 'repeat purchase mechanism'), as well as the loss of reputation in the marketplace caused by the contractual violation (the 'reputational mechanism'). The magnitude of the private sanction that can be imposed on a breaching party is defined by the transactor's brand name capital.

Klein and Leffler, therefore, predict that the amount of brand name capital a party possesses will determine the degree of incompleteness in their contractual arrangements. For example, parties with extremely limited brand name capital will tend to rely on 'thicker' contracts where transactors attempt to specify nearly all contingencies in a court-enforceable manner. Conversely, 'thin' contracts or handshake deals are more likely to be prevalent where substantial brand name capital is present.[4]

The key economic advantage of self-enforcement is flexibility. Brand name-enforced contracts allow transactors to efficiently use information accumulated during the course of the contractual relationship and permit transactors to more easily modify or breach the agreement. The primary benefit associated with this type of contractual flexibility is that transactors are assured that performance will take place over a broad range of possible ex post market conditions. The cost of this flexibility is the possibility that transactors 'hold up' their

---

3   Lott (1988) extends the Klein and Leffler model by introducing random cost or demand shocks. Bull (1987) and Levin (2003) present formal models of self-enforcement. For a discussion and other references, see Hermalin, Katz and Craswell (2007).

4   Brand name capital need not be exogenous. Klein and Leffler (1981) discuss advertising as one method by which firms can invest in increased brand name capital with expenditures on non-salvageable firm-specific assets. Similarly, transactors might establish and rely upon social networks to enhance the effectiveness of the reputation mechanism. For example, Greif (1993) considers contractual enforcement in the context of social networks that establish a reputation mechanism to prevent opportunistic behavior and facilitate performance in the absence of court enforcement. Hartmann and Gil (2007) demonstrate the role of ethnic and social networks in facilitating contractual performance in the dry cleaning industry.

trading partners by taking advantage of unspecified elements of performance and attempting to appropriate the available quasi-rents resulting from relationship-specific investment.

Both transacting parties consider the potential gain from this type of hold-up from breaching the underlying contractual understanding with the capital loss imposed by the private sanction. The magnitude of the private sanction that can be imposed in the case of non-performance defines what Klein refers to as the 'self-enforcing range' of the contractual relationship. While changes in market conditions might increase or decrease the value of specific investments and therefore make hold-up more or less profitable, a hold-up will only occur when the gain from doing so exceeds the private sanction that can be imposed if the breach is detected. When market conditions change in sufficient magnitude to render hold-up profitable despite the privately imposed sanction, the contract is outside the self-enforcing range and hold-up will occur.

Klein's self-enforcement framework has very different implications for the role of contract terms and contract law than the standard economic approach. The standard economic analysis of contract terms underlying much of the principal-agent and mechanism design literatures envisions contract terms as instruments to create optimal incentives on some court-enforceable proxy for performance.[5] This standard approach to contract theory, sometimes associated with the property rights theory of the firm,[6] incorporates contractual incompleteness by allowing for the possibility that rational transactors might omit contingencies because of failures to foresee and provide for those contingencies or the inability of courts to verify performance. This view is often contrasted with what the literature refers to as the 'transaction cost economics'(TCE) theory of the firm associated with Klein and Oliver Williamson (1975).[7] Klein (1996) describes the shortcomings of standard contract theory as follows:

> The problem with the standard economic framework is that court enforcement and private enforcement are considered as alternatives – firms will rely upon one or the other, but never both. Principal-agent models, for example, formulate the contracting problem as if transactors do not possess any private enforcement capital. Therefore, it is not surprising that these models have limited predictive value in explaining real world contract terms. On the other hand, standard economic models of reputational enforcement provide no role for contractual specification. However, given the fact that private enforcement capital is limited, transactors can be expected to use written contract terms and, hence, the assistance of the court, as a supplement to private enforcement.

The economics literatures on contracting and self-enforcement have generally proceeded on two parallel tracks without fully considering the complementary relationship between court and self-enforcement and its implications for both contract design and interpretation. The standard approach envisions the use of written terms solely as an instrument to create an

---

5   Indeed, enforcing contracts as written is the court's exclusive role in the conventional economic theory of contracts. For a survey of the principal-agent literature, see Hart and Holmstrom (1987).

6   See, for example, Grossman and Hart (1986), Hart and Moore (1988, 1990).

7   Gibbons (2005) describes the property rights theory of the firm as the 'inverse' of TCE. Where both rely on contractual incompleteness and asset specificity, '[TCE] envisions socially destructive haggling ex post, the property-rights theory assumes efficient bargaining, and where [TCE] is consistent with contractible specific investments ex ante, the property-rights theory requires non-contractible specific investments'.

incentive to perform with respect to some court-enforced, contractually specified measure of performance. The self-enforcement framework implies a complementarity between court enforcement and private enforcement, in the sense that the enforcement mechanisms are more effectively used in conjunction with one another than separately. Klein (1996) describes the purpose of contractual specification as an attempt to

> [e]conomize on the amount of private enforcement capital to make a contractual relationship self-enforcing by merely 'getting close' to desired performance in a wide variety of circumstances (without creating undue rigidity) and to let the threat of private enforcement move performance the remainder of the way to the desired level.

There are two ways contract terms can operate within this framework. The first is to directly control non-performance with written terms. Contract terms can specify court-enforceable measures of performance such as quantity, quality, price, color, or date of delivery. By using written terms to specify performance of these elements in a court-enforceable manner, the parties decrease the amount of private capital necessary to keep the relationship within the self-enforcing range. The second mechanism through which contract terms can broaden the self-enforcing range, and therefore reduce the probability of hold-up, is by shifting private enforcement capital between the parties. In other words, contract terms may be used to ensure that the private enforcement capital aligns with the parties' relative hold-up potentials, thereby ensuring that the party with the greater hold-up potential has more to lose by non-performance than his trading partner with less hold-up potential.

The use of exclusive territories in distribution relationships is an illustrative example of the major differences in approaches to a common contract term. The standard contract theory view of exclusive territories contemplates the grant of the territory as an attempt to create optimal incentives for franchisee performance as increasing the franchisee's exposure to repeat customers and therefore internalizing the externalities associated with dealer free-riding on the franchisor's brand name.[8] Applying the alternative self-enforcement approach, Klein and Murphy (1988) and Klein (1995) demonstrate how the exclusive territory also creates a premium stream for the franchisee and thus increases his costs of non-performance if the franchisor terminates the relationship. Instead of viewing contract terms as creating the correct performance incentives with respect to some contractually specified measure, the self-enforcement framework implies that transactors will select contract terms to economize on their scarce private enforcement capital and broaden the self-enforcing range to assure performance under the broadest possible range of likely ex post market conditions and thereby increase the parties' ability to flexibly adapt to changes in those conditions. Application of this framework in order to understand how the adoption of a particular contractual arrangement increases the self-enforcing range has been particularly valuable in explaining choices about organizational form and contractual choice.

3   The hold-up problem and the theory of the firm

Klein's most cited contributions to both economics and law and economics concern the theory of the firm. Kim et al. (2006) list KCA as the 30th most cited economics paper from

---

[8]   See Rey and Stiglitz (1995), Rey and Tirole (1986) for examples of the standard approach.

1970 to 2005 despite the fact that the article was not cited until 1980.[9] The vertical integration of General Motors and Fisher Body, originally offered as a motivating example in support of the theoretical framework presented in KCA, has become the paradigmatic example of the theory of the firm in action in textbooks, articles, and classrooms in law schools, business schools, and economics departments.[10] However, Klein's contributions to the theory of the firm are also part of a more general framework for understanding the role of contract terms and self-enforcement. The primary advantage of vertical integration within this framework is the increased flexibility that transactors gain by avoiding the use of rigid long-term contracts to supplement their reputational capital.

This section focuses on Klein's contributions to the literature examining the boundaries of the firm applying this framework, with emphasis on the relationship between those boundaries and asset specificity. Whinston (2003) has described the theoretical and empirical confirmation of the relationship between asset specificity and vertical integration as 'one of the great success stories in industrial organization over the last 25 years'.[11] To provide some context for these contributions, I will first discuss the origins and subsequent developments of the literature.

Coase (1937) first identified the relationship between transaction costs and the scope of the firm as a fundamentally important research question for industrial organization economics. Since Coase's seminal contribution, the same question has attracted the attention of many economists and legal scholars attempting to identify the determinants of firm scope. Thus, not surprisingly, there are several non-mutually exclusive 'theories of the firm' that emphasize different aspects of the vertical integration decision. The primary theories discussed in the literature are the TCE approach, generally associated with Klein and Williamson, and the modern property rights approach (PRT), developed by Grossman and Hart (1986) and Hart and Moore (1990).[12] While the TCE approach emphasizes the costs associated with ex post bargaining, PRT generally assumes efficient and costless ex post bargaining and emphasizes the choice of ownership structures in providing optimal incentives for ex ante investment.

While the distinction between ex ante incentives and ex post bargaining is somewhat useful in distinguishing the general features of the TCE and PRT approaches, there are also important similarities and more subtle differences that have led to some difficulty in identifying their distinguishing features. These difficulties have led some to re-examine the TCE and PRT approaches to distill their primary features into simple formal models. For example, Gibbons (2005) supplies basic formal models for four leading theories of the firm distilled from the work of Klein, Williamson, Hart, and Holmstrom:[13] (1) a 'rent-seeking theory', (2)

---

9   This measure likely underestimates the impact of KCA on law and economics for another reason: it does not the measure impact on legal scholarship and law and economics scholarship in legal journals. A Westlaw search of the JLR database reveals an additional 353 citations.

10   A Google search for 'Fisher Body' and 'General Motors' and 'Theory of the Firm' generates 1,310 hits (search conducted 03/06/2008).

11   The positive relationship between asset specificity and vertical integration is documented in several surveys of the empirical literature in Lafontaine and Slade (2007), Joskow (1988), Shelanski and Klein (1995), Crocker and Masten (1996), Lyons (1996), Coeurderoy and Quélin (1997), and Masten and Saussier (2000).

12   See also Hart (1995), Holmstrom and Milgrom (1991, 1994), Holmstrom and Tirole (1991) and Holmstrom (1999) for some key contributions to the PRT approach.

13   See also Whinston (2003).

a 'property rights theory' (PRT), (3) an 'incentive system' theory, and (4) an 'adaptation' theory.

Important similarities exist between the theories focusing on ex ante incentive alignment and ex post contractual governance. For example, the approaches have in common a central role for contractual incompleteness. While the 'rent-seeking' and 'adaptation' approaches emphasize the relationship between that incompleteness and the ability to hold up one's trading partner to increase their share of quasi-rents, PRT emphasizes physical ownership of assets and residual control rights that exist because of contractual incompleteness. Recent literature surveys somewhat incompletely characterize TCE approaches as emphasizing ex post contracting costs and largely ignoring ex ante incentives, while PRT approaches focus exclusively on ex ante incentives to invest and assume costless renegotiation.[14]

The 'rent-seeking' and 'adaptation' theories of the firm were developed by KCA (1978), Klein (1996, 2000, 2007), Klein and Murphy (1988, 1997), and Williamson (1971, 1985), and emphasize the role of integration in preventing socially destructive 'haggling' over 'appropriable quasi-rents'. While these simplifying labels come with some risk of obfuscating important and subtle differences between theories, they are useful for highlighting some of the critical features of the theories. For example, the 'rent-seeking' label correctly captures the fact that a hold-up involves attempts to redistribute wealth between parties, and that the resources parties expend in attempts to obtain and prevent these transfers also have allocative effects. Of course, the view that the TCE approach focuses exclusively on ex post contracting costs is overstated, as Klein (1996) and others have also emphasized ex ante contracting costs, where transactors engage in a wasteful search for an informational advantages over transacting partners during the negotiation process.[15]

Klein (1996, 2000, 2007) and Klein and Murphy (1988, 1997) also emphasize the role of vertical integration in facilitating coordination by reducing contractual specification, thus reducing reliance on court enforcement to enforce intentionally incomplete, imperfect, and rigid long-term contracts.[16] Gibbons (2005) calls this relationship between vertical integration and ex post contractual adjustment the 'adaptation' theory of the firm. The coordination advantages of integration within this framework stem largely from the avoidance of 'rigidity costs', including potential hold-up problems associated with rigid and imperfect long-term contracts. The costs saved by using integration rather than contract to avoid hold-up problems are not limited to negotiation and 'ink' costs. Rather, vertical integration avoids costs associated with using explicit terms in a long-term contract when market conditions are uncertain over time. This advantage in coordinating economic activities through integration, in turn, depends on the conditions that must be present for using long-term contracts in the first instance. For example, specific investments and insufficient reputational capital must be present because the parties could otherwise coordinate activities without long-term contracts.

---

[14] Lafontaine and Slade (2007) provide a very useful survey of the empirical evidence with respect to these theories. Gibbons (2005) focuses on theoretical contributions.

[15] See Schmitz (2007) for a recent attempt to include inefficient rent-seeking in a property rights model.

[16] Williamson (1971, 1973, 1975, 1991) also emphasizes the role of vertical integration in improving sequential decision-making as uncertainty is resolved over time. While Williamson (1975) focuses on the relationship between integration and relational adaptation within the firm, Gibbons (2005) distinguishes Klein's work as emphasizing the role of relational contracting between firms.

The most well-known example of the rigidity costs associated with contractual specification is the Fisher Body-General Motors case first discussed briefly in KCA (see also Klein 1988, 2000). The Fisher Body-General Motors case has become a classic example in economics, illustrating the relationship between asset specificity and vertical integration, a relationship that has been demonstrated empirically in many settings and industries. However, the primary economic significance is that Fisher Body and General Motors operated with a long-term exclusive dealing contract before that contractual arrangement was replaced in favor of vertical integration, and thus the case highlights the relative advantages and disadvantages of each arrangement.

There has been a great deal of subsequent discussion over the details of the relationship between Fisher Body and General Motors and the events that led to integration. Coase (2000, 2006), Freeland (2000), and Casadesus-Masanell and Spulber (2000) have offered alternative accounts of the integration story and argued Fisher Body did not hold up General Motors, integration was motivated by other considerations, and long-term contracts are always sufficient to resolve hold-up concerns. In some ways, it is difficult to know what to make of this literature challenging Klein's (1988, 2000) account of these events. Some of these accounts appear to challenge the entire empirical literature demonstrating the relationship between asset specificity and vertical integration by attacking this single example designed to illuminate how the mechanism could work in practice by generating greater market contracting costs, thus leading to greater vertical integration. After 30 years of debate about this particular example, this much is clear: Klein's theory of hold-up, and its primary prediction of a positive relationship between asset specificity and vertical integration, had held up quite well and has become one of the most well-documented economic phenomena in industrial organization economics.[17]

But this critical literature, and Klein's responses to it, have also served a productive purpose. The details of the Fisher Body hold-up are critical precisely because they provide an opportunity to understand the mechanism behind the failure of the long-term exclusive dealing contract in favor of vertical integration. This critical literature led by Coase has produced a better understanding of the events that led to Fisher Body's hold-up of General Motors and its execution. Indeed, the set of critical papers from Coase (2000, 2006) and others have led Klein (2000, 2007) to extend the analysis of the Fisher Body-General Motors case. For example, Klein (2007) provides additional evidence from the actual 1919 Fisher Body–General Motors contract, previously unavailable, to add to the substantial evidence of the economic relationship compiled in the Du Pont case record and other sources.[18] After 30 years of study and debate, the primary lesson of the Fisher Body-General Motors example remains the same:

---

[17]   See empirical literature cited supra n. 11.

[18]   Klein (2007) demonstrates that Fisher Body did not hold up General Motors by actually mis-locating plants or adopting an inefficient low-capital intensive production technology. While Fisher Body did threaten to mis-locate plants, Klein documents how Fisher Body accomplished its hold-up of General Motors by 'negotiating a highly favorable contractual adjustment in 1922 in response to General Motors' demand that Fisher Body's substantial new investment in additional capacity take the form of co-located body plants'. This contractual adjustment led to the previously observed substantial decrease in Fisher Body's capital-to-sales ratio. This explanation reconciles the existing evidence concerning threats of plant mis-location, the reduction in capital-to-sales ratio, and the contractual adjustment. Coase (2006) does not recognize that the 1922 contract renegotiation was made to overcome Fisher Body's threatened refusal to co-locate its plants.

transacting parties choose contract terms to economize on the reputational capital necessary to make the contractual relationship self-enforcing under the widest possible range of ex post circumstances. But, as the Fisher Body-General Motors' relationship illustrates, the contract terms parties choose can also result in additional hold-up potential.

Klein's emphasis on the role of contract terms within the self-enforcement framework is an important distinction between the contributions of Klein and Williamson.[19] While both adopt the TCE approach and have made fundamentally important contributions to both the theory of the firm and contractual choice, Klein's self-enforcement framework has generated a lens through which specific contractual arrangements can be examined to increase our understanding of how those terms broaden the self-enforcing range. The primary advantage of vertical integration within this framework is the increased flexibility transactors gain by avoiding the rigidity associated with long-term contracts. The framework is useful to explain vertical integration as a particular contractual arrangement that facilitates self-enforcement rather than a special case, and can be applied to explain a number of other contractual arrangements. Indeed, Klein (1996) notes that the self-enforcement framework 'should be judged by how much it assists us in explaining the particular contractual arrangements in the marketplace'. The fruits of Klein's application of the self-enforcement framework are discussed in Section 4.

4   The self-enforcement framework and contractual choice

The self-enforcement framework entails the combination of insights discussed in Sections 2 and 3 – the threat of loss of future sales and reputation and the role of contract terms in controlling hold-up behavior – and provides a productive framework for analyzing contractual arrangements. This section's primary purpose is to survey the application of this framework to a number of contractual arrangements.[20]

It is worth repeating that the role of contract terms within this framework is significantly different from the standard economic approach in ways critically important to the economic analysis of contract law.[21] The fundamental motivation for using court-enforced contract terms in the self-enforcing framework is to supplement self-enforcement. If sufficient reputational capital was available, transactors would generally choose to avoid the costs of contractual specification by relying exclusively on self-enforcement. However, because such capital is generally limited, parties must supplement the self-enforcement mechanism with written terms.

The self-enforcement framework generates two fundamental insights about contracting. The first is about the very nature of contract terms. Within the self-enforcement framework, contract terms may be thought of as accomplishing one of two goals: decreasing short-term gains achieved by not performing in a manner consistent with the contractual understanding (W1), or increasing the transactor's reputational capital (W2), the capital cost of the lost

---

[19]   A second difference involves some differences in the definition of hold-up. Williamson's (1975) definition of a hold-up includes moral hazard behavior, dishonesty, and surprise, whereas Klein (1996) argues that moral hazard is a form of contractual non-performance, not hold-up, because it is fully anticipated.

[20]   See also Masten (2000).

[21]   See infra Section 5 for a discussion of the advantages of the self-enforcement framework view of contract terms for contract interpretation.

expected future profit stream imposed upon a non-performing transactor upon termination. While the economic literature generally recognizes the role of contract terms in defining some element of performance, and therefore reducing W1 by controlling this element through court enforcement, within the self-enforcement framework the role of contractual specification is to render the residual W1, after all cost-effective contract terms are specified, less than W2. What is less well-recognized in both the economics and law and economics literatures is that contract terms may be used to shift expected future rents, and therefore reputational capital, between transactors. The economic rationale for utilizing contract terms to shift future rents is to more closely align each transactor's reputational capital with his potential expected gain from nonperformance. Some examples of the use of contract terms in this spirit are explored throughout this section.[22]

The second fundamental insight, explored in greater detail in Section 5, is that the self-enforcement framework demonstrates a fundamental complementarity between court enforcement and self-enforcement. Klein (1996) describes this complementarity as follows:

> The two enforcement mechanisms are substitutes in demand, in the sense of a positive cross elasticity of demand, so that an increase in the price of one mechanism leads to an increased use of the other mechanism. But the two mechanisms are complements in supply, in the sense of a positive cross elasticity of supply, so that an increase, for example, in the quantity of reputational capital leads to an increase in the marginal productivity of court enforcement. That is, the two mechanisms work better together than either of them do separately.

This complementarity has important implications for the role of contract law and contract interpretation in broadening the self-enforcing range of contracts.

The self-enforcement approach can be usefully contrasted with the contract design literature that I have described as the 'standard' or 'conventional' approach. This description is not meant to be entirely critical. This literature has been highly influential in economics, heavily cited by law and economics scholars, and has supplied some important insights about contracting behavior.[23] However, it cannot be avoided that this conventional approach to contracts envisions a different role for contract terms in assuring performance than the self-enforcement approach. Specifically, this literature examines the role of specific contract terms in minimizing malincentives, given that performance can only be contracted upon imperfectly. While his literature takes incomplete contracting very seriously, and has produced several fundamentally useful insights about contracting, it has the drawback of generally envisioning agreements as either court-enforced or self-enforced, but not both. In other words, the standard contract theory literature contemplates the purpose of contracts as fundamentally about creating optimal incentives for performance on some imperfect, but court-enforceable, measure.

The similarities and differences between these approaches should be apparent. Both approaches are anchored by a foundation which accepts the notion that contracts are incomplete. Both approaches also acknowledge the role of contracts terms in reducing the gains from non-performance that derive from contractual specification. But the mechanism through

---

22   See Goldberg (1976), Goldberg and Ericson (1987), and Crocker and Masten (1991) on the use of contract terms to facilitate self-enforcement and contractual flexibility, including the adjustment of prices as market conditions change over time.

23   See, for example, Posner (2003).

which specification affects performance is quite different between the two literatures. In the standard literature, specification can prevent high-value opportunism by using contract terms to provide a direct incentive to perform where non-legal sanctions are insufficient to facilitate performance. Alternatively, the self-enforcement approach models the contracting process as an attempt to use court-enforced terms as a *complement* to limited reputational capital in order to render an economic relationship self-enforcing over the broadest possible range of ex post market conditions. The standard approach leaves no room for the interaction between specification and reputational capital. Competing economic models should be judged by their predictive power of real world contractual arrangements. By this measure, the self-enforcement mechanism has been highly successful, whereas the principal-agent literature has been underwhelming in its ability to explain the content of contracts.[24]

The Fisher Body-General Motors exclusive dealing contract again illustrates the predictive power of the self-enforcement approach. Fisher Body had entered a long-term, cost-plus exclusive dealing contract. The purpose of this contract was to encourage Fisher to make General Motors-specific investments and protect Fisher from hold up by locking General Motors into Fisher. Instead, when market conditions changed dramatically, Fisher Body was able to hold-up General Motors and negotiate a significant side payment, and the parties eventually vertically integrated. The standard view cannot explain the original exclusive dealing/cost-plus arrangement the parties adopted, as they created a direct incentive for Fisher to increase the cost of auto bodies. However, the self-enforcement approach demonstrates why the terms Fisher Body and General Motors adopted were efficient when adopted and operated successfully for several years without Fisher Body attempting to hold up General Motors.

In addition to vertical integration, Klein has applied the self-enforcement framework to explain the role of a number of contractual arrangements with significant success over the past 30 years. These contributions have been highly influential in the literatures, as well as with judges. For organizational purposes, these contributions will be divided into two broad categories: (1) vertical restraints; and (2) franchising.

4.1 The economics of vertical restraints

Perhaps the most influential of these contributions has been the explanation of vertical restraints between manufacturers and retailers. For example, Klein and Murphy (1988) and Klein (1999) demonstrate the role of resale price maintenance (RPM) and exclusive territories in facilitating contractual performance and supply of the desired dealer services. Manufacturers use vertical restraints to decrease the short-run gain from cheating (W1) by limiting the ability to expand output and increase the long-run gain from performance (W2)

---

[24]   See, for example, Posner (2003) ('so far the literature has failed to predict the content of either contracts or legal doctrines'). Posner points out that this literature, which he overbroadly refers to as the literature on incomplete contracts without referencing work on self-enforcement, predicts contracts that are much more complex than those designed by real parties. Posner explains this gap between theory and evidence by suggesting that real-world parties are less rational than those in the economic literature. However, the real world observation of contracts less complex than those predicted by the principal-agent literature is also fully consistent with the self-enforcement approach, where contract terms are used to supplement reputational capital.

by creating a quasi-rent stream that will be lost if non-performance is detected.[25] This explanation of RPM in providing a premium stream to dealers in order to induce the supply of additional promotional services has successfully provided a pro-competitive explanation of RPM where the standard explanation of inter-dealer free-riding does not apply (Telser 1960). Indeed, Klein and Murphy's (1988) pro-competitive explanation of RPM as a method to facilitate the supply of promotional services was recently relied upon by the Supreme Court in *Leegin Creative Leather Product, Inc. v. PSKS, Inc.*, in overturning the longstanding per se prohibition against minimum RPM.[26]

Klein and Murphy's analysis of vertical contractual relationships also provides another fundamental insight concerning a pervasive incentive conflict between manufacturers and retailers with respect to the supply of promotional services. This insight has been the foundation for a number of analyses of contractual arrangements in the retail setting. Specifically, Klein and Murphy demonstrate that retailers will undersupply promotional services because manufacturers do not take into account the incremental profit margin earned by the manufacturer on promotional sales when some, but not all, consumers value the promotional service. RPM or other vertical restraints can create a premium stream for the retailer to induce provision of promotional services that would not otherwise be supplied under the threat of termination for non-performance. Retailers that fail to provide those services are 'free-riding' on the contractual arrangement by taking the compensation and failing to deliver the contracted for services.[27]

Consider the case of promotional shelf space. Klein and Wright (2007) apply the insight of the Klein and Murphy model to explain slotting contracts, shelf space contracts between manufacturers and retailers. Klein and Wright illustrate that when deciding how much promotional shelf space to provide a manufacturer's product, retailers will not take into account the manufacturer's profit margin on the incremental sales produced by the promotional shelf space. This problem is particularly significant when the manufacturer supplies a differentiated product where the wholesale price it receives is substantially greater than its marginal production cost. Thus, retailers will not find it in their interests to supply the promotional shelf space necessary to generate the manufacturer's profitable incremental sales. Manufacturers, therefore, must find a way to contractually incentivize retailers to supply their products the desired promotional shelf space. In the grocery retail setting, Klein and Wright show that the efficient form of compensation often involves a lump-sum per unit time slotting fee when inter-retailer competition on the particular product makes compensation with a lower wholesale price a more costly way to generate equilibrium retailer shelf space rents.

---

[25]   Klein and Murphy (1988) demonstrate how Coors implemented a combination of RPM with an exclusive territory to create a premium stream and encourage dealers to provide refrigeration and product rotation services for Coors beer that underwent a brewing process that did not include pasteurization and deteriorated quickly at room temperature.

[26]   In addition to the Supreme Court's reliance on the Klein and Murphy analysis of vertical restraints and RPM in *Leegin*, the analysis has also been widely cited in the legal literature for its implications for antitrust law, franchising, and contract law, including 77 citations in the JLR database.

[27]   This type of free-riding should be distinguished from what Klein refers to as the 'classic retailer free-riding' analysis popularized by Telser (1960). As Klein (1988, 1993) and others, such as Pitosfky (1983), have pointed out, the services full-service retailers provide in cases involving RPM generally do not involve this type of free-riding. Rather, the promotional services provided are those for which the free-riding consumers are unwilling to pay.

More generally, Klein has extended the analysis of the incentive conflict between manufacturers and retailers concerning promotional effort in a series of papers examining the role of exclusive dealing terms in distribution contracts. One theme that emerges from these recent analyses is that our current understanding of the potentially pro-competitive role of exclusive dealing in preventing dealer free-riding is unduly narrow. For example, Klein and Lerner (2007) offer an expanded economic analysis of free-riding that begins from the premise, discussed above, that manufacturers often want their dealers to supply more promotional effort than the dealers would independently provide. The contractual solution to this incentive conflict is to adopt a marketing arrangement under which the manufacturer compensates the retailer for these extra services. This can take place through the use of exclusive territories, RPM, slotting allowances, or other promotional payments. However, the creation of the necessary premium stream generated by this contractual solution can cause other problems associated with retailer free-riding on the marketing arrangement. Klein and Lerner (2007) identify three types of free-riding strategies to supplement the conventional economic analysis of retailer free-riding. Specifically, the retailer can 'free-ride' on the investments the manufacturer provides to sell rival products, by using the promotional efforts the manufacturer paid for to sell rival products, or by simply not supplying the increased level of brand-specific promotion for which the manufacturer paid.

Free-riding on manufacturer-supplied investments to sell rival products is the most frequently discussed in antitrust law and economics and by the courts. Marvel (1982) first identified the rationale for exclusive dealing contracts in preventing this sort of free-riding, which has been accepted in antitrust jurisprudence on the grounds that it promotes valuable investments.

Klein and Lerner (2007) expand on this analysis by debunking economists' claim that exclusive dealing could not prevent the other two types of free-riding. Indeed, exclusive dealing contracts can also prevent free-riding on paid for promotional efforts, even absent manufacturer-supplied investments that dealers can use to sell alternative products. When a manufacturer solves the promotional incentive conflict by compensating the dealer for providing additional promotional effort with an extra profit margin on the dealer's sales of the manufacturer's products, the dealer has the incentive to free-ride by switching their promotional efforts to alternative brands.

Further, Klein and Lerner (2007) present an economic rationale for the commonly claimed role of exclusive dealing in 'increasing dealer loyalty' by producing dedicated dealers, even absent any dealer switching behavior. While courts have long accepted the conventional wisdom that exclusive dealing could increase dealer loyalty, little was known about how exclusivity could induce greater promotional effort. Klein and Lerner (2007) demonstrate that exclusive dealing can prevent a third type of dealer free-riding, failing to supply paid for promotional effort, by increasing the marginal incentive for dealers to promote the manufacturer's products. Klein and Lerner also demonstrate that the exclusive dealing contracts in *Dentsply* were, at least, partially explained by a desire to prevent this third type of free-riding, and that the Third Circuit mistakenly relied upon the conventional economic wisdom in rejecting this rationale.

Separately, Klein and Murphy (2008) have shown that exclusive dealing can 'intensify' competition for distribution when a retailer commits to exclusively or primarily promote a single manufacturer's products. The fundamental economic insight of Klein and Murphy's analysis is that the exclusive dealing contract increases the elasticity of demand facing manufacturers bidding for the exclusive shelf space and access to the retailer's customer base. Thus, the competitive bidding process results in increased dealer compensation that, in turn, benefits consumers when payments are ultimately passed on to final consumers.[28] While exclusive dealing contracts inherently make some consumers worse off by reducing product variety within the store, Klein and Murphy demonstrate that competitive retailers enter these exclusive arrangements only when it allows them to compete in the marketplace by offering a combination of price and product variety which will be preferred by a sufficiently large group of consumers. In other words, failing to offer consumers a combination of price and variety in a competitive retail marketplace is unlikely to be profitable under these conditions because retailers will lose a substantial number of consumers and sales to rival supermarkets.

Klein and Murphy (2008) also consider a variety of contractual alternatives designed to intensify manufacturer competition for shelf space while accommodating consumer demand for product variety. These alternatives include 'partial exclusives' such as preferential shelf space contracts, market share contracts, and category management contracts, which delegate shelf space allocation input to a manufacturer. A reasonable economic interpretation of the implicit understanding under which a category captain operates is that it will stock other highly demanded brands, in addition to its own products, so as not to unnecessarily reduce overall retailer demand and profitability.[29] Collectively, the insights from Klein's recent work on the economics of exclusive dealing demonstrate that exclusive dealing, to use antitrust terminology, frequently involves 'competition on the merits' and is part of the normal competitive process.[30]

Klein's analysis of vertical restraints extends beyond contractual provisions facilitating retailer supply of promotional effort. For example, Klein and Kenney's (1983) seminal analysis of the block booking arrangement prevalent in the American motion picture industry demonstrates that block booking terms were used to reduce ex post opportunism. Klein and Kenney (1983) challenged the prevailing, and still influential, view that block booking arrangements were a form of price discrimination. Stigler (1963) had argued that block booking was a method distributors used to capture additional consumer surplus by price discriminating to exploit the variance in individual film valuations across cities. However, Klein and Kenney challenged this view by presenting evidence from the *Loew's* case suggesting that block prices were not uniform and varied across geographic markets. In addition, using a competitive auction mechanism to grant a single station in multiple station markets the exclusive rights to film distribution is inconsistent with the price discrimination motive, since the auction would reveal individual station values without resorting to block booking.[31]

---

28   Wright (2001) provides evidence that competition in the grocery retail sector has remained intense despite substantial increases in concentration over the past several decades. Klein and Wright (2007) provide evidence that retailer profitability has remained constant over this same time period during which slotting contracts and payments to supermarkets increased dramatically.

29   Wright (2009) applies the insights of Klein and Murphy's analysis of partial exclusives to the adoption of category management contracts in the retail sector. Specifically, Wright analyzed the competitive consequences of United States Tobacco's category management arrangement and implementation that were the basis for the *Conwood Co. v. United States Tobacco Co.* antitrust litigation.

30   Klein (2003) and Klein (2001) discuss the use of exclusive dealing contracts in the *Microsoft* litigation.

31   Kobayashi (2005) discusses the Klein and Kenney analysis as it relates to the economic literature on bundling.

Kenney and Klein then applied the self-enforcement framework to understand the use of block booking contract terms in the motion picture industry. Specifically, Kenney and Klein argue that block booking prevents buyers from rejecting part of a package of products that is average-priced. The economic rationale for average-pricing in the motion picture industry is to deter opportunism in the form of investments in informational advantages with little or no social value. For example, in *Paramount*, block booking was used to prevent buyers from picking through a subset of films after initial exhibition results became available.[32] Similarly, the block booking arrangement in *Loew's* discouraged wasteful searching for exceptional film values.

Klein and Kenney also apply this framework to De Beers' marketing arrangement for uncut diamonds. De Beers pre-sorted diamonds into relatively homogeneous categories to be sold in pre-selected blocks to pre-selected buyers. These pre-selected blocks were to be sold at non-negotiable prices and buyers' rejection of the sales offer would result in the withdrawal of future invitations to the buyer to purchase stones. In the De Beers arrangement, block booking prevents wasteful oversearching to identify the highest quality stones and leaving only low quality stones behind. These pre-purchase investments lead to wealth transfers between consumers and sellers but have little social value. Block booking prevents the wasteful costs of individually pricing the stones in each quality group and is enforced by a brand-name enforcement mechanism. Specifically, De Beers discourages buyers from 'cheating' on the arrangement by rejecting sights of lower than average quality by providing buyers with a premium stream that exceeds the rents from such rejection. The enforcement mechanism thus relies on De Beers' brand name because buyers expect they will receive a diamond sight from the underlying quality distribution upon which the average price is based. Similarly, because buyers will lose the premium stream associated with De Beers' pricing if they reject a sight that is less than average quality, the arrangement is self-enforcing.

Two overarching themes emerge from Klein's work on vertical restraints. The first is a commitment to increasing our economic understanding of these arrangements as they operate in the real world rather than assuming away the important institutional details of the arrangements for the purposes of analysis. For example, Klein's analysis of vertical restraints builds on the fundamental economic reality that the normal competitive process often results in manufacturers compensating retailers for the provision of shelf space and other promotional services. This insight builds upon what is a departure from the standard view of the economics of retail in the literature, where retailers merely passively transmit exogenous consumer preferences, and its only economic function is to reduce search costs. To the contrary, Klein's analytical framework begins in a world where the retailer operates in a competitive environment facing a downward-sloping demand, and has some discretion over its shelf space, promotion, and pricing decisions. Without building these two empirical regularities into the analytical framework, it would be nearly impossible to understand the fundamental incentive conflict over the provision of retail promotion such as shelf space, and therefore also impossible to understand the use of exclusive and partial exclusive contracts in this setting. The adoption of a more realistic framework for analysis that includes brand names, self-enforcement, and a more realistic account of retail competition allows for a more

---

[32]   Klein and Kenney (2000) provide evidence of opportunistic exhibitor rejection of films where exhibitors would cancel or shorten the run of 'overpriced' films and substitute films from competing distributors.

robust understanding of the way these contract terms operate and their competitive consequences.

4.2   The economics of franchising

Franchising is one of the most studied forms of organization in the economics literature. At
least legally, franchising is a unique form of contractual organization. For example, franchising is the subject of a thicket of state and federal regulations, whereas analytically similar
contractual arrangements are not subjected to special scrutiny. On the other hand, franchising
is just one of many distribution arrangements where manufacturers exercise control over their
exclusive retailers where these economic forces are present. Franchising has provided a set of
arrangements for understanding the role of contract terms in reducing transactions costs and
incentive conflicts.

The underlying economics of franchising are similar to the economics of vertical
restraints. The interesting economic questions concerning franchising are similar to those
concerning contractual choice in vertical relationships: what is the role of the particular
contractual terms adopted in the franchise contract, and what determines whether a franchise
is owned and operated by the franchisor rather than owned and operated by an independent
franchisee?

I will focus on three of Klein's key contributions to the law and economics of franchising:
(1) application of the promotional incentive conflict analysis originally articulated in Klein
and Murphy to franchising arrangements; (2) explaining contract terms franchisors and franchisees adopt to facilitate self-enforcement; and (3) applying the economic analysis of franchising to antitrust aftermarket claims to establish the legal and economic principle that
market power should be measured ex ante at the time of contracting rather than ex post.

The first economic question with respect to franchising is to understand why franchisor
and franchisee incentives do not coincide and thus require contractual restraints. If the incentives for performance were aligned, there would be no reason for contractually controlling
franchisee behavior. A number of reasons have been studied at great length in the economics
literature. For example, when franchisees jointly use a common brand name, each franchisee
can free-ride on the brand name by reducing quality, because the quality reduction results in
an 'across-the-board' reduction in future demand.[33] A second, well-known form of free-
riding, discussed above, involves franchisee supply of some pre-purchase service that
consumers can get free of charge at a full service franchisee before purchasing at a presumably lower price from a 'free-riding' franchisee who does not provide the service. This is what
Klein has referred to as the 'special services' free-riding problem originally articulated by
Telser (1960). A third form of incentive conflict involves 'successive monopoly' or 'double
marginalization'. Where the franchisee possesses some power over price, it is sometimes
claimed that franchise restraints are an attempt to control the franchisee's incentive to
increase price to reflect its market power.

A critical and distinguishing feature of Klein's analysis of franchising agreements is its
focus on a fourth incentive conflict: the supply of promotional services. This incentive
conflict is much more general and pervasive than the three 'special case' scenarios tend to

---

[33]   See Rubin (1978) and Klein (1980). Rubin (1978) provides an early transaction-cost econom-
ics-based explanation of franchising based upon the costs of monitoring employee-operated franchise
outlets.

suggest. All that is required, as discussed above in the context of vertical restraints, is that the franchisee control provision of some inputs that influence demand for the franchisor's product, and that the franchisor sells those products at a mark-up over its marginal cost. Attentive readers will recognize these conditions as analogous to those articulated by Klein and Murphy (1988) and Klein and Wright (2007) with respect to vertical restraints. The emphasis of this fourth promotional incentive conflict appears to explain the prevalence of vertical restraints in settings where special services free-riding, the use of common brand names, or successive monopoly problems are absent or insignificant.

Using the promotional malincentive problem as a starting point for the analysis, Klein applies the self-enforcement framework, discussed in greater detail above, to analyze the role of contract terms in franchise contracts. Again, the critical economic point is that contract terms can operate in two ways to facilitate performance. The first method is to provide the correct marginal incentive for franchisee performance by contractually specifying the desired performance to be enforced by a court. Contractual specification alone is generally insufficient to assure performance because it is impossible, or at least prohibitively costly, to fully specify a legally enforceable agreement documenting each element of performance. The second method contract terms can facilitate performance by creating sufficient franchisee rents so the threat of termination by the franchisor generates sufficient incentive to supply the desired behavior. The self-enforcement mechanism, as discussed in Klein and Leffler (1981) and Klein and Murphy (1988), requires the franchisor to monitor franchisee behavior and terminate the franchisee for non-performance. The important distinction is that the threat of termination, and not the threat of litigation to enforce the contract terms, produces the incentive to perform.

As with the Klein and Murphy (1988) analytical framework for vertical restraints, this view of franchising contract terms raises the question of how these terms create direct performance incentives or economic rents. For example, Klein and Murphy (1988) and Klein (1995) discuss the use of exclusive territories, RPM, and the number and spacing of outlets as alternative ways to create the franchisee premium stream.[34]

A second important economic question related to franchising involves when franchisors will rely on company ownership as opposed to the franchising of outlets. Economists have made significant efforts to theoretically and empirically identify the determinants of company-owned outlets and the content of franchise contract terms.[35] The self-enforcement framework also implies that the key determinant of vertical integration of outlets is the monitoring costs of franchisor-owned outlets relative to franchised outlets. This prediction is consistent with the empirical finding that state franchise laws prohibiting franchisee termination except for 'good cause' result in reduced welfare. For example, Klick, Kobayashi, and Ribstein (2007) find a positive relationship between state franchise termination restrictions and the fraction of franchisor-owned outlets, and a negative relationship between the regulations and the overall level of franchising.[36] Brickley and Dark (1987) also identify a negative relationship between distance of an outlet to the nearest franchise headquarters and franchisor

---

[34]   Kaufmann and Lafontaine (1994) provide evidence that McDonald's franchisees retain significant rents.

[35]   See, for example, Brickley and Dark (1987); Brickley, Dark and Weisbach (1991b); Bhattacharyya and Lafontaine (1995); Lafontaine (1992); Lafontaine and Shaw (1999).

[36]   See also Beales and Muris (1993); and Smith (1982).

ownership, though it is unclear whether this evidence strongly supports the relationship between franchisee-monitoring costs relative to the costs of monitoring a franchisor-owned outlet.[37]

A third key feature of Klein's analysis of franchise arrangements is its application to antitrust analysis of franchise-tying arrangements. In the typical franchise-tying claim, a franchisee challenges an underlying requirements contract as an illegal tie-in under the Sherman Act. A necessary element of a franchise-tying claim was that the franchisor possessed antitrust market power. Klein and Saft (1985) first recognized the key economic insight involving antitrust analysis of these franchise-tying cases: that franchisor market power should be measured, contrary to the legal presumption after *Siegel v. Chicken Delight*, during the pre-contract time period when franchisees make their decisions and competition between franchisors is reflected in contract terms. Klein (1999) motivates this analysis with the example of a law firm looking for office space to rent. From the perspective of the law firm contemplating a lease, and before making significant investments in its new office space, there is significant competition among potential building owners, as many close substitutes exist for the space the law firm is seeking. Building owners cannot and do not exercise power because of the competition between owners at the pre-contract stage. Therefore, Klein concludes, the presence of pre-contract competition can be expected to generate a competitive package price for the space and other contract terms such as parking rates, air conditioning rates, and other amenities.

The 'hold-up' problem at the root of most franchise-tying cases occurs only after the law firm has signed a long-term lease, made investments, and becomes 'locked in'. Prior to the Klein and Saft (1985) analysis, the legal presumption was that this type of post-contract hold-up was a monopoly problem associated with market power. But consider again the law firm who entered into a competitively negotiated package price. Defining market power ex post in such a case would necessarily mean that market power existed in each scenario, even when contract terms were negotiated in highly competitive markets where buyers make sunk investments. Similarly, Klein and Saft (1985) and Klein (1999) persuasively argued that antitrust laws associated with monopoly power should measure market power at the pre-contract stage. In sum, although the franchisor's ability to 'hold-up' the franchisee might result in bad outcomes for the franchisee, not all bad outcomes in all contracts are antitrust problems. Antitrust problems require the exercise of monopoly power, whereas the typical franchise-tying case does not. Conflating contract problems associated with imperfect buyer information or hold-up potential with the exercise of monopoly power threatens to cast the shadow of antitrust liability and treble damages over mundane contractual disagreements.

This insight has been extremely influential in antitrust analysis of franchise-tying arrangements and aftermarket tie-in claims. For example, at least nine federal courts have cited the Klein and Saft analysis in rejecting franchise-tying claims, including the Supreme Court in its landmark 1992 *Kodak* decision. While the *Kodak* decision was widely thought to have opened the door to 'aftermarket' franchise-tying claims, Goldfine and Vorrasi (2004) demonstrate, lower federal courts have all but completely rejected the invitation from *Kodak* to

---

[37]   Klein (1995) argues that distance of an outlet to the nearest franchisor headquarters is not a reasonable proxy for monitoring costs because if they are significant at all, these costs would also increase the costs of monitoring franchisor-owned outlets.

expand 'aftermarket lock-in' theory in the franchise setting or elsewhere. Courts commonly reject these theories based on the distinction, borne in Klein's analysis, between 'contract power' and 'antitrust power'. This sensible development in antitrust treatment of tying arrangements is owed in large part to the strength of the Klein and Saft (1985) and Klein (1999) arguments that (1) hold-up is a problem distinct from the exercise of monopoly power, (2) antitrust market power must be present at the pre-contract stage, and (3) transactors aware that they are entering an agreement without complete information and with the potential for hold-up will make arrangements to protect themselves (either with contractual terms or by dealing with firms with large reputations and much to lose by executing a hold-up). It should be pointed out that despite popular descriptions of *Kodak* as endorsing post-contract evaluation of antitrust market power, Klein (1999) correctly points out that *Kodak* approved the aftermarket hold-up logic only under limited circumstances, including the existence of an actual hold-up. The limitations adopted by the *Kodak* court carefully avoid the expansion of antitrust market power to all contracts signed in competitive markets where buyers have made sunk investments and therefore some modicum of hold-up potential exists. These limitations, along with the death of franchise tying and *Kodak* aftermarket claims in the lower courts, suggests that Klein's work in emphasizing the distinction between the economic forces associated with hold-up and those associated with antitrust market power have been highly influential in altering the path of antitrust jurisprudence in this area.

An additional key contribution of Klein and Saft (1985) is the economic explanation of tie-ins in economizing on monitoring costs of franchisees. For example, Klein and Saft demonstrate that a franchise tie-in might reduce the common brand name free-riding because it reduces the costs of policing and detecting franchisee cheating since the franchisor can identify cheating whenever he sees a non-authorized product in the franchisee outlet, rather than making more difficult quality comparisons. Klein and Saft also show that franchise tie-in arrangements might efficiently meter value across franchisees by placing an upcharge on inputs, rather than collecting the franchise fee on sales.[38] Klein and Saft (1985) conclude their analysis with the following observation concerning the potential implications for antitrust law: 'an understanding of these pro-competitive benefits is necessary before the court is likely to adopt an explicit rule of reason standard, rather than the extremely rough de facto rule of reason standard we now have'. While the Court has not taken the opportunity to overturn *Jefferson Parish* and explicitly adopt the rule of reason approach, lower federal courts have substantially clarified the analysis applied to franchise-tying cases and have been reluctant to impose antitrust liability on problems with adequate remedies in contract law.

5   Self-enforcement and optimal contract law

Posner (2003) has recently noted that 'economics fails to explain contract law' and that it 'provides little normative guidance for reforming contract law'. That diagnosis is rather bleak for the law and economics of contracts. And, according to Posner, the economists are at least partly to blame. Economists have produced models that 'focus on small aspects of contractual behavior or make optimal doctrine a function of variables that cannot be realistically observed,

---

[38]   Klein (1999) argues that the requirements contracts in *Chicken Delight* and *Kodak* are likely efficient components of a discriminatory metering arrangement. Klein (1999), Klein (1995), and Klein and Wiley (2003) argue that contractual arrangements that foster economic price discrimination enhance efficiency and should be immunized from antitrust liability.

measured, or estimated'. The incomplete contracts literature fails to describe contracts themselves as its models predict contracts that are far more complex than those observed in the real world. On top of failing to explain real world contracts, the economics literature also fails to explain contract doctrine.

Posner is correct in that much of what he describes as the incomplete contracts literature has failed to predict the content of actual contracts. Indeed, one recurring theme in this essay has been that the 'conventional' incomplete contracting approach is unlikely to predict contract terms because it ignores the potential for these terms to facilitate self-enforcement. On the other hand, Posner essentially ignores the work of Klein, Williamson, Goldberg and others who have emphasized self-enforcement and reputation in understanding the role of contract terms. By way of contrast with the conventional approach, the self-enforcement framework has generated significant economic understanding of a variety of contractual terms and complex distribution arrangements, including RPM, block booking, franchising, tying, slotting contracts, exclusive dealing, exclusive territories, and vertical integration. This literature provides a more optimistic view of the state and direction of the law and economics of contracts.

The key difference between the self-enforcement approach and the conventional approach is worth repeating yet again: the latter envisions the sole role of contract terms is to create the correct incentives for performance with respect to some contractually specified measure. Whereas, the self-enforcement framework implies that transactors will select contract terms to economize on their limited amounts of private enforcement capital and broaden the self-enforcing range to assure performance under the broadest possible range of likely ex post market conditions. Under the self-enforcement approach, contract terms not only are used to provide incentives to perform on some court-verifiable measure, but can also create rents that facilitate performance when coupled with the threat of termination. Because self-enforcement is an important feature of economic relationships, it is no surprise that the standard models have limited predictive value in explaining real-world contract terms. The standard approach continues, as a general matter, to proceed as if reputational enforcement is an 'all or nothing' choice, rather than understanding the complementary nature of self- and court-enforcement mechanisms.

The self-enforcement framework Klein has developed over the last 30 years also has important implications for optimal contract law. In the extreme case, the standard approach would render the content of contract law largely irrelevant since parties could presumably contract around inefficient doctrine in most circumstances. But contract law is not irrelevant in the real world. The content of the law matters because contracting parties largely accept it as given and do not 'opt out' of all inefficient doctrine, thereby saving significant resource costs by relying on what amounts to an exogenously imposed and impartial set of terms. And because the law matters, efficient contract doctrine sets rules that allow courts to identify terms parties would have adopted when contractual arrangements break down because some unspecified contingency occurs. In other words, efficient contract doctrine should set rules that allow the court to interpret an incomplete contract to reflect the terms the parties would have adopted ex ante had they contracted over those contingencies.

The self-enforcement framework might be especially useful for providing insights concerning the task of interpreting contracts. The economic approach to contracts poses a critical issue with respect to how judges should interpret intentionally incomplete contracts when the parties' intentions may deviate from the written terms. One proposal frequently raised in the law and economics literature, that judges should interpret contracts by filling in those terms parties would have adopted had they contracted over some contingency, is obviously a difficult task. Despite widespread recognition of the difficulties associated with this sort of judicial contractual gap-filling, the self-enforcement analysis discussed throughout this essay suggests that law and economics scholars may have actually underestimated the complexity of this task. This is because the role of contract terms goes beyond shifting risks and creating direct incentives to preventing hold-up risk. Klein (1995) illustrates this point with the example of a simple long-term fixed-price contract. The conventional approach suggests that the sole role of the fixed-price contract term is to insure against the risk of price volatility. However, the self-enforcement framework reveals that, in addition to allocating risk efficiently, fixed-price contracts can play an important role in reducing the probability of hold-up, thereby encouraging specific investment and performance. Klein (1980) demonstrates that in order to economize on the parties' reputational capital, efficient self-enforcing arrangements can often include seemingly 'unfair' and 'one-sided' contract terms that courts may have a tendency not to enforce.[39]

The self-enforcement framework implies that the primary role of contract law and interpretation in facilitating efficient economic exchange should, at least in principle, broaden the self-enforcing range. Contract law and interpretation doctrines can, in principle, be applied to minimize hold-up behavior by identifying attempts to hold up a transacting party and preventing parties from using the court to facilitate a hold-up. Some have argued that contract doctrine has developed in a manner consistent with this view. For example, Muris (1981) argues that 'when viewed through the lens of opportunism, many aspects of the law previously regarded as diverse in nature should be recognized as containing a common unifying principle' and that 'judges can, and often do, act to lower important costs of transacting'.[40]

The application of contract interpretation to broaden the self-enforcing range has some appeal. The court could, in principle, operate as a substitute for the parties' private reputational capital by going beyond literal interpretation methods to understand the context of the arrangement and parties' intent. In this sense, contextual methods of interpretation have some theoretical advantage over more formal and literal methods, which involve enforcing terms only as they are written. However, the potential for judicial lowering of transactions costs comes with the risk that judges might apply contract law in a manner that reduces the self-enforcing range and, therefore, increases the costs to transacting parties and the brand-name capital required to avoid hold-up. It is a difficult problem for contract theorists and economists to understand the purpose of the terms parties adopt in the context of a complex contractual arrangement. It is difficult to imagine that the task would not be overwhelming for a judge without expertise in the particular industry or in the economics of contracts. Applying flexible interpretation methods, as predicted in Klein (1980), might lead courts to refuse to enforce non-standard or apparently one-sided contract terms that actually are important in encouraging specific investments and facilitating self-enforcement by shifting private capital.[41]

---

[39] See also Posner and Bebchuk (2006) for a similar analysis.

[40] On the law and economics of contract interpretation, see Goetz and Scott (1981), Schwartz (1992), Hadfield (1994), Ben-Shahar (1999), Schwartz and Scott (2003), Katz (2004), Posner (2005), Posner (1998), and Posner, Eggleston and Zeckhauser (2000).

[41] Hadfield (1994); Katz (2004); Posner (2005); Posner (1998); Schwartz (1992).

One weakness with the law and economics literature surrounding contract interpretation is that it has traditionally had little to do with contracts themselves rather than specific doctrines as they relate to parties' disputes about contracts. But how are courts to enforce the intent of the parties when the self-enforcement framework suggests that the 'true' aims of the parties will often diverge, and possibly contradict, the contract's literal terms? The self-enforcement approach implies that if judicial efforts to align the true aims of the parties with written terms are ultimately erroneous, the result will be an increased strain on the parties' reputational capital and a more narrow self-enforcing range. The question of how willing courts are to enforce written contract terms, as well as how frequently judicial attempts to fill gaps result in errors that frustrate the parties' intent, is ultimately empirical. However, the self-enforcement framework does suggest a more subtle, and perhaps more complex, approach to understanding contract terms and filling contractual gaps. In the absence of evidence that judges can competently carry out this difficult task, one might draw the tentative conclusion that the self-enforcement framework provides the basis for an economic argument in favor of formal contract interpretation methods.

6 Conclusion

Klein has made a number of seminal contributions to the law and economics of contracting. The cumulative impact of these contributions on our economic knowledge of contractual arrangements is substantial. Klein's work has improved our knowledge of franchise contracts, block booking, RPM, exclusive dealing, shelf space contracts, exclusive territories, and vertical integration. These contributions have not only improved our economic state of knowledge about contracts, but significantly improved antitrust policy.

The sum of these individual contributions, however, understates the essence of Klein's contributions to law and economics. More important than any of these individual contributions is the analytical framework Klein developed to understand the role of contract terms in providing marginal incentives to perform against some court-enforceable proxy, and also to facilitate self-enforcement by creating a premium stream that will be lost upon termination. This framework reconciled two stylized 'facts' of contracting: (1) the ubiquity of incomplete contracts, and (2) the importance of private enforcement. Rather than assume away the critically important elements of contracting, Klein's work can be characterized as increasing our understanding of contractual arrangements in the real world. The same commitment to analysis of real world economics explains Klein's work in vertical restraints, and in particular, the rejection of the overly simplistic models of retail competition in the conventional economics literature in favor of a more realistic approach that grapples with important institutional details. It is this more realistic approach, embracing rather than assuming away the complexities associated with the reality, which has generated Klein's important economic insights about contractual relationships.

Contractual arrangements between sophisticated parties can be incredibly difficult to understand. This difficulty is further enhanced by understanding that contractual arrangements, including vertical integration, do not merely provide incentives to perform, but also shift reputational capital between parties to facilitate performance. Increasing our economic knowledge of contracts and their terms in this complex environment requires significant attention to detail, knowledge of the law and relevant institutions, an understanding of the industry in which the contracts are adopted, as well as the economic incentives of the parties. Meaningful contributions do not come easily or without significant investment. Klein's pioneering work over the past 30 years has not only left us with a much greater understanding of contractual arrangements, but also provides a model for law and economics scholars and economists motivated to explain real world phenomena, rather than merely producing blackboard insights.

References

Beales, J. Howard, and Timothy J. Muris. 1993. *State and Federal Regulation of National Advertising*. Washington DC: American Enterprise Institute.

Ben-Shahar, Omri. 1999. 'The Tentative Case against Flexibility in Commercial Law'. *Chicago Law Review* 66:781.

Bhattacharyya, Sugato, and Francine Lafontaine. 1995. 'Double-Sided Moral Hazard and the Nature of Share Contracts'. *Rand Journal of Economics* 26:761–78.

Brickley, James A., and Frederick H. Dark. 1987. 'The Choice of Organizational Form in the Case of Franchising'. *Journal of Financial Economics* 18:401–420.

Brickley, James A., Frederick H. Dark, and Michael S. Weisbach. 1991a. 'The Economic Effects of Franchise Termination Laws'. *Journal of Law & Economics* 34:101–32.

Brickley, James A., Frederick H. Dark, and Michael S. Weisbach. 1991b. 'An Agency Perspective on Franchising'. *Financial Management* 20.

Bull, Clive. 1987. 'The Existence of Self-Enforcing Implicit Contracts'. *Quarterly Journal of Economics* 102(1):147–60.

Casadesus-Masanell, Ramon and Daniel F. Spulber. 2000. 'The Fable of Fisher Body'. *Journal of Law & Economics* 43:67–104.

Coase, Ronald H. 2006. 'The Conduct of Economics: The Example of Fisher Body and General Motors'. *Journal of Economics & Management Strategy* 15 255–78.

Coase, Ronald H. 2000. 'The Acquisition of Fisher Body by General Motors'. *Journal of Law & Economics* 43:15–31.

Coase, Ronald H. 1937. 'The Nature of the Firm'. *Economica* 4:386–405.

Coeurderoy, Regis, and B. Quélin. 1997. 'Transaction Cost Economics: A Survey of Empirical Research on Vertical Integration'. *Revue d'Economie Politique*, 107:145–81.

Crocker, Keith J., and Scott E. Masten. 1996. 'Regulation and Administered Contracts Revisited: Lessons from Transaction-Cost Economics for Public Utility Regulation'. *Journal of Regulatory Economics* 9:5–39.

Crocker, Keith J., and Scott E. Masten. 1991. 'Pretia ex Machina? Prices and Process in Long-Term Contracts. *Journal of Law & Economics* 34:69–99.

Eisenberg, Theodore. 1990. 'Testing the Selection Effect: A New Theoretical Framework with Empirical Tests'. *Journal of Legal Studies* 19:337–58.

Freeland, Robert F. 2000. 'Creating Holdup through Vertical Integration: Fisher Body Revisited'. *Journal of Law and Economics* 43:33–66.

Froeb, Luke. 1993. 'The Adverse Selection of Cases for Trial'. *International Review of Law and Economics* 13:317–24.

Gibbons, Robert. 2005. 'Four Formal(izable) Theories of the Firm?'. *Journal of Economic Behavior & Organization* 58:200–245.

Goetz, Charles J., and Robert E. Scott. 1981. 'Principles of Relational Contracts'. *Virginia Law Review* 67:1089–1150.

Goldberg, Victor P. 1976. 'Toward an Expanded Economic Theory of Contract'. *Journal of Economic Issues* 10:45–61.

Goldberg, Victor P., and John R. Erickson. 1987. 'Quantity and Price Adjustments in Long-Term Contracts: A Case Study of Petroleum Coke'. *Journal of Law and Economics* 30: 369–98.

Goldfine, David A.J., and Kenneth M. Vorrasi. 2004. 'The Fall of the *Kodak* Aftermarket Doctrine: Dying a Slow Death in the Lower Court'. *Antitrust Law Journal* 72:209–31.

Granitz, Elizabeth, and Benjamin Klein. 1996. 'Monopolization by "Raising Rivals' Costs": The Standard Oil Case'. *Journal of Law and Economics* 39:1.

Greif, Avner. 1993. 'Contract Enforceability and Economic Institutions in Early Trade: The Maghribi Traders' Coalition'. *American Economic Review*, 83: 525–48.

Grossman, Gene M., and Michael L. Katz. 1983. 'Plea Bargaining and Social Welfare'. *American Economic Review* 73:747–57.

Grossman, S.J., and O.D. Hart. 1986. 'The Costs and Benefits of Ownership: A Theory of Vertical and Lateral Integration'. *Journal of Political Economy* 94:691–719.

Hadfield, Gilliam K. 1994. 'Judicial Competence and the Interpretation of Incomplete Contracts'. *Journal of Legal Studies* 23:159–84.

Hart, Oliver. 1995. 'Corporate Governance: Some Theory and Implications'. *Economic Journal* 105:678–89.

Hart, Oliver D., and Sanford J. Grossman. 1986. 'The Costs and Benefits of Ownership: A Theory of Vertical and Lateral Integration'. *Journal of Political Economy* 94:961–719.

Hart, Oliver D., and Bengt Holstrom. 1987. 'The Theory of Contracts' in *Advances in Economic Theory*, edited by Mauro Baranzini. Palgrave Macmillan.

Hart, Oliver D., and John Moore. 1988. 'Incomplete Contracts and Renegotiation'. *Econometrica* 56:755–785.

Hart, Oliver D., and John Moore. 1990. 'Property Rights and the Nature of the Firm'. *Journal of Political Economy* 98:1119–58.

Hartmann, Wesley R., and Richard Gil. 2007. 'Airing Your Dirty Laundry: Vertical Integration, Reputational Capital and Social Networks'. Working paper. http://faculty-gsb.stanford.edu/ hartmann/IntegrationAndNetworks.pdf.

Hermalin, Benjamin E., Avery W. Katz, and Richard Craswell. 2007. 'Contract Law' in *Handbook of Law and Economics*, edited by A. Mitchell Polinsky and Steven Shavell. Amsterdam: North Holland.

Holmstrom, Bengt. 1999. 'Managerial Incentive Problems: A Dynamic Perspective'. *Review of Economic Studies* 66:169–82.

Holmstrom, Bengt, and Paul Milgrom. 1991. 'Multitask Principal-Agent Analyses: Incentive Contracts, Asset Ownership, and Job Design'. *Journal of Law, Economics and Organization* 7:24-52.

Holmstrom, Bengt and Paul Milgrom. 1994. 'The Firm as an Incentive System'. *American Economic Review* 84:972–91.

Holmstrom, Bengt, and Jean Tirole. 1991. 'Transfer Pricing and Organizational Form'. *Journal of Law, Economics and Organization* 7:201–28.

Hylton, Keith N. 1993. 'Asymmetric Information and the Selection of Disputes for Litigation'. *Journal of Legal Studies* 22:187–210.

Joskow, Paul L. 1988. 'Asset Specificity and the Structure of Vertical Relationships: Empirical Evidence'. *Journal of Law, Economics and Organization* 4:95-117.

Katz, Avery. 2004. 'The Economics of Form and Substance in Contract Interpretation'. *Columbia Law Review* 104:496.

Katz, Michael A., and John E. Leonard. 2004. 'Predatory Pricing or Price Leadership: An Economic and Legal Analysis'. *Midwest Law Review* 19:85–95.

Kaufmann, Patrick J., and Francine Lafontaine. 1994. 'Costs of Control: The Source of Economic Rents for McDonald's Franchisees'. *Journal of Law & Economics* 37:417–53.

Kessler, Daniel, Thomas Meites, and Geoffrey Miller. 1996. 'Explaining Deviations from the Fifty-Percent Rule: A Multimodal Approach to the Selection of Cases for Litigation'. *Journal of Legal Studies* 25:233–59.

King, Brayden, and G. Gordon Smith. 2009. 'Contracts as Organizations'. *Arizona Law Review* 51:1–45.

Kim, E. Han, Adair Morse, and Luigi Zingales. 2006. 'What has Mattered to Economics Since 1970'. Working paper. Ross School of Business. http://papers.ssrn.com/sol3/ papers.cfm?abstract_id=927429.

Klein, Benjamin. 2007. 'The Economic Lessons of Fisher Body – General Motors'. *International Journal of the Economics of Business* 14:1–36.

Klein, Benjamin. 2003. 'Exclusive Dealing as Competition for Distribution "On the Merits".' *George Mason Law Review* 12:119–62.

Klein, Benjamin. 2001. 'The Microsoft Case: What Can a Dominant Firm Do to Defend Its Market Position?' *Journal of Economic Perspectives* 15:45–62.

Klein, Benjamin. 2000. 'Fisher-General Motors and the Nature of the Firm'. *Journal of Law & Economics* 43:105–41.

Klein, Benjamin. 1999. 'Market Power in Franchise Cases in the Wake of *Kodak*: Applying Post-Contract Hold-Up Analysis to Vertical Relationships'. *Antitrust Law Journal* 67:283–326.

Klein, Benjamin. 1996. 'Why Hold-Ups Occur: The Self-Enforcing Range of Contractual Relationships'. *Economic Inquiry* 34:444–63.

Klein, Benjamin. 1995. 'The Economics of Franchise Contracts'. *Journal of Corporate Finance* 2:9–37.

Klein, Benjamin. 1993. 'Market Power in Antitrust: Economic Analysis After *Kodak*'. *Supreme Court Economic Review* 3:43–92.

Klein, Benjamin. 1988. 'Vertical Integration as Organizational Ownership: The Fisher Body-General Motors Relationship Revisited'. *Journal of Law, Economics and Organization* 4:199–213.

Klein, Benjamin. 1980. 'Transaction Cost Determinants of "Unfair" Contractual Arrangements'. *American Economic Review* 70:356–62.

Klein, Benjamin, Robert G. Crawford, and Armen A. Alchian. 1978. 'Vertical Integration, Appropriable Rents, and the Competitive Contracting Process'. *Journal of Law & Economics* 21:297–326.

Klein, Benjamin, and Roy W. Kenney. 2000. 'How Block Booking Facilitated Self-Enforcing Film Contracts'. *Journal of Law and Economics* 43:427–35.

Klein, Benjamin, and Roy W. Kenney. 1983. 'The Economics of Block Booking'. *Journal of Law & Economics* 26:497–540.

Klein, Benjamin, and Keith Leffler. 1981. 'The Role of Market Forces in Assuring Contractual Performance'. *Journal of Political Economy* 89:615–41.

Klein, Benjamin and Andres V. Lerner. 2007. 'The Expanded Economics of Free-Riding: How Exclusive Dealing Prevents Free-Riding and Creates Undivided Loyalty'. *Antitrust Law Journal* 74:473–519.

Klein, Benjamin, and Kevin M. Murphy. 2008. 'Exclusive Dealing Intensifies Competition for Distribution'. *Antitrust Law Journal* 75:433–66.

Klein, Benjamin, and Kevin M. Murphy. 1997. 'Vertical Integration as a Self-Enforcing Contractual Arrangement'. *American Economic Review* 87:415–20.

Klein, Benjamin, and Kevin M. Murphy. 1988. 'Vertical Restraints as Contract Enforcement Mechanisms'. *Journal of Law and Economics* 31:265–97.

Klein, Benjamin, and Lester F. Saft. 1985. 'The Law and Economics of Franchise Tying Contracts'. *Journal of Law & Economics* 28:345–61.

Klein, Benjamin, and John Shepard Wiley. 2003. 'Competitive Price Discrimination as an Antitrust Justification for Intellectual Property Refusals to Deal'. *Antitrust Law Journal* 70:599–642.

Klein, Benjamin, and Joshua D. Wright. 2007. 'The Economics of Slotting Contracts'. *Journal of Law and Economics* 50:421–54.

Klick, Jonathan, Bruce H. Kobayashi, and Larry E. Ribstein. 2007. 'Incomplete Contracts and Opportunism in Franchising Arrangements'. *American Law & Economics Association Annual Meetings*, available at: http://works.bepress.com/ribstein/17

Kobayashi, Bruce. 2005. 'Does Economics Provide A Reliable Guide to Regulating Commodity Bundling By Firms? A Survey of the Economic Literature'. *Journal of Competition Law and Economics* 1:707.

Krier, James E., and Stewart J. Schwab. 1997. 'The Cathedral at Twenty-Five: Citations and Impressions'. *Yale Law Journal* 106:2121–48.

Laffont, Jean-Jacques, Patrick Rey, and Jean Tirole. 1998. 'Network Competition: I. Overview and Nondiscriminatory Pricing'. *Rand Journal of Economics* 29:1–37.

Laffont, Jean-Jacques, Patrick Rey, and Jean Tirole. 1998. 'Network Competition: II. Price Discrimination'. *Rand Journal of Economics* 29:38–56.

Lafontaine, Francine. 1992. 'Agency Theory and Franchising: Some Empirical Results'. *RAND Journal of Economics* 23:263–83.

Lafontaine, Francine, and Kathryn L. Shaw. 1999. 'The Dynamics of Franchise Contracting: Evidence from Panel Data'. *Journal of Political Economy* 107:1041–80.

Lafontaine, Francine, and Margaret Slade. 2007. 'Vertical Integration and Firm Boundaries: The Evidence'. *Journal of Economic Literature* 45:629–85.

Landes, William M., and Richard A. Posner. 1996. 'Heavily Cited Articles in Law'. *Chicago-Kent Law Review* 71:825–40.

Levin, Johnathan. 2003. 'Relational Incentive Contracts'. *American Economic Review* 93:835–57.

Lott, John R. 1988. 'Brand Names, Ignorance, and Quality Guaranteeing Premiums'. *Applied Economics* 20:165–76.

Lyons, Richard K. 1996. 'Optimal Transparency in a Dealer Market with an Application to Foreign Exchange'. *Journal of Financial Intermediation* 5:225–54.

Nalebuff, Barry. 1987. 'Credible Pretrial Negotiation'. *Rand Journal of Economics* 18:198–210.

Macaulay, Stewart. 1963. 'Non-Contractual Relations in Business: A Preliminary Study'. *American Sociological Review* 28:55–67.

MacLeod, W.B. and J.M. Malcomson. 1993. 'Investments, Holdup, and the Form of Market Contracts'. *American Economic Review* 83:811–37.

Marvel, Howard P. 1982. 'Exclusive Dealing'. *Journal of Law and Ecnomics* 25:1–26.

Masten, Scott E. 2000. 'Symposium: Empirical Research in Commercial Transactions' Comments on Miwa and Ramseyer's 'Rethinking Relationship-Specific Investments'. *Michigan Law Review* 98:2668–77.

Masten, Scott E., and Stéphane Saussier. 2000. 'Econometrics of Contracts: An Assessment of Developments in the Empirical Litterature of Contracting'. *Revue d'Economie Industrielle* 92:215–37.

McGee, John. 1958. 'Predatory Price Cutting: The Standard Oil (N.J.) Case'. *Journal of Law and Economics* 1:137.

Muris, Timothy. 1981. 'Opportunistic Behavior and the Law of Contracts'. *Minnesota Law Review* 65:521.

Muris, Timothy. 2003. 'Improving the Economic Foundations of Competition Policy'. *George Mason Law Review* 12:1.

Muris, T., and J.H. Beales. 1995. 'The Foundations of Franchise Regulation: Issues and Evidence'. *Journal of Corporate Finance* 2:157.

Pitofsky, Robert. 1983. 'In Defense of Discounters: The No-Frills Case for a Per Se Rule Against Vertical Price Fixing'. *Georgetown Law Journal* 71:1487–96.

Posner, E. 2003. 'Economic Analysis of Contract Law After Three Decades: Success or Failure?' *Yale Law Journal* 112:829.

Posner, E. 1998. 'The Parol Evidence Rule, the Plain Meaning Rule, and the Principles of Contractual Interpretation'. *Penn Law Review* 146:533.

Posner, E., K. Eggleston, and R. Zeckhauser. 2000. 'The Design and Interpretation of Contracts: Why Complexity Matters'. *Northwestern Law Review* 95:91.

Posner, Richard A. 2005. 'The Law and Economics of Contract Interpretation'. *Texas Law Review* 83:1581–614.

Posner, Richard A., and Lucian Bebchuck. 2006. 'One-Sided Contracts in Competitive Consumer Markets'. *Michigan Law Review* 104:827–36.

Priest, George L. 1987. 'The Current Insurance Crisis and Modern Tort Law'. *Yale Law Journal* 96:1521–90.

Priest, George L., and Benjamin Klein. 1984. 'The Selection of Disputes for Litigation'. *Journal of Legal Studies* 13:1.

Rey, P., and J. Tirole. 1986. 'The Logic of Vertical Restraints'. *American Economic Review* 76:921–39.

Rey, Patrick, and Joseph Stiglitz. 1995. 'The Role of Exclusive Territories in Producers' Competition'. *Rand Journal of Economics* 26:431–51.

Rubin, Paul H. 1978. 'The Theory of the Firm and the Structure of the Franchise Contract'. *Journal of Law and Economics* 21:223–33.

Schmitz, Patrick W. 2008. 'Incomplete Contracts, the Hold-up Problem, and Asymmetric Information'. *Economics Letters* 99:119–22.

Schwartz, Alan. 1992. 'Relational Contracts in the Courts: An Analysis of Incomplete Agreements and Judicial Strategies'. *Journal of Legal Studies* 21:271–318.

Schwartz, Alan, and Robert E. Scott. 2003. 'Contract Theory and the Limits of Contract Law'. *Yale Law Journal* 113:541.

Shapiro, Fred R. 1996. The Most-Cited Law Review Articles Revisited. *Chicago-Kent Law Review* 71:751–80.

Shavell, Steven M. 1995. 'Alternative Dispute Resolution: An Economic Analysis'. *Journal of Legal Studies* 24:1–28.

Shelanski, Howard A., and Peter G. Klein. 1995. 'Empirical Research in Transaction Cost Economics: A Review and Assessment'. *Journal of Law, Economics and Organization* 11:335–61.

Siegelman, Peter, and John J. Donohue III. 1995. 'The Selection of Employment Discrimination Disputes for Litigation: Using Business Cycle Effects to Test the Priest-Klein Hypothesis'. *Journal of Legal Studies* 24:427–62.

Smith, John Maynard. 1982. 'Evolution and the Theory of Games'. Cambridge University Press.

Spier, Kathryn E. 1992. 'The Dynamics of Pretrial Negotiation'. *The Review of Economic Studies* 59:93–108.

Stigler, George J. 1963. 'Public Regulation of the Securities Markets'. *Journal of Business* 37:117.

Telser, Lester G. 1960. 'Why Should Manufactureres Want Fair Trade?' *Journal of Law and Economics* 3:86–105.

Waldfogel, Joel. 1990. 'The Selection Hypothesis and the Relationship between Trial and Plaintiff Victory'. *Journal of Political Economy* 103:229–60.

Whinston, Michael D. 2003. 'On the Transaction Cost Determinants of Vertical Integration'. *Journal of Law, Economics, and Organization* 19:1–23.

Whinston, Michael D., and Ilya Segal. 2003. 'Robust Predictions for Bilateral Contracting with Externalities'. *Econometrica* 71:757–791.

Williamson, Oliver E. 1991. 'Strategizing, Economizing, and Economic Organization'. *Strategic Management Journal* 12:7594.

Williamson, Oliver E. 1971. 'The Vertical Integration of Production: Market Failure Considerations'. *American Economic Review* 61:112–23.

Williamson, Oliver E., and Michael Riordan. 1985. 'Asset Specificity and Economic Organization'. *International Journal of Industrial Organization* 3:365–78.

Williamson, Oliver E., Michael Wachter, and Jeffrey Harris. 1975. 'Understanding the Employment Relation: The Analysis of Idiosyncratic Exchange'. *The Bell Journal of Economics* 6:25078.

Williamson, Oliver E. 1973. 'Markets and Hierarchies: Some Elementary Considerations'. *American Economic Review* 63:316–25.

Wright, Joshua D. 2009. 'Antitrust Analysis of Category Management: *Conwood v. U.S. Tobacco*'. *Supreme Court Economic Review* 17.

Wright, Joshua D. 2007. 'Slotting Contracts and Consumer Welfare'. *Antitrust Law Journal* 74:439–66.

Wright, Joshua D. 2001. 'Vons Grocery and the Concentration-Price Relationship in Grocery Retail'. *UCLA Law Review* 48:543–79.

8   Buchanan and Tullock on law and economics
Robert D. Tollison

1   Introduction

A discussion of the contributions of James M. Buchanan and Gordon Tullock to the literature of law and economics requires some initial delineation of such an assignment. Both men have made voluminous contributions to economics and other disciplines that in one way or another could be said to be related to law and economics. Where does one draw the line in assessing what is relevant and what is not?

As a working rule, I define law and economics as the application of economic theory and method to explaining law and legal institutions. In this sense, Tullock has a body of work that is directly in the field of law and economics. He has, for example, an early book on the subject (Tullock 1971b). Buchanan's work is less directly connected to law and economics as such, although his work in other areas like public choice and philosophy is highly relevant to law and economics in general. This distinction between the work of the two scholars makes it easier to cover Tullock's contributions. Buchanan has a number of direct contributions, but his influence on law and economics derives basically from his enormously influential work in other areas. This distinction between the two authors and the issues it raises will become clearer as the chapter unfolds.

The chapter is organized simply. The joint contributions of Buchanan and Tullock are covered first. Then the individual contributions of each man, starting with Buchanan, are discussed. The general approach consists in not being copious or encyclopedic but aims to say enough about each topic to give the reader a good idea of what the essential contribution is. Adequate references will be provided for anyone wishing to dig deeper (see Brennan et al. 1999 and Rowley 2004).

2   Joint work

2.1   The Calculus of Consent

Buchanan and Tullock (1962) is a classic in the field of public choice, and is also a foundational work for associated efforts to expand the explanatory domain of modern economics in such areas as law and economics. The *Calculus* features a number of topics and results, including constitutional political economy, voting rules, logrolling (vote trading), and so on. There are two levels of analysis in the book. One is at the constitutional stage where the rules are selected. The other is the analysis of in-period politics (or how the sausage is made). There are various examples of concepts and analysis in the *Calculus* that are germane to law and economics. Let us start with a constitutional issue.

One of the central lessons of the *Calculus* is that there is nothing magic about simple majority rule. Depending on the costs and benefits, a constitutional decision maker could choose a more or less restrictive voting rule. For example, where the ultimate consequences of an adverse collective decision are high to the representative voter, stricter voting rules will be observed. One thus observes stricter voting rules for veto overrides, treaties, constitutional amendments, Security Council voting at the United Nations, and so forth. The *Calculus* offers a rationale for such voting rules as part of the architecture of democracy.

Of course, the prevalence of simple majority rule to govern in-period politics suggests the strong survival value of this institution. Nonetheless, Buchanan and Tullock (1962) provide a sound basis for the existence and appeal of stricter voting rules. Perhaps in a 1000 years citizens will live in polities featuring supermajority voting rules. Be this as it may, the relevance of voting rules to law and economics is transparent. At the appellate level, for example, judicial decision making embodies voting procedures featuring simple majority rule. To some extent, then, judicial behavior can be understood in terms of the normal analyses of coalition formation, logrolling, defection, and so on. The endless discussion of five–four Supreme Court decisions is a good example of this type of problem.

Turning to an issue affecting in-period politics, another central result in the *Calculus* is that simple majority rule (especially when combined with geographic representation) is a fertile breeding ground for logrolling and the passage of unproductive legislation (pork). You vote for my tariff, and I will vote for your new post office. The reason is simply that simple majority rule opens the door to taxing those outside the winning coalition to benefit the fortunate $N/2 + 1$. In the limit public investments will be about half as productive as alternative private investments. This part of the *Calculus* presages the modern interest-group theory of government in that is demonstrates how small groups of voters can win legislative support for their proposals. The few win at the expense of the many. Given that interest groups and their effects on economics is a central issue in law and economics, this part of the *Calculus* is clearly relevant to such work. Indeed, law and economics scholars (Landes and Posner 1975) have developed models of judicial behavior based on interest-group models.

Nonetheless, the choice of rules and institutions is a black box. To the extent that it has any content, one could observe that the people and groups that dominate normal politics would likely dominate constitutional politics, as was the case with the US Constitution (McGuire and Oshfeldt 1984). Various ideas about how to generate disinterested behavior at the constitutional stage of decision making have been proposed to get around this problem, but the issue of how to obtain better institutions and better people at the constitutional stage, if decision makers are not angels but ordinary mortals, remains with us as a practical manner. This approach naturally brings ethics into the discussion since disinterest is equated with fairness. This is a hallmark of Buchanan's work.

The US Constitution was a powerfully productive document, propelling a young nation along a path to prosperity and freedom. And it was crafted by individuals (Madison, Jay, Hamilton) who fit the general idea of disinterested actors. Yet it did nothing about slavery, and arguably, the individuals who wrote it wound up running the government they created for the next 30 to 40 years (capture?). The design of better institutions starts with the design of better institutions to choose the rules we live under. The difficulty of this problem cannot be understated. Think of it this way. Suppose we convened a constitutional convention today in the US? Who would participate? What would happen? What type of institutions would be selected?

We often forget that we abandoned a pretty good form of government when we adopted the Constitution, namely, the Articles of Confederation. After all, we fought and won the Revolutionary War under the Articles. This was a form of government in which power flowed from the bottom up. States could refuse to go along with policies with which they disagreed, thereby limiting moves by the central government that did not produce something like a consensus. For the most part the Articles have a bad reputation because of the issue of slavery and secession. But set aside social issues and consider economic issues such as tariffs or pork-barrel spending. It seems clear that the ability of lower units to opt out of policies that are not in their self-interest would deter tariffs and other costly policies. Viewed in this way, selective secession is not such a bad idea.

These are a limited number of examples of how the *Calculus* relates to the field of law and economics. Basically, it offers a rich understanding of the architecture of democracy: how the rules are chosen and how the sausage is made. There is much in the book that I have not covered, but I think the point is made. The *Calculus* is a foundational work for scholars in law and economics. I have not checked, but I dare say that the *Calculus* is a heavily cited reference in journals of legal scholarship, a type of market test for the importance of such a work.

2.2 Theory of regulation

Administrative law and regulation is an important topic in law and economics. The theory of regulation has emerged in a number of different directions since Stigler's (1971) paper on the subject. One important development in the theory is due to Buchanan and Tullock (1975), who offered a public choice explanation for why we observe firms sometimes seeking to impose costly regulations on their industry. They present a model of 'heterogeneous' firms in which some firms have a comparative advantage in dealing with such costly regulation and hence could under certain conditions benefit from seeing the costly regulation put in place. The process works this way. Some firms are low-cost producers. The regulation raises their costs, but it also raises rivals' costs, some of which will be forced to exit the industry, thereby forcing market price to rise. The increase in price exceeds the increase in costs for the low-cost firms, and the wealth of these firms increases. Firms in such situations will find it in their self-interest to lobby for costly regulation.

This insightful paper became the basis of subsequent work, such as Marvel's (1977) classic paper on the British Factory Acts and other contributions to the theory of regulation.

2.3 Other joint work

There are only a few other joint papers by the two men, some of which are well removed from a connection to law and economics. Two related papers are a paper on monopoly (Buchanan and Tullock 1968) and a paper on the growth of government (Buchanan and Tullock 1977). In the monopoly paper, they make the useful distinction that monopoly rents are capitalized so that existing owners of the monopoly only earn a normal rate of return on their investment. Antitrust attempts to break up the monopoly therefore pose a distributional issue, in that the original monopolist probably has long since cashed in his chips and moved to the south of France. The growth of government paper stresses the link between growth in the number of public employees and their salaries as a basic causal factor in the expansion of the public sector. The linkage is that public employees are much more likely to vote than other parts of the population.

3 Buchanan

Buchanan's contributions to law and economics are primarily found in basic works such as the *Calculus* and *The Limits of Liberty* (Buchanan 1975) and not in journal articles. For example, there are only five entries in his *Collected Works* listed under the category 'Economists,

Efficiency, and the Law'. I am thus left with the same problem as before of linking Buchanan's general work to law and economics. My plan is the following. I first discuss Buchanan's (1975) discussion of 'Law as Public Capital' (Chapter 7 in *The Limits of Liberty*). I then turn to individual papers related to law and economics including a paper on the Coase Theorem.

3.1   Law as a public good

The idea of law as a public good emerges in the broader analytical setting of *Limits* wherein Buchanan analyzes the general issue of how (or if) individuals can emerge from anarchical states into stable societies. In this regard, his basic point is that law-abiding behavior is a pure external economy; in essence, an individual only generates benefits for others if she plays by the rules. This means that the provision of law-abiding behavior is a public good, and faces the age-old issue of free (or cheap) riding and underprovision. In the limit there would be no compliance and no social order.

Buchanan recognizes that this is a model of a limiting case. For example, he stresses that smaller groups of individuals (traders) may follow rules because in addition to providing a public good to the group, such behavior is in the direct self-interest of the individual trader. Put more commonly, a reputation for keeping one's word is a valuable asset in itself. What, then, is the prediction of the model? Law-abiding behavior will emerge in small groups of traders who transact with one another on a regular basis. And this type of behavior is translated in a modern setting through institutions such as the markets for reputation and brand names. There is thus a route out of the jungle.

But this is a double-edged sword. In some cases the cost of rule compliance will be greater than the benefits, leading to anarchy. As Buchanan stresses, individuals can provide public bads as well as public goods. His crucial point is that laws and adherence to laws represent a form of public capital which is central to the maintenance of a social order. Economists are fond of saying that a society's resource base consists of land, labor, capital, and entrepreneurship. Buchanan's point is that we need to add legal institutions as a form of capital to this list. This is a well-recognized point today in the empirical study of economic growth, but it was not so widely appreciated in 1977.

In a way Buchanan teaches us in *Limits* that we live at the edge of the jungle. The fact that law-abiding behavior is a public good means that a society must be vigilant against deviations from this norm and that law enforcement is not simply a cost/benefit analysis for individual actors or law enforcers. If the maintenance of social order depends on law enforcement, then the benefits of law enforcement are always going to be high relative to the costs.

3.2   Buchanan on Posner

Buchanan (1974) wrote a review article about Posner's (1977) law and economics textbook. The title gives away the content -- 'Good Economics -- Bad Law'. Buchanan takes Posner to task for failing to recognize the limits of a legal regime in which the maximization of economic efficiency is the only goal. Not only are agents poorly motivated to do this, but the application of such a principle will not work where exchange is not voluntary (rape).[1]

---

[1]   I do not think that Posner considered forced exchange as a case where economic efficiency had any meaning.

Buchanan is basically worried that Posner wishes to have all other legal norms and precedents negated in favor of a voluntary exchange standard. As discussed above, Buchanan views these other norms and precedents as part of a public capital stock that plays an important role in society. The fact that such institutions persist means that they have passed a sort of 'test' of their reliability.

Actually, there would appear to be plenty of room for agreement between Buchanan and Posner. Posner wants judges to apply good economics in their work, and it is clear that this would be a good thing even to Buchanan. One does not have to view Posner's enterprise as a wholesale replacement of existing legal procedures. Rather it can be seen in a friendlier light that a little more economic commonsense at the margin would be helpful to the legal process. Hence, it is useful to instruct potential jurists, and even sitting jurists, in basic economics, and this is what Posner's textbook and the subsequent growth of law and economics courses in law schools has done. Better economics, better law, at the margin.

3.3   Buchanan on Coase
Buchanan (1973) has a little known paper about the Coase Theorem, a topic central to law and economics. His point is simple and important. In his view, neither Pigou nor Coase takes into account the institutional structure of an externality. In Coase the decision maker only has to assign property rights and all is well. In Pigou the decision maker must implement a liability rule in a value-maximizing fashion. Buchanan's point is that neither of these institutional assumptions is likely to hold in practice. In a world with rent seeking, logrolling, corruption, bureaucracy, majority rule, and so on, it is folly to think that Coase's allocation-neutral result is going to be easy to replicate. And Pigou's approach equally flounders on the shores of bureaucratic ineptitude and incentives. What is needed is more focus on the institutional structure of externality problems. How (auctions?) and under what conditions (administratively?) are property rights defined, assigned, and enforced? How does rent seeking affect the social costs of property rights assignments? I could go on, but I think the reader can see the importance of Buchanan's point.

3.4   Conclusion
I hope the reader will keep in mind that I have by no means covered the landscape of all of Buchanan's contributions to law and economics. I have focused on obvious cases and tried to give some idea of his general approach to the subject. In truth, virtually all of his work is foundational to law and economics. Perhaps the most striking characteristic of his work is the stress on the fairness and ethics of process rather than particular outcomes or policies.

4   Tullock
Tullock's work in law and economics came primarily at the beginning of the law and economics movement (Tullock 1971b, 1980). It is fair to say that along with Coase, Posner, and Becker, Tullock was a co-founder of law and economics.[2] Nonetheless, his work has had very little influence on the field, a subject well discussed by Goetz (1987). This paradox is unfortunate because it is the peculiarities of Tullock's approach and analysis that are interesting (more on this below). My approach will be to explain Tullock's approach and several

---

[2]   It is also worth noting that Tullock is trained as a lawyer not an economist.

prominent themes in his work in order to give the reader a general idea of Tullock's contributions in this area.

4.1   Method

Tullock is a utilitarian in his approach to legal processes, basically ruling out ethical considerations. In *The Logic of the Law*, he states that he will use the principles of modern welfare economics to evaluate legal systems. By this he means a 'loose' application of a Paretian logic in which parties will see fit to adopt 'better' legal processes because of the gains from trade.[3] In this spirit he applies novel cost/benefit analyses to various aspects of the legal system such as judges, juries, criminal behavior, common law, litigation, lawyers, and so on. His conclusions have upset many apple carts, which is a reason why his work has not penetrated the law and economics literature very much at all. None of this, however, goes to the merits of Tullock's work, which is endlessly fascinating and insightful. I would rather say that Tullock's work in this area is overlooked and underappreciated.

4.2   Optimal speed limits

The Benthamite in Tullock (1971b, pp. 140–146) can be easily demonstrated in his discussion of optimal speed limits. As always, Tullock is interested in minimizing the social costs of legal constraints such as a speed limit. This is fundamental to his approach to the law. Obviously, the choice of a speed limit can be reduced to such considerations. The lower the limit (if enforced), the fewer are traffic fatalities and the higher are the costs of traveling by car (unless the occupants enjoy the drive). The latter costs are simply the opportunity costs of the time spent driving (lost wages), and the former fatalities are the costs of human mortality and morbidity caused by automobile accidents due to speeding. Tullock argues that it is not a great feat to put numbers on these concepts so that an 'optimal' speed limit can be derived. This would obviously be at the point where the marginal costs of an increase in the limit just equaled the marginal benefits.

One can, of course, raise various practical objections to this approach. More accident-prone stretches of road will have lower speed limits (as they do now). And the calculation may be more complicated than it appears because accidents may not be a function of speed alone but speed plus the variance of speed across drivers along a given stretch of road.[4] But the point is not about speed limits; it is about minimizing the social costs of a law. Throughout *Logic* and his other work on law and economics, this is the way Tullock analyzes the law, with often novel and unusual conclusions. Jeremy Bentham is alive and well as Tullock goes about his calculations with only a minor bow to other considerations, such as ethics. It is also easy to see how this approach can be generalized to other legal constraints. Marginal deterrence, for example, is a key issue in discussions of the effectiveness of the death penalty in deterring murders, but surely not the only consideration.

---

[3]   His approach is analogous to the 'efficiency' result in Becker's (1983) model of interest groups.

[4]   Note the further complications due to the fact that roads are not privately owned and are typically not priced.

4.3 Judges

Tullock's analysis of judicial behavior is interesting but somewhat inconclusive (Goetz 1987). He addresses the issue in both *Logic* and *Trials on Trial* (1980).

Oddly enough, there is not a vast literature on the motivation of judges. Given that federal judges have life tenure and a fixed nominal wage, I suppose this is not surprising. Under such circumstances, economics would not predict that very much effort would be forthcoming from judges. Yet there is virtually no evidence to support shirking by federal judges any more than by college professors, some of whom have the same type of employment contract.

More to the point, Tullock stresses that judges may be subject to lack of motivation and to bureaucratic imperatives with respect to the decisions they reach. Consider the issue of prison crowding. When sentencing a convicted defendant, the judge has precious little incentive to take account of the size of the total prisoner population relative to available prison space. The judge is in what may be called a 1/N situation and behaves in accordance with his private costs rather than responding to external costs of prison crowding. Prison space is a 'commons', and the judge's incentives lead her to 'overuse' the commons.

Tullock (1971a) makes the same type of argument with respect to the crime rate. He argues that individual judges will free ride with respect to the overall level of criminal activity in their sentencing behavior and show too much leniency. He thereby offers a clear rationale for sentencing guidelines.

Tullock offers us no remedies for what he views as lapses in judicial incentives. As discussed below, Tullock (1971b) prefers an inquisitorial or continental legal system characterized by judicial rather than jury decision making, but he never quite explains how these more powerful judges would be motivated to overcome the issues discussed just above (Goetz 1987). He simply assumes that the costs of litigation would be lower in the inquisitorial system.

The problem is a good one, and I can only make a stab at possible answers. We could obviously raise judicial pay. This would not only attract more able candidates for the bench, but it would also deter free riding and corruption (Becker and Stigler 1974). We could also examine the behavior (at the state level in the US) of elected versus appointed judges. Elected judges tend to be more plaintiff-friendly, but their sentencing behavior in criminal cases bears a closer look.

Be all this as it may, the hallmark of Tullock's treatment of judges is the application of public choice principles to their behavior. As Goetz (1987) stresses, this was quite predictable and natural.

4.4 Common law

Tullock (1997) has extensively critiqued common law judicial institutions and procedures. As he says, he prefers Napolean to Blackstone. In this regard Tullock has extensively analyzed common law versus continental legal processes, and he makes a cogent argument that on most counts, the continental approach produces better outcomes at a lower total cost. He does not trust juries, and argues (based on evidence) that juries basically do not know what they are doing or even the facts of the case in front of them. Better to have a trained judge to sift through the arguments and evidence. In a statistical sense, Tullock is arguing that the trained judge will make fewer type II errors (accepting the null hypothesis when it is false) than a jury. Tullock's attitude toward the jury system can best be summarized by the old question, would you want your gall bladder taken out by a jury?

His basic objection to the common law system is that it proceeds on an adversarial basis and is therefore very expensive to operate. As such, he would argue that the common law system is a (much) more costly way to make legal decisions. Common law systems have more lawyers, more cases, and more resources devoted to legal argument than the continental system. Tullock envisages a legal system that more or less operates like a seminar where the judge is the professor, and the attorneys are graduate students presenting their research results at a seminar (using expert witnesses as needed), after which the judge assigns grades.

Tullock's concern is with reducing the costs of law enforcement. In his critique of common law procedures, one can see how his work in law and economics has remained outside the mainstream in law and economics. Common law jurists, attorneys, and law professors are not likely to be interested in work that, if implemented, would jeopardize their human capital. Nonetheless, I find rereading these papers and books to be refreshing, interesting, stimulating, and well worthwhile. After all, maybe he is right.

4.5 Rent seeking

Rent seeking (Tollison 1982) is the costly pursuit of wealth transfers. The concept was first introduced by Tullock (1967). His point was simple but profound. He argued that the use of real resources to capture a transfer is a social cost. The social cost is due to the fact that the resources used in this case have an opportunity cost in the economy with respect to engaging in positive-sum activities.

Tullock's point was simple, though full of potential pitfalls. He argued that expenditures made to capture a transfer were a form of social cost. The social cost arises because the resources used for transfer seeking have a positive opportunity cost somewhere else in the economy with respect to engaging in positive-sum activities. Transfer seeking is at best a zero-sum activity in that it simply shuffles dollars among people and groups and is probably negative-sum if traditional deadweight costs result as a by-product of such activities. Social costs clearly arise in the process by which resources are shifted from positive-to zero- and negative-sum activities. Rent seeking thus embodies a social cost in terms of the foregone product of the resources employed in rent seeking.

There have been numerous subsequent contributions to the theory and measurement of rent seeking (Tollison 1997). In positive economic terms the theory of rent seeking is the basis of the interest-group theory of government (McCormick and Tollison 1981, Becker 1983). Rent seeking in this regard is synonymous with lobbying. In normative economic terms, rent seeking represents an additional social cost of regulation, monopolies, and crime. This is primarily the sense in which Tullock introduced the concept and the way he has used it in his work on law and economics. For example, his treatment of the common law adversarial process stresses the waste of resources caused by legal argument as opposed to a judicial decision maker behaving as a disinterested (and lower cost) fact-finder. Rent seeking thus plays a pivotal role in Tullock's analysis of legal processes.

Tullock (1967) originally proposed the concept of rent seeking to apply to 'tariffs, monopolies, and theft'. Obviously, theft is a forced transfer in which victims will make costly investments in locks, police, and so on in order to control the level of criminal activity. Criminals will also spend resources to increase their criminal effectiveness and lower the probability of apprehension. The actual question to pose here is, however, do these expenditures represent a net social cost for the economy about which something could be profitably done?

Buying a lock is a response to the security of property rights in a society. This security can be produced in a variety of ways (including moral exhortation), but in the face of the relevant probabilities, buying a lock can hardly be seen as an unproductive investment. Given the prevailing ethos, a lock protects property rights, and the protection of property rights enhances the productivity of resources over what they could produce without the lock. To argue that one can be wealthier without locks and lawyers implies that there are feasible reforms in behavior that will reduce such costs. This is certainly believable, but this is exactly the burden that estimators of the costs of rent seeking face. The lock and the lawyer are only wasteful to the extent that these resources can be feasibly reallocated to more productive uses. Alternatively, contributions to churches should be regarded as substitutes for locks.

In principle, the cost of rent seeking is simply the increase in GDP that would result if a feasible way to reallocate resources from locks and lawyers to more productive uses could be found by a political entrepreneur. This figure could be high or low, but it is probably low given the ability of rent-seeking inputs to resist such reallocations. And the mere resistance of the inputs is yet another reason not to waste resources attempting such a reallocation.

The bias of the argument is apparent – the range and extent of feasible reform in the rent-seeking society is not large, and the logic of this argument is inherent in the theory of rent seeking. Reform will be resisted, and this resistance is, one-for-one, a social cost of reform.

Tullock's concept of rent seeking thus runs afoul of his welfare approach to evaluating legal reforms, such as the ones he proposes. The world is efficient, or so it seems. So the bottom line is that rent seeking is an important concept. It explains, for example, why monopolies are more costly than we thought they were when monopoly profits were treated as a transfer rather than a social cost. This is a major increase in our understanding of how the economy works, but in a normative sense it may not have much practical application in terms of the type of Paretian reform that undergirds Tullock's approach to law and economics. Indeed, entrenched interests will fight back against reform, making it all the more uncertain whether there are net social gains from, for example, deregulation.

5 Conclusion

This survey surely does not do justice to the work of these two men. Buchanan has other major work, especially in public finance and the theory of public goods which I have ignored. Tullock has major work on bureaucracy and social dilemmas which is not mentioned. Hopefully, I have said enough so that the interested reader has gotten a good idea of what each man is about and can use that as a guide to further reading of these authors. Over simplistically, Tullock is an unrepentant utilitarian, and Buchanan is a constitutional political economist. Tullock analyzes specific legal practices in cost/benefit terms. Buchanan is more concerned with the process and fairness with which these practices are selected. These two themes were joined in the *Calculus*, but over time each man's work represents the road not taken by the other.

References

Becker, Gary S. (1983), 'A Theory of Competition Among Pressure Groups for Political Influence', *Quarterly Journal of Economics*, 98, 371–400.

Becker, Gary S. and George J. Stigler (1974), 'Law Enforcement, Malfeasance, and the Compensation of Enforcers', *Journal of Legal Studies*, 3, 1–18.

Brennan, Geoffrey, Hartmut Kliemt, and Robert D. Tollison (eds) (1999), *The Collected Works of James M. Buchanan*, Indianapolis, US : Liberty Fund. 20 volumes.

Buchanan, James M. (1973), 'The Coase Theorem and the Theory of the State', *Natural Resources Journal*, 13, 579–94.

Buchanan, James M. (1974), 'Good Economics – Bad Law', *Virginia Law Review*, 60, 483–92.
Buchanan, James M. (1975), *The Limits of Liberty: Between Anarchy and Leviathan*, Chicago, US: University of Chicago Press.
Buchanan, James M. and Gordon Tullock (1962), *The Calculus of Consent: Logical Foundations of Constitutional Democracy*, Ann Arbor, US: University of Michigan Press.
Buchanan, James M. and Gordon Tullock (1968), 'The Dead Hand of Monopoly', *Anti-trust Law and Economic Review*, 1, 85–96.
Buchanan, James M. and Gordon Tullock (1975), 'Polluters' Profits and Political Response: Direct Controls Versus Taxes', *American Economic Review*, 65, 139–47.
Buchanan, James M. and Gordon Tullock (1977), 'The Expanding Public Sector: Wagner Squared' *Public Choice*, 31, 147–50.
Goetz, Charles J. (1987), 'Public Choice and the Law: The Paradox of Tullock', in Charles K. Rowley (ed.), *Democracy and Public Choice: Essays in Honor of Gordon Tullock*, Oxford, UK and New York, US: Basil Blackwell, pp. 171–80.
Landes, William M. and Richard A. Posner (1975), 'The Independent Judiciary in an Interest-group Perspective', *Journal of Law and Economics*, 18, 875–901.
Marvel, Howard P. (1977), 'Factory Regulation: A Reinterpretation of Early English Experience', *Journal of Law and Economics*, 20, 379–402.
McCormick, Robert E. and Robert D. Tollison (1981), *Politicians, Legislation, and the Economy: An Inquiry into the Interest-group Theory of Government*, Boston, US: Martinus Nijhoff.
McGuire, R.A. and R.L. Oshfeldt (1984), 'Economic Interests and the American Constitution: A Quantitative Rehabilitation of Charles A. Beard', *Journal of Economic History*, 44 (June), 509–19.
Posner, Richard A. (1977), *Economic Analysis of Law*, Boston, US: Little, Brown.
Rowley (ed.) (2004), *The Selected Works of Gordon Tullock*, Indianapolis, US: Liberty Fund. 10 volumes.
Stigler, George J. (1971), 'The Economic Theory of Regulation', *Bell Journal of Economics and Management Science*, 2, 3–21.
Tollison, Robert D. (1982), 'Rent Seeking: A Survey', *Kyklos*, 35, 575–602.
Tollison, Robert D. (1997), 'Rent Seeking', in Dennis C. Mueller (ed.), *Perspectives on Public Choice: A Handbook*, Cambridge, UK: Cambridge University Press, pp. 506–25.
Tullock, Gordon (1967), 'The Welfare Costs of Tariffs, Monopolies, and Theft', *Western Economic Journal*, 5, 224–32.
Tullock, Gordon (1971a), 'Public Decisions as Public Goods', *Journal of Political Economy*, 79, 913–16.
Tullock, Gordon (1971b), *The Logic of the Law*, New York, US: Basic Books.
Tullock, Gordon (1997), *The Case Against the Common Law*, Fairfax, US: Locke Institute.
Tullock, Gordon (1980), *Trials on Trial: The Pure Theory of Legal Procedure*, New York, US: Columbia University Press.

9 Henry Manne: intellectual entrepreneur
Larry E. Ribstein

Henry G. Manne's remarkable career has spanned path-breaking theorizing and writing, teaching, and organizing and has made him a seminal figure in law and economics. Manne began by forging the first detailed law and economics theory of the firm. But this formidable intellectual achievement was only the beginning of Manne's career. Manne understood that he needed to prepare an audience for his ideas.

Manne's second achievement was creating an extensive intellectual enterprise for the manufacture, promotion and dissemination of ideas. This included seminars bringing leading scholars together to create and discuss papers, law and economics education to train legal scholars and judges in basic economic principles and economists in basic legal principles, and a law school to create a long-term intellectual community and train tomorrow's lawyers and policymakers. Manne's influence rests at least as much on this entrepreneurial effort as on his intellectual achievements.

1. Manne's theory of the firm
In order to understand Manne's contributions to corporate theory, it is necessary to peek at the World Before Manne (WBM). In WBM, thinking about the corporation was dominated by *The Modern Corporation and Private Property* (Berle and Means 1932). Berle and Means found that each individual shareholder in the 200 largest non-financial corporations owned no more than a small fraction of the company's stock. They theorized that, given such small and scattered holdings, managers could virtually perpetuate themselves by using corporate funds to solicit proxies. Thus, a large chunk of private property in the US was controlled by non-owner managers who had little incentive to use it wisely. Berle and Means thought the solution to what they thought was a problem was to view the corporation as a political institution. The shareholders should act like good corporate citizens, think hard about how to use their vote, and certainly not sell it. In order to make shareholders into better corporate citizens, they should be given enough information to vote intelligently. Business leaders, entrusted like political leaders with large segments of the economy, should act like statesmen. And when managers and shareholders do not act as they are supposed to under this theory, they should be despised as mercenaries and banished from power.

Manne saw that missing from this picture was any appreciation of the role of markets. Berle and Means and their followers did not take account of the fact that, unlike citizens of a political entity, shareholders are not born into corporations. Rather, they willingly exchange their cash for securities at prices set in an active auction market. These prices depended on the existence of market mechanisms to constrain managers and empower the owners, giving firms a strong incentive to provide such protection. Since the corporation has survived for a long time in free markets, it makes more sense to identify the market devices that contribute to the corporation's survival than to assume that shareholders have for generations given themselves up as sheep to be shorn.

This insight motivated Manne's work throughout the 1960s and early 1970s. However, the existing theory of the firm offered Manne little help in finding the mechanisms that make corporations work. Coase (1937) had described the firm as a device for minimizing transaction costs in which control by a profit-motivated entrepreneur substituted for setting prices in markets. Coase's paper had received little attention by the time Manne started writing in the late 1950s. Moreover, Coase's theory was really no more than a sketch that posed more questions than it answered. For example, what is the source of the profit that the entrepreneur supposedly produces through his or its control? Alchian and Demsetz's (1972) theory of the entrepreneur's role in team production was a decade away when Manne started writing. What if there are many profit-sharers – how can they effectively control the manager? Jensen and Meckling's (1976) theory of agency costs was still a decade and a half away when Manne started writing. In light of these gaps in the theory of the firm, it is no wonder that Berle and Means's handy political analogy continued to dominate the field more than 40 years after these works were published.

Manne's background, which he discussed in a recent interview (Manne 2007), motivated him to look for things that made markets work rather than to doubt that they did. Manne had been raised in a commercial background and worked in his father's store in Memphis even before being exposed to the theory of free markets. He went to the University of Chicago Law School, a rare oasis in what was then the intellectual desert of American legal education. It was the home of Aaron Director, who was in turn linked by marriage to another important theoretician of free markets, Milton Friedman. Chicago was also a venue for the prominent libertarian thinker Friedrich A. Hayek, whose seminars Manne attended, and whose thinking was reflected very early in Manne's writing (Manne 1961). Manne's readings sustained him through uninspiring graduate studies at Yale, and he was prepared to hit the ground running when he entered legal academia. Though Manne entered a law teaching profession that was still solidly anchored in the tradition of law as an autonomous discipline, he was armed with theoretical tools that only much later (and partly because of his own efforts) became standard equipment for young law teachers.

Manne applied to corporations and corporate law the same rules that apply to other market institutions. As in all markets, securities markets can be expected to cause assets to flow to their highest and best use, including well-governed and well-managed firms. Business people who fail the market test, including by trying to be statesmen, will be unemployed. As we will see, by asking the right questions about what makes the firm work as a market institution, Manne was able to produce answers that were both provocative and plausible.

1.1   Early work

Very early in his career as a young legal scholar at St Louis University Manne was already discussing the themes that were to make his scholarly career. While he was still in his twenties, Manne was puncturing the prevailing myths of corporate governance. Manne (1956), reviewing a book by the manager of public relations research at General Electric advocating corporate charitable contributions, expressed the fear that

> [t]o the extent that business has moved out of its traditional profit-making function and into quasi-governmental and social welfare areas, fuel will be available to those in government who may wish to control this vast corporate power.

Manne (1958), reviewing J.A. Livingston's criticism of existing devices for disciplining managers, criticized Livingston's reliance on such self-appointed shareholder activists as Lewis Gilbert, and on improving the conscience of institutional investors. But in a discussion that provides an interesting glimpse into Manne's later work, Manne also criticizes Livingston for dismissing what Manne believes is the very important tool of the shareholder's right to sell his shares (ibid., p. 311). Manne for the first time discusses the market for control and its relationship to efficient stock markets:

> [Livingston] overlooks the obvious fact that a 'raider' in a proxy fight is not simply interested in gaining the votes of other shareholders. It may be and usually is a prerequisite to victory that he own or control a substantial block of shares. And nothing, absolutely nothing, will serve as quite the inducement for this venture as a relatively low price for the shares. This low price, of course, is often a direct result of the attitudes of many small shareholders, who, in their own infinitesimal fashion, by selling their shares, add to the probability of success of a raid on management.

Manne observed that, even if they occur infrequently, the mere threat of a proxy fight may have a 'substantial and often severe impact . . . on the management of the corporation'.[1] Later he notes that while the derivative suit may be a partial discipline, because of the business judgment rule 'the only solution to mild but continuing inefficiency will be an attempt to win corporate control. The fight for control is a mechanism by which the market operates to weed out the inefficient and less productive.'

Manne (1961) aggregated Manne's review of the prevailing paradigm of corporate governance, notably including Berle and Means (1932), and began his detailed criticism of it. This article was an important though little-noticed jumping off point for Manne's later theorizing. Manne mainly used the footnotes to weave his own views through the presentation of the views of others, and reiterated some of his points in the earlier book reviews.

Most importantly, Manne bemoaned 'the near silence of the economists' on the subject of the modern corporation (Manne 1961, p. 583). He discussed three exceptions. First, Lintner (1959), who Manne believed had 'undercut' the empirical foundation of Berle and Means by showing that capital markets do constrain corporate managers because managers rely on the capital markets rather than internally generated earnings to fund expansion (Manne 1961, p. 583). Second, Rostow (1959), as had Manne in his first book review, emphasized that corporations should maximize profits, and criticized (as Manne was often to do) the failure of managerialist theories of corporate governance 'to provide any substitute for the traditional economic defense of market allocation of scarce resources by utilization of a price mechanism' (Manne 1961, p. 584). Third, Manne discussed Friedrich Hayek's more detailed defense of the profit-maximization goal (ibid., pp. 585–8). Manne noted that, while most

---

1   Manne's discussion of whether corporate governance is actually failing as Livingston suggests includes an aside on executive compensation, which is interesting in view of the similar debates occurring fifty years later (Manne 1958, p. 313):

> One may question whether [executive compensation] is an area in which the market is operating to guarantee no more than a competitive return to the participants. The availability of managerial talent must be taken into consideration; it is a relatively scarce commodity. One wonders all the more when one sees Mr. Livingston's list of the 22 top paid corporate executives in the country, omitting stock option and deferred payment plans. Perhaps it is only envy which makes us concerned by these figures but they do not disturb.

writers saw a danger in corporate power, Hayek saw that the 'historical enemy of individual liberties has been political power' (ibid, p. 586).

Manne (1961) began by noting that Manne's footnote criticisms of the existing paradigm were 'not intended to present an integrated theory of the corporation', but that '[i]n time I hope to offer such a work'. Manne then concluded that 'the single weakest factor in the current intellectual development of a corporate philosophy is the lack of a coherent theory of how corporations should work when they have grown large' (ibid., p. 587). In this article, Manne offered some hints of what his complete theory would look like. In discussing Rostow's defense of the corporate raider, Manne notes (ibid., p. 584, n. 85), that '[t]he implication of his remarks is that there is need for an economic study of the "market" for corporate managers', as well as of the markets for capital and for shareholders' votes – the three markets that later were to form the foundation of the broad theory of the corporation in Manne (1967a).

In a paper published the following year, Manne began to deliver on his promise and fill the gap he had identified in corporate theory.

1.2   'The "Higher Criticism" of the Modern Corporation' (1962)

In 'Higher Criticism', Manne laid out his basic challenge to the prevailing wisdom concerning corporate law. Manne identified the problem with Berle and Means (1932) as their 'belief that the modern corporation could no longer be analyzed in traditional economic terms' (Manne 1962, p. 407). That insight had several important implications. First, Manne observed that there is a market for managers (ibid., p. 402, n. 10), and that this market determines how profits are allocated between managers and owners (ibid., p. 402).

Second, Manne challenged the notion in Berle and Means and elsewhere that the corporation should be analyzed as a political institution. Shareholders have purely economic incentives, and they may lack incentives to be informed (ibid., p. 412). It follows that they should be able to sell their votes (ibid., p. 411) – a significant basis of the market for control, which Manne developed in later articles.

Third, given the essentially market nature of the corporation and how it selects and compensates managers, it is absurd to conceive of corporate managers as statesmen (ibid., p. 414). Rather, Manne noted that they are best judged by their ability to earn profits for the firm (ibid., p. 415). The firms of managers who engage in charity rather than maximizing profits will be driven from competitive markets (id. pp. 416–17).

Fourth, this last observation suggests a reason why corporate managers should favor corporate social responsibility: it provides a public interest justification for monopoly power, and thus for insulating managers from market pressures (ibid., pp. 417–18).

Fifth, Manne again used the market perspective to criticize traditional notions that managers should be monitored by 'super boards' of directors or by institutional shareholders. Directors cannot analyze all aspects of managers' judgment, providing a significant basis for the business judgment rule (ibid., p. 422). Institutional investors should monitor through the market by selling their shares (ibid., p. 421).

In short, Manne showed how scholars had ignored the real economic constraints on firms. Scholars' emphasis on moral standards, constitutionalism, paternal watchdogs 'all represent disguised efforts to find an alternative to the price mechanism in economic matters.' (ibid., p. 431). Manne said:

It will be surprising if such matters as insider trading, derivative suits, cumulative voting, and many other aspects of corporation law cannot be fitted into a comprehensive economic analysis of the modern corporation. Such an analysis is needed for many reasons, but the most important advantage to be anticipated is a standard by which we may make improvements without inadvertently destroying the entire complex arrangement. Until we have developed a satisfactory body of theoretical analysis of the modern corporation, it perhaps behooves us to tread very slowly in the direction of change.

Over the next five years Manne developed the ideas in 'Higher Criticism', providing the comprehensive economic framework that had been missing from the corporate literature.

1.3 'Theoretical Aspects of Share Voting' (1964)

Manne's first step in completing the ambitious agenda set in 'Higher Criticism' was to demonstrate how voting in corporations differs from voting in politics. This paper also laid the foundation for Manne's next major article on the market for control.

In 'Share Voting', Manne continues his response to Berle and Means. They criticized corporate governance on the basis that apathetic shareholders ceded control to managers, thereby separating control from ownership. The regulatory response to the Berle and Means problem was the federal securities laws, and particularly the federal proxy rules, which gave the shareholders information in connection with corporate elections so they could act like owners. But Manne points out that, given the costs of processing information, it still may not be worthwhile for shareholders to be informed (Manne 1964, p. 1440). In other words, shareholders' apathy is rational. Giving them more to read does not significantly change the calculus.

The shareholders' solution to the apathy problem is relying on or selling their shares to those who have an incentive to incur the costs of being informed. Relying on larger shareholders is unlikely to expose the passive shareholders to harmful conflicts of interest because shareholders all have basically the same interests in maximizing profits (ibid., p. 1441). This observation was consistent with the capital assets pricing model, which was only then being developed. Even if shareholders generally have diverse preferences regarding payouts, they can invest in firms whose shareholders have compatible preferences (ibid., p. 1442).

In short, Manne saw that Berle and Means' political model of the corporation had overlooked the market forces that made the corporation work. Rather than relying on active participation by immobile shareholders, the corporation works because investments are mobile and therefore can flow easily from passive to active investors (ibid., p. 1445). Indeed, given these market forces, Manne concluded that 'the corporation is probably a far more democratic mechanism from the viewpoint of shareholders than is government from the point of view of voters' (ibid.). It follows that the federal proxy rules addressed a non-problem. Indeed, these rules may have made things worse by raising the costs of competing for corporate control, thereby subverting the control market as a solution to shareholder apathy (ibid., p. 1443).

1.4 'Mergers and the Market for Corporate Control' (1965)

Manne's most famous article is actually a 'companion article' to the share voting article discussed in the preceding section (Manne 1965, p. 110, n. 1). While the share voting article examines the sell side of the market for control, 'Mergers' discusses the buy side. This short article (only eleven pages in print) is a significant part of Manne's overall agenda in outlining an economic theory of the firm and includes several important and original insights. The article proceeds from the basic point Manne made in previous papers – corporations work as economic institutions because shareholders need not themselves actively participate in governance, but rather can sell to those who have the right economic incentives to maximize the value of control.

The paper's central point is that stock prices reflecting managerial inefficiency make takeovers attractive. Manne observes that compared to the disciplinary force of takeovers (citing the example of Louis Wolfson's fight for control of Montgomery Ward), 'the efforts of the SEC and the courts to protect shareholders through the development of a fiduciary duty concept and the shareholder's derivative suit seem small indeed' (ibid., p. 113).

An effective market for control presupposes an efficient securities market that accurately reflects the quality of a firm's management. This insight is contained in a notable footnote (ibid., p. 112, n. 10) that essentially encapsulates the efficient capital markets hypothesis, which was then only being developed and had not yet been tested. Manne began the footnote by noting that the correlation he was supposing 'would seem at first blush to raise an empirical question'. Indeed, a control market is a dubious proposition if share prices do not provide a reliable basis for testing management efficiency. But Manne was confident about proceeding without evidence of market efficiency because of 'compelling reasons. . . . for believing that this correlation [between stock prices and managerial efficiency] exists'. He theorized that profit-motivated insiders 'perform a kind of arbitrage function for their company's stock', thereby causing share prices to reflect management quality. While many uninformed shareholders also trade, these trades will be randomly distributed and therefore will not affect stock prices over time. More informed trades will influence stock prices, so that 'over some period of time it would seem that the average market price of a company's shares must be the "correct" one'.[2]

This footnote, which is merely a step in Manne's overall analysis, is remarkably prescient and original. It anticipates not only the efficient capital markets hypothesis (which itself relied on the still-developing capital assets pricing model), but also work on the mechanisms of market efficiency, synthesized twenty years later in Gilson and Kraakman's notable article (Gilson and Kraakman 1984)). The footnote also anticipates Manne's own work several years later on the economics of insider trading. And Manne even envisioned the invention of the event study by noting how the efficiency of the control market could be tested by seeing whether the price of an acquired company falls and the acquired company rises (Manne 1965) p. 119).

Manne observed that a takeover would not occur unless the premium for control was less than the cost of managerial inefficiency (ibid., p. 117). It follows that efforts to regulate the market for control may reduce the efficiency of corporate governance by raising the costs of takeovers. This observation anticipated Easterbrook and Fischel's famous takeover defenses article seventeen years later (Easterbrook and Fischel (1981)). In particular, antitrust doctrine reduces corporate efficiency to the extent that it discourages mergers. Manne noted that horizontal mergers between firms in the same industry have an important cost advantage because the competitor usually has information about the target that other firms lack

---

[2]   Manne (1964, p. 1435, and ibid., n. 23), had earlier discussed the relationship of the control market with securities markets in offering a brief but sophisticated explanation of the premium price of a tender offer.

(ibid., p. 118–19). This suggests a reason to be careful about prohibiting horizontal mergers, particularly where competitors have low costs of entry. Similarly, securities regulation may make proxy fights expensive, as, for instance, by forcing insurgents to guarantee the accuracy of statements about incumbent managers despite having little access to facts inside the corporation (ibid., p. 115, n. 18). And Berle's proposal to force control sellers to share their control premia with non-controlling shareholders would have the perverse effect of discouraging control transfers (ibid., p. 116).

1.5 'Cash Tender Offers for Shares' (1967b)

This article begins with the basic insights from the articles discussed immediately above: control is an economic good for which people compete, and information is valuable and subject to a market (Manne 1967b, p. 236). Because shareholders get 'fantastic protection' from the control market, interfering with this market may do 'profound injury' to investors (ibid., p. 237).

Manne emphasized the extent to which the market for control turns previous notions of corporate governance upside down. Though control purchasers who quickly sell the company are disparaged as 'liquidators', in fact they have an incentive to liquidate only if this is the best use of the assets. Manne suggested that 'garbagemen' would be more accurate than 'liquidators', adding, '[a]nyone for "corporate redeemer"?' (ibid., pp. 236–7, n. 14).

As in his 1965 'Mergers article', Manne praised the notorious corporate 'raider' Louis Wolfson, in a discussion that included important insights about securities markets and corporate governance, and specifically the precise mechanism by which the control market produces value (ibid., pp. 239–40, n. 23). Focusing on Wolfson's notorious takeover of Capital Transit, Manne observed that the most obvious problem with the target seemed to be its low dividend despite significant accumulated cash. However, consistent with Manne's observation about dividend policy in the 'Share Voting' article, Manne noted that low dividends alone could not affect corporate value because the firm could attract a clientele of shareholders who preferred this policy. Manne pointed out that Capital Transit's earnings had been declining for years, and that '[i]t is quite possible that accounting procedures obscured even greater losses'. Thus, the shareholders' only hope was that a savior like Wolfson would come along and buy control, thereby offering them more for their shares than they were worth under current management.

The Wolfsons of the world need the right incentive to work their magic in the control market. Because they are risk-taking entrepreneurs in the Schumpeterian sense, they are motivated by the sort of significant profit in the takeover that would justify the risk. Regulating takeovers would reduce the profits from taking control, thereby weakening the incentive that makes the control market work. In particular, Manne criticizes an article by Manuel Cohen (1966), then chair of the Securities and Exchange Commission (SEC), defending the proposed takeover legislation. Cohen's assertion that insurgents should be on an 'equal footing' with target shareholders ignored the incentives that make the control market work (Manne 1967b, p. 243). Manne said that '[m]oralistic aspirations for equality of wealth have nothing to do with rigorous analysis and clear understanding of the corporate field' (ibid., p. 241). Other proposed federal takeover regulations that would raise the costs of takeovers were similarly perverse, including requiring tendering shareholders to get the highest price (ibid., p. 248), and giving shareholders a seven-day option to withdraw (ibid., p. 251).

Instead of rules that frustrate the market for control, Manne suggested rules that would bolster the market by encouraging auctions, letting shareholders propose transactions, or forcing incumbent directors to show that they have explored feasible alternatives (ibid., p. 245).

1.6   Insider Trading and the Stock Market (1966)

This book applies Manne's basic insight that the corporation must be analyzed as an economic institution to trading in the firm's shares. Manne begins by challenging the ancient notion that insider trading should be illegal because it is immoral. Though Manne recognizes morality's role in making markets work, he emphasizes that this morality needs to be based on 'institutions, practices and consequences' (Manne 1966, p. 15). Interestingly, this idea contains the inkling of an economic theory of morality embedded in what people actually do and in the market-based consequences of their actions rather than in Kantian first principles.

Manne reviewed the slight extant economic theory of insider trading and found it wanting. The literature supposed that insider trading erodes investor confidence and thus causes investors to avoid the market (ibid., p. 8), and that it increases the risk of stock manipulation (ibid.). But there was no evidence supporting these notions. Indeed, the common law did not recognize a broad remedy for insider trading – only one based on fraud or breach of fiduciary duty (ibid., pp. 17–18, 24). Spurred more by emotion and rhetoric than evidence or analysis (ibid., pp. 8–10), Congress enacted a limited remedy for insider trading in §16(b) of the Securities and Exchange Act of 1934 (ibid., pp. 26–30). The SEC undertook no additional analysis when it later recognized an insider trading liability under its Rule 10b-5, disregarding the common law limitations on the duty (ibid., p. 46).

Manne embarked on the project that the SEC already should have done of analyzing the costs and benefits of insider trading. As in the footnote in 'Mergers', Manne hypothesized that insider trading moves transactions, and therefore prices, in the direction indicated by the information because the reservation prices of informed insiders change, while those of uninformed outsiders remain the same (ibid., p. 98). Outsiders who are in the market irrespective of price buy and sell at more accurate prices than would have existed in the absence of insider trading. Although those trading in the same direction as the insiders may be said to have been injured by higher purchase prices or lower sale prices, the winners balance the losers (ibid., p. 101). Only those who traded *because of* insider-trading-induced price fluctuations might be said to have been hurt by insider trading. But whether insider trading has caused net social losses depends in part on how many of these traders there are, and on whether the benefit to long-term investors of more accurate securities prices outweighs the losses to traders (ibid., pp. 102, 107).

Even if insider trading can be said to hurt some investors, this does not end the analysis under Manne's approach. That is because insider trading may be a valuable, if not the only, way to fully compensate entrepreneurs operating in large firms. Manne distinguished *capitalists*, who assumed and were paid for undertaking risk in the sense of predictable future variations, and *entrepreneurs* who Schumpeter viewed as *creating* uncertainty by disrupting the future (ibid., pp. 114–18, discussing Schumpeter 1942). If the entrepreneur's compensation is to adequately motivate his activity, it must reflect the profits he created (ibid., pp. 119–24). If large firms could not adequately compensate entrepreneurs, the latter would work elsewhere (ibid., p. 125).

The key to adequately compensating entrepreneurs in large firms, according to Manne, was to permit entrepreneurs to trade on inside information. Other forms of incentive compensation were more suited to those who merely manage risk rather than entrepreneurs who create uncertainty (ibid., p. 137). Salary and bonus could not isolate the entrepreneur's contribution, due partly to the limitations of accounting rules (ibid., p. 124). Profit-sharing rewards the payoffs from past investments rather than encouraging investments in the future (ibid., p. 135). Stock options had to be granted prior to the manager's innovation, so that the entrepreneur's gains depended on the number of shares he happened to own at the relevant time, not the value of the innovation (ibid., p. 136). If they cannot keep the profits from insider trading, entrepreneurs may be tempted to work for smaller companies, putting large firms at a competitive disadvantage (ibid., p. 144).

In sum, Manne showed how insider trading could be understood from the standpoint of an overall theory of the corporation. This effectively converts insider trading from a moral dilemma and item on the public regulatory agenda to a term in the corporate contract.

1.7   'Our Two Corporation Systems' (1967a)

This article ties the writings discussed above into the sort of comprehensive theory of corporate law that Manne had sketched in 'Higher Criticism'. The article includes many powerful insights concerning the function of corporate rules that were embraced in the later law and economics literature. In his analysis of differences between closely held and publicly held corporations, Manne demonstrates how the contrast between these two contexts highlights the important role of markets in shaping corporate law.

Manne situates the public corporation in three markets – for capital by entrepreneurs, the secondary market in corporate shares, and the market for control (Manne 1967a, p. 265). With respect to the first market, Manne describes the public corporation as basically a device by which entrepreneurs raise capital (ibid., p. 260). The entrepreneurs or promoters not only bring in capital but also select managers. Returning to the theme of 'Higher Criticism', Manne reiterates the inappropriateness of viewing the corporation as a political institution.

With respect to the secondary share market, Manne explains limited liability as facilitating capital-raising by enabling small investments (ibid., p. 262) – an explanation embraced by later commentators (Easterbrook and Fischel (1985), p. 96; Halpern et al. 1980, p. 130). Securities markets permit individual shareholders to express dissatisfaction with current management by selling their shares (Manne 1967a, p. 264). This avoids the need to facilitate dissolution by minority holders, which would frustrate other shareholders' need to rely on the stability of the corporation (ibid., p. 264) – an idea that Hansmann and Kraakman (2000) recently characterized as the 'essential' function of corporate law.

With respect to the market for control, Manne picks up on his observation in 'Mergers' that this market assumes efficient securities markets. Here Manne (1967a, p. 266) notes the point developed in more detail in 'Insider Trading' (1966) that prices accurately reflect reality because of trading by knowledgeable insiders.

These markets help explain many of the details of corporate law. For example, the business judgment rule, which prevents judges from second-guessing business decisions, is made possible by market discipline of managers, including the market for control (Manne 1967a, p. 273).

Analysis of the market context of public corporations assists in understanding close corporations, where these markets do not function. Manne speculates that corporation statutes dealt exclusively with public corporations because these statutes were conceived of as primarily regulatory (ibid., pp. 276–7). The corporation statutes were conscripted for use by closely held corporations as a device to avoid increasing personal income tax rates by sheltering income in corporations (ibid., p. 277). But this development caused fundamental differences between closely held and publicly held corporations to be 'overlooked' (ibid., p. 278). In contrast to the publicly held corporation, the close corporation was not a device by entrepreneurs to raise capital, but rather a way to aggregate owners' multifarious contributions. With respect to the secondary share market, owners were not passive capitalists and their management rights were not freely transferable. The absence of a ready market for shares impedes the operation of the market for control (ibid., p. 280).

The sharply different market context of close corporations leads to very different rules. With a less active market for control, the owners of closely held corporations would have less use for a hands-off business judgment rule (ibid., p. 280). They also would want restricted transferability, veto rights, direct control rights, some power to dissolve the firm, and devices for dealing with the deadlock that may result from direct shareholder power (ibid., p. 282–4).

In addition to explaining specific corporate rules, Manne sees lessons about the role and development of corporate law. He notes that the corporation evolved to meet business needs and should not be regarded as having been rooted in older business forms (ibid., p. 260). Manne attributes the permissiveness of corporate law to the ability to shop for law in a federal system (ibid., pp. 269–70, n. 20), thereby providing an early analysis of the importance of the market for corporate law. This permissiveness accommodated the needs of closely held firms by allowing them to opt out of public corporation norms (ibid., p. 284). Thus, in Manne's theory, the key to the corporation is not law but economic theory, with the federal system providing a mechanism for adapting law to theory. Manne closes with the observation that 'our general corporation laws seem to be in the process of becoming general close corporation laws with only incidental relevance to large companies' and that '[o]ne is almost tempted to suggest that the large corporation system could and would function substantially as it does if there were almost no state corporation statutes corporation statutes beyond provisions for corporation' (ibid., p. 284). These remarks anticipate Bernard Black's (1990) much later observations about the 'triviality' of state corporation law.

1.8   Wall Street in Transition (1974)

As discussed so far, Manne's theory demonstrates significant disparities between the regulatory view of the corporation and the contractual view that arises from economic theory. In *Wall Street in Transition,* Manne et al. provided a political explanation of why these disparities can arise, focusing on the important example of the federal securities laws.

Manne hypothesized that the securities laws resulted, not from investors pushing for protection from fraud, but from firms pushing for protection from competition. The anticompetitive effect of disclosure laws may not seem obvious, since they apply to all publicly traded firms. Moreover, by providing a mechanism by which firms can 'bond' their disclosure and by subsidizing the work of securities analysts, the securities laws would seem to help smaller firms compete for capital with more well-known and trusted larger firms. But Manne argued that the securities laws actually favor larger firms because of economies of scale of disclosure, and because disclosure is more burdensome for higher-risk firms, which are likely to be smaller and newer (Manne et al. 1974, p. 49). For example, rules requiring 'hot issues' to disclose their plans of operation hurt newer firms whose initial plans are unreliable (ibid., p. 52). Indeed, Manne turns on its head the rationale for the securities laws that they are necessary to reduce risk. He notes that some investors prefer risk (ibid., p. 50) and that it is the riskier firms (such as, for example, the mining industry in its infancy) that drive the economy. The securities laws, by discriminating against riskier firms, protect the established and politically influential firms from the competition they most fear – the 'unorthodox invader' that does not merely marginally affect prices or costs, but can drive existing firms (and of course their managers) out of business (ibid., pp. 31–5).

Manne suggests that we might find evidence of his theory by asking whether after the enactment of the securities laws, the rate of return of larger firms rose more than that of their competitors (ibid., p. 36), or whether private placements increased (ibid., p. 47). Interestingly, the strongest evidence of Manne's theory has come more than thirty years later with the Sarbanes-Oxley Act. Just as Manne predicted, this increase in disclosure requirements disproportionately hurt smaller firms (Kamar et al. 2006). This may help explain the observed flight of small firms from US public securities markets following the enactment of Sarbanes-Oxley.

The political explanation of securities regulation becomes more plausible given the questionable value of federal disclosure laws. Manne debunks the standard argument for securities laws as necessary to increase investor confidence in the markets: Losses, not fraud, drive investors out of the markets (Manne et al. 1974, p. 64). Manne observes that most of the information the securities laws provide is historical and therefore has little value to investors (ibid., pp. 38, 65–6). The subsidy for information gathering is unnecessary because market participants can capture the value of the information (ibid., p. 43). Worse, the securities laws interfere with firms' property rights in information (ibid., p. 33) and accordingly reduce incentives to produce information (ibid., p. 41). Evidence supporting these arguments about the net costs of securities disclosures includes the fact that shares were not revalued in the wake of the additional disclosures required by the Securities and Exchange Act of 1934 (ibid., p. 63).

Wall Street in Transition includes additional Manne observations on the economics of information and securities markets, following up on his work in *Insider Trading* and initial insights in 'Mergers'. Manne put his theories in the context of recent evidence of market efficiency and the 'random walk' of securities prices (Manne et al. 1974, p. 66). This work shows that information moves market prices (ibid., p. 77). As he first observed in 'Mergers' and later developed in *Insider Trading,* the ability to profit on information, including through insider trading, helps keep stock prices efficient (1974, p. 83). It is difficult to provide direct evidence of efficiency by correlating the occurrence and importance of an event with stock price movement because the movement itself indicates that a material event has occurred (ibid., p. 81–2). Here Manne anticipated the emergence of cumulative average return studies in determining securities liability and damages.

Manne concluded his analysis of securities regulation by describing the powerful forces preserving the status quo, among them the specialized securities bar. These practitioners gain from new rules that make more work for lawyers in general, and securities lawyers in particular (Manne et al. 1974 pp. 93–5). Securities lawyers are in a particularly good position to exploit the benefits of securities regulation through their close working relationship with federal securities regulators. Government bureaucrats and lawyers have strong incentives to promote regulation, have persuaded themselves of the social desirability of their objectives, and have significant clout.

Though Manne seems to paint a dismal prospect, he concludes on a hopeful note by observing, with Schumpeter, that 'it is the business of intellectuals to question the established order' (ibid., p. 96). Indeed, as discussed below in Section 3, Manne's chief influence lay in spurring intellectuals to pursue their 'business'.

2   An evaluation of Manne's scholarship

This section puts Manne's work into broader intellectual perspective. Sub-section 2.1 summarizes Manne's intellectual innovations. Sub-section 2.2 discusses some qualifications of Manne's analysis and framework that scholars have put forward in the wake of Manne's theories. However, as discussed in Sub-section 2.3, Manne has shown in his recent work how these apparent qualifications actually fit well into his general framework.

2.1   Manne's contributions

Section 1 presents an impressive list of intellectual achievements. Most importantly, Manne formulated a broad economic framework of the corporation that explains the corporation's success and effectively answers Berle and Means, whose criticism of the public corporation had dominated discourse for thirty years. This framework gave Manne a rich opportunity for theorizing that gave rise to several seminal observations:

(1)   The market for control protects dispersed and passive shareholders from inefficient managers.

(2)   In the context of this market, shareholders' voting power is essentially exercised in the stock market rather than by voting as in a political election. Thus, efforts to legislate 'shareholder democracy' are fundamentally misguided.

(3)   The efficient stock market plays a key role in the economic theory of the corporation by, among other things, accurately discounting the value of incumbent management and thereby providing the foundation of the market for control.

(4)   Given the important role of the market for control in disciplining managers, regulation that increases the costs of takeovers can injure shareholders.

(5)   Publicly traded shares and the market for control provide an economic rationale for many of the details of corporate governance, including the business judgment rule.

(6)   This economic framework explains the structure not only of public corporations, but also of closely held firms, where legal rules must adjust for the absence of the public securities markets.

(7)   Insider trading can be understood as a mechanism of market efficiency and a way to reward entrepreneurial activity by managers of large firms.

(8)   The structure of corporate law could be explained by political as well as efficiency considerations. Competition among the states can erode inefficient mandatory state corporation laws, while interest groups may cause federal regulation of securities markets to diverge from efficiency.

2.2   Qualifications of Manne's analysis

Although Manne's body of work was a considerable achievement, his framework left room for debate about the details. Manne's theories can best be viewed as hypotheses for which many of the tools of modern empirical analysis, including event studies (which Manne was arguably the first to envision), had not even been invented when Manne wrote. Moreover, even if Manne was correct across the board in 1965, one would expect that corporations would change, creating a need for new theories and the qualification of existing ones. In other words, Manne's framework was necessarily contingent on a particular state of the world. But the framework nevertheless holds up well because it provides tools that remain useful even in a complex and dynamic environment.

With that perspective in mind, it is worth noting some of the qualifications of Manne's theories that have emerged since he wrote in the 1960s and early 1970s. First, some scholars have raised issues concerning both the costs and benefits of the market for control. Just as Manne argued that property rights were essential to encourage the production of information and efficient securities markets, so managers need to have property rights in their jobs in order to have the incentive to develop job-specific expertise (Haddock et al. 1987). Also, there are alternatives to the market for control for addressing the free rider problem of dispersed ownership. In particular, we might expect to see more concentrated ownership when the control benefits of such ownership outweigh the costs, including foregone risk diversification (Demsetz and Lehn 1985). There are also alternative control structures such as private equity that might address the agency problems of particular types of firms better than relying on the market for control (Jensen 1989; Ribstein 2004).

Second, by the late 1980s, the combined effects of federal and state takeover regulation arguably reduced the role of hostile tender offers in corporate governance. Indeed, some of these impediments to takeovers result from the very managerial power that Manne argued was essential. Manne argued that the strong business judgment rule, which tells courts not to interfere with corporate management, is backed by the disciplinary force of the market for control (Manne 1967a, p. 280). Yet this very business judgment rule made room for the poison pill and other takeover defenses. Manne argued that increased costs of takeovers would reduce their effectiveness. This raises a question whether the market for control as it exists today can support all of the corporate governance implications that Manne argued for.

Third, Manne recognized that an efficient stock market was a necessary prerequisite of the market for control, and by extension of Manne's theory. Yet Manne had to posit the existence of such a market in the absence of reliable data. In a recent interview, Manne (2007) remarked that it was '[g]reat fun to do a piece where you weren't relying on data, but had locked up the logic and it was something new'. There is today significant evidence of market efficiency. However, there is also a vast literature on behavioral finance that raises questions about market efficiency.

Fourth, Manne theorized that insider trading was necessary to encourage entrepreneurial efforts in large corporations. Yet insider trading in the classic sense of managers trading in the shares of their firms continues to be illegal. Does it follow that large corporations are not entrepreneurial? Manne's economic framework suggests that we may need to find a substitute for the incentive effects of insider trading.

Fifth, Manne only briefly touched on an important aspect of the market context of corporations, the market for corporate law. However, the post-Manne scholars such as Winter (1977) who pioneered the study of this area owe much to Manne's market-oriented approach. For example, while Cary's (1974) theory of the race to the bottom in corporate law was in the spirit of Berle and Means's theory of helpless dispersed shareholders, Winter responded with the Manne-esque observation that it was unlikely such behavior would survive in vigorous capital markets.

2.3 Manne's recent work

In recent years, particularly following his retirement from full-time teaching and administration, Manne has written a series of articles that help put recent scholarship and developments, including some of those discussed in Sub-section 2.2, in the perspective of Manne's economic theory of corporate law.

First, in an article in a symposium on behavioral finance (Manne 2006), Manne discussed the implications of behavioral finance theory. He argued that behavioral economics is just another of the many attacks on neoclassical economics that have ultimately strengthened the discipline by eliciting a theoretical response. Just as Coase answered the challenge of externalities to classical market economics, so Manne answered Berle and Means' challenge to the corporation. Manne argues that the law and economics response to behavioral finance is likely to be a deeper theory of price formation. For example, this theory may help determine the relationship between efficient market prices and the number of irrational or fully informed traders in a market.

Second, Manne (2005) returned to the topic of insider trading. Manne revised his theory to recognize insider trading's role in communicating enterprise information that assists in managing the firm. Manne also wondered why, in light of the importance of insider trading, it did not elicit a strong corporate response. The answer is that markets adjust. Some insider trading 'went underground', outside the law's reach. Moreover, Manne suggests that if regulation does make insider trading more costly, we would expect other market devices to arise to deal with the problem. An important candidate is prediction markets that operate outside the SEC's jurisdiction over stock markets. Manne argued (ibid., p. 185):

> If the stock market cannot itself be used to gain certain information because of insider trading restrictions, then managers . . . can create a virtual market to provide some of that same information. Virtual markets even have some benefits the actual stock market does not, such as the ability to segregate specific causes of share-price changes . . . [T]hese markets can ameliorate some of the costs of the SEC's campaign against insider trading, and we can expect them to flourish.

Third, Manne (2003), writing in the wake of Enron and Sarbanes-Oxley, took the opportunity to challenge extensive regulation of markets just as Congress was enacting the broadest securities laws since 1934. Manne returned to his theories about the market for control and insider trading to show that they could support efficient corporate governance without extensive regulation, that the demand for regulation reflected interest groups rather than public interest. In other words, Manne's lessons are still valid; we have only to learn them.

3   The impact of Manne's ideas: the intellectual as entreprenuer

How influential was Manne's work? William Carney (1999) has shown that Manne's works, and particularly his 'Mergers' article, have been very widely cited. But such citation studies tend to establish *recognition*. The *influence* of Manne's work is harder to show (Priest 1999). This section addresses Manne's influence in two ways. Section 3.1 looks beyond scholarly impact to attempt a qualitative analysis of the real world impact of Manne's theories. Section 3.2 then focuses on Manne's strongest contribution – his importance as an intellectual entrepreneur and network builder.

3.1   Real world impact

As shown in Section 1, Manne provided a thorough and convincing rejoinder to the Berle-Means paradigm that had prevailed since the 1930s. Many commentators accepted the conclusions of Berle and Means that the corporation was a dysfunctional institution in need of regulatory assistance, that managers functioned as quasi-public servants, and that corporate governance was to be modeled after the political institutions of democracy. Manne responded that the corporation had to be understood in the context of markets, that it was an economic and not a political institution, and that the market for control provided the discipline that was missing from the Berle-Means model. Because these ideas were original and ran totally counter to the prevailing wisdom, the emergence of these ideas in the real world and in popular discourse provides an indication of Manne's influence.

The precise extent of Manne's influence is hard to measure. It is certainly possible that law and economics in general, and its application to corporate governance in particular, would have happened without Manne. Yet it is noteworthy that while many of the ideas that Manne drew on had been expressed by Hayek, Coase, Schumpeter and others, nobody prior to Manne had brought these ideas into the legal literature. And this was no accident. After all, Manne was bucking a paradigm that had a great deal of influence in the legal academy, and on which many prominent scholars had staked their careers.

The prevailing paradigm's power is reflected in the legal academy's reluctance for many years to admit Manne's theories into the mainstream and the heavy criticism he faced from the legal academic establishment. Notably, Manne's market for control article (Manne 1965), though written by a law professor, was published in a finance journal. Much of the criticism leveled at Manne stemmed from his temerity in defending insider trading. Manne (1966) sparked significant negative commentary from law professors and prompted Manne to publish a defense (Manne 1970). As Jonathan Macey has commented (Macey 1999, p. 271):

> Perhaps even more important than the nature of Dean Manne's discourse about insider trading was the sheer moral courage Manne displayed. Legal academia is a club, and to be ostracized by its elite can curtail or ruin a young academic's career, even a career with Manne's stellar credentials. I wonder how many people in academics today would have the courage to risk everything to write what they want to write, to reach the conclusions they think are justified, and then to stand by those conclusions in the midst of the unprecedented criticism that Dean Manne initially received for his work. I am sure that the number is not very large. For this alone, Dean Manne deserves recognition.

Manne's theories were not only original and creative, but had the significant attraction of creating a comprehensive framework for corporate law. Established scholars may have been tempted to ignore Manne as a challenge to their life's work. But after Manne wrote, scholars, particularly younger scholars, had little temptation to ignore the edifice Manne had constructed. Instead, they could, and did, proceed to empirically test the theories as Manne repeatedly invited them to do, criticize or reject them on theoretical grounds, or share in the attention the theories were generating by elaborating on them. Manne therefore set the agenda for much future work in corporate scholarship. It is certainly plausible that corporate theory would have proceeded very differently but for his work.

Manne was also, in a sense, lucky in that his ideas became well known just at the time they started playing out on the public stage (Carney 1999). Manne's theories therefore provided a handy explanation for current events. Indeed, Manne even seems to have seeped into popular culture. Consider the film *Other People's Money* (1991), in which a corporate raider responds to criticism that he is a destroyer of firms by telling the shareholders, 'Who cares [about you shareholders]? . . . Me. I'm your only friend. I'm making you money; that's the only reason you became shareholders.' The echo from Manne (1967b)'s praise of corporate 'garbagemen' seems more than coincidental.

If Manne's views were seeping into the public consciousness they might also be influencing public policy. In the 1960s, takeover artists like Louis Wolfson could appeal only to their self-interest, while profligate corporate managers could wrap themselves in the public good.

By the 1980s, Manne had provided a public interest justification for takeovers and for view-ing the corporation in economic terms that made it easier to resist calls for tighter takeover regulation.

However, takeovers ultimately were regulated. Similarly, the old views of the unfairness of insider trading and image of the corporation as a political democracy still hold consid-erable sway today, both in politics and in scholarship. Congress ignored Manne's lessons in the regulatory frenzy that followed Enron and culminated in the Sarbanes-Oxley Act. Seventy years after adopting the federal securities laws, legislators again forgot about dynamic capital markets and the strong incentives they give firms to provide effective governance (Ribstein 2002). Another massive federal law had been enacted ostensibly to 'restore investor confidence', but actually to hobble newer and more entrepreneurial competitors.

While the persistence of the Berle-Means paradigm testifies to the power of popular distrust of large corporations, there has been a change that may owe something to Henry Manne. After Sarbanes-Oxley, unlike in the 1930s, a substantial group of leading legal scholars immediately questioned the reforms, a larger group of finance economists had the theories and tools to test their costs and effectiveness, and there was a large audience in academia, think tanks, Congress and the SEC for this theory and evidence. The skeptics of regulation are playing an increasing role in the public debate.

To be sure, it is hard to argue that one individual caused a change in the regulatory envi-ronment. One might argue that, given the work of other pioneers of law and economics, scholars writing in this vein eventually would have turned to the economics of corporate governance, and eventually would have come to similar conclusions. After all, part of the power of Manne's work is that he was so often right, which suggests that others would have come to the same conclusions on their own. But as discussed in the next section, the accep-tance of law and economics itself owed much to Manne's entrepreneurial efforts.

3.2   Manne as entrepreneur

Manne saw that the quality of ideas alone may not be enough to make them influential. Once people have become convinced of a particular point of view, it is hard to change their minds. That is particularly so for scholars who have invested a career in the point of view. Yet scholars hold an important key to public opinion. Contending interest groups may be tarred in the public view by their self-interest. Interest groups therefore can increase their clout by turning to the apparently disinterested intellectual elites who float above partisan squabbles. Moreover, under the right circumstances, scholars can be influenced to change their minds. After all, outside the prevailing wisdom lie the substantial rents accruing to originality. Manne had both an incentive and an opportunity to make scholars more recep-tive to his views.

Manne influenced mainly through the seminars, many supported by the Liberty Fund, and the law and economics educational programs for law professors, economists and judges. The warm sun, vigorous walks, pleasant golf and good food helped to soften stub-born minds and make them receptive to the morning and afternoon lectures, papers and discussions. Manne may have nudged things along by tweaking the agenda to at least slightly stack the intellectual deck (Priest 1999). And the relationships formed during these programs helped germinate an intellectual network that leveraged the effect of these programs (Rubin 1999).

These efforts could be viewed as interventions in the distribution chain. Manne saw the importance of getting involved in the manufacturing process – in law school, where legal minds were formed. Manne noted at the beginning of his insider trading book lawyers' tendency to focus on individuals and one-to-one unfairness, while economists consider the general allocation of resources (Manne 1966, p. 3). Before lawyers would accept Manne's theories, they had to learn to think more like economists. Thus, after many years of working outside of the legal education establishment, Manne's career led almost inevitably back into legal education and to his deanship at George Mason University School of Law.

George Mason was a natural fit. The President of George Mason University, George Johnson, was seeking a quick route to prominence and therefore had more tolerance than the usual university administrator for an entrepreneurial dean (interview 2007). Moreover, located within sight of Washington, DC, a public policy role for George Mason Law School seemed appropriate. At any rate, the symbolism was apt: Manne, who had begun his working life in his family's dry goods store, now found himself managing a law school out of a former department store (Demsetz 1999).

Manne believed that both law schools and law students should specialize. For the law school, Manne focused hiring on law and economics scholars and integrated economics into the whole law school curriculum. Until Manne's efforts at GMU, law and economics had been consigned to (at most) a one or two-person outpost at most schools and to a special 'law and economics' elective course. Within the law school, Manne instituted specialization through several specialty 'tracks', through which students could concentrate on developing expertise in fields like corporate law and intellectual property (Adams 1999).

GMU Law School ended up being less important in training lawyers than as part of the intellectual network Manne had established with the seminars and programs. The specialty tracks garnered some attention, but ultimately there was not enough demand for the sort of full-blown specialization in law school that Manne had envisioned. Manne's approach to intellectual specialization in legal education has not yet caught on, and its graduates do not seem to have played an important role in promoting the use of law and economics. On the other hand, the intellectual specialization of the law faculty paid rich dividends. GMU gave a critical mass of scholars an opportunity to write and teach together on a long-term basis. Both those who remain at George Mason and the 'diaspora' of scholars who left for other schools form a significant body of law and economics scholarship.

GMU Law School was also important because of the entrepreneurial spirit Manne brought to it. Before the mid-1980s when Manne came to GMU, there was no real culture of competition among law schools. Indeed, law schools really did not have distinct products to sell. But competition and a distinctive product was exactly what Manne had in mind for GMU as part of his plan for creating a market for his ideas. The sudden visibility that Manne brought to GMU, and the fact that it was able to vault from nowhere to the first tier of law schools in only a few years, created a model for other law schools. It helped that around the same time US News and World Reports started ranking law schools, and that an early ranking announced the arrival of GMU Law as a top 'up and coming' school.

The new competition among law schools, plus the advent of law school rankings, have now created an opportunity for the kind of product differentiation that Manne hoped to bring to legal education. Law schools have more incentive than ever to be distinctive, and there is still a chance that might include the specialization that Manne advocated. The biggest impediment to this sort of development is the internal governance structure of universities in general, and law schools in particular. Manne (1993) pointed out that universities are run as non-profit institutions under a board of trustees, a system in which nobody has a property right in the institution's success. Power therefore has devolved to university faculties. This is complicated in the case of law schools by the lawyer cartel's significant control over legal education. In other words, unlike the corporations that Manne studied, universities and law schools are not basically market institutions. Thus, even if the market demanded specialization and product differentiation, it is not clear that the governing bodies of universities would respond to this demand. Instead, schools could be expected to continue to make things comfortable for their tenured faculties. There is no market for control to deal with recalcitrant university administrators.

4   Concluding remarks

Henry Manne has had a remarkable career. Writing when there was a theory vacuum at the heart of legal academia, Manne breathed life into corporate law by using economic principles to formulate a sweeping new theory of the corporation. Then he took his show on the road with seminars, programs and ultimately a law school to create a market for his ideas.

Manne was an entrepreneur in two important respects – not only in the literal sense of bringing people and ideas together, as discussed in Sub-section 3.2, but also in the sense discussed in Manne's work on insider trading – that is, more than merely a manager of existing ideas, but an active participant in the creative destruction of the existing paradigm.

Manne's career demonstrates that a single scholar can leave noticeable ripples in the stream of intellectual history. Even the most innovative thinkers make only incremental contributions that are difficult to isolate from the general ferment of ideas. But because of both the originality of his work and the network that he created for disseminating his ideas, Manne was unusually influential. By demonstrating that corporations, and by inference other important institutions, are best analyzed in market terms, and by creating an intellectual market for these and other economic ideas, Manne changed the way scholars, judges, regulators and others think about the role of law in society.

Bibliography

Adams, William H. (1999), 'The George Mason Experience', *Case Western Reserve Law Review* **40** (Winter), 431–43.
Alchian, Armen A. and Harold Demsetz (1972), 'Production, Information Costs, and Economic Organization', *American Economic Review* **62** (5), 777–95.
Berle, Adolf A. and Gardiner C. Means (1932), *The Modern Corporation and Private Property*, New York: Macmillan.
Black, Bernard (1990), 'Is Corporate Law Trivial? A Political and Economic Analysis', *Northwestern University Law Review* **84** (2), 542–97.
Butler, Henry N. and Larry E. Ribstein (2006), *The Sarbanes-Oxley Debacle*, Washington, DC: AEI Press.
Carney, William J. (1999), 'The Legacy of "The Market For Corporate Control" and the Origins of the Theory of the Firm', *Case Western Reserve Law Review* **50** (Winter) 215–44.
Cary, William (1974), 'Federalism and Corporate Law: Reflections Upon Delaware', *Yale Law Journal* **83** (4), 663–705.
Coase, Ronald H. (1937), 'Nature of the Firm', *Economica* **4** (New Series) (16), 386–405.
Cohen, Manuel (1966), 'A Note on Takeover Bids and Corporate Purchases of Stock', *Business Law* **22** (1), 149–57.
Demsetz, Harold and Kenneth Lehn (1985), 'The Structure of Corporate Ownership: Causes and Consequences', *Journal of Political Economy* **93** (6) 1155–77.
Demsetz, Harold (1999), 'Henry Manne: Scholar, Academic, Entrepreneur, and Friend', 50 *Case Western Reserve Law Review* 253.

Easterbrook, Frank H. and Daniel Fischel (1985), 'Limited Liability and the Corporation', *University of Chicago Law Review* **52** (1), 89–117.

Easterbrook, Frank H. and Daniel Fischel (1981), 'The Proper Role of a Target's Management in Responding to a Tender Offer', *Harvard Law Review* **94** (6), 1161–204.

Gilson, Ronald J. andd Reinier Kraakman (1984), 'The Mechanisms of Market Efficiency', *Virginia Law Review* **70** (4), 549–644.

Haddock, David, Jonathan Macey and Fred McChesney (1987), 'Property Rights in Assets and Resistance to Tender Offers', *Virginia Law Review* **73** (4), 701–46.

Halpern, Paul, Michael Trebilcock and Stuart Turnbull (1980), 'An Economic Analysis of Limited Liability in Corporation Law', *University of Toronto Law Journal* **30** (2), 117–50.

Hansmann, Henry and Reinier Kraakman (2000), 'The Essential Role of Organization Law', *Yale Law Journal* **110** (3), 387–440.

Hayek, Friedrich A. (1960), 'The Corporation in a Democratic Society: In Whose Interest Ought it and Will it be Run?', in M. Anshen and G.L. Bach (eds) (1985), *Management and Corporations*, New York: McGraw-Hill, pp. 99–117.

Jensen, Michael C. (1989), 'Eclipse of the Public Corporation', *Harvard Business Review* **67** (September–October (5), 61–74.

Jensen, Michael C. and William Meckling (1976), 'Theory of the Firm: Managerial Behavior, Agency Costs and Capital Structure', *Journal of Financial Economics* **3** (4), 305–60.

Kamar, Ehud, Pinar Karaca-Mandic, and Eric Talley (2006), 'Going-Private Decisions and the Sarbanes-Oxley Act of 2002: A Cross-Country Analysis', http://papers.ssrn.com/sol3 /papers.cfm?abstract_id=901769, USC CLEO Research Paper No. C06-5, USC Law School Legal Studies Paper No. 06-10.

Lintner, John (1959), 'The Financing of Corporations', in Edward S. Mason (ed.) *The Corporation in Modern Society*, Cambridge, MA: Harvard University Press, pp. 166–201.

Macey, Jonathan R. (1999), 'Securities Trading: A Contractual Perspective', *Case Western Reserve Law Review* **50** (Winter) 269–89.

Manne, Henry G. (2007), 'Conversation with Henry Manne', Liberty Fund Intellectual Portrait Series (DVD).

Manne, Henry G. (2006), 'Remarks on The Lewis & Clark Law School Business Law Forum: Behavioral Analysis of Corporate Law: Instruction or Distraction?', *Lewis & Clark Law Review* **10** (Spring), 169–76.

Manne, Henry G. (2005), 'Insider Trading: Hayek, Virtual Markets, and the Dog that Did Not Bark', *Journal of Corporate Law* **31** (Fall), 167–85.

Manne, Henry G. (2003), 'A Free Market Model of a Large Corporation System', *Emory Law Journal* **53** (Summer), 1381–400.

Manne, Henry G. (1993), 'Comment on Peter Byrne's 'Academic Freedom And Political Neutrality', *Journal of Legal Education* **43** (September), 340–45.

Manne, Henry G. (1970), 'Insider Trading and the Law Professors', *Vanderbilt Law Review* **23** (3), 547–90.

Manne, Henry G. (1967a), 'Our Two Corporation Systems: Law and Economics', *Virginian Law Review* **53** (March), 259–84.

Manne, Henry G. (1967b), 'Cash Tender Offers for Shares: A Reply to Chairman Cohen', *Duke Law Journal* **16** (2), 231–53.

Manne, Henry G. (1966), *Insider Trading and the Stock Market*, New York: Free Press.

Manne, Henry G. (1965), 'Mergers and the Market for Corporate Control', *Journal of Political Economy* **73** (2), 110–20.

Manne, Henry G. (1964), 'Some Theoretical Aspects of Share Voting: An Essay in Honor of Adolf A. Berle', *Columbia Law Review* **64**, 1427–45.

Manne, Henry G. (1962), 'The "Higher Criticism" of the Modern Corporation', *Columbia Law Review* **63** (March), 399–432.

Manne, Henry G. (1961), 'Current Views on the 'Modern Corporation', *University of Detroit Law Journal* **38** (5), 559–88.

Manne, Henry G. (1958), 'Review of *Livingston, The American Stockholder*', *St Louis University Law Journal* **5** (2) 309–16.

Manne, Henry G. (1956), 'Review of *Eels, Corporation Giving in a Free Society*', *University of Chicago Law Review* **24** (1), 194–202.

Manne, Henry G., Ezra Solomon and Kalman J. Cohen (1974), *Wall Street in Transition: The Emerging System and its Impact on the Economy*, New York: New York University Press.

Priest, George L. (1999), 'Henry Manne and the Market Measure of Intellectual Influence', *Case Western Reserve Law Review* **50** (Winter), 325–31.

Ribstein, Larry E. (2004), 'Why Corporations?' *Berkeley Business Law Journal* **1** (2),183–232.

Ribstein, Larry E. (2002), 'Market v. Regulatory Responses to Corporate Fraud', *Journal of Corporate Law* **28** (Fall) 1–67.

Rostow, Eugene V. (1959), 'To Whom and for What Ends is Corporate Management Responsible?', in Edward S. Mason (ed.), *The Corporation in Modern Society*, Cambridge, MA: Harvard University Press, pp. 46–71.
Rubin, Paul H. (1999), 'Henry G. Manne, Network Entrepreneur', *Case Western Reserve Law Review* **50** (Winter), 333–7.
Schumpeter, Joseph A. (1942), *Capitalism, Socialism, and Democracy*, New York: Harper & Row.
Winter, Ralph (1977), 'State Law, Shareholder Protection, and the Theory of the Corporation', *Journal of Legal Studies* **6** (2), 251–92.

10 Gary Becker's contributions to law and economics
John F. Pfaff*

To write about Gary Becker's influence on law and economics is a surprisingly difficult task. It is akin to asking how Isaac Newton changed physics: before Newton there was one paradigm, and after him simply another. Likewise with Becker. And as with Newton, an intellectual history of Becker's contributions runs the risk of being either trivial or impossible – trivial if it simply retells the well-known story of a seismic shift, impossible if it tries to trace out all the shift's implications. I will do my best to weave between these two.

Though some may disagree, I do not think it an overstatement to claim that no one – and I include here Ronald Coase and Richard Posner – has shaped contemporary law and economics more than Gary Becker. This is perhaps a surprising claim, given how little he has written that falls directly within the traditional bounds of legal scholarship: a book on discrimination (Becker 1971 [1957]), and a few articles on crime (Becker 1968a), enforcement (Becker and Stigler 1974), and drug addiction (Becker and Murphy 1988a; Becker et al. 2006, 1994, 1991). The rest of his work, such as his writings on the family (Becker 1991a) and human capital (Becker 1993a), is certainly relevant to the law but falls outside its primary focus. Becker himself admits that his involvement in law and economics is, at best, only tangential (Roundtable 1997).

But his work, both within and without the legal field, has exerted a tremendous influence on legal scholarship in general, not just on law and economics. And it has done so in at least two ways. First, and more important, it fundamentally redefined what it meant to 'do economics', or to be an economist. The common theme that unites all of Becker's work is its assertion that all human behavior, not just market behavior, can be productively described using an economic model of rational choice. Becker's central contribution has been to point out, repeatedly and in numerous contexts, that prices exist everywhere, and that they shape behavior in consistent ways. Everyone, economists and non-economists alike, is comfortable stating that the production and consumption of bananas changes in predictable ways with their dollar price. Then why not the production of children (where prices include direct expenditures and foregone income) or of crime (where guilt and the expected time in prison act as prices)? The price-tag may be more explicit for bananas, but that does not make the prices, or their effect on behavior, any different for any other choice. As a result of this broad, all-encompassing definition of 'economics', questions that traditionally fell within the realm of sociology and political science now lay open to economists, both inside and outside the legal academy. To use Medema's (2008) apt phrase, Becker ushered in the shift from 'law and economics' to the 'economic analysis of law'. Prior to Becker, legal economists primarily

*   Associate Professor of Law, Fordham Law School. My thanks to Gary Becker, Sheila Foster, Caroline Gentile, Jake Gersen, Jae Lee, and Tom Miles for helpful comments.

studied how legal rules affected economic outcomes; after, they used economic tools to examine the legal rules themselves.[1]

Second, Becker's writings have directly shaped debates in numerous areas of legal scholarship and policy. Legal work on crime and discrimination continues to probe and wrestle with the implications of his writings in these fields. And topics ranging from divorce and inheritance law to contracts benefit from his insights on, for example, the family and human capital.

Becker's primary contribution was thus to fully introduce the rational actor to the study of law. His work has forced scholars to take into account the rational decisions of criminals, malfeasants, bigots, and even drug addicts. More generally, by exploring the implications of rational choices concerning marriage and divorce, child-birth and child-raising, college attendance, and even suicide, he paved the way for economists and rational-choice scholars in political science and sociology to examine the interactions between choice of any sort and the legal regime.

A key reason for the power, tractability, and widespread applicability of Becker's rational choice framework is its relative simplicity. Becker's methodology rests on just three core assumptions: that (1) people maximize, (2) preferences are stable, and (3) markets clear.[2] Two benefits flow from these. First, they lead to clear, testable predictions. As Lazear (2000) points out, economics has been successfully 'imperialistic' because it has survived the market test. Many of its ideas and claims have been both provocative and verified. Second, the assumptions can be easily operationalized; many of Becker's most interesting and counter-intuitive results have come from little more than a spare utility function, first-order conditions, and comparative statics. The widespread adoption of Becker's approach surely arose in part because it could be learned easily and adapted quickly to any new problem. There are no complex theoretical underpinnings to learn, no dense forest of equations to hack through.

Thanks in large part to Becker, all of human behavior, and thus all of law, opened itself to economic analysis. Economists are now comfortable writing about issues ranging from the effect of abortion policy on fertility decisions (Levine et al. 1999) to the relationship between government support of religion and public religiosity (Iannaccone et al. 1997) to the rationality of engaging in suicide bombing (Wintrobe 2003). By now, many of these papers may cite Becker only in passing, if at all; but each rests on his pioneering work of applying economic insights to 'non-economic' questions (a phrase that has lost almost all meaning).

This chapter is organized as follows. Section 1 provides a brief biographical sketch of Becker's economic career, and it examines and discusses his general methodological approach. Though powerful, Becker's fundamental assumptions are not without their critics, and it is essential to appreciate both their strengths and weaknesses.

Section 2 then takes a deeper look at Becker's writings on the two topics directly relevant to law and economics: crime (Becker 1968a; Becker and Murphy 1988a; Becker and Stigler

---

[1]   Becker's reformulation of what it means to be an economist makes the word 'economic' difficult to use in some cases. It can refer both to the study of the market economy (the pre-Becker definition) and to the study of any act of constrained maximization. When it is not clear from the context, I will refer to the former type of study as 'market economics'.

[2]   Becker himself has argued that his approach rests on a fourth prong, namely the importance of efficiency (Roundtable 1997:1135). Unlike the first three, however, efficiency is a normative concept, not a positive one.

1974; Becker et al. 2006, 1991) and discrimination (Becker 1971 [1957], 1968b). It lays out the basic premises and explores how these articles shaped, and continue to shape, the relevant intellectual debates. As one would expect with work that is over three decades old, not all of Becker's assertions survive – while Becker suggested that an optimal punishment strategy would often entail setting sanctions very high and the probability of apprehension low, advances in our understanding of criminal behavior are beginning to suggest the opposite – but the core insight of rationality remains highly relevant. Many criminologists may not agree that criminals are as rational as Becker suggested, for example, but it is clear that they still perceive that the burden remains on them to explain why criminals are not so (see, for example, Robinson and Darley 2004). Using crime and discrimination as examples, this section also considers the wider implications of Becker's work (such as that on the family and human capital) for law and economics and legal scholarship more generally.

Section 3 turns to a less obvious, but no less important, area of contribution: Becker's personal role. Becker has often personally encouraged the growth of law and economics in general, and of legal economists in person. Given the strong effect he has had on, and the continuing relationships he has with, such leading law and economics figures as Richard Posner and William Landes, this could be one of his greatest influences.

1 Becker and his methodology

1.1 A brief biography

As one would expect for an economist of Becker's stature, his intellectual biography has been told many times before, so I will recount it here only briefly.[3] From the very beginning of his economic career, Becker was drawn to questions that did not fall within the scope of market economics, at one point coming close to leaving the discipline altogether. While an undergraduate economics major at Princeton, Becker found himself losing interest in the field due to its detachment from important social issues. At the encouragement of one of his professors, he looked towards sociology, in particular the work of Talcott Parsons. This experience led him to remain in economics, and after graduation he enrolled at the University of Chicago as a graduate student. It was there, in Milton Friedman's introductory microeconomics course, that Becker realized the full potential economics had to address myriad social issues.[4]

Though his earliest work fell within the confines of market economics, such as international trade (Becker 1952) and monetary theory (Becker and Baumol 1952; Friedman and Becker 1957), it did not take long for Becker to turn his attention to less traditional issues. His dissertation, published by the University of Chicago Press in 1957, set forth his basic model of discrimination. Though his application of economics to such non-market behavior faced some resistance, strong support from the Chicago faculty encouraged him to continue applying economic models outside their usual home.

The result is well known. Becker has been a leading pioneer in the fields of human capital and the economics of the family. He has used economic models to examine crime and drug addiction, fertility and divorce, household production, education and intergenerational mobility,

---

[3] Most notably, by Becker himself, in Becker (1993b) and in Swedberg (1990), from which much of this discussion comes.

[4] It is fitting that Becker inherited the course from Friedman and, teaching it to this day, continues to instill that same feeling in Chicago graduate students.

and interest-group competition.[5] Impressively, more than fifty years into his career Becker continues to write on the edge of economic thought, recently turning his attention to issues such as social interactions and preference formation (Becker 1996; Becker and Murphy 2000; Becker et al. 2005), and the economics of happiness (Rayo and Becker 2007a, 2007b).[6] And importantly, Becker's focus has always been on important social issues – discrimination, crime, the family, education. His work stands in stark contrast to the lament of his mentor, Milton Friedman (1999): 'economics has become increasingly an arcane branch of mathematics rather than dealing with real economic problems'.

For his pioneering work, Becker received the John Bates Clark Medal in 1967. In 1992, he was awarded the Nobel Prize in Economics 'for having extended the domain of micro-economic analysis to a wide range of human behaviour and interaction, including nonmarket behaviour'. And in 2006, the University of Chicago renamed its Initiative on Chicago Price Theory the Becker Center on Chicago Price Theory; as Edward Snyder, Dean of Chicago's Graduate School of Business, said, '[e]conomics, but for Gary Becker, would be a much less exciting discipline, less relevant, and much more narrow' (Goddu 2006). Becker has also been presented with the National Medal of Science (in 2000) and the Presidential Medal of Freedom (in 2007).

Levitt and Chiappori (2003), in an article measuring the extent to which particular theorists influence current empirical work, provide compelling evidence of Becker's consistent ability to produce seminal papers. Looking at all empirical microeconomic papers published in the top three economic journals (*American Economic Review*, *Journal of Political Economy*, and the *Quarterly Journal of Economics*) between 1999 and 2001, Levitt and Chiappori count how many times a particular theorist is cited as the inspiration for the empirical undertaking. Of the 149 studies in their sample, Becker is cited in fifteen of them; no other theorist is cited more than ten times (and of these there are only two). And as evidence of the vitality of his research, work from every decade of his career, back to his 1957 dissertation, is cited, and his fifteen citations include thirteen different papers.

1.2   Becker's methodology

At the core of Becker's approach are three fundamental assumptions: people are rational, their preferences are stable, and markets clear. These are assumptions which economists have long employed when studying the market economy; what sets Becker apart is his willingness to apply them far more widely. It is not surprising that his approach encountered – and encounters still, if to a much lesser extent – stiff resistance, both within and (especially) outside of economics. Perhaps most famously, Coase (1988) has argued that economics should limit itself to the study of the market economy and not take on the mantle of studying human choice more broadly. That said, due in no small part to Becker, economics' imperialist ambition appear to be a well-established feature of the discipline.

---

5   Becker's (1958) paper on interest groups was written in 1952 but not published until 1958. As Becker recounts (Swedberg 1990), the 1952 version had been rejected by the *Journal of Political Economy* and, stung by the rejection, Becker waited before submitting a different version of it. In the interim, Downs (1957) published his seminal work on the economics of politics.

6   It should be pointed out that Becker (1974) examined the importance of social interaction effects decades before most economists addressed the issue, although he confronted it again only briefly (Becker 1991b) before returning to it recently.

While generally accepted within economics, at the very least as necessary evils that provide theoretical tractability, none of these assumptions is without controversy. A vast literature, for example, has grown attacking the rationality assumption. Its roots are deep: Veblen (1898) challenged it over one hundred years ago, sarcastically criticizing the neo-classical *homo economicus* as someone who is 'a lightning calculator of pleasure and pains, who oscillates like a homogeneous globule of desire of happiness under the impulse of stimuli that shift him about the area, but leave him intact'. More recently, behavioral economists have started to examine when and where decision-makers make systematic 'errors' (as compared to their wholly rational theoretical counterparts).[7]

Becker confronted some concerns with rationality early in his career. In Becker (1962), he demonstrates that many of the standard economic theorems, such as the downward-sloping demand curve, hold even if people behave irrationally (which he defines as either randomly or unresponsively). But the current critiques of rationality take a slightly different tack: it is not that people are randomly irrational, but rather systematically irrational. Certain cognitive biases, such as the availability heuristic, loss aversion, and framing effects cause people to make decisions in *non*-randomly irrational ways. And these biases have the ability to undermine some of the policy recommendations that flow from Becker's rational-choice models.

Consider, for example, Becker's (1968a) suggestion that optimal criminal policy at times involves setting the sanction very high and the probability of arrest and conviction very low, perhaps as close to zero as possible. If people misperceive the probability randomly, then the average person assesses the probability correctly and, on average, people respond as if their perceived probability is the true probability. But the availability heuristic states that people treat low-probability events as zero-probability events; this is a systematic error, not a random one. And if it is right, then a close-to-zero probability of arrest and conviction will not deter crime.

What these findings indicate, however, is not a need to move away from the rational actor model, but to use a more sophisticated version of it, something Becker himself has long advocated. From the very beginning he has acknowledged that the economic model of human behavior has much to learn from anthropology, psychology, and sociology (Becker 1976). It is essential for economists to think deeply about people's motivations and decision-making processes, and to account for the fact that such decision-making is influenced in part by lack of information and 'calculating capacity' (Becker 1993a). While behavioral adjustments may undermine certain policy recommendations produced by older rational choice models, they do not change the fundamental approach of modeling people as choosing as best they can subject to the constraints that they face. At most, they force economists to acknowledge that 'mental' budget constraints can be just as important as financial or – as Becker (1965) makes

---

7   A footnote trying to summarize this literature would take up the entire chapter; good discussions can be found in Jolls et al. (1998), Korobkin and Ulen (2000), and Sunstein (2000). The importance of behavioralism was made clear in 2002 when one of its leading proponents, Daniel Kahneman, became the first psychologist to win the Nobel Prize in Economics. Posner (1998a) provides a cogent (partial) rebuttal to the current enthusiasm, at least within law, for behavioral models. Fudenberg (2006) also raises several valid concerns, in particular that behavioralism, at least for now, is more a set of *ad hoc* patches to the rational actor model than a self-sustaining alternative model; as such, it runs the risk of turning tautological. Nonetheless, he concludes that it is 'unwise and inefficient to do economics without paying *some* attention to good psychology'.

so clear – temporal budget constraints. And by providing a clearer picture of how those constraints operate, behavioralism advances, not undermines, the rational actor model.[8]

Though the other two assumptions – stable preferences and equilibrium – are generally discussed less often, both have also recently faced sustained criticism. Consider first the assumption that preferences are stable (Stigler and Becker 1977). A model allowing for constantly shifting preferences would be incapable of making predictions or falsifiable claims. Becker's commitment to this assumption is seen most dramatically in his work on rational addiction (Becker and Murphy 1988a; Becker et al. 2006, 1994, 1991; Stigler and Becker 1977), a theory which has withstood frequent empirical evaluation. That is not to say that tastes and preferences emerge exogenously, and Becker has recently turned his attention to examining how preferences are in fact formed (Becker 1996; Becker and Murphy 2000).

The most recent attack on the stable-preferences assumption has been the 'situationist' critique (Hanson and Benforado 2005; Hanson and Kysar 1999a, 1999b; Hanson and Yosifon 2004, 2003). The central claim of situationalism – which aggressively defines itself in opposition to the 'dispositionalism' of the standard economic model of behavior – is that any choice we make depends critically on the contextual situation in which we are operating. In other words, actors' preferences are not stable across situations.[9] Thus someone who believes himself to be disposed against sadism, and who generally acts in compassionate ways, may subject a victim to extreme electrical shocks when instructed to do so by someone in (or perceived to be in) a position of authority or expertise; this is what happened in Milgram's famous electroshock experiment. Situationalists argue that however disposed the actors were against torture, that disposition was overridden by the situational pressures of being told by an authority figure that they had to impose high-voltage shocks.

The situationalists are surely correct to draw our attention to the importance of context and setting. Early economics relied on a model of human behavior that was too atomistic. And there are certainly plenty of circumstances in which the manipulation of situational cues can influence people's behavior: the entire advertising industry is built on this principle. That context can act powerfully on decision-makers, however, does not mean rational choice is a flawed approach.[10] Any well-designed rational-choice model should acknowledge the relevant social and psychological pressures at play; the solution likely does not lie down the road of abandoning the stable preferences assumption altogether, but rather in developing more sophisticated models that explicitly account for context. Again, as Becker and Murphy (1993) point out, a model of shifting (unstable) tastes lacks a theory of consumer choice and thus cannot make clear predictions.

---

[8]   Though it may seem so at first blush, this argument does not reduce rational choice to a tautology. Adjusting the rational actor model to account for observed patterns in decision-making methods differs fundamentally from, say, positing a 'taste' for framing effects. Most important, many of the these behavioral heuristics have been observed in experimental settings. That is not to say, of course, that they cannot be misused in ex post, ad hoc ways.

[9]   Hanson and Yosifon (2004:1) argue that their model is designed to 'retire' the rational-actor model. Their claim, however, is less that people do not maximize, but rather that their perception of the constraints they face depends critically on the situations in which they are located. As such, it is much more a disagreement about the stability of preferences than about rationality more generally.

[10]   Becker and Murphy (1993), for example, account directly for context in their discussion of advertising.

Like that of stable preferences, the assumption of equilibrium – examining comparative statics taken from first-order conditions, for example – is generally accepted within economics. Nonetheless, some economists, loosely aggregated under the term 'heterodox', have attacked (among other things) the extent to which 'orthodox' neo-classical economics focuses on equilibrium behavior; see, for example, Lawson (2006, 2005).[11] Examining behavior at equilibrium, however, is necessary for deriving meaningful (and testable) results. Equilibrium assumptions are essentially efforts to reduce large-scale problems to their more manageable constituent pieces. To reject equilibrium analysis is to reject formal modeling altogether, and the significant advances in economics have not come from rejecting formalism but rather from improving its underlying assumptions (Backhouse 2004; see also Robinson 1974).

Becker himself has asserted a fourth element to his approach, namely efficiency analysis (Roundtable 1997). This component, however, differs fundamentally from the other three: where those are positive, efficiency is normative. In other words, the first three generate predictions about how people will respond to changes in legal rules and are thus useful to anyone who wishes to make policy decisions, regardless of ideological or normative bent. Efficiency, however, is a normative criterion for assessing whether a particular behavioral outcome is desirable.[12] Any complete policy analysis requires a normative standard by which to measure success, but efficiency is but one of many possible options. And tying economic analysis too closely to efficiency concerns allows unsolvable[13] normative debates to overshadow the power and effectiveness of positive economic analysis. Though this is certainly not a position shared by all economists, I agree with Frank Knight's (alleged) statement: 'As an economist, I cannot tell you whether you should adopt food price controls. I can tell you, if you do, you should expect widespread hunger.' (Mashaw 1999:2.)

This is more than a philosophical debate. As Hirsch and Osborne (1992) point out, the blurring of the line between positive and normative analysis has led those with different normative views to attack the entire law and economics endeavor, normative and positive alike. Posner (1998b:31) looked to a future in which law and economics 'become[s] so deeply woven into the fabric of law that it ceases to be visible as a distinct field'. That clearly has not happened, and support for, or opposition to, it is often (though by no means always) roughly split along ideological lines. While Posner (2007) is right to point out that there are many law and economics scholars whose normative conclusions lean to the left, that the discipline retains the aura of being 'conservative' is likely not coincidental: its relatively individualistic, utilitarian view of efficiency accords more closely with conservative normative goals than more liberal ones. This close relationship between economics and efficiency certainly predates Becker. It is, instead, a long-run intellectual tradition within both economics and law and economics. Overlooked in the debate about efficiency, however, is the fact that economics' behavioral models are useful to anyone who wishes to make consequentialist (which by no means equals utilitarian) policy recommendations.

---

[11]   A very interesting debate between 'orthodox' and 'heterodox' economists was held on-line in June 2007 at tpmcafe.com. See http://bookclub.tpmcafe.com/book_title/hip_heterodoxy.

[12]   Conceivably, one could adopt a definition of efficiency that is agnostic as to the policy goal: a more efficient result is any outcome that is closer to an ideal point, anyway defined, than the initial point. Within the economics literature, however, efficiency generally adopts either a utilitarian or, at least in the case of some of Posner's (1981, 1979) work, a wealth-maximizing focus.

[13]   As Leff (1974) puts it well, '[n]ormative premises are just that; they don't get any more proved by being talked about'.

That, briefly, is the big picture. We can now turn to two specific applications of Becker's methodology: his studies of crime and discrimination. Both provide clear case-studies of the effects of his work on law and economics scholarship in particular, and legal scholarship more generally.

2   Crime and discrimination

Very little of what Becker has written falls explicitly within the standard confines of law and economics, although very little of his work lacks legal implications. Two early projects of his, however, are clearly legal in nature: his studies of discrimination (Becker 1971 [1957]) and crime (Becker 1968a; Becker and Stigler 1974). Conveniently, both shed light on Becker's direct and indirect contributions to law and economics, and to legal scholarship more generally. Directly, each influenced and continues to influence the debate within its field. Indirectly, each reflects Becker's willingness to apply the tools of economics beyond their traditional scope.

2.1   The economic analysis of crime

Over the past forty years, Becker has written several articles relating to criminal justice, examining the behaviors of criminals (Becker 1968a), enforcers (Becker and Stigler 1974), and drug users and other addicts (Becker and Murphy 1988a; Becker et al. 2006, 1991). Each of these articles has influenced how law and economics scholars, as well as sociologists and criminologists, study criminal behavior. Furthermore, each (Becker 1968a in particular) has expanded people's conceptions of what constitutes an 'economic question' in general. This section considers the significance of Becker's models to each of these three topics.

Crime and punishment   In many ways, Becker's seminal work on the economics of crime can be seen as a restoration: by emphasizing the rationality of potential offenders, Becker brought the ideas of Beccaria (1995 [1764]) and Bentham (2004 [1811], 1970 [1789]) back to criminology. Between the classical era of Beccaria and Bentham and its revitalization under Becker, models of criminal behavior had been shaped by various flavors of deterministic positivism, theories which left little room for individual decision-making.[14] Biological determinists such as Ferri (1897), Goring (1919 [1913]), and Lombroso (1918 [1899]) looked to physiological factors; psychological determinists such as the Glueck and Glueck (1950) to mental states; and sociological determinists such as Shaw and McKay (1942) and Merton (1938) to social disorder and social strains. Becker's key insight was to return to the forefront the criminal as an autonomous decision-maker.

(There is a potential irony here. By forcing criminologists to think of the criminal as a decision-maker, the rational-choice model of crime may have played a role in the revival of retributivism, a philosophy often cast as the alternative to consequentialist models like Becker's. After all, if the criminal is not a rational actor but instead a slave to deterministic

---

[14]   This discussion of the history of positivist thinking in criminology draws heavily on Gottfredson and Hirschi (1990). Ironically, Gottfredson and Hirschi chastise Becker for being an economic reductionist. They argue that the economic analysis of crime treats crime too much like another labor market option. This, of course, fundamentally misstates Becker's contribution, which is to treat criminal behavior as a form of *non-market* decision-making.

impulses, how can his decision to offend be morally wrong? How can there be any autonomy to respect if the offender is not autonomous?[15])

The origin of Becker's paper is well-known. Running late to a student's oral exam when teaching at Columbia, Becker could not find a convenient legal parking space. He realized he faced a choice: drive further to a legal lot, or park illegally and risk getting a ticket. Deciding that the probability of getting a ticket was sufficiently low, given the size of the potential fine he faced, he parked illegally (and managed to avoid getting ticketed). Walking in to the exam, Becker realized that many criminals must surely engage in a similar calculus, roughly weighing the expected punishment against the gains from the crime. Unfortunately for the student, Becker proceeded to grill him about this new theory during the exam.[16]

Becker's model rests on three simple components. First, the cost of enforcing the law, C, is a function of the number of arrests a, the probability of conviction p, and the number of offenses O. Second, the supply of crime, O, is determined by p, the magnitude f of the sanction, and a catchall term u to account for idiosyncratic factors such as outside opportunities and direct utility or disutility from committing crime. These crimes yield gains of $G(O)$ to offenders and losses of $H(O)$ to the victims, for a net social harm of $D = G - H$. And third, the social cost of punishment is equal to bf, where b depends on the nature of the sanction. For fines, $b \approx 0$, while $b > 1$ for punishments such as prison. With these terms, Becker is able to construct a social loss function $L = L(D, C, bf, O)$.

The rest of the article traces out how the government should optimally minimize the social loss L. Most famously, Becker argues that, under certain (and important) conditions, optimal policy entails setting p as close to zero as possible and f as high as possible.[17] He notes too that p and f should be chosen so that the elasticity of offending with response to the former is greater than that with respect to the latter; he cites some empirical evidence (Ehrlich 1967; Smigel 1965) indicating that this may in fact be the case. The nature of people's elastic responses to changes in p and f also sheds light on why we treat premeditated crimes, as well as crimes perpetrated by the young or the insane, differently. Furthermore, he establishes that, when offenders are risk-loving, the optimal p and f for a particular crime both rise with its marginal social cost. This too accords with real-world practice, where the harshest crimes face both the highest risk of conviction and the stiffest sanctions.

No paper can address every possible issue, and a large literature has developed to fill in the gaps of the model and explore the implications of some of its assumptions.[18] Polinksy and Shavell, for example, have fleshed out the optimal balance between the probability of conviction and the magnitude of fines, taking into account risk aversion (Polinsky and Shavell 1979; see also Kaplow 1992), various types of enforcement costs (Polinsky and Shavell 1992), and

---

[15]   Of course, one should be careful about overstating the tension between determinism and retribution. See, for example, Morse (2004).

[16]   The student passed.

[17]   The conditions are that offenders are risk neutral, that fact-finders' willingness to convict does not move inversely with the size of the sanction, and that the sanction is (relatively) costless to impose. These assumptions allow a decline in p to be perfectly compensated by an increase in f. If offenders are risk-preferrers, if sanctions are relatively expensive, or if conviction becomes more difficult for higher punishments (if $\partial p / \partial f < 0$), then Becker demonstrates that optimality may require a more interior solution.

[18]   It should be noted, though, that Becker touches on almost every extension to and critique of his model throughout his original paper, either in passing in the text or in a footnote.

differences in individuals' wealth (Polinksy and Shavell 1991). Others have considered broader optimality conditions, such as when incarceration should replace fines in the presence of judgment-proofness (Shavell 1985) or when unknown defendant wealth makes the calibration of fines difficult (Polinsky 2004). Still others have looked at the optimal sanction for recidivists (Polinsky and Rubinfeld 1991; Polinsky and Shavell 1998) and for attempts (Shavell 1990), the implications of imperfect information about enforcement (Bebchuck and Kaplow 1992; Kaplow 1990; Sah 1991; Shavell 1987), the extent to which juries are less willing to convict in the presence of high sanctions (Andreoni 1991), and the importance of social interaction effects (Rasmusen 1996). And Mookherjee and Png (1994) and Shavell (1992) have considered the issue of marginal deterrence: if the maximum penalty cannot deter all crime, then perhaps gradations of sanctions are needed to prevent offenders from committing more serious crimes.[19]

Though perhaps influential within the confines of the economic examination of crime, it is not immediately apparent how much this theoretical literature has directly shaped the broader study of crime; especially within the legal academy, many are hostile to its basic arguments.[20] But, as Rosen (1993) points out, that detractors seem hostile to the theory does not mean they are not influenced by it. And Becker's theory has had at least two significant effects.

The first, and perhaps more specific, is the robust empirical exploration into the deterrent effect of criminal law it inspired. Starting with Ehrlich's pioneering works looking at the effect of incarceration (Ehrlich 1972) and, more famously, the death penalty (Ehrlich 1975), economists, sociologists, criminologists, psychiatrists, and legal academics have debated, redebated, and then debated some more the extent to which criminals respond to changes in the probability of punishment and to changes in its severity. Two key limitations have made it difficult to test the economic/deterrent model of crime. First, it is hard to separate any deterrent effects of harsher punishments from their incapacitative effects (Levitt 1998a), and incapacitation should reduce crime regardless of the rationality of offenders. Second, empirical models of deterrence face serious problems of endogeneity. More police, for example, should lead to less crime, but more crime leads to more police. Not surprisingly, the cities with the highest crime rates tend to have the largest police forces. Failure to account for this type of endogenous relationship can bias estimates, even to the point of changing the sign of the effect (Levitt 1997).[21]

---

[19]   This is, for example, a possible argument against the felony-murder rule, which can make a felon (such as a bank robber) liable for any death that occurs during that felony, even if caused by someone else. The felony-murder rule should reduce the number of felonies resulting in a death, but once a death occurs, no legal sanction can deter the felon from committing more murders, so the number of deaths per felony-resulting-in-a-death should rise. The net effect of the felony-murder rule on murders is thus unclear, and unfortunately the data are such that unambiguous results cannot be empirically established (Malani 2002).

[20]   A personal anecdote is, I think, indicative. Shortly before entering the job market for a law school teaching position, I was warned that as an economist who studied criminal law, I had to make it clear to criminal law faculties that I did more than 'that p and f stuff'.

[21]   One interesting result of this endogeneity problem has been a small but insightful literature looking at the effect of league-imposed exogenous shocks to the number of sports referees on the number of fouls or penalties committed (Allen 2002; Hutchinson and Yates 2007; Levitt 2002b; McCormick and Tollison 2007, 1984).

But despite some dissenting voices (Doob and Webster 2003; Robinson and Darley 2004), the developing consensus within the empirical literature is that criminals, on average though certainly not always, respond rationally to changes in expected punishments. They commit fewer crimes when more police are deployed (Levitt 2002a, 1997), and when sentences are longer (Kessler and Levitt 1999; Levitt 1998b, 1996; Shepherd 2002a, 2002b). One high-profile exception to these findings, however, appears to be the death penalty: despite myriad studies examining the issue (Ehrlich 1975; Dezhbakhsh et al. 2003, Katz et al. 2003; Mocan and Gittings 2003; Zimmerman 2004), Berk (2005), Cohen-Cole et al. (2007), and Donohue and Wolfers (2005) have ably demonstrated that problems with the data render it essentially impossible to identify any deterrent effect (or its absence).[22]

Not only do we have evidence that criminals respond to incentives, but we have developed more nuanced and sophisticated views on *how* they respond to them. And while some of these findings suggest different policy solutions than those implied by Becker's basic model, they do not detract from the core idea that much can be gained by modeling the rational behavior of potential offenders. We understand, for example, that offenders tend to be more responsive to changes in the certainty, rather than the severity, of punishment (Nagin 1998). This could be because offenders are exceptionally impetuous and thus heavily discount changes in sentence length (Gottfredson and Hirschi 1990), or because a significant portion of the total sanction imposed for a conviction comes from informal, non-state punishments such as stigmatization and loss of income (Lott 1992; Nagin and Waldfogel 1998; Waldfogel 1994). We know too that while fines may be relatively cheap to impose, they are also politically unpopular: perhaps perceived as simply 'pricing crime', they lack a sufficiently expressive edge to retain much popularity (Kahan and Posner 1999) – although it should be pointed out that the US Sentencing Commission relied extensively on fines when developing the federal sentencing guidelines in part due to Becker's work (Posner 1993a). And some critics of deterrence have recently suggested that offenders may be rational but do not know about changes in the law (Doob and Webster 2003; Robinson and Darley 2004); it seems hard, however, to reconcile this claim with the evidence that comes from ethnographic studies of high-crime communities (for example, Bourgois 2003).

Perhaps the most important extension to Becker's model is the current effort to explore the importance of social interactions, norms, and informal social sanctions.[23] While Becker focused on the state supplied sanction *pf*, evidence indicates that crime is motivated, at least in part, by forces such as peer pressure and norm internalization (for example, guilt).[24] Economists have recently, if belatedly, begun to develop more social models of human behavior. Bar-Gill and Harel (2001), for example, examine how shifts in crime rates can influence the magnitude of punishment by changing the social stigma for crime. And Glaeser et al. (1996) use a model of social interactions to explain the strong geographic clustering of

---

[22]   Becker (2006) himself, however, maintains that the evidence of a deterrent effect is sufficient to justify the continued use of the death penalty.

[23]   Becker's original model made room for this option: recall the offender's objective function was $O = O(p, f, u)$, where u reflected any other possible sanction. The original model, however, focused solely on p and f and, like the models of the day, treated individuals as relatively atomistic.

[24]   Gaviria and Raphael (2001), for example, provide a good overview of the peer-effects literature and its empirical difficulties (such as separating causal peer effects from self-selection into certain peer groups).

offenses in the United States. Ludwig and Kling (2006) also explore the importance of social effects, exploiting data from the Moving to Opportunity (MTO) program run by the federal Department of Housing and Urban Development. MTO relocates randomly selected families from high-crime housing complexes to more stable environments to examine the importance of social settings on, among other things, crime; Ludwig and Kling, however, find little effect of MTO on crime rates.

It should be expected that today's model of the criminal does not look exactly like that set forth by Becker three decades ago. If anything, what should be surprising is how similar it remains. The criminal is more impetuous (perhaps, if DiIulio 1996 is right, remarkably so), and he cares more about his friends, environment, and upbringing, but he is still rational. The main contribution of Becker's model to criminology remains, even if some of its policy recommendations do not: it is essential for investigators to think carefully about how (potential) criminals respond to the incentives before them. As we develop richer and deeper understandings of human behavior, our views on how to properly shape and manage those incentives will change. But the underlying thought, that criminals respond predictably to changing incentives, remains vital.

The second important contribution of Becker's model of crime, besides its effect on the study of criminal behavior, has been its influence on that of 'deviant' behavior broadly defined. Though Becker's paper focused exclusively on crime, linking its theoretical findings to rough data on criminal behavior in the United States, the model applies to any situation in which one party seeks to engage in conduct that another party wants to prevent. It should therefore come as no surprise that Becker's model motivates examinations of violations of antitrust law (Easterbrook 1981; Landes and Posner 1981), environmental regulations (Langbein and Kerwin 1985), and safety recalls (Bromily and Marcus 1989), as well as studies of bureaucratization (Wintrobe 1982), terrorism (Landes 1978; Sandler and Enders 2004), and compliance with everything from tax laws (Dubin et al. 1987) to oil cartels (Danielsen 1976) to speed limits (Graves et al. 1989).

Finally, Becker's article has had at least one other indirect, and little-known, effect. Calabresi and Melamed's (1972) famous article on the proper use of property and liability rules – which launched a literature of its own across property, contracts, and torts – was written in response to Becker's crime piece (Posner 1993a). Becker's paper can be read to imply that the optimal sanction for theft should leave the offender indifferent between stealing the good and buying it. Calabresi and Melamed believed that property rights should be used to tip the scales in favor of trade over theft, at least when transactions costs are low, and they wrote their article to stress this point.

The economics of enforcement   Deterrent policies work only if those charged with enforcing the laws actually uphold them. It is thus not surprising that Becker next turned his attention to the incentives of the police (Becker and Stigler 1974). Enforcers of all types face constant temptation, such as bribery and shirking, and it is essential to structure their incentives to encourage them to remain honest. Becker and Stigler's solution is a contract with three parts: a bond the enforcers post roughly equal to the value of temptation, an annual income premium equal to the returns on the bond, and a large pension that returns the value of the bond at the end of employment. The large pension, which is forfeited in full if the enforcer is caught misbehaving at any point, along with the income premium, discourage misbehavior; the up-front bond ensures that the markets clear (without it, the wage premium would lead to a surplus supply of labor). In some cases, the initial bond is replaced by under-paying the enforcer early in his career and overpaying him later.

It is easy to see the wide applicability of the model, since employees of all types face the temptation to misbehave. As Becker and Stigler acknowledge, their model is relevant for 'purchasing agents, sales personnel, soldiers, physicians, lawyers, managers', and many others. Their basic insight has been applied to a wide range of situations, including franchising (Brickley et al. 1991), general corruption (for example, Acemoglu and Verdier 2000), and pension plans (Ippolito 2001, 1985). At least in the pension setting, Ippolito (2001:18) has argued that 'all subsequent pension-incentive papers are variants of [Becker and Stigler's] simple model'.

The overall empirical support for the model, however, is mixed. As Bulow and Summers (1986) and Dickens et al. (1989) note, several real-world restrictions limit the applicability of these sorts of 'bonding' contracts. Liquidity constraints can thwart the use of bonds, and legal restrictions such as minimum wages the use of low early wages. Bonds also introduce moral hazard problems (the employer has an incentive to improperly terminate the employee in order to seize the bond) and increase the effort (and thus costs) with which employees resist termination. As a result, investigators have put forth the idea of efficiency wages, in which an employee is simply paid above-average wages to induce good behavior, resulting in labor markets that do not clear (Baker et al. 1988). Proving the existence of efficiency wages has been difficult (Prendergast 1999), but it does appear that bonds and other up-front payments are used only in specific settings, particularly franchising and pensions.

Drug use and other addictive behaviors   Perhaps Becker's most ambitious effort to extend his rational choice methodology is his work on rational addiction (Becker and Murphy 1988a; Becker et al. 2006, 1994, 1991). The intuition, though controversial,[25] is straight-forward. Rational addicts, like all other rational people, are forward-looking utility maximizers with stable preferences. What separates addictive consumption from regular consumption is not that it changes tastes or eliminates choice, but that the marginal utility of consuming the addictive good today is a function of the total amount of the good consumed in the past. Specifically, the more of the good consumed in the past, the greater its marginal utility today; this is referred to as 'adjacent complementarity'.[26] Furthermore, rational addicts pay attention to the lifetime expected value of the 'full price' of consumption, which includes both direct monetary expenditures and any utility losses (from harmful addictive goods) or gains (from beneficial ones). The model is sophisticated enough to account for the decision to quit cold turkey, for turning to drugs in times of stress, and for differing degrees of future-mindedness. Subsequent work has even allowed for time preferences to arise endogenously (Becker and Mulligan 1997). Thus even forward-looking rational actors can become addicted (although the propensity for addiction may rise the more myopic the consumer).

The model generates at least two policy implications, one positive, the other normative. From a positive perspective, its results indicate, contrary to widely asserted conventional wisdom, that long-run addictive behavior responds to changes in the permanent price of the

---

[25]   Perhaps the bluntest statement of disapproval is the title to Rogeberg (2004): 'Taking Absurd Theories Seriously: Economics and the Case of Rational Addiction Theories'.

[26]   Note that rising *marginal* utility is consistent with tolerance effects, in which higher levels of past consumption lower the *total* utility of a given level of current consumption.

addictive good.[27] Normatively, the theoretical findings provide a strong argument against government regulation of addictive goods, at least beyond imposing Pigouvian taxes to account for any externalities: if users rationally account for future disutility from consumption, then any additional prohibition only increases their disutility (since it raises the price). If addicts are rational, then regulation beyond that advocated by Pigou implicates the general utilitarian dislike of paternalism.[28]

A theory of this sort demands empirical validation. And despite the sometimes vitriolic attacks on the rationality assumption, empirical tests have often, though certainly not always, yielded results consistent with the theory's predictions. It should perhaps be expected that the consumption of addictive but non-'mind altering' substances, such as cigarettes (Becker et al. 1994; Chaloupka 1991; Gruber and Közegi 2001; Chaloupka and Warner 2000 provides a good summary of the empirical literature) and caffeine (Olekalns and Bardsley 1996) exhibit rational-addiction patterns. Gruber and Közegi (2001), for example, examine smoking behavior in the time between an announced hike in cigarette taxes and the actual implementation of the new taxes; they find that cigarettes purchases rise (since cigarettes are weakly durable) but consumption falls in preparation of reduced future consumption, precisely what the rational-addict theory predicts.

But the results extend to substances more often thought to substantially impair rational decision-making. Tests returning results consistent with rational addiction have looked at cocaine use by the young (Grossman et al., 1998a), gambling (Mobilia 1993), and alcohol (Grossman et al., 1998b; Klick 2002). Klick (2002) is particularly interesting because it looks at a non-monetary change: when states make access to treatment easier and less expensive, people engage more in addictive behavior. The policy implications are clear – greater access to treatment may not reduce consumption – and set forth starkly the importance of the rational addict model. The results, however, are not uniform. Liu et al. (1999), for example, finds evidence that opium use in Taiwan did not follow the patterns suggested by rational addiction theory.

Despite finding support for the rationality assumption, however, some recent work casts doubt on the non-interventionist policy recommendations that emerge from Becker and Murphy (1988a). Gruber and Közegi (2001) update the rational addict model to account for time-inconsistent preferences, specifically hyperbolic discounting of the sort defined by Laibson (1997). Though they are unable to develop an empirical test capable of separating hyperbolic- from non-hyperbolic discounting, their theoretical results indicate that, if present, hyperbolic discounting induces strong 'internalities' (intraperson intertemporal externalities) which actually argue in favor of government regulation beyond Pigouvian levels.

Thus, no matter what the choice, people respond to the prices and incentives they face. If this holds true for addiction, it is hard to imagine the behavior for which it does not. Improved behavioral models, such as those which incorporate hyperbolic discounting, may reach differ-

---

[27]   Other predictions regarding price are that responses will be greater for anticipated rather than unanticipated changes in price and for permanent rather than temporary changes.

[28]   Becker et al. (2006) provides another argument against enforcing drug laws drawn from rational-offender theory. Interdiction policies attempt to drive down drug use by using fear of incarceration to drive up drug prices. If supply or demand is relatively inelastic, such policies are generally socially wasteful in many situations. Excise taxes, however, appear to be much more effective.

ent policy recommendations than those which rely on older assumptions,[29] but they remain fundamentally rational models and demonstrate the power of such approaches.

2.2 The economics of discrimination

From the very beginning of his career, Becker pushed the boundaries of economic analysis. His dissertation, later published by the University of Chicago Press as *The Economics of Discrimination* (1971 [1957]), was an ambitious effort to explain the presence of racial discrimination. Like his work on crime, Becker's theory of discrimination continues to play an important role in the research on the topic.

The model is straight-forward. First, rather than assuming that firms maximize profit, Becker assumes they maximize utility; or, more precisely, that their owners and managers do so. Some have described this deviation from profit-maximization to utility-maximization as 'troubling' (Schwab 2000), but it is unclear to me why this is the case. Firms are not conscious entities themselves, but are instead made up of (utility-maximizing) people. Why should we believe that managers or owners who maximize utility in all their decisions suddenly decide to maximize only profits when it comes to a business entity? If anything, what should be troubling is any departure from *utility* maximization. It could be that market discipline sets a price on discrimination higher than what the manager is willing to pay, driving him to 'purchase' only profit-maximizing behavior, but that claim differs qualitatively from one saying that firm-owners are inherently profit-maximizing.

Second, discrimination arises from a taste for racial animus.[30] Thus a racist white employer who pays a black employee a wage w feels like he is paying the wage $w(1 + d)$, where d is a parameter reflecting his degree of racism. Similarly, a racist white employee earning the wage w while working for a black employer would feel like his earnings are $w(1 - d)$.[31] Consumer discrimination is modeled identically, replacing the wage w with the price p. From these basic elements, Becker extracts several hypotheses, such as that discrimination lowers the net income of both the discriminators and the discriminated, that the discriminated-against minorities lose more than the discriminating majorities, and that the minorities lose even more if they attempt to retaliate. Perhaps most controversially, he argues that under certain conditions (a limitation that is often overlooked) market forces should drive discriminating owners from the market.

Not surprisingly, this model has generated a significant amount of attention and criticism.[32] Early on, the model was attacked by Arrow (1972:192) for its claim that market forces

---

[29]   As Gruber and Közegi (2001) themselves admit, there is no empirical evidence either for or against hyperbolic discounting, although they point out that experimental evidence has yet to confirm that people discount exponentially rather than hyperbolically.

[30]   At the time Becker wrote his dissertation, racial animus was, in many circles, openly held and freely expressed; the prevalence of such views has certainly diminished since then. That does not mean, however, that animus is any less important. The Implicit Association Test, for example, suggests that most whites and almost half of all blacks subconsciously prefer 'white' to 'black'. See, for example, Jolls and Sunstein (2006). Becker's model captures both sources of bias.

[31]   Epstein (1992) builds on this part of Becker's model, arguing that employment discrimination arises when employers, motivated by profit instead of animus, try to hire relatively homogeneous workforces in the name of workplace stability. In other words, it is the racism of the employees, not the employers, that leads to segregated workplaces.

[32]   Donohue (1998), Gersen (2007), and Schwab (2000) all provide good overviews.

could drive discriminators out of business; it was a theory that 'predicts the absence of the phenomenon it was designed to explain', and one that was inconsistent with the discrimination clearly present in the 1950s. This, however, mischaracterizes the model. Market forces drive out discrimination only under specific circumstances, such as when firms exhibit constant return to scale technology.[33] When one firm can expand indefinitely, the most efficient firm will undersell all others: unless a discriminator possesses unique entrepreneurial skill, he will be unable to pay the 'price' for his discrimination.[34] As Heckman (1998:112) notes, Becker's model implies no discrimination only if 'the supply of entrepreneurship is perfectly elastic in the long run at a zero price, so entrepreneurs have no income to spend to indulge their tastes, or if there are enough nonprejudiced employers to hire all blacks'. These are clearly strong conditions. As Schwab (2000) points out, a prejudiced owner who otherwise could be earning 10 per cent on his investment can maintain an 8 per cent return to satisfy his prejudice indefinitely. He will face more pressure than an unbiased owner to sell his company, perhaps, and so on the margin competition should reduce the presence of racism, but this is a far more constrained statement than the claim normally attributed to Becker's model.

It should also be noted that the market-forces claim applies only to employer-based discrimination. If discrimination originates from animus held by either employees or customers, then long-run market pressures need not eliminate discrimination unless the market is large enough to be wholly segregated.[35] And these sources of discrimination are likely more empirically significant than employer animus (Becker 1993a).

The reliance on an assumed taste for discrimination, however, should raise some concerns. Assuming particular tastes to explain patterns in the data risks turning rational-choice models into tautologies. Whatever behavior is observed can be explained by assuming a taste for that behavior; as Moran (2003:2386) suggests, imputing tastes runs the risk of turning rationality into 'phlogiston', and Becker himself has admitted that positing changes in taste is 'the economist's admission of defeat' (Fuchs 1994:184). But, at least in this context, the introduction of a taste parameter is not entirely problematic. The existence of a taste for discrimination leads to testable claims that differ from those that arise under the assumption of the taste's absence. In other words, here we can explicitly test for the taste's presence, thus avoiding the pitfalls of tautology. Moreover, assuming a taste for racism may be qualitatively different than assuming one for driving on the right-hand side of the road.

---

[33]   Constant returns to scale implies that a firm's marginal costs do not change as it grows. A firm is thus as efficient at producing one widget as ten as a hundred as one thousand. This allows the most efficient firm to provide for the entire market, since it can expand without any loss of efficiency. A firm exhibiting diminishing returns to scale, however, becomes less efficient as it grows. If the market is sufficiently large, the non-discriminating firm will expand until its (diminished) marginal productivity equals that of the less efficient discriminating firm, and both will exist side by side.

[34]   Becker (1968b) makes an entrepreneurial argument of this sort. Donohue (1998), at least, is not persuaded, arguing that entrepreneurial talent was likely in sufficient supply in the South during the 1950s, 'unless the scarce skill was knowing how to [hire minorities] without having one's mill burned down by the Ku Klux Klan'.

[35]   Charles and Guryan (2007) point out that the distinction between employer and employee is not exogenous: a given individual can choose whether to be one or the other, and that choice may be influenced by racial attitudes. They find evidence that self-employed owners, who tend to have few or no employees, exhibit higher degrees of racism than other owners.

Nonetheless, the response within economics has been to look for rational reasons to discriminate even in the absence of any animus.[36] One result has been the theory of statistical discrimination (Aigner and Cain 1977; Arrow 1973; Phelps 1972). The intuition is simple: employers use, say, race as a proxy for other relevant but unobservable variables. If employers know that members of group *A* exhibit, on average, higher values of an unobservable trait *x* than members of group *B*, it may be profit-maximizing to discriminate against members of group *B* even if the employer feels no animus of any sort.[37] Of course, profit-maximizing need not imply normative appealing. Most obviously, by looking at average values rather than marginal ones, statistical discrimination discourages members of group *B* from investing in, for example, human capital development (Lundberg and Startz 1983).

A second non-taste-based approach has been to look beyond the individual actor to broader social contexts.[38] McAdams (1995), for example, has asserted that Becker's discriminator is too atomistic: people are social animals, and group-level forces can influence their behavior. In particular, McAdams looks at the relationship between discrimination and group status, arguing that group *A* can elevate itself by discriminating against group *B*. Arrow (1998) points to a different social concern, that jobs are often acquired through informal social networks rather than impersonal 'job markets', and that failure to account for these paths to employment leaves economic models of labor discrimination incomplete. And signaling theorists such as Lessig (1995) take a third approach, suggesting that discrimination can be used by people lacking animus to signal their willingness to cooperate with (discriminatory) social norms in general. Lessig then suggests that anti-discrimination laws are effective because they cloud the signal behind non-discriminatory acts: are they anti-cooperative or law-abiding?

These competing theories are often difficult to isolate empirically. Some recent productive efforts, however, seem to suggest that the taste theory explains some, though certainly not all, of the observed patterns of discrimination. Levitt (2004), for example, takes advantage of the strategic structure of a television game-show, *The Weakest Link*. Due to the way prize money is awarded, the behavior of a taste-based discriminator and a statistical discriminator should be similar at the start of the game but different at the end. Levitt exploits this exogenous shift in incentives to uncover evidence of both taste-based and statistical discriminatory behavior. Gersen's (2007) analysis of data from filings before the Equal Employment Opportunity Commission yields results consistent with taste-based-, statistical-, and status-based discrimination. In particular, he finds that taste plays a more important role in sex discrimination, statistical- and status-based discrimination a more important role in racial discrimination. And Charles and Guryan (2007), using data from the General Social Survey on racial sentiment, report that racial differences in wages are positively correlated with both the average

---

[36]   Perhaps ironically, some of the challenges to Becker's model are more in keeping with Becker's approach than his own model – statistical discrimination, for example, relies on a purer form of the rational actor model than one incorporating a taste for discrimination.

[37]   Here, discrimination would mean that the employer would favor an applicant from group *A* over one from group *B* when the two applicants possess identical observable traits (or when those of the group-*B* applicant are better).

[38]   Becker's work in this area, Becker and Murphy (2000) in particular, has focused less on discrimination and more on how social interactions, such as the desire to live near certain types of neighbors, can lead to segregation even in the absence of discrimination.

level of racism in a region as well as the racism of the marginal discriminator. Both claims are consistent with Becker's theory. But the findings are not uniform. List (2004), for example, develops several field experiments which he uses at trading-card shows to examine the offers made to minorities; his results are more consistent with statistical than taste-based discrimination.

Some of Becker's work on other aspects of human behavior has also shed light on the origins of discriminatory (or seemingly discriminatory) behavior. His theory of human capital, for example, explains some observed disparities in wages between the sexes. The theory implies that people invest more in training for tasks they expect to do more often. If women do not plan to work as much as men, they will invest less in human capital and, since their marginal productivity will be lower, earn less. These lower earnings, however, are not (at least to an economist) discriminatory. This theory, however, runs into an empirical problem: as women entered the labor force in large numbers in Western countries, their wages did not converge to men's as quickly as theory predicted. Becker (1985) suggests that the explanation rests, at least in part, on a sexual division of labor. Even as women enter the workforce, there is a domestic division of labor between married (or otherwise coupled) men and women, with women taking on a larger share of household work. With a relatively large share of their time devoted to household labor, women will invest less in human capital and self-select into less time-demanding (and thus lower-paying) occupations. Empirical evidence supports this claim to some extent, though not unambiguously (see, for example, Neumark and McLennan 1995). At the very least, the theory forces us to consider more carefully the rational tradeoffs that may be causing disparities seen in the data.

It is thus clear that Becker's book still shapes the analysis of discrimination fifty years after it was written. Most important, the model has survived half a century of rigorous empirical testing. The taste for discrimination clearly does not explain all of the discrimination observed in the data, but it certainly explains some of it, and Becker's insistence that discrimination be viewed through the prism of rational choice continues to pay dividends.

2.3   Crime, malfeasance, and discrimination: the case of racial profiling

Issues of race and crime are intimately intertwined in the United States, and so it is not surprising that Becker's work in these two areas at times intersects. It does so most dramatically, perhaps, when it comes to the police practice of racial profiling. Racial profiling raises several important questions: When police officers rely on racial profiling, are they engaging in statistical- or animus-based discrimination? If the former, how do criminals rationally respond to it? If the latter, or if an example of inefficient statistical discrimination, how do we confront another example of enforcer malfeasance? Whether profiling is in fact effective policing has become an important issue since the terrorist attacks of September 11, 2001, which made profiling – a practice which implicates historical tensions between the police and minority communities – much more politically tenable.

Knowles et al. (2001) (KPT) developed the first systematic theoretical and empirical investigation into racial profiling, using searches for drugs incident to traffic stops as their key example. In broad terms, their model consists of three pieces: in the absence of profiling, minorities (following KPT, I will refer to these as A) offend more than majorities (W), non-racist police officers seek to maximize the number of successful searches, and offenders respond to changes in search intensities. If offenders were non-responsive, then the police would maximize the number of successful searches simply by searching A every time. But rational offenders change the calculus: as the police search A-types relatively more, members of A will transport drugs less often while members of W will do so more often.

Thus, in equilibrium, the police should distribute their searches so that their 'hit rates' (the fraction of stops that produce successful searches) are equal across both groups. If the hit rate for A is greater than that for W, police should search more members of A. This substitution will drive down the hit rate of searches of A (since, facing greater risks, fewer As will carry drugs), and drive up that of searches of W (since more will now transport contraband in light of lower expected punishment). Note that given differences in the propensity to offend across groups, equal hit rates need not imply equal searching intensity in equilibrium.

Thus this theory yields a testable hypothesis. If it is correct (an issue dealt with shortly), police engaged in statistical discrimination will have equal hit rates, those profiling out of racial animus unequal rates. In particular, racist police will have lower hit rates for searches of group A (since they will 'over-search' them). Using data from the Maryland State Police gathered as part of a lawsuit concerning its alleged use of racial profiling, KPT find little evidence in general of animus-based discrimination: hit rates are relatively equal across whites and blacks, although the results are consistent with racial discrimination against Hispanics.

The KPT model has faced numerous criticisms. Anwar and Fang (2006), for example, point out that the KPT model implies that in equilibrium race wholly determines the probability of carrying contraband – the probability does not depend on any other trait observable to the police – and that the model assumes no variation in discriminatory preferences across police officers. Anwar and Fang's revised model, which does not rely on either assumption, nonetheless fails to detect evidence of animus motivating search decisions (using data from Florida). Bjerk (2007) draws attention to the same point and demonstrates that if police observe both an offender's race and an imperfect signal of offending, then in equilibrium statistically discriminating police will stop more members of A than members of W, will be relatively more successful when searching members of A, and will stop more innocent members of A. Like Anwar and Fang, Antonovics and Knight (2004) similarly exploit data (this time from Boston) on the race of both the stopping officer and the person stopped, but they produce results that are consistent with race-based animus. Persico and Todd (2006) summarize sixteen studies looking at police stops across different jurisdictions. They claim that the results suggest that hit rates are roughly similar for whites and blacks, though those for blacks are generally lower than those for whites; where available, those for Hispanics are often significantly lower.

Even if we accept as a given that the police are not indulging in tastes for discrimination, however, it is unclear what equal hit rates say about the policy implications of racial profiling. Harcourt (2007) and Persico (2002) point to a fundamental concern with hit rates, namely that police behavior equalizing hit rates need not reduce crime, and in fact may increase it. Key to their argument is the plausible claim that if group A offends more than W in the absence of profiling, then As likely respond to changes in enforcement patterns less elastically than Ws. If so, equalizing hit rates does not minimize crime: shifting one stop from W to A will reduce offending by the less-elastic A *less* than it will increase offending by the more-elastic W. As a result, restrictions on profiling need not conflict with socially optimal policing strategies.

Which brings us to the third issue of profiling. If profiling is improper, either because it is motivated by racial animus or because equalized hit rates lead to inefficient outcomes, how can we discourage the police from engaging in profiling? The solution, of course, is data – the more data we have on stops and searches, the more police departments will be able to discipline malfeasant officers. However, as Dominitz (2003) points out, this is not necessarily as easy as it may appear. If offending differs by race, then it is impossible to simultaneously ensure that five proposed definitions of 'equal treatment' are satisfied: equal search rates, equal find rates, equal thoroughness of search, equal rates of detention of innocent parties, and equal arrest rates of the guilty. And the work by Harcourt (2007) and Persico (2002) further implies that the relationships between these definitions of equality and crime rates are not immediately clear as well. Legislatures and courts have not yet wrestled deeply with the difficult normative choices they thus face.

Resolving the debate over racial profiling is clearly beyond the scope of this chapter. What is most relevant here is that it again shows the power of Becker's framework. Simple assumptions about the motivations of offenders and enforcers lead to testable hypotheses, and these help us to start searching for answers to difficult but important questions of social policy.

2.4   Further forays into rational choice

Though Becker's work on discrimination and crime fall most explicitly within the realm of 'law and economics', much of his other work has had important implications for the field as well. As Posner (1993a) points out, Becker's writings on human capital, the household, and the family have been used to explain everything from the efficiency of contracting at will (Epstein 1984) to the behavior of federal judges (Posner 1993b). It is not surprising that in his efforts to apply rational choice widely and unrelentingly Becker has touched on innumerable topics with legal implications.

Consider, for example, his work on the family. Most famous is his model of marital stability. By assuming that marital decisions are, like all decisions, made rationally, Becker (1991a) is able to apply the Coase Theorem to marriages. If the Coase Theorem conditions hold – with the assumption that transactions costs are low perhaps appearing to be a *very* strong claim when it comes to divorce – the choice of a legal divorce rule (fault- or no-fault divorce) should not affect the number of divorces. And there is empirical evidence roughly along these lines. Friedberg (1998) finds evidence that shifts from fault- to no-fault divorce rules did not contribute significantly to patterns in US divorce rates, with the rule change explaining about one-sixth of the increase. Wolfers (2006) replicates Friedberg's results and describes a slightly more complex picture: the shift to unilateral divorce laws leads to a short-run spike that dissipates over time, with no apparent effect ten years out. Though the results are not wholly consistent with the Coasean model – the short-run spike technically refutes the theory – Wolfers argues that they are more consistent with the rational-bargaining model than with its strict alternatives.

Though perhaps not as well-known as his theory of divorce, Becker's work on the family has been relevant in many other areas of family law as well. Becker (1991a), Becker and Murphy (1988b), and Becker and Tomes (1986), for example, examine how skills and wealth are passed from generation to generation, how parents adjust investments in their children's human capital in response to public expenditures of education, and how old-age support programs such as social security influence internal family cohesion. That these models have implications for tax law, estate law, education law, and a host of other disciplines is immediately obvious.

There is no need to belabor the point. Becker's career has been defined by extending the rational-choice model to cover all human behavior. And there are few if any spheres of human behavior which are wholly unregulated (or at least uninfluenced) by the law. Becker's models – and at the very least his methodological approach – thus have applications in all areas of law. No longer do legal economists simply consider how legal rules influence market outcomes. Instead, they examine the behavioral implications of legal changes for all aspects of life. To (re)quote Medema (2008), Becker's work laid the foundation for the transition from 'law and economics' to 'the economic analysis of the law'.

3   Becker's personal contributions

Becker's intellectual efforts have contributed significantly to contemporary law and economics. But it is important to realize that his personal efforts have played a vital role as well. Becker has not only shaped the field through the articles he has written, but also through the people he has affected and the institutions he has developed.

Consider his influence on two of the other central pioneers of law and economics, Richard Posner and William Landes. As Posner (1993a:214) recounts, it was Becker who 'helped solidify [his] own commitment to law and economics by signing [him] up as a research associate of the National Bureau of Economic Research'. Medema (2008) makes this point even more forcefully, pointing out that Posner's work prior to his time at the NBER focused on classical law and economics topics such as antitrust and government regulation. It was only after moving to the NBER and becoming (as Medema puts it) 'Beckerized' that Posner turned his attention to a wider range of questions. And the importance of Posner's time at the NBER points to another of Becker's contributions. That the NBER even had a section dedicated to law and economics in the first place was, to at least a significant degree, the result of Becker's effort to expand the range of issues addressed by the Bureau (Fuchs 1994).

Becker also played an important role in Landes's career. He supported Landes, for example, when Landes's early foray into law and economics (Landes 1971) was met with distaste and suggestions that he quickly focus on more 'relevant' lines of research for the good of his career. And according to Posner (1993a), Becker encouraged Posner to work with Landes; the result is perhaps one of the most fruitful pairings in law and economics. Since their first joint effort in 1975, Landes and Posner have co-authored at least thirty-four articles together (and sometimes with third parties), of which only a small representative sample are Landes and Posner (2003, 2001, 1987, 1981, 1975).

These two high-profile examples of Becker's influence are by no means the only ones. I have no doubt that many of Becker's former students can attest to his encouragement of and influence on their work. Speaking personally, I can still pinpoint the moment in Becker's first-year graduate microeconomics course when I realized I would focus on law and economics.

4   Conclusion

It is remarkable to compare the tables of contents of the *Journal of Political Economy* of 1951 to those of 2001. The articles from 1951 are on what one would think of as classically 'economic' topics: income transfers, utility functions, interest rate issues, labor and wages, tax policy.[39] And certainly the *Journal* of 2001 still addresses such core economic issues,

---

[39]   See, for example, Baumol (1951: utility functions), Boulding (1951: interest rates, along with Metzler 1951b, 1951c), Campbell (1951: tax policy, along with Lent 1951), Metzler (1951a: income transfers), and Stigler (1951: labor and wages, along with Jasny 1951, Lewis 1951, and Rees 1951).

with articles on labor and wages, banks and liquidity, price variability, and utility functions.[40] But much of the 2001 *Journal* covered themes that can only be described as 'Beckerian': spousal leisure decisions, the racial bias of police vehicle searches, guns and crime, political correctness, war and democracy, and educational attainment outcomes.[41] Even if uncited, Becker's influence permeates all these articles.

Not surprisingly, the transformative effect he had on economics extends to law and economics; we can apply this same crude empiricism to the *Journal of Law and Economics*. The 1968[42] volume of the *Journal* addressed such 'law and economics' topics as utilities and regulation, mergers, insurance, and antitrust.[43] By 2006, the shift to 'the economic analysis of law' is clear: articles in the *Journal* examine the origins of democracy; the effect of religion, teen pregnancy, or gun access on crime; the proper structure of plea bargains; the effect of crime on employment; the drivers of teacher quality; and abortion and drug use.[44] Again, 'traditional' topics – mergers, regulation, contracting – remain,[45] but the overall nature of the articles has clearly shifted. The *Journal of Law and Economics* has changed just like the *Journal of Political Economy*.

Duxbury (1995), like Tolstoy (1982 [1869]), cautions against a great-man-of-history view of law and economics. The modern law and economics movement – the economic analysis of law – has many founders: not just Becker, but everyone discussed in this book, and many more besides. But while it is important to not overstate the role of one particular person, it is equally important to not understate it. And the modern transformation of economic-legal scholarship in many ways owes its deepest debt to Gary Becker.

A final anecdote provides an example of the extent to which Becker's work can transform the way we think about legal questions. When I began work on this chapter, I believed that Becker's (1968a) work on crime – though certainly transformative within economics, and to some extent law and economics – had not had a large impact within legal scholarship more broadly. It may have inspired the large literature discussed above, by people like Kaplow, Polinsky, and Shavell, but its effect within the law literature had always struck me as slight. While Becker focused on fines, for example, the criminal justice system uses prison; and the

---

[40]   See, for example, Diamond and Rajan (2001: liquidity), Robson (2001: utility functions), Saint-Paul (2001: labor and wages, along with Acemoglu and Angrist 2001), and Silver and Ioannidis (2001: prices).

[41]   See, for example, Cameron and Heckman (2001: educational outcomes, along with Bedard 2001), Duggan (2001: guns and crime), Fong and Zhang (2001: spousal leisure), Hess and Orphanides (2001: war and democracy), Knowles et al. (2001: police searches), and Morris (2001: political correctness).

[42]   The *Journal of Law and Economics* did not begin until 1958, and for several of its early years published only one number per year. I opted, then, to begin with its second decade of publication.

[43]   See, for example, Kitch (1968: regulation, along with Peterman 1968, Levin 1968, Demsetz 1968), Pashigian (1968: monopoly and antitrust, along with Maule 1968), and Rowley (1968: mergers), Kunreuther (1968: insurance).

[44]   See, for example, Bar-Gill and Ayal (2006: plea bargains), Charles and Stephens (2006: abortion and drugs), Fleck and Hanssen (2006: origins of democracy), Heaton (2006: religion and crime), Hunt (2006: teen births and crime), Ihlanfeldt (2006: crime and employment, along with Holzer et al. 2006), Lakdawalla (2006: teacher quality), and Mocan and Tekin (2006: guns and juvenile crime).

[45]   See, for example, Brickley et al. (2006: contracting), Gagnepain and Marín (2006: regulation), and Peters (2006: mergers).

substitutability of p and f seemed to go against evidence of criminal impetuousness and juror reluctance to convict when sanctions are high.

Of course, the article is a seminal one, not just because of its broader implications for economic imperialism, but because of its influence on criminal law in particular. And, somewhat ironically, my under-appreciation of this was the result of its importance. It is true that, forty years later, some of its assumptions have been found wanting. But the core insight, an idea that had been forgotten essentially since Beccaria and Bentham, was to treat criminals as rational actors. And on this point, the paper was revolutionary and revolutionizing. Researchers might disagree about the optimal balance of certainty and severity, about the impulsiveness of criminals, about the limits of their rationality, about the social costs of various sanctioning regimes. But Becker's paper forced them to wrestle with the maximizing behavior of the offenders. So thoroughly did Becker change the nature of the debate that, by the time I started law school in the late 1990s, the rough rationality of the offender was taken as essentially a given.

Bibliography

Acemoglu, Daron, and Joshua D. Angrist. 2001. 'Consequences of Employment Protection? The Case of the Americans with Disability Act'. *Journal of Political Economy* 109: 915–57.

Acemoglu, Daron, and Thierry Verdier. 2000. 'The Choice Between Market Failures and Corruption'. *American Economic Review* 90: 194–211.

Aigner, Dennis, and Glen Cain. 1977. 'Statistical Theories of Discrimination in the Labor Markets'. *Industrial & Labor Relations Review* 30: 175–87.

Allen, W. David. 2002. 'Crime, Punishment, and Recidivism: Lessons from the National Hockey League'. *Journal of Sports Economics* 3: 39–60.

Andreoni, James. 1991. 'Reasonable Doubt and the Optimal Magnitude of Fines: Should the Penalty Fit the Crime?' *RAND Journal of Economics* 22: 385–95.

Antonovics, Kate L., and Brian G. Knight. 2004. 'A New Look at Racial Profiling: Evidence from the Boston Police Department'. NBER Working Paper No. 10634.

Anwar, Shamena, and Hanming Fang. 2006. 'An Alternative Test of Racial Prejudice in Motor Vehicle Searches: Theory and Evidence'. *American Economic Review* 96: 127–51.

Arrow, Kenneth. 1998. 'What Has Economics to Say about Racial Discrimination?' *Journal of Economic Perspectives* 12: 91–100.

Arrow, Kenneth. 1973. 'The Theory of Discrimination'. In *Discrimination in Labor Markets*, edited by Orley Ashenfelter and Albert Rees. Princeton: Princeton University Press.

Arrow, Kenneth. 1972. 'Some Mathematical Models of Race in the Labor Market'. In *Racial Discrimination in Economic Life*, edited by A.H. Pascal. Lexington: Lexington Books.

Backhouse, Roger E. 2004. 'History and Equilibrium: A Partial Defense of Equilibrium Economics'. *Journal of Economic Methodology* 11: 291–305.

Baker, George P., Michael C. Jensen, and Kevin J. Murphy. 1988. 'Compensation and Incentives: Practice vs. Theory'. *Journal of Finance* 43: 593–616.

Bar-Gill, Oren, and Oren Gazal Ayal. 2006. 'Plea Bargains Only for the Guilty'. *Journal of Law and Economics* 49: 353–64.

Bar-Gill, Oren, and Alon Harel. 2001. 'Crime Rates and Expected Sanctions: The Economics of Deterrence Revisited'. *Journal of Legal Studies* 30: 485–501.

Baumol, William J. 1951. 'The Neumann-Morgenstern Utility Index – An Ordinalist View'. *Journal of Political Economy* 59: 61–66.

Bebchuck, Lucien A., and Louis Kaplow. 1992. 'Optimal Sanctions When Individuals are Imperfectly Informed about the Probability of Apprehension'. *Journal of Legal Studies* 21: 365–70.

Beccaria, Cesare. 1995 [1764]. *On Crimes and Punishments and Other Writings*. Cambridge: Cambridge University Press.

Becker, Gary S. 2006. 'On the Economics of Capital Punishment'. *The Economists' Voice* 3: 3(4).

Becker, Gary S. 1996. *Accounting for Tastes*. Cambridge: Harvard University Press.

Becker, Gary S. 1993a. 'Nobel Lecture: The Economic Way of Looking at Behavior'. *Journal of Political Economy* 101: 385–409.

Becker, Gary S. 1993b. 'Gary Becker'. In *Les Prix Nobel 1992*, edited by Tore Frangsmyr. Philadelphia: Coronet Books.

Becker, Gary S. 1991a. *A Treatise on the Family: Enlarged Editions*. Cambridge: Harvard University Press.

Becker, Gary S. 1991b. 'A Note on Restaurant Pricing and Other Examples of Social Influences on Price'. *Journal of Political Economy* 99: 1109–16.

Becker, Gary S. 1985. 'Human Capital, Effort, and the Sexual Division of Labor'. *Journal of Labor Economics* 3: S33–S58.

Becker, Gary S. 1976. *The Economic Approach to Human Behavior*. Chicago: University of Chicago Press.

Becker, Gary S. 1974. 'A Theory of Social Interactions'. *Journal of Political Economy* 82: 1063–93.

Becker, Gary S. 1971 [1957]. *The Economics of Discrimination*. Chicago: University of Chicago Press.

Becker, Gary S. 1968a. 'Crime and Punishment: An Economic Approach'. *Journal of Political Economy* 76: 169–217.

Becker, Gary S. 1968b. 'Discrimination, Economic'. In *The International Encyclopedia of the Social Sciences*, edited by David L. Sills. New York: Macmillan.

Becker, Gary S. 1965. 'A Theory of the Allocation of Time'. *Economic Journal* 75: 493–517.

Becker, Gary S. 1962. 'Irrational Behavior and Economic Theory'. *Journal of Political Economy* 70: 1–13.

Becker, Gary S. 1958. 'Competition and Democracy'. *Journal of Law and Economics* 1: 105–9.

Becker, Gary S. 1952. 'A Note on Multi-Country Trade'. *American Economic Review* 42: 558–68.

Becker, Gary S., and William Baumol. 1952. 'The Classical Monetary Theory: The Outcome of the Discussion'. *Economica* 19: 355–76.

Becker, Gary S., Michael Grossman, and Kevin Murphy. 2006. 'The Market for Illegal Goods: The Case of Drugs'. *Journal of Political Economy* 14: 38–60.

Becker, Gary S., Michael Grossman, and Kevin Murphy. 1994. 'An Empirical Analysis of Cigarette Addiction'. *American Economic Review* 84: 396–418.

Becker, Gary S., Michael Grossman, and Kevin Murphy. 1991. 'Economics of Drug: Rational Addiction and the Effect of Price on Consumption'. *American Economic Review: Papers and Proceedings* 81: 237–41.

Becker, Gary S., and Casey B. Mulligan. 1997. 'The Endogenous Determination of Time Preference'. *Quarterly Journal of Economics* 112: 729–58.

Becker, Gary S., and Kevin Murphy. 2000. *Social Economics: Market Behavior in a Social Environment*. Cambridge: Harvard University Press.

Becker, Gary S., and Kevin Murphy. 1993. 'A Simple Theory of Advertising as a Good or Bad'. *Quarterly Journal of Economics* 108: 941–64.

Becker, Gary S., and Kevin Murphy. 1988a. 'A Theory of Rational Addiction'. *Journal of Political Economy* 96: 675–700.

Becker, Gary S., and Kevin Murphy. 1988b. 'The Family and the State'. *Journal of Law and Economics* 31: 1–18.

Becker, Gary S., Kevin M. Murphy, and Ivan Werning. 2005. 'The Equilibrium Distribution of Income and the Market for Status'. *Journal of Political Economy* 113: 282–310.

Becker, Gary S., and George Stigler. 1974. 'Law Enforcement, Malfeasance, and Competition of Enforcers'. *Journal of Legal Studies* 3: 1–18.

Becker, Gary S., and Nigel Tomes. 1986. 'Human Capital and the Rise and Fall of Families'. *Journal of Labor Economics* 4: S1–S39.

Bedard, Kelly. 2001. 'Human Capital versus Signaling Model: University Access and High School Dropouts'. *Journal of Political Economy* 109: 749–75.

Bentham, Jeremy. 2004 [1811]. *The Rationale of Punishment*. Honolulu: University Press of the Pacific.

Bentham, Jeremy. 1970 [1789]. *An Introduction to the Principles of Morals and Legislation*. London: Athlone Press.

Berk, Richard. 2005. 'New Claims about Executions and General Deterrence: Déjà Vu All Over Again?' *Journal of Empirical Legal Studies* 2: 303–30.

Bjerk, David. 2007. 'Racial Profiling, Statistical Discrimination, and the Effect of a Colorblind Policy on the Crime Rate'. *Journal of Public Economic Theory* 9: 521–46.

Bourgois, Philippe. 2003. *In Search of Respect: Selling Crack in El Barrio*. Cambridge: Cambridge University Press.

Boulding, Kenneth E. 1951. 'M. Allais's Theory of Interest'. *Journal of Political Economy* 59: 69–73.

Brickley, James A., Federick H. Dark, and Michael S. Weisbach. 1991. 'The Economic Effects of Franchise Termination Laws'. *Journal of Law and Economics* 34: 101–32.

Brickley, James A., Sanjog Misra, and R. Lawrence van Horn. 2006. 'Contract Duration: Evidence from Franchising'. *Journal of Law and Economics* 49: 173–96.

Bromily, Philip, and Alfred Marcus. 1989. 'The Deterrent of Dubious Corporate Behavior: Profitability, Probability and Safety Recalls'. *Strategic Management Journal* 10: 233–50.

Bulow, Jeremy I., and Lawrence H. Summers. 1986. 'A Theory of Dual Labor Markets with Application to Industrial Policy, Discrimination, and Keynesian Unemployment'. *Journal of Labor Economics* 4: 376–414.

Calabresi, Guido, and A. Douglas Melamed. 1972. 'Property Rules, Liability Rules, and Inalienability: One View of the Cathedral'. *Harvard Law Review* 85: 1089–128.

Cameron, Stephen V., and James J. Heckman. 2001. 'The Dynamics of Educational Attainment for Black, Hispanic, and White Males'. *Journal of Political Economy* 109: 455–99.

Campbell, Colin D. 1951. 'Are Property Tax Rates Increasing?' *Journal of Political Economy* 59: 434–42.

Chaloupka, Frank J. 1991. 'Rational Addictive Behavior and Cigarette Smoking'. *Journal of Political Economy* 99: 722–42.

Chaloupka, Frank J., and Kenneth E. Warner. 2000. 'The Economics of Smoking'. In *Handbook of Health Economics*, edited by A. J. Culyer and J. P. Newhouse. Cambridge: National Bureau of Economic Research.

Charles, Kerwin K., and John Guryan. 2007. 'Prejudice and the Economics of Discrimination'. Unpublished manuscript.

Charles, Kerwin K., and Melvin Stephens, Jr. 2006. 'Abortion Legalization and Adolescent Substance Use'. *Journal of Law and Economics* 49: 481–506.

Coase, Ronald. 1999. 'Interview with Ronald Coase'. *Newsletter of the International Society for New Institutional Economics* 2.

Coase, Ronald. 1988. *The Firm, the Market, and the Law*. Chicago: University of Chicago Press.

Coats, A. W. 1968. 'Political Economy and the Tariff Campaign of 1903'. *Journal of Law and Economics* 11: 181–229.

Cohen-Cole, Ethan, Steven Durlauf, Jeffrey Fagan, and Daniel Nagin. 2007. 'Model Uncertainty and the Deterrent Effect of Capital Punishment'. Unpublished manuscript.

Danielsen, Albert L. 1976. 'Cartel Rivalry and the World Price of Oil'. *Southern Economic Journal* 42: 407–15.

Demsetz, Harold. 1968. 'Why Regulate Utilities?' *Journal of Law and Economics* 11: 55–66.

Dezhbakhsh, Hashem, Paul H. Rubin, and Joanna M. Shepherd. 2003. 'Does Capital Punishment Have a Deterrent Effect? New Evidence from Postmoratorium Panel Data'. *American Law and Economics Review* 5: 344–76.

Diamond, Douglas W., and Raghuram G. Rajan. 2001. 'Liquidity Risk, Liquidity Creation, and Financial Fragility: A Theory of Banking'. *Journal of Political Economy* 109: 287–327.

Dickens, William T., Lawrence F. Katz, Kevin Lang, and Lawrence H. Summers. 1989. 'Employee Crime and the Monitoring Puzzle'. *Journal of Labor Economics* 7: 331–47.

Dilulio, Jr., John J. 1996. 'Help Wanted: Economists, Crime, and Public Policy'. *Journal of Economic Perspectives* 10: 3–24.

Dominitz, Jeff. 2003. 'How Do the Laws of Probability Constrain Legislative and Judicial Efforts to Stop Racial Profiling?' *American Law & Economics Review* 5: 412–32.

Donohue, John J. 1998. 'Discrimination in Employment'. Peter Newman, ed. New Palgrave Dictionary of Economics and the Law (London: Macmillan Reference Limited). 615–24.

Donohue, John J., and Justin Wolfers. 2005. 'Uses and Abuses of Empirical Evidence in the Death Penalty Debate'. *Stanford Law Review* 58: 791–846.

Doob, Anthony N., and Cheryl M. Webster. 2003. 'Sentence Severity and Crime: Accepting the Null Hypothesis'. *Crime and Justice* 30: 143–96.

Downs, Anthony. 1957. *An Economic Theory of Democracy*. New York: Harper & Row.

Dubin, Jeffrey A., Michael J. Graetz, and Louis L. Wilde. 1987. 'Are We a Nation of Tax Cheaters? New Econometric Evidence on Tax Compliance'. *American Economic Review* 77: 240–45.

Duggan, Mark. 2001. 'More Guns, More Crime'. *Journal of Political Economy* 109: 1086–114.

Duxbury, Neil. 1995. *Patterns of American Jurisprudence*. Oxford: Clarendon Press.

Easterbrook, Frank. 1981. 'Predatory Strategies and Counterstrategies'. *University of Chicago Law Review* 48: 263–337.

Ehrlich, Isaac. 1975. 'The Deterrent Effect of Capital Punishment: A Question of Life and Death'. *American Economic Review* 65: 397–417.

Ehrlich, Isaac. 1972. 'The Deterrent Effect of Criminal Law Enforcement'. *Journal of Legal Studies* 1: 259–76.

Ehrlich, Isaac. 1967. 'The Supply of Illegal Activities'. Unpublished manuscript, Columbia University, New York.

Epstein, Richard. 1992. *Forbidden Grounds: The Case Against Employment Discrimination Law*. Cambridge: Harvard University Press.

Epstein, Richard. 1984. 'In Defense of the Contract at Will'. *University of Chicago Law Review* 51: 947–82.

Ferri, Enrico. 1897. *Criminal Sociology*. New York: D. Appleton and Company.

Fleck, Robert K., and F. Andrew Hanssen. 2006. 'The Origins of Democracy: A Model with Application to Ancient Greece'. *Journal of Law and Economics* 49: 115–46.

Fong, Yuk-fai, and Junsen Zhang. 2001. 'The Identification of Unobservable Independent and Spousal Leisure'. *Journal of Political Economy* 109: 191–202.

Friedberg, Leora. 1998. 'Did Unilateral Divorce Raise Divorce Rates? Evidence from Panel Data'. *American Economic Review* 88: 608–27.

Friedman, Milton. 1999. 'Conversation with Milton Friedman'. In *Conversations with Leading Economists: Interpreting Modern Macroeconomics*, edited by Brian Snowden and Howard R. Vane. Cheltenham and Northampton, MA: Edward Elgar.

Friedman, Milton and Gary S. Becker. 1957. 'A Statistical Illusion in Judging Keynesian Models'. *Journal of Political Economy* 65: 64–75.

Fuchs, Victor R. 1994. 'Nobel Laureate: Gary S. Becker: Ideas about Facts'. *Journal of Economic Perspectives* 8: 183–92.

Fudenberg, Drew. 2006. 'Advancing Beyond *Advances in Behavioral Economics*'. *Journal of Economic Literature* 44: 694–711.

Gagnepain, Philippe, and Pedro L. Marín. 2006. 'Regulation and Incentives in European Aviation'. *Journal of Law and Economics* 49: 229–48.

Gaviria, Alejandro, and Steven Raphael. 2001. 'School-Based Peer Effects and Juvenile Behavior'. *Review of Economics and Statistics* 83: 257–68.

Gersen, Jacob. 2007. 'Markets and Discrimination'. *New York University Law Review* 82: 101–48.

Glaeser, Edward L., Bruce Sacerdote, and Jose A. Scheinkman. 1996. 'Crime and Social Interactions'. *Quarterly Journal of Economics* 111: 507–48.

Glueck, Sheldon, and Eleanor T. Glueck. 1950. *Unraveling Juvenile Delinquency*. Cambridge: Harvard University Press.

Goddu, Jennifer Q. 2006. 'Gift Names The Becker Center on Chicago Price Theory, Founded by Richard O. Ryan'. University of Chicago News Office.

Goring, Charles. 1919 [1913]. *The English Convict*. London: His Majesty's Stationery Office.

Gottfredson, Michael R., and Travis Hirschi. 1990. *A General Theory of Crime*. Stanford: Stanford University Press.

Graves, Philip E., Dwight R. Lee, and Robert L. Sexton. 1989. 'Statutes versus Enforcement: The Case of the Optimal Speed Limit'. *American Economic Review* 79: 932–36.

Grossman, Michael, Frank J. Chaloupka, and Charles C. Brown. 1998a. 'The Demand for Cocaine by Young Adults: A Rational-Addiction Approach'. *Journal of Health Economics* 17: 427–74.

Grossman, Michael, Frank J. Chaloupka, and Ismail Sirtalan. 1998a. 'An Empirical Analysis of Alcohol Addiction: Results from the Monitoring the Future Panels'. *Economic Inquiry* 36: 39–48.

Gruber, Jonathan, and Botond Közegi. 2001. 'Is Addiction "Rational"? Theory and Evidence'. *Quarterly Journal of Economics* 116: 1261–303.

Hanson, Jon, and Adam Benforado. 2005. 'The Costs of Dispositionism: The Premature Demise of Situationist Law and Economics'. *University of Maryland Law Review* 64: 24–84.

Hanson, Jon, and Doug Kysar. 1999a. 'Taking Behavioralism Seriously: Some Evidence of Market Manipulation'. *Harvard Law Review* 112: 1420–572.

Hanson, Jon, and Doug Kysar. 1999b. 'Taking Behavioralism Seriously: The Problem of Market Manipulation'. *New York University Law Review* 74: 632–749.

Hanson, Jon, and David Yosifon. 2004. 'The Situational Character: A Critical Realist Perspective on the Human Animal'. *Georgetown Law Journal* 93: 1–179.

Hanson, Jon, and David Yosifon. 2003. 'The Situation: An Introduction to the Situational Character, Critical Realism, Power Economics, and Deep Capture'. *University of Pennsylvania Law Review* 152: 129–346.

Harcourt, Bernard. 2007. *Against Prediction: Profiling, Policing, and Punishing in an Actuarial Age*. Chicago: University of Chicago Press.

Heaton, Paul. 2006. 'Does Religion Really Reduce Crime?' *Journal of Law and Economics* 49: 147–72.

Heckman, James J. 1998. 'Detecting Discrimination'. *Journal of Economic Perspectives* 12: 101–16.

Hess, Gregory D., and Athanasios Orphanides. 2001. 'War and Democracy'. *Journal of Political Economy* 109: 776–810.

Hirsch, Werner Z., and Evan Osborne. 1992. 'Law and Economics – Valuable but Controversial'. *Law and Social Inquiry* 17: 521–37.

Holzer, Harry J., Steven Raphael, and Michael A. Stoll. 2006. 'Perceived Criminality, Criminal Background Checks, and the Racial Hiring Practices of Employers'. *Journal of Law and Economics* 49: 451–80.

Hunt, Jennifer. 2006. 'Do Teen Births Keep American Crime High?' *Journal of Law and Economics* 49: 533–66.

Hutchinson, Kevin P., and Andrew J. Yates. 2007. 'Crime on the Court: A Correction'. *Journal of Political Economy* 115: 515–19.

Iannaccone, Laurence R., Roger Finke, and Rodney Stark. 1997. 'Deregulating Religion: The Economics of Church and State'. *Economic Inquiry* 35: 350–64.

Ihlanfeldt, Keith R. 2006. 'Neighborhood Crime and Young Males' Job Opportunity'. *Journal of Law and Economics* 49: 249–84.

Ippolito, Richard A. 2001. 'Pension Incentives and Sorting Effects'. Paper presented at the Institute for the Study of Labor Conference on 'Pension Reform and Labor Markets'.

Ippolito, Richard A. 1985. 'The Economic Function of Underfunded Pension Plans'. *Journal of Law and Economics* 28: 611–51.

Jasny, Naum. 1951. 'Labor and Output in Soviet Concentration Camps'. *Journal of Political Economy* 59: 405–19.

Jolls, Christine M., and Cass. R. Sunstein. 2006. 'The Law of Implicit Bias'. *California Law Review* 94: 969–96.

Jolls, Christine M., Cass R. Sunstein, and Richard Thaler. 1998. 'A Behavioral Approach to Law and Economics'. *Stanford Law Review* 50: 1471–550.

Kahan, Dan, and Eric Posner. 1999. 'Shaming White-Collar Criminals: A Proposal for Reform of the Federal Sentencing Guidelines'. *Journal of Law and Economics* 42: 365–92.

Kaplow, Louis. 1992. 'The Optimal Probability and Magnitude of Fines for Acts that Definitely are Undesirable'. *International Review of Law and Economics* 12: 3–11.

Kaplow, Louis. 1990. 'Optimal Deterrence, Uninformed Individuals, and Acquiring Information about Whether Acts are Subject to Sanctions'. *Journal of Law, Economics, and Organization* 6: 93–128.

Katz, Lawrence, Steven D. Levitt, and Ellen Shustorovich. 2003. 'Prison Conditions, Capital Punishment, and Deterrence'. *American Law and Economics Review* 5: 318–43.

Kessler, Daniel, and Steven Levitt. 1999. 'Using Sentence Enhancements to Distinguish Between Deterrence and Incapacitation'. *Journal of Law and Economics* 42: 343–63.

Kitch, Edmund J. 1968. 'Regulation of the Field Market for Natural Gas by the Federal Power Commission'. *Journal of Law and Economics* 11: 243–80.

Klick, Jonathan. 2002. 'Have a Drink on Us: Mental Health Parity, Rational Addiction, and Off-Setting Behavior'. Unpublished manuscript, available on-line at http://ssrn.com/abstract=338200.

Knowles, John, Nicola Persico, and Petra Todd. 2001. 'Racial Bias in Motor Vehicle Searches: Theory and Evidence'. *Journal of Political Economy* 109: 203–29.

Korobkin, Russell B., and Thomas S. Ulen. 2000. 'Law and Behavioral Science: Removing the Rationality Assumption from Law and Economics'. *California Law Review* 88: 1051–144.

Kunreuther, Howard. 1968. 'The Case for Comprehensive Disaster Insurance'. *Journal of Law and Economics* 11: 133–64.

Laibson, David. 1997. 'Golden Eggs and Hyperbolic Discounting'. *Quarterly Journal of Economics* 112: 443–77.

Lakdawalla, Darius. 2006. 'The Economics of Teacher Quality'. *Journal of Law and Economics* 49: 285–330.

Landes, William. 1978. 'An Economic Study of U.S. Aircraft Hijacking, 1961–1976'. *Journal of Law and Economics* 21: 1–31.

Landes, William. 1971. 'An Economic Analysis of the Courts'. *Journal of Law and Economics* 14: 61–107.

Landes, William, and Richard Posner. 2003. *The Economic Structure of Intellectual Property Law*. Cambridge: Harvard University Press.

Landes, William, and Richard Posner. 2001. 'Harmless Error'. *Journal of Legal Studies* 30: 161–92.

Landes, William, and Richard Posner. 1987. 'Trademark Law: An Economic Perspective'. *Journal of Law and Economics* 30: 265–309.

Landes, William, and Richard Posner. 1981. 'Market Power in Antitrust Cases'. *Harvard Law Review* 94: 937–96.

Landes, William, and Richard Posner. 1975. 'The Private Enforcement of Law'. *Journal of Legal Studies* 4: 1–46.

Langbein, Laura, and Cornelius M. Kerwin. 1985. 'Implementation, Negotiation, and Compliance in Environmental and Safety Regulation'. *Journal of Politics* 47: 854–80.

Lawson, Tony. 2006. 'The Nature of Heterodox Economics'. *Cambridge Journal of Economics* 30: 483–505.

Lawson, Tony. 2005. 'The (Confused) State of Equilibrium Analysis in Modern Economics: An Explanation'. *Journal of Post Keynesian Economics* 27: 423–44.

Lazear, Edward. 2000. 'Economic Imperialism'. *Quarterly Journal of Economics* 115: 99–146.

Leff, Arthur A. 1974. 'Economic Analysis of Law: Some Realism about Nominalism'. *Virginia Law Review* 60: 451–82.

Lent, George E. 1951. 'Excess-Profit Taxation in the United States'. *Journal of Political Economy* 59: 481–97.

Leontief, Wassily. 1984. 'Academic Economics'. *Science* 217: 104–107.

Lessig, Lawrence. 1995. 'The Regulation of Social Meaning'. *University of Chicago Law Review* 62: 943–1045.

Levin, Harvey J. 1968. 'The Radio Spectrum Resource'. *Journal of Law and Economics* 11: 433–502.

Levine, Phillip B., Douglas Staiger, Thomas J. Kane, and David J. Zimmerman. 1999. '*Roe v. Wade* and American Fertility'. *American Journal of Public Health* 89: 199–203.

Levitt, Steven. 2004. 'Testing Theories of Discrimination: Evidence from *Weakest Link*'. *Journal of Law and Economics* 47: 431–52.

Levitt, Steven. 2002a. 'Using Electoral Cycles in Police Hiring to Estimate the Effects of Police on Crime: Reply'. *American Economic Review* 94: 1244–50.

Levitt, Steven. 2002b. 'Testing the Economic Model of Crime: The National Hockey League's Two-Referee Experiment'. *Contributions to Economic Analysis & Policy* 1.

Levitt, Steven. 1998a. 'Why Do Increased Arrest Rates Appear to Reduce Crime: Deterrence, Incapacitation, or Measurement Error?' *Economic Inquiry* 36: 353–72.

Levitt, Steven. 1998b. 'Juvenile Crime and Punishment'. *Journal of Political Economy* 106: 1156–85.

Levitt, Steven. 1997. 'Using Electoral Cycles in Police Hiring to Estimate the Effects of Police on Crime'. *American Economic Review* 87: 270–90.

Levitt, Steven. 1996. 'The Effect of Prison Population Size on Crime Rates: Evidence from Prison Overcrowding Litigation'. *Quarterly Journal of Economics* 111: 319–51.

Levitt, Steven, and Andre Chiappori. 2003. 'An Examination of the Influence of Theory and Individual Theorists on Empirical Research in Microeconomics'. *American Economic Review* 93: 151–5.

Lewis, H. Gregg. 1951. 'The Labor-Monopoly Problem: A Positive Program'. *Journal of Political Economy* 59: 277–87.

List, John. 2004. 'The Nature and Extent of Discrimination in the Marketplace: Evidence from the Field'. *Quarterly Journal of Economics* 119: 49–89.

Liu, Jin-Long, Jin-Tan Liu, James K. Hammitt, and Shin-Yi Chou. 1999. 'The Price Elasticity of Opium in Taiwan, 1914–1942'. *Journal of Health Economics* 18: 795–810.

Lombroso, Cesare. 1918 [1899]. *Crime: Its Causes and Remedies*. New York: Little, Brown.

Lott, Jr., John R. 1992. 'An Attempt at Measuring the Total Monetary Penalty from Drug Convictions: The Importance of an Individual's Reputation'. *Journal of Legal Studies* 21: 159–87.

Ludwig, Jens, and Jeffrey R. Kling. 2006. 'Is Crime Contagious?' Unpublished manuscript.

Lundberg, Shelly, and Richard Startz. 1983. 'Private Discrimination and Social Intervention in Competitive Labor Markets'. *American Economic Review* 73: 340–47.

Malani, Anup. 2002. 'Does the Felony-Murder Rule Deter Crime? Evidence from FBI Crime Data'. Unpublished manuscript.

Mashaw, Jerry L. 1999. *Greed, Chaos, and Governance*. New Haven: Yale University Press.

Maule, C.J. 1968. 'Antitrust and the Takeover Activity of American Firms in Canada'. *Journal of Law and Economics* 11: 423–32.

McAdams, Richard H. 1995. 'Cooperation and Conflict: The Economics of Group Status Production and Race Discrimination'. *Harvard Law Review* 108: 1003–84.

McCormick, Robert E., and Robert D. Tollison. 2007. 'Crime on the Court, Another Look: Reply to Hutchinson and Yates'. *Journal of Political Economy* 115: 520–21.

McCormick, Robert E., and Robert D. Tollison. 1984. 'Crime on the Court'. *Journal of Political Economy* 92: 223–35.

Medema, Steven G. 2008. 'From Dismal to Dominance? Law and Economics, and the Values of Imperial Science'. In *Norms and Values in Law and Economics*, edited by Aristides Hatzis. London: Routledge.

Metzler, Lloyd A. 1951a. 'A Multiple-Country Theory of Income Transfers'. *Journal of Political Economy* 59: 14–29.

Metzler, Lloyd A. 1951b. 'The Rate of Interest and the Marginal Product of Capital: A Correction'. *Journal of Political Economy* 59: 67–68.

Metzler, Lloyd A. 1951c. 'Wealth, Saving, and the Rate of Interest'. *Journal of Political Economy* 59: 93–116.

Merton, Robert K. 1938. 'Social Structure and Anomie'. *American Sociological Review* 3: 672–82.

Mobilia, Pamela. 1993. 'Gambling as Rational Addiction'. *Journal of Gambling Studies* 9: 121–51.

Mocan, H. Naci, and R. Kaj Gittings. 2003. 'Getting Off Death Row: Commuted Sentences and the Deterrent Effect of Capital Punishment'. *Journal of Law and Economics* 46: 453–78.

Mocan, H. Naci, and Erdal Tekin. 2006. 'Guns and Juvenile Crime'. *Journal of Law and Economics* 49: 507–32.

Mookherjee, Dilip, and I.P.L. Png. 1994. 'Marginal Deterrence in Enforcement of Law'. *Journal of Political Economy* 102: 1039–66.

Moran, Rachel F. 2003. 'The Elusive Nature of Discrimination'. *Stanford Law Review* 55: 2365–418.

Morris, Stephen. 2001. 'Political Correctness'. *Journal of Political Economy* 109: 231–65.

Morse, Stephen J. 2004. 'New Neuroscience, Old Problems'. In *Neuroscience and the Law*, edited by Brent Garland. New York: Dana Press.

Nagin, Daniel S. 1998. 'Criminal Deterrence Research at the Outset of the Twenty-First Century'. *Crime and Justice* 23: 1–42.

Nagin, Daniel, and Joel Waldfogel. 1998. 'The Effect of Conviction on Income through the Life Cycle'. *International Review of Law and Economics* 18: 25–40.

Neumark, David, and Michele McLennan. 1995. 'Sex Discrimination and Women's Labor Market Outcomes'. *Journal of Human Resources* 30: 713–40.

Olekalns, Nilss, and Peter Bardsley. 1996. 'Rational Addiction to Caffeine: An Analysis of Coffee Consumption'. *Journal of Political Economy* 104: 1100–104.

Pashigian, B. Peter. 1968. 'Market Concentration in the United States and Great Britain'. *Journal of Law and Economics* 11: 299–320.

Persico, Nicola. 2002. 'Racial Profiling, Fairness, and Effectiveness of Policing'. *American Economic Review* 95: 1472–97.

Persico, Nicola, and Petra Todd. 2006. 'Generalizing the Hit Rates Test for Racial Bias in Law Enforcement, with an Application to Vehicle Searches in Wichita'. *The Economic Journal* 116: F351–F367.

Peterman, John L. 1968. 'The Clorox Case and the Television Rate Structures'. *Journal of Law and Economics* 11: 321–422.

Peters, Craig. 2006. 'Evaluating the Performance of Merger Simulation: Evidence from the U.S. Airline Industry'. *Journal of Law and Economics* 49: 627–50.

Phelps, Edmund. 1972. 'A Statistical Theory of Racism and Sexism'. *American Economic Review* 62: 659–61.

Polinsky, A. Mitchell. 2004. 'The Optimal Use of Fines and Imprisonment when Wealth is Unobservable'. NBER Working Paper 10761.

Polinsky, A. Mitchell, and Daniel L. Rubinfeld. 1991. 'A Model of Optimal Fines for Repeat Offenders'. *Journal of Public Economics* 46: 291–306.

Polinsky, A. Mitchell, and Steven Shavell. 1998. 'On Offense History and the Theory of Deterrence'. *International Review of Law and Economics* 18: 305–24.

Polinsky, A. Mitchell, and Steven Shavell. 1992. 'Enforcement Costs and the Optimal Magnitude and Probability of Fines'. *Journal of Law and Economics* 35: 133–48.

Polinsky, A. Mitchell, and Steven Shavell. 1991. 'A Note on Optimal Fines when Wealth Varies Among Individuals'. *American Economic Review* 81: 618–21.

Polinsky, A. Mitchell, and Steven Shavell. 1979. 'The Optimal Tradeoff between the Probability and Magnitude of Fines'. *American Economic Review* 69: 880–91.

Posner, Richard. 2007. *Economic Analysis of Law* (7th ed.). New York: Aspen Law and Business.

Posner, Richard. 1998a. 'Rational Choice, Behavioral Economics, and the Law'. *Stanford Law Review* 50: 1551–75.

Posner, Richard. 1998b. *Economic Analysis of Law* (5th ed.). New York: Aspen Law and Business.

Posner, Richard. 1993a. 'Gary Becker's Contributions to Law and Economics'. *Journal of Legal Studies* 22: 211–15.

Posner, Richard. 1993b. 'What Do Judges Maximize? (The Same Thing Everybody Else Does)'. *Supreme Court Economic Review* 3: 1–41.

Posner, Richard. 1981. *The Economics of Justice*. Cambridge: Harvard University Press.

Posner, Richard. 1979. 'Utilitarianism, Economics, and Legal Theory'. *Journal of Legal Studies* 8: 103–40.

Prendergast, Canice. 1999. 'The Provision of Incentives in Firms'. *Journal of Economic Literature* 37: 7–63.

Rasmusen, Eric. 1996. 'Stigma and Self-Fulfilling Expectations of Criminality'. *Journal of Law and Economics* 39: 519–43.

Rayo, Luis, and Gary S. Becker. 2007a. 'Evolutionary Happiness and Efficiency'. *Journal of Political Economy* 115: 302–37.

Rayo, Luis, and Gary S. Becker. 2007b. 'Habits, Peers, and Happiness: An Evolutionary Perspective'. *American Economic Review* 97: 487–91.

Rees, Albert. 1951. 'Wage Determination and Involuntary Unemployment'. *Journal of Political Economy* 59: 143–53.

Robinson, Joan. 1974. 'History Versus Equilibrium'. *Indian Economic Journal* 21: 202–13.

Robinson, Paul H., and John M. Darley. 2004. 'Does Criminal Law Deter? A Behavioral Science Investigation'. *Oxford Journal of Legal Studies* 24: 173–205.

Robson, Arthur J. 2001. 'Why Would Nature Give Individuals Utility Functions?' *Journal of Political Economy* 109: 900–914.

Rogeberg, Ole. 2004. 'Taking Absurd Theories Seriously: Economics and the Case of Rational Addiction Theories'. *Philosophy of Science* 71: 263–85.

Rosen, Sherwin. 1993. 'Risks and Rewards: Gary Becker's Contribution to Economics'. *Scandinavian Journal of Economics* 95: 25–36.

Roundtable Discussion. 1997. 'The Future of Law and Economics: Looking Forward'. *University of Chicago Law Review* 64: 1129–65.

Rowley, C.K. 1968. 'Mergers and Public Policy in Great Britain'. *Journal of Law and Economics* 11: 75–132.

Sah, Raaj K. 1991. 'Social Osmosis and Patterns of Crime'. *Journal of Political Economy* 99: 1272–95.

Saint-Paul, Gilles. 2001. 'On the Distribution of Income and Worker Assignment under Intrafirm Spillovers, with an Application to Ideas and Networks'. *Journal of Political Economy* 109: 1–37.

Sandler, Todd, and Walter Enders. 2004. 'An Economic Perspective on Transnational Terrorism'. *European Journal of Political Economy* 20: 391–16.

Schwab, Stewart. 2000. 'Employment Discrimination'. In *Encyclopedia of Law and Economics*, edited by Boudewijn Boukaert and Gerrit De Geest. Cheltenham and Northampton, MA: Edward Elgar.

Shavell, Steven. 1992. 'A Note on Marginal Deterrence'. *International Review of Law and Economics* 12: 345–55.

Shavell, Steven. 1990. 'Deterrence and the Punishment of Attempts'. *Journal of Legal Studies* 19: 435–66.

Shavell, Steven. 1987. 'A Model of Optimal Incapacitation'. *American Economic Review* 77: 107–10.

Shavell, Steven. 1985. 'Criminal Law and the Optimal Use of Nonmonetary Sanctions as a Deterrent'. *Columbia Law Review* 85: 1232–62.

Shaw, Clifford R., and Henry D. McKay. 1942. *Juvenile Delinquency and Urban Areas*. Chicago: University of Chicago Press.

Shepherd, Joanna. 2002a. 'Police, Prosecutors, Criminals, and Determinate Sentencing: The Truth about Truth-in-Sentencing Law'. *Journal of Law and Economics* 45: 509–34.

Shepherd, Joanna. 2002b. 'Fear of the First Strike: The Full Deterrent Effect of California's Two- and Three-Strike Legislation'. *Journal of Legal Studies* 31: 159–201.

Silver, Mick, and Christos Ioannidis. 2001. 'Intercountry Differences in the Relationship between Relative Price Variability and Average Prices'. *Journal of Political Economy* 109: 355–74.

Smigel, Arleen. 1965. 'Crime and Punishment: An Economic Analysis'. Unpublished Master's thesis.
Stigler, George J. 1951. 'The Division of Labor is Limited by the Extent of the Market'. *Journal of Political Economy* 59: 185–93.
Stigler, George J., and Gary S. Becker. 1977. '*De Gustibus Non Est Disputandem*'. *American Economic Review* 67: 76–90.
Sunstein, Cass, ed. 2000. *Behavioral Law and Economics*. Cambridge: Cambridge University Press.
Swedberg, Richard. 1990. *Economics and Sociology*. Princeton: Princeton University Press.
Tolstoy, Leo. 1982 [1869]. *War and Peace*. Translated by Rosemary Edmunds. London: Penguin Press.
Veblen, Thorstein. 1898. 'Why is Economics not an Evolutionary Science?' *Quarterly Journal of Economics* 12: 373–97.
Waldfogel, Joel. 1994. 'The Effect of Criminal Conviction on Income and the Trust "Reposed in the Workmen."' *Journal of Human Resources* 29: 62–81.
Wintrobe, Ronald. 2003. 'Can Suicide Bombers be Rational?' Unpublished manuscript.
Wintrobe, Ronald. 1982. 'The Optimal Level of Bureaucratization within a Firm'. *Canadian Journal of Economics* 15: 649–68.
Wolfers, Justin. 2006. 'Did Unilateral Divorce Laws Raise Divorce Rates? A Reconciliation and New Results'. *American Economic Review* 96: 1802–20.
Zimmerman, Paul R. 2004. 'State Executions, Deterrence, and the Incidence of Murder'. *Journal of Applied Economics* 7: 163–93.

11 Pioneers of law and economics: William M. Landes and Richard A. Posner

Thomas S. Ulen[1]

Law and economics has been the most significant innovation in legal scholarship of the past 100 years. Its success may be judged in part by the fact that it has grown from being an intriguing but niche novelty in the early 1980s to becoming the default method of legal scholarship in almost every area of academic specialization. But the impact of law and economics has gone beyond the academy and has reached the formation of public policy, the manner and substance of judicial decisions, the practice of law, and more.

No two people have had a more profound impact on this revolution that William M. Landes and Richard A. Posner. As individual authors, as joint authors, and, in the case of Judge Posner, as a federal appeals court judge, Landes and Posner have helped to define the field and to elucidate our understandings of some of the most important areas of law and economics. Indeed, I can call to mind only six other authors who write together in teams and separately who might claim to have had the same status and impact as have Landes and Posner: Charles Goetz and Bob Scott, Mitch Polinsky and Steve Shavell, and Frank Easterbrook and Daniel Fischel.[2]

As the bibliographies of Judge Posner's work, Professor Landes's work, and their joint work appended to this piece indicate, Landes and Posner have produced near-miraculous amounts of scholarship since their first collaboration in the early 1970s. A review that sought to give a full sense of their individual contributions would be book-length and might, even then, do a merely glancing job of indicating the breadth of their scholarly concerns. I shall not seek to do that here, although I shall briefly mention some of their early, independent, seminal work in the field. My focus will be on their jointly authored work and, principally, on just a few of what I believe to be their most significant contributions to the field of law and economics.

I begin with brief biographies of Landes and Posner. Then I discuss their early collaborative articles. Finally, I discuss their books on tort and intellectual property law.

1 Biographies

William M. Landes received his BA in economics from Columbia University in 1960 and his Ph.D. in economics, also from Columbia University, in 1966, where he studied with the future Nobel Laureate and pioneer in law and economics, Gary Becker. Landes taught in the Economics Departments of Stanford University, Columbia University, the Graduate Center

---

[1]   Swanlund Chair, University of Illinois at Urbana-Champaign; Professor of Law, University of Illinois College of Law; and Director of the Illinois Program in Law and Economics.

[2]   There is nothing to be gained from comparing these three sets of scholars with respect to their impact on the field. Rather, this seems to be an appropriate point at which to remark on the fact that the field of law and economics has attracted an astonishing number of extremely talented scholars.

of the City University of New York, and the University of Chicago and at the Fordham University School of Law before joining the faculty of the University of Chicago Law School in 1980. At the law school, Landes serves as the Clifton R. Musser Professor of Law and Economics and teaches courses on the economic analysis of law, art law, and intellectual property and directs the Olin Program in Law and Economics. In addition to his seminal work in law and economics, Landes has also written extensively on antitrust matters. He has served as President of the American Law and Economics Association, has appeared as an expert before courts, administrative agencies, and committees of Congress, and has served as co-editor of the *Journal of Legal Studies*. He is an avid collector of art and has served on the board of the Smart Museum of Art at the University of Chicago. Landes and his wife, Elisabeth, also a distinguished law-and-economics scholar, endowed the Elisabeth and William M. Landes Gallery within the Smart Museum.

Richard A. Posner graduated with a BA in English from Yale University in 1959 and graduated with an LLB from Harvard Law School, where he was President of the *Harvard Law Review*, in 1962. He then clerked for Justice William J. Brennan Jr, during the 1962–3 US Supreme Court term. From 1963 to 1965 Posner served as assistant to Commissioner Philip Elman of the Federal Trade Commission. For the next two years he was assistant to the solicitor general of the United States and then served as general counsel of the President's Task Force on Communications Policy. Posner's first academic appointment, as associate professor, was to the faculty of the Stanford Law School in 1968. He moved to the University of Chicago Law School in 1969, and was Lee and Brena Freeman Professor of Law prior to his appointment in 1981 as a judge of the US Court of Appeals for the Seventh Circuit. He was the chief judge of the court from 1993 to 2000.

Judge Posner founded the first journal devoted exclusively to law-and-economics scholarship, the *Journal of Legal Studies*, in 1972. His scholarly output has been – as the bibliography appended to this chapter indicates – extraordinary. Posner has retained a position as Senior Lecturer at the University of Chicago Law School since his appointment to the federal bench in 1981 and has taught courses in administrative law, antitrust, economic analysis of law, history of legal thought, conflict of laws, regulated industries, law and literature, the legislative process, family law, primitive law, torts, civil procedure, evidence, health law and economics, law and science, and jurisprudence. During 1995–6 Posner served as President of the American Law and Economics Association and was, with Orley Ashenfelter, the founding editor of the *American Law and Economics Review*. He is an Honorary Bencher of the Inner Temple and a corresponding fellow of the British Academy. He has received a number of awards, including the Thomas Jefferson Memorial Foundation Award in Law from the University of Virginia in 1994, the Marshall-Wythe Medallion from the College of William and Mary in 1998, the 2003 Research Award from the Fellows of the American Bar Foundation, the 2003 John Sherman Award from the US Department of Justice, the Learned Hand Medal for Excellence in Federal Jurisprudence from the Federal Bar Council in 2005, and, also in 2005, the Thomas C. Schelling Award from the John F. Kennedy School of Government at Harvard University.

Judge Posner has received honorary doctorates in law from Harvard University (1986), Syracuse University (1987), Duquesne University (1993), Georgetown University (1995), the University of Ghent (1996), Yale University (1997), the University of Pennsylvania (2000), Brooklyn Law School (2001), Northwestern University (2002), the Aristotle University of Thessaloniki (2002), and the University of Athens (2002).

Judge Posner is one of the most prolific federal judges ever. His opinions are collected at Project Posner, www.projectposner.org. He has for years co-authored a blog with Gary Becker, the Becker-Posner blog, available at www.becker-posner.com.

2 Early collaboration

William M. Landes began his scholarly career as a labor economist, writing his first professional articles about fair employment laws and their effects. His first foray into the field of what would become law and economics was 'An Economic Analysis of the Courts', 14 *Journal of Law and Economics* 61 (1971). Although the article's central concern is criminal complaints, the factors with which Landes worked are general enough that the article can confidently be said to have begun the modern literature on suit versus settlement in the civil context.

Landes begins with the observation that the vast majority of criminal complaints do not result in a trial. They are, rather, settled by plea bargains. He asks why this should be the case and proposes a simple model of the choice between settlement by plea bargain and trial. In particular, he is interested in the relationships among the criminal defendant's wealth, the expected value of the criminal sanction (the probability of conviction times the value of the sanction), the workings of the bail system, and the extent of court delay on the decision to settle or proceed to trial.[3]

The second part of Landes's seminal article is an empirical analysis, in which he confronts the hypotheses regarding the choice of trial or settlement with data on criminal prosecutions and concludes that there is statistically significant evidence in favor of his model.

It is worth noting, I believe, that Landes's initial article on what would become a central topic in law and economics contained both theoretical and empirical sections. While it is becoming commonplace to perform empirical work on legal topics (or at least to allude to the importance of doing empirical work to supplement the theoretical work), Landes's inclusion of empirical work in his discussion of a legal issue in the early 1970s was prescient. However standard it has long been among economists to follow the scientific method of supplementing theoretical with empirical work and to do (or plan to do) empirical work, the commitment to empirical work on legal issues is of much more recent coinage. Landes was, in 1971, far ahead of his time.

Let me make two more points about this early commitment on Landes's part to empirical work regarding legal matters. First, this is a commitment that has remained at the core of Landes's work for the past 40 years. Indeed, I am hard pressed to think of another prominent law-and-economics scholar who has so consistently performed both first-rate theoretical and empirical work and who has always combined the two halves of the scientific method in his scholarship.

Second, Landes's commitment to exploring the empirical implications of theoretical work clearly had a strong impression on his co-author, Judge Posner. Their joint work, as we shall see. has always followed the 'first the theory, then the evidence' model of scientifically minded scholarship. Moreover, Judge Posner's early scholarly writing in law and economics clearly was influenced by Landes's commitment to empirical work. See, for example,

---

[3] The first appendix in the paper adapts the paper's model to a discussion of the factors influencing suit and settlement in civil cases.

Posner's 'A Theory of Negligence', 1 *Journal of Legal Studies* 29 (1972); the article begins with a model of the negligence liability system and then surveys late 19th century tort litigation to see if the theory is borne out by the reported cases.

The first article that Landes and Posner worked on together was 'The Private Enforcement of Law', 4 *Journal of Legal Studies* 1 (1975). This article was, in part, a response to the suggestion made by Gary Becker and George Stigler (in 'Law Enforcement, Malfeasance, and Compensation of Enforcers', 3 *Journal of Legal Studies* 1 (1974)) in favor of the privatization of most law-enforcement efforts. In contrast, Landes and Posner argue that a gradual replacement of private enforcement service by public law enforcement services was the distinctive trend of the 19th century and that this was, by and large, a good and efficient thing. Indeed, they argue that although there are still important pockets of private enforcement, the current division of responsibility between public and private enforcers may be optimal. The article is notable for its sophisticated modeling and its use of telling examples – as in its discussion of blackmail and bribery.[4]

Landes and Posner next published 'The Independent Judiciary in an Interest-Group Perspective', 18 *Journal of Law and Economics* 875 (1975). This article argues that economic analysis holds the key to explaining why an independent judiciary stands apart from the push and pull of interest-group politics that does and should characterize much of our governmental institutions.

> The existence of an independent judiciary seems inconsistent with – in fact profoundly threatening to – a political system in which public policy emerges from the struggle of interest groups to redistribute the wealth of the society in their favor, the view of the political process that underlies much of the recent economic work, as well as an older political-science literature, on the political system. The outcomes of the struggle can readily be nullified by unsympathetic judges – and why should judges be sympathetic to a process that simply ratifies political power rather than expresses principle? The Supreme Court's policy toward economic legislation during a period of roughly 50 years ending in the late 1930's illustrates the power and proclivity of an independent judiciary to nullify the legislative results of interest-group politics.[5]

The novelty of the Landes-Posner hypothesis is that the independent judiciary is an essential part of the implicit bargain between constituents and the legislature. Interest groups 'purchase' legislation from the legislature through campaign contributions and other forms of support. But once enough legislators have committed to further the political agenda of an interest group, what is to prevent them (or their successors in the legislature) from reneging on the deal in a future session? Indeed, could crafty legislators not strategically threaten to renege so as to elicit continuing streams of financial and other commitments from the various interest groups who desire legislative services? Is there any mechanism that can see to it that once an interest group has successfully persuaded the legislature to enact favorable statutes, the legislature will not easily reverse itself in the near future?

---

[4]   I am also deeply struck, when I examine the articles in the early issues of the *Journal of Legal Studies*, by the exuberance of the scholarship that is on display there. It was a marvelous time when a new and obviously fruitful and important area of scholarly inquiry was being born.

[5]   Landes and Posner, 'Independent Judiciary', at 876.

There are, the authors say, two mechanisms that help to prevent legislative deals from being unstable. The first is the voting rules of the legislature itself. At a minimum, the legislature requires that action be taken by majority vote, and in some instances by supermajority vote. Given the press of other business, it is not likely that capricious enacting and repealing will be able to command legislative majorities as part of a scheme to whipsaw hapless interest groups. But there are other procedural safeguards: the seniority system, 'bicameralism, the committee system, and filibusters', among others.

The second element in securing legislative interest-group deals is the independent judiciary. This is best seen by imagining the opposite. Suppose that the judiciary were perfectly beholden to the legislature – that it rules in disputes so as to capture, perfectly, the desires of the legislature. And further suppose that the legislature has, as the authors hypothesize, succumbed to pressure from the dairy industry and enacted a special tax on margarine in year 1. In year 2, the margarine manufacturers desire to have the tax repealed and are prepared to 'pay' to have the tax repealed. They can do their best to induce the legislature to rescind its actions of year 1, or they can bring an action against the tax before the judiciary. If the judiciary is serving as perfect agents of the current legislature and the current legislature would like to accommodate the margarine manufacturers but cannot get around to repeal because of the press of other business, the judiciary can stop collection of the tax just as effectively as if the entire tax had been revoked.

But suppose that the judiciary does not simply do the bidding of the current legislature. Rather, suppose that the judiciary is independent of the current legislature and seeks to adhere to the desires of the enacting legislature (when asked to stay the collection of the margarine tax). If so, 'it follows that an independent judiciary facilitates, rather than, as conventionally believed, limits the practice of interest-group politics'.[6]

The authors make clear that they are not speaking of a venal judiciary, nor are they supporting the view of those who perceive judges as simply politicians in black robes.

> Where we differ from these commentators is in not venerating the courts as repositories of some special wisdom, integrity, morality, or commitment to principle. In our view the courts do not enforce the moral law or ideals of neutrality, justice, or fairness; they enforce the 'deals' made by effective interest groups with earlier legislatures. Of course, since the judges are independent, an appeal to principles may be effective courtroom or law-review advocacy.[7]

This conclusion is everything to which legal scholarship should aspire: insightful; a counterintuitive result that couldn't possibly be right, but then, on reflection, just might be; a result that is, while contrary to prevailing, comfortable learning, dazzlingly enlightening; and full of empirical suggestions.

Finally, let me note the third joint effort of these authors: 'Legal Precedent: A Theoretical and Empirical Analysis', 19 *Journal of Law and Economics* 249 (1976). The authors examined a dataset of federal appellate court opinions from the years 1974 and 1975 to see the extent to which the citation practices of the federal courts illustrate the use of legal precedent as a form of judicial capital. The theoretical insight that motivates the empirical work is the perception that legal precedents are a form of capital, and that the economic theory of investment in the

---

6   Landes and Posner, 'Independent Judiciary', at 879.
7   Landes and Posner, 'Independent Judiciary', at 894.

formation of capital and the depreciation of capital stock is a useful method of examining how courts make use of precedent:

> We treat the body of legal precedents created by judicial decisions in prior periods as a capital stock that yields a flow of information services which depreciates over time as new conditions arise that were not foreseen by the framers of the existing precedents. New (and replacement) capital is created by investment in the production of precedents.[8]

There are, as the appended bibliography indicates, more early articles by Landes and Posner that bear rereading and fresh explication.

3   Later collaboration

Landes and Posner have continued to collaborate since those first articles of the mid-1970s. Rather than comment on each of those articles, I prefer to focus on what I believe to have been the two central contributions of the later phase of their collaboration – to tort law and intellectual property law.

Although they have produced many articles together, these two colleagues have produced only two books together: *The Economic Structure of Tort Law* (1987) and *The Economic Structure of Intellectual Property Law* (2003). Much of what is in those books was foreshadowed by a series of articles. But because the books brought together most of what was in those articles and added new material, I shall devote my attention mostly, but not exclusively, to the content of the books.

3.1   Tort law

Beginning with the marvelous article of John Prather Brown in 1973,[9] the economic analysis of tort liability is one of the great accomplishments of modern legal scholarship. One important aspect of that literature has been to move the central focus of tort law away from the sometimes arid discussions of what justice demands in a particular accidental context and toward a more productive discussion of how best to induce strangers to take other-regarding and socially optimal amounts of precaution so as to minimize the social costs of accidents.

The early editions of Posner's magnificent *Economic Analysis of Law* (7th edition, 2007) developed the famous 'least cost avoider' theory of assigning tort liability. That theory, attractive as it seemed at the time and as appropriate as it may be in limited circumstances, is not suitable for the general case in which potential victim and injurer cannot make precaution-cost comparisons *ex ante* an accident and in which precaution is a continuous, not a lumpy or discrete variable. Rather, following Brown's model, the modern view is that tort law must influence precautionary and activity-level decisions 'behind a veil of ignorance': the decision maker will not know whether he will be the victim or the injurer or whether the person he injures or who injures him will be complying with the legal duty of care, impecunious, or a psychopath. The theoretical task for the modern economic theory of tort liability is to explain how and why the law can compel reasonable people to confer benefits (in the form of increased precaution) on others when they (the decision makers) do not know whether they will injure or be injured. Moreover, all of this has to be explained *ex ante* an

---

8   Landes and Posner, 'Legal Precedent', at 250–51.
9   J.P. Brown, 'Toward an Economic Theory of Liability', 2 *Journal of Legal Studies* 323 (1973).

accident or litigation, and the parties must reasonably anticipate what would happen if there is an accident and if there is litigation. And if there is litigation, one cannot now be sure what liability standard the court will use, nor how accurately the court will evaluate one's precautionary actions, nor how accurately the court will measure damages and award compensation.

The criticisms of the early Posnerian tort liability model were mooted by the exposition in *The Economic Structure of Tort Law* (1987). There, Landes and Posner laid out the more modern understanding of tort law (in which attempts to avoid liability induce potential victim and potential injurer to take optimal care independently of one another) and elaborated on that model.[10] The book is highly readable and is supplemented with highly informative footnotes; the references to the literature are exhaustive; and the legal points are ably illustrated by reference to actual cases.[11]

Landes and Posner elaborate what they call the 'positive economic theory of tort law':

> This theory holds that the rules of the Anglo-American common law of torts are best explained as if designed to promote efficiency in the sense of minimizing the sum of expected damages and costs of care; or, stated differently, that the structure of the common law of torts is economic in character.[12]

In the first ten chapters, the authors explore the doctrines of tort law to see the extent to which those doctrines contribute to the minimization of the social costs of accidents (the standard articulation of the economic goal of exposure to tort liability). Generally speaking, Landes and Posner prefer the negligence as the default tort liability standard, preferring to reserve strict liability for situations of so-called 'unilateral precaution' or situations where there are significant activity-level effects that the negligence standard might miss.

Landes and Posner are generally optimistic about the ability of the appropriate liability standard to induce efficient behavior. They make this point with particular effectiveness in a long chapter that examines the law of product-related accidents. A noteworthy theme in that chapter is the extent to which socioeconomic variables can explain the principal changes in tort law over the last half century or so. For example, Landes and Posner test the hypothesis that the year in which states dropped the privity requirement in products liability actions is determined by the state's degree of urbanization, its per capita income, the population per registered automobile, the percentage of the population that is illiterate, the percentage of the state labor force that is employed in agriculture, and so on. As I have repeatedly noted in this chapter, I enthusiastically applaud this sophisticated empirical attempt to explain an important legal change. Empirical work of this sort is clearly the direction in which law and economics must move.

Needless to say, the economic analysis of tort law has continued to develop since the publication of *The Economic Structure of Tort Law* in 1987. But in the intervening 20 years those changes have been relatively modest by comparison to the ferment of discovery that culminated in this book (and Shavell's contemporaneous treatise of the same subject).

---

[10]   The Landes and Posner book appeared at about the same time – and from the same publisher, Harvard University Press – as Steve Shavell's *Economic Analysis of Accident Law* (1987), which presented a more formal treatment of the issues.

[11]   Some of the material in this section comes from T.S. Ulen, 'The Economics of Tort Law', 23 *Law & Society Review* 939 (1989).

[12]   Landes and Posner, *The Economic Structure of Tort Law*, at 312.

3.2   *Intellectual property law*

In the late 1980s and early 1990s, Landes and Posner co-authored a series of articles about intellectual property issues that importantly redefined the economics of that area of the law. (See 'Trademark Law: An Economic Perspective', 30 *Journal of Law and Economics* 265 (1987); 'The Economics of Trademark Law', 78 *Trademark Reporter* 267 (1988); 'An Economic Analysis of Copyright Law', 18 *Journal of Legal Studies* 325 (1989); and 'Some Economics of Trade Secret Law', 5 *Journal of Economic Perspectives* 261 (1991) (also co-authored with David D. Friedman).) Prior to this series of articles, the prevailing economic view of intellectual property law was that it was not substantially different from the economic analysis of real property law. Just as secure, predictable property interests were necessary to induce efficient investment in improvements to real property, so too were secure, predictable property interests necessary for investment in the discovery of new, useful, and non-obvious inventions and innovations and in creative and expressive works. Beyond that core identity of real and intellectual property interests, there was nothing particularly intriguing about intellectual property. The Landes-Posner articles on intellectual property (IP) changed much of that.

The central insight of the articles was the recognition that what most needed explaining about IP (by comparison to real property) was why IP rights are time-limited (and real property interests are, generally, not so limited). In so far as there was a standard economic explanation of the limitation of patent rights, it was that the exclusive grant of right to a patent holder could be a grant of a monopoly interest. Because monopolies impose social costs (in that the monopolist limits output in order to raise price), the limitation on the duration of patent rights was said to limit the potential social costs that would follow if the patent turned out to be a monopoly.[13] Because it is difficult to tell *ex ante* whether any given patent is going to be a monopoly, the only prudent course of action is to limit the duration of them all.[14]

While that argument might be reasonably well known with respect to patents, what still required explanation is why there are time limitations on copyrights and none on trademarks and trade secrets. And, moreover, why the time limitation on patents has remained more or less constant for over 200 years while that on copyrights has generally grown longer and longer over the same time period. Landes and Posner provided answers to these and other questions.

Their explanation of why there are limitations on the duration of copyright and of why those limitations have been increasing is ingenious. The central insight is the existence of 'tracing costs', which they define as the costs to a current expressive innovator of checking existing creative works to make reasonably certain that he is not explicitly using someone else's copyrighted material. To illustrate, suppose that a librettist desires to write an opera about star-crossed lovers: the young woman is a Palestinian Muslim from the West Bank, and

---

[13]   Of course, not all patents are monopolies. While all patents are grants of exclusive right, in some (perhaps, many) instances it is easy for innovators to develop substitutes for a given patent. Consider pharmaceuticals for treating erectile dysfunction. Cialis, Viagra, and Levitra are all patented but are substitutes for one another.

[14]   This is not, of course, strictly true. One could, for example, give patent holders an indefinite patent life but with rising annual renewal fees scaled to approximate the social costs of continuing the patent for another year. Or the state could take the patent interest and pay just compensation. Or the legislature could selectively extend the patent life of certain items, as Congress has done with respect to so-called 'orphan drugs'.

the young man is a Jew from one of the settlements on the West Bank. Their families, long-standing enemies, are violently opposed to their involvement and put many impediments in the lovers' way. What obligations would the librettist have to make sure that this story did not infringe on another's copyright? Clearly, he or she has an obligation to make sure that the work does not make inappropriate use of material from *West Side Story* or any other modern rendering of the Romeo-and-Juliet or Pyramus-and-Thisbe story.[15] But simply because the story has been told before does not mean that the modern librettist cannot retell the story in a new setting. He or she must make sure that this rendering is, however, original.

The costs of tracing can be high. Indeed, the longer that an expressive artist has copyright protection for his work, the greater the tracing costs to subsequent artists will be. If, for example, copyright extends for 20 years, then a new artist's obligation is to look backward 20 years and no more. If the copyright extends for 100 years, then the obligation is look backward for 100 years. Because these tracing costs can be substantial, there is an argument to be made for limiting them. One reason, therefore, for limiting the duration of copyright is to limit the period backward that current artists must look in order to minimize the chances of infringement.

But there are offsetting arguments in favor of extending copyright for a greater period. Presumably, current artists will be encouraged to devote additional resources to expressive work if the period of exclusivity is longer – just as longer patent life (and more secure patent rights) will encourage an increase in inventive and innovative activity. But Landes and Posner go beyond this relatively trivial point to make a far more telling one: the spread of literacy and of new technologies for copying have increased the demand for expressive works. Not only has there been an increase in the demand for legitimate expressive works; there is also an increase in the demand for illegitimate expressive works. If someone would like a copy of an expressive work, they may be tempted by the lower price of illegitimately copied works, such as those made on photocopiers or electronically. The presence of these illegitimately copied expressive works might reduce the earnings of expressive artists and thereby diminish the incentive to engage in creative work.

Landes and Posner argue, therefore, that the spread of literacy and the rise in average income (both of which increase the demand for copyrightable works) and the simultaneous rise of difficult-to-monitor copying technologies make a strong argument in favor of longer copyright protection.

The actual optimal length of copyright protection is, therefore, the result of a periodically recalibrated balance between the desire to minimize, reasonably, tracing costs and maximize the incentive to engage in creative and expressive work. Landes and Posner argue that this rebalancing has generally resulted in an increase in the duration of copyright protection. They do not go so far as to contend that today's standard of the 'author's life plus 70 years' is optimal under current copying technologies, wealth, and rates of literacy. They fully recognize that there are other considerations at issue, such as the push and pull of political forces in state and the national legislatures and a desire to have a US standard that is nearly identical to that in the rest of the developed world (on the theory that expressive activity, like nearly everything else, is becoming globalized).

---

[15]   Landes and Posner have a delightful section in *The Economic Structure of Intellectual Property Law* about the value of modern artists' updating older works, as Shakespeare did with Ovid's story from *The Metamorphoses* and Bernstein did with Shakespeare's play.

Landes and Posner have argued – both in their book on IP and in a stand-along article – for fundamental reform of copyright. This reform is premised on the view that the factors that they have previously identified – tracing costs and creation of the appropriate incentives for expressive activity – are still the right ones to be balanced. But they are prepared to argue for a different regime to accomplish that balance. Their proposal is for a regime of 'indefinitely renewable copyright'. The gist of the reform is for a fixed period of initial copyright coverage – say, 20 years – with an option to renew the coverage for additional 20-year periods.

The argument in favor of this proposal is straightforward and pragmatic: the prospect of indefinite renewal will preserve the strong incentive to engage in creative and expressive work but would obviate the necessity for periodic legislative tinkering with the duration of copyright. The duration of copyright would be within the control of the copyright holder him- or herself and would presumably be made on the basis of sensible economic calculations. For example, we might imagine that the potential renewer will ask, 'Is the cost of renewal justified by the prospect of continued profits from sales over the next 20-year period?'[16]

There are two possible criticism that one might make of the proposal. The first is that the Constitution instructs Congress to grant copyright for 'limited Times'. Clearly, whatever else that phrase may mean, it does not mean 'perpetual'. Arguably, Landes's and Posner's proposal stops short of perpetuity by using the adjective 'indefinite'.

Nonetheless, the second, related criticism is that indefinite renewal might amount to perpetuity. Landes and Posner appeal to empirical work to address this possibility. They note that while a small fraction of copyrights might renew repeatedly and thereby stretch the meaning of 'limited Times', the vast majority of copyrights will lapse within a reasonably short period of time. Their evidence for this assertion comes from an examination of renewal practices when, between 1883 and 1964, copyright was granted for an initial period of 28 years and could be renewed for another 28-year term for a nominal fee. They find that only 11 percent of all copyright holders renewed their copyrights during that period. Additionally, they find that of all the books published in 1930, only 1.7 percent are still in print.[17] So, the dangers of perpetual copyright through infinite renewal would seem to be minimal.

As sensible and attractive as this proposed reform seems, I am skeptical that Congress will adopt anything of the sort in the near future. Well-reasoned reform proposals have almost never been adopted simply on the strength of their seeming to be a good idea. So, how could the Landes-Posner proposal in favor of indefinitely renewable copyright become law? What seems to me to be required to get the attention of the Congress is an empirical study that demonstrates the feasibility and advisability of the proposal. I cannot imagine what sort of demonstration is possible. Surely no country is willing to lend its copyright law for an experiment to test the Landes-Posner model. That leaves as the only possibility something artificial – a simulation perhaps. The exercise would be well worth whatever care would be required to design a plausible experiment to test the proposition.

The insights of the articles on intellectual property of the late 1980s and early 1990s – articles then extended in *The Economic Structure of Intellectual Property Law* (2003) – include a now-standard economic treatment of trademark law. Trade- and servicemarks reduce the

---

16   As we shall see shortly, this is precisely the calculation that a trademark holder is presumed to make in deciding whether to continue to enforce his or her trade- or servicemark.

17   See Landes and Posner, 'Indefinitely Renewable Copyright', 70 *University of Chicago Law Review* 471, 473–4 (2003).

search costs for consumers: having settled on the output of a particular firm as being more desirable than that of other producers, the trade- or servicemark of the desirable producer makes it inexpensive for consumers to identify the output of that producer. From this foundational point, Landes and Posner then show that most of the doctrines of trademark law fit within this economic model. For instance, the statutory provision that allows treble damages for trademark infringement makes sense: without supracompensatory damages, the small likelihood of detection may tempt trademark infringers to mimic the more expensive output of others. And the provision that forbids receiving a trademark on a product class is clearly designed to make monopolization more difficult.

One of the most interesting aspects of trademark law to which Landes and Posner draw attention is that, unlike patents and copyrights, trademarks have no time limitation. They explain that there are neither social costs (other than those of monopolization, which we have already discussed) nor tracing costs associated with trademarks. Rather, a trademark is valuable to its holder only to the extent that it has value to consumers. As a result, social and private interests are precisely aligned: the trademark holder will continue to enforce his or her mark only so long as the anticipated benefits from doing so exceed the costs. The holder will, therefore, determine the appropriate duration of his or her trademark.

Finally, Landes and Posner brought the economics of trade secrets squarely within the ambit of IP law. They noted – in 'Some Economics of Trade Secret Law', 5 *Journal of Economic Perspectives* 261 (1991) (also co-authored with David D. Friedman) – that trade secret law was simply an alternative method to the patent system of securing the benefits of innovative and inventive activity. The innovator could seek the time-limited protection of the patent regime (in exchange for which he would have to publish his invention or innovation) or seek to profit from the invention by using it himself or licensing it to others. In the latter case, the innovator would seek to secure the benefits of the innovation through contract law – by, for example, licensing his innovation but only if the licensee is willing to sign a non-disclosure agreement. Similarly, the inventor who abjured patent in favor of trade secret would also require his employees to sign non-disclosure agreements, so that if they left his employment, they could not reveal his innovation to subsequent employers or customers.

Landes and Posner (and Friedman) also noted that under trade secrets there are some privacy protections for the innovator (making it illegal, for instance, to fly over a rival's factory in an effort to discover details of a manufacturing process), but that these are limited. Most notably, rivals may purchase the innovator's output and 'reverse engineer' the product in an effort to discover what innovations have been incorporated into the product.[18]

These factors make the choice between patent law and trade secret law a relatively straightforward economic calculation. If an innovator believes that non-disclosure agreements can be effective, that reverse engineering is likely to be ineffectual, and that the potential economic life of the innovation exceeds 20 years, then he ought to prefer trade secret law to patent law. In principle, trade secret law gives a much longer time period of protection than does patent. The telling example of the effectiveness of trade secret law is Coca-Cola.

The upshot of these articles (and of *The Economic Structure of Intellectual Property Law*) is a comprehensive economic theory of intellectual property. There will, of course, be additional

---

[18]   The first scholarly discussion of the topic of reverse engineering did not appear until more than 10 years after the Landes-Posner-Friedman article in the *Journal of Economic Perspectives*. See Pamela Samuelson, 'The Law and Economics of Reverse Engineering', 111 *Yale Law Journal* 1575 (2002).

insights about intellectual property law in the future. But Landes's and Posner's articulation of a thorough, satisfying, and insightful economic theory of intellectual property is a noteworthy accomplishment.

4   Conclusion

The field of law and economics has prospered in the last 30 years in part because of the forcefulness and importance of the insights that the field has brought to the study of law. But it has also prospered because of the remarkably talented group of people who have written in the field. There is an unavoidable chicken-and-egg problem in trying to sort out which came first – the brilliant expositors or the attractive manner of analyzing the law. Far more likely was a simultaneity of attractive scholarship and brilliant scholars. In whichever order they appeared, they have effected a revolution in the way we look at, analyze, and seek to reform the law.

Of the notable partnerships among brilliant scholars who pioneered the economic analysis of law, none has been more productive and important than that between William M. Landes and Richard A. Posner. Beginning in the early 1970s and continuing through today, they have produced some of the most original and important scholarship in this field. I have surveyed some of their early writing so as to indicate the novelty of their early work and their two books to demonstrate their comprehensive and original treatments of two prominent areas of law – torts and intellectual property. I hope that I have adequately stressed how innovative and important this collaboration has been. In reviewing this work, the attribute of their work that has struck me most forcefully has been their commitment to combine theoretical insight and empirical hypothesis-testing in every article and book that they have produced. I have long felt that the most lasting innovation that law and economics will be seen to have brought to the study of law is the importation into legal scholarship of the scientific method of theorization, hypothesis-articulation, and empirical work.[19] I had not realized how perfectly and consistently Landes and Posner had practiced that radical methodological innovation.

William Landes and Richard Posner Bibliography

Books
The Economic Structure of Intellectual Property Law (Harvard University Press, 2003).
The Economic Structure of Tort Law (Harvard University Press, 1987).

Articles
'An Empirical Analysis of the Patent Court', 71 *University of Chicago Law Review* III (Winter 2004).
'The Political Economy of Intellectual Property Law', American Enterprise Institute-Brookings Joint Center for Regulatory Studies (2004).
'Indefinitely Renewable Copyright', University of Chicago Law & Economics, Olin Working Paper No. 154.
'Indefinitely Renewable Copyright', 70 *University of Chicago Law Review* 471 (2003).
'Harmless Error', 30 *Journal of Legal Studies* 161 (January 2001).
'Citations, Age, Fame and the Web', 29 *Journal of Legal Studies* 319 (January 2000).
'The Economics of Legal Disputes over the Ownership of Works of Art and Other Collectibles', in *Essays in the Economics of the Arts*, V.A. Ginsburgh and P.-M. Menger, eds (Elsevier Science, 1996).
'Heavily Cited Articles in Law', 7 *Kent Law Review* No. 3 (1996).
'The Economics of Anticipatory Adjudication', 23 *Journal of Legal Studies* 683 (June 1994).

---

[19]   See T.S. Ulen, 'A Nobel Prize in Legal Science: Theory, Empirical Work, and the Scientific Method in the Study of Law', 2002 *University of Illinois Law Review* 875.

'The Influence of Economics on Law: A Quantitative Study', 36 *Journal of Law and Economics* 385 (April 1993).

'Some Economics of Trade Secret Law', 5 *Journal of Economic Perspectives* 61 (Winter 1991) (with David Friedman).

'An Economic Analysis of Copyright Law', 18 *Journal of Legal Studies* 325 (June 1989).

'The Economics of Trademark Law', 78 *Trademark Reporter* 267 (May/June 1988).

'Trademark Law: An Economic Perspective', 30 *Journal of Law and Economics* 265 (October 1987); reprinted in the *Intellectual Property Review* (1988).

'New Light on Punitive Damages', *Regulation* 33 (September/October 1986).

'A Positive Economic Analysis of Products Liability', 14 *Journal of Legal Studies* 535 (December 1985).

'Tort Law as a Regulatory Regime for Catastrophic Personal Injuries', 13 *Journal of Legal Studies* 417 (August 1984).

'Causation in Tort Law: An Economic Approach', 12 *Journal of Legal Studies* 109 (January 1983).

'An Economic Theory of Intentional Torts', 1 *International Review of Law and Economics* 127 (December 1981).

'The Positive Economic Theory of Tort Law', 15 *Georgia Law Review* 851 (Summer 1981).

'Market Power in Antitrust Cases', 94 *Harvard Law Review* p937 (March 1981).

'Contribution Among Antitrust Defendants: A Legal and Economic Analysis', 23 *Journal of Law and Economics* 331 (October 1980) (with Frank H. Easterbrook).

'The Economics of Passing On: A Reply to Harris and Sullivan', 128 *University of Pennsylvania Law Review* 1274 (May 1980).

'Joint and Multiple Tortfeasors: An Economic Analysis', 9 *Journal of Legal Studies* 517 (June 1980).

'Legal Change, Judicial Behavior and the Diversity Jurisdiction', 9 *Journal of Legal Studies* 367 (March 1980).

'Benefits and Costs of Airline Mergers: A Case Study', 11 *The Bell Journal of Economics* 65 (Spring 1980) (with Dennis W. Carlton).

'Should Indirect Purchasers Have Standing to Sue under the Antitrust Laws? An Economics Analysis of the Rule of *Illinois Brick*', 46 *University of Chicago Law Review* 602 (Spring 1979).

'Adjudication as a Private Good', 8 *Journal of Legal Studies* 235 (March 1979).

'Altruism in Law and Economics', 68 *Papers and Proceedings of the American Economic Review* 417 (May 1978).

'Should We Tax Virgin Materials to Finance Waste Disposal?' *Waste Age* (March 1978).

'Salvors, Finders, Good Samaritans, and Other Rescuers: An Economic Study of Law and Altruism', 7 *Journal of Legal Studies* 83 (January 1978).

'Legal Precedent: A Theoretical and Empirical Analysis', 19 *Journal of Law and Economics* 249 (September 1976).

'The Independent Judiciary in an Interest Group Perspective', (Universities–National Bureau Conference on Economic Analysis of Political Behavior), 18 *Journal of Law and Economics* 875 (December 1976).

'The Private Enforcement of Law', 4 *Journal of Legal Studies* 1 (January 1975).

William Landes Bibliography

Books

Essays in the Economics of Crime and Punishment (National Bureau of Economic Research, 1974) (edited with Gary S. Becker).

Articles

'The Economic Analysis of Art Law', in 1 *Handbook of the Economics of Art and Culture* 212, Victor A. Ginsburg and David Throsby, eds (Elsevier B.V., 2006) (with Daniel B. Levine).

'The Test of Time: Does 20th Century American Art Survive?', in *Contributions to Economic Analysis: The Economics of Art and Culture,* Victor Ginsburgh, ed. (Elsevier Science, 2004).

'Indirect Liability for Copyright Infringement: An Napster and Beyond', *Journal of Economic Perspectives* (Spring 2003) (with Douglas Lichtman).

'The Empirical Side of Law and Economics', 70 *University of Chicago Law Review* 167 (2003).

'Indirect Liability in Copyright: An Economic Perspective', 17 *Journal of Economic Perspectives* 113 (2003) (with Douglas Lichtman).

'Acts of Terror with Guns: Multiple Victim Shootings', in *The Bias Against Guns*, John Lott, ed. (Regnery, 2003) (with John Lott).

'Copyright', in *The Handbook of Cultural Economics*, Ruth Towse, ed. (Edward Elgar, 2002).

'What Has the Visual Artist's Rights Act of 1990 Accomplished?', 25 *Journal of Cultural Economics* 283 (November 2001).

'Harmless Error', 30 *Journal of Legal Studies* 161 (January 2001) (with Richard A. Posner).

'Copyright, Borrowed Images and Appropriation Art: An Economic Approach', 9 *George Mason Law Review* 1 (2000).

'The Social Market for the Great Masters and Other Collectibles', in *Social Economics: Market Behavior in a Social Environment* (Harvard University Press, 2000) (with Gary S. Becker and Kevin M. Murphy).

'Winning the Art Lottery: The Economic Returns to the Ganz Collection', in *Recherches Economiques de Louvain* (forthcoming).

'Introduction to Interpreting Legal Citations', 29 *Journal of Legal Studies* 319 (January 2000).

'Citations, Age, Fame and the Web', *Journal of Legal Studies* (January 2000) (with Richard A. Posner).

'Gary S. Becker Biography', entry in *The New Palgrave Dictionary of Economics and the Law* (1998).

'Sequential and Bifurcated Trials', entry in *The New Palgrave Dictionary of Economics and the Law* (1998).

'Judicial Influence: A Citation Analysis of Federal Courts of Appeals Judges', *Journal of Legal Studies* (June 1998) (with Lawrence Lessig and Michael Solimine).

'The Art of Law and Economics: An Autobiographical Essay', 41 *The American Economist*, No. 1 (Spring 1997), reprinted in *Passion and Craft, Economists at Work*, Michael Szenberg, ed. (Michigan University Press, 1998).

'Counterclaims: An Economic Analysis', *International Review of Law & Economics* (September 1994).

'The Economics of Anticipatory Adjudication', 23 *Journal of Legal Studies* 683 (June 1994) (with Richard A. Posner).

'The Influence of Economics on Law: A Quantitative Study', 36 *Journal of Law and Economics* 385 (April 1993) (with Richard A. Posner).

'Sequential and Unitary Trials: An Economic Approach', *Journal of Legal Studies* (January 1993).

'Copyright Protection of Letters, Diaries and Other Unpublished Works: An Economic Approach', *Journal of Legal Studies* (January 1992).

'Insolvency and Joint Torts: A Comment', *Journal of Legal Studies* (June 1990).

Review of Ronald Coase, *The Firm, The Market and The Law*, University of Chicago Law School Record (Fall 1988).

'The Economics of Trademark Law', 78 *Trademark Reporter* 267 (May/June 1988) (with Richard A. Posner).

'Harm to Competition: Cartels, Mergers and Joint Ventures', 52 *Antitrust Law Journal* 625. Reprinted in *Antitrust Policy in Transition: The Convergence of Law and Economics,* E. Fox and J. Halverson, eds (American Bar Association, 1984).

'Optimal Sanctions for Antitrust Violations', *University of Chicago Law Review* (Spring 1983); reprinted in 26 *The Journal of Reprints for Antitrust Law and Economics* 79 (1996).

'An Introduction to the Economics of Antitrust', an appendix in Richard A. Posner and Frank H. Easterbrook, *Antitrust: Cases, Economic Notes and Other Materials*, 2nd ed. (West, 1980).

'Contribution Among Antitrust Defendants: A Legal and Economic Analysis', 23 *Journal of Law and Economics* 331 (October 1980) (with Frank H. Easterbrook and Richard A. Posner).

'Benefits and Costs of Airline Mergers: A Case Study', 11 *The Bell Journal of Economics* 65 (Spring 1980) (with Dennis W. Carlton and Richard A. Posner).

'An Economic Study of U.S. Aircraft Hijacking, 1961–1976', *Journal of Law and Economics* (April 1978).

'Legality and Reality: Some Evidence on Criminal Procedure', *Journal of Legal Studies* (June 1974).

'Foreign Criminal Procedure: A Comment', *The Economics of Crime and Punishment,* conference volume of the American Enterprise Institute for Public Policy Research (1973).

'The Bail System: An Economic Approach', *Journal of Legal Studies* (January 1973). Reprinted in Becker and Landes, *Essays in the Economics of Crime and Punishment* (Columbia University Press, 1974).

'Compulsory Schooling Legislation: An Economic Analysis of Law and Social Change in the Nineteenth Century', *Journal of Economic History* (March 1972) (with Lewis Solomon).

'Law and Economics', *National Bureau of Economic Research – 51st Annual Report* (September 1971).

'An Economic Analysis of the Courts', 14 *Journal of Law and Economics* (April 1971). Reprinted in Becker and Landes, *Essays in the Economics of Crime and Punishment* (1974).

'Roundtable on the Allocation of Resources to Law Enforcement', 59 Papers and Proceedings of the *American Economic Review* (May 1969).

'The Economics of Fair Employment Laws', 76(4) *Journal of Political Economy* (July/August 1968).

'The Effect of State Fair Employment Law on the Economic Position of Non-Whites', Papers and Proceedings of the 79th Annual Meeting 57 *Am. Econ. Rev.* 578.

Richard A. Posner Bibliography

Books

Economic Analysis of Law, 7th ed. (Aspen Law & Business, 2007).

Countering Terrorism: Blurred Focus, Halting Steps (Hoover Studies in Politics, Economics and Society) (Rowman & Littlefield).

The Little Book of Plagiarism (Pantheon Press, 2007).

Not a Suicide Pact: The Constitution in a Time of National Emergency (Oxford University Press, 2006).

Uncertain Shield: The U.S. Intelligence System in the Throes of Reform (Hoover Institution and Rowman & Littlefield, 2006).

Remaking Domestic Intelligence (Hoover Institution, July 2005).

Preventing Surprise Attacks: Intelligence Reform in the Wake of 9/11 (Hoover Institution and Rowman & Littlefield, 2005).

Catastrophe: Risk and Response (Oxford University Press, 2004).

Public Intellectuals: A Study of Decline (Harvard University Press, paperback edition 2003 (new Preface and Epilogue)).

Law, Pragmatism, and Democracy (Harvard University Press, 2003).

Economic Analysis of Law, 6th ed. (Aspen Law & Business, 2003).

Economic Foundations of Private Law (Edward Elgar Publishing Ltd, 2002) (co-edited with Francesco Parisi).

Breaking the Deadlock: The 2000 Election and the Courts (Princeton University Press, 2001).

Antitrust Law (second edition of *Antitrust Law: An Economic Perspective*) (University of Chicago Press, 2001).

Public Intellectuals: A Study of Decline: A Critical Analysis (Harvard University Press, 2001).

The Economic Structure of the Law: The Collected Economic Essays of Richard A. Posner (3 vols), Francesco Parisi, ed. (Edward Elgar Publishing Ltd, 2001).

Frontiers of Legal Theory (Harvard University Press, 2001).

An Affair of State: The Investigation, Impeachment, and Trial of President Clinton (Harvard University Press, 1999).

The Problematics of Moral and Legal Theory (Harvard University Press, 1999).

Economic Analysis of Law, 5th ed. (Aspen Law & Business, 1998).

Law and Literature (Harvard University Press, 1998) (enlarged and revised edition).

Law and Economics (3 vols) (Edward Elgar Publishing Ltd, 1997) (co-edited with Francesco Parisi).

Essays of Richard A. Posner on Economic Analysis of Law (2 vols), Francesco Parisi, ed. (Edward Elgar Publishing, Ltd. 1997).

Law and Legal Theory in England and America (Clarendon Press/Oxford University Press, 1996).

The Federal Courts: Challenge and Reform (Harvard University Press, 1996) (second edition of *The Federal Courts: Crisis and Reform*).

A Guide to America's Sex Laws (University of Chicago Press, 1996) (with Katharine Silbaugh).

Aging and Old Age (University of Chicago Press, 1995).

Overcoming Law (Harvard University Press 1995).

Private Choices and Public Health: The AIDS Epidemic in an Economic Perspective (Harvard University Press, 1993) (with Tomas J. Philipson).

Economic Analysis of Law, 4th ed. (Little, Brown, 1992).

Sex and Reason (Harvard University Press, 1992).

The Essential Holmes: Selections from the Letters, Speeches, Judicial Opinions, and Other Writings of Oliver Wendell Holmes, Jr. (University of Chicago Press, 1992).

Cardozo: A Study in Reputation (University of Chicago Press, 1990).

The Problems of Jurisprudence (Harvard University Press, 1990).

Law and Literature: A Misunderstood Relation (Harvard University Press, 1988).

The Economic Structure of Tort Law (Harvard University Press, 1987) (with William M. Landes).

Economic Analysis of Law, 3rd ed. (Little, Brown, 1986).

The Federal Courts: Crisis and Reform (Harvard University Press, 1985).

Tort Law: Cases and Economic Analysis (Little, Brown, 1982).

The Economics of Justice (Harvard University Press, 1981).

Economics of Corporation Law and Securities Regulation (Little, Brown, 1981) (with Kenneth E. Scott).

Antitrust: Cases, Economic Notes, and Other Materials, 2nd ed. (West, 1980) (with Frank H. Easterbrook); with 1984–5 Supplement.

The Economics of Contract Law (Little, Brown, 1978) (with Anthony T. Kronman).

Economic Analysis of Law, 2nd ed. (Little, Brown, 1977).

The Workload of the Supreme Court (American Bar Foundation, 1976) (with Gerhard Casper).

Antitrust Law: An Economic Perspective (University of Chicago Press, 1976).

Antitrust: Cases, Economic Notes, and Other Materials (West, 1974).

Economic Analysis of Law (Little, Brown, 1973).

Articles and article-length monographs

'Catastrophic Risk: A Social Scientific Approach', *American Interest* (forthcoming).

'Brandeis and Holmes, Business and Economics, Then and Now', *Review of Law and Economics* (forthcoming).

'Norms and Values in the Economic Approach to Law', *Economic Analysis of Law: A European Perspective*, Aristides N. Hatzis, ed. (forthcoming).

'Indefinitely Renewable Copyright', 70 *University of Chicago Law Review* 471 (with William M. Landes).

'Relations between Law and Literature' *Irish Jurist* (forthcoming).

'Past-Dependency, Pragmatism, and Critique of History in Adjudication and Legal Scholarship', *University of Chicago Law Review* (forthcoming).

'Tribute to Ronald Dworkin', 63 *New York University Annual Survey of American Law* 9 (2007).

'The New Market for Federal Judicial Law Clerks', 74 *University of Chicago Law Review* 447 (Spring 2007) (with Christopher Avery, Christine Jolls and Alvin E. Roth).

'In Memoriam: Bernard D. Meltzer (1914–2007)', 74 *University of Chicago Law Review* 435 (Spring 2007).

'A Note on Rumsfeld v. Fair and the Legal Academy', 2006 *Supreme Court Review* 47.

'In Defense of Prometheus' (unpublished, February 2007).

'Are American CEOs Overpaid, and, if So, What if Anything Should be Done about it?' (February 2007).

'Cognitive Theory as the Ground of Political Theory in Plato, Popper, Dewey, and Hayek', in *Cognition and Economics* 253, Elisabeth Krecke, Carine Krecke, and Roger G. Koppl, eds. (JAI Press, 2006).

'Censorship versus Freedom of Expression in the Arts', in 1 *Handbook of the Economics of Art and Culture* 309, Victor A. Ginsburgh and David Throsby, eds. (North Holland, 2006) (with Tun-Jen Chiang).

'The Role of the Judge in the Twenty-First Century', 86 *Boston University Law Review* 1049 (2006).

'Suicide and Risk-Taking: An Economic Approach' (unpublished, April 2006) (co-authored with Gary S. Becker).

'Demand and Supply Trends in Federal and State Courts over the Last Half Century', 8 *Journal of Appellate Practice and Process* 133 (2006).

'Efficient Responses to Catastrophic Risk', 6 *Chicago Journal of International Law* 511 (2006).

'Antitrust in the Not-for-Profit Sector', National Bureau of Economic Research Working Paper 12132 (March 2006) (with Tomas J. Philipson).

'The Reorganized U.S. Intelligence System after One Year', National Security Outlook (Special Edition) (American Enterprise Institute, April 2006).

'Judicial Autonomy in a Political Environment', 38 *Arizona State Law Review* 1 (2006).

'Common Law Economic Torts: An Economic and Legal Analysis', 48 *Arizona Law Review* 735 (2006).

'One-Sided Contracts in Competitive Consumer Markets', 104 *Michigan Law Review* 827 (2006) (with Lucian A. Bebchuk).

'Law School Rankings', 81 *Indiana Law Journal* 13 (2006).

'Efficient Responses to Catastrophes' (unpublished, December 2005).

'Public Policy toward Catastrophes' (unpublished, December 2005).

'The Law and Economics Movement: From Bentham to Becker', in *The Origins of Law and Economics: Essays by the Founding Fathers* 328, Francesco Parisi and Charles K. Rowley, eds. (Edward Elgar Publishing 2005).

'The Supreme Court, 2004 Term: Foreword: A Political Court', 119 *Harvard Law Review* 31 (2005).

'Intelligence Reform since 9/11: An Organizational Economics Perspective', *Journal of Economic Perspectives* 151 (Fall 2005) (with Luis Garciano).

'The Romance of Force: James Fitzjames Stephen on Criminal Law', (unpublished, April 2005).

'Vertical Restraints and Antitrust Policy', 72 *University of Chicago Law Review* 229 (2005).

'Catastrophic Risks, Resource Allocation, and Homeland Security', *Journal of Homeland Security* (November 1, 2005).

'Hayek, Law, and Cognition', 1 *New York University Journal of Law & Liberty* 147 (2005).

'Judicial Behavior and Performance: An Economic Approach', 32 *Florida State University Law Review* 1259 (2005).

'The Law and Economics of Contract Interpretation', 83 *Texas Law Review* 1581 (2005).

'The Federal Trade Commission: A Retrospective', 72 *Antitrust Law Journal* 761 (2005).

'Intellectual Property: The Law-and-Economics Approach', *Journal of Economic Perspectives* 57 (Spring 2005).

'Guido Calabresi's The Costs of Accidents: A Reassessment', 64 *Maryland Law Review* 12 (2005).

'The Evolution of Economic Thinking about Legislation and its Interpretation by Courts', in *Theory and Practice of Legislation: Essays in Legisprudence* 53, Luc J. Wintgens, Philippe Thion, and Melanie Cury eds (Ashgate Publishing, 2005).

'The Effect of U.S. Tort Law, and of Tort-Law Reform, on the Reinsurance Industry' (unpublished, September 2004).

'Legal Pragmatism', in *The Range of Pragmatism and the Limits of Philosophy* 144, Richard Shusterman, ed. (Wiley-Blackwell, 2004).

'Torture, Interrogation, and Terrorism', in *Torture: A Collection* 291, Sanford Levinson, ed. (Oxford University Press, 2004).

'Law and Economics in Common-Law, Civil-Law, and Developing Nations', 17 *Ratio Juris* 66 (2004).

'Federalism and the Enforcement of Antitrust Laws by State Attorneys General', in *Competition Laws in Conflict: Antitrust Jurisdiction in the Global Economy* 252, Richard A. Epstein and Michael S. Greve, eds. (AEI Press, 2004).

'The 2000 Presidential Election: A Statistical and Legal Analysis', 12 *Supreme Court Economic Review* 1 (2004).

'The Impeachment and Trial of William Clinton' (unpublished, August 2003).

'Fair Use and Statutory Reform in the Wake of Eldred', 92 *California Law Review* 1639 (2004) (co-authored with William F. Patry).

'Legal Pragmatism', 35 *Metaphilosophy* 147 (2004).

'Pragmatic Liberalism versus Classical Liberalism', 71 *University of Chicago Law Review* 659 (2004).

'The Constitutionality of the Copyright Term Extension Act: Economics, Politics, Law, and Judicial Technique in Eldred v. Ashcroft', *Supreme Court Review* 143 (2004).

'John Dewey and the Intersection of Democracy and Law', in *Dewey, Pragmatism, and Economic Methodology* 167, Elias L. Khalil, ed. (Routledge, 2004).

'Animal Rights: Legal, Philosophical, and Pragmatic Perspectives', in *Animal Rights: Current Debates and New Directions* 51, Martha C. Nussbaum and Cass R. Sunstein, eds (Oxford University Press, 2004).

'The Long-Run Growth in Obesity as a Function of Technological Change', *Perspectives in Biology and Medicine* S87 (Summer 2003 Supplement) (with Tomas J. Philipson).

'The Law and Economics Movement: From Bentham to Becker', (unpublished, December 2003).

'Censorship and Free Speech: First Amendment Issues in the Visual Arts' (unpublished, September 2003) (with T.J. Chiang).

'How Long Should a Copyright Last?' 50 *Journal of the Copyright Society of the U.S.A.* 1 (2003).

'Misappropriation: A Dirge', 40 *Houston Law Review* 621 (2003).

'Reply: The Institutional Dimension of Statutory and Constitutional Interpretation', 101 *Michigan Law Review* 952 (2003).

Law, Economics, and Democracy: Three Lectures in Greece' (University of Athens Department of History and Philosophy of Science, 2002).

'Behavioral Law and Economics: A Critique', *Economic Education Bulletin* (American Institute for Economic Research, August 2002).

'Formal versus Substantive Economic Theories of Law' (unpublished, July 2002).

'Comment réguler?' (unpublished, May 2002).

'Legal Scholarship Today', 115 Harvard Law Review 1314 (2002).

'Bush v. Gore as Pragmatic Adjudication', in *A Badly Flawed Election: Debating Bush v. Gore, the Supreme Court, and American Democracy* 187, Ronald Dworkin, ed. (New Press, 2002).

'Pragmatism versus Purposivism in First Amendment Analysis', 54 *Stanford Law Review* 717 (2002).

'The Economics of Presidential Pardons' (unpublished, December 2001) (with William M. Landes).

'Regulation and Deregulation in the United States' (unpublished, May 2001).

'Antitrust and the New Economy', 68 *Antitrust Law Journal* 925 (2001).

'Bush v. Gore: Prolegomenon to an Assessment', 68 *University of Chicago Law Review* 719 (2001).

'Florida 2000: A Legal and Statistical Analysis of the Election Deadlock and the Ensuing Litigation', *Supreme Court Review* (2000) 1.

'On Liberty: A Reevaluation' (unpublished, August 2000).

'Rorty on Law and Public Policy', (unpublished, August 2000).

'Dworkin, Polemics, and the Clinton Impeachment Controversy', 94 *Northwestern University Law Review* 1023 (2000).

'The Market for Federal Judicial Law Clerks' (unpublished, January 2000) (with Christopher Avery, Christine Jolls, and Alvin E. Roth).

'Cost-Benefit Analysis: Definition, Justification, and Comment on Conference Papers', 29 *Journal of Legal Studies* 1153 (2000).

'Orwell versus Huxley: Economics, Technology, Privacy, and Satire', 24 *Philosophy and Literature* 1 (2000).

'Market Signaling of Personal Characteristics' (unpublished, January 2000) (with Gertrud M. Fremling).

'An Economic Analysis of the Use of Citations in the Law', 2 *American Law and Economics Review* 381 (2000).

'Is the Ninth Circuit Too Large? A Statistical Study of Judicial Quality', 29 *Journal of Legal Studies* 711 (2000).

'Savigny, Holmes, and the Law and Economics of Possession', 86 *Virginia Law Review* 535 (2000).

'Citations, Age, Fame, and the Web', 29 *Journal of Legal Studies* 319 (2000) (with William M. Landes).

'The Effects of Deregulation on Competition: The Experience of the United States', 23 *Fordham International Law Journal* S7 (2000).

'Values and Consequences: An Introduction to Economic Analysis of Law', in *Chicago Lectures on Law and Economics* 189, Eric A. Posner, ed. (West Publishing Co., 2000).

'The Law and Economics of the Economic Expert Witness', *Journal of Economic Perspectives* 91 (Spring 1999).

'An Economic Approach to the Law of Evidence', 51 *Stanford Law Review* 1477 (1999).

'Employment Discrimination: Age Discrimination and Sexual Harassment', 19 *International Review of Law and Economics* 421 (1999).

'The Law and Economics Movement: From Bentham to Becker' (unpublished, September 1999).

'The Demand for Human Cloning', 27 *Hofstra Law Review* 579 (1999) (with Eric A. Posner).

'The Long-Run Growth in Obesity as a Function of Technological Change' (unpublished, November 1999) (with Tomas J. Philipson).

'Harmless Error' (unpublished, November 1999) (with William M. Landes).

'Status Signaling and the Law, with Particular Application to Sexual Harassment', 147 *University of Pennsylvania Law Review* 1069 (1999) (with Gertrud M. Fremling).

'Creating and Enforcing Norms, with Special Reference to Sanctions', 19 *International Review of Law and Economics* 369 (1999) (with Eric B. Rasmusen).

'The Speech Market and the Legacy of Schenck' (unpublished, July 1998).

'Emotion versus Emotionalism in Law', in *The Passions of Law* 309, Susan Bandes, ed. (NYU Press, 1999).

'Against Ethical Criticism: Part Two', 22 *Philosophy and Literature* 416 (1998).

'Rational Choice, Behavioral Economics, and the Law', 50 *Stanford Law Review* 551 (1998).

'Reply to Critics of "The Problematics of Moral and Legal Theory,"' 111 *Harvard Law Review* 1796 (1998).

'Bentham's Influence on the Law and Economics Movement', 51 *Current Legal Problems* 425 (1998).

'Professionalisms', 40 *Arizona Law Review* 1 (1998).

'Against Constitutional Theory', 73 *New York University Law Review* 1 (1998).

'The Problematics of Moral and Legal Theory', 111 *Harvard Law Review* 1637 (1998).

'Social Norms, Social Meaning, and Economic Analysis of Law: A Comment', 27 *Journal of Legal Studies* 553 (1998).

'The Demand for Human Cloning', in *Clones and Clones: Facts and Fantasies about Human Cloning* 233, Martha C. Nussbaum and Cass R. Sunstein, eds (W.W. Norton & Company, 1998) (with Eric A. Posner).

'Creating a Legal Framework for Economic Development', *World Bank Research Observer* 1 (February 1998).

'Conceptions of Legal "Theory": A Response to Ronald Dworkin', 29 *Arizona State Law Journal* 377 (1997).

'Narrative and Narratology in Classroom and Courtroom', 21 *Philosophy and Literature* 292 (1997).

'Against Ethical Criticism', 21 *Philosophy and Literature* 1 (1997).

'Social Norms and the Law: An Economic Approach', 87 *American Economic Review Papers and Proceedings* 365 (May 1997).

'Are We One Self or Multiple Selves? Implications for Law and Public Policy', 3 *Legal Theory* 23 (1997).

'Explaining the Variance in the Number of Tort Suits across U.S. States and between the United States and England', 26 *Journal of Legal Studies* 477 (1997).

'The Future of Law and Economics in Europe', 17 *International Review of Law and Economics* 3 (1997).

'The Economic Approach to Homosexuality', in *Sex, Preference, and Family: Essays on Law and Nature* 173, David M. Estlund and Martha C. Nussbaum, eds (Oxford University Press, 1997).

'Equality, Wealth, and Political Stability', 13 *Journal of Law, Economics, and Organization* 344 (1997).

'The Economics of Legal Disputes over the Ownership of Works of Art and Other Collectibles', in *Essays in the Economics of the Arts* 177, Victor A. Ginsburgh and Pierre-Michel Menger, eds (North Holland, 1996) (with William M. Landes).

'The Cost of Rights: Implications for Central and Eastern Europe-and for the United States', 32 *Tulsa Law Journal* 1 (1996).

'Heavily Cited Articles in Law', 71 *Chicago-Kent Law Review* 825 (1996) (with William M. Landes).

'Pragmatic Adjudication', 18 *Cardozo Law Review* 1 (1996).

'Sexual Behavior, Disease, and Fertility Risk', 1 *Risk Decision and Policy* 91 (1996) (with Tomas J. Philipson).

'Wealth Maximization and Tort Law: A Philosophical Inquiry', in *Philosophical Foundations of Tort Law* 99, David G. Owen, ed. (Oxford University Press, 1996).

'Euthanasia and Health Care: Two Essays on the Policy Dilemmas of Aging and Old Age', in 17 *The Tanner Lectures on Human Values*, 13, Grethe B. Peterson, ed. (University of Utah Press, 1996).

'The Economic Epidemiology of Crime', 39 *Journal of Law and Economics* 405 (1996) (with Tomas J. Philipson).

'The Costs of Enforcing Legal Rights', *Eastern European Constitutional Review* 71 (Summer 1995).

'Judicial Biography', 70 *New York University Law Review* 502 (1995).

'The Sociology of the Sociology of Law: A View from Economics', 2 *European Journal of Law and Economics* 265 (1995).

'Judges' Writing Styles (And Do They Matter?)', 62 *University of Chicago Law Review* 1421 (1995).

'The Microeconomics of the AIDS Epidemic in Africa', 21 *Population and Development Review* 835 (1995) (with Tomas J. Philipson).

'A Theoretical and Empirical Investigation of Public Health Subsidies for STD Testing', 105 *Quarterly Journal of Economics* 445 (1995) (with Tomas J. Philipson).

'Economics, Time and Age: Twenty Fifth Geary Lecture', Economic and Social Research Institute of Ireland (1994).

'What Do Judges and Justices Maximize? (The Same Thing Everybody Else Does)', 3 *Supreme Court Economic Review* 1 (1994).

'The Economics of Anticipatory Adjudication', 23 *Journal of Legal Studies* 683 (1994) (with William M. Landes).

'Public Spending on AIDS Education: An Economic Analysis', 37 *Journal of Law and Economics* 17 (1994) (with Tomas J. Philipson).

'The Radical Feminist Critique of Sex and Reason', 25 *Connecticut Law Review* 515 (1993).

'Legal Scholarship Today', 45 *Stanford Law Review* 1627 (1993).

'The Material Basis of Jurisprudence', 69 *Indiana Law Journal* 1 (1993).

'Cross-Cultural Differences in Family and Sexual Life: An Economic Analysis', 5 *Rationality and Society* 421 (1993) (with Gary S. Becker).

'Richard Rorty's Politics', 7 *Critical Review* 33 (1993).

'The New Institutional Economics Meets Law and Economics', 149 *Journal of Institutional and Theoretical Economics* 73 (1993).

'Ronald Coase and Methodology', 7 *Journal of Economic Perspectives* 197 (Fall 1993).

'The Influence of Economics on Law: A Quantitative Study', 36 *Journal of Law and Economics* 385 (1993) (with William M. Landes).

'Blackmail, Privacy, and Freedom of Contract', 141 *University of Pennsylvania Law Review* 1817 (1993).

'Legal Reasoning from the Top Down and from the Bottom Up: The Question of Unenumerated Constitutional Rights', 59 *University of Chicago Law Review* 433 (1992).

'When Is Parody Fair Use?', 21 *Journal of Legal Studies* 67 (1992).

'Foreword', in James Fitzjames Stephen, *Liberty, Equality, Fraternity* 7 (University of Chicago Press, 1992).

'Democracy and Distrust Revisited', 77 *University of Virginia Law Review* 641 (1991).

'Some Economics of Trade Secret Law', 5 *Journal of Economic Perspectives* 61 (Winter 1991) (with David D. Friedman and William M. Landes).

'Bork and Beethoven', 42 *Stanford Law Review* 1365 (1990).

'What Has Pragmatism to Offer Law?', 63 *University of Southern California Law Review* 1653 (1990).

'Art for Law's Sake', 58 *American Scholar* 513 (1989).

'The Depiction of Law in The Bonfire of the Vanities', 98 *Yale Law Journal* 1653 (1989).

'The Future of Law and Economics: A Comment on Ellickson', 65 *Chicago-Kent Law Review* 57 (1989).

'Philistinism in Law', 16 *Northern Kentucky Law Review* 515 (1989).

'Legislation and its Interpretation: A Primer', 68 *Nebraska Law Review* 431 (1989).

'An Economic Analysis of Sex Discrimination Laws', 56 *University of Chicago Law Review* 1311 (1989).

'The Ethics and Economics of Enforcing Contracts of Surrogate Motherhood', 5 *Journal of Contemporary Health Law and Policy* 21 (1989).

'Coping with the Caseload: A Comment on Magistrates and Masters', 137 *University of Pennsylvania Law Review* 2215 (1989).

'Conservative Feminism', *University of Chicago Legal Forum* 191 (1989).

'A Comment on Weisberg's Interpretation [of Billy Budd]', 1 *Cardozo Studies in Law and Literature* 71 (1989).

'On Theory and Practice: Reply to "Richard Posner's Praxis"', 49 *Ohio State Law Journal* 1077 (1989).

'An Economic Analysis of Copyright Law', 18 *Journal of Legal Studies* 325 (1989) (with William M. Landes).

'An Economic Approach to Issues of Religious Freedom', 56 *University of Chicago Law Review* 1 (1989) (with Michael W. McConnell).

'Hegel and Employment at Will: A Comment', 10 *Cardozo Law Review* 1625 (1989).

'Interpreting Law, Interpreting Literature (II)', 8 *Raritan: A Quarterly Review* 59 (Summer 1988).

'The Economics of Trademark Law', 78 *Trademark Reporter* 267 (1988) (with William M. Landes).

'The Jurisprudence of Skepticism', 86 *Michigan Law Review* 827 (1988).

'Interpreting Law, Interpreting Literature', 7 *Raritan: A Quarterly Review* 1 (Spring 1988).

'The Ethics of Wealth Maximization: Reply to Malloy', 36 *Kansas Law Review* 261 (1988).

'Conventionalism: The Key to Law as an Autonomous Discipline?', 38 *University of Toronto Law Journal* 333 (1988).

'The Efficiency and the Efficacy of Title VII', 136 *University of Pennsylvania Law Review* 513 (1987).

'The Constitution as an Economic Document', 56 *George Washington Law Review* 4 (1987)

'What Am I? A Potted Plant?' *The New Republic* 23 (September 28, 1987).

'Trademark Law: An Economic Perspective', 30 *Journal of Law and Economics* 265 (1987) (with William M. Landes).

'The Justice of Economics', 1 *Economia delle Scelte Pubbliche* 15 (1987).

'The Law and Economics Movement', 77 *American Economic Review Papers and Proceedings* 1 (May 1987).

'The Regulation of the Market in Adoptions', 67 *Boston University Law Review* 59 (1987).

'Legal Formalism, Legal Realism, and the Interpretation of Statutes and the Constitution', 37 *Case Western Reserve Law Review* 179 (1987).

'The Decline of Law as an Autonomous Discipline: 1962–1987', 100 *Harvard Law Review* 761 (1987).

'New Light on Punitive Damages', *Regulation* 33 (September/October 1986) (with William M. Landes).

'Law and Literature: A Relation Reargued', 72 *Virginia Law Review* 1351 (1986).

'Free Speech in an Economic Perspective', 20 *Suffolk Law Review* 1 (1986).

'The Ethical Significance of Free Choice: A Reply to Professor West', 99 *Harvard Law Review* 1431 (1986).

'Law and the Theory of Finance: Some Intersections', 54 *George Washington Law Review* 159 (1986).

'The Summary Jury Trial and Other Methods of Alternative Dispute Resolution: Some Cautionary Observations', 53 *University of Chicago Law Review* 366 (1986).

'Wealth Maximization Revisited', 2 *Notre Dame Journal of Law, Ethics, and Public Policy* 85 (1985).
'Can Lawyers Solve the Problems of the Tort System?', 73 *California Law Review* 747 (1985).
'An Economic Theory of the Criminal Law', 85 *Columbia Law Review* 1193 (1985).
'A Positive Economic Analysis of Products Liability Law', 14 *Journal of Legal Studies* 535 (1985) (with William M. Landes).
'Wealth Maximization and Judicial Decision-Making', 4 *International Review of Law and Economics* 131 (1984).
'Some Economics of Labor Law', 51 *University of Chicago Law Review* 988 (1984).
'Tort Law as a Regulatory Regime for Catastrophic Personal Injuries', 13 *Journal of Legal Studies* 417 (1984) (with William M. Landes).
'The Meaning of Judicial Self-Restraint', 59 *Indiana Law Journal* 1 (1983).
'Statutory Construction in the Classroom and in the Courtroom', 50 *University of Chicago Law Review* 800 (1983).
'Will the Federal Courts Survive Until 1984? An Essay on Delegation and Specialization of the Judicial Function', 56 *University of Southern California Law Review* 761 (1983).
'Causation in Tort Law: An Economic Approach', 12 *Journal of Legal Studies* 109 (1983) (with William M. Landes).
'Toward an Economic Theory of Federal Jurisdiction', 6 *Harvard Journal of Law and Public Policy* 41 (1982).
'Excessive Sanctions for Governmental Misconduct in Criminal Cases', 57 *Washington Law Review* 635 (1982).
'Economics, Politics, and the Reading of Statutes and Constitutions', 49 *University of Chicago Law Review* 263 (1982).
'The Positive Economic Theory of Tort Law', 15 *Georgia Law Review* 851 (1982) (with William M. Landes).
'Rethinking the Fourth Amendment', *Supreme Court Review* 49 (Philip B. Kurland, et al., eds) (1981).
'The Present Situation in Legal Scholarship', 90 *Yale Law Journal* 1113 (1981).
'An Economic Theory of Intentional Torts', 1 *International Review of Law and Economics* 127 (1981) (with William M. Landes).
'A Reply to Some Recent Criticisms of the Efficiency Theory of the Common Law', 9 *Hofstra Law Review* 775 (1981).
'Divestiture, Deconcentration, and Antitrust Policy', in *Kontroll von Marktmacht nach deutschen, europaischem und amerikanischen Kartellrecht* 58 (FIW-Schriftenreihe, Heft 98, 1981).
'Lawyers as Philosophers: Ackerman and Others', *American Bar Foundation Research Journal* 231 (1981).
'The Concept of Corrective Justice in Recent Theories of Tort Law', 10 *Journal of Legal Studies* 187 (1981).
'Market Power in Antitrust Cases', 94 *Harvard Law Review* 937 (1981) (with William M. Landes).
'The Economics of Privacy', 71 *American Economic Review Papers and Proceedings* 405 (May 1981).
'The Next Step in the Antitrust Treatment of Restricted Distribution: Per Se Legality', 48 *University of Chicago Law Review* 6 (1981).
'Social Investing and the Law of Trusts', 79 *Michigan Law Review* 72 (1980) (with John H. Langbein).
'Contribution among Antitrust Defendants: A Legal and Economic Analysis', 23 *Journal of Law and Economics* 331 (1980) (with Frank H. Easterbrook and William M. Landes).
'The Economics of Passing On: A Reply to Harris and Sullivan', 128 *University of Pennsylvania Law Review* 1274 (1980) (with William M. Landes).
'Joint and Multiple Tortfeasors: An Economic Analysis', 9 *Journal of Legal Studies* 517 (1980) (with William M. Landes).
'The Value of Wealth: A Comment on Dworkin and Kronman', 9 *Journal of Legal Studies* 243 (1980).
'Optimal Sentences for White Collar Criminals', 17 *American Criminal Law Review* 409 (1980).
'The Ethical and Political Basis of the Efficiency Norm in Common Law Adjudication', 8 *Hofstra Law Review* 487 (1980).
'Retribution and Related Concepts of Punishment', 9 *Journal of Legal Studies* 71 (1980).
'Legal Change, Judicial Behavior, and the Diversity Jurisdiction', 9 *Journal of Legal Studies* 367 (1980) (with William M. Landes).
'Benefits and Costs of Airline Mergers: A Case Study', 11 *Bell Journal of Economics* 65 (1980) (with Dennis W. Carlton and William M. Landes).
'Anthropology and Economics', 88 *Journal of Political Economy* 608 (1980).
'A Theory of Primitive Society, with Special Reference to Law', 23 *Journal of Law and Economics* 1 (1980).
'The Uncertain Protection of Privacy by the Supreme Court', *Supreme Court Review* 173 (Philip B. Kurland and Gerhard Casper, eds) (1979).
'Information and Antitrust: Reflections on the Gypsum and Engineers Decisions', 67 *Georgetown Law Journal* 1187 (1979).
'Should Indirect Purchasers Have Standing to Sue under the Antitrust Laws? An Economic Analysis of the Rule of *Illinois Brick*', 46 *University of Chicago Law Review* 602 (1979) (with William M. Landes).
'Epstein's Tort Theory: A Critique', 8 *Journal of Legal Studies* 457 (1979).
'Some Uses and Abuses of Economics in Law', 46 *University of Chicago Law Review* 281 (1979).
'Privacy, Secrecy, and Reputation', 28 *Buffalo Law Review* 1 (1979).

'The Chicago School of Antitrust Analysis', 127 *University of Pennsylvania Law Review* 925 (1979).

'The Antitrust Decisions of the Burger Court', 47 *Antitrust Law Journal* 819 (1979).

'The Bakke Case and the Future of "Affirmative Action,"' 67 *California Law Review* 171 (1979)

'Utilitarianism, Economics, and Legal Theory', 8 *Journal of Legal Studies* 103 (1979).

'The Federal Trade Commission's Mandated-Disclosure Program: A Critical Analysis', in Harvey J. Goldschmid, ed., *Business Disclosure: Government's Need to Know* 331 (McGraw-Hill, 1979).

'The Homeric Version of the Minimal State', 90 *Ethics* 27 (1979).

'Adjudication as a Private Good', 8 *Journal of Legal Studies* 235 (1979) (with William M. Landes).

'An Approach to the Regulation of Bank Holding Companies', 51 *Journal of Business* 379 (1978) (with Fischer Black and Merton H. Miller).

'An Economic Theory of Privacy', *Regulation* 19 (May/June 1978).

'The Right of Privacy', 12 *Georgia Law Review* 393 (1978).

'Altruism in Law and Economics', 68 *American Economic Review Papers and Proceedings* 417 (May 1978) (with William M. Landes).

'The Economics of the Baby Shortage', 7 *Journal of Legal Studies* 323 (1978) (with Elisabeth M. Landes).

'Salvors, Finders, Good Samaritans, and Other Rescuers: An Economic Study of Law and Altruism', 7 *Journal of Legal Studies* 83 (1978) (with William M. Landes).

'The Rule of Reason and the Economic Approach: Reflections on the Sylvania Decision', 45 *University of Chicago Law Review* 1 (1977).

'The Caseload of the Supreme Court: 1975 and 1976 Terms', *Supreme Court Review* 87 (Philip B. Kurland and Gerhard Casper, eds) (with Gerhard Casper) (1977).

'Gratuitous Promises in Economics and Law', 6 *Journal of Legal Studies* 411 (1977).

'Impossibility and Related Doctrines in Contract Law: An Economic Analysis', 6 *Journal of Legal Studies* 83 (1977) (with Andrew M. Rosenfield).

'Market Funds and Trust-Investment Law: II', *American Bar Foundation Research Journal* (with John H. Langbein) (1977).

'Market Funds and Efficient Markets: A Reply', 62 *American Bar Association Journal* 1616 (1976) (with John H. Langbein).

'Legal Precedent: A Theoretical and Empirical Analysis', 19 *Journal of Law & Economics* 249 (1976) (with William M. Landes).

The Robinson-Patman Act: Federal Regulation of Price Differences (American Enterprise Institute, 1976).

'The Revolution in Trust Investment Law', 62 *American Bar Association Journal* 887 (1976) (with John H. Langbein).

'Blackstone and Bentham', 19 *Journal of Law & Economics* 569 (1976).

'The Rights of Creditors of Affiliated Corporations', 43 *University of Chicago Law Review* 493 (1976).

'Oligopolistic Pricing Suits, the Sherman Act, and Economic Welfare (Symposium): A Reply to Professor Markovits', 28 *Stanford Law Review* 903 (1976).

'The Prudent Investor's Powers and Obligations in an Age of Market (Index) Funds', in *Evolving Concepts of Prudence* 19 (Financial Analysts Research Foundation, 1976); also in 5 *Journal of Contemporary Business* 85 (Summer 1976).

'Market Funds and Trust-Investment Law', *American Bar Foundation Research Journal* 1 (with John H. Langbein) (1976).

'The Independent Judiciary in an Interest-Group Perspective', 18 *Journal of Law & Economics* 875 (1976) (with William M. Landes).

'The Supreme Court and Antitrust Policy: A New Direction?' 44 *Antitrust Law Journal* 141 (1975).

'A Comment on No-Fault Insurance for All Accidents', 13 *Osgoode Hall Law Journal* 471 (1975).

'The Social Costs of Monopoly and Regulation', 83 *Journal of Political Economy* 807 (1975).

'The Economic Approach to Law', 53 *Texas Law Review* 758 (1975).

'Antitrust Policy and the Supreme Court: An Analysis of the Restricted Distribution, Horizontal Merger and Potential Competition Decisions', 75 *Columbia Law Review* 282 (1975).

'The Private Enforcement of Law', 4 *Journal of Legal Studies* 1 (1975) (with William M. Landes).

'Power in America: The Role of the Large Corporation', in J. Fred Weston, ed., *Large Corporations in a Changing Society* 91 (New York University Press, 1975).

'The DeFunis Case and the Constitutionality of Preferential Treatment of Racial Minorities', *Supreme Court Review* 1 (Philip B. Kurland ed.) (1974).

'A Study of the Supreme Court's Caseload', 3 *Journal of Legal Studies* 399 (1974) (with Gerhard Casper).

'Exclusionary Practices and the Antitrust Laws', 41 *University of Chicago Law Review* 506 (1974).

'Problems of a Policy of Deconcentration', in Harvey J. Goldschmid et al.. eds., *Industrial Concentration: The New Learning* 393 (Little, Brown, 1974).

'Theories of Economic Regulation', 5 *Bell Journal of Economics & Management Science* 155 (1974).

'Certificates of Need for Health Care Facilities: A Dissenting View', in Clark C. Havighurst, ed., *Regulating Health Facilities Construction* 113 (American Enterprise Institute Press, 1974).

'An Economic Analysis of Legal Rulemaking', 3 *Journal of Legal Studies* 257 (1974) (with Isaac Ehrlich).

'Truth in Advertising: The Role of Government', in Yale Brozen, ed., *Advertising and Society* 111 (New York University Press, 1974).

'The Probable Effects of Pay Cable Television on Culture and the Arts', in Richard Adler and Walter S. Baer, eds, *The Electronic Box Office: Humanities and Arts on the Cable* 79 (Praeger Publishers Inc., 1974).

Regulation and Advertising by the FTC (American Enterprise Institute 1973).

'Economic Justice and the Economist', *Public Interest* 109 (Fall 1973).

'An Economic Approach to Legal Procedure and Judicial Administration', 2 *Journal of Legal Studies* 399 (1973).

'Reflections on Consumerism', *University of Chicago Law School Record* 19 (Spring 1973).

'Strict Liability: A Comment', 2 *Journal of Legal Studies* 205 (1973).

'The Appropriate Scope of Regulation in the Cable Television Industry', 3 *Bell Journal of Economics & Management Science* 98 (1972).

Market Transfers of Water Rights: Toward an Improved Market in Water Resources, National Water Commission, Legal Study No. 4, Final Report, July 1 (National Technical Information Service, 1972) (with Charles J. Meyers).

'The Behavior of Administrative Agencies', 1 *Journal of Legal Studies* 305 (1972); also in Gary S. Becker and William M. Landes, eds., *Essays in the Economics of Crime and Punishment* 215 (Columbia University Press, 1974).

'A Theory of Negligence', 1 *Journal of Legal Studies* 29 (1972).

'Killing or Wounding to Protect a Property Interest', 14 *Journal of Law & Economics* 201 (1971).

'Regulatory Aspects of National Health Insurance Plans', 39 *University of Chicago Law Review* 1 (1971).

'Taxation by Regulation', 2 *Bell Journal of Economics & Management Science* 22 (1971).

'A Program for the Antitrust Division', 38 *University of Chicago Law Review* 500 (1971).

'Natural Monopoly and its Regulation: A Reply', 22 *Stanford Law Review* 540 (1970).

'A Statistical Study of Antitrust Enforcement', 13 *Journal of Law & Economics* 365 (1970).

'Antitrust Policy and the Consumer Movement', 15 *Antitrust Bulletin* 361 (1970).

Cable Television: The Problem of Local Monopoly, RAND Memorandum RM-6309-FF (May 1970).

'Conglomerate Mergers and Antitrust Policy: An Introduction', 44 *St John's Law Review* (special edition) 259 (1970).

'The Provision of Data-Processing Services by Communications Common Carriers', in R. Dunn, *Policy Issues Presented by the Interdependence of Computer and Communications Services* (Stanford Research Institute Report No. 7379B-1, February 1969).

'The Federal Trade Commission', 37 *University of Chicago Law Review* 47 (1969).

'Advertising and Product Differentiation', 2 *Antitrust Law & Economics Review* 47 (1969).

'Oligopoly and the Antitrust Laws: A Suggested Approach', 21 *Stanford Law Review* 1562 (1969).

'Natural Monopoly and Its Regulation', 21 *Stanford Law Review* 518 (1969).

Book reviews, comments, and miscellaneous

'In Memoriam: Bernard D. Meltzer', *University of Chicago Law Review* (forthcoming).

'A Tribute to Ronald Dworkin – And a Note on Pragmatic Adjudication', *New York University Annual Review of American Law* (forthcoming).

'Fair Use after Eldred: Debate with Alex Kozinski', *Journal of the Copyright Society of the U.S.A.* (forthcoming).

'Community and Conscription', in *Rethinking Commodification: Readings in Law and Culture* (forthcoming).

'Democracy and Judiciary: A Comment on Aulis Aarnio, The Court System and Democracy', *Ratio Juris* (forthcoming).

'Clinical and Theoretical Approaches to the Teaching of Evidence and Trial Advocacy', *Quinnipiac Law Review* (forthcoming).

'Legal Theory', in *Encyclopedia Britannica* (forthcoming).

'Enlightened Despot', *The New Republic* 53 (April 23, 2007) (Review of Aharon Barak, *The Judge in a Democracy* (2006)).

'Time to Rethink the FBI', *Wall Street Journal* A13 (March 19, 2007).

'Penal Theory in Paradise Lost', 105 *Michigan Law Review* 1049 (2007) (with Jillisa Brittan).

'In Defense of Plagiarism: No Harm, No Foul is What the Law Ought to Be', *Forbes* 32 (January 29, 2007).

'How to Make the Poor Poorer', *Wall Street Journal* A22 (January 26, 2007) (with Gary S. Becker).

'"How to Skip the Constitution" – An Exchange', *New York Review of Books* 63 (January 11, 2007) (with David Cole).

'Essay: Law Reviews', 46 *Washburn Law Journal* 155 (Fall 2006).

'The Constitution in a Time of National Emergency: An Interview with Judge Richard Posner' (James Landman, interviewer), 70 *Social Education* 446 (2006).

American Constitution Society: Debate Series: 'Posner Responds to Stone Proposal' (September 21, 2006), 'Posner Responds to Stone Responding to Posner' (September 25, 2006).

'Foreword', Richard E. Levy, *The Power to Legislate: A Reference Guide to the United States Constitution* xiii (Praeger Publishers, 2006).

'The Constitution vs. Counterterrorism', *Wall Street Journal* A12 (August 22, 2006).

'We Need Our Own MI5', *Washington Post* A13 (August 15, 2006).

'What Is Law and Economics Today? An American View', 1 *New Frontiers of Law and Economics* 89 (2006).

Debate with Geoffrey R. Stone on Civil Liberties and National Security, University of Chicago Faculty Blog (June 19, 2006).

'The Lessons of Toronto and Domestic Intelligence', *Chicago Tribune* C21 (June 8, 2006).

'Our Intelligence Quotient', *Wall Street Journal* A14 (May 15, 2006).

Panel Discussion, 'Panel One: The State of the Debate', in 'Presidential Powers: An American Debate' (Center on Law and Security, New York University School of Law, April 25, 2006).

'The Economics of Capital Punishment', *The Economists' Voice* (March 2006).

'The Courthouse Mice', Review of Todd C. Peppers, *Courtiers of the Marble Palace: The Rise and Influence of the Supreme Court Law Clerk* (2006), and Artemus Ward and David L. Weiden, *Sorcerers' Apprentices: 100 Years of Law Clerks at the United States Supreme Court* (New York University Press, 2006), *New Republic* 32 (June 5 and 12, 2006).

'How I Work', *Fortune* 82 (March 20, 2006).

'A New Surveillance Act: A Better Way to Find the Needle in the Haystack', *Wall Street Journal* A16 (February 15, 2006).

'Tap Dancing: A TNR Online Debate with Philip B. Heymann', *New Republic Online* (January 31, 2006, February 2, 2006, February 5, 2006).

'Review of Steven Shavell, Foundations of Economic Analysis of Law (2004)', 44 *Journal of Economic Literature* 405 (2006).

'Justice Breyer Throws Down the Gauntlet', Review of Stephen Breyer, *Active Liberty: Interpreting Our Democratic Constitution* (2005), 115 *Yale Law Journal* 1699 (2006).

'Wire Trap: What If Wiretapping Works?' *New Republic* 15 (February 2, 2006).

'Our Domestic Intelligence Crisis', *Washington Post* A31 (December 21, 2005).

'Transaction Costs and Antitrust Concerns in the Licensing of Intellectual Property', in *Direito Empresarial: Aspectos Atuais de Direito Empresarial Brasileiro e Comparado* 519, Ecio Perin Junior, Daniel Kalansky, and Luis Peyser, eds (Guilherme Ferreira, 2005).

'Our Incompetent Government', *New Republic* 23 (November 14, 2005).

'Community and Conscription', in *Rethinking Commodification: Cases and Readings in Law and Culture* 128, Martha C. Ertman and Joan C. Williams, eds (NYU Press, 2005).

'What's Wrong with the Patriot Act?', *Legal Affairs* (October 2005) (debate with Geoffrey R. Stone).

'Do We Have Too Many Intellectual Property Rights?', 9 *Marquette Intellectual Property Law Review* 173 (2005).

'The Importance of Property Rights in the Common Law Tradition', *Economic Education Bulletin* 67 (May 2005).

'Bad News', *New York Times Book Review* 1 (July 31, 2005).

'Danger in "Fixing" CIA', *Los Angeles Times* B13 (May 24, 2005).

'Intelligence Critique Fatigue', *Washington Post* A19 (April 6, 2005).

'Surprise Attacks and the Limits of Intelligence', *Commentary* 50 (April 2005).

'Important Job, Impossible Position: Why No One Wants to Be Director of National Intelligence', *New York Times* A27 (February 8, 2005).

'Vertical Restrictions and Fragile Monopoly', 50 *Antitrust Law Bulletin* 499 (2005).

'The Probability of Catastrophe . . .', *Wall Street Journal* A12 (January 4, 2005).

'Constitutional Law from a Pragmatic Perspective', Review of David M. Beatty, *The Ultimate Rule of Law* (2004), 55 *University of Toronto Law Journal* 300 (2005).

'Blinkered', Review of Malcolm Gladwell, *Blink: The Power of Thinking without Thinking*, New Republic 27 (January 24, 2005).

'Murder They Wrote', Review of Stephen Kern, *A Cultural History of Causality: Science, Murder Novels, and Systems of Thought* (2004), 306 *Science* 2193 (2004).

'Foreword', in Francisco González de Cossio, *Competencia Económica: Aspectos Jurídicos y Económicos* xi (Editorial Porrua, 2005).

'The Becker-Posner Blog', http://becker-posner-blog.com/.

Guest Blogger, 'Leiter Reports', View Blog Online.

'Eldred and Fair Use', The Economists' Voice (September 2004) http://www.bepress.com/ev/vol1/iss1/art3.

'CSI: Baker Street', Review of *The New Annotated Sherlock Holmes*, Leslie S. Klinger, ed. (2004), New Republic (October 11, 2004).

Guest Blogger, 'Lessig Blog', August 23–9, 2004, http://www.lessig.org/blog/archives/2004_08.shtml.

'The 9/11 Report: A Dissent', Review of Final Report of the National Commission on Terrorist Attacks upon the United States, *New York Times Book Review* 1 (August 29, 2004).
'Law, Pragmatism, and Democracy: A Response to Ilya Somin', 16 *Critical Review* 465 (2004).
'Against the Law Reviews', *Legal Affairs* (November/December 2004).
'The People's Court', Review of Larry D. Kramer, *The People Themselves: Popular Constitutionalism and Judicial Review* (2004), *New Republic* 32 (July 19, 2004).
'Misjudged', *New Republic* 4 (May 17, 2004).
'No Thanks, We Already Have Our Own Laws: The Court Should Never View a Foreign Legal Decision as a Precedent in Any Way', *Legal Affairs* 40 (July/August 2004).
'Richard Posner Replies [to Evan Gerstmann]', *New Republic* 5 (February 16, 2004).
'Pragmatic Liberalism Defended', 71 *University of Chicago Law Review* 683 (2004).
'Smooth Sailing', *Legal Affairs* 40 (January/February 2004).
'Civil Liberties and National Security: The Pragmatic Approach' (unpublished, December 2003).
'Wedding Bell Blues', Review of Evan Gerstmann, *Same-Sex Marriage and the Constitution* (2004), *New Republic* 33 (December 22, 2003).
'Foreword', in Aspasia Tsaoussis-Hatzis, *The Greek Divorce Law Reform of 1983 and Its Impact on Homemakers: A Social and Economic Analysis* ix (2003).
'The End Is Near', Review of Margaret Atwood, *Oryx and Crake* (2003), *New Republic* 31 (September 22, 2003).
'Law and Economics in Common Law and Civil Law Nations', 7 *Associations: Journal for Legal and Social Theory* 77 (2003).
'Hayek, the Mind, and Spontaneous Order: A Critique', *Transactional Viewpoints* 1 (Summer 2003).
'Desperate Times, Desperate Measures', Review of Daniel Farber, *Lincoln's Constitution*, New York Times Book Review 20 (August 24, 2003).
'Richard A. Posner Replies [to William A. Galston]', *New Republic* 5 (July 28 and August 4, 2003).
'An Army of the Willing: Why Conscription Does Not Serve Community', *New Republic* 27 (May 19, 2003).
'The Anti-Hero', Review of Bruce Allen Murphy, *Wild Bill: The Legend and Life of William O. Douglas* (2003), *New Republic* 27 (February 24, 2003).
'The Oligarch', Review of Daniel Kelly, *James Burnham and the Struggle for the World: A Life* (2002), *New Republic* 39 (December 23, 2002).
'Dewey and Democracy: A Critique', *Transactional Viewpoints* 1 (Summer 2002).
'The Economics of Business Scandals and Financial Regulation', unpublished (October 2002).
'Richard A. Posner Replies [to Laurence H. Tribe]', *New Republic* 4 (October 14, 2002).
'Reflections on an America Transformed', *New York Times* (national edition) (September 8, 2002).
'The Best Offense', Review of Alan M. Dershowitz, *Why Terrorism Works* (2002) *New Republic* 28 (September 2, 2002).
'Public Intellectual Par Excellence', Review of Christopher Hitchens, *Why Orwell Matters* (2002), *Wilson Quarterly* 111 (Autumn 2002).
'Foreword', in *Antitrust Law*, 2d ed. (2001; Korean translation forthcoming).
'How I Approach the Decision of an ERISA Case', *New York University Review of Employee Benefits and Executive Compensation* 141 (2002).
'The University as Business', *Atlantic Monthly* 21 (June 2002).
'Capital Crimes', Review of Stuart Banner, *The Death Penalty: An American History* (2002), *New Republic* 32 (April 1 and 8, 2002).
'On Plagiarism', *Atlantic Monthly* 23 (April 2002).
'Bush v. Gore: Reply to Friedman', 29 *Florida State University Law Review* 871 (2001).
'Richard A. Posner Replies', *Atlantic Monthly* 16 (March 2002).
'In Over their Heads', *Boston Globe* C1 (January 27, 2002).
'Diary', *Slate* (January 14–18, 2002).
'The Professors Profess', *Atlantic Monthly* 26 (February 2002).
'Strong Fiber After All', *Atlantic Monthly* 22 (January 2002).
'Security versus Civil Liberties', *Atlantic Monthly* 46 (December 2001).
'The Accidental Jurist', Review of R. Kent Newmyer, *John Marshall and the Heroic Age of the Supreme Court* (2001)), *New Republic* 36 (December 17, 2001).
'Legal Writing Today', 8 *Scribes Journal of Legal Writing* 25 (2001–2).
'The Law and Economics of Intellectual Property', *Daedalus* 5 (Spring 2002).
'Opinion', in Symposium: At the Crossroads of Law & Technology: Second Annual, 14 *Loyola of Los Angeles Law Review* 1345 (2001).
'Preface', in *The Law and Economics of the Environment* xv, Anthony Heyes, ed. (Edward Elgar Publishing, 2001).
'Against Footnotes', *Court Review* 24 (Summer 2001).
'Dialogue: Animal Rights', *Slate* (June 12–15, 2001) (with Peter Singer).
'Dialogue: The Supreme Court and the 2000 Election', *Slate* (July 2–3, 6, 9, 2001) (with Alan Dershowitz).

'Comment on Lempert on Posner', 87 *Virginia Law Review* 1713 (2001).

'Foreword', in Michael J. Whincop and Mary Keyes, *Policy and Pragmatism in the Conflict of Laws* xiv (Ashgate Publishing, 2001).

'Forum: The Triumph of Expedience: How America Lost the Election to the Courts', Discussion with Pamela Karlan, *Harper's Magazine*, 31 (May 2001).

'Sex, Economics, and Other Legal Matters: An Interview with Richard A. Posner', *Reason* 36 (April 2001) (interview by Steve Kurtz).

'Bush v. Gore: Prolegomenon to an Assessment', 68 *University of Chicago Law Review* 719 (2001).

'Liberalismo e mercato', in *La Liberta dei Moderni tra Liberalismo e Democrazia: Atti del Convegno di Societa Milano* 151617 Ottobre 1999, 152 (October 2000).

'Prologo', in *Derecho y Economa: Una Revisin de la Literatura* 9, Andres Roemer, ed. (Fouda de Cultura Economica USA, 2000).

'The Ethics of Judicial Commentary: A Reply to Lubet', *Court Review* 6 (Summer 2000).

'Against Medical Privacy' (unpublished, October 2000).

'The Law of the Beholder', Review of Anthony G. Amsterdam and Jerome Bruner, *Minding the Law* (2000), *New Republic* 49 (October 16, 2000).

'What Has Modern Literary Theory to Offer Law?' Review of Guyora Binder and Robert Weisberg, *Literary Criticisms of Law* (2000) (unpublished, August 2000).

'Eguaglianza economica e liberta politica', *Biblioteca della liberta*, No. 153, p. 3 (2000).

'Let Them Talk', Review of Peter Brooks, *Troubling Confessions: Speaking Guilt in Law and Literature*, *New Republic* 42 (August 21, 2000).

'Mediation' (unpublished, June 2000).

'On the Alleged "Sophistication" of Academic Moralism', 94 *Northwestern University Law Review* 1017 (2000).

Review of Steven M. Wise, *Rattling the Cage: Toward Legal Rights for Animals* (unpublished, June 2000).

'"An Affair of State": An Exchange', *New York Review of Books* 60 (April 27, 2000) (with Ronald Dworkin).

'Foreword', in *Encyclopedia of Law and Economics, vol. I: The History and Methodology of Law and Economics* xii, Boudewijn Bouckaert and Gerrit De Geest, eds (Edward Elgar Publishing, 2000).

'Prologo', in *Derecho y Economia: Una Revision de la Literatura* 9, Andres Roemer, ed. (2000).

Review of Jeremy Waldron, *Law and Disagreement* (1999), 100 *Columbia Law Review* 582 (2000).

'Let Employers Insist if Three Years of Law School is Necessary', *Los Angeles Daily Journal* 6 (December 15, 1999).

'The Moral Minority', Review of Gertrude Himmelfarb, *One Nation, Two Cultures* (1999), *New York Times Book Review* 14 (December 19, 1999).

'Ask, Tell', Review of William N. Eskridge, Jr, *Gaylaw: The Apartheid of the Closet* [1999], *New Republic* 52 (October 11, 1999).

'Analisi economica del diritto pubblico e penale: una rassegna', *Biblioteca della liberta*, No. 149, p. 37 (1999) (with Francesco Parisi).

'Cultural Studies and the Law', Review of Paul W. Kahn, *The Cultural Study of Law: Reconstructing Legal Scholarship* (1999), Raritan 42 (Fall 1999).

'Appeal and Consent', Review of Mark Tushnet, *Taking the Constitution away from the Courts* (1999), *New Republic* 36 (August 16, 1999).

'Judicial Case Management', *Inner Temple Yearbook* 58 (1999–2000).

'Analisi economica del diritto privato e commerciale: una rassegna', *Biblioteca della liberta*, No. 148, p. 3 (1999) (with Francesco Parisi).

'In the Fraud Archives', Review of Janet Malcolm, *The Crime of Sheila McGough*, *New Republic* 29 (April 19, 1999).

'Preface' to *Natural Monopoly and its Regulation – 30th Anniversary Edition* (Cato Institute, 1999).

'Corrective Justice', in 2 *The Philosophy of Law: An Encyclopedia* 163, Christopher Berry Gray, ed. (Routledge, 1999).

'Trials without Truth, Sentencing without Justice', Review of William T. Pizzi, *Trials without Truth: Why Our System of Criminal Trials Has Become an Expensive Failure and What We Need to Do to Rebuild It*, and Kate Stith and Jose A. Cabranes, *Fear of Judging: Sentencing Guidelines in the Federal Courts*, *Times Literary Supplement* 9 (February 26, 1999).

'Introduction to Baxter Symposium', 51 *Stanford Law Review* 1007 (1999).

'From the Bench: Convincing a Federal Court of Appeals', *Litigation* 3 (Winter 1999).

'Scuole e tendenze nell'analisi economica del diritto', *Biblioteca della liberta*, No. 147, p. 3 (1998) (with Francesco Parisi).

'Remarks on "Women in the Legal Struggle over the Public/Private Divide"' (unpublished March 1998).

'This Magic Moment', Review of Bruce Ackerman, *We the People, vol. 2: Transformations*, *New Republic* 32 (April 6, 1998).

'Law School Should be Two Years, Not Three', *Harvard Law Record* 9 (January 16, 1998).

'Optimism about AIDS Is Premature', *Wall Street Journal* A22 (February 4, 1998) (with Tomas J. Philipson).

'Privacy', in 3 *The New Palgrave Dictionary of Economics and the Law* 103, Peter Newman, ed. (1998).

'Oliver Wendell Holmes, Jr.', in 2 *The New Palgrave Dictionary of Economics and the Law* 244, Peter Newman, ed. (Palgrave Macmillan, 1998).

'Max Weber', in 3 *The New Palgrave Dictionary of Economics and the Law* 684, Peter Newman, ed. (Palgravbe Macmillan, 1998).

'In Memoriam: William J. Brennan', 111 *Harvard Law Review* 9 (1997).

'Holmes: Foreword', 63 *Brooklyn Law Review* 7 (1997).

'The Skin Trade', Review of Daniel A. Farber and Suzanna Sherry, *Beyond All Reason: The Radical Assault on Truth in American Law*, *New Republic* 40 (October 13, 1997).

'The Future of Law and Economics: Looking Forward', roundtable discussion with Gary Becker, Ronald Coase, Richard Epstein, and Merton Miller, 64 *University of Chicago Law Review* 1132 (1997).

'The Rise and Fall of Administrative Law', 72 *Chicago-Kent Law Review* 953 (1997).

'What Gets Better with Age?', *Across the Board: The Conference Board Magazine* 39 (March 1997).

'Bad Faith', Review of Duncan Kennedy, *A Critique of Adjudication (Fin de Siècle)* (1997), *New Republic* 34 (June 9, 1997).

'The Path Away from the Law', 110 *Harvard Law Review* 1039 (1997).

'Should There Be Homosexual Marriage? If So, Who Should Decide?', Review of William N. Eskridge, Jr, *The Case for Same-Sex Marriage*, 95 *Michigan Law Review* 1578 (1997).

'Legal Narratology', *Review of Law's Stories: Narrative and Rhetoric in the Law*, Peter Brooks and Paul Gewirtz, eds, 64 *University of Chicago Law Review* 737 (1997).

Review of *Holmes and Frankfurter: Their Correspondence, 1912–1934*, Robert M. Mennel and Christine L. Compston, eds, *New York Times Book Review* 16 (December 15, 1996).

'Response to Martha Nussbaum, "Platonic Love and Colorado Law: The Relevance of Ancient Greek Norms to Modern Sexual Controversies"', in *The Greeks and Us: Essays in Honor of Arthur W. H. Adkins* 218, Robert B. Louden and Paul Schollmeier, eds. (University of Chicago Press, 1996).

'The Immoralist', Review of Leo Katz, *Ill-Gotten Gains: Evasion, Blackmail, Fraud, and Kindred Puzzles of the Law*, *New Republic* 38 (July 15 and 22, 1996).

'"Rational Choice, Public Policy, and AIDS": A Comment', 8 *Rationality and Society* 498 (1996) (with Tomas J. Philipson).

Foreword, *Corporate Bankruptcy: Economic and Legal Perspectives* xi, Jagdeep S. Bhandari and Lawrence A. Weiss, eds. (Cambridge University Press, 1996).

'Law's Reason', Review of Jurgen Habermas, *Between Facts and Norms: Contributions to a Discourse Theory of Law and Democracy*, *New Republic* 26 (May 6, 1996).

'Recht is de broze vernislaag van een booming industry: Interview met Richard A. Posner', *Nederlands Juristenblad*, afl. 45/46, 1625 (December 15, 1995) (J.F. Bruinsma and N. J. H. Huls, interviewers).

'Economics of Law: An Interview with Judge Posner', *Litigation* 23 (Fall 1995) (Jeffrey Cole, interviewer).

'Response to Clark Freshman, "Were Patricia Williams and Ronald Dworkin Separated at Birth?"' 95 *Columbia Law Review* 1610 (1995).

'The Most Punitive Nation', *Times Literary Supplement* 3 (September 1, 1995).

'Working within the Confines of Our Current Judiciary', in *Symposium on Law Clerks: The Transformation of the Judiciary, The Long Term View: A Journal of Informed Opinion* 32 (Spring 1995).

'Annual Dinner Address' (May 18, 1995), in *The American Law Institute: Remarks and Addresses: 72nd Annual Meeting* 39 (American Law Institute, 1995); also in *The Bar Examiner* 9 (August 1996).

'The Future of the Student-Edited Law Review', 47 *Stanford Law Review* 1131 (1995).

'Juries on Trial' (Review of Jeffrey Abramson, *We, the Jury: The Jury System and the Ideal of Democracy* and Stephen J. Adler, *The Jury: Trial and Error in the American Courtroom*), *Commentary* 49 (March 1995).

'The Hand Biography and the Question of Judicial Greatness', 104 *Yale Law Journal* 511 (1994).

'Barflies' (Review of Mary Ann Glendon, *A Nation under Lawyers: How the Crisis in the Legal Profession is Transforming American Society*), *New Republic* 40 (October 31, 1994).

'The Judging Game', Review of Stanley Fish, *There's No Such Thing as Free Speech and it's a Good Thing Too*, *Times Literary Supplement* 14 (July 15, 1994).

'The Law's Leaden Muse', Review of Fred R. Shapiro, *The Oxford Dictionary of American Legal Quotations*, *American Scholar* 449 (Summer 1994).

'Executive Detention in Wartime', Review of A.W. Brian Simpson, *In the Highest Degree Odious*, 92 *Michigan Law Review* 1675 (1994).

'The Economic Approach to AIDS', *Issues in Science and Technology* 33 (Spring 1994) (with Tomas J. Philipson and John H. Wright).

'Obsession', Review of Catharine A. MacKinnon, *Only Words*, *New Republic* 31 (October 18, 1993).

'How I Write', 4 *Scribes Journal of Legal Writing* 45 (1993).

'Gary Becker's Contributions to Law and Economics', 22 *Journal of Legal Studies* 211 (1993).

'The Deprofessionalization of Legal Teaching and Scholarship', 91 *Michigan Law Review* 1921 (1993).

'Reply [to Coase and Williamson]', 149 *Journal of Institutional and Theoretical Economics* 119 (1993).

'Law as Politics: Horwitz on American Law, 1870–1960', Review of Morton J. Horwitz, *The Transformation of American Law: 1870–1960, The Crisis of Legal Orthodoxy*, 6 *Critical Review* 559 (1992).

Review of Bruce Ackerman, *The Future of Liberal Revolution*, in *East European Constitutional Review* 35 (Fall 1992).

'The Strangest Attack Yet on Law and Economics', 20 *Hofstra Law Review* 933 (1992).

'Remarks on Law and Literature', 23 *Loyola University Chicago Law Journal* 181(1992).

'From Von's to Schwinn to the Chicago School: Interview with Judge Richard Posner, Seventh Circuit Court of Appeals', *Antitrust* 4 (Spring 1992).

'Democracy and Dualism', Review of Bruce Ackerman, *We the People, vol. 1: Foundations, Transition* 68 (No. 56 Summer 1992).

'Ms. Aristotle', 70 *University of Texas Law Review* 1013 (1992).

'Medieval Iceland and Modern Scholarship', Review of William Ian Miller, *Bloodtaking and Peacemaking: Feud, Law, and Society in Saga Iceland*, 90 *Michigan Law Review* 1495 (1992).

'Courting Evil', Review of Ingo Müller, *Hitler's Justice: The Courts of the Third Reich*, *New Republic* 36 (June 17, 1991).

'The Uncertain Future of Legal Education', *Proceedings of the Association of American Law Schools* 132 (1991).

'Duncan Kennedy on Affirmative Action', *Duke Law Journal* 1155 (1990).

'A Tribute to Justice William J. Brennan, Jr.', 104 *Harvard Law Review* 13 (1990).

'Us v. Them', Review of Minow, *Making All the Difference: Inclusion, Exclusion, and American Law*, *New Republic* 47 (October 15, 1990).

'100 Years of Antitrust', *Wall Street Journal* A10 (June 29, 1990).

'The Separation of Powers', in *Politics and the Constitution: The Nature and Extent of Interpretation* 41 (American Studies Center, May 1990).

'Introduction to Federal Courts Symposium', *Brigham Young University Law Review* 1 (1990).

'Rebuttal to Malloy', 24 *Valparaiso Law Review* 183 (1990).

'Law and Economics is Moral', 24 *Valparaiso University Law Review* 163 (1990).

'Law and Literature', in *The Guide to American Law Supplement 1990* 171 (West Publishing Company, ed., 1990).

Review of Novick, *Honorable Justice: The Life of Oliver Wendell Holmes*, *Wall Street Journal* A9 (August 9, 1989).

Foreword, in *Essays in Law and Economics: Corporations, Accident Prevention and Compensation for Losses* 5, Michael Faure and Roger Van den Bergh, eds. (Antwerp: MAKLU, 1989).

'Gregor Samsa Replies', 83 *Northwestern University Law Review* 1022 (1989).

Review of Eskridge and Frickey, *Cases and Materials on Legislation: Statutes and the Creation of Public Policy*, 74 *Virginia Law Review* 1567 (1988).

'Law and Literature', *University of Chicago Law School Record* 18 (Fall 1988).

'Comment on Donohue', 22 *Law and Society Review* 1927 (1988).

'Comment: Responding to Gordon Tullock', 2 *Research in Law and Policy Studies* 29 (1988).

'A Manifesto for Legal Renegades', *Wall Street Journal* 17 (January 27, 1988).

'Die Deregulierungsbewegung in den USA', *Neue Archer Zeitung* 31 (December 22, 1987); also in *Wo Regeln Bremsen: Deregulierung und Privatisierung im Vormarsch*, Gerhard Schwarz, ed. (1988).

Panel Discussion on 'Constitutional Scholarship: What Next?', 5 *Constitutional Commentary* 13, 17 (1988).

'Jurisprudential Responses to Legal Realism', 73 *Cornell Law Review* 326 (1988); and Discussion thereof, 73 *Cornell Law Review* 341 (1988).

'The Insignificance of Macroeconomics in Patent Antitrust Law: A Comment on Millstein', 9 *Cardozo Law Review* 1203 (1988).

'From Billy Budd to Buchenwald', 96 *Yale Law Journal* 1173 (1987).

'Goodbye to the Bluebook', 53 *University of Chicago Law Review* 1343 (1986).

'The Constitution as Mirror: Tribe's Constitutional Choices', 84 *Michigan Law Review* 551 (1986).

'In Memoriam: Henry J. Friendly', 99 *Harvard Law Review* 1724 (1986).

'The Crisis in the Courts', 5 (2) *Manhattan Report* 3 (1985) (roundtable discussion).

Review of Kellogg, *The Formative Essays of Justice Holmes*, and Pohlman, *Justice Oliver Wendell Holmes & Utilitarian Jurisprudence*, 53 *George Washington Law Review* 870 (1985).

'Comment on "On the Economic Theory of Crime,"' in XXVII *Criminal Justice: Nomos* 310, J. Roland Pennock and John W. Chapman, eds. (1985).

Review of Parrish, *Felix Frankfurter and his Times: The Reform Years*, 67 *Minnesota Law Review* 292 (1982).

'Tribute to Mr. Justice Brennan', *Annual Survey of American Law* xi (1981).

'Introduction to Conference on the Law and Economics of Privacy', 9 *Journal of Legal Studies* 621 (1980).

'Should We Tax Virgin Materials to Finance Waste Disposal?', *Waste Age* 12 (March 1978) (with William M. Landes).

'Monopoly in the Marketplace of Ideas', 86 *Yale Law Journal* 567 (1977).

Affirmative Action: The Answer to Discrimination? (American Enterprise Institute Round Table 1975) (with Ralph K. Winter, Jr., Owen Fiss, Vera Glaser, William Raspberry and Paul Seabury).

'Some Thoughts on Legal Education', *University of Chicago Law School Record* 19 (Winter 1972).

'Volume One of the Journal of Legal Studies – An Afterword', 1 *Journal of Legal Studies* 437 (1972).

Panel Discussion, in Martin Greenberger, ed., *Computers, Communications, and the Public Interest* 242 (Baltimore: John Hopkins Press, 1971).

'Power in America – A Review Essay', 25 *Public Interest* 114 (Fall 1971).

'The Closed Enterprise System – Nader on Antitrust', *New Republic* 11 (June 26, 1971).

Review of Sutherland, *The Monopolies Commission in Action*, 44 *Journal of Business* 236 (1971).

Review of Calabresi, *The Costs of Accidents: A Legal and Economic Analysis*, 37 *University of Chicago Law Review* 636 (1970).

Separate Statement of Richard A. Posner, in *Report of the ABA Commission to Study the Federal Trade Commission* 92 (September 15, 1969).

Review of Alexander, *Honesty and Competition*, 56 *California Law Review* 928 (1968).

Review of Myres McDougal et al., *Law and Public Order in Space*, 77 *Harvard Law Review* 1370 (1964).

12 Putting law first: Richard Epstein's contribution to law and economics
*Andrew P. Morriss**

Summarizing Richard Epstein's impact on law and economics (or just on law) is a task of the same order of magnitude as summarizing the impact of China on the world's economy today, describing the Colorado River with only a glass of water to use as an illustration, or coming up with a fresh metaphor to describe his impact without having the literary imagination of a Dickens. Attempting to do so in a mere book chapter is an act so foolhardy that the reader would be justified in thinking the likelihood of a valuable result to be so low that there is little point in reading further. After all, in the time it has taken me to write these first few sentences (or you to read them), it is possible (and even likely) that Epstein has written several paragraphs of an article or book that will shape the future course of discussion in yet another area of the law, as he has done so often. As one measure of the breadth of Epstein's scholarship, it struck me as completely plausible when my initial search for books by Epstein unearthed *The Theory of Gambling and Statistical Logic*, first published in 1967 by 'Richard A. Epstein', that this was an early work written as the result of an undergraduate encounter with a poorly taught statistics course. Closer examination revealed what the author-title data did not, however, that the author was part of the Aerospace Group, Space Systems Division, Hughes Aircraft Company. While it would not be a total shock to discover that Epstein has been simultaneously writing, teaching, and designing aircraft, I was relieved to confirm that there are two people named Richard A. Epstein writing books.

Rather than attempt to summarize the entire body of Epstein's work and then assess its impact, I will focus on four areas that I contend exemplify how his work has changed law and economics. These four areas illustrate a broader theme reflected in the title of this chapter and the major argument made here, that Richard Epstein's most significant contribution to law and economics as a discipline has been to insist that it is *law* and economics, not simply the economic analysis of law, which matters in the end. The law part matters, for Epstein is first and foremost a lawyer in the classical sense. He believes that there is law out there and that while economics (and psychology, sociology, history, political science, and philosophy) can help us make sense of it, we must wrestle directly with the law if we are to have anything useful to say at the end of the day.

After some brief, but critically important, discussion of the origins of his approach, I will address three major areas of Epstein's work: his employment law scholarship, particularly his groundbreaking article 'In Defense of the Contract at Will' (1984), his takings clause scholarship, particularly his extraordinary book *Takings* (1985); and his constitutional analysis, as

---

*   Thanks to Roger Meiners for comments on an earlier draft and to Jonathan Adler, who organized, and the participants in the Liberty Fund symposium on takings in February 2007 for an insightful exploration of *Takings* and the response to it.

captured in his recent book *How Progressives Rewrote the Constitution* (2006a). This choice is somewhat arbitrary, of course, as it leaves out his work on patent law, torts, and a host of other subjects and it does not deal in detail with the multiple works addressing even these subjects, but it has the virtue of capturing the broad sweep of Epstein's impact without requiring a multi-volume set.

1   Roman origins

Richard Epstein took an unconventional path to the study of law. Rather than beginning with a law degree at an American university or with a stopover in England to study politics, economics, or philosophy, he went from his undergraduate studies at Columbia College to Oriel College, Oxford and studied law for two years there before enrolling at Yale with advanced standing as the result of the Oxford studies. As Epstein put it in a 1997 lecture, 'I was out of phase in both educational systems, a condition that has not yet righted itself' (Epstein 1997, p. 243). As a result, Epstein began his legal studies not with the American first-year canon of Property, Torts, Contracts, Criminal Law, Civil Procedure, and Constitutional Law but with Roman Law. His first legal writing assignment was not a memo in a legal research and writing class but a paper 'on the development of the contract of stipulation from the time of the Twelve Table to the time of Justinian' (ibid.). His first law teacher was not a Chicago-trained economist or a legal philosopher steeped in contemporary legal theory but Alan Watson, the great Roman law scholar of the second half of the twentieth century, making his exposure not just to Roman law but to the highest level of scholarship on the subject. And his thoughts about law formed as the result of 'read[ing] a bunch of stuff and then talk[ing] to a tutor for an hour' and then repeating the process. 'The only direction I got was being told to read the 19th-century judicial opinions' (Chapman 1995). As a result, by the time he got to Yale Law School and was exposed to modern American thinking about law, Epstein already had ideas of his own about law (ibid.). As Epstein noted, this unusual beginning had 'long term significance for the entire way [he has] come to view law and legal history' ever since (Epstein 1997, p. 243).

It would be a major error not to take seriously the Roman and English common law origins of Epstein's approach to law and economics. As Epstein noted in his own reflection on Roman law's impact on modern law, these origins simultaneously provided him with evidence of a set of rules and institutions that worked extraordinarily well but also revealed that the rules were 'defended in a manner that most of us were not likely to find very persuasive' (Epstein 1997, p. 245). As a result, 'the first influence' from his study of Roman law was 'to pose the question of how to supply a pattern of justification for a set of rules that looks to be well-established on the one hand and somewhat arbitrary on the other' (Epstein 1997, p. 246). It is hard to think of a better general description for Richard Epstein's vast body of work than the quest for a 'pattern of justification' for such rules.

It is also important that the quest begins with law – the reader finds in Epstein's work a constant concern to get the details right about what the rules were and how they have been changed before venturing to offer an explanation. As he noted in his discussion of the 1900 Supreme Court case *Ohio Oil Co. v. Indiana (No. 1),* '[a]s ever, wisdom lies in the details' (Epstein 1997, p. 255). This is in contrast to the approach of at least some law and economics scholars, as the lengthy debate over comparative and contributory negligence that played out in the 1970s and contrasting that debate with Epstein's work is a useful way to see the consequences of the differences in approach.

Brown (1973), as well as less formal analyses by Calabresi (1970) and Posner (1972), set out the original law and economics case for contributory negligence by focusing on the optimal sharing of the burden of taking care between a potential tortfeasor and victim. A second wave of law and economics scholarship took on the issue with a more sophisticated understanding of the details of the law and produced a more nuanced set of conclusions about the relative efficiency of the two rules under various conditions (Haddock and Curran 1985, p. 54; Cooter and Ulen 1986, p. 1067; Shavell 1987, p. 294). The evolution of the law and economics analysis of comparative and contributory negligence is the evolution of an economic analysis. The model begins with a relatively simple set of assumptions about what the legal rules are, applies economics, and produces a result. The next model modifies the assumptions to incorporate a new feature of interest and compares the result to the original. Each iteration builds toward a model of sufficient complexity to capture the relevant aspects of the legal institution. This is a productive and useful methodology and one that has yielded considerable insights into the functioning of legal institutions. It is not sufficient, however, and here is where the discipline has benefited from Epstein's influence.

Two examples well illustrate the impact of Roman law on the development of Epstein's thinking. First is his assessment of the rule of capture and the modern modifications of it in the context of oil and gas (Epstein 1997, pp. 244–58). Roman lawyers 'had very decided views' on property and Epstein begins with their statement of the rule of capture. He then traces the development of their views on circumstances under which capture did not apply, finding that the body of law which developed 'contemplated certain systems which were communal and others that were private and worried about the interactions that could take place between them when the two systems came together' (Epstein 1997, p. 245). Here is a concern that runs throughout Epstein's work and in which we can see clearly the benefits of an analysis that begins with attempting to understand how centuries of property law work before attempting to decide how it ought to work.

Capture worked well in the ancient world, but it does not work as well in a world in which the technology of capture is more efficient and there are more people doing the capturing. We thus find ourselves in a world in which 'major resource losses' occur and so we can justify shifting to a more complex and costly rule (ibid., 250–51). In the case of oil and gas, capture produces just such losses because it encourages inefficient rates of exploitation. When oil and gas are mixed, the problem is that those with rights to the oil will waste the gas. And in *Ohio Oil Co.* the state of Indiana provided a remedy by requiring those extracting oil to limit their waste of gas. Once we drill down to the details of the production of oil and gas in Indiana in 1900, however, we find that this is not simply a case of requiring cooperation to maximize production but a reallocation of resources from one group (the oil rights holders) to another (the gas rights holders) because the release of the gas was a necessary part of the production of the oil. And the story is complicated further by the conflict being between Indiana residents (with gas rights) and out-of-state interests (with oil rights). Suddenly the picture is not so clear. 'In this picture it is not possible to see the statute as a way to prevent overconsumption of a common pool resource for the benefit of all. Instead, it becomes a one-sided effort in which local producers get the better of their out-of-state rivals . . .' (Epstein 1997, p. 256).[1]

---

[1]   As Epstein notes (1997, p. 255), he had given a more optimistic account of the state's role in *Takings* (1985, pp. 219–23) but had reassessed his view in light of the details of oil and gas production.

Not only does this knock out the possible efficiency justification of the law as implicitly compensating for losses by making everyone better off, as it would if it increased recovery of both oil and gas, but it adds public choice considerations because now we have a law showing favoritism to one group over another and it raises Commerce Clause issues as it favors in-state interests at the expense of out-of-state interests. And once again, 'Roman conceptions come back to help us' (Epstein 1997, p. 257). If we start with the first possession rule, we can see that when something is redistributed from the Ohio Oil Company, compensation is required. If we apply Roman ideas of quasi-contract, we find a baseline of requiring state action be justified by actual increases in wealth to both parties. Once we see the problem clearly through the lens of the Roman legal concepts, the justification for the Supreme Court's deference to the Indiana legislature is exposed for the 'intellectual Jell-O' it is (Epstein 1997, pp. 256, 258). There has been a taking and compensation is needed to ensure that we do not fall victim to special interest manipulation of the state.

Roman legal concepts are not simply useful in the context of first possession rules, however. Epstein (2005b) also uses them to untangle the law of cyberspace, in what he terms an example of 'the extent to which an appreciation of traditional legal learning often helps us to navigate our way through tricky modern problems' (p. 103). The problem is straightforward: should the tort of conversion be available to govern misappropriation of domain names? To answer this question, Epstein unpacks the decision by Judge Alex Kozinski in *Kremen v. Cohen*, which dealt with the misappropriation of a domain name by Stephen Cohen, a 'third-party knave', by tricking Network Solutions, Inc., the domain name registrar, into reassigning the domain name 'sex.com' to him from Gary Kremen, the initial registrant of the name. Which of the two innocents, Kremen or Network Solutions, must bear the costs of Cohen's theft?

Judge Kozinski answered the question by first determining that this was not a case of contract. If it was not contract, and there was no contract between Kremen and Network Solutions, that resolved the issue because Network Solutions did not require consideration from Kremen in exchange for registering the domain name, and the applicable law must be tort. If the applicable law is tort, then the answer must be that Network Solutions, which gave away Kremen's property to Cohen, must bear the loss rather than Kremen, who did nothing.

Roman legal concepts suggest an alternative analysis because they do not require consideration to produce contractual liability – consideration is sufficient but not necessary for a contract. As a result, Epstein notes, ancient law is better than modern American law in accurately describing business relationships:

> the consideration requirement does a poor job in tracking the requirements of trade in a variety of transactions that lie at the periphery of commercial law. The addition or subtraction of a single term, or surety, or any alteration in the price often take place without consideration. A firm offer may be held open as a business matter for a short period of time without consideration, in order to prompt the potential buyer or seller to give it more serious examination. Free samples and replacement parts are routinely promised in the course of long-term business relationships, wholly without any immediately binding quid pro quo. (Epstein 2005b, pp. 114–15)

Roman contract law included numerous forms of contracts in which consideration is merely 'a test of executor enforcement' rather than as a 'test of contractual validity' (ibid., p. 117). Now, using Roman legal concepts, a court could let Network Solutions off the hook (if the standard for gratuitous transactions is bad faith) or hold it liable (if the standard is gross negligence).

But the one solution that is clearly wrong is the one embraced by Judge Kozinksi. Nowhere does a strict liability standard ever get paired up with a gratuitous transaction, which is what the result that Judge Kozinski's contraction of the law of contract necessarily creates. The choice of the wrong boundary between contract and tort has powerful consequences. (ibid., p. 118)

It is important to appreciate that Epstein's analysis of *Kamen* is first and foremost a legal analysis, not an economic analysis. The distinction is not based on the absence of equations and graphs – plenty of law and economics from Posner's seminal *Economic Analysis of Law* (1998) to Ellickson's landmark *Order Without Law* (1991) rely minimally or not at all on such technical tools. The economics comes in to add clarity to the law, not supplant it or direct it. Economics serves as the salt to the main dish of law – it enhances the flavor without dominating it – and the meal is not overly salty. This matters because the tricky bits come in just where the law has a comparative advantage over economics. Epstein concludes his cyberlaw analysis by noting that

> The chief difficulty with the classic libertarian framework is that it does not have a secure place to take into account the rule of forced exchanges and interconnections, which is surely a critical issue in structuring the overall internet, just as it was critical in dealing with the organization of railroads and communications systems before it. But the issues that we have here involve the allocation of the risk of loss in a broken-down transaction. The differential treatment of stranger and contractual transactions is as old as the law itself, and it continues to maintain its vitality in newer areas. Those who do not master the basic principles are prone to fall into serious error. In one sense that is the key lesson to take away from the sorry saga of *Kremen v. Cohen*. (Epstein 2005b, p. 120)

We cannot quite substitute 'economic' for 'classic libertarian' in the above quote and retain Epstein's original meaning, but there is an analogous but somewhat different problem when we do. Libertarianism runs into trouble when it confronts situations where contract is too expensive a solution to a problem. Economics generally, and law and economics in particular, can readily identify such situations, but both veer perilously close to the edge of allowing judges to assume the role of the economic model's hypothetical omniscient social planner. Richard Posner, for example, makes this leap in his embrace of Hans Kelsen over Friedrich Hayek because 'Kelsen's philosophy of law opens a space for economic analysis, and in particular for the use of economics by judges in a wide range of cases that come before them but that Hayek's philosophy of law closes that space, forbids judges to have anything to do with economics' (Posner 2003, p. 251). Epstein avoids this trap, however, by starting with the law and making incremental moves based on a rich understanding of institutional detail with the aid of economics, rather than beginning with the economics as much of law and economics seems to do.

Moreover, the economics in Epstein's work is different from the economics in the work of some of the other pioneers discussed in this volume. There is not the overriding concern with efficiency that pervades much law and economics but rather a sense that some economics helps understand the issues and illuminate the tradeoffs. I recall what must be a long-forgotten comment by Epstein at a lecture many years ago. Confronted with an economic argument for a serious infringement on liberty, he said (in more or less these words): 'It is a good thing that freedom of contract and association and property rights happen to yield more material goods than restrictions on freedom, but if I have to choose between increasing liberty and increasing wealth, I choose liberty'.

A second difference between the economics brought to bear by Epstein and that brought to bear by some of the other pioneers is that Epstein takes seriously the work of Friedrich Hayek. Unlike Posner, who wrote in 2001 that he had 'read little of Hayek's work' (Posner 2003, p. 2), even a brief perusal of Epstein's body of work turns up considerable evidence of a sophisticated and nuanced reading of Hayek (for example, Epstein 1999, 2002, 2005c, 2006b). Much as Hayek did, although with some significant differences at times, Epstein articulates a case for caution in meddling with the institutions built from contract, tort and property that we have inherited from England, and from Rome, not because those institutions are necessarily efficient ones or otherwise desirable ones but because the limits to our knowledge make it hard to improve on private ordering without careful analysis and deep understanding.

To what do we owe this difference in emphasis? A strong case can be made that it stems in large part from that initial training at Oxford. Epstein entitled his discussion of his early study of Roman and English common law 'A Misspent Youth' (Epstein 1997, p. 243). This is one of the rare occasions on which I must disagree completely with him. I think we are all the richer for his early exposure to Roman law.

2   Employment law

Epstein's work on employment and labor law has covered a wide range of topics, from employment discrimination statutes (Epstein 1992) to the National Labor Relations Act (Epstein 1983a, 1983b, 1985a) to employment at will (Epstein 1984). His work has been influential by any measure. For example, *Forbidden Grounds* has been cited more than 600 times by articles in the Westlaw JLR database, and not only because it caused apoplectic reactions among many law professors and is virtually the only serious scholarship questioning the merits of antidiscrimination laws. What was unique in Epstein's scholarship when it appeared, and still remains relatively rare in legal scholarship, was his willingness to start from first principles. No one had undertaken an assessment of antidiscrimination law, labor law, or even employment law from the ground up when he wrote his work in those areas. By going back to the initial common law doctrines, taking careful note of how both the common law and the statutes that displaced it actually worked, Epstein raised important questions about the law of the workplace.

We can see both Epstein's methods and his impact through 'In Defense of the Contract at Will'. The article's impact can be seen from the more than 260 citations to it in the Westlaw JLR database. (To put that into perspective, keep in mind that approximately 40 percent of law review articles are not cited *at all*.[2]) It can also be seen from its appearance at a time when virtually no one could be found to say anything positive about contracts at will. The employment at-will rule was under siege in the academy, where it came in for virtually universal condemnation, and the courts, which were busy eroding it with a variety of exceptions (public policy, implied contract, implied covenant of good faith and fair dealing) throughout the 1970s and 1980s (Morriss 1994, pp. 680–81). Epstein's defense changed the debate from a one-sided race to condemn the rule as an antiquated relic to a serious discussion of the merits of the rule. Perhaps coincidentally, but then again, perhaps not, the trend in the courts

---

[2]   Professor Thomas Smith of the University of San Diego is investigating citation patterns using data from Lexis/Nexis. His preliminary results are reported on the blog, 'The Right Coast', at http://therightcoast.blogspot.com/2005/07/voice-crying-in-wilderness-and-then.html (accessed February 16, 2008) and discussed in his working paper, 'The Web of Law', which is available on SSRN at http://papers.ssrn.com/sol3/papers.cfm?abstract_id=642863.

reversed in the second half of the 1980s, bringing the common law back from the expansive decisions of the 1970s and early 1980s. (Because the reversal of direction came about not because courts abandoned their earlier positions outright but through reinterpretation of earlier precedents in more restrictive ways, few of the reversals were explicitly acknowledged by the courts making them and so it is impossible to directly assess whether Epstein's arguments played a role by examining the court opinions.)

The employment at will doctrine is generally traced back to *Payne v. Western & Atlantic R.R.*,[3] an 1884 Tennessee case that did not involve a wrongful dismissal case at all (Epstein 1984, p. 949 n. 3). Beginning with a 1967 attack on the rule by Professor Laurence Blades, the attack on the at-will rule from academic quarters came largely from labor law professors (for example, those who teach the law of unionization rather than the law of employment based on individual contracts). Like Blades, most of the commentators saw the at-will rule as an archaic relic of pre-NLRA workplace law, a vehicle for employer victimization of employees, and an obstacle to a workplace built around collective bargaining. In making their assessments, the critics rarely looked beyond the language of the rule itself and courts' reports of decisions in wrongful discharge suits involving the rule. Not only are wrongful discharge cases an unrepresentative sample of employment relations, but the procedural posture of most of these cases (on appeal of a dismissal for failure to state a claim because the relationship had been found to be at will) meant that the appellate courts took the facts as alleged in the plaintiffs' complaints as true for the purposes of examining the legal issue, yielding a sample of facts biased heavily toward the sensationalistic. For example, one of the earliest cases eroding the at-will rule dealt with a claim that the employer had fired the employee for serving on a jury.[4] Such events are clearly not typical of the day-to-day experience of the vast majority of American employers and employees.

One of Epstein's crucial innovations in the field was to ask how the at-will rule related to the run-of-the-mill employment relationship. To do so he looked first to an area where at-will relationships were firmly established but the inequality of bargaining power that triggered alarm bells for the labor law professoriate spearheading the attack on employment at will were absent: partnership law. The business problem for partnerships is comparatively simple to state. The partners must agree on how to divide the proceeds of their joint efforts, they must find a way to mutually satisfy themselves that each partner is contributing the appropriate level of effort, and the partners must not enrich themselves at the partnership's expense (Epstein 1984, p. 959). Making things more difficult, partners' contributions to partnerships are generally in the form of labor, meaning that each partner's 'eggs are in a single basket' (Epstein 1984, p. 961). The at-will rule in the partnership context gives each a threat point that deters some, but not all, abuses by the other partners since it allows comparatively easy exit by any partner who suspects his confederates of slacking or cheating. 'The provision for at-will dissolution of the partnership helps stabilize the arrangement after formation and thus tends to be in the interest of both parties at formation' (Epstein 1984, p. 962).

Having established the economic function of an at-will rule in one context, Epstein then moved to apply it to the employment context. An employee, unlike a partner, is not a residual claimant. But an employee, like a partner, poses monitoring issues in both directions. The

---

  3   81 Tenn. 507 (1884) (overruled on other grounds) *Hutton v. Watters*, 132 Tenn. 527 (1915).
  4   *Nees v. Hocks*, 536 P.2d 512 (Ore. 1975).

employee is vulnerable to abuse by the employer, the employer is vulnerable to slacking by the employee.

> The parallels to the partnership situation are instructive, for the at-will arrangement is, if anything, even more effective between employers and employees. As with partnerships, the threat, be it of discharge or resignation, becomes more effective the greater the level of employee or employer abuse; it is thus an effective if informal means of encouraging self-restraint. . . . There is no need to resort to any theory of economic domination or inequality of bargaining power to explain at-will contracting, which appears with the same tenacity in relations between economic equals and subordinates and is found in many complex commercial arrangements, including franchise agreements, except where limited by law. (Epstein 1984, p. 965)

Moreover, from an abused employee's point of view, the threat of resignation 'turns out to be most effective when the employer's opportunistic behavior is the greatest because the situation is one in which the worker has the least to lose' (Epstein 1984, p. 967). Employees also impose reputational losses on employers when they quit or are fired unjustly, which hampers the ability to hire in the future and harms relations with the ex-employee's co-workers (Epstein 1984, p. 968). There are other advantages as well.

The problem thus reduces to a question of whether the inequality of bargaining power in the employment relationship requires a different rule from the partnership context. Again, Epstein does a reality check and notes that we observe both wages above subsistence and an employee right to quit in employment contracts, suggesting that employers' ability to force employees down to subsistence wages is absent. Turnover costs are borne by both employers and employees, and the costs to employers are non-trivial (Epstein 1984, pp. 973–4). The real issue then is who is going to get the larger share of the surplus created by the employment contract? If the surplus grows as the employment relationship lengthens, as a result of human capital investment by the employee for example, the employee may do quite well in the division of the surplus. Even if he does not, however, the employee will earn no less than he would in his next best employment (where he lacks human capital). Any intervention in the division of the surplus is unlikely to come cheaply, and the net gains from intervention are thus likely to be small (Epstein 1984, p. 976).

This argument is elegant in its simplicity and grounded in a thorough understanding of what labor economics tells us about the workplace. The economics informs the legal analysis, but the analysis is structured the way a good transactional lawyer approaches his job. What is the client trying to accomplish? What are the pitfalls we can contract against and what are the pitfalls that it is too expensive to write contractual language to deal with? What are the costs of enforcing an agreement? How can the transactions costs of accomplishing our joint objective be accomplished? Armed with a contract lawyer's view of the transaction, Epstein is then able to see what had eluded critics of the at-will rule from Blades in 1967 (and continues to elude many of them to this day): we need a rule for the vast majority of employment contracts that do not result in lawsuits, not a rule for the tiny minority which do. (The small number of outliers where employers do things like discharge employees for serving on juries can be dealt with directly by statute, as indeed virtually every state has done.)

Applying this analysis produces a different view of some of the landmark cases. Epstein directly addresses the leading case of *Fortune v. National Cash Register Co.*,[5] in which the

---

5   364 N.E.2d 1251 (Mass. 1977).

Massachusetts Supreme Judicial Court faced a claim by an employee that he had been discharged by his employer just before a portion of a large commission was to be paid. The court determined that there was an implied covenant of good faith and fair dealing in the employment contract that the employer would pay the commissions in good faith and that the claim that the employee had been discharged just before the commission payment would become due was sufficient grounds to state a claim and reach a jury trial. What the court missed, Epstein pointed out, was that the contractual structure of commission payments had a purpose – to match payment to effort where more than one person was involved in closing the deal – and that the firm's behavior was consistent with that purpose. Indeed, the commission allegedly owed the plaintiff had not been retained by the firm but paid to his successor.

> The court in *Fortune* did not try to understand the commission structure that it was prepared to condemn; instead, it made the chronic mistake of thinking that what it intuited to be an unfortunate business outcome invalidated the entire contractual structure. In its enthusiastic meddling in private contracts, the court nowhere suggested an alternative commission structure that would have better served the joint interests of the parties at the time of contract formation. Here, as in so many cases, an unquestioning adherence to the principle of freedom of contract would have yielded results both simpler and superior to those generated after an extensive but flawed judicial examination of the basic terms. (Epstein 1984, p. 981–2)

'In Defense of the Contract at Will', together with Epstein's work on labor law and anti-discrimination laws, made multiple contributions. The most relevant of these for our purposes is that together these articles set out a comprehensive case for freedom of contract as a baseline norm in fields of law where the idea of freedom of contract itself was seen as laughable at best. In the early 1980s, before Epstein wrote these pieces, no one in the legal academy took seriously the idea that freedom of contract was even relevant to discussions of labor and employment law. The legal academics in the field were largely drawn from the union side of labor law (for reasons that would require a separate article to explore), there was no separate field of 'employment law' yet, and employment discrimination law was largely a field of doctrinal statutory interpretation. Epstein's work shook the field, producing much better work on all sides of the issues in response, by taking seriously the insights of economics into the workplace and then considering the problem as a good lawyer would. Getting the law back into the law and economics of labor and employment law has made all the difference in producing a serious body of scholarship.

3 Takings

Among Richard Epstein's many contributions to law and economics (and to just plain 'law', as well as to political science, to American politics, and probably much more as well), one of the most influential has been his scholarship on the issue of takings and eminent domain. With his 1985 book *Takings: Private Property and the Power of Eminent Domain*, Epstein played the major role in reviving discussion of the Constitution's Takings Clause and the subsequent debate over eminent domain that continues to flourish in journals, in state legislatures, and in the courts. Before 1985, for example, Westlaw's JLR database contains just twelve articles with 'takings' in the title and just 84 with 'eminent domain' in the title (the vast majority of which are practitioner-oriented articles). By contrast, after 1985 the database has 1,137 documents with 'takings' in the title and 385 with 'eminent domain', and a whopping 1,070 articles that cite to Epstein's book.[6] Even taking into account the greater coverage of post-1985 journal articles in the database, this is a major shift. Of course, the shift is due in part to the Supreme Court's greater interest in takings issues after 1985.[7] But it is unlikely that the Supreme Court would have shown such interest had Epstein not written *Takings*, and the debate today would be quite different and less centered on the issues Epstein raised there in the absence of his work. In short, there simply was little real debate on takings before *Takings* and none on the scale that there was afterwards. The amount of intellectual firepower brought to bear on the issues by those who disagreed with Epstein, as well as by those drawn into the debate on the same side, on takings issues before and after *Takings* is simply not of the same order of magnitude.

Takings had an important impact in the public sphere just a few years after its publication when Senator Joseph Biden questioned Supreme Court nominee Clarence Thomas about the book on national television.

> [T]he proceedings began with [Biden] waving a copy of Epstein's *Takings* before the cameras, and asking Thomas if the book had been on his reading list: '[There is] a new, fervent area of scholarship that basically says: Hey, look, we, the modern-day court, have not taken enough time to protect people's property, the property rights of corporations, the property rights of individuals, the property rights of businesses,' Biden said. 'And so what we have to do is we have to elevate the way we've treated property, we have to elevate that to make it harder for governments to interfere . . .'
>
> Biden wondered what would happen 'were Mr. Epstein's views to take hold.' If the property rights of businesses were to be respected, making it 'harder for the government to regulate them without paying them,' then that would be a 'multi-million dollar change in the law,' he worried (correctly). (Bethell 1998, pp. 181–2).

One key measure of Epstein's success in changing the public debate can be seen in the differences between the questions on *Takings* during Clarence Thomas's confirmation hearings and those raised in later nominees' hearings. As Epstein himself put it during a 1995 interview,

> 'I took some pride in the fact that [Sen.] Joe Biden (D-Del.) held a copy of *Takings* up to a hapless Clarence Thomas back in 1991 and said that anyone who believes what's in this book is certifiably unqualified to sit in on the Supreme Court. That's a compliment of sorts,' says Epstein. 'But I took even more pride in the fact that, during the Breyer hearings, there were no such theatrics, even as the

---

6   All searches updated as of January 20, 2008.

7   The most significant takings/eminent domain cases immediately prior to 1985 were *Berman v. Parker*, 348 US 26 (1954) and *Hawaii Housing Authority v. Midkiff*, 467 US 229 (1984), while the most recent regulatory takings case had been *Ruckelshaus v. Monsanto Company*, 467 US 986 (1984) and *Penn Central Transportation Co. v. New York City*, 438 US 104 (1978). *Midkiff* was an opinion remarkable only for the wide scope it gave to the government to exercise the power of eminent domain and *Monsanto* and *Penn Central* were notable primarily for the space they gave to regulatory takings with a doctrine the Court itself admitted was 'an ad hoc factual inquiry' rather than a legal one. *Ruckelshaus*, 467 US 986, 1005. Since 1985, the Court has decided eight cases involving various aspects of takings jurisprudence: *Kelo v. City of New London, Conn.*, 545 US 469 (2005); *Lingle v. Chevron USA*, 544 US 528 (2005); *Tahoe-Sierra Preservation Council, Inc. v. Tahoe Regional Planning Agency*, 535 US 302 (2002); *Palazzolo v. Rhode Island*, 533 US 606 (2001), *Lucas v. South Carolina Coastal Council*, 505 US 1003 (1992), *Keystone Bituminous Coal Ass'n v. DeBenedictis*, 480 US 470 (1987); *Nollan v. Cal. Coastal Comm'n*, 483 US 825 (1987); *First English Evangelical Lutheran Church of Glendale v. County of L.A., Cal.*, 482 US 304 (1987). To be sure none of these are decisions that resemble what might have been written by a Justice Epstein.

nominee was constantly questioned on whether he agreed with the Epstein position on deregulation as if that position could not be held by responsible people.' (Chapman 1995)

Clearly the public view of *Takings* changed significantly over time. Indeed, *Takings'* reception in the legal academy was extraordinarily hostile. I cannot improve on Eric Claeys's summary of the initial reaction in a 2006 assessment of *Takings'* legacy (which I quote here without the accompanying footnotes):

> In prominent reviews, by respectable and otherwise quite thoughtful scholars, *Takings* was called 'a disturbing book,' a 'patent and howling failure,' and an 'intellectual wasteland.' Peg Radin described its style of argument as 'philosophical camel-swallowing.' Frank Michelman dismissed the kind of property theorizing associated with Epstein's project as 'obtuseness.'
>
> And those criticisms are the quick dismissals, not the jeremiads. 'The book's only useful contribution,' Mark Kelman decried, 'may be to expose more fully the moral venality and intellectual vacuity of formal, legalized libertarianism.' Kelman's hostility paled in comparison to that of leading property theorists, who intuited that *Takings* unsettled how legal scholars have talked about property for generations. Joseph Sax sputtered that Epstein is a 'prisoner of an intellectual style so confining and of a philosophy so rigid that he has disabled himself from seeing problems as beyond the grasp of mere formalism.' And, for my personal favorite, Thomas Grey fulminated that *'Takings* belongs with the output of the constitutional lunatic fringe, the effusions of gold bugs, tax protestors, and gun-toting survivalists.' (Claeys 2006, pp. 439–40)

Not everyone reacted with hostility, of course. *Takings* received some favorable reviews from classical liberals in the academy. Professor James Huffman cited Epstein's 'sturdy house of bricks' to replace 'the flimsy house of straw that is current takings law' (Huffman 1986, p. 154). Philosopher Ellen Frankel Paul praised *Takings* for its 'wide ranging scope and its vast improvement over the takings muddle that our courts have wrought' even as she lamented that Epstein too readily accepted 'Social Security, zoning, and welfare transfers' as so embedded in our society as to make their abolition impossible (Paul 1986, pp. 177–8). But these positive assessments in the academy were few and far between.

Takings is a major accomplishment in law and economics, and not just in law, and Epstein's methodology exemplifies how his methods contribute to the economic approach while retaining the primacy of law. As he notes in the book's first sentence, *Takings* 'is an extended essay about the proper relationship between the individual and the state' (Epstein 1985b, p. 1). It is not an extended essay about economic efficiency, reducing transactions costs, or constrained optimization – the more normal subjects of work in law and economics – although it does rely on all three from time to time in support of its arguments.

To assess *Takings'* impact, we need to examine how Epstein makes his case. The book begins with 'A Tale of Two Pies', a straightforward economic argument that compares total wealth in the state of nature and in a world with some government. The world with government has more wealth than the world without and therein lies the sole justification for the state: 'All government action must be justified as moving a society from the smaller to the larger pie' (Epstein 1985b, p. 4). Two problems stand in the way of moving to the larger pie. First, is the 'inability to control private aggression' in the absence of a state. Second, people will not sufficiently fund the police power voluntarily, and so we need to overcome transaction costs, holdouts, and free riders, problems that 'are insuperable when the conduct of a large number of individuals must be organized'. This is mother's milk to economists, and one can easily imagine a reader with an economics Ph.D. from one of the top, mathematically oriented Ph.D. programs firing up his or her copy of Mathematica™ to start some modeling exercises. But Epstein makes a quite different move after defining the problem. He points out that this 'simple structure' of the problem of government will work only 'if we have a very clear sense of what counts as individual rights and of why government is called upon to protect them' (Epstein 1985b, p. 5). The crucial question then becomes to find an explanation for rights that can provide that clear sense. Thus rather than delve into a model that might examine nuances of the tradeoffs between the police power and protection of individual liberty, Epstein instead takes the reader on a first principles examination of Hobbes and Locke.

But the philosophical inquiry leads not into extended speculation on the origins of rights. Epstein is quite content to leave the ultimate basis of the rights indeterminate because the source of the rights is not determinative of the question at hand. The source may be divine, libertarian, or utilitarian – what matters is that the source is *before* the state. This is a thoroughly lawyerly approach: to know whether Jones wins his claim for Blackacre against Smith, we need know only whether Jones's claim is stronger than Smith's, not whether Jones' claim is also stronger than Walker's or Johnson's. Indeed Jones may prevail against Smith today and lose against Walker tomorrow. Thus to examine questions of state power we need not resolve the question of where they come from if we know that the individual's claim is stronger than the state's.

The combination of the clear statement of the justification for the state in economic terms as the solution to the Hobbesian problem and the rights-based analysis leads us to a thoroughly practical discussion of the right way to interpret Constitutional text. The Constitution includes many undefined terms: 'private property, taken, just compensation, and public use' among them. These terms are used in 'sentences of great power but of equally great abstraction'. To read these, Epstein says, we must look to '[t]he community of understanding' that arises from 'the way these words are used in ordinary discourse by persons who are educated in the normal social and cultural discourse of their own time' (Epstein 1985b, p. 20).

We can contrast this, as Epstein does, with Thomas Grey's philosophical approach that denies that words such as 'private property' can have a uniform meaning. Epstein quotes from Grey's argument that there can be no uniform definition of property because there are tensions within the meaning in different contexts, leading up to Grey's conclusion that '[i]t seems fair to conclude from a glance at the range of current usages that the specialists who design and manipulate legal structures of the advanced capitalist economies could easily do without using the term "property" at all' (Epstein 1985b, p. 21 quoting Grey 1980, p. 163). To this, Epstein's response is simple: 'Try it' (Epstein 1985b, p. 21).

Epstein is right that Grey's argument is impracticable. Rejecting a word with 'well-nigh universal usage in the English language', Grey leaves us with nothing to take its place and we find ourselves without an effective limit to the state's power (a power necessary to solve the original problem of moving to the bigger pie.) Property works, albeit imperfectly and not always with the theoretical elegance desired by philosophers, but it does work. This is ultimately a lawyerly objection, rather than an economist's or a philosopher's. Grey's argument fails on lawyers' terms because it does not work in everyday life.

Yet the analysis here is not simply a lawyer's objection to a philosopher's speculation. For the next problem Epstein addresses comes from the lawyers. What about the difficult cases where the principles clash? 'A's occupation is prior to B's, but B has fenced first. A's deed is first in time, but B's deed may be first recorded.' Here Epstein pulls back, avoiding 'an

acute attack of lawyers' disease' by recognizing that '[m]arginal cases are the stuff of litigation; they are not the stuff of basic human arrangements'. There may be plenty of 'doctrinal
murkiness' about, but the legal rules almost always make it clear who owns what (Epstein
1985b, 23–4). 'Lawyers can speak with precision about legal problems even though language
is vague and messy at the edges' (Epstein 1985b, p. 24).

The final piece of the argument is developing a framework for understanding constitutional texts. What authority does the text have and what sources should we examine to deci-
pher it? These are a lawyer's questions, not an economist's. The answers too are those of a
lawyer steeped in the historical roots of the common law – we should look to the writers of
the time for guidance, but balance our assessment of history with the recognition that the
Framers wrote in general terms precisely to avoid being limited to the specific historical
examples that motivated their concern with particular problems. (Indeed, throughout the book
Epstein's arguments are deeply rooted in law, and he draws heavily on arguments, precedent,
practice, and experience under both English common law and Roman law.) '[T]he framers
were as aware of the problem of legislative innovation as we are. They knew that they could
not know the future and drafted accordingly' (Epstein 1985b, p. 29).

In just over thirty pages at the start of *Takings*, Epstein has sketched all the material
summarized here and set out a comprehensive theory that embraces not only a method of
constitutional interpretation but a theory of the state as well. In many respects, the remaining
three hundred and some pages are simply working out the details as the key points of the
theory are thoroughly developed in this first section. It yields four questions that must be
answered to understand takings:

1. Is there a taking of private property?
2. Is there any justification for taking that private property?
3. Is the taking for a public use?
4. Is there any compensation for the property so taken? (Epstein 1985b, p. 31).

Answering these questions is quite a different enterprise from answering the question of
whether or not a particular interpretation of the takings clause is going to produce an efficient
outcome or not. These questions sketch out a lawyer's case in chief in a suit against the state
for compensation for the loss of his client's property. That is not to say that the answers do
not involve economic analysis, for they do, or that the answer is merely a matter of doctrinal
development, for it is not. But these questions do approach the problem of takings in a way
that is quite different from the methods of most law and economics scholarship. Yet there is
much to be gained by Epstein's method.

Consider, for example, the ongoing debate over the relevance of legal scholarship
launched by Judge Harry Edwards (1992), complaining that modern legal scholarship, particularly the 'law and . . .' approaches and critical legal studies, had moved academic work away
from doctrinal analysis and made it so that 'judges, administrators, legislators, and practitioners have little use for much of the scholarship that is now produced by members of the
academy' (1992, p. 35). What concerned Edwards was the appearance in 'elite' law faculties
of 'significant contingents of "impractical" scholars who are "disdainful of the practice of
law"' and whose work amounts to 'abstract scholarship that has little relevance to concrete
issues, or addresses concrete issues in a wholly theoretical manner' (ibid.).

One answer to Edwards is scholarship like *Takings* which applies the tools of economics,
along with more traditional tools of legal scholarship, to illuminating an area of the law that

previously was obscure. While I doubt that Edwards had *Takings* in mind when he called for more relevant legal scholarship, Epstein's work in the area of takings (or elsewhere) is not vulnerable to the critique Edwards offered precisely because it is rooted in the law. One may disagree with particular points of history or legal interpretation, as some of Epstein's critics have done, but it is not possible to argue that Epstein's points are not well within the realm of legal argument. Reading *Takings* requires just the sort of 'fluency with legal texts and concepts' that Edwards insisted was missing from legal education and legal scholarship. (Edwards 1992, p. 39).

But, of course, no court has yet embraced *Takings'* analysis. Does that mean that the argument has failed? No. *Takings*, and Epstein's work generally, are legal arguments first and foremost but they are not legal arguments addressed primarily to a court. Epstein himself asked at the end of the book whether *Takings* was likely to produce a change in the law of the Takings Clause itself.

> The question then arises whether there is a political will to carry out these reforms, either by the courts or the legislature. The short answer is that there is not. And there may never be. The long answer is perhaps more instructive. One reason why the will is wanting is because the dominant intellectual trend has been heavily against the positions taken here. Private property is thought to be a conclusory label; ad hoc considerations are thought to dominate the analysis of takings problems. Political deals are thought to be the essence of democracy. Undermining the conventional respectability of intellectual skepticism may in the long run help to rehabilitate the political will, even if it does not revive the constitutional doctrine. (Epstein 1985b, p. 329).

It seems certain that if the intellectual trend is ever reversed, the reversal will trace its roots to the publication of *Takings*.

It is all well and good to try cast Epstein as a prophet crying in the legal wilderness or even as a Moses leading American constitutional theory toward a classical liberal promised land, but neither role fits his actual impact. *Takings'* impact is threefold. First, it serves as an example of law *and* economics, of engaging in analysis using the tools provided by economics (and philosophy) in pursuit of the answer to a practical question: When does the state owe compensation to Smith when it acts to reduce the value of Smith's property? It is impossible to read *Takings* without coming away with an appreciation of what the imperfect, often vague, and sometimes contradictory mass of legal doctrine can accomplish when someone carefully and thoroughly explores the details of the doctrine and works through the implications of surprisingly straightforward and simple principles. (I should note that these principles are revealed as simple and straightforward only when a lawyer of Epstein's caliber has explained them. They escaped earlier commentators even if they now seem obviously relevant.) Second, *Takings* recast the terms of the debate. The Supreme Court may not have embraced Epstein's theories, but, as noted earlier, *Takings* is no longer Exhibit A at confirmation hearings as part of a litmus test for radical beliefs. The power of Epstein's elegantly simple argument has begun to erode the intellectual trend, and the intellectual discourse about takings today must include consideration of the arguments made in *Takings* to be taken seriously. Without *Takings,* it seems safe to say, there would not have been the flourishing of eminent domain and Takings Clause scholarship that there has been over the past thirty years. Along these same lines, James Ely recently argued persuasively that Epstein was the primary intellectual force in changing the terms of debate over property in the constitutional order. Once dismissed for advancing strange ideas that contradicted the conventional wisdom, Professor Epstein has seen his views resonate more widely than his critics expected. The subordination of property, once taken for granted, is now open to discussion. No thoughtful scholar can address the topic of regulatory takings without coming to grips with Epstein's arguments. Specifically, his work has been the catalyst for an outpouring of scholarship on the origins and history of the Takings Clause. It is not too much to conclude that Professor Epstein's work has triggered a national dialogue on the role of property in American constitutionalism. The vigor with which critics assail Epstein's views – he has been compared to Thomas Malthus and derided as a radical reactionary – is a backhand testament to their intellectual appeal and impact. (Ely 2006, p. 426).

Finally, *Takings* was a major part of a broader revival of classical liberal legal scholarship that now includes scholars such as Eugene Volokh and Randy Barnett. It has helped to make topics like property rights intellectually respectable enough that the legal academy has been forced to acknowledge that such ideas can sit at the table with the rest of legal scholarship.

We must not underestimate the scope of the change. Tom Bethell's (1998) tracing of property rights through history begins with an account of property rights' 'fall from grace'. Bethell notes that

> In the 1950s, when Encyclopedia Britannica Inc. published its *Great Books of the Western World*, property was not among the 102 topics in its index of 'great ideas.' Arnold Toynbee overlooked property in his 12-volume *Study of History*. . . . William H. McNeill's *Rise of the West* and Oswald Spengler's *Decline of the West* likewise found property dispensable. Fernand Braudel's three-volume *Civilization and Capitalism, Fifteenth to Eighteenth Century*, paid scant attention to property or law, as did *A History of Civilizations*, by the same author. (Bethell 1998, p. 7)

And it was not just historians who paid no attention to property rights for most of the twentieth century. 'Between 1928 and 1974, the [US Supreme] Court refused to hear a single zoning case' and 'best-selling [economics] textbooks by Paul Samuelson and others either skirted questions of ownership or relegated them to a paragraph under the rubric of "capitalist ideology."' (Bethell 1998, p. 8). The change in attention to property rights in recent years has been dramatic, and is surely due in significant part to Epstein's work, including *Takings*. Indeed, when historian Richard Pipes chose the epigrams for the chapter in *Property and Freedom* on the twentieth century, he used quotes from *Takings* and from Charles Reich's 1964 article 'The New Property' (reportedly the most cited article in the history of the *Yale Law Journal* (Bethell 1998, p. 178)) (Pipes 1999, p. 209). No better contrast between property theorists can be imagined than between Epstein and Reich, between the old property derived from centuries of history and the new derived from armchair theorizing, and there is no better indication of the change in intellectual climate than that as Reich's work has begun to appear ever more dated and irrelevant, Epstein's work has moved from the sidelines to the center of the debate.

To give just one personal anecdotal example of how much things have changed just in the last fifteen years, when I entered the legal teaching market in the early 1990s, I was asked whether as an economist I was 'like Richard Epstein' during more than one job interview. Using my lawyer's training (or perhaps it was my viewing of *Sesame Street's* 'which of these things is not like the other' programming during my formative years), I was able to truthfully answer 'no', while mentally completing the sentence 'because I'm not nearly as smart or productive'. I cannot imagine that anyone asks such a question of candidates today, unless they are looking for a 'yes' answer.

One reason Epstein was able to start a debate over property rights is that he began by looking at issues as a lawyer does. Had he been in economics graduate school during the 1960s, for example, it is unlikely he would have heard much about property rights for the reasons Bethell describes. But because he started with law in an English legal program (as opposed to an American one), he started with Roman law and English common law, and both are deeply concerned with property. Indeed, during the long period when property was out of intellectual fashion, it was professors, not lawyers, who had lost interest in property rights. Without a renewed legal focus, it strikes me as doubtful that interest in property rights would have revived as quickly or as deeply.

4   Constitutional analysis

If *Takings* was an initial assault on contemporary constitutional analysis, Epstein's later constitutional work has been a sustained campaign to set constitutional law on a firmer footing as law derived from a consistent set of principles. In *How the Progressives Rewrote the Constitution* (2006a), Epstein pulled together his thoughts on interpreting constitutions and the history of the interpretation of the US Constitution in the hands of the Supreme Court. (The book is the written version of the B. Kenneth Simon Lecture in Constitutional Thought lecture Epstein delivered at the Cato Institute in 2004.) The book, and Epstein's constitutional writings generally, make many important points about constitutional law. What is important here are two points relating to law and economics.

The first contribution the book makes is a convincing argument that we must assess the impact of constitutional doctrines by reference to reality. We have data on the state of the world and we can use that data to assess whether the received wisdom of constitutional history is correct or not. Thus, for example, the change in constitutional jurisprudence between the pre-New Deal Supreme Court and the post-New Deal Supreme Court must be assessed, in part, by examining data on the state of the world before and after the change. And, Epstein notes, progressive reformers like Louis Brandeis explicitly made their case for changes in constitutional law on the grounds that changes in social conditions demanded it.

Epstein takes the task seriously, quoting Brandeis's claim that corporate economic power meant a rise in inequality of bargaining power that demanded legal reform to meet new 'social needs' (Epstein 2006a, pp. 4–5 quoting Brandeis). The Progressives' claims are thus capable of being evaluated by looking to data. While Brandeis did not offer any empirical support for his argument about the impact of this loss of bargaining power, Epstein does offer 'some rudimentary numbers, readily available today' that show declining child labor, a shortening work week, rising wages, and increasing life expectancy (Epstein 2006a, pp. 5–6). If the Progressives' arguments were correct, then we should have observed the reverse.

Epstein argues, convincingly, that rather than rely on data the Progressive argument was built around an assumption that active government was good government. 'Predictably, their theory of good government generated a compatible constitutional theory. Thus, any constitutional doctrine that stood in the way of comprehensive reforms had to be rejected or circumvented' (Epstein 2006a, p. 7). This argument in *How the Progressives Rewrote the Constitution* is an elaboration on the two pies with which Epstein opened *Takings*. We can tell whether particular policies or methods of constitutional interpretation are correct by examining their consequences. Indeed, we must make such an examination if we are to understand whether the policies are constitutional because government is only justified when it moves us from the smaller to the larger pie. By introducing an empirical element into debate, Epstein offers an alternative to contemporary constitutional law's fascination with penumbras, emanations from penumbras, and other abstract debates. There has not been a sweeping embrace of empiricism in constitutional law as a result (at least not yet), but the elaboration of an alternative is a step in the right direction for those who find contemporary constitutional law to be drifting into results-oriented, ahistorical expressions of the preferences of the justices. The growing interest in constitutional political economy owes a considerable debt to Epstein's introduction of these themes in his larger body of work.

The second contribution to law and economics of Epstein's constitutional analysis is to put discussion of the pre-New Deal constitutional law on a sounder historical footing. Too often, contemporary constitutional law proceeds from the notion that under the 'now discredited' *Lochner* era approach, a court of *laissez faire* ideologues sat athwart all social progress. As Epstein shows, however, 'a fair assessment of the Old Court [the pre-New Deal court] finds it allowing state action to control standard tort-like externalities, and even trumping the common law with respect to industrial accidents [through workers' compensation laws]' (Epstein 2006a, p. 50). What mattered, Epstein argues, is that the 'Old Court' got it right on where it mattered most, striking efforts to interfere with 'the operation of ordinary competitive labor markets' and seeing that the common law was adequate 'so long as free entry was allowed on both sides of labor and product markets' (ibid.) Understanding constitutional law's development is not possible so long as we are in the grip of misconceptions about the historical record. This is crucial for law and economics, and not just for law or legal history, because an accurate description of the institutions under study is a prerequisite for a coherent analysis of those institutions, whether by modeling or by empirical analysis. Most importantly, an accurate understanding of the development of Progressive constitutional thought is necessary to understanding 'the great doctrinal divide that has dominated constitutional law to the present day': the distinction between economic rights and 'matters of speech, religion, and race' (Epstein 2006a, p. 112).

There is a coherent and powerful theme connecting virtually all of Epstein's work on constitutional issues: that economic liberties are no different from political, religious, or other forms of liberty. Epstein is certainly not the only person to make such a claim, either in modern times or in earlier ones. James Ely, Jr, for example, took the title of his history of the treatment of property in constitutional law, *The Guardian of Every Other Right* (2007), from a comment by Virginian Arthur Lee, a member of the Continental Congress. But Epstein is the leading exponent of the argument today and has articulated it with greater specificity and clarity than anyone else. As with the specific arguments advanced in *Takings*, this general point has not yet persuaded a majority of the Court or of the legal academy. But as with *Takings*, its influence is going to be felt more by shifting the frame of reference in the debate itself than in next year's Supreme Court docket.

Epstein's approach is more in tune with what the population at large thinks about the Constitution, as could be seen in the backlash to the Supreme Court's 2004 decision in *Kelo v. City of New London*. A survey of the popular reaction to *Kelo* found not only the deep outrage at the idea that private property could be taken by governments to be transferred to favored developers, but a fairly nuanced view of takings generally that supported the use of eminent domain for more traditional uses such as road and school construction (Nadler et al. 2008). Public opinion may not translate into immediate remedial legislation (Somin 2008;

Morriss 2008), but Ilya Somin's analysis of post-*Kelo* reform legislation found that citizen-initiated referenda were the most likely to move eminent domain toward a position similar to that advocated by Epstein (Somin 2008). The idea that economic rights are entitled to protection comparable to that given to other rights is one with a strong resonance in the popular understanding of the Constitution's protection of property rights.

These two contributions are of particular importance for law and economics in part because they open the door to future work by others. Epstein's framework for evaluating government as requiring justification for the exercise of public power as enhancing welfare (that is, each move must take us from the smaller to the larger pie) provides both a metric for evaluating particular features of government (the just compensation clause as a means of ensuring that takings do indeed increase welfare) and opens the field of constitutional law to serious economic inquiry. And treating economic liberties on an equal footing with other liberties demands thorough economic analysis of constitutional doctrine. For example, Epstein offers a concise explanation of when government action can move us to the larger pie:

> The key insight is this: competition is a positive-sum game, while aggression is a negative-sum game. For that social reason, and not for any fascination with the 'possessive individualism' that the Progressives denounced, the former should be favored and protected while the latter is deplored and restricted. Individual control over one's labor and property should be governed, therefore, by the principle that competition and aggression are polar opposites. Competition enhances social welfare. Aggression diminishes it. (Epstein 2006a, pp. 15–16)

As a practical matter, what this demands is careful economic analysis of just when government action promotes or diminishes competition and of where opportunities for rent-seeking transform lobbying into thinly disguised aggression. In short, Epstein has sketched an agenda for the next generation of law and economics scholarship on constitutional law.

5   Concluding thoughts

While the preceding pages have barely begun to discuss Epstein's body of work, I hope they have captured the essence of what distinguishes Epstein's contribution to law and economics from the contributions of the other pioneers recognized in this volume. Epstein's work has put the law first and that has made a significant difference in his scholarship. The result has influenced the discipline not merely by advancing clear, logical arguments about particular points but by demonstrating over and over that one must understand the law before being able to do economic analysis of the law. Unlike, for example, his fellow Chicagoan Richard Posner, Epstein has not attempted to provide us with an overarching philosophy or a metric to be used to analyze every case. And unlike the contributions of pioneers like Steven Shavell, Epstein has not provided us with formal economic modeling. Rather, with the approach of a lawyer in a common law court, Epstein has carefully taken each problem apart, identified the principles, examined the evidence, and then built a case for a solution that, more often than not, yields an outcome of the same order of economic efficiency as those that might come from Posner's analysis or Shavell's models.

In academic writing there is an impulse to say something critical, to mark off territory of one's own, and to prove one's intellectual chops by snapping at the heels of the master. It is almost necessary to do so to be credible, for otherwise one risks appearing to fawn. There have been times when I found myself in disagreement with something Epstein has written.

There are even a few where I still disagreed after further reflection. Elaborating on these few instances would add nothing to assessment of Epstein's scholarly impact, however.

Epstein's influence goes well beyond the academic world. He has participated in a number of amici and other briefs to the Supreme Court in a variety of cases and he has engaged in public debate on behalf of his ideas in numerous fora. One anecdote about those debates gives a flavor of their impact. During the litigation in the 1990s by a coalition of plaintiffs' attorneys and state attorneys general against the major US tobacco companies, Mississippi Attorney General Michael Moore and his law school classmate Richard 'Dickie' Scruggs led the coalition's efforts to persuade various nonprofits to accept the terms of the settlement (Yandle et al. 2008). Returning from 'a critical reception' before health interest groups unimpressed with the deal, Moore called Scruggs to describe his experience. 'At a litigation conference earlier in the year, Scruggs endured a critical grilling from University of Chicago law professor Richard Epstein, who wouldn't let up as Scruggs wilted. "Man, I've just had an Epstein on steroids," Moore told his friend"' (Mollenkamp et al. 1998, p. 191). It is hard to imagine a higher accolade from two of the best trial lawyers and politicians in America than being the reference standard for a thorough dissection of one's position.

One final matter needs mention to capture Richard Epstein's impact on law and economics. His writing is extraordinary in its breadth and depth, but to talk only of his writing would be to fail to capture the full range of Epstein's influence since it would neglect three crucial unwritten avenues. First, Epstein has served on the law faculty at the University of Chicago for more than three decades. In that time he has taught thousands of students in courses from Torts to Federal Income Tax to Patents to Roman Law. More than a few of those students have gone on to become law professors themselves. Just as his first course in Roman Law shaped his subsequent career, so the impact of his teaching is likely to be as significant as, if harder to measure than, the impact of his writing.

Second, Epstein has had an impact on Chicago through his service to the university and the law school, serving on important university committees and even as interim dean from February to June 2001 at Chicago. No one who has discussed Chicago with him can come away without being impressed by his devotion to the school. Law and economics would not be where it is today without Chicago and Chicago would not have been what it has been without Epstein's contributions to the institution, as well as his scholarship.

Finally, Epstein's impact on the academy has gone far beyond Chicago. He has generously given his time to mentor would-be and young faculty with little or no connection to Chicago (including me). Working with organizations such as the Institute for Humane Studies, he has helped steer young law and economics scholars toward the appropriate path to a successful career, whether or not they agreed with him on particular issues or even on broader methodological grounds. As he noted in a symposium piece addressing the comments of others on *Takings*, 'As one grows more senior in the profession, it becomes ever more apparent that we pay our debt to our own teachers by trying to help, in whatever way we can, the next generation of scholars and students. And in one sense, the highest praise is to take seriously younger scholars when they chase after you' (Epstein 2005a, p. 418). He has been free with the praise of taking younger scholars seriously and if they all repay him by doing the same for the next generation, Richard Epstein will deserve credit for moving legal scholarship toward a genuine exchange of ideas among people who can disagree politely and reasonably on many topics yet remain colleagues in a broader enterprise.

References

Bethell, Tom. 1998. *The Noblest Triumph: Property and Prosperity through the Ages*. New York: St Martin's Griffin.

Blades, Lawrence E. 1967. 'Employment at Will v. Individual Freedom: On Limiting the Abusive Exercise of Employer Power'. *Columbia Law Review* 67: 1404–35.

Brown, John Prather. 1973. 'Toward an Economic Theory of Liability'. *Journal of Legal Studies* 2: 323–49.

Calabresi, Guido. 1970. *The Cost of Accidents*. New Haven, Conn.: Yale University Press.

Chapman, Steve. 1995. 'Takings Exception'. *Reason* (April). Available at http://www.reason.com/news/show/29662.html.

Claeys, Eric and Richard A. Epstein. 2006. 'Takings: An Appreciative Retrospective'. *William and Mary Bill of Rights Journal*, 15: 439–55.

Cooter, Robert D. and Thomas S. Ulen. 1986. 'An Economic Case for Comparative Negligence'. *New York University Law Review* 61: 1067–110.

Edwards, Harry T. 1992. 'The Growing Disjunction between Legal Education and the Legal Profession'. *Michigan Law Review* 91: 34–78.

Ely, James W., Jr. 2007. *The Guardian of Every Other Right: A Constitutional History of Property Rights*. New York: Oxford University Press (3rd ed.).

Ely, James W., Jr. 2006. 'Impact of Richard Epstein,' *William and Mary Bill of Rights Journal* 15: 421–8.

Epstein, Richard A. 2006a. *How the Progressives Rewrote the Constitution*. Washington, DC: Cato Institute.

Epstein, Richard A. 2006b. 'Intuition, Custom, and Protocol: How to Make Sound Decisions with Limited Knowledge'. *New York University Journal of Law and* Liberty 2: 1–27.

Epstein, Richard A. 2005a. 'Taking Stock of Takings: An Author's Retrospective'. *William and Mary Bill of Rights Journal* 15: 407–20.

Epstein, Richard A. 2005b. 'The Roman Law of Cyberconversion'. *Michigan State Law Review* 2005: 103–20.

Epstein, Richard A. 2005c. 'The Uses and Limits of Local Knowledge: A Cautionary Note on Hayek'. *New York University Journal of Law and Liberty* 1: 208–209.

Epstein, Richard A. 2002. 'Does Literature Work as Social Science?'. *University of Colorado Law Review* 73: 987–1011.

Epstein, Richard A. 1999. 'Hayekian Socialism'. *Maryland Law Review* 58: 271–99.

Epstein, Richard A. 1997. 'The Modern Uses of Ancient Law'. *South Carolina Law Review* 48: 243–65.

Epstein, Richard A. 1992. *Forbidden Grounds: The Case against Employment Discrimination Laws*. Cambridge, Mass.: Harvard University Press.

Epstein, Richard A. 1985a. 'Agency Costs, Employment Contracts, and Labor Unions', in *Principals and Agents: The Structure of Business*, J. Pratt and R. Zeckhauser, eds. Cambridge, MA: Harvard University Press.

Epstein, Richard A. 1985b. *Takings: Private Property and the Power of Eminent Domain*. Cambridge, MA: Harvard University Press.

Epstein, Richard A. 1984. 'In Defense of the Contract at Will'. *University of Chicago Law Review* 51: 947–81.

Epstein, Richard A. 1983a. 'A Common Law for Labor Relations: A Critique of the New Deal Labor Legislation'. *Yale Law Journal* 92: 1357–408.

Epstein, Richard A. 1983b. 'Common Law, Labor Law, and Reality: A Rejoinder to Professors Getman and Kohler'. *Yale Law Journal* 92: 1435–41.

Grey, Thomas. 1980. 'The Disintegration of Property,' in *Property*, J. Roland Pennock and John W. Chapman, eds. NOMOS monograph no. 22.

Haddock, David and Christopher Curran. 1985. 'An Economic Theory of Comparative Negligence'. *Journal of Legal Studies* 14: 49–72.

Huffman, James L. 1986. 'A Coherent Takings Theory at Last: Comments on Richard Epstein's *Takings: Private Property and the Power of Eminent Domain*'. *Environmental Law* 17: 153–79.

Mollenkamp, Carrick, Joseph Karl Menn, Adam Levy, and Joseph Menn, 1998. *The People vs. Big Tobacco*. Princeton, NJ: Bloomberg Press.

Morriss, Andrew P. 2009. 'Symbol or Substance? An Empirical Assessment of State Responses to *Kelo*'. *Supreme Court Economic Review* 2009: 237–78.

Morriss, Andrew P. 1994. 'Exploding Myths: An Empirical and Economic Reassessment of the Rise of Employment at Will'. *Missouri Law Review* 59: 679–773.

Nadler, Janice, Shari Seidman Diamond and Matthew M. Patton. 2008. 'Government Takings of Private Property: *Kelo* and the Perfect Storm', in Nathaniel Persily, Jack Citrin and Patrick Egan (eds) *Public Opinion and Constitutional Controversy*.

Paul, Ellen Frankel. 1986. 'Moral Constraints and Eminent Domain: A Review Essay of Richard Epstein's *Takings: Private Property and the Power of Eminent Domain*'. *George Washington Law Review* 55: 152–78.

Pipes, Richard. 1999. *Property and Freedom*. NY: Knopf.

Posner, Richard A. 2003. 'Kelsen versus Hayek: Pragmatism, Economics, and Democracy', in *Law, Pragmatism, and Democracy*. Cambridge, Mass.: Harvard University Press.

Posner, Richard A. 1972. 'A Theory of Negligence'. *Journal of Legal Studies* 1: 29–96.

Reich, Charles A. 1964. 'The New Property'. *Yale Law Journal* 73: 733–87.

Shavell, Steven. 1987. *Economic Analysis of Accident Law*. Cambridge, Mass.: Harvard University Press.

Somin, Ilya. 2008. *The Limits of Backlash: Assessing the Political Response to* Kelo, George Mason University Law and Economics Research Paper Series, No. 07-14 (January).

Yandle, Bruce, Joseph A. Rotondi, Andrew Dorchak and Andrew P. Morriss. 2008. 'Bootleggers, Baptists, and Televangelists: Regulating Tobacco by Litigation'. *University of Illinois Law Review* 1225–84.

13 Calabresi's influence on law and economics
Keith N. Hylton*

No lecture on the foundations of modern law and economics would be complete without some discussion of Guido Calabresi's work.[1] In this essay, I will focus on the influence of two contributions from Calabresi; his book, *The Costs of Accidents*,[2] and his article with Douglas Melamed on property rules and liability rules.[3]

Guido Calabresi has authored a large number of articles, so there is much more to examine than simply the book and the Calabresi-Melamed article. However, the book and the article are by far the most important pieces by Calabresi in terms of impact on law and economics scholarship. The book and the article have had profound and permanent effects on law and economics scholarship, providing fundamental templates for later research.

Calabresi's *Costs* alone has had an enormous influence on law and economics. Modern law and economics, as we see it practiced today, had its start with Ronald Coase's article on transaction costs, Gary Becker's article on crime[4] and Guido Calabresi's book. Calabresi's article on property rules did not have the same impact as the book initially, but it may have a bigger impact in the long run.

The book and the article represent different models of law and economics scholarship, both highly successful in Calabresi's case. The book is an example of grand thesis scholarship. The article is an example of normal science: an effort to set out a general model that explains important features of the law. Grand thesis scholarship tends to grab more attention than normal science, which appears to be true of Calabresi's contributions. My suspicion, however, is that normal science advances a field of research further in the long run than grand thesis scholarship.

I will try to identify and trace the vein of thought represented by Calabresi's scholarship, both backward in time to examine its sources, and forward to its impact on current scholarship. I will start with an effort to locate Calabresi's book within the history of economic analysis of law. After that, I will focus on three broad topics: positive versus normative law and economics; positivist versus anti-positivist in law and economics, and the assumption of rationality in the economic analysis of law.

---

* Professor of Law and Paul J. Liacos Scholar in Law, Boston University, knhylton@bu.edu.

[1] I have surveyed a substantial part of Calabresi's contributions earlier in Keith N. Hylton, 'Calabresi and the Intellectual History of Law and Economics', 64 *Maryland Law Review* 85 (2005). This essay borrows heavily from the arguments I made in my earlier article.

[2] The complete citation is Guido Calabresi, *The Costs of Accidents: A Legal and Economic Analysis* (New Haven: Yale University Press, 1970).

[3] Guido Calabresi and A. Douglas Melamed, 'Property Rules, Liability Rules, and Inalienability: One View of the Cathedral', 85 *Harvard Law Review* 1089 (1972).

[4] Gary S. Becker, 'Crime and Punishment: An Economic Approach', 76 *Journal of Political Economy* 169 (1968).

Calabresi and the history of law and economics

Within a span of two years, Calabresi published *Costs* (1970) and his essay on property rules (1972), two pieces that would permanently alter the landscape of law and economics scholarship. Before Calabresi's *Costs*, one would have to go back to Holmes's *The Common Law*, published in 1881,[5] to find an examination of tort law of comparable depth and sophistication. Before the publication of his essay on property rules, there were very few pieces of normal-science law and economics of comparable scope. Two pieces that clearly meet this test are Coase's article on transaction costs[6] and Gary Becker's article on crime.[7] Guido Calabresi's article on risk distribution in tort law is one of the earliest contributions to law and economics,[8] but its scope is much narrower than the Coase and Becker articles. Buchanan's article on products liability is also an important early contribution,[9] but its scope is also narrow in comparison to the Coase and Becker articles.

Law and economics consists of two major branches; grand thesis scholarship and normal science. If one were tracing the roots of Calabresi's article on property and liability rules, one might justifiably identify the starting point of normal science scholarship in law and economics, which is probably Coase's article on transaction costs, as the prime source. Calabresi's *Costs*, however, as part of the grand thesis branch, has much older roots.

In this section I will focus on the grand thesis branch and trace the broad current of law and economics thought up to Calabresi's *Costs*. The significance of Calabresi's work is better understood by considering the law and economics writing that preceded him.

A brief overview of the intellectual history of law and economics

Law and economics views law from an instrumentalist perspective. That is a perspective that seeks to determine the function of law and the manner in which it solves the social problems thrown before it. Bentham is the most obvious source that comes to mind for this approach. Bentham's core contribution to legal theory was a rejection of the view that law should be understood as emanating from or growing out of some set of a priori fundamental rights. Blackstone had led students to think of the law in this way, and Bentham, as one of those students, staked his career on overturning this view. He succeeded; though Blackstone was a more complicated thinker than Bentham's early caricature suggests.

Blackstone himself incorporated instrumentalist reasoning in parts of his *Commentaries*.[10] His volume on criminal law both refers to and shows the influence of Beccaria's utilitarian writing on punishment.[11] Taking the sum of his views as a theorist, Blackstone presents a muddled picture. He comes across as utilitarian in his treatment of criminal law, and a promoter of non-consequentialist, fundamental-rights theory in other parts of the

---

5   Oliver Wendell Holmes, Jr, *The Common Law* (1881) (Boston: Little Brown & Company).

6   R.H. Coase, 'The Problem of Social Cost', 3 *Journal of Law and Economics* 1 (1960).

7   Becker, *supra* note 4.

8   Guido Calabresi, 'Some Thoughts on Risk Distribution and the Law of Torts', 70 *Yale Law Journal* 499–553 (1961).

9   James M. Buchanan, 'In Defense of Caveat Emptor', 38 (1) *The University of Chicago Law Review* 64–73 (Autumn 1970).

10   William Blackstone, *Commentaries on the Laws of England* (Chicago: University of Chicago Press, 1979) (1765–9).

11   Cesare Beccaria, *On Crimes and Punishments*, Henry Paolucci ed. (Indianapolis: Bobbs-Merrill, 1963).

Commentaries; especially when he discusses the most basic protections provided by the common law – of life, liberty, property.[12]

As I have suggested, the instrumentalist or functionalist approach to law typically identified with Bentham makes some appearances in the theoretical literature that predates Bentham. The case of Beccaria I have already mentioned. Beccaria's theory that punishment should be set at a level that wipes out the expected gains of the criminal actor, and not above that level, formed the basis of his influential critique of criminal law enforcement published in 1764. Beccaria's critique served as the chief source of theoretical insights for Blackstone's treatment of criminal law, and also likely served as the chief inspiration for Bentham's work on criminal law. While Blackstone provided a negative inspiration for Bentham, a figure that Bentham would caricature, ridicule, and hold up as an example of all that is wrong with legal theory,[13] Beccaria provided a positive inspiration.

Almost at the same time as Beccaria was writing, Adam Smith lectured on jurisprudence to a class at Glasgow University. Notes from those lectures are published under the title *Lectures on Jurisprudence*.[14] Smith's lectures, seldom discussed in the law and economics literature, provide the first sustained treatment of law from an economic perspective. Smith provides especially detailed discussions of property and criminal law. His lectures on criminal law, anticipating Becker, argue that criminal penalties tend to be inversely related to the probability of detection. Smith's work has never received the attention showered on Bentham, which I find puzzling.

Immediately before Beccaria and Smith, one finds Hume's discussion of property and norms, which treats property law as the result of an implicit contract that develops over time within a society.[15] While Hume influenced Smith, he appears not to have influenced Bentham. Before Hume, one finds Hobbes's discussion of the common law, arguing that the king should have a strong hand in interpreting the law, and, more importantly, suggesting that the law's purpose is to maximize social welfare.[16]

Although Bentham is generally viewed as the source of instrumentalism in legal theory, I think the starting point is Hobbes. At the core of instrumentalism is the notion that the law's purpose should be understood from the perspective of what an economist would call a social planner or what a philosopher might call a Platonic philosopher-king. Hobbes is probably the fundamental source for the argument that law should not be understood or justified only on its own terms, or, equivalently, rejecting the notion that law can only be understood or justified by a lawyer steeped in the intricacies of legal opinions and terminology. Law and

---

12   Another reason Blackstone's perspective as a theorist is unclear is that he shows influences from Hobbes in parts of his discussion. His perspective may be closer to utilitarian than is commonly recognized.

13   See Jeremy Bentham, *A Comment on the Commentaries: A Criticism of William Blackstone's Commentaries on the Laws of England*, Charles W. Everett, ed. (1928), (Oxford: Clarendon Press). For an illuminating discussion of Bentham and Blackstone, see Richard A. Posner, *The Economics of Justice* 13–47 (Cambridge: Harvard University Press, 1983).

14   Adam Smith, *Lectures on Jurisprudence: The Glasgow Edition*, R.L. Meet et al. eds (Oxford University Press, 1978) (1762–5).

15   David Hume, *Treatise of Human Nature* 484–501 (Buffalo, NY: Prometheus Books, 1992) (1737).

16   Thomas Hobbes, *A Dialogue Between a Philosopher and a Student of the Common Laws of England*, Joseph Cropsey ed. (Chicago: University of Chicago Press, 1971) (1681).

economics practitioners make the argument frequently today; the first wave of legal realists, including Holmes, made the argument several generations ago. Bentham preceded the realists by roughly 100 years. All of them are partly in debt to Hobbes.

I am not suggesting that Bentham is not the key or most important source for instrumentalism. He clearly is, especially for the law and economics school. However, being the most important source is not the same thing as being the starting point. The starting point for instrumentalism in law is the notion of *detachment*; that the law should be justifiable to a detached spectator who is not committed to maintaining some set of perceived logical connections among legal doctrines. Once that notion is accepted, we have the groundwork set for all instrumentalist theories of law.

Now let's move back up to Bentham, in whose work we see a purposive and goal-oriented marriage of instrumentalism and utilitarianism, and consider the development of law and economics from this point. After Bentham, roughly 100 years passed before Holmes wrote *The Common Law*, presenting a utilitarian justification for the law. But there are big differences from Bentham's approach. Holmes backs away from the detachment of Hobbes and Bentham: he wants us to understand the law and its internal logic. Holmes backs away from the role of independent critic or censor. He sets out to justify the law as it is.

Calabresi's *Costs* (and Becker's 'Crime')

Following Holmes, we find another dry spell up to the roughly simultaneous publications of Calabresi's *Costs* and Becker's article on crime.[17] This 'dry spell' includes Ronald Coase's famous article on transaction costs. Coase's article delivers what has come to be known as the Coase Theorem; that is, if transaction costs are zero, the allocation of legal entitlements will not stand in the way of an efficient allocation of resources. The Coase Theorem justifiably has become a starting point for analysis in law and economics. Of course, this raises the question why I would locate Coase's article within a dry spell of the law and economics literature. The reason is that the Coase article lays out fundamental tools for economic analysis of law, but does not push a grand thesis about the nature of law – for example, whether it is efficient or socially optimal.[18] The tools provided by the Coase article have turned out to be enormously helpful to researchers. Indeed, the Coase article is the starting point of normal science law and economics. However, as is often the case in academic scholarship, important developments in scientific capital are overshadowed by work that pushes an ambitious thesis.

---

[17]   I refer to this period as a dry spell only because there does not appear to be anything as ambitious in scope as we see at the endpoints (Holmes on one end, Calabresi on the other). However, there were novel and important contributions to law and economics over this period. The best known is that of Ronald Coase; see Coase, *supra* note 6 (setting out the 'Coase Theorem', which holds that if transaction costs are low, individuals will bargain their way to an efficient arrangement, whatever the liability rule). While the Coase Theorem has become perhaps the key starting point for any economic analysis of law, I have not focused on it here because it is not associated with a broad school of thought in law and economics. Other important contributions are those of Aaron Director, probably the founder of 'Chicago School' antitrust analysis, and Ward Bowman. The institutional economics of John R. Commons is another important contribution.

[18]   Coase's discussion of nuisance indicates that he thought it was economically efficient, though he did not take the time to present a positive theory of nuisance law in the article. Coase suggested that the judges were balancing economic considerations appropriately in their decisions. In spite of this, Coase made no effort in his article to argue that common law was efficient or inefficient.

There are interesting similarities between Calabresi's *Costs* and Becker's 'Crime'. Both Becker and Calabresi step into the role of detachment, following the tradition of Hobbes and Bentham. Neither thinks it is important for his reader to understand the law from the perspective of a specialist in the common law. This is obviously natural for Becker, since he had no training as a lawyer. For Calabresi, Hobbesian detachment is a bit tougher to explain. After all, Calabresi had distinguished himself as one of the best trained lawyers of his generation. Yet, there we find him in *Costs*, proceeding as if the law were of secondary importance at best.

Indeed, one could describe the personality reflected in Calabresi's *Costs* as one of hyper-detachment. The book describes itself as a 'legal and economic analysis', which it most assuredly is. But Calabresi takes a position of detachment from both the law and the economics. He prefaces his economic remarks in several parts of the book with comments such as 'an economist would say',[19] to remind us that he does not necessarily agree with them. He tells us early on that economics is good for solving certain problems, but not all problems, especially those involving basic questions of identity or morality.[20] In spite of this, he conducts an economic analysis that appears to be on the highest level of sophistication that one could imagine for the topic at hand. And as Michelman noted in his review,[21] Calabresi shows a greater awareness of the machinery of law and government, and the limits of human rationality, than even the best economists would have brought to the task.

Calabresi's book and Becker's article are in the tradition of Bentham. Like Bentham, both Calabresi and Becker apply utilitarianism in an effort to promote sweeping reforms of vast areas of the law. In Calabresi's case, his ultimate goal is to replace the 'fault system' (or negligence regime) of tort law with one based on strict liability for injury-causing activities. Becker, on the other hand, aims to change the goal of criminal punishment from completely deterring criminal acts to internalizing costs to offenders. Both reforms are so ambitious that neither author seriously could have expected to see them implemented within his lifetime.

Also like Bentham, the reforms suggested by Calabresi and Becker would have the effect of undermining established law in their chosen research areas, to the point of making it irrelevant. Calabresi's approach is most clearly similar to Bentham's, as his reforms would have required abandoning the negligence rule and all of the complicated law that has grown out of it. Calabresi's approach would have replaced the core of tort doctrine with simpler, more direct, liability rules that, on a statistical basis, would have loaded liability on the most appropriate actors (the cheapest cost avoiders). Becker's approach would have resulted in a Bentham-like revolution in an indirect manner. By changing the system of penalties to ones based on cost-internalization, it would no longer be necessary under Becker's regime to know whether you had violated the law. If we could calculate the external costs of your actions accurately, we could impose those costs on you, and the law, whatever it says, would eventually wither away.

The skeptical view toward law, and specifically the claim that law could be simplified drastically or reduced to insignificance, is central to some of the best known normative theo-

---

[19]   See, for example, Calabresi, *supra* note 2, at 72 (discussing optimal pricing based on social cost).

[20]   Calabresi, *supra* note 2, at 18.

[21]   Frank I. Michelman, 'Pollution as a Tort: A Non-Accidental Perspective on Calabresi's *Costs*', 80 *Yale Law Journal* 647 (1971) (book review).

ries of government. Plato would make the law wither away by reorganizing society so that you could not tell whether a stranger was in fact your brother. Marx would make law wither away by removing the profit-incentive from our actions. The Pigovian approach reflected in Becker and Calabresi would make law wither away by internalizing external costs to the source. Each of these grand theories fails, in some degree, to take into account the problem of rent-seeking. Removing the law as an independent constraint on government action makes it easier for interest groups to use government as a path toward wealth or privilege. Perhaps this explains why the most successful grand theory of legal skepticism, that of Marx, has had tragic consequences.

Admittedly, a reference to Marx, even one as oblique as the preceding one, is an excessive and heavy-handed way of pointing to the downside of grand thesis-driven scholarship. Moreover, it distracts attention away from the important contributions to scientific capital in Calabresi's *Costs*, some of which will be explored later in this essay. One important contribution that should be noted here is Calabresi's analysis of the incentives effects of strict liability and negligence. The notion that strict liability differs from negligence largely in its impact on entry, exit, scope, and scale decisions – decisions that we refer to as *activity level* decisions – appears to have been first explored by Calabresi. This is a basic distinction in the analysis of incentives in law and economics.

Posner's book and the Calabresi-Melamed article

The next major developments following Calabresi's book and Becker's article were the near simultaneous publications of the first edition of Richard Posner's *Economic Analysis of Law* and the Calabresi-Melamed article on property rules.[22] Since Posner's book had a greater immediate impact, I will focus on it first.

Just as Holmes bought into utilitarianism but rejected the reform efforts of Bentham, Posner bought into economic analysis and rejected the reform efforts of Calabresi and Becker. Like Holmes, Posner defended the law as it is. However, Posner is much more explicit in his adoption of economic theory than Holmes. Posner claims that the common law aims to maximize wealth, which is distinguishable from utilitarianism, largely in the sense that wealth maximization makes no effort to take into account differences in individual preferences, except in so far as those differences are expressed in the market through prices. Wealth maximization, as an objective, yields a result that is probably identical to that of Adam Smith's impartial spectator, who also made no effort to take into account differences in individual preferences when he decided whether some allocation was appropriate. Holmes, on the other hand, was writing at a stage when there was far less scientific capital to use in his own work, and speaking to a somewhat different audience. In addition, he appears to be more of a utilitarian, and more Hobbesian, in the sense that he believes that laws must be 'living and armed',[23] or backed up by the preferences of a forceful group.

The Calabresi–Melamed article has to some extent suffered the same fate as Coase's article on transaction costs. Both articles are foundational pieces of normal-science law and economics. Like Coase's article, the Calabresi–Melamed article provides a set of tools that

---

[22]   Posner, Richard, *Economic Analysis of Law* (Boston: Little Brown & Company, 1972). Calabresi and Melamed, *supra* note 3.

[23]   Hobbes, *supra* note 16, at 59 (Hobbes makes the point in his dialogue that real laws are 'living and armed' and therefore distinguishable from the laws of 'reason' promoted by the philosopher).

are enormously helpful to law and economics researchers. But important advances in scientific capital are often overshadowed by scholarship that makes ambitious claims.

The Calabresi–Melamed article argues that legal rules can be classified as property rules, liability rules, or inalienability rules. The first two categories turn out to be much more important than the last. Property rules enable those protected by them to enjoin threatened invasions of their interests and to seek compensation for invasions that occur. Liability rules enable those protected to seek compensation only. The property versus liability rule distinction is at the core of understanding the rationales for compensatory and punitive damages, and for trespass and negligence law.[24] The distinction is also key to understanding the boundary between tort law and criminal law: Posner's article on the economics of criminal law, which identifies market-bypassing as a core rationale for criminal prohibitions, is essentially a derivative work based on Calabresi-Melamed.[25]

Calabresi and Melamed build directly on Coase's contribution by pointing to the existence of transaction costs as a key determinant of legal rules. While the Coase Theorem shows us that the law does not matter when transaction costs are zero, the Calabresi-Melamed framework shows us how the law responds to transaction costs. It is a sparse, general model that explains vast areas of the common law. Sparsity is a desirable trait in a model because it constrains the author from attempting to include all sorts of ad hoc components to immunize the model against failure. As ad hoc immunizing components are added to a model, it eventually ceases being a model and becomes a journalistic description of the events the author is attempting to explain. In spite of its simplicity, the Calabresi-Melamed framework is virtually unmatched in its explanatory power by any other positive theory of common law rules.

The Calabresi-Melamed analysis runs as follows. Property rules are generally preferable to liability rules because they protect both subjective and objective components of valuation against expropriation. Liability rules are used instead of property rules largely because high transaction costs make it infeasible to have property rules as a barrier against every threatened invasion of an interest protected by the law (that is, an entitlement). The prohibitory function of property rules is also preferable, as Calabresi-Melamed suggest late in their article, when individuals engage in activities that are always socially undesirable in the sense that the gain to the offender is considerably less than the harm to the victim.

Property rules are desirable in low transaction cost settings and liability rules are desirable in high transaction cost settings. Since property rules prevent takings, they force actors who desire some entitlement of another person to use the market – that is, to bargain – for possession of the entitlement rather than take it. This ensures that transfers that take place in low transaction cost settings will be efficient in the sense that the valuation attached to the entitlement by the acquiring party exceeds that of the transferring party. In the case of a socially undesirable activity, property rules are preferable because the activity is one that reduces social wealth no matter the scale at which is carried out. For example, playing with a live hand grenade in a crowded area is an activity that reduces social wealth in any objective assessment. To such an activity a property rule should be applied because it prohibits the

---

24   Keith N. Hylton, 'Property Rules and Liability Rules, Once Again', *Review of Law and Economics*, Article 1 (2006).
25   Richard A. Posner, 'An Economic Theory of the Criminal Law', 85 *Columbia Law Review* 1194 (1985). For discussion of the link between Posner's article and Calabresi and Melamed, see Hylton, 'Property Rules', *supra* note 24.

activity altogether rather than simply attempting to internalize the harms suffered by victims to the actor.

Obviously, the claim about socially undesirable activities generates the response that a property rule may not be desirable in that setting because a particular actor may experience nearly infinite utility from engaging in an activity that harms thousands of people at one time. This is an old complaint that law and economic theorists through several generations have attempted to dismiss through various devices. Adam Smith used the concept of the impartial spectator to set aside any concern for the interests of utility monsters. Bentham had no patience for the utility monster proponents and asserted that utility is essentially equivalent to wealth. Posner has adopted wealth maximization as the objective of the law. Each of these devices reflects a sense that legal rules have to be based on statistical averages to some extent, and not on some rare, unusual, and unobserved exceptional case.

These devices for dismissing utility monsters may fall short of theoretical persuasiveness, but they are a necessary part of the positive law and economics enterprise – and a large part of normal science in law and economics consists of positive analysis. A theoretically persuasive dismissal of utility monsters may be beyond our reach. As in the cases of fairies and elves, we have no way of disproving their existence. Still, critics of positive law and economics would offer this as a major flaw. But positive law and economics has to explain the law and legal institutions, and the incentives they create and respond to. Its success should be measured by this criterion, not by whether the theory is capable of accounting for some possibly non-existent creature. In other words, positive law and economics is a work horse that should not be judged according to its shape or beauty; it should be judged according to how well it performs its task. While it is the habit of philosophically minded law professors to criticize law and economics for failing to display theoretical perfection, this is a lot like criticizing a work horse for failing to display some aesthetically desired level of muscular symmetry.

Perhaps it was because of the looming utility-monster (or inter-personal comparison of utility) critique that the Calabresi-Melamed article shows such reticence in asserting the argument for using property rules when conduct is always socially undesirable. The argument, as I noted earlier, appears late in their article, and much of it is buried in footnotes.

The Calabresi-Melamed article provides a simple explanation for the basic distinction in the law between trespass and negligence liability. Trespass law, understood broadly to incorporate all of the claims that would have been asserted under the common law writ of trespass (for example, trespass to real property, assault and battery), is a category of laws which operate as property rules. Moreover, trespass law is observed in low transaction cost settings: for example, adjacent landowners. Negligence law, on the other hand, operates under the liability rule model. It is typically observed in high transaction costs settings, such as accidents on the roads or on the seas.

The property versus liability rule framework of Calabresi-Melamed is a powerful device for evaluating the social desirability of remedial or punishment schemes, as well as providing the core rationale for the differences between tort and criminal law. Both the Coase article and the Calabresi-Melamed article are highly cited and are recognized as fundamental building blocks of law and economics today. Still, neither article offers a grand thesis about the shape or direction of the law. For that reason each has had less influence, in comparison to grand thesis-driven contributions such as Posner's book, on the directions taken by follow-on researchers. The articles have influenced the practice of normal science of scholarship, to be sure. But I do not think they have had a big impact on the direction which researchers have chosen.

Perhaps reflecting the underappreciated status of the Calabresi-Melamed article, a series of articles employing asymmetric information models published in the 1990s questioned the basic propositions of the Calabresi-Melamed model.[26] On a closer read, these articles appear to be reconcilable with the Calabresi-Melamed framework, and do not contradict it.[27] The asymmetric information models illustrate the relatively underdeveloped state of the literature on transaction costs. They suggest that a three-part distinction of high, low, and intermediate transaction cost settings would provide a better model of property and liability rule categories.[28]

Since the purpose of this essay is to examine the contributions of Calabresi to law and economics, I will not continue to go forward tracing the general development of law and economics. I have said enough here in my effort to locate Calabresi's work within the broad current of thought in law and economics. I will turn now to consider some of the tensions between different approaches in law and economics and how Calabresi's work has affected these approaches.

Positive versus normative law and economics

Students of economics are familiar with the distinction between *positive economics* and *normative economics*. Positive economics seeks to explain institutions or conventions that exist. Normative economics seeks to tell us how institutions or conventions should be designed. The same distinction applies to law and economics. Positive law and economics seeks to explain the law, or the legal system, as it is. Normative law and economics seeks to describe how the law or the legal system should be.

Calabresi's two major works are foundational studies in both the normative and positive economic analysis of law. The building blocks provided in Calabresi-Melamed are likely to be used long after *Costs* has receded into the background. In the long run, the Calabresi-Melamed article may turn out to be the most influential of Calabresi's writings. Still, for the present, *Costs* is the work that most clearly defines Calabresi's contributions, and especially to the tension between positive and normative analysis. I will start with a focus on the influence of *Costs* on the positive versus normative divide in law and economics.

Costs, with its criticism of the negligence regime and argument that it should be replaced by simpler rules based on strict liability, is clearly in the normative category. Calabresi's approach puts him firmly in the camp of Bentham, who wanted to scrap the common law, and replace it with a simpler set of rules that would be easier to follow and lead to more predictable outcomes. Indeed, normative law and economics begins more or less with Bentham, and then has its next most significant advance in Calabresi's *Costs*. Probably the majority of modern articles on law and economics are normative analyses, especially among the pieces based on mathematical modeling.[29]

---

[26]   Louis Kaplow and Steven Shavell, 'Property Rules versus Liability Rules: An Economic Analysis' 109 (4) *Harvard Law Review* 713–90 (1996). Ian Ayres and Eric Talley. 'Solomonic bargaining: Dividing an Entitlement to Facilitate Coasean Trade', 104 *Yale Law Journal*, (1995).

[27]   Hylton, 'Property Rules', *supra* note 24.

[28]   Ibid.

[29]   See, for example, A. Mitchell Polinsky and Steven Shavell, 'Punitive Damages: An Economic Analysis', 111 *Harvard Law Review* 869 (1998); Keith N. Hylton, 'Welfare Implications of Costly Litigation under Strict Liability', 4 *American Law and Economic Review* 18 (2002). I describe these papers as 'normative' because they set out mathematical models of optimal legal regimes without attempting to use those models to provide a justification for existing legal doctrine in the areas examined.

Positive law and economics, on the other hand, arguably begins with Adam Smith's lectures, though they appear to have had no clear influence on anyone. Although one can find instances in which scholars have rediscovered points discussed in Smith – for example, the notion that an efficient system would impose higher penalties when the probability of detection is low; or the notion, stressed by Holmes, that the criminal law has its roots in vengeance – it is quite difficult to find citations to Smith's lectures. The next step along the positive path, roughly 100 years after Smith, is Holmes's *The Common Law*. That is followed, again after another 100 years, by Posner's *Economic Analysis of Law*. Today, positive economic analysis of law continues to be published, though it seems to be less attractive to scholars than normative analysis.

A normative economic analysis typically begins with the derivation and specification of an objective function, which the analyst then argues is optimized by his particular policy prescription. In Calabresi's analysis, he describes the objective function as the sum of the injury and avoidance costs associated with accidents (primary costs), risk-spreading costs (secondary costs), and administrative costs (tertiary costs).[30] This description of the tort system's objective is now the standard approach to evaluating the operational efficiency of the tort system. The core of Calabresi's argument for reform is that a system of strict liability rules, directed at the appropriate activities, comes much closer to minimizing the sum of primary, secondary, and tertiary costs than does the fault system.

In view of the greater popularity of normative law and economics among today's scholars, Calabresi's *Costs* has to be considered a success in terms of inspiring the work of generations that followed. In addition to the inspiration provided by Calabresi, the reasons for this success are several. First, normative law and economics does not require a huge investment in learning the details of legal doctrine. Thus, a normative scholar should find it easier to work across disciplines and to gain the interest of scholars in other disciplines. Second, given the view in most law faculties that economics is a conservative mode of thought, normative work may appear especially attractive to law professors who do not specialize in economics (that is, the majority of law professors) and to law students as well.

The question lurking beneath this is whether the relative advantage enjoyed by normative law and economics is a desirable result. Is it a good thing for legal scholarship, or scholarship in general, that the Bentham-Calabresi line of law and economics scholarship is now more popular than the Smith-Holmes-Posner line?

I think there is a case to be made that it is not a good thing, and that law and economics scholarship and legal scholarship generally will suffer in the long term as a result. The case begins with the view espoused by Karl Popper and Milton Friedman on the relative value of positive analysis in economics.[31] The Popper-Friedman argument is that economic analysis is most valuable when it is helping us solve existing puzzles, to understand institutions or conventions that exist, and less valuable when used to design new institutions.

The argument behind the Popper-Friedman position is as follows. When we approach complicated social institutions or conventions, like the law, we are looking at a system that has evolved over time, and has along the way adapted to constraints and solved problems. The

---

[30]   Calabresi, *supra* note 2, at 26–9.
[31]   Karl R. Popper, *The Open Society and its Enemies*, vol. 2, p. 95 (Princeton: Princeton University Press, 1966); Milton Friedman, *Essays in Positive Economics* 5 (Chicago: University of Chicago Press, 1953).

analyst often cannot easily discover the information that is embodied within the system's design. Economic analysis, however, can be quite useful in this discovery process. In a similar fashion, normative analysis that attempts to redesign a social system from scratch – for example, redesigning the law of torts – is at a disadvantage for the same reason; the analyst may not understand all of the information embodied in the existing system.

This argument applies to economic analysis of law. Indeed, the argument applies most strongly here, if it applies anywhere. If there is any validity at all to the Popper-Friedman view, that validity must surely be observed in the case of the legal system, and particularly the common law. The common law is a system that has evolved – a 'grown order' in Hayek's terms[32] – responding at various times to constraints that may no longer be obvious. With such systems, the analyst with a reformist agenda should show some humility.

Humility and self-doubt are very much on display in Calabresi's *Costs*. Still, even when doubts are expressed openly, there is no getting around the problem of uncertainty and limited knowledge. The normative law and economics approach, from Bentham to Calabresi to modern analysts, reflects at bottom an arrogant belief in the power of theory to provide useful policies for reforming complicated institutions. And law certainly qualifies as a complicated social institution. This may seem to be a harsh assessment. However, what should one say about the implicit assumption underlying a substantial part of the normative project, when an analyst claims to have found a reform that solves a complicated systemic problem that has bedeviled countless individuals participating in the system for many years, many of whom are quite as thoughtful as the normative analyst?

The common law is full of puzzles in the form of doctrines whose functions are generally not understood. Economic analysis of law, at least to the Popper-Friedman sympathizers, serves its most useful purpose when it is helping us solve those puzzles. If positive analysis is useful in discovering the information hidden in a social institution, such as the law, then it would appear reasonable to ask law and economics analysts to try to uncover that information before proposing grand legislative reforms of the common law.

Calabresi and positive law and economics

As I said at the outset, law and economics scholarship can be divided into grand thesis and normal science branches, and Calabresi's influence on both has been enormous. *Costs* is largely a normative project, but it also offers important insights for positive law and economics as well. The Calabresi-Melamed article is a strictly positive project.

The grand thesis of *Costs* overshadowed both its contributions to normal science and the contributions of the Calabresi-Melamed article. But I think in the long run, the contributions to positive law and economics will have the greatest impact on future research. The two contributions I will focus on here are the activity versus care-level distinction explored in *Costs* and the property versus liability rule framework of Calabresi-Melamed.

Activity versus care levels

It has now become commonplace for law and economics scholars, especially within the field of torts, to distinguish care and activity-level effects of liability. The care-level effect of

---

[32]   F.A. Hayek, *Law, Legislation, and Liberty: Rules and Order* 35–54 (Chicago: University of Chicago Press, 1973); Hayek, *The Constitution of Liberty* 160 (Chicago: University of Chicago Press, 1960) (using the term 'spontaneous order').

liability is the effect on an actor's instantaneous level of precaution. For example, if an actor drives more carefully because of the threat of liability under the negligence rule, then one could say that liability has caused the actor to increase his level of care. The activity-level effect refers to the frequency with which an actor engages in some conduct that might give rise to liability. For example, if the threat of liability causes an actor to drive less frequently, then one could say that liability has caused the actor to reduce his activity level.

The distinction between care and activity-level effects has become central to the analysis of strict liability and negligence. Shavell's article on strict liability was the first to formally analyze the effects of strict liability and negligence on care and activity levels.[33] However, the idea that strict liability differs from negligence because of its activity level effects appears to have been introduced, or first explored at length, in Calabresi's *Costs*.[34]

As I said earlier, before Calabresi's *Costs* one would have to go back to Holmes's *The Common Law* to find an analysis of tort law of comparable sophistication. However, Holmes devoted little attention to the analysis of strict liability. Although Holmes provided a largely utilitarian defense of the common law of torts (and other subjects as well), he appeared to be reluctant to offer a detailed defense of the law on strict liability. His chapters on tort law focus on trespass, negligence, and intentional torts such as fraud. Holmes's discussion of *Rylands v. Fletcher* is limited to less than two pages,[35] though what he has to say is largely consistent with modern economic analyses of strict liability.

The distinction between activity and care levels introduced in Calabresi played a substantial, though sometimes overlooked, role in the development of the positive economic theory of torts. First, the distinction was a part of Posner's economic defense of the negligence system.[36] Posner argued that since the negligence rule is sufficient to bring about reasonable care, strict liability would operate primarily as a tax on activity. Second, the distinction between activity and care levels has provided the foundation for a positive theory of strict liability doctrine.

Holmes noted in *The Common Law* that the strict liability principle varies in 'different jurisdictions, as the balance varies between the advantages to the public and the dangers to individuals from the conduct in question'.[37] This insight can be translated into economic terms. Every activity will carry with it external costs and external benefits, and the balance of those externalities will depend on the jurisdiction. Storing large quantities of water externalizes risk to adjacent landowners, but the same activity may externalize substantial benefits in areas where water storage is crucial for the survival of industry.[38] Given that people will take reasonable care under both negligence and strict liability, the path to understanding strict liability doctrine can be found by analyzing the balance of external costs and external benefits connected to activities.[39] Where the external costs (of an activity) substantially exceed the

---

[33]   Steven Shavell, 'Strict Liability versus Negligence', 9 *Journal of Legal Studies* 1 (1980).

[34]   And Calabresi's arguments in *Costs* were based on arguments set out in his article on risk distribution and torts, *supra* note 8.

[35]   Holmes, *supra* note 5, at 156–7.

[36]   Richard Posner, 'A Theory of Negligence', 1 *Journal of Legal Studies* 29 (1972).

[37]   Holmes, *supra* note 5, at 156.

[38]   *Turner v. Big Lake Oil*, 96 SW2d 221 (1936).

[39]   Keith N. Hylton, 'A Missing Markets Theory of Tort Law', 90 *North Western University Law Review* 977 (1996).

external benefits, the law will impose strict liability.[40] Where external costs are less than or roughly in balance with external benefits, the negligence rule will be observed.

Property rules versus liability rules

The Calabresi-Melamed article contributes greatly to the resolution of many puzzles in the common law. Indeed, in spite of the many years since its publication, not all of the useful insights have been mined out of it.

Of course, an impressive list of insights into the common law have already been mined out of Calabresi-Melamed. I have already mentioned the functional distinction between trespass and negligence doctrine, which is explained by the Calabresi-Melamed model.

Another important distinction explained by Calabresi-Melamed is the tort–criminal law boundary. Posner's economic theory of criminal law is essentially a spin-off of the Calabresi-Melamed article. Posner rejects Becker's internalization goal and argues that criminal law should aim for complete deterrence by removing gains from criminal activity. His explanation boils down to the argument that the core common law crimes are versions of takings that occur in low transaction cost settings – instances of bypassing the market. The crimes that do not fit in this category involve types of conduct that are socially inefficient at all times. Given this, internalization is not the appropriate goal of the criminal law. This is an argument that follows directly from Calabresi-Melamed, and is more or less stated in the footnotes and text toward the end of the article. It is a fundamental insight into criminal and tort doctrines.

I have suggested elsewhere that the Calabresi-Melamed framework is useful in gaining a sense of the meaning of criminal intent.[41] Criminal prohibitions cover categories of conduct involving takings in low transaction cost settings and socially undesirable activity. Criminal intent is a doctrine that serves to distinguish these categories from others in which tort doctrine alone applies. Criminal intent exists when the actor attempts to *take* something from or *impose* a cost on the victim in a setting in which the actor easily could have gained consent; and when the actor engages in activity that indicates *indifference* to the welfare of others. When the objective evidence of the defendant's conduct is consistent with either of these objectives, the law says that the defendant had the requisite criminal intent.

The Calabresi-Melamed analysis forms the groundwork of an objective theory of criminal intent. Much of the work in formulating a positive theory of criminal intent is found in explaining how courts can infer criminal intent from the defendant's words and conduct. Holmes gave considerable attention to this question in his chapter on criminal law in *The Common Law*. A modern effort to explain criminal intent doctrine, from an objectivist perspective, would combine Holmes's observations on inference with the Calabresi-Melamed framework. It is unfortunate that most modern criminal law scholarship on intent today is from the subjectivist school, which has poor prospects of ever developing a positive theory of criminal law.

Merrill's analysis of nuisance law is derived largely from Calabresi-Melamed. Merrill argues that nuisance is a hybrid setting in which the parties can engage in bargaining ex ante, as in the typical low-trespass trespass scenario, but that the cost of evaluating the entitlements

---

[40]   Id.

[41]   Keith N. Hylton, 'The Theory of Penalties and the Economics of Criminal Law', 1 (2) *Review of Law and Economics*, Article 1 (2005).

is too high to make bargaining convenient. Given this, nuisance law adopts a mixture of property and liability rules.

Merrill's model of nuisance law can be used to illustrate the usefulness of a more careful division of transaction cost regimes. Nuisance law does not fit easily into the Calabresi-Melamed framework at first sight. Nuisance is a hybrid property-liability rule regime in the sense that courts sometimes award injunctions and at other times only award damages. At first this may seem jarring because nuisance often occur in the context of adjacent landowners. Adjacent landowners should be able to bargain easily. This raises the question why nuisances are not treated the same as trespasses.

The key reason nuisances are not treated the same as trespasses, identified by Merrill, is that nuisances are actually high transaction cost settings. The relevant property right at stake in a nuisance dispute is often something hard to define, such as clean air or freedom from noise. Although adjacent landowners may be face-to-face on a daily basis, it might be quite difficult for them to negotiate the terms of some agreement on the level of clean air that one owner is entitled to. In view of this, typical nuisances such as air pollution should be viewed as high transaction cost situations. Under the Calabresi-Melamed analysis, the liability rule is preferable to the property rule.

It should be clear from Merrill's analysis that transaction costs are a bit more complicated than the high versus low distinction suggests. One can distinguish transaction costs into the costs of meeting ex ante (before the accident) and the costs of reaching an agreement. Transactions costs are clearly high or prohibitive where the cost of meeting is extremely high. That is often true of accidents on the roads or on the seas. But as Merrill's nuisance example illustrates, there are settings in which the cost of meeting is low and the cost of reaching agreement is high. In these settings, one finds hybrid regimes in which property rules and liability rules are both observed. Calabresi and Melamed suggest that eminent domain should be treated as a hybrid regime.

The theory of damages is another category of scholarship that leans heavily on the Calabresi-Melamed framework.[42] Property rules should be observed in settings in which transaction costs are low or the underlying activity is socially undesirable. But if property rules fail to completely prohibit the conduct of the actor in these settings, damages have to be set at a level that carries out the function of the property rules.

How should damages be set in order to carry out the function of property rules? At a minimum, the damages should eliminate any gain experienced by the actor. Since property rules protect subjective evaluations, it would also be desirable that the damages serve that function too by compensating for both objective and subjective losses. However, since no measure exists for subjective damages, it appears that the primary goal should be to eliminate any prospect of gain on the part of the actor.

This theory implies that punitive damages should be observed in cases involving takings (in low transaction cost settings) and activities that are always socially undesirable. Moreover, it implies that punitive damages should be designed to ensure that the actor enjoys no gain from his activity. This theory, which has its roots in Calabresi and Melamed, provides a better positive account of the punitive damages case law than alternative theories, such as the internalization theory of Polinsky and Shavell.[43]

---

[42] Hylton, 'Property Rules', *supra* note 24.
[43] Polinsky and Shavell, *supra* note 29.

For example, suppose the actor wants to use his neighbor's garage in order to shelter his car from the weather. The actor has an expensive car; he is willing to pay $100 a day for the garage. The neighbor loses only $1 a day by not having access to his garage. Suppose the actor 'takes' the garage – simply parks his car in the neighbor's garage without seeking permission. Under the property rule framework, this is a taking in a low transaction cost setting. The proper damage amount would eliminate any gain on the part of the taker. That implies a damage award that is equivalent to $100, at a minimum, for each day that the actor uses his neighbor's garage. In terms of actual damages awarded at trial, this suggests that a court should award the neighbor $1 in compensatory damages (for each day), and a minimum of $99 in punitive damages (for each day). The internalization approach urged by Polinsky and Shavell would result in a damage award of $1 (for each day).

The number of possible applications of the property rules framework is large, and I have touched on just a few of the best known here. Wachter and Cohen applied the framework to labor law.[44] Its application to constitutional law has recently been explored by Eugene Kontorovich.[45]

Calabresi and rationality in law and economics
The next topic I will consider is the role played by the rationality assumption in law and economics and Calabresi's influence on that role. I will return to a focus on Calabresi's *Costs*, which deals at some length with the rationality issue.

A brief overview of rationality in the law and economics literature
Law and economics is often criticized, especially in the law journals, for adhering too strongly to the rational actor model. Critics have argued that people do not always behave as rational actors, that they do not carefully and accurately weigh the costs and benefits of their anticipated actions.

The critique of rationality in law and economics is difficult to assess and may collapse into triviality. The process of natural selection should make some responses to external events strong enough to overwhelm our attempts to calculate, and yet these inborn tendencies do not prove that man is never a rational actor. Alternatively, someone may calculate the immediate costs and benefits of a particular action carefully, and then after realizing that it would be costly to reveal to others that he had done so, lie about his motives or take an irrational act. By his words, or perhaps by his actions, he would not appear to be rational. Finally, some minimal degree of rationality must be accepted even by critics of the rationality assumption. For if actors are completely or always irrational, laws are pointless.

In any event, the rational actor assumption that critics have in mind is one of an individual who *always* weighs the costs and benefits of his anticipated actions, and always takes the act with the greatest net benefit (benefit in excess of cost). The rational actor fails to take care when the cost of taking care is greater than the benefits he captures, or the liability he avoids, through care. The rational actor breaches a contract whenever the benefit from breaching

---

[44]   Michael L. Wachter and George M. Cohen, 'The Law and Economics of Collective Bargaining: An Introduction and Application to the Problems of Subcontracting, Partial Closure, and Relocation', 136 *University of Pennsylvania Law Review* 1349, 1353 (1988).
[45]   Eugene Kontorovich, 'The Constitution in Two Dimensions: A Transaction Cost Analysis of Constitutional Remedies', 91 *Virginia Law Review* (2005).

exceeds the cost. The rational actor commits a crime whenever the benefit from the criminal act exceeds the expected penalty. These benefits and costs are typically reduced to dollars so that the rational man can make an apples-to-apples comparison.[46]

This version of the rational man actor is a relatively recent feature of the law and economics literature. Bentham held to a version of the rational actor assumption. He argued that all men calculate, even the insane. However, Bentham made some allowance for departures from the extreme or strong rationality assumption. His suggestions for outrageous punishments imply a belief that criminals often did not attempt to foresee and calculate the consequences of their actions, and so it was necessary to design penalties that would attract their attention.[47] For example, suppose the typical prospective rapist does not rationally convert his expected hedonic gains and anticipated punishment into a common denominator, such as dollars. He might find these different expectations incommensurable, and given this inability to convert gains and losses into the same terms, may discount the losses from punishment entirely.[48] A punishment such as castration, which has the flavor of Bentham, might be superior in its deterrent effect because the prospective rapist finds it easier to evaluate the punishment in precisely the same terms as he evaluates his hedonic gains.

Given his utilitarian approach, Holmes must have believed that men were rational and would respond rationally to penalties. However, Holmes did not have a clear need to assume a strong form of rationality. He was concerned with explaining the logic of the law, not with analyzing its deterrent impact.

Becker and Calabresi represent a fork in the road in the development of the rationality assumption in the law and economics literature. Becker presents a model in which criminals are rational actors. It makes sense in Becker's model, to reduce the probability of capture to near zero and increase the fine to near infinity, because this maintains a high expected penalty and at the same time saves the state the costs of frequent enforcement efforts. This is the sort of prescription that could only come from a model that assumes a strong form of rationality. Studies of behavior and psychology – for example, those of B.F. Skinner[49] – suggest, contrary to Becker's model of deterrence, that people learn best through frequent rewards or penalties in connection with desired or undesired acts.

---

46   This description of the rational actor suggests that what is really special about the assumption is that it places severe restrictions on the actor's utility function. One could imagine an individual who enjoys breaching contracts. His utility function should take into account his taste for breach. Given those preferences, one could say that his tendency to always breach, even in cases where the net monetary payoff is negative, is rational. But the rational actor model excludes such cases. This is a basic definitional issue that runs throughout this chapter's discussion of rationality, and the rationality debate in law and economics generally.

47   For Bentham's suggested punishments, see Jeremy Bentham, *The Rationale of Punishment*, Book 1, chapter 8, section 3, 60–61 ('punishment of "offending member"'); Book 2, chapter II, sections 1–3, 76–93 (deformation and mutilation as possible punishments) (London: Robert Heward, 1830).

48   Bentham said that in order to encourage the potential offender to take his prospective penalty into account before committing an offense, a punishment should have some 'characteristic' relating it to the offense. See Jeremy Bentham, *The Principles of Morals and Legislation* 192 (Amherst: Prometheus Books, 1988) (1781) ('Punishment cannot act any farther than in as far as the idea of it, and of its connection with the offence, is present in the mind. The idea of it, if not present, cannot act at all ... Now, to be present, it must be remembered, and to be remembered it must have been learnt ... When this is the case with a punishment and an offence, the punishment is said to bear an *analogy* to, or to be *characteristic* of, the offence.)'

49   B.F. Skinner, *Science and Human Behavior* (New York: The Free Press, 1953).

Calabresi, on the other hand, allows for less than perfect rationality and the need for the state to act paternalistically at times. In particular, Calabresi describes four important deviations from the strong form of rationality.[50] First, people may not have enough information to make rational decisions. Second, even if given sufficient information, they may suffer from an optimism bias – a belief that bad things will happen only to other people. Third, they may be judgment proof, so that an increase in the amount of liability in excess of their assets has no marginal effect on their incentives for care. Fourth, and most interesting, Calabresi argues that people are likely to do poorly in comparing short-term benefits and long-term costs – a problem he describes in terms of the Faustian bargain. Part of the problem may be free-riding, or a version of the familiar Prisoner's Dilemma. Knowing that society will not want to see me suffer in my old age, I may not save today, expecting society to help me out when I reach poverty in my later years. This is perfectly rational behavior at an individual level, but irrational on an aggregate level. Another part of the problem is time-inconsistency in preferences. Looking at his overall preferences, Ulysses knows that he should pay no attention to the Sirens. However, at the point at which he hears their song, he can only see clearly the part of his preference map directly in front of him. Because our preferences are dependent upon the perspective from which we view them, we may rationally choose to take actions in the short run that are welfare-reducing in the long run.

To be sure, both Becker and Calabresi assumed that men are rational. The difference between their approaches is in the degree of rationality posited. Becker assumes rationality in its strongest form. His argument that deterrence could be maintained under a program that reduces the frequency of punishment while increasing its severity assumed a degree of rationality that had never received support from behavioral studies in the social sciences. Famous studies by Skinner and others that long predated Becker's paper suggested that people do not behave as rationally as Becker's model assumed.[51] Calabresi, in contrast, assumes a weak form of rationality; that actors are basically rational subject to some pretty consistent deviations.

From this fork in the road, with Becker adopting strong-form rationality and Calabresi a weak form, the law and economics literature seems to have taken Becker's path. Posner, whose name is virtually synonymous with the Chicago School, adhered to Becker's approach to rationality, and the strong rationality assumption has since become a defining characteristic of Chicago-School Law and Economics.

It should be clear that things did not need to go this way. There is nothing special about the strong-form rationality assumption that makes it a necessary feature of the economic analysis of law. The scholars, largely Chicago-School, who immediately followed Becker and Calabresi could have chosen to follow Calabresi's example rather than Becker's. If that path had been followed, there would be far less criticism of law and economics. The behavioral law and economics school, still in its infancy, would have been old by now.

It should also be clear that Calabresi's description of weak rationality anticipated the behavioral law and economics school by a generation. The behavioral school has identified an expanding list of deviations from strong-form rationality: over-optimism,[52] framing

---

[50]   Calabresi, *supra* note 2, at 55–60.

[51]   For example, Skinner, *supra* note 49; C.B. Ferster and B.F. Skinner, *Schedules of Reinforcement* (New York: Appleton-Century-Crofts, 1957).

[52]   See, for example, Linda Babcock and George Loewenstein, 'Explaining Bargaining Impasse: The Role of Self-Serving Biases', 11 *Journal of Economic Perspectives* 109–26 (1997).

effects,[53] endowment effects,[54] ignorance of base-line probabilities,[55] and others.[56] The behavioral literature has expanded, in terms of scientific capital, far beyond where it stood when Calabresi wrote *Costs*, with Daniel Kahneman and Amos Tversky providing a significant part of that expansion.[57] Still, in the end, it appears that the behavioral school's message leaves us in the same position as where Calabresi had started, viewing men as weakly rational – that is, rational, subject to some pretty consistent deviations.

Calabresi's analysis shows that the behavioralist position is not a critique of a deep flaw in law and economics. It is a reaction to a particular strong-form version of rationality that emerged with Becker and the Chicago School. Economic analysis of law can easily incorporate the behavioralist position, as we observe in *Costs*. The question is whether it would be desirable, as a general matter, to incorporate the behavioralist view in economic analysis of law.

This is partly an empirical question. Given my bias toward the Popper-Friedman view, I would ask whether incorporation of the behavioralists' results improves the ability of economics to either explain the law or predict its effects. I do not think that there are great stakes connected to this issue. It is not a big question about methodology. It is a small question about how quickly the law-and-economics analyst should reach for Occam's razor.

The other perspective on the question whether behavioral analysis promises a substantial methodological change in law and economics starts with asking *why* we see substantial deviations from strong-form rationality. The most plausible explanation is that evolution has shaped our responses to certain stimuli in ways that depart from the rationality model. The role of evolution has not received much attention in the behavioral law and economics literature, but this may be its area of greatest potential. An over-optimism bias, for example, may appear to be a departure from rationality on an individual level, yet it may be rational on an aggregate level because it imparts an evolutionary advantage.[58] Modifying the model of rationality to take into account the ways in which natural selection may have encouraged nonrational behavioral or thought tendencies could lead us to a better understanding of the social desirability of some legal constraints.

There is, of course, the broader question whether actors are largely rational or largely irrational. I have not dealt with it because it is not an issue between the rationalists and the

---

[53]   Jeffrey J. Rachlinski, 'Gains, Losses, and the Psychology of Litigation', 70 *Southern California Law Review* 113 (1996).

[54]   See, for example, Richard Thaler, *The Winner's Curse* 63 (Princeton: Princeton University Press, 1994).

[55]   Amos Tversky and Daniel Kahneman, 'Judgment Under Uncertainty: Heuristics and Biases', 185 *Science* 1124 (1974).

[56]   David Laibson, 'Golden Eggs and Hyperbolic Discounting', 112 *Quarterly Journal of Economics* 443–77 (1997) (hyperbolic discounting of future payoffs); Robert H. Frank, Thomas D. Gilovich, and Dennis T. Regan, 'Does Studying Economics Inhibit Cooperation?' 7 *Journal of Economic Perspectives* 159–71 (1993) (empirical study suggesting that studying economics makes you less likely to cooperate).

[57]   Daniel Kahneman and Amos Tversky, 'Prospect Theory: An Analysis of Decision Under Risk', 47 *Econometrica* 263 (1979); Tversky and Kahneman, *supra* note 49.

[58]   In a competitive environment, an optimism bias could be beneficial to one group that has to compete against another. Indeed, the inculcation of an optimism bias seems to be a central part of what coaches aim to do with their teams. The evolutionary explanation for an optimism bias may be similar to that for altruism.

behavioralists. Both sides buy into the assumption that men are largely rational. And as I noted before, if men are largely irrational, laws are pointless. Much of our lives are built around the assumption that people behave rationally. We assume that people will follow traffic patterns rather than simply choose their preferred direction on any road; that they will drive over bridges rather than jump off of them or blow them up. The difficulty with irrationality is that there are so many ways in which it can be expressed. If the number of irrational individuals within a society becomes sufficiently large, the level of public order and coordination necessary for a functioning society collapses.

Calabresi's influence on the rationality debate

The foregoing examination suggests some parameters on Calabresi's influence on the treatment of rationality in the law and economics literature. The influence could not possibly be great, because the different positions taken by responsible scholars on the question of rationality are not far apart. The behavioral school appears to accept the position that people are fundamentally rational. The arguments that exist are over the degree of rationality; whether it is a strong form of the sort implied in Becker's analysis of crime, or a weaker form of rationality. Moreover, in assessing influence, one has to put some weight on the time at which a scholar appears. Even if later scholars do not refer explicitly to an earlier scholar in their work, ideas set out earlier are still capable of having an influence on later scholarship.

With these parameters in mind, Calabresi deserves a considerable degree of credit, from the behavioral law and economics school, as the first prominent law and economics scholar to address the question of rationality in economic analysis of law, in a manner that allows for some departures from strong-form rationality. He appears to have lost out in the short term to the strong-form rationality posited in the writing of Becker and of Posner. However, the behavioral school has grown in importance and continues to grow as part of the law and economics literature. Many of the arguments of the behavioral school, as well as its practical message for law, were anticipated by Calabresi in *Costs*. In many respects, it would not be an exaggeration to say that the literature is catching up to the point at which Calabresi began.

In any event one should not exaggerate the importance of the rationality debate within law and economics. Calabresi took a position early on which appears to be where the literature has come to today. In the end the rationality issue is a question of the level of detail the analyst wants to build into his model. Still, it is hard to resist the conclusion that law and economics, as a field of research, would be better off today if it had followed the early example of Calabresi more closely on the rationality issue.

For example, the analysis of discrimination is one topic within law and economics that probably would have benefited from theorists incorporating weak-form rationality assumptions from the start. Adam Smith, puzzling over the question why slavery persisted in his day even though it seemed to be inefficient, suggested that it might be due to a not-entirely-rational and deeply-ingrained preference among humans to impose status hierarchies.[59] Although bargaining is rational and can lead to an efficient Coasean solution, most people prefer to give orders rather than bargain.[60] And the winners in a status hierarchy will often prefer to maintain the hierarchy rather than permit efficient arrangements to destroy it. Incorporating these

---

59   Adam Smith, *Lectures on Jurisprudence*, *supra* note 14, at 186.
60   Ibid.

weak-form rationality assumptions into the framework of law and economics would have improved its capacity to analyze discrimination and the laws responding to it.

I see no reason to believe that the weakly rational actor is less self-interested than the strongly rational actor. It is common in the legal academy for professors to criticize the rationality model on the ground that it ignores the internal sense people often feel of an obligation to comply with the law. This internal viewpoint is often contrasted with that of the rational man, who complies with the law only when the gain from compliance exceeds its cost. But if one chooses to dismiss the rational man model, then one must recognize that men may depart from strong-form rationality and yet still be self-interested. An actor who generally is moved by an internal sense of obligation to comply with the law may behave in a self-interested and socially destructive manner in a setting in which he does not think that the obligation applies.

Calabresi and positivism versus anti-positivism

The last topic I will consider is Calabresi's influence on positivism and anti-positivism in law and economics. The term *positivism*, to lawyers, refers to the view that the only laws that exist are those in the statute books or likely to be enforced by the state. An *anti-positivist* would argue that laws also include norms or conventions that people respect, even if they are not in a law book anywhere or the state is unlikely to enforce them. One version of anti-positivism is the classical common law theory of Blackstone, which views the law as resulting from the norms of 'reasonable conduct' adopted within society.[61]

There have been debates in the law between positivist and anti-positivist schools of thought for a long time, sometimes spilling into the case law. The most famous in American law is that between Holmes and Cardozo over the law of contributory negligence in railroad crossing accidents. Most law students are introduced in their first year to the famous Supreme Court cases *Baltimore and Ohio Railroad v. Goodman*[62] and *Pokora v. Wabash Railway*.[63] Holmes took the position in *Goodman* that a firm rule of contributory negligence must be set for all cases in which the plaintiff fails to stop, look, and listen at the crossing. Cardozo, later in *Pokora*, rejected this position and argued that law must always be flexible to facts and existing customs.

Hume is the first to bring the anti-positivist approach to the economic analysis of law.[64] Hume argued that we determine through long experience that certain acts are harmful to social welfare, and society develops norms discouraging those acts.[65] Over time, those norms become publicly asserted as law. Somewhat later, Hayek argued that the law evolves from norms that develop through social intercourse.[66] Bruno Leoni extended this line of reasoning to provide one of the early arguments for the economic efficiency of common law.[67]

Calabresi does not take a clear position on the positivism versus anti-positivism debate. However, because his approach is so similar to Bentham's, it is implicitly positivist. The most basic component of that approach is what I have referred to as detachment, the notion that one

---

61 Blackstone, *Commentaries*, *supra* note 10, vol. 1, 63–92.
62 *Baltimore and Ohio R.R. v. Goodman* 275 US 66 (1927).
63 *Pokora v. Wabash Ry.* 292 US 98 (1934).
64 Hume, *supra* note 15.
65 Ibid.
66 Hayek, *Law, Legislation, and Liberty*, *supra* note 32.
67 Bruno Leoni, *Freedom and the Law* 59–96 (Princeton, New Jersey: D. Van Nostrand, 1961).

does not feel a need to study or explain the law in great detail in order to evaluate it. While one can be detached in this sense, and not positivist, it seems to me that one must be a positivist if detached. The reason is that if the detached analyst does not need to explain or work through the legal doctrines carefully in order to reach an assessment of the law, he clearly will perceive no need to study norms as generators of legal doctrine. Hence, the detached analyst is never an anti-positivist. On the other hand, if the analyst is evaluating the law, he must have some minimal sense of what it consists of, which would seem to require a positivist's conception of law.

I doubt that any anti-positivist, or believer in norms as important sources of law, could ever be detached in the sense of Bentham and Calabresi. If you believe that norms are an important source – let's say, the most important source – of common law, then you probably also think that those norms develop over time through implicit contracts. It follows that you would see it as important to understand precisely how these norms meet the expectations of the parties. Consider the contract analogy. If you were looking at a contract between an employer and employee, would you evaluate the desirability of a specific contract term by analyzing its incentive effects, or by trying to determine if the term made sense in terms of the expectations of the parties? The anti-positivist position seems to rule out detachment because it requires a careful examination of common law doctrine.

Anti-positivism has not fared well in the law and economics literature. I suspect that the influence of Calabresi's *Costs* is one of the reasons anti-positivism has been in the shadows of law and economics. Neither Becker nor Calabresi made any references to Leoni, Hayek, or Hume in their contributions. Perhaps their examples had some influence on Posner, who does not discuss or even cite any of the anti-positivist literature that preceded his book. Modern generations of scholars, raised on Becker, Calabresi, and Posner, seem to be largely unaware of this strand of law and economics.

The one difference in this trend is represented by the new 'norms' literature.[68] This literature has not, so far, returned to the original direction of the early anti-positivist law and economics literature. The new norms literature, for the most part, has not attempted to provide a deeper understanding of the common law, or suggested significant reasons to question the positivist approach in the modern literature. The one exception to this statement is Ellickson's study of ranchers in California, which is a ground-level examination of norms that sometimes deviate from law on the books.

The study of norms should consist primarily of empirical or sociological studies of the actual law-like rules adopted in various societies as norms. Classical common law theory views common law as the tip of an iceberg resting on a thick substratum of norms. By studying the development of real norms and their transference or evolution into rules of law, anti-positivist law and economics could give us a better sense of how common law develops, the different paths that it could take, and the advantages of the common law relative to the civil law process.

---

68   Robert D. Cooter, 'Decentralized Law for a Complex Economy: The Structural Approach to Adjudicating the New Law Merchant', 144 *University of Pennsylvania Law Review* 1643 (1996); Robert Ellickson, *Order Without Law: How Neighbors Settle Disputes* (Cambridge: Harvard University Press, 1991); Richard H. McAdams, 'The Origin, Development, and Regulation of Norms', 96 *Michigan Law Review* 338 (1997); Eric A. Posner, *Law and Social Norms* (Cambridge: Harvard University Press, 2000).

The anti-positive approach probably will return and grow as a piece of the law and economics literature, just as the behavioral approach is growing today. Its most promising direction is likely to be found in historical and anthropological studies. The rules adopted by ancient societies or of relatively isolated populations offer insights into the development of law through implicit contracts.

Conclusion

I have focused on a relatively small portion of Guido Calabresi's total body of work: just his book *The Costs of Accidents* and his article on property rules. However, either of these contributions alone would exceed the impact of the life's work of most scholars. And Guido Calabresi's influence on law and economics is largely explained by the book and the article.

The book and the article are foundational pieces in the two major branches of law and economics: grand thesis scholarship and normal science. The book belongs in the category of grand thesis classics on tort law such as Holmes's *The Common Law*, but it makes contributions to the normal science project as well.

Calabresi's *Costs* laid the groundwork for economic analysis of law as a discipline within law schools, and established a template for modern economic analysis of law that is normative, positivist, and assumes weak-form rationality. Indeed, any modern analysis of the operational efficiency of the legal system must borrow heavily from Calabresi. At least in part because of the influence of Calabresi, the combination of normative economic analysis and legal positivism appears to have become the dominant approach in law and economics. However, any template has the negative consequence of displacing alternative approaches. In the case of Calabresi's *Costs*, the positive analysis reflected in the earlier work of Smith and Holmes, and the anti-positivist approach of Hume, Hayek, and Leoni, were displaced. Positive economic analysis of law quickly returned with Posner's work, but the anti-positivist literature remains largely in the shadows. The assumption of weak rationality has only recently begun to return to the forefront of law and economics.

The Calabresi-Melamed article has been overshadowed by *Costs*, but may in the long run prove to have the greater impact. The property rules framework offers as an extremely rich and general positive theory of law. Calabresi and Melamed used the framework to explain fundamental portions of tort and criminal law. Other scholars have extended the framework and applied it to new areas. My sense is that there is much more to be mined from the property rules framework than scholars have attempted so far.

14 Easterbrook and Fischel

Katherine V. Litvak

1 Introduction

Easterbrook and Fischel made three central contributions to law and economics: one conceptual, one methodological, and one substantive. Conceptually, they helped push law and economics away from its early preoccupation with seeking economic justifications for existing laws, and toward its modern form of using economic analysis to study the effects of laws. Methodologically, they were among the first (preceded perhaps only by Henry Manne) to incorporate new tools of finance (portfolio selection theory, capital structure irrelevance theories, capital asset pricing model) and economics (transaction costs economics and agency costs theory) into legal analysis. Substantively, they systematically explored, and tested the limits of, the contractarian, 'nexus of contracts' model of the corporation, spearheading the development of modern corporate law scholarship.

1.1 Conceptual contribution: from 'Find the pattern' to 'Justify the pattern' to 'Find consequences of the pattern'

Easterbrook and Fischel's conceptual push toward applying the standard of modern social-science research to legal analysis would perhaps seem unimpressive to economists, but it was a critical part of a painful transformation in the legal academy. The classic pre-law-and-economics mode of legal scholarship involved the search for patterns in cases, statutes, and regulations, with the aim to explain past decisions and predict/prescribe future ones. A creative scholar was one who could classify messy precedents in a way that would illuminate the hidden logic behind them. To evaluate the quality of a legal theory, critics asked whether a theory was able to parsimoniously explain past decisions without resorting to endless ad hoc excuses for aberrant outcomes. Once a traditional scholar found a plausible set of proxies to classify past decisions (say, by announcing that a proxy for the applicable damage rule was the defendant's intent, or adequacy of proof, or excessiveness of compensation), a scholar wasn't normally required to explain rigorously why that proxy was 'better' than any other proxy, and what the consequences of using that proxy could be. To be sure, a successful traditional theory had to have a coherent rationale (a classification based on the alphabetic order of parties, even if supported by case law, would not have been a hit), but the rationale itself had to pass a rather low threshold of not being patently ridiculous.

The first wave of law and economics research made a critical step of moving beyond the search for patterns, and asked why the rules were the way they were. Of course, law and economics scholars weren't the only ones who asked this question – legal realists earlier, and critical legal theorists later, also sought to explain the existing patterns, rather than merely describe them. The law and economics niche was to look for the intended purposes served by legal rules, rather than for societal forces that led to the introduction of such rules and the 'purpose' analysis was normally defined as a blend of incentive effects and price effects.

The 'intended purpose' approach, however, was still a victim of the same problem that led to the demise of the traditional search for patterns. When the explicit goal of a theory is to explain the existing pattern, announcing the pattern to be wrong undermines the endeavor. For the traditional legal scholarship, the danger of running into 'wrong' precedents provided an incentive to cherry-pick favourable ones. For the 'intended purpose' scholarship, inconvenient precedents created the temptation to seek excuses for existing rules, rather than evaluate those rules dispassionately. Indeed, the effort to justify existing rules on efficiency grounds produced a widely discussed weakness of the early law and economics work – the inconsistent use of assumptions, which rendered some early law and economics theories unfalsifiable. The early work of Richard Posner fits this mold.[1]

Of course, Easterbrook and Fischel were not entirely free of this weakness – they were children of their times, and sometimes explicitly announced that their research agenda was to look for efficiency justifications for existing rules (for example, in their work on mandatory disclosure and insider trading). Still, unlike many of their predecessors, they routinely asked whether the consequences of existing rules matched the rules' intended purposes, and happily announced mismatches when they found them (as in their analysis of takeovers). In addition – and as a natural consequence of their social-scientific research approach – they relentlessly asked why we need a rule in the first place, and why private actors cannot get to the right outcome for themselves. This inquiry, rooted in skepticism about whether government knows best, foreshadowed later work in law-and-economics, which built on positive political theory.

1.2 Methodological contribution: the introduction of finance into legal analysis
The shift from seeking justifications for existing legal rules toward studying the effects of rules required the use of new analytical techniques. Modern finance and the new economic theories of the firm provided those tools, and the growing body of work in empirical economics and finance guided the basic intuitions behind this new mode of legal analysis. Easterbrook and Fischel were among the first legal academics who competently used this literature. The insights from modern finance theory were critical for Easterbrook and Fischel's famous push to analyze the effects of legal rules on diversified shareholders, rather than on shareholders of a particular firm. Likewise, economic theory of the firm was a stepping stone for Easterbrook and Fischel's innovative take on fiduciary standards in corporate acquisitions.

1.3 Substantive contribution: innovations in the analysis of corporate law
Easterbrook and Fischel's substantive contributions grew out of their broader conceptual insights and methodological innovations. A conventional understanding of the corporation in, say, 1970, was roughly as follows. Shareholders owned the corporation; their ownership claims, called shares, were governed by corporate law. Creditors lent money to the corporation, their loans were regulated by contract. Employees worked for the corporation, but usually did not invest in it; their claims for pay were also largely contractual.

In the 1970s, this view changed radically. Law and economics scholars reconceived the business enterprise as a creature of contract at its core, and shareholders as merely one more group of contracting parties. The central early moves in this reconceptualization were by

---

[1]   Landes, William M. and Posner, Richard A. *The Economic Structure of Tort Law* (1987); Posner, Richard A. *Economic Analysis of Law* (1st ed. 1972).

Alchian and Demsetz in 1972, and by Jensen and Meckling in 1976.[2] Jensen and Meckling were apparently the first to use the term 'nexus of contracts' to describe a firm.

By 1980, the concept that a corporation was a creature of contract was largely accepted by law and economics scholars. But what this meant had yet to be explored. Enter Frank Easterbrook, merely a year into his first (and only) academic position at the University of Chicago Law School, and Daniel Fischel, who had just started at Northwestern. In a series of articles from 1981 through 1986, they undertook to explore the implications of this new model for corporate law, relentlessly addressing one area after another:

- Corporate takeovers in 1981 and 1982;[3]
- Interaction between the regulation of takeovers and antitrust laws in 1982;[4]
- Shareholder voting in 1983;[5]
- Mandatory disclosure in 1984;[6]
- Limited shareholder liability in 1985;[7]
- Damages in securities lawsuits in 1985;[8] and
- Non-public corporations in 1986.[9]

After that, the burst was over. Their first 1981 article on defensive tactics in response to hostile takeover bids remains, according to one reputable source, 'the most heavily cited corporate law article in legal scholarship'.[10] Frank Easterbrook became a federal judge in 1985, and is today widely considered one of the most influential judges in the country.[11] Dan Fischel drifted off into litigation consulting, as a principal in Lexecon, though 'drifted' is perhaps not the right word for a fabulously successful enterprise. They wrote one more overview article in 1989, for a symposium inspired by their work.[12] They combined and

---

2   Alchian, Armen A. and Demsetz, Harold (1972), 'Production, Information Costs, and Economic Organization', *American Economics Review*, 62, 777; Jensen, Michael C. and Meckling, William H. (1976), 'Agency Costs and the Theory of the Firm', *Journal of Financial Economics*, 3, 305.

3   Easterbrook, Frank H. and Fischel, Daniel R. (1981), 'The Proper Role of a Target's Management in Responding to a Tender Offer', *Harvard Law Review*, 94, 1161; Frank Easterbrook and Daniel R. Fischel (1982), 'Corporate Control Transactions', *Yale Law Journal*, 91, 737; Frank Easterbrook and Daniel R. Fischel, (1982) 'Auctions and Sunk Costs in Tender Offers', *Stanford Law Review*, 35, 1.

4   Easterbrook, Frank H. and Fischel, Daniel R., 'Antitrust Suits by Targets of Tender Offers', 80 *Michigan Law Review* 1155 (1982).

5   Easterbrook, Frank H. and Fischel, Daniel R. (1983) 'Voting in Corporate Law', *Journal of Law and Economics*, 26, 395.

6   Easterbrook, Frank H. and Fischel, Daniel R. (1984), 'Mandatory Disclosure and the Protection of Investors', *Virginia Law Review*, 70, 669.

7   Easterbrook, Frank H. and Fischel, Daniel R. (1985), 'Limited Liability and the Corporation', *University of Chicago Law Review*, 52, 89.

8   Easterbrook, Frank H. and Fischel, Daniel R. (1985), 'Optimal Damages in Securities Cases', *University of Chicago Law Review*, 52, 611.

9   Easterbrook, Frank H. and Fischel, Daniel R. (1986), 'Close Corporations and Agency Costs', *Stanford Law Review*, 38, 271.

10   Wikipedia entry for Frank Hoover Easterbrook, www.wikipedia.org, visited January 12, 2008.

11   Choi, Steven J. and Gulati, Mitu G. (2005), 'Mr. Justice Posner? Unpacking the Statistics', *New York University Annual Survey of American Law*, 61, 19–43.

12   Easterbrook, Frank H. and Fischel, Daniel R. (1989), 'The Corporate Contract', *Columbia Law Review*, 89, 1416, in Symposium, Contractual Freedom in Corporate Law.

condensed their articles into a book in 1991.[13] At least on corporate law, they together wrote no more.

1.4 Some general thoughts in the hindsight

What might we say today about their approach, with the aid of more than 20 years of hindsight? First, it was bold. There wasn't much empirical evidence then on what really mattered in corporate law. The field we today call law and finance did not exist. The lack of data slowed Easterbrook and Fischel hardly at all. They happily marshaled evidence to support their positions in the few cases where it was available, and happily speculated where it was not.

Second, they never hid their views about what was, and wasn't, good law, which for them meant law that minimized transaction costs, harmful avoidance strategies, perverse incentives to misbehave, administration and enforcement costs, and other losses. They stated their preferred hand directly, acknowledged the second without dwelling on it, and if their views would sometimes turn out to be wrong in hindsight, that was an expected cost of clear positions, bluntly stated.

Third, contrary to the popular perception, and contrary to their own pronouncements of allegiance to the nexus-of-contracts model of the corporation, they were not instinctively anti-regulation. Quite to the contrary: they supported heavy existing regulatory schemes (like mandatory disclosure and punishment for insider trading) and even proposed their own regulation (the prohibition against defensive tactics in takeovers) that went against the observable patterns in voluntary private contracts. Their regulatory position – the use of mandatory rules to strengthen market institutions – is still a subject of heated debate among academics and policymakers.

Fourth, many of their core ideas still seem right, or close to right, or at least plausible and not clearly wrong. The contractarian perspective continues to dominate corporate law scholarship at major schools today. Even when it is tweaked or modified, it offers a starting place – freedom of contract, in this case the corporate charter – as the base position, and requires all regulation to be justified. Their endorsement of an active takeover market, announced when hostile bids were just taking off in the United States, is broadly accepted by the corporate law academy today, even if many might not agree that takeover defenses should be limited as strictly as Easterbook and Fischel proposed. Their views on the national regulation of disclosure are likewise broadly accepted in the modern legal academy, to the chagrin of deregulation advocates, who subsequently articulated alternative positions.[14]

Fifth, the empirical revolution in corporate law, and in legal scholarship more generally, has changed the way we evaluate bold statements about what the world is, or what it ought to be. Empiricists, myself included, are trained to be cautious in what we say, and never to venture too far beyond what data can tell us. In reading Easterbrook and Fischel's work today, questions like 'what is the evidence?' and 'isn't that really an empirical question?' come often. Easterbrook and Fischel's failure to address those questions wasn't entirely their fault – in their time, relevant empirical work was often thin, and much of the legal academy was

---

[13]   Easterbrook, Frank H. and Fischel, Daniel R. (1991), *The Economic Structure of Corporate Law* (Cambridge, Mass.: Harvard Univesity Press).

[14]   Romano, Roberta (1998), 'Empowering Investors: A Market Approach to Securities Regulation', *Yale Law Journal* 107, 2359–430.

unimpressed by attempts to incorporate empirical analysis into law review articles. To their credit, Easterbrook and Fischel took more care to discuss then-available empirical evidence than most of their contemporaries – and certainly more than contemporaries outside a small group of law-and-economics scholars working in corporate law (such as Lucian Bebchuk, Ronald Gilson, and Alan Schwartz).

Sixth, Easterbrook and Fischel's work was – characteristically for their times – parochial. Cross-country analysis was a decade away, and cross-country empirical studies lay still further in the future. Comparative corporate law in its current quantitative form was non-existent. They wrote at a time when the United States was the unquestioned model for how corporations should behave and corporate law should evolve. They assumed that dispersed ownership was optimal, and addressed its characteristic problems. Today, we would say that dispersed ownership relies instead on an extensive set of institutions, including some of the mandatory laws that Easterbrook and Fischel supported. Like most of their contemporaries, they assumed that the dominant agency problem of the large public corporation was how to make managers work well and hard. Today, we would say that controlling insider self-dealing is the second major agency problem of the large corporation – and in much of the world, the more important one.

Seventh, they had no crystal ball. They addressed the major corporate law issues of their day. Some problems are the same today, but some are not. Were they writing today, for example, they would almost certainly have to address the topic of executive compensation. In their book, the topic not only does not merit its own chapter, it does not even merit a mention in the index.

In order not to be too broad brush, I will focus below on three areas where I find their contributions to be most impressive or most characteristic of the rest of their work: the regulation of takeovers, mandatory disclosure, and limited liability. For each, I will explore what their views were, what we know today, and where Easterbrook and Fischel seem right, wrong, or incomplete.

2   The regulation of takeovers and the market for corporate control

One of Easterbrook and Fischel's best known contributions was a series of papers on regulation of hostile takeovers.

Shareholders of publicly traded firms normally transfer their shares freely, in relatively low volumes, and individual trades have no impact on the firm's management and operations. However, occasionally, a single party acquires enough shares to be able to elect a new board of directors, replace management, and introduce dramatic changes to the firm. To buy enough shares for this purpose, a buyer normally has to offer current shareholders a significant premium over the market price. Sometimes, a bidder offers to buy all shares, again normally at a significant premium over the pre-bid market price. As a result, shareholders of the target firm benefit from the offer, while its managers stand to lose their jobs. The question is: should managers be allowed to impede shareholders' ability to sell their shares at a premium to whomever they please, if the likely consequence of the sale is that managers will be fired?

Posing the question this way highlights the fundamental conflict of interest inherent in the takeovers debate. Understandably, the usual response from the target managers was that they opposed takeovers because doing so was in the best interest of shareholders. Showing such 'best interest', however, turned out to be difficult because it required the explanation for why it's a bad idea to sell something that is effectively a commodity at above market price. One popular explanation was (and still is) a simple assertion that market prices do not fully reflect all relevant information, and that the target's management is either unable to credibly convey such information to the market or that the immediate release of such information is not in the best interests of shareholders because, for example, it might prematurely hurt a firm's competitive position. The call was essentially to trust self-interested managers, rather than markets.

The second way to support managers' defensive stance was to assert that the original bid, while representing a premium over market price, was not the maximum that the potential acquirer, or another acquirer, was willing to pay. Because dispersed shareholders cannot bargain with the acquirer directly, they have incentives to sell at the first offered price, so long as it is above market.[15] In this view, the job of the target management is to stop direct sales by shareholders and bargain with the acquirer for better terms or search for alternative buyers who would be willing to pay more.

Rapid, hostile acquisitions of large stakes first emerged in the 1960s, and prompted federal intervention through the Williams Act, to slow the process down and ensure that the target's management had time to respond to a bid. But until Easterbrook and Fischel entered the debate over target management's proper role, the debate in the legal academy was almost entirely static: it centered around the efforts to increase the bid once a bid was made. Easterbrook and Fischel challenged that.[16] Their first key observation was that the target's effort to increase the bid reduces acquirer's profits and therefore reduces acquirer's incentives to engage in search and bidding in the first place. What the target's shareholders need to maximize is not the size of a final bid, but the expected value of a bid – the size of a final bid multiplied by the probability that such a bid will occur. Under plausible assumptions, a defensive tactic that increases the size of the final bid may still harm target shareholders if it substantially reduces the chance that the bid will be made or completed.

The second key insight advanced by Easterbrook and Fischel was to shift the discussion from a single-firm approach to a broader view of shareholders as a class.[17] When the bidder and the target are both public companies, a diversified shareholder has a roughly similar chance of being on either side of the transaction. Therefore, while ex post, target shareholders might well prefer a rule that produces higher prices for the bids that are made, thus benefiting targets, ex ante, diversified shareholders prefer the rule that increases the joint wealth of target and acquirer shareholders. The inquiry, then, moves whether defensive tactics benefit target shareholders, taking into account the effect of such tactics on acquirers' incentives to bid. Rather, the right question is whether diversified shareholders prefer higher or lower levels of takeover activity in general.

---

15   Herzel, Leo, Schmidt, John R. and Davis, Scott J. (1980), 'Why Corporate Directors Have a Right to Resist Tender Offers', *Corporation Law Review*, 3, 107; Lipton, Martin (1979), 'Takeover Bids in the Target's Boardroom', *Business Lawyer*, 35, 101–33.

16   Easterbrook and Fischel, 'The Proper Role of a Target's Management', *supra* note 2, 1161–201; Easterbrook and Fischel, 'Auctions and Sunk Costs', *supra* note 2, 1–21.

17   Some of these ideas were developed earlier or contemporaneously, mostly by economists, but were almost entirely ignored by legal academics until Easterbrook and Fischel's powerful intervention. See Sanford J. Grossman and Oliver D. Hart (1980), 'Takeover Bids, The Free Rider Problem, and the Theory of the Corporation', *Bell Journal of Economics*, 11, 42–64; Jarrell, Gregg A. and Bradley, Michael (1980), 'The Economic Effects of Federal and State Regulations on Cash Tender Offers', *Journal of Law and Economics* 23, 371–407.

On this issue, Easterbrook and Fischel joined a growing group of finance and economics scholars who argued that higher takeover activity is beneficial to shareholders as a class because takeovers serve as a powerful tool constraining managerial misbehavior and incompetence.[18] The catchphrase, coined by Henry Manne, was that takeovers and proxy fights together comprised a 'market for corporate control'. In that maket, takeovers had important advantages over proxy fights. The intuition behind this view was as follows. Small dispersed shareholders have little incentive to monitor management and little chance to influence managerial behavior through voting. Large blockholders have more incentives and ability to act, but, because they bear all of the costs of monitoring while receiving only a portion of benefits, they would still under-supply monitoring effort. One way to overcome this collective action problem is to concentrate costs and benefits of monitoring in the same hands. This is effectively what a takeover does.

If a diversified shareholder, deciding ex ante and under the veil of ignorance as to whether he will end up on the target or acquirer side, would prefer unimpeded takeovers as a means of corporate governance, the appropriate legal rule should be for the target's management to do nothing. This insight was the basis of Easterbrook and Fischel's famous proposal to prohibit all defensive tactics by the target's management including delaying or otherwise obstructing the first bid to seek a higher price, either from the first bidder or a second bidder.

One interesting set of objections had to do with designing a regime that would increase the chances that the target will ultimately end up in the hands of the highest valuator.[19] Even if one agrees with Easterbrook and Fischel's broader view that the appropriate level of analysis is diversified shareholders ex ante, rather than shareholders of targets ex post, the question still remains whether unimpeded takeovers hurt allocative efficiency. If the first bidder values the target less than some other potential acquirer does (for example, because of different synergies), a rule that prevents the target's management from shopping for a higher bidder may result in misallocation of a valuable asset.

Not a problem, Easterbrook and Fischel respond. If the second bidder truly values the target more, it can simply buy the target from the first bidder. This is surely the case in a world with minimal transaction costs, information asymmetries, agency problems, disruptions to the target's business, and so forth. But what if one of the above conditions does not hold? If transaction costs are sufficiently high (or if each acquisition substantially disrupts the target), the higher-valuing second bidder may be unable to buy the target through a subsequent transaction with the first bidder, even though it would have been able to outbid the first bidder in the original takeover contest. Likewise, high transaction costs may result in reducing the ultimate value of the target below what it would have been (to anyone) if the target held an auction, presumably won by the second bidder.

---

[18]   Manne, Henry (1965), 'Mergers and the Market for Corporate Control', *Journal of Political Economy*, 73, 110–20; Jensen, Michael C. and Meckling, William H. (1976), 'Theory of the Firm: Managerial Behavior, Agency Costs and Ownership Structure', *Journal of Financial Economics*, 3, 305–60; Fama, Eugene F. (1980), 'Agency Problems and the Theory of the Firm', *Journal of Political Economy*, 88, 288–307; Jensen, Michael C. and Ruback, Richard S. (1983), 'The Market for Corporate Control: The Scientific Evidence', *Journal of Financial Economics* 11, 5–50.

[19]   Gilson, Ronald (1982), 'Seeking Competitive Bids versus Pure Passivity in Tender Offer Defense', *Stanford Law Review*, 35, 51–67; Gilson, Ronald (1981), 'A Structural Approach to Corporation: The Case against Defensive Tactics in Tender Offers', *Stanford Law Review*, 33, 819–91.

This debate ultimately rests on empirical questions. How high, on average, are transaction costs of initial and subsequent bids and acquisitions? Are those costs interdependent? Do they relate to some target/acquirer/industry characteristics? What is the marginal impact of the first-bidder's odds of success on acquirers' incentives to search and bid? What is the marginal impact of the increase in search and acquisition activity on the improvement in managerial performance of potential targets?

Most of these questions are still unanswered. Partly, the answers might be hard to come by, under any legal regime. But a further reason is that we never had such a natural experiment: no US jurisdiction has ever adopted a regime that precluded takeover defenses. No US state has even gone as far as the UK and banned defenses designed to block the first bidder altogether, rather than facilitate an auction. Thus, we don't know whether a no-defense world would result in serial acquisitions; whether such serial acquisitions would harm targets and/or acquirers; whether potential acquirers could develop a system of bargaining with target shareholders over price without the participation of the conflicted management of the target, and so forth.

However, many of Easterbrook and Fischel's early predictions found subsequent empirical support, and many of their assumptions turned out to be correct. We now have substantial evidence that firms that adopt anti-takeover defenses experience losses in value,[20] as do firms subject to state anti-takeover laws.[21] Firms with staggered boards (the most powerful takeover defense, when combined with a poison pill) have lower market value than firms without staggered boards (although causation here is not easily ascertainable).[22] When managers remove

---

[20]   Ryngaert, Michael (1988), 'The Effects of Poison Pill Securities on Shareholder Wealth', *Journal of Financial Economics*, 20, 377–411; Mahoney, James M., Sundaramurthy, Chamu, and Mahoney, Joseph T., (1996), 'The Differential Impact on Stockholder Wealth of Various Antitakeover Provisions', *Managerial and Decision Economics*, 17, 531–49; Jarrell, Gregg A., Brickley, James A., and Netter, Jeffry M. (1988), 'The Market for Corporate Control: The Empirical Evidence since 1980', *Journal of Economic Perspectives*, 2, 49–68; DeAngelo, Harry and Rice, Edward M. (1983), 'Antitakeover Charter Amendments and Stockholder Wealth', *Journal of Financial Economics* 11, 329–59; Jarrell, Gregg A. and Poulsen, Annette B. (1987), 'Shark Repellents and Stock Prices: The Effect of Antitakeover Amendments since 1980', *Journal of Financial Economics*, 19, 127–68; Barnhart, Scott W., Spivey, Michael F., and Alexander, John C. (2000), 'Do Firm and State Antitakeover Provisions Affect How Well CEOs Earn their Pay?', *Managerial and Decision Economics*, 21, 315–28. John Coates, however, criticized some of these studies for getting the law wrong; see Coates, John C. (2000), 'The Contestability of Corporate Control: A Critique of the Scientific Evidence on Takeover Defenses', *Texas Law Review*, 79, 271–382.
[21]   Szewczyk, Samuel H., and Tsetsekos, George P. (1991), 'State Intervention in the Market for Corporate Control: The Case of Pennsylvania Senate Bill 1310', *Journal of Financial Economics*, 31, 3–24; Karpoff, Jonathan M. and Malatesta, Paul H.. (1989), 'The Wealth Effects of Second Generation Takeover Legislation', *Journal of Financial Economics*, 25, 291–322; Karpoff, Jonathan M. and Malatesta, Paul H. (1995), 'State Takeover Legislation and Share Values: The Wealth Effects of Pennsylvania's Act 36', *Journal of Corporate Finance*, 1, 367–82; Ryngaert, Michael and Netter, Jeffry (1988), 'Shareholder Wealth Effects of the Ohio Antitakeover Law', *Journal of Law, Economics, and Organization*, 4, 373; Schumann, Laurence (1989), 'State Regulation of Takeovers and Shareholder Wealth: The Case of New York's 1985 Takeover Statutes', *Rand Journal of Economics*, 19, 557–67; Ryngaert, Michael and Netter, Jeffry (1990), 'Shareholder Wealth Effects of the 1986 Ohio Antitakeover Law Revisited: Its Real Effects', *Journal of Law, Economics, and Organization*, 6, 253–62; Robert Daines (2001), 'Do Staggered Boards Affect Firm Value? Massachusetts and the Market for Corporate Control', working paper, Stanford Law School.
[22]   Bebchuk, Lucian Arye and Cohen, Alma, (2005), 'The Costs of Entrenched Boards', *Journal of Financial Economics*, 78, 409–33.

staggered boards, firm value increases.[23] The hypothesis of the disciplining role of takeovers is supported as well: targets that prior to the takeover were significantly underperforming other firms in their industry are more likely to replace managers after the completion of the takeover.[24] Firms in states with an active takeover market are more profitable.[25]

Easterbrook and Fischel were also correct in suggesting that takeovers create value by undoing value-destroying transactions put together by incompetent or disloyal corporate managers. We now know, for example, that managers who build empires ostensibly to create value through diversification are more likely to destroy shareholder wealth;[26] that bad acquisitions increase the chance that a firm will become the target of a subsequent takeover itself,[27] and that nearly half of all acquired targets are subsequently divested.[28] Poorly managed firms are more likely to be targets of takeovers,[29] and bidders earn higher returns when they target poorly managed firms.[30] Firms that have lost more value due to diversification are most likely to be taken over.[31]

The opponents of Easterbrook and Fischel, who disputed the disciplining value of takeovers and asserted that takeovers merely transfer wealth from other constituencies (employees, bondholders, consumers), turned out to be mostly wrong. As to employees: Takeovers do not result in job losses, save at target headquarters, and the losses there are offset, on average, by gains elsewhere.[32] There is no evidence that takeovers often breach

---

23   Olubunmi, Faleye (2005), 'Classified Boards, Firm Value, and Managerial Entrenchment', *Journal of Financial Economics*, 83, 501–29; Ganor, Mira (2008), 'Why Do Managers Dismantle Staggered Boards?', *Delaware Journal of Corporate Law*, vol 33, p. 1.

24   Martin, Kenneth J. and McConnell John, (1991), 'Corporate Performance, Corporate Takeovers, and Management Turnover', *Journal of Finance*, 46, 671–87.

25   Mary S. Schranz (1993), 'Takeovers Improve Firm Performance: Evidence from the Banking Industry', *Journal of Political Economy*, 101, 299–326.

26   Berger, Philip G. and Ofek, Eli. (1995), 'Diversification's Effect on Firm Value', *Journal of Financial Economics*, 37, 39–65; Lang, Larry H.P. and Stulz, Renee E. (1994), 'Tobin's q, Corporate Diversification and Firm Performance', *Journal of Political Economy*, 102, 1248–80; Servaes, Henry (1996), 'The Value of Diversification During the Conglomerate Merger Wave', *Journal of Finance*, 51, 1201–25.

27   Mitchell, M. and Lehn, Kenneth (1990), 'Do Bad Bidders Become Good Targets?' *Journal of Political Economy*, 98, 372–98.

28   Kaplan, Steven and Michael Weisbach (1992), 'The Success of Acquisitions: Evidence from Divestitures', *Journal of Finance*, 47, 107–38; Lichtenberg, Frank and Siegel, Donald (1987), 'Productivity and Changes in Ownership of Manufacturing Plants', *Brooking Papers on Economic Activity*, 643.

29   Hasbrouck, Joel (1985), 'The Characteristics of Takeover Targets: Q and Other Measures', *Journal of Banking and Finance*, 9, 351–62; Morck, Randall, Shleifer, Adrei and Vishny, Robert (1988), 'Characteristics of Targets of Hostile and Friendly Takeovers', in Alan J. Auerbach, ed., *Corporate Takeovers: Causes and Consequences* (Chicago: University of Chicago Press); Barber, Brad, Palmer, Donald, and Wallace, James (1995), 'Determinants of Conglomerate and Predatory Acquisitions: Evidence from the 1960s', *Journal of Corporate Finance*, 1, 283–318.

30   Lang, Larry H.P., Stulz, Renee E. and Walking, Ralph A. (1989), 'Managerial Performance, Tobin's Q, and the Gains from Successful Tender Offers', *Journal of Financial Economics*, 24, 137–54; Servaes, H. (1991), 'Tobin's Q and the Gains from Takeovers', *Journal of Finance*, 46, 409–19.

31   Philip G. Berger and Eli Ofek, 'Bustup Takeovers of Value-Destroying Diversified Firms', *Journal of Finance*, 51, 4, 1175–200 (1996).

32   Kaplan, Steve (1989), 'The Effect of Management Buyouts on Operations and Value', *Journal of Financial Economics*, 24, 217–54; Brown, Charles and Medoff, James L. (1988), 'The Impact of

implicit contracts between the firm and workers or suppliers.[33] Plant closings are not associated with takeovers.[34] Wages of blue collar employees in plants subject to takeovers were found to grow after takeovers. However, wages of white collar employees decline after takeovers, supporting the view that takeovers hurt middle managers of targets.[35] Union wages slightly increase after successful hostile takeovers.[36] The sole evidence of breach of implicit contracts between firms and employees is the finding that takeovers result in wealth transfers from firms' pension funds to shareholders.[37]

There is no evidence that shareholder gains came from losses to the treasury. Tax bill reductions are small and cannot on average account for most of the takeover premium.[38]

The evidence on transfers from bondholders to shareholders is mixed, but the studies that find declines in bondholder wealth report magnitudes substantially lower than takeover premia, too small to explain shareholder gains by wealth transfers. Following the announcements of leveraged buyouts, abnormal returns to nonconvertible debt are approximately zero.[39] There is no correlation between the size of shareholder gains and the amount of pre-transaction outstanding debt.[40] Average bondholder losses are small.[41]

There is also no evidence that takeovers involve transfers from consumers.[42]

Subsequent commentators proposed more objections to Easterbrook and Fischel's no-takeover-defense view. One line of arguments is based on the idea that the threat of a takeover may encourage myopic behavior on the part of a target's management. If stock prices do not

---

Firm Acquisitions on Labor', in Auerbach, A., ed., *Corporate Takeovers: Causes and Consequences*, (Chicago: University of Chicago Press).

[33]   Lichtenberg, Frank (1992), *Corporate Takeovers and Productivity*, p. 43. MIT Press, Cambridge, Mass; Gokhale, Jagadeesh, Groshen, Erica and Neumark, David (1995), 'Do Hostile Takeovers Reduce Extramarginal Wage Payments?' *Review of Economics and Statistics*, 77, 470–85.

[34]   Blackwell, David, Marr, Wayne and Spivey, Michael (1990), 'Plant-Closing Decisions and the Market Value of the Firm', *Journal of Financial Economics*, 26, 277–88.

[35]   Lichtenberg, Frank and Siegel, Donald (1990), 'The Effect of Ownership Changes on the Employment and Wages of Central Office and Other Personnel', *Journal of Law and Economics*, 33, 383–408.

[36]   Rosett, Joshua (1990), 'Do Union Wealth Concessions Explain Takeover Premiums? The Evidence on Contract Wages', *Journal of Financial Economics*, 27, 263–82.

[37]   Pontiff, Jeffrey, Shleifer, Andrei, and Weisbach, Michael S. (1990), 'Reversions of Excess Pension Assets after Takeovers', *RAND Journal of Economics*, 21, 600–13.

[38]   Auerbach, Alan J. and Reishus, David (1988), 'The Effects of Taxation on the Merger Decision', in A. Auerbach, ed., *Corporate Takeovers: Causes and Consequences* (Chicago: University of Chicago Press); Bhagat, Sanjay, Shleifer, Andrei, and Vishny, Robert (1990), 'Hostile Takeovers in the 1980s: The Return to Specialization', *Brookings Papers on Economic Activity: Microeconomics*, 1–72.

[39]   Marais, Laurentius, Schipper, Katherine and Smith, Abbie (1989), 'Wealth Effects of Going Private for Senior Securities', *Journal of Financial Economics*, 23, 155–91.

[40]   Lehn, Kenneth and Poulsen, Annette (1988), 'Leveraged Buyouts: Wealth Created or Wealth Distributed?' in Murray Weidenbaum and Kenneth Chilton, eds., *Public Policy Towards Corporate Takeovers* (New Brunswick, NJ: Transaction Publishers) p. 46.

[41]   Dennis, Debra K. and McConnell, John J. (1986) 'Corporate Mergers and Security Returns', *Journal of Financial Economics*, 16, 143–87; Warga, Arthur and Welch, Ivo (1990), 'Bondholder Losses in Leveraged Buyouts', First Boston Working Paper Series FB 90–04; Paul Asquith and Thierry A. Wizman (1991) 'Event Risk, Wealth Redistribution and the Return to Existing Bondholders in Corporate Buyouts', *Journal of Financial Econonomics*, 27, 195–214.

[42]   Eckbo, B. Espen (1983), 'Horizontal Mergers, Collusions and Stockholder Wealth', *Journal of Financial Economics*, 11, 241.

accurately reflect all private information known to managers, firm managers that face the prospect of easy replacement might take a short-term view – overinvesting, underinvesting, investing in the wrong things – because they concentrate on stock prices instead of long-term firm value. One well-known model predicts that firms that erect takeover defenses should be able to increase profitable long-term investments, such as research and development, which investors might undervalue.[43] This prediction, however, is not supported empirically: firms that introduce takeover defenses were found to reduce R&D intensity.[44] Another version of this argument is that managers who are unable to defend through traditional means may engage in alternative defensive tactics that are not easily regulable, but more harmful to a firm, than the current legal defenses.[45] To my knowledge, no empirical study directly tests this proposition.

Perhaps the most interesting line of criticism involves references to observed patterns of contracting. If takeover defenses are harmful to shareholders, one would expect not to see defenses in corporate charters, or at least not to see them in IPO charters, where the costs of anti-takeover provisions are likely to be internalized by the parties that take firms public. Indeed, in the early 1980s, Easterbrook and Fischel announced, without empirical support, that IPO charters do not contain takeover defenses; they believed that defenses were introduced in the midstream by disloyal managers.

Subsequent evidence showed this assertion to be wrong: most IPO charters of firms that went public in the mid-1990s contained anti-takeover provisions, and over 60 percent contained a particularly noxious provision – staggered board – that strengthens the power of poison pills.[46] Further, the proportion of firms going public with staggered boards increased nearly threefold during the 1990s, the decade of shareholder activism and heightened awareness of harms that defenses may cause to shareholder wealth. Corporate law allows firms to protect shareholders from midstream managerial opportunism by including, during the IPO stage, explicit provisions that restrict the board's authority to adopt anti-takeover provisions in the future, most notably the potent poison pill defense. No company was found to do so.[47] Anti-takeover provisions are also ubiquitous in charters of spinoffs.[48] This is indeed a puzzle. If anti-takeover provisions are harmful to shareholders, it is not clear why IPO charters would overwhelmingly contain some provisions and permit midstream adoption of others. A separate uncomfortable question is why the institutional investors which showered corporations with demands to remove takeover defenses in the 1990s remained silent when private firms in which those same institutions were invested were taken public with defenses in their charters.

---

43   Stein, Jeremy C. (1988), 'Takeover Threats and Managerial Myopia', *Journal of Political Economy* 96, 61–80.
44   Meulbroek, Lisa K., Mitchell, Mark L., Mulherin, Harold J., Netter, Jeffry M., and Poulsen, Allette B. (1990), 'Shark Repellents and Managerial Myopia: An Empirical Test', 98 *Journal of Political Economy* 5, 1108–17.
45   Jennifer Arlen and Eric Talley (2003), 'Unregulable Defenses and Perils of Shareholder Choice', *University of Pennsylvania Law Review*, 152, 577–666.
46   Daines, Robert and Klausner, Michael (2001), 'Do IPO Charters Maximize Firm Value? Antitakeover Protection in IPOs', *Journal of Law, Economics, and Organization*, 17, 84–120.
47   Coates, John C. (2001), 'Explaining Variation in Takeover Defenses: Blame the Lawyers', *California Law Review*, 89, 1301–421.
48   Daines, Robert and Klausner, Michael (2004), 'Agents Protecting Agents: An Empirical Study of Takeover Defenses in Spinoffs', working paper.

Interestingly, the Easterbrook-Fischel wave of takeover literature concentrated almost exclusively on the conflict between managers and shareholders, debating whether anti-takeover defenses represent a wealth transfer from shareholders to managers. Years later, scholars recognized that some forms of takeover defenses may involve wealth transfers from one group of shareholders to another. Dual class recapitalizations, for example, typically provide one group of shareholders with voting control, compensating the other group with dividends. Such voting control can be a powerful anti-takeover device, particularly pernicious when management retains a substantial portion of voting shares. Consistent with Easterbrook and Fischel's view, companies whose voting rights are controlled by a single party were found to trade at a discount.[49] However, the evidence is unclear on whether dual-class recapitalizations (which can be thought of as adoptions of anti-takeover defenses) result in aggregate shareholder loss. Some studies find no effect of recapitalizations on aggregate shareholder wealth;[50] others find a positive effect;[51] yet others find a significant negative effect.[52] These studies, however, do not directly test Easterbrook and Fischel's early hypotheses: recall that the key question raised by Easterbrook and Fischel was whether takeover defenses benefit diversified shareholders as a class. So long as we cannot measure the private benefits of control that holders of voting stock receive from recapitalizations, we cannot tell whether shareholders as a class have benefited or not. So long as recapitalizations involve the exchange of money for voting power, the measurable changes in shareholder wealth may simply reflect whether holders of non-voting stock were adequately compensated during the recapitalization.

As mentioned before, one important feature highlighted by Easterbrook and Fischel's takeovers work is that they were not eager to rely on markets in the face of perceived market failure. Quite to the contrary: they explicitly suggested overwriting private contracts – corporate charters – by law for the greater good of shareholder wealth. Since nothing in corporate charters prohibited managers from engaging in defensive tactics, and since shareholders at the time did not oppose charter amendments to adopt takeover defenses in the midstream (and still don't oppose them in the IPO stage), Easterbrook and Fischel's ban on behavior of target managers view, places more trust in their economic intuitions than in markets. People screening the legal academy for thoroughly anti-regulation free-marketeers will come away disappointed.

3 Mandatory disclosure

Three years after their first takeover defense article, Easterbrook and Fischel published another influential article that still continues to generate ire among the anti-regulation crowd.

---

49   Kunz, Roger M. and Angel, James J. (1996), 'Factors Affecting the Value of the Stock Voting Right: Evidence from the Swiss Equity Market', *Financial Management*, 25, 7–20.
50   Partch, M. Megan (1987), 'The Creation of a Class of Limited Voting Common Stock and Shareholder Wealth', *Journal of Financial Economics*, 18, 303–39; Shum, Connie M., Davidson, Wallace N., and Glascock, John L. (1995), 'Voting Rights and Market Reaction to Dual Class Common Stock Issues', *The Financial Review*, 30, 275–287.
51   Cornett, Marcia M. and Vetsuypens, Michael R. (1989), 'Voting Rights and Shareholder Wealth: The Issuance of Limited Voting Common Stock', *Managerial and Decision Economics*, 10, 175–88.
52   Jarrell, Gregg A. and Poulsen, Annette B. (1987), 'Shark Repellents and Stock Prices: The Effect of Antitakeover Amendments since 1980', *Journal of Financial Economics*, 19, 127–68.

They asked whether there was a public-interest rationale for the survival of federal securities laws and, in particular, mandatory disclosure.[53]

Their answer was yes, but not for the reasons popular in the legal academy of the early 1980s. Easterbrook and Fischel's first move was to reject the then-dominant view that the purpose of mandatory disclosure was to curb fraud and protect unsophisticated investors. They pointed out that fraud is, and has long been, illegal under state laws, and thus the burden is on the proponents of federalization to show why a particular type of fraud (in the sale of securities) should be selected for federal treatment. As to unsophisticated investors, Easterbrook and Fischel reminded us that share prices are set by informed traders, and the rest of the world free rides on their efforts. At the same time, Easterbrook and Fischel weren't willing to concede that the adoption and survival of federally mandated disclosure was merely a product of interest-group politics.

Easterbrook and Fischel's search for the public-interest justification for mandatory disclosure left them with two questions: first, why disclosure should be regulated at all, and second, why it should be regulated on the federal, rather than state, level. Their answer to both questions was essentially the same: market failure.

As to the need for mandatory disclosure in general: the issue was whether firms have sufficient incentives to disclose information on their own. The opponents of regulation pointed out that firms can reduce their cost of capital if they can credibly disclose information that investors value; since silence would inevitably be interpreted as a signal of bad news, even the firms with less than glorious information have incentives to disclose it. To make disclosures more believable, firms can (and do) engage information intermediaries – accountants, lawyers, bankers – to verify the news. Further, even if investors, left to their own devices, would either under- or overproduce information, the Coase Theorem tells us that firms and investors can strike deals, on a firm-by-firm basis, for the disclosure of appropriate amounts of information. If different firms benefit from different disclosures, the system of tailored disclosure by private contract might be more efficient than one-size-fits-all system of disclosure mandated by regulators.

Easterbrook and Fischel's main response was to point to third-party effects. If some disclosures give a competitive advantage to a firm's competitors, it may not be in the best interests of the investors of some firms to contract for such disclosures. And yet the issue, as in the takeovers debate, is not the welfare of the shareholders of a particular firm, but the welfare of diversified shareholders as a class. If a diversified shareholder stands a roughly similar chance of being invested in a firm that benefits from a competitor's disclosure and in a firm that is hurt by such a disclosure, a shareholder should choose the rule that maximizes benefits across the board. In Easterbrook and Fischel's view, such an aggregate wealth-maximization regime may not emerge from autonomous firm-level contracts, thus warranting regulation.[54]

---

53   Easterbrook, Frank H. and Fischel, Daniel R. (1984), 'Mandatory Disclosure and the Protection of Investors', *Virginia Law Review*, 70, 669.

54   In a contemporaneous paper, John Coffee offered additional arguments in support of mandatory disclosure, exloring other sources of market inability to produce efficient amounts of disclosure. Coffee, John C. (1984), 'Market Failure and the Economic Case for a Mandatory Disclosure System', *Virginia Law Review*, 70, 717–53.

Their argument rests on empirical assertions that have not yet been shown to be correct (or incorrect). On the firm level: to argue that voluntary disclosure would under-supply information because of third-party effects, one needs to show that the benefits to a firm from voluntary disclosure (lower cost of capital) would be systematically lower than the costs to a firm created by competitive disadvantage. So far, no such showing has been made. Could the relevant competitively sensitive elements of disclosure be isolated for a narrow regulation, leaving the rest to private contracting? Does the answer depend on industry or firm characteristics? Does mandatory disclosure in fact produce enough competitively-sensitive information (that would otherwise not have been produced) to justify the costs of regulation? Or does mandatory disclosure instead result in costly avoidance schemes – operational, financial, accounting? Does it reduce firms' incentives to invest in projects whose value can be diminished through mandatory disclosure? Does it push some types of projects into private (non-disclosing) firms? Does the required release of competitively sensitive information reduce competition? In short, how do the full costs of mandatory disclosure compare with the full benefits? We still don't know.

Even if one concludes that disclosure should be regulated, the next question is why it should be regulated nationally, rather than by states. Here, Easterbrook and Fischel's answer is the perils of interstate competition: if states are given the power to regulate disclosure of out-of-state firms (potential defendants) for the benefit of in-state shareholders (potential plaintiffs), we may end up with a race to the bottom, with too much disclosure, and likely inconsistent disclosure, mandated by different states. Easterbrook and Fischel also have a second answer: efficiency of enforcement. Under a federal regime, all claims involving a particular transaction can be brought in one case, rather than fifty separate cases, reducing litigation costs.

This answer is not entirely satisfactory. Federal regulation is not the only alternative to the downward spiral of state competition to transfer wealth from out-of-staters to in-staters, or to the risk of serial litigation of the same claim. Another alternative is choice-of-law reform that would require consolidation of all nationwide claims in a single action, and would send the litigation to the jurisdiction specified ex ante by the issuer, much like today's system for corporate-law class actions.[55] So long as the applicable jurisdiction can be selected by issuers upfront, and so long as markets can decently price corporations' choice of law (we have evidence that they do so for corporate law),[56] states will have incentives to draft securities laws that benefit investors, instead of drafting laws that benefit in-state plaintiffs at the expense of out-of-state defendants. Several subsequent commentators have proposed reforms of the current federal system to allow jurisdictional competition for securities disclosure regimes.[57]

---

[55]   Romano, Roberta (1998), 'Empowering Investors: A Market Approach to Securities Regulation', *Yale Law Journal*, 107, 2359–430.

[56]   Daines, Robert M. (2001), 'Does Delaware Law Improve Firm Value?', *Journal of Financial Economics*, 62, 525–58.

[57]   Romano, Roberta (1998), 'Empowering Investors: A Market Approach to Securities Regulation', *Yale Law Journal*, 107, 2359–430; Choi, Stephen J. and Guzman, Andrew T. (1996), 'The Dangerous Extraterritoriality of American Securities Law', *Northwestern Journal of International Law and Business*, 17, 207; Choi, Stephen J. and Guzman, Andrew T. (1998), 'Portable Reciprocity: Rethinking the International Reach of Securities Regulation', *Southern California Law Review*, 71, 903.

The debate, again, hinges on empirical questions. To justify the superiority of federal regulation over competitive state laws, one needs to show that the net benefits of federal regulation are higher than those of the alternative system. Here, Easterbrook and Fischel made a notable departure from the then-standard in the legal academy practise of speculating about the world without evidence. Instead, they wrote a section on available empirical work, complete with criticisms of prior economic research, concluding that the evidence was not informative enough to affect their position. Despite its modest ambitions, their review of prior empirical work was perhaps even more impressive than their substantive contribution. While other legal scholars at the time also moved to incorporate basic finance and economic theory into their analysis, it was rare for a legal academic to provide a detailed discussion of empirical evidence.

Sadly, empirical evidence is still too thin to support a definitive position on federal regulation of disclosure. Two studies have looked at the effects of the 1933 Act. One study found no effect on medium-term annual returns of affected firms, although there was some evidence that there were changes over longer time periods. Post-Act firms were found to be less risky, but it is not clear whether the Act caused the reduction in risk or drove riskier firms out of public markets.[58] A later study concluded that mandatory disclosure provided useful information when issuer reputation or third-party bonding (trading on the New York Stock Exchange (NYSE)) were not available to create incentives for voluntary disclosure.[59]

Turning to the 1934 Act: firms that voluntarily disclosed sales information prior to the Act and the firms that first disclosed sales because of the Act did not have significantly different abnormal returns.[60] The Act did not make a measurable difference for companies that already had high standards of financial disclosure.[61] Across all NYSE firms, high disclosing and not, new disclosures did not reduce informational asymmetry; neither did they make earnings more informative.[62]

Two studies inspect the effects of the 1964 extension of mandatory disclosure to large public firms traded over-the-counter. Both find positive abnormal returns, and one finds declines in investor forecast errors.[63] Finally, one study examined the effect of a December 1980 change in the Securities and Exchange Commissions' (SEC's) disclosure rule, requiring disclosure of additional information of financial results. Share prices were found to become more accurate following the adoption of the rule.[64]

---

[58]   Stigler, George J. (1964), 'Public Regulation of the Securities Markets', *Journal of Business*, 37, 117–42.

[59]   Simon, Carol J. (1989), 'The Effect of the 1933 Securities Act on Investor Information and the Performance of New Issues', *American Economic Review*, 79, 295–318.

[60]   Benston, George J. (1973), 'Required Disclosure and the Stock Market: An Evaluation of the Securities Exchange Act of 1934', *American Economic Review*, 63, 132–55.

[61]   Daines, Robert and Jones, Charles M. (2005), 'Mandatory Disclosure, Asymmetric Information and Liquidity: The Impact of the 1934 Act', working paper.

[62]   Mahoney, Paul and Mei, Jiangping (2007), 'Mandatory *vs.* Contractual Disclosure in Securities Markets: Evidence from the 1930s', working paper.

[63]   Greenstone, Michael, Oyer, Paul, and Vissing-Jorgensen, Annette (2004), 'Mandated Disclosure, Stock Returns, and the 1964 Securities Acts Amendments'. *Quarterly Journal of Economics*, 121, 399–460 (1006); Ferrell, Allen (2004), 'Mandated Disclosure and Stock Returns: Evidence from the Over-the-Counter Market', working paper.

[64]   Fox, Merritt B., Durnev, Art, Morck, Randall, and Yeung, Bernard Yin (2003), 'Law, Share Price Accuracy and Economic Performance: The New Evidence', *Michigan Law Review*, 102, 331–53.

Overall, the evidence suggests that there can be some value from disclosure rules, but is inconclusive on how much, and whether the rules should be set at the national level. Unlike the debate over hostile takeovers, which over the years was shaped by dozens if not hundreds of empirical papers, the debate over mandatory disclosure is still at the speculative stage.

Perhaps, in their writing on disclosure, Easterbrook and Fischel were influenced by the tendency in early law-and-economics scholarship to search, possibly too hard, for efficiency explanations for what the law then was. For takeover regulation, they called for law to change, to impose radical restrictions on takeover defenses. For disclosure, they seem, in contrast, to look for reasons to explain the regulatory scheme we have.

4 Limited liability

Easterbrook and Fischel's work on limited liability is one of their most consequential, if underappreciated, contributions. This work often gets overshadowed by their more famous papers on takeovers and disclosure. Limited liability simply didn't occupy evening news and economics journals as much as takeovers, and had less powerful policy implications.

To appreciate the extent of Easterbrook and Fischel's innovation in the study of limited liability, one needs to remember the state of the world before their arrival. With limited exceptions,[65] legal scholars treated limited liability as a gift from the government to equity investors of certain types of business enterprises (corporations), but not other types (say, general partnerships or sole proprietorships). When debts of a general partnership exceed firm's assets, creditors can pursue the personal assets of individual partners. As a result, a small investment may expose a partner to large personal losses, in theory wiping out all his personal wealth. In contrast, when the debts of a corporation exceed business assets, creditors are barred from pursuing the personal assets of shareholders. An investor buying $100 worth of corporate stock risks at most losing $100. Such a great gift from the government, in the traditional view, had to come with a payback – in return, the corporation had to submit to government regulation.

The traditional argument was a non-sequitur. Even if we view limited liability as a government's 'gift' to shareholders, we need to recognize that such a gift is of a different type than, say, a tax break or a direct subsidy. The transfer here is not from the government's coffers to shareholders, but rather from third parties (creditors) to shareholders. Even if we adopt the early view that such governmentally mandated wealth transfer is an entirely unpriced windfall for shareholders, one would think that the appropriate response should be a targeted regulation benefiting the most likely losers (creditors) in the amount sufficient to compensate them for their losses, rather than a blanket mandate to regulate corporations as to matters that have nothing to do with creditors' welfare. One could extend this argument further by noticing that limited liability affects different classes of creditors, and creditors of different types of firms, differently, based on their exposure to non-collection risks. A proper payback for the benefits of limited liability, then, would have to involve corporate laws that differ with the firm's bankruptcy risks and the types of creditors it had. However, corporate law does not contain any such targeted approaches.

---

65   Manne, Henry G. (1967), 'Our Two Corporate Systems: Law and Economics', *Virginia Law Review*, 53, 259–84; Posner, Richard A. (1976), 'The Rights of Creditors of Affiliated Corporations', *University of Chicago Law Review*, 43, 499–526; Halpern, Paul J., Trebilcock, Michael J. and Turnbull, Stuart M. (1980), 'An Economic Analysis of Limited Liability in Corporation Law', *University of Toronto Law Journal*, 30, 117–50.

Despite many obvious flaws, the 'payback' view of limited liability dominated legal scholarship for decades. Easterbrook and Fischel delivered one of the first blows to it. They challenged the basic premise of the 'gift' argument – that the governmentally created wealth transfer is unpriced. Following earlier work, Easterbrook and Fischel observed that the price of credit normally reflects the risk of non-collection. A borrower with a volatile income and a limited history of prior repayment will have to pay higher interest than a stable borrower. A firm whose borrowing is effectively secured by the personal wealth of its investors should command a lower interest rate than an identical firm that does not provide such a cushion. Since the cost of credit incorporates the presence (or absence) of limited liability, there is no reason to think that limited liability results in a wealth transfer.[66] Limited liability is not a 'gift' from the government any more than, say, a default rule announcing that all corporate debt is unsecured unless a contract specifically states otherwise.

An important point here is that limited liability is a default, rather than mandatory, rule. A firm that would like to lower its cost of credit can renounce limited liability wholesale (either by saying so in a corporate charter or by choosing a non-corporate organizational form); it can also cherry-pick individual contracts for unlimited liability treatment, by allowing individual shareholders to pledge their personal assets as a collateral (a common practice in close corporations). The question, then, is why limited liability is a sensible default rule, and why public corporations rarely vary from this default rule.

Easterbrook and Fischel's answer is that limited liability allows for the best specialization of different corporate constituencies. Limited liability reduces the need for shareholder monitoring of managers and other shareholders. It promotes the free transfer of shares, which improves capital markets and markets for corporate control. By divorcing the value of the firm's assets from the identity of its shareholders, limited liability improves the markets' capacity to value the firm's assets. Because unlimited liability creates a risk that a shareholder's personal assets will be exposed, and the more firms one invests in, the greater the risk is, limited liability promotes investor diversification.[67]

As discussed below, the link between limited liability and the irrelevance of shareholder identity (and the broad benefits associated with such irrelevance) turn out to be more complicated than at first appears. However, even if one accepts Easterbrook and Fischel's view that shareholders' personal assets must be protected to facilitate the transferability of shares and the proper functioning of capital markets, one still needs to ask why limited liability, rather than insurance, is the best way to achieve that result. After all, limited liability is simply an insurance policy sold by creditors to shareholders.[68] Why is it systematically more efficient

---

[66]   Posner, Richard A. (1976), 'The Rights of Creditors of Affiliated Corporations', *University of Chicago Law Review*, 43, 499–526; Halpern, Paul J., Trebilcock, Michael J. and Turnbull, Stuart M. (1980), 'An Economic Analysis of Limited Liability in Corporation Law', *University of Toronto Law Journal*, 30, 117–50.

[67]   Some of these observations were introduced well before Easterbrook and Fischel by Henry Manne. See Manne, Henry G. (1967), 'Our Two Corporate Systems: Law and Economics', *Virginia Law Review*, 53, 259–84. See also Woodward, Susan (1985), 'Limited Liability in the Theory of the Firm', *Journal of Institutional and Theoretical Economics*, 141, 601–11.

[68]   The very same benefits have been listed as benefits of corporate purchase of insurance. Louis De Alessi, 'Why Corporations Insure', *Economic Inquiry*, 1987, 25, 429–38 ('insurance encourages specialization in ownership, increasing the returns to monitoring and lowering shareholders' demand for a more diversified portfolio; it enhances the credibility of specific capital as a performance bond; and it

to purchase such insurance from parties who are not normally in the business of providing insurance?

Here Easterbrook and Fischel fall into the 'justify the current regime' trap which plagued the first wave of law and economics, effectively announcing that the existing pattern must be optimal because it is the pattern we observe. They list various hypotheses explaining the preference for limited liability over outside insurance; all rest on unsupported and questionable empirical claims. Their main explanation is that creditors are cheaper providers of insurance because they have better information about the firm and are in a better position to monitor the firm's operations to reduce the moral hazard problem. It is not clear why this has to be the case at all times. Some information about a firm's risks might be credibly conveyed only to insiders (including creditors) but not outsiders (such as insurance companies), making creditors better insurers.

But this simple observation is not sufficient. First, many potential risks might be known to all parties equally, and it isn't clear whether conveyable or non-conveyable risks dominate, and whether the pattern of domination varies across firms. Second, if information about a firm's risk of failure is not credibly conveyable to some outsiders (insurance companies), it may not be credibly conveyable to creditors either. After all, many creditors are not close insiders (for example, trade creditors and investors in public bonds often are not), and, in fact, the need to reduce creditor monitoring costs is one of the benefits of shareholder control that Easterbrook and Fischel themselves suggest. Meanwhile, limited liability requires that all creditors participate in the insurance scheme, even the ones who are unlikely to receive information unavailable to outside insurers, and even though there is no obvious correlation between a creditor's exposure to risks of non-payment and his capacity to learn relevant information. Third, some risks might be better ascertainable by professional actuaries through data-mining than by creditors, and again, there is no evidence that such risks are systematically dominated by the risks non-conveyable to third parties. The same may be said about Easterbrook and Fischel's claim that creditors are more able to monitor the moral hazard problem than insurance companies are. Both limited liability and outside insurance give rise to moral hazard; it is not clear why outside insurers are always uniquely disadvantaged in dealing with this problem.

Contemporaneous and subsequent literature disputed much of Easterbrook and Fischel's analysis of limited liability. First, the Coase Theorem implies that the default rule allocating liability to a particular corporate constituency should not matter, at least for voluntary creditors, because a firm's participants will contract with each other over the optimal allocation of risk.[69] Thus, if limited liability is merely a voluntary (and priced) insurance scheme, we should expect a wide variety of liability regimes across firms, perhaps with the pattern tracking firm, shareholder, or creditor characteristics. The fact that we don't see much variety suggests that transaction costs or other common Coasean problems either (a) make limited liability a universally optimal choice; or (b) preclude firm-level bargaining over the optimal allocation of liability; or (c) make overriding the default prohibitively expensive. In either case, the burden is on the proponents of the 'limited liability as an insurance purchased from

---

lowers the cost to shareholders of compensating other members of the team for investing in firm-specific assets').

69   Meiners, Roger E., Mofsky, James and Tollison, Robert D. (1979), 'Piercing the Veil of Limited Liability', *Delaware Journal of Corporate Law*, 4, 351–67.

creditors' hypothesis to specify these costs. An argument that the emerged order must be optimal, or else it would have been changed, is unsatisfactory.

Second, and more importantly, most of the problems attributed by Easterbrook and Fischel to unlimited liability (the need for inter-shareholder monitoring; reduced transferability of shares; harm to the market's ability to separate the value of firms' assets from the value of shareholders' private wealth; impediments to shareholder diversification, and so on) are true for joint and several liability, but not for proportional liability.[70] Under joint and several liability, each shareholder is liable for the entire amount of corporate obligation in excess of firm assets. Under proportional liability, each shareholder is liable only for a pro rata portion of the excess liability. Strictly speaking, even a joint and several liability can approximate proportional liability: the usual arrangement is to combine joint and several liability with a contribution rule that allows a shareholder who paid more than his pro rata share of damages to sue other shareholders for a proportional contribution. In a world without transaction costs and insolvency risks, the two regimes would yield identical results. However, litigation costs and difficulties in collecting judgments often make subsequent litigation impracticable for the shareholder who paid originally, and virtually guarantee that the two regimes do not produce identical results. In effect, the difference between joint and several liability with contribution and proportionate liability is in who bears the transaction costs of collection and risks of insolvency. With joint and several liability, the costs and risks fall on individual wealthy shareholders; with proportionate liability, they fall on creditors.

Under the proportional liability rule, shareholders do not need to monitor each other's wealth because each shareholder is responsible for a pre-specified portion of excess liability that does not depend on others' ability to pay. Likewise, the transferability of shares, and the resulting efficiency of capital markets, markets for corporate control, and investor diversification, are not impeded because the personal wealth of fellow shareholders does not affect one's liability and chances of being sued. To be sure, some of these savings in transaction costs to shareholders will be offset by higher costs to creditros, who now *will* care who the shareholders are.

Since the costs of a proportional liability regime might not be as high as Easterbrook and Fischel suggest in their general defense of limited liability, the question is whether proportional liability might produce sufficient benefits to justify the costs. One benefit of unlimited liability, recognized by Easterbrook and Fischel, as well as others, is the improvements in the tort system. The preceding discussion concentrated on voluntary creditors – lenders, trade creditors, employees – with respect to whom limited liability is not likely to produce large externalities. But tort creditors are different: while sometimes, they could in theory contract ex ante for optimal allocation of the risk of nonpayment (say, in product liability or medical malpractice cases), often, such ex ante contracting is not feasible (say, in cases of pollution or street accidents). In those cases, unpriced limited liability undermines the deterrence function of tort liability because it induces firms to take too much risk and invest too little in precautions.[71] In addition, limited liability induces corporations to shield their assets by shift-

---

[70]   David W. Leebron (1991), 'Limited Liability, Tort Victims, and Creditors', *Columbia Law Review*, 91, 1565–650.

[71]   Tort liability is not the only possible way to force corporations to internalize costs or risky activity. We could instead tax such activities directly and leave unlimited liability in place. See Banerjee, Anindya and Besley, Timothy (1990), 'Moral Hazard, Limited Liability and Taxation: A

ing risky operations to subsidiaries or other parties, which might be an otherwise inefficient arrangement.[72]

This has led to the suggestion that proportional unlimited liability may be superior to both the current limited liability regime and joint and several unlimited liability.[73] The objections to this proposal were centered around its benefits and administrability. First, while proportionate liability may improve the functioning of the tort system, the benefits might be modest because, as mentioned before, many tort claims, such as product liability, arise from prior contractual relationships between tortfeasors and victims. Some claims are priced ex ante, much like claims of financial or trade creditors, incorporating the fact of limited liability. Second, litigation costs and the difficulty of collection will limit tort victims to pursuing only the wealthiest and largest investors, who would still have incentives to sell their shares in distressed firms to other shareholders who would not be worth chasing. As a result, victims might remain largely under-compensated and tortfeasors underdeterred; the extent of additional deterrence may well be insignificant enough to warrant intervention to override the limited liability pattern which is apparently preferred by shareholder and creditors combined.

Third, the current rules of civil litigation further reduce the attractiveness of proportionate liability by impeding efforts to obtain jurisdiction over individual shareholders.[74] If proportionate liability were introduced, we could expect a rise in litigation arbitrage, which would help shareholders judgment-proof themselves by investing through limited liability shell companies or moving their assets to inaccessible jurisdictions. Fourth, a similar arbitrage could develop in capital markets, with a rise in judgment-proof investors specializing in holding the equity of risky companies.[75] Finally, firms would likely develop novel means of judgment-proofing.[76]

Ultimately, the advantage of limited liability is an empirical question. The empirical literature, however, is thin and hardly supports Easterbrook and Fischel's view. The best available natural experiment involved the introduction of limited liability in California in 1931.[77] There is no evidence that California's switch from proportionate liability to limited liability affected incorporation rates or shareholder wealth. While California's exchange-traded firms could opt into the limited liability regime by simply amending their name, most eligible firms

---

Principal-Agent Model', *Oxford Economic Papers*, 42, 46–60. Another option is to regulate dangerous activities, rather than tax them; most law-and-economics scholars, including Easterbrook and Fischel, believe that normally, both tort and tax are more efficient than direct regulation.

[72] Roe, Mark J. (1986), 'Corporate Strategic Reaction to Mass Tort', *Virginia Law Review*, 72, 1–59.

[73] Hansmann, Henry B. and Kraakman, Reinier H (1991), 'The Uneasy Case for Limiting Shareholder Liability in Tort', *Yale Law Journal*, 101, 1879–934.

[74] Alexander, Janet Cooper (1992), 'Unlimited Shareholder Liability through a Procedural Lens', *Harvard Law Review*, 106, 387–445.

[75] Joseph A. Grundfest (1992), 'The Limited Future of Unlimited Liability: A Capital Markets Perspective', *Yale Law Journal*, 102, 387–425; Woodward, Susan (1985), 'Limited Liability in the Theory of the Firm', *Journal of Institutional and Theoretical Economics*, 141, 601–11.

[76] LoPucki, Lynn M. (1996), 'The Death of Liability? A Systems/Strategic Analysis', *Yale Law Journal*, 106, 1–92.

[77] Weinstein, Mark (2003), 'Share Price Changes the Arrival of Limited Liability in California', *Journal of Legal Studies*, 32, 1–25; Weinstein, Mark (2006), 'Limited Liability in California: 1928–1931', *American Law and Economics Review*, 8, 1, 33–61.

chose not to do so. Share prices of affected California firms did not significantly change in response to the introduction of the new liability regime or thereafter.

Another natural experiment was the switch by the American Express Company, the last publicly traded firm with unlimited liability, to the corporate form with limited liability in 1965.[78] The change did not significantly effect firm value, but appears to have reduced both the systematic and unsystematic risk of the company. Both findings are consistent with the view that, in a Coasean world, switching to limited liability does not create value.

Overall, current finance theory and evidence suggest that limited liability is for the most part irrelevant, and early claims of its superiority might have been overstated. Nevertheless, Easterbrook and Fischel deserve significant credit for helping to push the issue away from the old paradigm of the 'gift from the government' to a rigorous world of law and finance.

---

[78]   Weinstein, Mark (2006), 'Don't Leave Home Without It: Limited Liability and American Express', working paper.

15 The path breaking contributions of A. Mitchell Polinsky and Steven Shavell to law and economics

Nuno Garoupa* and Fernando Gómez-Pomar**

1 Introduction

Writing a short essay on the path-breaking contributions of A. Mitchell Polinsky and Steven Shavell to Law and Economics is a difficult and challenging task. It is difficult because their productivity is remarkable, the scope of their work is impressive. We have surveyed more than 150 articles (written over 30 years or so) with applications to almost all fields of law and economics. The challenging part is to provide a flavor of their highly influential work in a single chapter. Furthermore, these two scholars are still very much in the business of producing new insights and high quality scholarly work. Hence this essay will surely be outdated by the time it is published.

Mitch Polinsky and Steve Shavell are two well-known scholars for anyone who has been interested by law and economics and they are among the most cited authors in the field. Mitch Polinsky is the Josephine Scott Crocker Professor of Law and Economics, Stanford Law School. An economist by training (BA Economics from Harvard, PhD Economics from MIT, and MSL from Yale Law School), Mitch Polinsky joined Stanford Law School in 1979. Steve Shavell has been the Samuel R. Rosenthal Professor of Law and Economics, Harvard Law School since 2000. Also an economist by training (AB Mathematics and AB Economics from Michigan, PhD Economics from MIT), Steve Shavell moved to Harvard Law School as a professor in 1980.

Polinsky and Shavell's contributions to law and economics have been acknowledged by the profession in several ways.[1] They are former presidents of the American Law and Economics Association (Mitch in 1993–4; Steve in 2001–2) and currently Steve Shavell serves as co-editor of the *American Law and Economics Review*. Their deep and profound understanding of law and economics, as shown in their scholarly record, has also served them well in book writing. Polinsky has produced an excellent textbook which is the standard introduction to the entire field of law and economics for a wide and diverse audience (Polinsky 1983a, and later editions). Shavell, in turn, has densely put together almost thirty years of scholarly effort, by him, and by many others, on the fundamental areas of the law, on a treatise in law and economics that could be labeled, not misleadingly, as the 'pure theory' of law and economics, and which will provide a reference point to scholars in law and economics, and to analysts of legal matters in general, for years to come (Shavell 2004). Very recently, they have edited together the extensive, authoritative and much needed – by the economics

*   Professor of Law, University of Illinois College of Law. Email: ngaroupa@law.uiuc.edu.
**   Professor of Law, Universitat Pompeu Fabra School of Law. Email: fernando.gomez@upf.edu.

[1]   Their first joint collaborations go back to the mid 1970s, though not in law and economics (Polinsky and Shavell 1975 and 1976).

profession mostly, sometimes not entirely aware of the now very large body of formal analysis of the legal system and other institutional matters – *Handbook of Law and Economics* (2007).[2]

The two authors of this chapter should disclose from the start the highest admiration for Mitch Polinsky and Steve Shavell. We honestly think that our enormous appreciation for their work has not reduced our ability to appraise their contribution objectively. However, since both of us have worked extensively with their contributions and have cited their papers innumerable times, we feel that Mitch Polinsky and Steve Shavell are truly giant scholars who have played a pivotal role in advancing law and economics to a new level of knowledge and influence.

The chapter surveys the contributions by Mitch Polinsky and Steve Shavell to the analysis of the law. They have made crucial contributions to the development of law and economics in the fundamental spheres of law and legal theory. Law enforcement, tort and product liability law, contract law, legal procedure, adjudication and lawyering, the protection of legal entitlements, and the role of fairness and distribution in legal policy are but some of the areas and topics in which their analytical skills have been put to work. Without any claim to being exhaustive, we will try to synthesize their main contributions in the fields outlined above. We start by looking at the economics of law enforcement, where Mitch Polinsky and Steve Shavell have worked in co-authorship for many years. Then, we turn to other areas of the law: torts, contracts, property, litigation, intellectual property, tax and welfare economics, and so on, where they have produced very important contributions, but usually not as a joint production exercise. Even if these lines of research have been largely independently pursued, occasionally with different co-authors, a common flavor in modeling the relevant issues, and the formal and comprehensive approach to legal problems as a way of doing law and economics remain, however, equally unaltered in both their respective separate work. This chapter concludes with some brief final remarks.

2   The economics of law enforcement[3]

We can easily say that Mitch Polinsky and Steve Shavell are the founding fathers of the law and economics of enforcement. It is true that the first seminal article is the well-known piece by Gary Becker, in 1968.[4] There, Becker presents an economic theory of deterrence based on the standard theory of demand (crime rates respond to risks and benefits). The probability and the severity of punishment deter offenses (in the general sense of violations of the law, and not in the particular legal sense of crime). Therefore, Becker concludes, the fine should be maximal since it is a costless transfer whereas the probability of detection and conviction is costly.[5] Polinsky and Shavell have developed an original economic model to assess Becker's claim in a variety of situations. In fact, the standard model of the economics of law enforcement (assessing the extent to which sanctions should be maximal and other legal implica-

---

2   Apart from important contributions to encyclopedias and dictionaries on law and economics (such as Shavell 2001, Kaplow and Shavell 2002a or Polinsky and Shavell 2008).

3   This section has benefited from Garoupa (1997).

4   The origins of the law and economics of enforcement go back to Beccaria and Bentham more than two hundred years ago.

5   Maximal sanctions are probably not the most important contribution of Becker (1968), but certainly the one that has attracted most attention.

tions) is now the so-called Polinsky-Shavell framework. This model has been developed throughout a long series of papers, not necessarily with the aim of establishing a unified theory of law enforcement, but more as an economic assessment of multiple problems encountered by scholars and policymakers in law enforcement. Although their work concentrates on public enforcement (they have surveyed the literature to which they have contributed so much in Polinsky and Shavell 2000a and 2007), we should not neglect their contributions to important issues in private enforcement. Also, the so-called Polinsky-Shavell framework is a model of optimal deterrence, but incapacitation has not been neglected (Shavell 1987a).[6]

The Polinsky-Shavell model is based on a couple of important assumptions. First, individuals are rational utility-maximizing agents choosing in conditions of risk. They compare the benefit from not complying with the law with the corresponding costs. Second, optimal enforcement of the law should be derived from the maximization of social welfare as the objective of public policy. The social welfare function is given by the sum of the benefits minus the costs for everyone. It is usually assumed that the gains from non-compliance should be considered when determining efficient law enforcement.

One important conclusion by Polinsky and Shavell is that there are many circumstances, as we will see, where non-maximal sanctions are efficient. In other words, albeit seminal, Becker's results apply under a very limited set of assumptions. Under richer assumptions, increasing the probability and decreasing the sanction could actually be the efficient policy. We can say that the main results offer interesting insights concerning the probability and severity of punishment in a multitude of situations.

Let's start with the most basic version of the Polinsky-Shavell model. Risk-neutral individuals choose whether to commit an act that benefits the actor by b and harms society by h. This act is punished with a sanction f and a probability p. A risk-neutral individual compares the gain b with the expected sanction pf. Everyone with a benefit higher than the expected sanction is not deterred; everyone with a benefit lower than the expected sanction is deterred. From a social perspective, all acts that generate more harm than benefit should be deterred; all acts that generate more benefit than harm should not be deterred. Therefore, if the expected sanction equals the harm, the private decision by each individual is socially efficient. However, this result presupposes that the probability and the severity of punishment are costless.

Let us assume that the distribution of parties by type is described by a density function $g(b)$ with a cumulative distribution $G(b)$; the distribution is known by the policymaker. The benefit b lies in the interval $[0,B]$. The probability of punishment p is costly, whereas the sanction is not (a fine in the simplest example). The cost function for the probability is $x(p)$ satisfying standard convexity properties. The maximum feasible sanction is F, which can be interpreted as the maximum wealth of individuals.

Risk-neutral individuals commit an offence if and only if b is greater than the expected fine, pf. Given individuals' decision to be honest or dishonest, social welfare is given by the sum of benefits minus costs:

---

6   Optimal incapacitation should be determined by comparing the marginal cost of incapacitating an individual with the marginal benefit of the future crimes that will not take place.

$$W = \int_{pf}^{B} (b - h)g(b)db - x(p)$$

Social welfare is maximized in the probability and in the fine. Immediately recognizing that the probability is marginally costly whereas the fine is not, we conclude that the optimal fine is maximal. The optimal probability satisfies the following condition:

$$Wp = (h - pF)g(pF)F - x_p = 0$$

There are two important results to be highlighted here:

(i)   The optimal probability is based on the harm caused by the offense and not by the illegal gain generated by non-compliance; that's because the objective is efficient deterrence and not full deterrence (further discussion by Polinsky and Shavell 1994b);
(ii) The optimal expected sanction is less than the harm caused by the offense (there is under-deterrence); that's because enforcement is costly.

$$pF = h - x_p/Fg(pF)$$

When punishment is costly, the results are a bit more complicated. Suppose if an individual engages in the harmful activity, he faces some probability of being caught and fined and/or imprisoned. Imprisonment is costly. Therefore, the optimal fine is still maximal (since it is costless), but it could be efficient to supplement a fine with an imprisonment term (when the maximal fine is not very large due to lack of assets by offenders or when the marginal cost of imprisonment is reasonably small). The reason for this result is that the fine is socially costless, hence it is advantageous to use it to its limits before using socially costly means of enforcement (Polinsky and Shavell 1984; Shavell 1985a).

The set-up developed by Polinsky and Shavell since their early 1979 paper has addressed several of the shortcomings of the most basic model.[7]

2.1   Individuals are identified by the harm they cause

Let us assume now that the courts can observe h (they still cannot determine the illegal gains b); in particular, individuals are identified by the harm they cause to society but only *ex post*. Consequently, the sanctioning function is given by $f(h)$ but the probability cannot be conditioned on the harm as in the basic model. Then there is a threshold for the expected sanction below which the optimal sanction equals h/p and above which the maximal fine prevails. Those individuals who cause a reasonably small harm face a non-maximal fine and are optimally deterred; only those who cause a positive net benefit commit the act. Those individuals who cause a sufficiently large harm face the maximal fine and are partially deterred as before (that is, there is under-deterrence). Less harmful crimes should be penalized with

---

[7]   Another interesting property of the model is studied by Lando and Shavell (2004). When resources are constrained, that is, $x(p)$ is constrained by a budget, focusing law enforcement on a subset of the population is the optimal legal policy.

smaller fines, whereas more harmful crimes should be penalized with larger fines. This result also suggests that it is easier to deter less harmful crimes than more harmful crimes (Polinsky and Shavell 1992).

An interesting extension of this line of reasoning is to consider the possibility that law enforcement is examined in a model with specific enforcement effort (effort devoted toward apprehending individuals who have committed a single type of harmful act) and general enforcement effort (effort devoted toward apprehending individuals who have committed any of a range of harmful acts).

The probability of apprehension p is determined by enforcement effort. Specific enforcement effort raises the probability of apprehension for those who commit a specific type of crime identified by h. General enforcement effort raises the probability of apprehension of all individuals who commit harmful acts. Let $z(h)$ be the enforcement effort specific to apprehending those who commit acts causing harm h and k the general enforcement effort. The probability of apprehension is now designated by $p(z(h),k)$. If enforcement effort is specific only, optimal sanctions are extreme for all acts. If enforcement is general only, optimal sanctions tend to rise with the harmfulness of acts and reach the extreme only for the most harmful acts. If enforcement is mixed, these two results should be combined in an efficient way following Shavell (1991a).

2.2   Individuals are identified by the gains they get from crime

If courts have perfect information about b and h for the parties who are apprehended, then under the optimal system of deterrence (Shavell 1987b): (1) parties whose acts are undesirable and who can be deterred will be deterred by the threat of a positive sanction; such sanctions will equal the maximum possible sanction, F; (2) parties whose acts are undesirable and who cannot be deterred (because the gain is too large), and also parties whose acts are desirable ($b>h$), will face no sanction and will commit their acts; (3) sanctions will therefore never actually be imposed.

If the private gain is larger than the social loss, then this act should not be deterred since the benefits more than compensate the harm. By consequence, only an act that satisfies $b<h$ should be deterred. The sanction to deter individuals from committing such act is obviously b/p. However this sanction is upper bounded by F. If b/p is greater than F, then the act cannot be deterred (that is, it is always committed). Thus, since it is costly to impose a sanction, if $b>pF$, the optimal sanction is zero. It is immediately obvious that sanctions will never be applied: this is so because those who are supposed to pay are always deterred.

Consequently, perfect information about b and h is socially valuable. The optimal sanction depends on both b and h in a non-trivial way. Previous results are therefore second-best due to asymmetric information. In fact, if courts cannot obtain perfect information about parties who are apprehended, then under the optimal system of deterrence (again Shavell 1987a): (1) there will generally be parties who commit acts and who are sanctioned. These parties will generally include those whose acts both are and are not desirable; (2) also, some parties will generally be discouraged from committing desirable acts; (3) the optimal sanction must be the maximum, F, for some parties; if the optimal sanction is neither zero nor F, it will be such that the marginal cost of raising sanctions, in terms of sanctions actually imposed, equals the net marginal social benefits due to deterrence of additional parties. The implications of these results are of the utmost importance, and point to the fact that it is rational for the law to look at the *purpose and motive of bad acts* when, as is often true, we are contemplating criminal sanctions or where sanctions are otherwise socially costly.[8]

2.3   Wealth varies among individuals

Recall that the maximal fine was interpreted as the entire wealth of an individual, all individuals having the same wealth. However, usually wealth varies among individuals (Polinsky and Shavell 1991). Suppose each individual is identified by the harm he causes by committing the act and by his wealth (w). We should immediately recognize that the optimal fine equals an individual's wealth for every individual with wealth less than h/p; for all other individuals who can afford to pay the expected value of the harm they create, the optimal fine should be h/p, which is less than their wealth w.

To understand this result, consider why the argument associated with Becker cannot be applied when wealth varies. Suppose that the fine is less than the wealth of the highest-wealth individuals. If the fine is raised and the probability of detection is lowered proportionally, it is true that those who can pay the higher fine are deterred to the same extent. However, those who cannot pay the higher fine are deterred less. Consequently, generally speaking, it is not optimal to raise the fine to the highest possible level.

Further complications arise if wealth varies across individuals and cannot be verified by the courts. In this case, courts can audit convicted offenders, but the technology of auditing usually allows for imperfect verification of the level of assets and is costly. The optimal probability and severity of punishment for the underlying offense vary with the cost of auditing and the fine for cheating on wealth (Polinsky 2006a).

2.4   Risk aversion

When individuals are risk averse, there are two important considerations. First, for a given probability, a lower sanction could achieve the same level of deterrence than would be obtained with the maximal fine if individuals were risk neutral. That is due to the risk premium. Second, imposing the combination of probability and fine obtained when individuals are risk neutral induces over-deterrence in this context. There are individuals for whom the gains from crime are greater than the disutility of punishment and yet they comply with the law. The problem is that the risk premium borne by criminals is a social cost. That is so because all individual costs are included in social welfare. In general, the risk premium is strictly increasing in the fine (the loss of the lottery), but not in the probability (as the probability approaches zero or one, uncertainty is reduced and the risk premium goes down). The government might want to decrease the fine and increase the probability as a way of balancing the risk premium against the net gains in deterrence. In other words, the maximal fine might not be optimal anymore (Polinsky and Shavell 1979).

Related to the issue considered here is the extent to which individuals exhibit different preferences with respect to fines and with respect to imprisonment. The way the disutility of imprisonment varies with the length of imprisonment shapes efficient enforcement. For example, suppose the disutility of imprisonment is very high in the first period but is negligible in the following periods. Then, from a deterrence perspective, the limited role of lengthy imprisonment terms must be balanced against the social cost. When there is information

---

8   A point emphasized by Shavell (1985a) and Shavell (2004, chapters 21 and 24).

about the shape of the disutility function, it should be used to determine efficient deterrence (Polinsky and Shavell 1999).

2.5 Issues in marginal deterrence including repeat offenses

In a seminal paper, Stigler (1970) has noticed that individuals choose over a set of possible actions. Therefore, not only general deterrence matters (compliance with the law), but also marginal deterrence (if an individual does not comply with the law, then he should commit the least serious offense). In other words, when faced with the possibility of committing several harmful acts, individuals should have clear incentives to choose the least harmful act. The important trade-off is that the marginal deterrence principle induces individuals to commit acts with lower harm (since they entail a lower expected sanction), but more individuals are induced to commit the act in the first place. Suppose, for example, that individuals may commit two acts if they are willing to. Some individuals may prefer to commit only one of them, but others certainly prefer to commit both. Repeat offenses could be framed in this context (although usually they are not discussed as a pure marginal deterrence problem).

A maximal fine should only be imposed on those who commit two offenses in order to satisfy the principle of marginal deterrence as explained by Polinsky and Rubinfeld (1991) in a nice application to recidivism. Polinsky and Shavell (1998b) have a twist on the argument for enhancing penalties for recidivism based on the existence of records of prior convictions: When an individual contemplates committing an offense in the first period, he will realize that if he is punished, not only will he bear an immediate fine but a record will be issued (thus making him bear in the second period a sanction higher than it would be otherwise).

Another version of the model of marginal deterrence looks at situations where individuals have to choose between act one or act two; they cannot commit both. Marginal deterrence issues arise as long as enforcement is general. If enforcement is specific to the act, then fines should be maximal and the probabilities chosen in the appropriate way. However, if enforcement is general, the optimal probability will be the same for both acts, and hence the fines should reflect this interdependence (Shavell 1992a).

2.6 Self-reporting behavior

A commonly observed feature of law enforcement is self-reporting of behavior: the reporting by parties of their own harm-producing actions to an enforcement authority. Offenders are offered a discount on the sanction in return for self-reporting. Kaplow and Shavell (1994a) show that the optimal self-reporting scheme is superior to the optimal scheme without self-reporting. In their model, self-reporting has two major advantages: first, enforcement resources are saved because those who commit harmful acts are induced to report their behavior; no enforcement effort is wasted in identifying them. Second, when individuals are risk averse, risk-bearing costs are eliminated because those who commit harmful acts report their behavior and pay a certain amount.

2.7 Providing evidence to legal tribunals

The evidence provided by individuals who face a court is a fundamental source of information for law enforcement. Without such evidence, it is more difficult to gather accurate information. Suppose that all that is directly observable is whether individuals engage in the activity (the harm h is not directly observable). Consider first the situation where individuals who engage in the activity definitely know h. It is intuitive that if an individual engages in the activity and is caught, he should be provided with incentives to provide *h*. However, in many cases, an individual is not able to know with certainty the harm he causes. Then, as shown by Shavell (1989a), the expected sanction for not providing such evidence should be less than maximal.

2.8   Settling out-of-court: the basics of plea-bargaining

Suppose that if an individual is caught and goes to trial, he will incur litigation costs and, with some probability, will be found liable and have to pay a fine. Alternatively, the individual may settle out of court and pay a settlement fine. The maximal fine should apply in order to induce the settlement. However, it is not clear whether settlements and litigation costs will tend to increase or decrease the optimal probability of detection. Settlements and litigation costs can substantially alter the optimal system of law enforcement and should not be neglected (Polinsky and Rubinfeld 1989).

2.9   Looking at Type I and Type II errors

The basic model neglects the possibility of miscarriage of justice (false positives) and the consequent need for greater accuracy. In reality, individuals may be mistakenly found liable for acts they did not commit (false positives – Type I error) and they may be exonerated when, in fact, they did commit the act in question (false negatives – Type II error). Compliance with the law is certainly affected, not only by the extent to which the law is enforced, but also by the accuracy of legal enforcement. Assume the cost devoted to enhancing accuracy is *k*. There is a probability $q(k)$ that individuals who have committed the act and who are detected will erroneously escape sanctions. There is a probability $r(k)$ that individuals who have not committed the act and who are detected will erroneously bear sanctions. Both functions decrease with *k* and the usual convexity assumptions hold.

In this extension of the basic model, individuals who commit the harmful act obtain an expected net benefit of $b - p(1 - q)f$, and those who do not commit the act bear an expected sanction of *prf*. Thus, an individual will not comply with law as long as the illegal gain is greater than $(1 - q - r)pf$. Immediately, we can observe that the possibility of false positives and false negatives dilutes deterrence.

The optimal sanction is still the maximal sanction *F*; nevertheless, the optimal effort on enhancing accuracy is always positive. Kaplow and Shavell (1994b) capture the point that spending money in enforcement (apprehension) and in accuracy are to be regarded as substitutes in achieving deterrence. Accuracy and enforcement effort are alternative ways of increasing deterrence. The optimal fine is the maximal sanction because it is a costless transfer, even though an error may occur.

The possibility of legal error also influences the decision to prosecute. Legal policies that reduce legal error or correct information problems might have important effects on the quality of prosecution (Polinsky and Shavell 1989).[9]

2.10   Punishment of attempts

An attempt is defined to be a potentially harmful act that does not happen to result in harm.

---

[9]   Notice that this article is broader than the point we emphasize. It explains how legal error shapes litigation and discusses corrective legal policies.

If an individual commits an act, he will obtain a benefit and he will suffer a sanction with a probability that depends on whether or not he causes harm. Let us say that with probability q an act will result in harm. Hence, with probability $1 - q$, the act is only an attempt. Suppose that the fine for a crime is f and for an attempt is s. Also, the probability of apprehension for a crime is p and for an attempt is r. The expected sanction faced by an individual who commits an act is $qpf + (1 - q)rs$.

Punishing attempts increases deterrence by raising the probability of effectively imposing sanctions. Punishing attempts thus increases deterrence by expanding the set of circumstances in which sanctions are imposed. By the usual argument, there is an upper bound to sanctions. Once that bound has been set, the only way to deter is by raising the probability of punishment. Therefore, punishing attempts is socially valuable.

However, in many circumstance, courts cannot determine the probability of harm. Shavell (1990) shows that sanctions for attempts and for causing harm are uniquely determined in this scenario: (i) the sanction for attempts is never larger than the sanction for causing harm; (ii) both are non-decreasing with the potential harm h.

2.11   Corruption
Corruption in law enforcement is a serious problem. It can include the payment of bribes or kickbacks to enforcers, threats to frame innocent individuals to get money from them (extortion), and actual framing (entrapment). In all these forms, corruption reduces deterrence and should be discouraged. One possibility is to make corruption a crime, thus creating a typical case of marginal deterrence. A second possibility is to reward enforcers for reporting violations; however, this might create serious incentives to engage in entrapment and extortion. Hence the appropriate reward should balance the benefits of reducing bribery against the cost of expanding extortion and entrapment (Polinsky and Shavell 2001).[10]

2.12   Private precaution
One problem generated by private precaution is that it aims to maximize not social welfare but individual welfare (of potential victims of non-compliance with the law). As a consequence, there is a serious divergence between the private choice of precaution and the socially efficient choice of precaution. This divergence might justify state intervention. It will also determine the optimal choice of severity and probability of punishment (Shavell 1991b).

2.13   Corporate liability
In the basic model, offenses are committed by individuals. In reality, many offenses result from the cooperation of different individuals. A particular and important example is corporate crime. One major question in the context of corporate or cooperative crime is how to assign liability: should the passive party (employers, shareholders) be criminally liable for the offense or violation of the law committed by the active party (employees, managers). Two arguments should be considered (Polinsky and Shavell 1993; Shavell 1997a): (i) in the absence of transaction costs, it is irrelevant to whom liability should be assigned (if liability is assigned to the employer *ex post*, salaries will be negotiated in such a way that the employee will pay for liability *ex ante*); (ii) with transaction costs (limited assets, asymmetry

---

10   More work on threat includes Shavell (1993b) and Spier and Shavell (2002).

of information), liability should be apportioned between the parties in order to maximize social welfare.

2.14   Fairness considerations
In Polinsky and Shavell (2000b), the authors incorporate notions of fairness concerning sanctions in the basic model (that is, individuals have preferences over the effective sanction borne by offenders). The optimal fine is usually not maximal due to fairness concerns. The probability of punishment must be adjusted as a consequence. However, it is not always the case that the probability goes up because a lower sanction reduces the effectiveness of enforcement and therefore makes it relatively more expensive.

2.15   Particular issues in private enforcement
Polinsky (1980a) has extended the model of optimal law enforcement to private firms. He argues that a comparison between private and public enforcement must take into account the structure of the costs of enforcement. Taking into account these differences, private enforcement leads, in a wide range of circumstances, to less enforcement rather than more in comparison with a system of ideal public enforcement. Public enforcement is socially preferable to private enforcement in many cases even when public enforcement is much costlier due to a strategic effect (private enforcers have an incentive not to enforce too high fines that create too much deterrence from a profit-maximizing perspective). In fact, in general, regulating private enforcers by paying them something different than the fine for each violator detected can achieve the socially most preferred outcome in a competitive environment (where the strategic effect disappears due to the standard zero profits constraint), but not in a monopolistic situation.

2.16   The general structure of law enforcement
Efficient law enforcement can be achieved by multiple legal instruments. Compliance with the law is determined by a combination of criminal, civil (tort and contract), administrative (including taxation) measures as well as moral conduct. This combination should be resolved by (i) the adequate level of punishment (fine, non-monetary sanctions, extra-legal sanctions); (ii) the least costly technology of enforcement depending on economies of scale and information asymmetries (public prosecution, private prosecution, regulation, management of social norms); and the appropriate timing of intervention (*ex ante facto*, *ex post facto*). Public law enforcement is clearly more apt when the adequate level of punishment is high (requiring for example non-monetary sanctions) and public prosecution is more effective (Shavell 1985a, 1993a and 2002).

3   Torts and product liability
In the early 1970s the thinking about tort law, one of the basic ingredients of law and legal education, was revolutionized by the work of Calabresi (1970) and Posner (1972), who changed the prevailing view of the subject in terms of compensation for the victim of harm, and of corrective justice to undo wrongdoings, altering the pre-existing status quo in legal entitlements. The approach was economic in spirit, emphasizing incentives and reduction and adequate distribution of the social costs of accidents in modern societies. Brown (1973) formalized this fundamental change in a model of unilateral and bilateral accidents, and liability rules, that has become the standard in the law and economics literature ever since. In

his path-breaking contribution, Brown showed that both potential injurers and potential victims are induced to take optimal levels of precautions under the set of liability rules that most modern legal systems tend to employ – albeit often in different factual scenarios: strict liability, negligence, and the rules that take into account the behavior of the victim (contributory and comparative negligence).

Steve Shavell, in a series of articles in the early and mid 1980s developed fundamental enhancements of this model that have become the essential building blocks of the standard economic theory of accidents and liability, together with the Brown framework. Those contributions were extended and presented in book form in Shavell (1987c), which still remains the classical reference book on the economic model of legal liability for accidents.[11]

3.1 Care vs. activity

In Shavell (1980a), the distinction between levels of precaution and levels of activity appears in the literature, and the advantage of strict liability over negligence in terms of adequately controlling the amount of risky activities by the injurer is shown – as well as the reverse for activity decisions by victims. The simple but powerful idea is clear when one thinks that negligence implicitly involves a subsidy to the injuring party, as long as he evades footing the bill of accidents caused when due care is used in the activity. The distinction clearly corresponds to real world difficulties for courts in determining the social desirability of decisions by individuals and firms about whether to engage in an activity, and how much of it to carry out, given that an overall welfare analysis would be required for the task. It must be noted, however, that sometimes the decisions concerning the 'activity' dimensions of the injurer's behavior are verifiable by the courts (the number of flying hours of a plane, for instance) and an estimate of optimal levels is not exceedingly costly, thus making the distinction one about the dimensions of behavior that can, or cannot, be included in a negligence determination.[12] In an independent article, Mitch Polinsky developed a similar argument but in the context of liability against firms (Polinsky 1980d).

3.2 The role of risk-aversion and insurance

In Shavell (1982a), the author systematically and comprehensively explores the relevance for liability for accidents of attitudes towards risk and the availability of both accident and liability insurance, and the ability of insurers to observe or not the behavior of the insured parties. In the latter case, moral hazard, a topic to which Shavell had already contributed in the more general principal-agent setting – namely, with Shavell (1979a) – becomes relevant. It is exhaustively shown how optimal levels of care, and of risk-bearing, may or not be achieved depending on the market for insurance, on moral hazard considerations, and on the liability rule in place. Shavell returned more specifically to various specific issues of relevance in tort law concerning accident insurance, and especially liability insurance, both in his 1987 treatise (Shavell 1987c), and in a later paper (Shavell 2000): the efficiency of subrogation clauses, the efficiency of excluding voluntary and quasi-voluntary events from coverage, and the social desirability of liability insurance and the effects of different regulatory policies

---

[11]   Also benefiting from work by Polinsky (1980d).

[12]   See also Shavell (1980c, 1985b and 2007c) for scope of liability and causation issues as well as Polinsky and Shavell (1994a) and the points discussed by Salvador et al. (2009), and Dari Mattiacci (2005).

concerning this branch of insurance (from prohibition to a legal mandate to buy liability insurance).[13] This analysis sheds light on the social desirability of liability insurance, historically contested by many – and by some even today – by pointing to the insurance policy-related incentives (premiums linked to behavior, deductibles, observation of care by insurers, and so on) that serve as a substitute for tort law incentives.

3.3   The combined use of liability and regulation

Liability and public regulation are commonly viewed as alternative means to correct externalities, yet most real world legal systems contain a varied mix of both kinds of instruments addressing the same set of risky activities. Shavell (1984b) is the starting point in the literature on the complementary use of liability and regulation. In this paper, it is shown how liability cannot achieve first-best in controlling externalities due to insufficient assets on the part of potential injurers. Public regulation equally fails given that a single standard is used for all potential injurers, while these may diverge in terms of the amount of harm they can produce with their actions. It is further shown that the combined use of both instruments can be more efficient than the separate use of one or other instrument when liability is enforced imperfectly and injurers escape full liability with some probability. When liability and regulation are jointly used, the paper also shows how the regulatory standard should be optimally set at a lower level than the level that would be desirable when regulation alone is in force.[14] The alternative scenario (liability and regulation as substitutes), however, was not forgotten, and was subject to extensive analyses of its comparative weaknesses and strengths in Shavell (1984c and 1987c, chapter 12).

3.4   Judgment-proofness

Since tort liability is an instrument based on money damages, its deterrent effect seems intuitively to depend on the level of assets of the potential injurer. The issue was explored by Summers (1983), and Steve Shavell himself dealt with it in the context just described in the previous subsection. But in Shavell (1986), a full-fledged analysis of the consequences of limited wealth, under alternative liability rules, for taking care, and for buying liability insurance, is presented.

The model uses a framework characterized by a safety technology in which the choice of care by the potential injurer affects external accident costs only through the probability of the accident, and by a care variable that does not affect the level of assets that can be seized by the courts in case the defendant is held liable (non-monetary care). Shavell shows that limited assets tend to reduce the incentive to take care under both strict liability and negligence. In the case of strict liability, when the asset constraint is lower than the level of harm, the injurer takes inefficiently low care. In the case of negligence, there is a critical threshold of assets, strictly lower than the level of harm, above which the potential injurer takes efficient care, and below which the latter opts for sub-optimal care. Thus, in some regions of the level of assets, they both equally underperform compared to the social optimum, and in others, negligence leads to a socially efficient level of care while strict liability does not. Shavell then

---

[13]   See Shavell (1992b) for an extension on liability and incentives to acquire information.

[14]   This result was later confirmed by Kolstad et al. (1990), and shown also, in a setting of perfect enforcement but heterogeneous wealth of injurers, by Schmitz (2000).

extends the analysis to the choice of activity levels, and to liability insurance coverage. Concerning the latter, it is shown that judgment-proofness distorts the incentives to buy liability insurance, and this, in turn, affects incentives to take care, and to engage in risky activities, depending on whether insurers can or cannot observe the choice of care of insured parties.

This early contribution gave rise to a flourishing branch of literature, expanding these initial results along several lines, in terms of both the accident setting explored and the alternative legal rules and policies subject to analysis.[15] Finally, Shavell himself has revisited the judgment-proofness issue, analyzing two policy options typically used by legal systems in the presence of risky activities with participants who may have limited assets, namely compulsory liability insurance, and the legal requirement to possess a minimum amount of assets in order to undertake an activity. Shavell (2005) determines the optimal conditions for the combined use of both instruments for a given activity, and presents an efficiency comparison between the joint use of compulsory liability insurance and a minimum asset requirement, and the latter alone.

3.5   Tort and incentive to sue

The effectiveness of tort liability as an instrument for deterring undesirable risky actions and activities may be thought to depend on the likelihood of the injurer being sued when an accident occurs. It is thus natural to think about the incentives to sue and use the legal system in the tort context. Shavell (1982b, 1997b) shows how the private incentive for the victim to sue the injurer in court fundamentally diverges from the social incentive. The former is based solely on the difference between the cost to the plaintiff of bringing the suit, and the expected amount of damages to be obtained. The social incentive, however, is given by the difference between the deterrence benefit of the suit (how much the choice of care by injurers improves if they are sued and have to pay damages) and the social costs of suit and trial (including the plaintiff's, the defendant's, and societal costs). Given this divergence, and depending on the parameters, the level of suits can be socially excessive or socially insufficient. Shavell himself extends the analysis by incorporating the possibility of settlement into the divergence

---

[15]   Beard (1990) considers monetary care expenditures (precautionary measures that reduce the assets of the potential injurer available to pay a damage award in case an accident materializes). In this setting, under-investment in precaution need not necessarily result from limited wealth and a strict liability rule of the potential injurer, because he may have an incentive to increase expenditure on care in order to reduce the assets that the victim will be able to appropriate to obtain compensation for harm incurred. Boyd and Ingberman (1994) extend the analysis of judgment-proof problems to alternative precaution and accident technologies. They consider safety measures that reduce the size of the accidental loss (pure magnitude technology), and safety measures that affect both the probability and the size of the loss (joint probability-magnitude technology). Dari Mattiacci and De Geest (2002) consider limited assets under a fourth accident technology, which they label the separate-probability-magnitude model. Strict liability induces for this technology either optimal precaution above a high threshold of assets, zero magnitude-reducing precaution and over or optimal probability-reducing precaution above an intermediate threshold, and zero magnitude-reducing precaution and sub-optimal probability-reducing precaution otherwise. Ganuza and Gomez (2008) show that when there is a problem of limited assets, the optimal negligence rule is not the ordinary negligence rule that uses the first-best level of care as the legally required due level of care. The second-best optimal rule identified selects as due care the minimum of first-best care and a level of care that takes into account the wealth of the injurer, and such a modified negligence rule maximizes the precautionary effort.

of private and social incentives to sue, in Shavell (1999), and assesses non-monetary judgments, in Shavell (1993c).[16]

In a similar vein, Mitch Polinsky has also addressed the problem of deterrence and litigation costs. The first approach works through adjustments in the amount of damages to achieve deterrence while minimizing litigation costs. Polinsky and Rubinfeld (1988a) show that, in the presence of risky activities and liability requiring litigation costs, by increasing or decreasing the damage award over the compensatory level by an appropriate amount, it is possible to optimally balance the incentives for care by the injurer (by raising damages, when incentives would otherwise be too low, and the reverse when they would be too high) and the incentives to sue of the victim (by reducing the award to reduce the need to incur suit and litigation costs).[17] The second approach works through the use of decoupling schemes that separate what the plaintiff receives as damages, and what the defendant pays as damages. Polinsky and Che (1991) show how decoupling damages may improve social welfare: instead of having just one policy variable (damages equal to harm caused) to control two different choices – the choice of care by the injurer, and the choice of bringing suit by the victim – we would have two variables. In the paper, they first derive what is the optimal choice of monetary payment to be imposed on the injurer, and show that it corresponds to the level of assets of the defendant (a result that has the flavor of a Beckerian maximum sanction, so the caveats in Section 2 could also be applicable here). Then, the optimal award to the victim is chosen by balancing the marginal costs and marginal benefits of the award, namely the costs of care and litigation costs, on the one side, and the improved deterrence effect, on the other side.[18]

3.6   Punitive damages and other issues on damages

Punitive damages, that is, damages awarded to the plaintiff that exceed – sometimes considerably – the amount necessary to compensate the harm suffered by the plaintiff, are one of the most characteristic features of American tort law (even in common law jurisdictions, punitive damages are seldom, if at all, used outside the US). Polinsky and Shavell (1998a) provide both a deterrence rationale for punitive damages, and normative prescriptions for their use. Punitive damages can serve a positive deterrence function, in the form of a multiplier reflecting the true probability of potential injurers facing the consequences of their actions. Injurers may escape liability for a number of reasons: the circumstances of the accident make it easy for the injurer to avoid being detected and identified; the causal link with the injurer's activity may be hard to establish, both for lack of evidentiary material, or due to weak statistical correlation; where the harm is small or dispersed, which creates substantial hurdles for the victims in suing; the passage of time between the action and the harm; insufficient assets on the part of the injurer to pay for the harm. If this is the case, deterrence through the tort system

---

[16]   See Shavell (1989b) for a discussion on the incentive to share information prior to settlement or litigation. On the value of silence, see also Shavell (1989c).

[17]   On the deterrence effect of settlements and trials, see Polinsky and Rubinfeld (1988b). On optimal awards when the probability of prevailing varies across plaintiffs, see Polinsky and Rubinfeld (1996). On frivolous lawsuits, see Rosenberg and Shavell (1985 and 2006) and Polinsky and Rubinfeld (1993). For a special case of lawsuits brought by shareholders against managers, see Kraakman et al. (1994). Finally, see Shavell (1996) to understand why any probability of the plaintiff prevailing at trial is possible, and not the classical 50 per cent.

[18]   Some of these concerns were discussed in Polinsky (1986).

is diluted. The use of a multiplier may help to restore the optimal amount of deterrence in some of the latter circumstances (though obviously not in all: punitive damages are generally of little use, except maybe when harm is stochastic, in remedying the underdeterrence created by the insolvency of defendants). If the probability of avoiding liability is q, and the amount of harm caused is H, the optimal amount of damages to impose on the defendant would be $H/q > H$. The fraction of this amount exceeding H would constitute deterrence-based punitive damages. Normatively, Polinsky and Shavell reject the notion that punitive damages should also reflect non-deterrence-related considerations, such as the reprehensibility of the injurer's behavior, or the benefit or gain obtained by the injurer through his harmful behavior. From a social welfare perspective, those factors should not weigh in the assessment of punitive damages.[19] In an experimental setting, however, even using University of Chicago Law School students, the probability of escaping liability, and thus deterrence considerations, have been shown to play a minimal role in the actual calculation of punitive damages by juries.[20]

Not entirely unrelated to this topic of punitive damages, Polinsky and Shavell (1994b) have argued on efficiency grounds in favor of the use of harm-based measures of liability (with a multiplier, if necessary) over those using restitution of gain as the basis for establishing the amount of liability. The reason for this lies in the fact that gain-based liability, or disgorgement of profits, is much more vulnerable to mistakes made by the courts or adjudicators in the calculation of the relevant amounts. Even very minor mistakes can produce extremely undesirable outcomes, whereas when the amount of liability is grounded on the extent of harm, the effects are much more attenuated. Both Polinsky and Shavell have explored independently other issues relating to imperfect information on the level of harm resulting from an accident. Polinsky (1987) analyzes when it would be desirable for courts to add to or subtract from the level of compensatory damages, to respond to imperfect information available to the injurer concerning harm to the victim. Kaplow and Shavell (1996a) explore how the private value for plaintiff and defendant of establishing with accuracy the real loss of the victim from the accident exceeds the social value of accuracy, when injurers, while making choices on care, only know the distribution of losses of the population of victims they may encounter. This analysis is extremely relevant for the use of scheduled or predetermined average damages, as used in several areas of the law (for transport and industrial accidents, and even for automobile accidents in some countries).

3.7   Product liability

The Brown-Shavell standard economic model of accidents and liability deals, at least originally, with accidents between strangers (car and pedestrian, polluting factory and property owners, and so on). But many harmful events occur among non-strangers, typically affecting individuals who are in a relationship with a firm. Among these, the most important fraction – at least in terms of the legal development of the field – comprises accidents caused by products manufactured by firms to consumers of such products. Shavell (1980a) shows how when victims are in a contractual relationship with manufacturing firms, consumers' perception of risk becomes the crucial dimension for the performance of alternative legal regimes. If consumers have perfect information about the risks of harm associated with the products of

---

[19]   See further discussion by Polinsky (1997) and Shavell (2007b).
[20]   See Sunstein et al. (2002).

each manufacturer, then a no liability regime, strict manufacturers' liability, and a negligence rule – maybe the one resulting from the risk-utility test in US product liability law – can all implement first-best safety in products. When consumers are only able to perceive the average risk of injury – across manufacturers of the same product – a no liability regime results in a level of product safety that is sub-optimal. And this holds, even if, in equilibrium, as it turns out, consumers' estimates of risk are accurate, and equal to the low level of safety common to all brands of the same product. Liability, be it strict, or negligence-like (if properly applied by courts) would, however, induce optimal levels of product safety. Nevertheless, this does not mean that legal intervention in the form of tort liability should be mandatory in this scenario, given that manufacturers would voluntarily offer warranties to cover product risks, if consumers can determine the coverage under the warranty provided by each individual manufacturer.

If consumers systematically underestimate product risks, a no liability system – even if warranties are available – would distort the choice of product safety level, and also the total quantity purchased, which would be inefficiently large (a result resonating of the care versus activity problem). Strict liability can, though, induce optimal levels of both product safety and product use, a result that has found resonance in the more recent literature defending a broad principle of enterprise liability based on market manipulation by firms (Hanson and Kysar 1999).

The former results hold in a competitive industry structure. Polinsky and Rogerson (1983) analyze the situation of consumer misperceptions of product risks, but with market power on the producer's side. Here, a shift in the liability rule from strict liability – the most efficient given underestimation of risk and competitive firms – to negligence, and then to no liability, may improve social welfare by inducing a manufacturer with market power to increase output in order to benefit from the reduction in costs – greater, due to the underestimation of risk, than the shift in consumer demand – produced by the move towards lower levels of liability. Thus, industry structure may have a bearing on the optimal design of product liability law.

Polinsky and Shavell have recently revisited in a co-authored paper the area of product liability, specifically the issue of disclosure of product risks by firms *vis-à-vis* consumers. In Polinsky and Shavell (2006), they compare mandatory versus voluntary disclosure under three alternative liability regimes. Under no liability, voluntary disclosure would imply that firms would only reveal positive information with respect to the baseline expectations of consumers, which has an obvious downside – any negative information acquired will be concealed – and a less obvious upside – the value of acquiring information about product risks increases, thus the incentive to obtain such information is also higher. The comparison with mandatory disclosure is then less straightforward, depending on the overall impact of the two effects. Under a perfectly functioning negligence regime, no liability will be imposed in equilibrium, thus making the outcome similar to the first regime. When there is perfect strict liability, given *ex post* full compensation of losses, consumers are indifferent to product risks, and mandatory and voluntary disclosure produce equivalent results.

4   Contract law

Contract law is one of the fundamental areas of law, and one in which, almost naturally – albeit, quite surprisingly, until fairly recently this has not been the case – the interplay with economic theory seems most immediate, given that contract law is probably, at least in large and open societies, the most powerful external mechanism to promote cooperation in economic exchange. Economists have sometimes downplayed the importance of contract law in the functioning of economic cooperation. When individuals can write a complete contract that determines contractual behaviour in the whole set of possible circumstances, and the basis of each contractual determination can be verified by the legal enforcer, typically, a court, the role of the legal system in economists' eyes is essentially mechanistic: its role would substantially be equivalent to blind enforcement of each and every term in the complete contract set out by the parties.

But even economic theorists find numerous factors to support the proposition that contractual incompleteness is the rule and not the exception: the prevalence of asymmetric information, and of non-verifiable information concerning many relevant contractual behaviors; the inevitability of imperfect specification of actions that will take place in the future, and in all possible states of the world in the future; difficulties in measuring and evaluating the cooperativeness of contractual behaviors, given the multidimensionality and complexity of many of them; all mean that, under certain circumstances, internal motivators for cooperation have an advantage over external mechanisms such as formal and legally enforceable contracts. Law and economics has added other factors to the long list of reasons that make drafting complete contracts chimerical in our imperfect world, basically the unavoidable ambiguities and uncertainties brought about by the use of ordinary language, in which contracts are written; bounded rationality on the part of the parties, that prevents them from perfectly anticipating all future contingencies, or fully exploiting the gains from trade between the parties in all future states of the world; transaction costs in drafting fully contingent contracts and the savings to the parties from leaving gaps in the contract.

Law and economics scholarship (first, and paradigmatically, Polinsky and Shavell) has systematically shown, in addition, how legal rules and doctrines can be thought of as substitutes for a complete set of contract specifications. In turn, this implies that rules and doctrines in contract law may be fruitfully analyzed as mechanisms to induce behavior in the contracting parties that can be assessed against the benchmark of a complete contract.

4.1 Remedies for breach

Remedies for breach of contract are the most powerful legal instruments to induce certain contractual actions by the parties.[21] Shavell, who contributed earlier in his career to principal-agent theory (Shavell 1979a, 1979b), and using the framework of that literature, initiated formal economic modeling of the effects of damage measures for breach (expectation damages, reliance damages, restitution damages) in two fundamental contractual decisions, the choice to perform or to breach, on the one side, and the choice of the level of (selfish or non-cooperative as they ended up being labeled later) relation-specific investments. Concerning the first decision, Shavell (1980b) shows how the expectation measure is able to exactly replicate the breach decision in a complete contingent contract, and thus induces an optimal level of breach by the performing party. The reliance measure induces sub-optimal performance (that is, excessive breach), and restitution damages induce an even lower level of contract performance. As for reliance investment decisions, the paper addresses two scenarios. The first is the one in which the investing party is the victim of breach. It is then shown that expectation damages induce excessive specific investment by the potential

---

[21]   The extent to which breach should be contemplated is discussed by Shavell (2006c).

victim of breach. The reason for this effect of overreliance lies in the fact that expectation damages fully insure the investing party against the possibility of losing the return on his investment, more than is optimal from the point of view of the joint welfare of the parties. Reliance damages perform even worse than expectation damages, that is, they induce even more over-investment. The reason is that to the full insurance motive to overrely (reliance damages fully insure the investing party because in all possible future states of the world, he obtains at least restitution of the cost of the investment) now has to be added a performance inducement function: by investing more in specific assets, the party directly increases the damage award the other party has to pay in case of breach, thus increasing the incentives of the latter to perform. Restitution damages, in turn, induce efficient reliance, given the – inefficiently low – level of performance under this measure of damages. These results have been to an important degree confirmed by experimental tests of contracting behavior in a controlled laboratory setting.[22]

The second scenario appears when the investing party is the one that can take the decision to breach or to perform the contract. In this case, expectation damages induce efficient investment: the breaching party is the residual claimant of the value of the investment (the reduction in cost of production, for instance), because the damage award he has to pay (the value of performance to the other party) does not depend on the level of investment. Reliance damages also perform worse than expectation damages, although in a different direction than in the first scenario. Given that reliance damages induce too little performance with respect to the efficient level, the investing party will receive a less than optimal return on the specific investment, and therefore the incentives to invest will be too low. Restitution damages perform in the same way as in the first scenario.

The superiority of expectation over reliance damages over these two dimensions (breach, and selfish reliance investments) was shown initially by Shavell for a scenario that rules out contract renegotiation. It was later shown to be valid with costless renegotiation by Rogerson (1984). In a later paper (Shavell 1984a), Steve Shavell introduced the analysis, in a similar scenario to the one just described, of specific performance as a remedy, the role of renegotiation, and the distinction between production contracts and contracts for the transfer of possession, which he exploited later as essential ingredients in a full-fledged comparative analysis of contract remedies, most particularly of specific performance and expectation damages as basic remedies against breach of contract; see Shavell (2004, chapters 15 and 16, and 2006a).

Polinsky has concentrated on the risk allocation properties of legal remedies for breach of contract. In Polinsky (1983b), he considers two potential sources of risk affecting the parties. One is a potential higher offer from a second buyer in a contract for transfer of possession. Here, it is shown that specific performance would optimally allocate risk if the seller is risk averse, and the buyer is risk neutral; expectation damages would be optimal only if the seller is risk neutral and the buyer is risk averse (exactly the converse of the previous scenario); reliance and restitution damages can never determine an optimal risk allocation; finally, liquidated damages can be optimal, if parties are free and rational to determine the optimal risk allocation amount. The second scenario is uncertainty concerning the production costs of the seller in a production contract. In this setting, specific performance can never achieve opti-

---

22   See Sloof et al. (2003).

mal risk allocation (given that the optimal payment for risk allocation can never exceed the buyer's expectation); expectation damages can be optimal in terms of risk allocation only when the seller is risk neutral and the buyer is risk averse; reliance and restitution damages can determine an optimal risk allocation only by coincidence, and where there are no a priori reasons why they could achieve it; as before, there remains the liquidated damages remedy as an optimal risk allocation device if the parties have the information to craft the remedy accordingly. The parties have an incentive to do so, but the courts may be reluctant to enforce the contract term allocating risk.

4.2 Asymmetric information

One of the major functions of contract law is to provide the contracting parties with a set of default terms to fill the gaps left in the contract in the formation period (in order to save transaction costs or for other reasons). One of the most famous of such defaults is the rule of *Hadley v. Baxendale*, a venerable Victorian English case – and a fixed star in the jurisprudential firmament, according to Grant Gilmore, the noted contract scholar. The rule – which, by the way, is of civil law origin, and imported into the common law through this decision – stipulates that damages for breach of contract will not provide full indemnity for all losses suffered by the aggrieved contracting party, but will be limited to those losses that were foreseen by the parties at the time of contracting, or were foreseeable at that time. The rule, according to traditional legal thinking, was rooted in the implied consent of the parties, and the prudent measure of avoiding potentially crushing liability on promisors.

Ayres and Gertner (1989) used this rule as the main illustration of their theory of penalty defaults (contrary to the majoritarian defaults that were uniquely favored by commentators at the time), which may be more efficient in settings of asymmetric information at the contracting stage. Bebchuk and Shavell (1991) independently offered a theory of limited liability in contract based on asymmetry of information about the level of losses resulting from breach. In this celebrated article, the underlying rationale for the rule is simple: when promisees have private information about the consequences of breach (their valuation, or vulnerability to breach), a rule of limited liability to foreseeable damage – thus excluding extraordinary or infrequent losses – would more efficiently channel information to the promisors at the contracting stage if this would increase the joint welfare of the contracting parties. Assuming that the majority of promisees only suffer ordinary, foreseeable losses, it is more efficient that the minority with high vulnerability identify themselves when signing the contract asking – and paying – for complete coverage of their higher level of harm. This is the incentive created by the Hadley rule. The opposite rule of full indemnity, on the contrary, would force the majority to identify at the contracting stage and ask for a waiver or limitation of liability in order to avoid being pooled with the high-loss promisees.[23]

Asymmetry of information at the contracting stage is nowadays the standard rationale for imposing disclosure duties in many fields of the law, ranging from general contract law, to consumer protection law, and to securities law. In Shavell (1994), we find a thorough analysis of how contract law creates incentives for acquisition and disclosure of contractually relevant

---

[23]   This contribution gave rise to later literature, analyzing in the same setting issues of market power (Johnston 1990) and stochastic damages (Adler 1999) – a paper that generated a reply in Bebchuk and Shavell (1999) – and assessing experimentally the stickiness of the Hadley default (Korobkin 1998a, 1998b).

information. The paper distinguishes between information with and without social value, and the role of legal rules should be to discourage the acquisition of the latter, and adequately encourage the acquisition of the former. This can be done, in most circumstances, by rules forcing disclosure possessed by the party with private information. The rules work differently, however, for the seller and for the buyer. If the seller is forced to disclose his private information, the incentive to acquire socially valuable information is not eliminated, as long as the truth of the positive information can be contractually warranted by the seller or otherwise credibly communicated and verified. Disclosure duties, however, erase the incentive for the seller to acquire socially worthless information. The incentive problem for the buyer is more complicated, because disclosure requirements would eliminate the incentive to invest in obtaining information without social value, which is efficient, but they would also negatively affect the incentive to acquire information that it is efficient to obtain. Even if the rule can discriminate among both types of information, the incentive problem for the buyer cannot be optimally solved through disclosure rules on socially valuable information.

4.3   Other topics in contract law

One particular type of contract that has deserved the attention of Steve Shavell is deferred gifts (Shavell 1991c). By making sense of altruism as well as opportunistic behavior, he explains why such contracts should be enforced under certain conditions even if they require only unilateral performance.

Recently, Steve Shavell has covered other important areas of contract law. The first is interpretation of contracts by courts or other adjudicators. How the parties draft contracts anticipating the interpretive and gap-filling strategies of courts, and conversely, how the latter should optimally read, complete and enforce contract terms are among the most interesting recent developments in current research on contract matters.[24]

Shavell (2006b) contains a general theory of the conditions that make court interpretation (that is, not blind enforcement of terms) optimal, as well as several important elements of interpretive strategy by courts, such as interpreting specific and general terms, filling voluntary gaps in contracts, and allowing extrinsic evidence to guide interpretation of terms for certain contingencies. The second is the hold-up problem as it appears in circumstances known in legal terms as duress as a cause of contract unenforceability. The topic was addressed in economic terms by Bar-Gill and Ben-Shahar (2004, 2005) as essentially one of separating credible from non-credible threats, and the need not to deter non-staged credible threats. Shavell (2007a) underlines the substantial inefficiencies associated with a contractual hold-up, in terms of both wasteful investments in preparing and defending against hold-up, as well as exposure to undesirable risk due to the hold-up. He points out, however, that the traditional legal remedy of voiding a contract for duress may be undesirable in situations in which the need of one contracting party and the advantage of the other are not artificial, but the result of uncontrollable events. He shows how a legal policy of limiting price may better serve efficiency, although this may be difficult for the courts to implement. Finally, the paper explains several regulatory restrictions on price (taxis, hotels) in terms of the principle of avoiding inefficient hold-ups through price controls.

---

24   See Posner (2005), Scott and Triantis (2006), Hermalin (2008), and Gomez (2008).

5 Nuisance and the protection of entitlements

Nuisance law and externalities are the birthplace of law and economics (Coase 1960), and the Calabresi-Melamed framework of legal instruments to protect rights and entitlements continues to shape our thinking about the structure of legal rules. Polinsky and Shavell have also made remarkable contributions to this field of research.[25]

A series of articles (Polinsky 1979, 1980b, 1980c) by Mitch Polinsky presents the most thorough and refined analysis of the complex set of issues arising from nuisance disputes. He compares the performance, in the presence of parties bargaining in the shadow of a legal solution, of the most important instruments (property rules and injunctions, liability rules and damages, and public law tools of tax and subsidy) in terms of both efficiency in the use of resources, and the distributional dimensions of the resulting outcomes. In the latter, more particularly, such as how the initial distribution of resources determined by collective choice (and assumed to be the socially desired one) is distorted by the different instruments. Different settings and factors are included in the analysis, from the number of parties involved in the conflict, to imperfect information on the part of the decision-maker, asymmetric information held by the parties, and redistribution costs.

In Kaplow and Shavell (1996b), we find the most comprehensive analysis of the advantages and disadvantages of protecting entitlements with property and liability rules. The initial organizing division of the analysis is the distinction between externalities and takings. For the former area, there is a general advantage of liability rule protection, even when transaction costs are relatively low: parties also bargain around liability rules. Several factors, extensively analyzed, should be weighed against this initial attractiveness: court mistakes in assessing harm – although to a lesser extent than generally thought, because average estimation also works most of the time; moral hazard; and limited wealth on the part of the originator of the externality. As far as takings of property are concerned, property protection is generally superior, although for reasons that diverge from the common rationale for channeling transactions through the market: the open-ended nature of the potential taker under a liability rule, the risk of arms races in reciprocal takings, and *ex-ante* unproductive investments in taking and to prevent takings.

The stream of literature flowing from these contributions by Polinsky and Shavell, in the wake of Coase, and Calabresi and Melamed, has been too numerous to cite.[26]

6 Lawyering, litigation costs and courts

Two important issues concerning the legal profession have merited the attention of Mitch Polinsky and Steve Shavell: the most adequate way to compensate lawyers and the extent to which legal advice is efficient. Concerning both issues, private incentives are misaligned with the social optimum and therefore might require some form of corrective policy.

---

[25] See also Polinsky (1980e) and Polinsky and Shavell (1982) for a discussion of Pigovian taxation. In Kaplow and Shavell (2002c), the authors defend the claim that corrective taxes are superior to quantity regulation in controlling externalities.

[26] Some of the most recent analyses have emphasized more complex types of rules (put option like, such as in Ayres and Balkin (1996); Ayres (2005); hybrid rules with switches leading from one to another simple rule, as in von Wangenheim and Gomez (2005)), *ex-ante* investments (Bebchuk (2001, 2002); Pitchford and Snyder (2004)), or both (von Wangenheim and Gomez (2005)).

With respect to legal fees, Polinsky and Rubinfeld (2003) show that contingent fees can be used to align the interests of lawyers and clients but need some form of modification. A third party is required to compensate the lawyer for a certain fraction of his costs, in return for which the lawyer would pay that party an up-front fee. In this way, the client will not bear any costs, even if the case is lost, just as under the conventional contingent fee system. In a related paper, Polinsky and Rubinfeld (2002) show that under the common contingent fee system, contrary to conventional wisdom, the lawyer might have an incentive to settle too few cases (once one takes into account the fact that lawyers might not litigate the case in court in the most efficient way).

As to legal advice, the divergence between private and social motives is notable. Legal advice can be used to avoid the law or undermine compliance; it can also reduce asymmetries of information and facilitate the understanding of the law. In all cases, for the lawyer, it is a matter of improving the standing of the client. However, from a social perspective, legal advice that undermines compliance is not a good thing. A distinction should be made between *ex ante facto* (Kaplow and Shavell 1988 and 1992) and *ex post facto* legal advice (Kaplow and Shavell 1989 and 1990). An important conclusion is that the regulation of legal advice should exhibit an important and serious dissimilarity between these two types of legal advice. The reality, however, does not always seem to do so.

With respect to litigation and civil procedure, an important question studied by Shavell (1982c) and Polinsky and Rubinfeld (1998) is the extent to which the American rule (each side pays her own litigation costs) is better than the English – or, probably more accurately, the European – rule (the loser pays all) in terms of deterrence, settlement and trial. The broad conclusion is that, depending on the parameters of the model, it could go either way. This result has important policy implications since it implies that reforms of civil procedure should be carefully evaluated.

The fashionable topic of alternative dispute resolution mechanisms (ADRs) has been addressed by Shavell (1995a). His tone is much less enthusiastic than that expressed by many economists. *Ex ante facto* ADR agreements have significant cost advantages for the parties but they might undermine deterrence and therefore are not necessarily adequate from a social perspective. However, *ex post facto* ADR agreements raise more serious concerns: they do not take into consideration the effect on prior behavior and might therefore hurt at least one of the parties. The conclusion of Steve Shavell's work on ADRs is that the widespread development of ADRs requires a more thorough analysis than just looking at cost reduction for the parties.

With respect to courts, Steve Shavell has developed a very important insight into the appeal process as a mechanism to correct errors (Shavell 1995b). He compares two alternatives, allowing appeals to a second instance court or improving the quality of adjudication by a first instance court. In the paper, he presents a compelling argument for why the appeal solution might actually be cheaper for society. Furthermore, he explains why litigants should be able to take the initiative to appeal rather than appeal courts having the right to reconsider decisions by first instance courts (if litigants know when errors were made, the appeals system naturally harnesses their information, since they will tend to make appeals only when they are likely to win). In a more recent paper (Shavell 2006d), Shavell looks at incentives for adjudicators in this context. His argument is that the appeals process disciplines adjudicators and makes them more likely to comply with socially desirable decisions at low cost for society (because they anticipate the behavior of appeal courts). His conclusions are reinforced by yet another paper (Shavell 2007d) where adjudicators enjoy discretion as a solution to the trade-off between opportunism and use of specific knowledge.

7 Intellectual property law

Steve Shavell has also worked on intellectual property law. In Shavell and van Ypersele (2001), the authors compare a public reward system with intellectual property rights (patents and copyrights). Their important conclusion is that an appropriately designed reward system – ideally, one that equates the reward to the entire social value of the innovation – may generate the right incentives to innovate – something that the intellectual property rights system is unable to do generally, at least without perfect price discrimination, as Arrow showed – but eliminating the monopoly power of intellectual property rights. There is an important difficulty, namely the amount of information required to determine the rewards to be paid by the government. Hence, a mixed or optional system (under which innovators choose between rewards and intellectual property rights) is shown to be superior.

8 Tax law and distribution

With Louis Kaplow, Steve Shavell has also addressed substantive issues in tax theory. In a series of papers (Kaplow and Shavell 1994c and 2000b), they argue that legal rules should not be used to play the role of income tax and redistribute wealth (in fact, a result very much on the topic of and fundamentally popularizing a previous article, Shavell 1981). The distortions imposed on the economy by empowering the legal system with a redistributive role are more costly than achieving the desired income equality by taxation. In a second paper, Kaplow and Shavell respond to criticism by Sanchirico (2000) on why heterogeneity across agents (with respect to taking care to avoid accidents) might justify the use of the legal system to favor the poor. The argument there is that the conditions under which such heterogeneity would reverse their result are hardly practical. These conclusions are of the utmost importance; after all, they imply that the commonly heard arguments that the distributional consequences of legal rules must be considered – how they will hurt this or that group of poor or middle class people– should be rejected, since the income tax system revision is a socially better alternative policy.

9 Welfare economics and the law

More recently, Steve Shavell has worked with Louis Kaplow to address a significant methodological controversy: the use of welfare economics as the unique criterion to assess legal policy. In a by-now famous book, Louis Kaplow and Steve Shavell discuss the advantages of welfare economics for legal policy assessment and the shortcomings of alternative philosophical approaches (Kaplow and Shavell 2001a and 2002b). One main issue tackled by the authors is the extent to which fairness or distributive justice criteria endorse legal policies that are inconsistent with the Pareto principle (Kaplow and Shavell 1999, 2000a, 2001b and 2003). In more detail, Kaplow and Shavell show that *any* welfare criterion that is not solely a function of the profile of people's utilities – that depends in *any* way on an independent principle of fairness or any other non-utility-based factor – will sometimes make all individuals worse off. This work has been extensively cited and criticized (Kaplow and Shavell 2004a and 2004b), not least because many scholars disliked the legal implications of these strong results. Although contentious, there is no doubt that this work is a fundamental point of reference for any meaningful discussion within economics and philosophy concerning the appraisal of legal policy.

10   Conclusion

Mitch Polinsky and Steve Shavell are two of the most accomplished scholars in the field, and this chapter is proof of the extensive nature of their path-breaking contributions to law and economics. Their work has provided us with important instruments to improve the economic analysis of legal institutions throughout the world. Since they are prolific and highly productive, we are pretty sure that a future revision of this chapter will enlist even more substantive references to the work they are producing just now.

References

Adler, B. (1999), 'The Questionable Ascent of Hadley v. Baxendale', *Stanford Law Review*, 51: 1547–90.
Ayres, I. (2005), *Optional Law: The Structure of Legal Entitlements*, Chicago: University of Chicago Press.
Ayres, I. and J.M. Balkin (1996), 'Legal Entitlements as Auctions: Property Rules, Liability Rules, and Beyond', *Yale Law Journal*, 106: 703–50.
Ayres, I. and R. Gertner (1989), 'Filling Gaps in Incomplete Contracts: An Economic Theory of Default Rules', *Yale Law Journal*, 99 (1): 87–130.
Bar-Gill, O. and O. Ben-Shahar (2004), 'The Law of Duress and the Economics of Credible Threats', *Journal of Legal Studies*, 33 (2): 391–430.
Bar-Gill, O. and O. Ben-Shahar (2005), 'Credible Coercion', *Texas Law Review*, 83 (3): 717–80.
Beard, T.R. (1990), 'Bankruptcy and Care Choice', *Rand Journal of Economics*, 21: 626–34.
Bebchuk, L. (2001), 'Property Rights and Liability Rules: The Ex Ante View of the Cathedral', *Michigan Law Review*, 100 (2): 601–39.
Bebchuk, L. (2002), 'Ex Ante Investments and Ex Post Externalities', Discussion Paper No. 397, John M. Olin Center for Law, Economics and Business, Harvard Law School.
Bebchuk, L. and S. Shavell (1991), 'Information and the Scope of Liability for Breach of Contract: The Rule of Hadley v. Baxendale', *Journal of Law, Economics and Organization*, 7 (2): 284–312.
Bebchuk, L. and S. Shavell (1999), 'Reconsidering Contractual Liability and the Incentive to Reveal Information', *Stanford Law Review*, 51 (6): 1615–27.
Becker, G.S. (1968), 'Crime and Punishment: An Economic Approach', *Journal of Political Economy*, 76: 169–217.
Boyd, J. and D.E. Ingberman (1994), 'Noncompensatory Damages and Potential Insolvency', *Journal of Legal Studies*, 23: 895–910.
Brown, J.P. (1973), 'Toward an Economic Theory of Liability', *Journal of Legal Studies*, 2 (2): 323–49.
Calabresi, G. (1970), *The Cost of Accidents: A Legal and Economic Analysis*, New Haven: Yale University Press.
Coase, R. (1960), 'The Problem of Social Cost', *Journal of Law and Economics*, 3 (1): 1–44.
Dari Mattiacci, G. (2005), 'On the Optimal Scope of Negligence', *Review of Law and Economics*, 1 (3): 331–64.
Dari Mattiacci, G. and G. De Geest (2002), 'An Analysis of the Judgment Proof Problem Under Different Tort Models', German Working Papers in Law and Economics.
Ganuza, J. and F. Gomez (2008), 'Realistic Standards: Optimal Negligence with Limited Liability', *Journal of Legal Studies*, 37 (2): 577–94..
Garoupa, N. (1997), 'The Theory of Optimal Law Enforcement', *Journal of Economic Surveys*, 11 (3): 267–95.
Gomez, F. (2008), 'The Charms of Vagueness in Contracts: Comments on Hermalin', *Journal of Institutional and Theoretical Economics*, 164: 99–105.
Hanson, J. D. and D.A. Kysar (1999), 'Taking Behavioralism Seriously: The Problem of Market Manipulation', *New York University Law Review*, 74 (3): 630–749.
Hermalin, B. E. (2008), 'Vague Terms: Contracting when Precision in Terms is Infeasible', *Journal of Institutional and Theoretical Economics*, 164: 76–94.
Johnston, J.S. (1990), 'Strategic Bargaining and the Economic Theory of Contract Default Rules', *Yale Law Journal*, 100: 615–64.
Kaplow, L. and S. Shavell (1988), 'Legal Advice about Contemplated Acts: The Decision to Obtain Advice, its Social Desirability and Protection of Confidentiality', *Journal of Legal Studies*, 17 (1): 123–50.
Kaplow, L. and S. Shavell (1989), 'Legal Advice about Information to Present in Litigation: Its Effects and Social Desirability', *Harvard Law Review*, 102 (3): 565–615.
Kaplow, L. and S. Shavell (1990), 'Legal Advice about Acts Already Committed', *International Review of Law and Economics*, 10 (2): 149–59.
Kaplow, L. and S. Shavell (1992), 'Private versus Socially Optimal Provision of Ex Ante Legal Advice', *Journal of Law, Economics and Organization*, 8 (2): 306–20.
Kaplow, L. and S. Shavell (1994a), 'Optimal Law Enforcement with Self-Reporting of Behavior', *Journal of Political Economy*, 102: 583–606.

Kaplow, L. and S. Shavell (1994b), 'Accuracy in the Determination of Liability', *Journal of Law and Economics*, 37 (1): 1–15.

Kaplow, L. and S. Shavell (1994c), 'Why the Legal System is Less Efficient than the Income Tax in Redistributing Income', *Journal of Legal Studies*, 23 (2): 667–81.

Kaplow, L. and S. Shavell (1996a), 'Accuracy in the Assessment of Damages', *Journal of Law and Economics*, 39 (1): 191–210.

Kaplow, L. and S. Shavell (1996b), 'Property Rules versus Liability Rules: An Economic Analysis', *Harvard Law Review*, 109 (4): 713–90.

Kaplow, L. and S. Shavell (1999), 'The Conflict between Notions of Fairness and the Pareto Principle', *American Law and Economics Review*, 1 (1): 63–77.

Kaplow, L. and S. Shavell (2000a), 'Notions of Fairness versus the Pareto Principle: On the Role of Logical Consistency', *Yale Law Journal*, 110 (2): 237–49.

Kaplow, L. and S. Shavell (2000b), 'Should Legal Rules Favor the Poor? Clarifying the Role of Legal Rules and the Income Tax in Redistributing Income', *Journal of Legal Studies*, 29 (2): 821–35.

Kaplow, L. and S. Shavell (2001a), 'Fairness versus Welfare', *Harvard Law Review*, 114 (4): 961–1388.

Kaplow, L. and S. Shavell (2001b), 'Any Non-Welfarist Method of Policy Assessment Violates the Pareto Principle', *Journal of Political Economy*, 109 (2): 281–6.

Kaplow, L. and S. Shavell (2002a), 'Economic Analysis of Law', in the *Handbook of Public Economics*, vol. 3 (edited by Alan J. Auerbach and Martin Feldstein), Cambridge, MA: Elsevier.

Kaplow, L. and S. Shavell (2002b), *Fairness versus Welfare*, Cambridge, MA: Harvard University Press.

Kaplow, L. and S. Shavell (2002c), 'On The Superiority of Corrective Taxes to Quantity Regulation', *American Law and Economics Review*, 4 (1): 1–17.

Kaplow, L. and S. Shavell (2003), 'Fairness versus Welfare: Notes on the Pareto Principle, Preferences, and Distributive Justice', *Journal of Legal Studies*, 32 (1): 331–62.

Kaplow, L. and S. Shavell (2004a), 'Any Non-Welfarist Method of Policy Assessment Violates the Pareto Principle: A Reply', *Journal of Political Economy*, 112 (1): 249–51.

Kaplow, L. and S. Shavell (2004b), 'Reply to Ripstein: Notes on Welfarist versus Deontological Principles', *Economics and Philosophy*, 20: 209–15.

Kolstad, C.D. T.S. Ulen and G.V. Johnson (1990), 'Ex Post Liability for Harm versus Ex Ante Safety Regulation: Substitutes or Complements?', *American Economic Review*, 80 (4): 888–901.

Korobkin, R. (1998a), 'The Status Quo Bias and Contract Default Rules', *Cornell Law Review*, 83: 608–87.

Korobkin, R. (1998b), 'Inertia and Preference in Contract Negotiation: The Psychological Power of Default Rules and Form Contracts', *Vanderbilt Law Review*, 51: 1583–651.

Kraakman, R. H. Park and S. Shavell (1994), 'When Are Shareholder Suits in Shareholder Interests?', *Georgetown Law Review*, 82 (5): 1733–75.

Lando, H. and S. Shavell (2004), 'The Advantage of Focusing Law Enforcement', *International Review of Law and Economics*, 24 (2): 209–18.

Pitchford, R. and C. Snyder (2004), 'Coming to the Nuisance: An Economic Analysis from an Incomplete Contracts Perspective', *Journal of Law, Economics and Organization*, 19 (2): 491–516.

Polinsky, A.M. (1979), 'Controlling Externalities and Protecting Entitlements: Property Right, Liability Rule, and Tax-Subsidy Approaches', *Journal of Legal Studies*, 8 (1): 1–48.

Polinsky, A.M. (1980a), 'Private Versus Public Enforcement of Fines', *Journal of Legal Studies*, 9 (1): 105–27.

Polinsky, A.M. (1980b), 'On the Choice Between Property Rules and Liability Rules', *Economic Inquiry*, 18 (2): 233–46.

Polinsky, A.M. (1980c), 'Resolving Nuisance Disputes: The Simple Economics of Injunctive and Damage Remedies', *Stanford Law Review*, 32 (6): 1075–112.

Polinsky, A.M. (1980d), 'Strict Liability vs. Negligence in a Market Setting', *American Economic Review: Papers and Proceedings*, 70 (2): 363–7.

Polinsky, A.M. (1980e), 'The Efficiency of Paying Compensation in the Pigovian Solution to Externality Problems', *Journal of Environmental Economics and Management*, 7 (2): 142–8.

Polinsky, A.M. (1983a), *An Introduction to Law and Economics* (Boston: Little, Brown and Company; second edition: Boston: Little, Brown and Company, 1989; third edition: New York, NY: Aspen Publishers, 2003).

Polinsky, A.M. (1983b), 'Risk Sharing through Breach of Contract Remedies', *Journal of Legal Studies*, 12 (2): 427–44.

Polinsky, A.M. (1986), 'Detrebling versus Decoupling Antitrust Damages: Lessons from the Theory of Enforcement', *Georgetown Law Journal*, 74 (4): 1231–6.

Polinsky, A.M. (1987), 'Optimal Liability When the Injurer's Information about the Victim's Loss is Imperfect', *International Review of Law and Economics*, 7 (2): 139–47.

Polinsky, A.M. (1997), 'Are Punitive Damages Really Insignificant, Predictable, and Rational? A Comment on Eisenberg et al.', *Journal of Legal Studies*, 26 (2): 663–77.

Polinsky, A.M. (2006a), 'Optimal Fines and Auditing when Wealth is Costly to Observe', *International Review of Law and Economics*, 26 (4): 323–35.

Polinsky, A.M. (2006b), 'The Optimal Use of Fines and Imprisonment when Wealth is Unobservable', *Journal of Public Economics*, 90 (3): 823–35.

Polinsky, A.M. and Y.K. Che (1991), 'Decoupling Liability: Optimal Incentives for Care and Litigation', *Rand Journal of Economics*, 22 (4): 562–70.

Polinsky, A.M. and W.P. Rogerson (1983), 'Products Liability, Consumer Misperceptions, and Market Power', *Bell Journal of Economics*, 14 (2): 581–9.

Polinsky, A.M. and D.L. Rubinfeld (1988a), 'The Welfare Implications of Costly Litigation for the Level of Liability', *Journal of Legal Studies*, 17 (1): 151–64.

Polinsky, A.M. and D.L. Rubinfeld (1988b), 'The Deterrent Effects of Settlements and Trials', *International Review of Law and Economics*, 8 (1): 109–16.

Polinsky, A.M. and D.L. Rubinfeld (1989), 'A Note on Optimal Public Enforcement with Settlements and Litigation Costs', *Research in Law and Economics*, 12: 1–8.

Polinsky, A.M. and D.L. Rubinfeld (1991), 'A Model of Optimal Fines for Repeat Offenders', *Journal of Public Economics*, 46: 291–306.

Polinsky, A.M. and D. L. Rubinfeld (1993), 'Sanctioning Frivolous Suits: An Economic Analysis', *Georgetown Law Journal*, 82 (2): 397–435.

Polinsky, A.M. and D.L. Rubinfeld (1996), 'Optimal Awards and Penalties When the Probability of Prevailing Varies Among Plaintiffs', *Rand Journal of Economics*, 27 (2): 269–80.

Polinsky, A.M. and D.L. Rubinfeld (1998), 'Does the English Rule Discourage Low-Probability-of-Prevailing Plaintiffs?' *Journal of Legal Studies*, 27 (2): 519–35.

Polinsky, A.M. and D.L. Rubinfeld (2002), 'A Note on Settlements under the Contingent Fee Method of Compensating Lawyers', *International Review of Law and Economics*, 22 (2): 217–25.

Polinsky, A.M. and D.L. Rubinfeld (2003), 'Aligning the Interests of Lawyers and Clients', *American Law and Economics Review*, 5 (1): 165–88.

Polinsky, A.M. and S. Shavell (1975), 'The Air Pollution and Property Value Debate', *Review of Economics and Statistics*, 57 (1): 100–104.

Polinsky, A.M. and S. Shavell (1976), 'Amenities and Property Values in a Model of an Urban Area,' *Journal of Public Economics*, 5 (1–2): 119–29.

Polinsky, A.M. and S. Shavell (1979), 'The Optimal Trade-off between the Probability and Magnitude of Fines', *American Economic Review*, 69: 880–91.

Polinsky, A.M. and S. Shavell (1982), 'Pigovian Taxation with Administrative Costs', *Journal of Public Economics*, 19 (3): 385–94.

Polinsky, A.M. and S. Shavell (1984), 'The Optimal Use of Fines and Imprisonment', *Journal of Public Economics*, 24: 89–99.

Polinsky, A.M. and S. Shavell (1989), 'Legal Error, Litigation and the Incentive to Obey the Law', *Journal of Law, Economics and Organization*, 5 (1): 99–108.

Polinsky, A.M. and S. Shavell (1991), 'A Note on Optimal Fines when Wealth varies Among Individuals', *American Economic Review*, 81 (3): 618–21.

Polinsky, A.M. and S. Shavell (1992), 'Enforcement Costs and the Optimal Magnitude and Probability of Fines', *Journal of Law and Economics*, 35 (1): 133–48.

Polinsky, A.M. and S. Shavell (1993), 'Should Employees be Subject to Fines and Imprisonment Given the Existence of Corporate Liability', *International Review of Law and Economics*, 13 (3): 239–57.

Polinsky, A.M. and S. Shavell (1994a), 'A Note on Optimal Cleanup and Liability After Environmentally Harmful Discharges', *Research in Law and Economics*, 16: 17–24.

Polinsky, A.M. and S. Shavell (1994b), 'Should Liability be Based on the Harm to the Victim or the Gain to the Injurer?', *Journal of Law, Economics and Organization*, 10 (2): 427–37.

Polinsky, A.M. and S. Shavell (1998a), 'Punitive Damages: An Economic Analysis', *Harvard Law Review*, 111: 869–962.

Polinsky, A.M. and S. Shavell (1998b), 'On Offense History and the Theory of Deterrence', *International Review of Law and Economics*, 18 (3): 305–24.

Polinsky, A.M. and S. Shavell (1999), 'On the Disutility and Discounting of Imprisonment and the Theory of Deterrence', *International Review of Law and Economics*, 28 (1): 1–16.

Polinsky, A.M. and S. Shavell (2000a), 'The Economic Theory of Public Enforcement of Law', *Journal of Economic Literature*, 38 (1): 45–76.

Polinsky, A.M. and S. Shavell (2000b), 'The Fairness of Sanctions: Some Implications for Optimal Enforcement Policy', *American Law and Economics Review*, 2 (2): 223–37.

Polinsky, A.M. and S. Shavell (2001), 'Corruption and Optimal Law Enforcement', *Journal of Public Economics*, 81 (1): 1–24.

Polinsky, A.M. and S. Shavell (2006), 'Mandatory Versus Voluntary Disclosure of Product Risks', NBER Working-Paper 12776.

Polinsky, A.M. and S. Shavell (2007), 'The Theory of Public Enforcement of Law', in the *Handbook of Law and Economics* (edited by A.M. Polinsky and S. Shavell), Oxford: Elsevier.

Polinsky, A.M. and S. Shavell (2008), 'Law and Economics', in the *New Palgrave Dictionary of Economics* (edited by Lawrence Blume and Steven Durlauf) London; Palgrave Macmillan.

Posner, R. (1972), 'A Theory of Negligence', *Journal of Legal Studies*, 1: 29–96.

Posner, R. (2005), 'The Law and Economics of Contract Interpretation', *Texas Law Review*, 83: 1581–614.

Rogerson, W. (1984), 'Efficient Reliance and Damage Measures for Breach of Contract', *Rand Journal of Economics*, 15 (1): 39–53.

Rosenberg, D. and S. Shavell (1985), 'A Model in which Suits are Brought for their Nuisance Value', *International Review of Law and Economics*, 5: 3–13.

Rosenberg, D. and S. Shavell (2006), 'A Solution to the Problem of Nuisance Suits: The Option to Have the Court Bar Settlement', *International Review of Law and Economics*, 26 (1): 42–51.

Sanchirico, C. W. (2000), 'Taxes versus Legal Rules as Instruments for Equity: A More Equitable View', *Journal of Legal Studies*, 29 (2): 797–820.

Salvador, P., N. Garoupa and C. Gomez-Ligüerre (2009), 'Scope of Liability: The Vanishing Distinction between Negligence and Strict Liability', *European Journal of Law and Economics*, forthcoming.

Schmitz, P.W. (2000), 'On the Joint Use of Liability and Safety Regulation', *International Review of Law and Economics*, 20 (3): 371–82.

Scott, R.E. and G.G. Triantis (2006), 'Anticipating Litigation in Contract Design', *Yale Law Journal*, 115: 814–79.

Shavell, S. (1979a), 'On Moral Hazard and Insurance', *Quarterly Journal of Economics*, 92: 541–62.

Shavell, S. (1979b), 'Risk Sharing and Incentives in the Principal and Agent Relationship', *Bell Journal of Economics*, 10 (1): 55–73.

Shavell, S. (1980a), 'Strict Liability versus Negligence', *Journal of Legal Studies*, 9 (1): 1–25.

Shavell, S. (1980b), 'Damage Measures for Breach of Contract', *Bell Journal of Economics*, 11: 466–90.

Shavell, S. (1980c), An Analysis of Causation and the Scope of Liability in the Law of Torts', *Journal of Legal Studies*, 9 (2): 463–516.

Shavell, S. (1981), A Note on Efficiency vs. Distributional Equity in Legal Rulemaking: Should Distributional Equity Matter Given Optimal Income Taxation?', *American Economic Review*, 71: 414–18.

Shavell, S. (1982a), 'On Liability and Insurance', *Bell Journal of Economics*, 13 (1): 120–32.

Shavell, S. (1982b), 'The Social versus the Private Incentive to Bring Suit in a Costly Legal System', *Journal of Legal Studies*, 11: 333–9.

Shavell, S. (1982c), 'Suit, Settlement, and Trial: A Theoretical Analysis under Alternative Methods for the Allocation of Legal Costs', *Journal of Legal Studies*, 11: 55–81.

Shavell, S. (1984a), 'The Design of Contracts and Remedies for Breach', *Quarterly Journal of Economics*, 99: 121–48.

Shavell, S. (1984b), 'Liability for Harm versus Regulation of Safety', *Journal of Legal Studies*, 13 (2): 357–74.

Shavell, S. (1984c), 'A Model of the Optimal Use of Liability and Safety Regulation', *Rand Journal of Economics*, 15: 271–80.

Shavell, S. (1985a), 'Criminal Law and the Optimal Use of Nonmonetary Sanctions as a Deterrent', *Columbia Law Review*, 85: 1232–62.

Shavell, S. (1985b), 'Uncertainty over Causation and the Determination of Civil Liability', *Journal of Law and Economics*, 28 (2): 587–609.

Shavell, S. (1986), 'The Judgment Proof Problem', *International Review of Law and Economics*, 6 (1): 45–58.

Shavell, S. (1987a), 'A Model of Optimal Incapacitation', *American Economic Review*, 77: 107–10.

Shavell, S. (1987b), 'The Optimal Use of Nonmonetary Sanctions as a Deterrent', *American Economic Review*, 77: 584–92.

Shavell, S. (1987c), *Economic Analysis of Accident Law*, Cambridge, MA: Harvard University Press.

Shavell, S. (1989a), 'Optimal Sanctions and the Incentive to Provide Evidence to Legal Tribunals', *International Review of Law and Economics*, 9: 3–11.

Shavell, S. (1989b), 'Sharing of Information Prior to Settlement or Litigation', *Rand Journal of Economics*, 20 (2): 183–95.

Shavell, S. (1989c), 'A Note on the Incentive to Reveal Information', *Geneva Papers on Risk and Insurance*, 14 (1): 66–74.

Shavell, S. (1990), 'Deterrence and the Punishment of Attempts', *Journal of Legal Studies*, 19 (2): 435–66.

Shavell, S. (1991a), 'Specific versus General Enforcement of Law', *Journal of Political Economy*, 99: 1088–108.

Shavell, S. (1991b), 'Individual Precautions to Prevent Theft: Private versus Socially Optimal Behavior', *International Review of Law and Economics*, 11 (2): 123–32.

Shavell, S. (1991c), 'An Economic Analysis of Altruism and Deferred Gifts', *Journal of Legal Studies*, 20 (2): 401–21.

Shavell, S. (1992a), 'A Note on Marginal Deterrence', *International Review of Law and Economics*, 12 (4): 345–55.
Shavell, S. (1992b), 'Liability and the Incentive to Obtain Information about Risk', *Journal of Legal Studies*, 21 (2): 259–70.
Shavell, S. (1993a), 'The Optimal Structure of Law Enforcement', *Journal of Law and Economics*, 36 (1): 255–87.
Shavell, S. (1993b), 'An Economic Analysis of Threats and their Illegality: Blackmail, Extortion and Robbery', *University of Pennsylvania Law Review*, 141 (5): 1877–903.
Shavell, S. (1993c), 'Suit versus Settlement when Parties Seek Nonmonetary Judgments', *Journal of Legal Studies*, 22 (1): 1–13.
Shavell, S. (1994), 'Acquisition and Disclosure of Information Prior to Sale', *Rand Journal of Economics*, 25 (1): 20–36.
Shavell, S. (1995a), 'Alternative Dispute Resolution: An Economic Analysis', *Journal of Legal Studies*, 24 (1): 1–28.
Shavell, S. (1995b), 'The Appeals Process as a Means of Error Correction', *Journal of Legal Studies*, 24 (2): 379–426.
Shavell, S. (1996), 'Any Frequency of Plaintiff Victory at Trial is Possible', *Journal of Legal Studies*, 25 (2): 493–501.
Shavell, S. (1997a), 'The Optimal Level of Corporate Liability Given the Limited Ability of Corporations to Penalize their Employees', *International Review of Law and Economics*, 17 (2): 203–13.
Shavell, S. (1997b), 'The Fundamental Divergence Between the Private and the Social Motive to Use the Legal System', *Journal of Legal Studies*, 26 (2): 575–612.
Shavell, S. (1999), 'The Level of Litigation: Private versus Social Optimality', *International Review of Law and Economics*, 19 (1): 99–115.
Shavell, S. (2000), 'On the Social Function and the Regulation of Liability Insurance', *Geneva Papers on Risk and Insurance, Issues and Practice*, 25 (2): 166–79.
Shavell, S. (2001), 'Law and Economics', in the *International Encyclopedia of the Social and Behavioral Sciences*, vol. 12 (edited by Neil J. Smelser and Paul B. Baltes), New York, NY: Elsevier.
Shavell, S. (2002), 'Law versus Morality as Regulators of Conduct', *American Law and Economics Review*, 4 (2): 227–57.
Shavell, S. (2004), *Foundations of Economic Analysis of Law*, Cambridge, MA: Belknap Press of Harvard University Press.
Shavell, S. (2005), 'Minimum Asset Requirements and Compulsory Liability Insurance as Solutions to the Judgment-Proof Problem', *Rand Economic Journal*, 36 (1): 63–77.
Shavell, S. (2006a), 'Specific Performance versus Damages for Breach of Contract: An Economic Analysis', *Texas Law Review*, 84 (4): 831–76.
Shavell, S. (2006b), 'On the Writing and Interpretation of Contracts', *Journal of Law, Economics and Organization*, 22 (2): 289–314.
Shavell, S. (2006c), 'Is Breach of Contract Immoral?', *Emory Law Journal*, 56: 439–60.
Shavell, S. (2006d), 'The Appeals Process and Adjudicator Incentives', *Journal of Legal Studies*, 35 (1): 1–29.
Shavell, S. (2007a), 'Holdup, Contracts, and Legal Intervention', *Journal of Legal Studies*, 36 (2): 325–54.
Shavell, S. (2007b), 'On the Proper Magnitude of Punitive Damages: Mathias V. Accor Economy Lodging', *Harvard Law Review*, 120: 1223–7.
Shavell, S. (2007c), 'Do Excessive Legal Standards Discourage Desirable Activity?', *Economics Letters*, 95 (3): 394–7.
Shavell, S. (2007d), 'Optimal Discretion in the Application of Rules', *American Law and Economics Review*, 9 (1): 175–94.
Shavell, S. and T. van Ypersele (2001), 'Rewards versus Intellectual Property Rights', *Journal of Law and Economics*, 44 (2): 525–47.
Sloof, R., E. Leuven, H. Oosterbeek and J. Sonnemans (2003), 'An Experimental Comparison of Reliance Levels under Alternative Breach Remedies', *Rand Journal of Economics*, 34 (2): 205–22.
Spier, K.E. and S. Shavell (2002), 'Threats without Binding Commitment', *Topics in Economic Analysis and Policy*, 2 (1): article 2.
Stigler, G.J. (1970), 'The Optimum Enforcement of Laws', *Journal of Political Economy*, 78: 526–36.
Summers, J. (1983), 'The Case of the Disappearing Defendant: An Economic Analysis', *University of Pennsylvania Law Review*, 132: 145–85.
Sunstein, C.R., D. Kanehman, R. Haiste, D.A. Schkade, J.W. Payne and W.K. Viscusi (2002), *Punitive Damages: How Juries Decide,* Chicago: The University of Chicago Press.
Wangenheim, G. von. and F. Gomez (2005), 'The Complex Economics of Nuisance Law: The Tragedy of Bargaining under Property and Liability Rules', Working Paper, University of Kassel-Pompeu Fabra University.

Index